D1736857

Police Management

Third Edition

Roy Roberg
San Jose State University

Jack Kuykendall
San Jose State University

Kenneth Novak
University of Missouri-Kansas City

New York   Oxford
OXFORD UNIVERSITY PRESS

Oxford University Press, Inc., publishes works that further Oxford University's
objective of excellence in research, scholarship, and education.

Oxford   New York
Auckland   Cape Town   Dar es Salaam   Hong Kong   Karachi
Kuala Lumpur   Madrid   Melbourne   Mexico City   Nairobi
New Delhi   Shanghai   Taipei   Toronto

With offices in
Argentina   Austria   Brazil   Chile   Czech Republic   France   Greece
Guatemala   Hungary   Italy   Japan   Poland   Portugal   Singapore
South Korea   Switzerland   Thailand   Turkey   Ukraine   Vietnam

Copyright © 2002 by Oxford University Press, Inc.

Published by Oxford University Press, Inc.
198 Madison Avenue, New York, New York 10016
http://www.oup.com

Oxford is a registered trademark of Oxford University Press

ISBN 978-0-19-533011-3

Printed in the United States of America
on acid-free paper

Dedication
To our favorite managers, Arlene, Mary, and Jill;
as well as our future managers, Alyssa and Casey.

Acknowledgements

We would like to acknowledge and thank Claude Teweles, Publisher of Roxbury Publishing Company, whose strong support, wit, humor, and insights have continued to make the writing process enjoyable and rewarding. Renee Ergazos, our project manager, also deserves special recognition. Her stellar effort has been invaluable and has significantly enhanced the final product. In addition, we would like to thank the rest of the staff at Roxbury who contributed to the text, including Arlyne Lazerson, Pauline Piekarz, and Dawn VanDercreek.

We further extend our appreciation to Tad Hughes, University of Louisville, and Erin Nelson Serrano, San Jose State University, for their valuable insights and assistance on several chapters. Finally, we would like to extend a special thanks to Marie Simonetti Rosen, Publisher of *Law Enforcement News*, for permitting us to reprint numerous articles that enhance the realistic view of police management as practiced by agencies throughout the United States.

Contents

Preface

The Third Edition of *Police Management* adheres to the general approach of the first two editions; namely, it is interdisciplinary in nature and applies general, police organization, and management theories to police departments. The book presents a balance between the theory and practice of modern police management and its application in a democratic society. A central theme of the text is describing and analyzing the transition from traditional to community policing from a managerial perspective.

An important new chapter on civil liability has been added to this edition and the remaining chapters have been substantially updated with contemporary research and real-life policing examples. Some of the new significantly expanded topics include broken windows policing and zero tolerance; neighborhood building; police-community expectations; racial profiling; cultural diversity; change and innovation; technology; police goals and measurement; control and accountability; job redesign and performance evaluation in a community policing context; police culture; and leadership and motivation.

Police Management shows students how to apply police research and contemporary management principles to the challenges of running today's complex police organizations—integrating theory with practice. We emphasize an analytical, rather than a purely descriptive approach, to understanding critical issues in police organization and management, and further recommend possible solutions. This is accomplished by utilizing an expectation-integration model, suggesting that effective police management is a function of how well expectations from employees, the community, and the organization are balanced. Finally, the text also offers a historical framework for understanding contemporary police management—putting students in touch with the foundations of modern law-enforcement management.

Case Study boxes introduce the student to recent data and research relevant to police management and provide sources to police-related research. *Inside Management* boxes describe real-life managerial problems and exemplary programs in police organizations. A revised Instructor's Manual/Testing Program is also available.

We would like to thank the many police officers, managers, and students with whom we have interacted over the years. Their experiences and insights have given us the basis for many of our ideas. We hope that the book increases the understanding of organization and management concepts, the "best practices" available, and the difficult role facing police managers.

Roy Roberg
Jack Kuykendall
Kenneth Novak

Chapter One

Police Management: An Introduction

CHAPTER OUTLINE

This text on the management of police organizations in a democratic society presents general theories of management and organization and their application to police departments while attempting to assess police management practices and problems. The book also attempts to provide a balance between theoretical and applied research and between conceptual and practical perspectives on police management. The authors hope that this text will enhance the student's understanding of the police and the way "good" management can make a difference in employee attitudes and behavior and in accomplishing organizational goals and objectives.

❖ ❖ ❖ ❖   ## Managerial Role and Organizational Environment

Police managers must try to formulate goals and design organizations to meet the expectations and needs of employees, clients (i.e., members of the community), and various other groups and individuals that may be affected by police activities, such as private police, court and correctional agencies, business and industry, other governmental agencies, and political leaders. Individual employees, as well as the organization (i.e., supervisors and managers), have certain expectations of one another. For instance, on the one hand, the organization expects employees to adequately perform their assigned tasks and uphold their responsibilities, abide by the rules, learn new skills, take the initiative, and (when appropriate) be able to work independently. On the other hand, employees expect the organization to treat them fairly and in a dignified manner and to provide adequate pay, benefits, and working conditions. Some employees may expect even more, depending on their desire for security, social interaction, status, power, and the opportunity to reach their full potential. For many individuals, their self-esteem is closely related to their success at work.

An *organization* may be defined as social groupings of two or more persons who are interdependent and work in a coordinated manner to achieve common goals. The purpose of management is to work toward the attainment of these goals by responding to the changing needs of employees, customers, and other influential individuals and organizations. One of management's primary responsibilities is to work toward the integration of individual and organizational needs, so that the organization can accomplish its goals. Full and complete integration for all parties in an organization is rarely, if ever, achieved. However, the ongoing attempt at integration creates an environment in which maximum productivity is possible.

Managerial and behavioral science research (see Macy and Mirvis, 1976) suggests that employees are more likely to come to work and stay with an organization if they are satisfied in their jobs, and they are more likely to be productive in terms of quality and quantity if they receive rewards, such as interesting and challenging tasks and recognition for good work. Satisfaction and rewards are influenced by the work environment, which includes the nature of the work itself, relations in the work group, organizational structure, managerial style, and the actual provision of valued rewards. Managers have a significant influence on the type of work environment.

To illustrate, assume that the typical police officer is working at about 60 to 70 percent of capacity, in terms of both the quality and quantity of work done. If by changing the work environment, this figure could be increased to 80 or 90 percent, the police department would actually have about 20 percent more resources, without necessarily requiring an additional investment of funds. The authors believe that many police departments in the United States could substantially increase both the quality and quantity of work performed if they were more effectively managed.

Although the work environment in an organization is critically important, it must be stressed that it does not mean that everything in the organization is perfect for all employees. It is important for both managers and workers to realize that each must exercise some give and take in achieving a mutually beneficial relationship. Employees need to come to work ready to do their best, and managers must strive to create a work environment in which employees can thrive.

Organizational successes should be shared and appreciated; organizational failures, unless they are deliberate, must be viewed as problems to be corrected rather than as the fault of people to be identified, blamed and punished. Neither managers nor workers can legitimately fix the blame or take the credit for life inside the organization. In general, however, a fix-the-problem managerial philosophy may be difficult for police departments to adopt, because they have a long history of blame-and-punishment management. Such an approach does not always result from a lack of education and training for managers; rather, it is a product of a political environment in which only punishment for a perceived police abuse will satisfy the public. Blame-and-punishment management is an abuse of managerial authority and is a major cause of inadequate employee performance and the development of a code of silence in police departments. Employees who are criticized and punished for nondeliberate mistakes may treat citizens in a similar fashion, try to avoid difficult situations and people, and band together to protect one another from what they consider to be arbitrary and unfair treatment.

Major Themes

The purpose of this book is to provide the reader with an understanding of how police organizations work, how people in them behave, and how individuals and groups can be effectively managed. To this end, **police management** may be defined as police organizational practices, including individual, group, organizational, and environmental processes, undertaken for the purpose of producing knowledge that can be used continuously to improve employee satisfaction and organizational performance.

This book's approach to understanding police organizations and management incorporates seven major themes. These themes are identified as follows in Table 1.1.

The first theme is **humanitarian orientation,** which recognizes the importance of human resources in police organizations. A concern for the employee (and the customer, or citizen) is a critical part of any successful managerial process. Compassion and concern for others are essential to effective police work. Managers must treat their employees the way they expect their employees to treat the customers of the organization.

The second theme is awareness of the **environment** in which police organizations must function. Just as managers must integrate the expectations of the employee with those of the organization, the expectations of the organization (including those of the employee) must be integrated with those of the environment (that is, the community). The community environment of police organizations is made up not only of individual citizens, interest groups, and neighborhoods but also of other governmental agencies, political and administrative leaders, businesses, other criminal-justice agencies, and private police organizations.

The third theme is understanding the **interdisciplinary nature** of the study of police management. Relevant organizational and management theories, along with important research from policing and other well-established disciplines, will be discussed. Because most of the rigorous empirical research and development of theory in organizational behavior and management have taken place in the behavioral sciences (especially psychology and sociology) and in the management field, this book attempts to blend these findings with current policing research.

Table 1.1	Major Themes of Police Management	
Theme	**Characteristics**
Humanitarian Orientation	The importance of the humane treatment of employees and citizens is emphasized.
Environment	The expectations of the organization must be integrated with those of the community.
Interdisciplinary Nature	Relevant principles, models, and theories from the social and behavioral sciences are utilized.
Scientific Method	Research studies using the scientific method are incorporated. A clinical scientist perspective is used to create a learning organization.
Four Levels of Analysis	Individuals, groups, the organization, and the organizational environment are analyzed.
Systems Theory and ContingencyTheory	The interrelated and interdependent parts of a system are related to the whole and to the environment. Management practices vary as circumstances and problems change.
Integrity	An organizational climate that fosters integrity for all employees is established.

The fourth theme is the importance of ***research and the scientific method*** for effective management. Empirical research helps managers to identify and understand important variables and relationships in the study of police organizations. In using the scientific method, managers become, in part, ***clinical scientists***, a term that has been used in social work for several decades (Brian, 1979: 132–133). To be clinical scientists, police managers should be trained to:

1. Use the police strategies, methods, programs, policies, and so on that are empirically known to be the most effective, that is, based on well-designed research that has been replicated.

2. Evaluate continuously the results associated with using strategies, methods, programs, and policies.

3. Participate in the discovery, testing, and reporting on the effectiveness of various innovative approaches to solving problems and addressing different situations.

4. Use untested approaches with great caution and only with adequate control and concern for their impact on citizens and organizational employees.

5. Communicate the results of research and evaluation to others.

Police departments in which managers adopt a clinical scientific perspective become ***learning organizations*** in which a continuous process of experimentation and evaluation provides the basis for a climate of innovation. When an organization has an innovative climate, it is easier for it to adapt to changing circumstances and new ideas.

The fifth theme is to use *four levels of analysis* to promote better understanding of the complex nature of organizational behavior (see Figure 1.1). The first level or basic building block of any organization is the **individual.** The next level of analysis is the **work group** (i.e., unit, team, shift, or program), a collection of individuals who work together to accomplish various tasks and objectives. The third level is the **organization,** made up of a collection of groups attempting to accomplish organizational goals. The final level of analysis is the **environment,** which was discussed above.

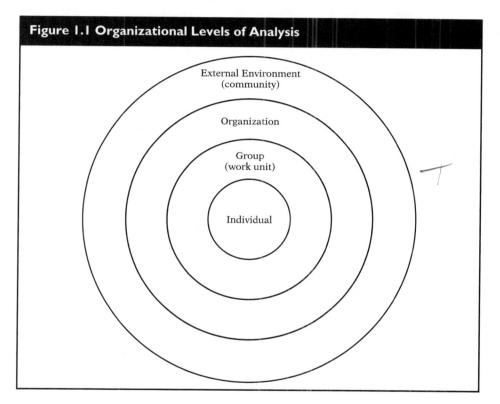

Figure 1.1 Organizational Levels of Analysis

External Environment
(community)

Organization

Group
(work unit)

Individual

The sixth theme is to apply **systems theory and contingency theory** to the study of police organizations. Using the four levels of analysis just described, one is in effect utilizing **general systems theory,** which views a system as a whole composed of interrelated and interdependent parts or subsystems. Police organizations can be thought of as **open systems,** which are a subsystem of a community, of its government, and of the criminal-justice system (including the police, courts and correctional institutions). By itself, a police organization can also be conceptualized as a system that has patrol, investigation, and communication subsystems, as well as other subsystems, such as day, evening, and midnight shifts. General systems theory provides a useful way to conceptualize police organizations and how they relate to their environment.

A more pragmatic approach to the study of organizations than general systems theory is contingency theory, which is specific in applying appropriate management concepts and methods to organizational circumstances. Contingency management studies the variables that influence the organization and employees. In other words, as circumstances and problems change, it may be necessary to change police management practices and employee responses in order to maintain or improve effectiveness.

The seventh theme in this book is ***promoting integrity*** throughout the organization. Although employee integrity is important in all organizations, it is crucial to police departments because of their role in a democratic society. In the authors' opinion, integrity is the single most important factor in policing. Without candor and sincerity, there is a lack of trust between manager and employee or between the police and citizens. An organizational climate that fosters integrity begins with leaders. Unfortunately, the police in the United States have had a long history of unethical and illegal behavior. Police managers must work hard to become role models of integrity for their officers and for the community, and officers must become role models for citizens.

Management

Managers differ from other organizational members in the work that they do. ***Management*** may be defined as the process of working with people in a humane way to achieve organizational goals and objectives as efficiently and effectively as possible. First, the idea of working with people rather than through them connotes a mutual participation between managers and employees, thus emphasizing a positive attitude toward employee involvement in the organization.

Second, the idea of humaneness is an integral part of the definition. The Funk and Wagnall's dictionary (1953, 575) defines humane as "having or showing kindness and tenderness; compassionate." It lists several synonyms—benevolent, charitable, gracious, merciful, and sympathetic—and several antonyms—barbarous, cruel, fierce, inhuman, merciless, and selfish. By promoting a humane approach to management, the authors believe that human dignity will be increased in the organization, the quality of the work environment will be improved, and employees will become more humane when dealing with community members.

Third, the definition also incorporates the importance of accomplishing goals and objectives. ***Goals*** are general statements of purpose that tend to be long range. Goals may be, and often are, used to identify the role or mission of the police (e.g., to reduce crime or the fear of crime or to improve citizen attitudes toward the organization and officers). However, goals may also be more specific. For example, a police department may have as a goal the reduction of property crimes for the next calendar year.

Objectives are usually more specific than goals and tend to be time-bounded and quantifiable. They should be consistent with the organization's goals. For example, an objective might be to reduce residential burglaries by 5 percent in the next six months. Thus, the objective is specific (refers to a specific type of crime), time-bounded (six months), and quantifiable (5 percent). It is also possible to develop other related objectives concerning the personnel, resources, training, and specific tactics associated with efforts to reduce residential burglaries. For example, all patrol officers assigned to des-

ignated high-crime areas will receive four hours of burglary-prevention
training within the next 30 days, and all homes in designated high-crime
areas will undergo security checks within the next 90 days. These objectives
are also consistent with a more general organization goal of preventing or
reducing crime, or a more specific goal of reducing the number of property
crimes in the next year.

Two other important terms in the definition of management are efficiency and effectiveness. However, before discussing them, it is first necessary to distinguish between outputs and outcomes in policing. **Outputs** are
what the police department does, for example, patrolling, making arrests,
writing tickets, helping citizens with problems, exercising discretion, behaving in a certain manner. **Outcomes** are what happens, at least in part, as a
consequence of police activities and behavior (e.g., changes in the crime rate,
citizen fearfulness, and degree of satisfaction with police service). Both outputs and outcomes are often discussed as the results or products of policing,
but it is important to remember that there is a difference between police
activities and behavior (outputs) and the impact or consequence of that activity and behavior (outcomes).

Police goals and objectives can be developed for both outputs and outcomes. For example, a general output goal might be to improve the quality of
police investigations (a police activity). A specific objective related to this
goal might be to increase the number of criminal cases accepted for prosecution by 20 percent during the next year. An outcome goal might be to reduce
the crime rate in the community. An objective related to this goal might be to
decrease the number of robberies by 10 percent during the next year.

Efficiency is concerned with the relationship between resources and
outputs. How much time and money were invested in the effort required to
accomplish a specific output goal or objective? To become more efficient, an
organization must accomplish output goals and objectives at a reduced cost
in time or money (which is usually the same thing in police work) or obtain
greater outputs or effectiveness at the same cost. **Effectiveness** is the degree
to which goals or objectives are accomplished. To become more effective, an
organization must have an increase in the number of goals and objectives
accomplished or come closer to realizing them. It is important to remember
that an organization can become more efficient without becoming more
effective, and vice versa.

In policing, the concept of **productivity** is often used instead of either
efficiency or effectiveness. However, productivity may also be used to characterize the relationship between police resources and outcomes. As noted previously, possible police outcome measures include the crime rate, citizen fear
levels, and citizen attitudes. When productivity is determined based on outcomes, an improvement in any of these areas would mean that the organization is more productive, unless the resources invested were disproportionate
given the outcomes achieved (e.g., a substantial increase in resources results
in only marginal improvements).

The concepts of quantity and quality are also related to efficiency, effectiveness, and productivity. **Quantity** simply means the amount of something
(e.g., arrests, traffic citations) expressed in numbers, percentages, rates, and
so forth. **Quality** is more ambiguous and therefore more difficult to define. It
is used here to mean an improvement over that which existed. For example, if
citizen satisfaction increased as a result of a new approach to conducting

traffic stops, this would be an improvement in quality. Or quality would be improved if a new report form for certain types of criminal investigation resulted in the gathering of more useful information, or if officers could complete investigations more quickly without a decline in citizen satisfaction.

The *process* that determines police outputs includes selection and training of officers, organization design, managerial practices, leadership, and community expectations. Police managers have more influence over outputs than outcomes. Basically, all police outcomes are related to *attitudes* (e.g., citizens' fear levels and opinions of the police) and *behavior* (e.g., active citizen cooperation and crimes attempted and committed). Many variables outside police control influence both attitudes and behavior. When outcome goals and objectives are established without a substantial understanding of the relationship between a particular police activity (output) and results (outcome) obtained, any changes that occur may be misleading. And any outcome goals and objectives achieved may or may not be the result of police activities and the behavior of officers.

As more is learned about the output-outcome relationship, the police will become more effective in setting and achieving outcome goals and objectives. Managers, however, can make substantial changes in police outputs, particularly in relation to the activities and behavior of officers. Even if the police in a democracy, regardless of what they lawfully do, may not always be able to have a significant and sustained impact on crime, police employees can still be honest, competent, and responsible.

The Managerial Process

Managers in every organization perform four essential functions: organizing, leading, planning, and controlling. Although managers perform each function, the time involved in each one varies according to the manager's level in the organization. For instance, people at higher levels, such as an assistant chief, spend a greater proportion of their time in organizing and planning, while those at lower levels, such as sergeants, spend more time supervising, which is one aspect of leading and controlling. The time spent in various functions is also influenced by the size of the organization. In a small police department, a sergeant may function both as an assistant chief and as a supervisor. Each managerial function is briefly described in the following paragraphs, and the remainder of the book explores these functions in more detail.

Planning is often considered the first function of managers, because ideally all other functions must be planned. The authors believe, however, that organizing (i.e., making decisions about purpose, structure, job design, and allocation of resources) is the first step in managing any organized endeavor, whereas leading (motivating and guiding employees) is the second. Therefore, organizing has been placed first, leading second, and planning third. Nevertheless, the order in which functions are listed is not critical in understanding the processes involved.

Organizing is the process of arranging personnel and physical resources to carry out plans and accomplish goals and objectives. Organizational structure, job design, group working arrangements, and individual work assignments are subject to the organizing process. Although all managers are involved in organizing, once again, the degree and scope differ, depending on their level within the organization. The patrol supervisor is more concerned with work assignments; the chief is more concerned with the structure of the organization and the overall distribution of personnel and physical resources.

Leading is motivating others to perform various tasks that will contribute to the accomplishment of goals and objectives. Motivating others is a difficult and complex process, especially in civil-service organizations where managers have less control over fiscal resources, such as base salaries and pay incentives, than in the private sector. How well a manager motivates employees to perform depends on the use of both extrinsic rewards, such as pay, promotion, and praise, and intrinsic rewards, such as job satisfaction and feelings of accomplishment. Intrinsic rewards are related to the nature and structure of the work performed, group processes, and managerial style.

Leading and *managing* are often used to mean the same thing, but they can be defined differently. Police leaders, particularly at the higher levels, are concerned with managing the relationship between the police and the community and other important organizations, such as government agencies. In this regard, leadership can mean more than engaging in the various managerial functions; it can also mean taking positions on important public issues, such as gun control, the drug problem, or the role of the police in a democratic society.

Planning is the process of preparing for the future by setting goals and objectives and developing courses of action for accomplishing them. The courses of action involve such activities as conducting research, identifying strategies and methods, developing policies and procedures, and formulating budgets. All managers engage in planning, but again the scope and nature of the activity differ considerably, depending on the managerial level within an organization. For instance, while a patrol supervisor may develop work schedules and operating activities for the upcoming week, a police chief may plan activities and changes for the upcoming year. In general, the higher the managerial level, the broader the scope of planning and the longer the time frame for the plans.

Controlling is the process by which managers determine how the quality of organizational systems and services can be improved, if goals and objectives are being accomplished, whether or not operations are consistent with plans, and if officers follow the policies and procedures of the organization. Efficiency, effectiveness, productivity, and both the concepts of quantity and quality are important in this phase of management. A manager's approach to controlling is strongly influenced by his or her perspective on dealing with individuals and performance problems. Does controlling mean to fix blame and punish, or is it to work with employees to analyze and solve problems?

If goals or objectives are not realized, or plans, policies, and procedures are not being followed, or there seems to be a qualitative problem with an organization's system or service, managers must determine why and take action. Controlling may be the most troublesome managerial function because it may be difficult to determine why a system, subsystem, or service is inadequate, why performance failures occur, and what to do to change and improve them. For example, police corruption and brutality continue to be serious performance problems, despite frequent attempts to determine their causes and correct them.

❖ ❖ ❖ ❖ Public, Private, and Police Management

It is not uncommon for public organizations and their managers to be criticized for being inefficient and ineffective when compared with many private organizations. Although such criticism may be valid in some circumstances, the authors suggest that managing an organization that is responsible for such things as crime and justice, education, and social welfare is more difficult, complex, and controversial than managing an organization that makes cars or computers. In addition, many public organizations differ from private organizations in terms of their time perspective, performance measurement, personnel constraints, equity, and openness (Allison, 1983).

Because of the political nature of their jobs, many public managers tend to have a shorter time perspective; therefore, they may do less long-term planning than do managers in the private sector. Because there is generally greater diversity in the community's or client's expectations of public organizations, performance measures may be vague, that is, more qualitative (or intangible) than quantitative, in the absence of a clearly identified bottom line in terms of profits or market share. For instance, it is easier to measure the quality of an assembled car than the quality of justly administered laws.

Because in democratic societies public scrutiny of the behavior of government officials is part of the political process, public managers tend to operate with more constraints on personnel and policy. As a result of merit-based selection processes, affirmative action, civil-service rules, and the political interest in the welfare of public employees, these managers have less flexibility in terms of who is employed and how those employees are treated. Accordingly, there tends to be a greater concern for equity in the public sector, even beyond the ways in which employees are selected and treated. For example, does a public agency have a diverse work force that is representative of the community? Are resources distributed appropriately? Do policies and procedures result in disparate results; for example, are more blacks than whites injured by police?

Police organizations are not only different from private organizations but also from other public organizations in regard to conflicts inherent in the role of the police in a democratic society. Ideally, democratic governments exist to represent and serve citizens. Yet, the police provide services that many in the society do not want, such as a traffic ticket or an arrest, but cannot always avoid. Although citizens, in the abstract, may agree to be governed, in practice, they often resist government intervention. To be successful, a democratic government must be based on a consensus among the inhabitants of a society; but when that consensus fails, the police are often the initial representatives of government that respond.

Democracy is also associated with some degree of freedom. Although complete freedom is not allowed in any society, at least a democracy permits participation in deciding how and when individual freedom will be restricted; however, the policies of police organizations and the decisions of individual police officers do not always consider citizen input. Consequently, the exercise of police authority tends to reflect an authoritarian orientation in an otherwise "free" society. Police are a constant reminder that freedom is limited.

Another important consideration in a democracy is equality, yet the citizen and the police officer are not equals. The police officer has the power to compel the citizen to observe laws and ordinances. He or she may even use coercion, including deadly force in some situations, if necessary to secure citizen compliance (Berkeley, 1969: 1–5).

All these factors indicate why the opposite of a democratic state is often called a police state. Democracy represents consensus, freedom, participation, and equality, whereas the police represent restriction and the imposition of the authority of government on the individual. That is why the police in a democracy are often confronted with hostility, opposition, and criticism, no matter how efficient, effective, or equitable they may be.

The tension between the police and a democratic society has resulted in an ongoing debate about the role of the police in the United States. This tension has resulted in a cycle of failure and reform that is probably inevitable. The police have periodically been perceived, by both the public and political leaders, to have failed in some significant way. Study of these failures results in recommendations for changes, some of which lead to other problems that eventually spawn yet another spate of reform. Community policing represents the latest solution for the appropriate place of police in democratic society. Eventually, a new approach or model will emerge, in part as a result of criticisms of community policing.

Attempts to manage the police-democratic conflict has resulted in the development of several police models (discussed in Chapter 3). Not only are these models concerned with the police-democratic conflict, they also include differing perspectives on how police organizations should be managed. In the abstract, managing is a generic process common to all organizations. In practice, managing is unique relative to environmental context, organizational culture, and the recurring problems addressed. In the next section, an expectation-integration model is used to provide a framework to understand police management.

The Expectation-Integration Model

What should the police do and how should they do it? The answer to this question varies by time and place as expectations change concerning the police role in a democracy. Expectations are derived from the community, the police organization, and the individual employee. These are used in Figure 1.2 to depict an expectation-integration model, which indicates the degree to which expectations are shared and integrated. The greater the degree of integration, the fewer the managerial problems. However, even with a substantial degree of integration of expectations, there will be numerous organizational problems that require management's attention. Recurring types of problems, such as scheduling work, obtaining and allocating resources, evaluating personnel, and so on, are intrinsic to all organizational endeavors. As the degree of integration of expectations declines, these problems become more difficult for managers to cope with, because dissatisfaction among employees or a substantial segment of the community results in reduced cooperation, which leads to greater expenditure of the manager's time and energy. The resulting problems may become so time-consuming that more basic managerial endeavors, such as long-term planning or organizational change, may be ignored to the detriment of the vitality and productivity of the organization. Organizations that seem to be plagued by crisis management have given insufficient attention to the management of expectations.

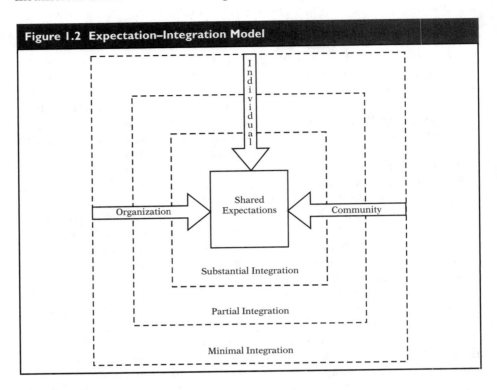

Figure 1.2 Expectation–Integration Model

Community Expectations

Community expectations of the police result from changing societal trends and problems (e.g.,rapid growth in population, economic recession, drug or gang problems) and the legal framework in which police function. The term *community* also has different meanings—not only the legally incorporated area of a city or county but also individuals who live in the same area or neighborhood, work for the same organization, or share common concerns (e.g., members of an ethnic group or a particular religion). Each community is also made up of individual citizens, who can interact with a police officer in at least five ways: as a suspect (including recipients of a traffic ticket), a victim, a witness, a bystander, or a citizen interested in influencing police policies and practices. In each of these five roles, the individual's expectations of the police may differ; for example, a victim's expectations differ somewhat from those of a suspect.

Legal expectations of the police are derived from substantive and procedural criminal laws and legal requirements that have resulted from civil suits. These laws provide the basic framework within which the police are supposed to function. Laws are intended to be rational rules that structure the relationship between individuals and between the individual and government. The rule of law is crucial to effective policing in a democratic society. The significance of the rule of law to democracy and the police is described in a Royal Commission Report on the British police:

... Liberty does not depend, and never has depended, upon any particular form of police organization. It depends upon the supremacy of ... the rule of law. The proper criterion (to determine if a police state exists) is whether the police are answerable to the law and ultimately, to a democratically elected [government]. (1962: 45)

Organizational Expectations

Organizational expectations come from both the formal and informal organization. *Formal expectations* are derived from leaders, supervisors, training programs, and organizational goals, objectives, policies, procedures, and regulations. The legal framework that is part of community expectations is incorporated into the expectations of individual officers. Organizational goals and objectives and policies and procedures are often influenced by community concerns. *Informal expectations* are derived from officers' peers and work groups. Officers are strongly influenced by their work experiences and the way they adjust to the emotional, psychological, intellectual, and physical demands of police work. Officers must attempt to do their job in a manner that is acceptable to both the police department and their peers; they must try not to be injured or killed or allow other officers or citizens to be injured or killed; and their conduct must not promote citizen complaints.

Individual Expectations

Police employees' *individual expectations* refer to their perspectives concerning the degree to which their needs are met by the organization and their working environment. All employees expect to be treated fairly and adequately rewarded. They usually develop strong opinions about how police work should be done; that is, what laws should be enforced, how they should be enforced, how to exercise their discretion, and so on. Each individual, with his or her needs and opinions, and the expectations of both the formal and informal organization, combine to create an organizational culture in which basic values and attitudes about the police role, effective police strategies and methods, and appropriate behavior are determined.

Expectation Integration

Managers are concerned primarily with two expectation-integration issues: community and organization, and organization and individual. Both areas are discussed, including several of the more important expectation-integration problems.

Community-Organizational Expectations

Community expectations of police departments are usually concerned with one or more of the following: (1) how police officers behave toward individuals, (2) how officers exercise their discretion, (3) how police departments utilize their resources, (4) specific policies and procedures in sensitive areas like recruitment, promotion, use of force, and so on, and (5) the performance of the police in dramatic (often well-publicized) incidents (e.g., the Rodney

King beating). Unfortunately, many citizens are not aware of what the police actually do, and they often expect them to do things they cannot or should not do. In this regard, sharing their expectations with citizens is often an educational process for the citizens.

Where integration of expectations tends to break down is when the police view the sharing of expectations as limited to this educational process. Sharing should work both ways. Some individuals and communities have good ideas and real concerns about police activity and behavior. In police departments across the United States, some officers do things daily that they should not do, such as waste valuable time and engage in inappropriate activities. Often, community expectations or concerns, if listened to, can result in improved police performance. And the community may also have valuable information about how to solve problems and may be willing to get involved in the problem-solving process. Two of the most important problems in community-organization expectation integration are related to the output-outcome relationship and police behavior.

Output-Outcome Relationship

The **outcome goals** of policing include both attitudes and behavior, that is, to reduce crime and disorder while maintaining or improving citizen trust and support. Essentially, the output-outcome relationship is one of cause and effect. What causes individuals to commit crime and to have either positive or negative attitudes about the police?

Conceptually, there are at least four distinct police strategies based on one or more crime causation assumptions (or theories). The **law enforcement strategy** invokes the formal sanctions of government (i.e., stopping suspicious persons, enforcing truancy and curfew laws, issuing citations, conducting investigations and making arrests). The **presence strategy** involves the police being visible, or identifiable, in the community; that is, wearing uniforms, patrolling in marked vehicles, and so on. Both strategies are based on the assumption that offenders calculate the risk of being caught by the police before they act. The higher the perceived risk, the less likely that a crime will be committed. The resource allocation plan of a police department determines the "normal" level of presence, and both the organization and the officer determine the extent to which laws are enforced (i.e., discretion). Higher levels, or the intensification (also called an increase in dosage), of presence and law enforcement are periodically used by the police in high-crime areas (e.g., saturation tactics, crackdowns, aggressive policing, crime control policing); however, this combination of strategies may also have a negative affect on citizen attitudes toward the police because there is an increase in the frequency of police-citizen conflict.

For actual and potential victims of crime, the **education strategy** involves providing knowledge and skills that, if utilized, may reduce the likelihood that individuals will be victimized. Again, this strategy is based on the assumption that offenders compare the risk of being caught with the possible rewards of a successful crime. The more difficult the target (location or person), the greater the perceived risk.

Police departments may also engage in educational activities for prospective and actual offenders (e.g., drug and gang prevention programs). While part of this education process may include a discussion of morality, it almost always includes information about the possible consequences of criminal behavior for both the offender and those they victimize. These consequences include not only those associated with the criminal justice system but also the shame and guilt offenders may feel if family members and friends learn of their behavior. Often, but not always, education programs for offenders come after involvement in the criminal justice system, and they may or may not involve the police.

When police engage in the fourth strategy, ***community building***, they are attempting, along with members of the community, to enhance the informal social controls of that community. The police do this by attempting to involve residents in various activities (e.g., develop a community association, neighborhood cleanup projects) and recreational and social events (e.g., block parties, sporting activities). As community members become more active, they may become more concerned about area problems. If a sense of community develops, it may have a significant influence on the socialization process and the behavior of residents, who may become more watchful and concerned about their neighbors, whom they are less likely to betray or victimize. In addition, the increased interest of citizens enhances both the presence and law enforcement strategies. Citizens who observe and report crime and disorder are an important part of the policing process.

The community building strategy requires that both police officers and managers assume a leadership role in the community. Police officers become managers as they engage in planning, organizing, and controlling activities with citizens, and, at times, with other public and private organizations.

There are problems associated with each strategy, but perhaps most problematic is the "proactive, prediction, pretext, policing process" that may be part of the law enforcement strategy. Reactive police work is the result of a citizen request for police assistance. Being proactive refers to police-initiated citizen encounters (e.g., traffic stop). When using the law enforcement strategy, proactive police work requires that the police have either "probable cause" (to arrest or cite) or "reasonable suspicion" (to temporarily detain for investigation) that a crime or infraction has been committed. An officer may observe (e.g., officer observes the illegal act) or be provided information (e.g., a description of a suspect) that establishes the legal basis for the police intervention.

When police officers engage in proactive law enforcement, they do so because they believe they have evidence that a crime has been committed. Or, they use the law as a pretext to stop individuals they predict are most likely to be involved in criminal activity. In general, the purpose of the stop is to ask the "suspect" questions, run a records check, look inside the automobile (if one is involved) for possible contraband, and obtain consent to search the vehicle.

An officer's decision to stop a "suspicious" person is based on a combination of variables that may include area (level of crime and disorder), time (of year, day, shift), appearance, number of persons, type of automobile (if one is involved), socioeconomic status, race/ethnicity, age, gender, prior knowledge (what the officer may know about the person or persons), public concern about a particular problem, organizational and supervisory expectations, whether the police officer is in a specialized unit designed to respond to certain types of problems (e.g., a gang unit), peer group expectations (i.e., the police culture), and officer variables (e.g., age, education, race/ethnicity, experience).

This use of a legal pretext is a long-standing practice in policing that is sometimes referred to as "getting pc" (probable cause). More recently, the term ***profiling*** has been associated with this practice. A profile is a combination of variables (e.g., age, appearance, gender, race/ethnicity, area, police experience, and so on) that predict individuals who police target with respect to crime-related incidents. Some of the variables used by the police to predict who to stop are more controversial than others. For example, if profiling by the police is perceived to be based primarily, or substantially, on the race or ethnicity, or age or gender, or socioeconomic status of the person stopped, some members of the community become concerned. It is often difficult to determine the extent to which race/ethnicity, or any other democratically sensitive variable, is significant in police decision making and if its use is a result of organizational or personal bias.

This "aggressive" or "crime control" or "crackdown" or "saturation" type of policing, if done frequently enough, may be effective in obtaining substantial but not necessarily permanent, declines in the crime rate; however, it is also likely to result in more citizen resentment and an increase in complaints. This may be the most sensitive issue in managing the democratic-police conflict and in integrating organizational-community expectations. The chapters on police behavior and resource utilization discuss this area in more detail.

Police Behavior

What is a democratic policing style? That is, how should police officers behave when interacting with community members? And how and when should that behavior (or style) change? In police-citizen encounters with suspects, victims, and witnesses, the goal of the officer is to secure information and cooperation without, if possible, using coercive techniques (e.g., implicit and explicit threats, use of some type of nonlethal or lethal force). Based on the initial assessment (potential for difficulty or danger), the officer selects a style and changes, or escalates or deescalates, as the situation changes, that is, as the degree to which cooperation and information are secured.

Which persons and situations are potentially difficult or dangerous? What assumptions are made concerning the risk to officers based on the initial, and subsequent, assessment? If the police stop a "suspicious" person, at night, in a location with minimal visibility, and this person reaches into his or her pocket, retrieves an object and raises his/her hand toward the officer(s), what is the probability that the object is a gun? Is it reasonable for the police to assume that the object might be a gun and respond with deadly force? Or is it more reasonable for the police to assume it is not a gun, and select another alternative (e.g., possibly retreat until the situation is more clearly determined)?

What should the basic democratic policing style be? Friendly? Business-like? Forceful? If cooperation/information is not secured, what style should the officer adopt? And how quickly should the new style be adopted? In general, the range of possible police responses include explanations for police action, asking questions, persuading (reasoning, humor), issuing commands or orders, making verbal threats, some type of hands-on response, use of nonlethal weapons, and use of deadly force. Only a small percentage of police-citizen encounters move beyond the explanation and "asking questions" stage. But if they do, the most critical decision is related to the use of some type of coercion (e.g., threats, force). While essential in some situations, the frequency of the use of coercion by the police is related to citizen attitudes toward the police. The more the police rely on coercive methods to secure information and cooperation, the more likely that citizens will question the legitimacy of the police and their activities. The selection and training of individuals who are both willing and capable relative to the use of coercion (including deadly force), yet are reluctant to do so, is a significant managerial challenge.

To what degree should police managers attempt to control basic style and escalation patterns? To what degree should it be left to the discretion of each officer? The organization attempts to influence style and escalation through training, policy, procedures, and supervision. The police culture is also important in this regard. Deciding when to rely on coercion to achieve goals and how to respond to difficult and dangerous persons is a critical management problem.

Another important subject is police ***discretion***. Police officers exercise discretion when they have the ability to choose from courses of action or inaction (Davis, 1969). More narrowly, it refers to the variables that influence the decisions that police officers make (e.g., arrest, citation, use of force). The comments above about "profiling" suggest that there are a number of possible variables involved in the police decision-making process. The exercise of discretion is critical to managing the police-democratic conflict because it is closely related to the public perception of the extent to which the police engage in preferential treatment or discrimination. Ideally, in a democracy, only one's actual behavior should be the basis for police action, but in reality there are many other variables that are influential (see profiling comments above). Both ***preferential treatment*** (e.g., officers not issuing traffic citations to other officers) and ***discrimination*** (e.g., the poor are more likely to be arrested than the rich) have been, and continue to be, serious problems in policing.

Limited resources and public expectations complicate the effective management of this problem. The police do not have the resources to enforce all laws, nor does the community want all laws enforced. And while citizens usually do not mind receiving preferential treatment, they often do not want it given to others. And no citizen wants to be discriminated against. In this regard, discrimination not only refers to the potential influence on discretion of sensitive variables like race and gender; it also refers to being selectively stopped, cited, or arrested. For example, when the police decide to enforce a law that is rarely enforced (e.g., "jaywalking"), those cited may believe that they are being discriminated against.

Organizational-Individual Expectations

As suggested earlier, in order to establish a high-quality work environment, the individual employee and the organization must strive to cooperate with and complement each other. In other words, what does each party expect from the other? Are their needs and goals similar? Do they feel comfortable with each other? What about the future? An initial sharing of expectations can greatly enhance this discovery process.

If an honest and trustworthy association between individual and organization can be fostered from the beginning, life within the organization is more likely to be rewarding and fulfilling. When the individual and the manager both strive toward the integration of expectations, relationships will improve as sources of discontent decrease because each knows what is expected of the other. Each party is then aware of the adjustments, the give and take, that are necessary for a mutually satisfying association. Simultaneously, many of the dysfunctions that can develop within organizations due to irresponsible or indifferent behavior by either party are diminished.

It may not be feasible to always obtain substantial integration of expectations, but each party should strive to reach this goal. In addition, it is crucial to understand that both conformity and deviance are found within organizations. A certain degree of conflict and deviancy is necessary and desirable for improvement to occur. Lengthy periods of quiet operation could be a sign of organizational stagnation or internal repression of legitimate concerns, which may lead to employee discontent. Continuous improvement in an organization is often the result of conflicting views about how things are currently done. In order to achieve integration of expectations, channels of communication must be opened, allowing for constructive input of deviant or contrary viewpoints. Managers may need to listen carefully to deviant individuals, because they may represent the cutting edge of organizational change.

Three of the most important issues in managing individual-organizational expectations are integrity, competence, and productivity. Each issue is introduced below and also addressed in other chapters.

Integrity

Integrity, or *honesty*, in policing is determined by the various types of standards or guidelines that define appropriate and inappropriate behavior. These include a code of ethics; criminal law and procedure; organizational policies, procedures, rules, goals, and objectives; the values and norms of the police culture, and expectations of the community. Behavior not in accordance with these standards may be considered deviant or inappropriate. Of course, some types of deviant behavior (e.g., accepting payoffs) is more serious than others (e.g., using profanity). But the manager's responsibility is essentially the same if the manager believes a response is necessary. Who is involved? How often does it happen? When does it happen? What are the causes? How can the behavior be changed?

At times, standards are in conflict. The community may have unreasonable expectations concerning how the police should respond, or should have responded, to a person or problem (e.g., shoot to wound rather than to kill). There is also a recurring tension between *ends versus means* in policing. In some instances the police may decide that the ends or goal is so desirable (e.g., obtain a confession), they may utilize illegal means (e.g., psychological or physical coercion) to do so. At times both the community and the police culture value ends more than means.

Even the ethical code of conduct in policing may provide conflicting guidelines for the organization and the officer. Ethical frames of reference can be *formalistic*; that is, demanding strict interpretation of the standards. Or a standard may be *utilitarian*; that is, if the ends are "just," the means used are acceptable. Finally, what is and is not ethical can be considered from a *relativistic* perspective; that is, right and wrong must be judged relative to the cultural context in which the behavior occurs.

Competency

Police competency includes task proficiency, problem-solving ability, and officer style. The competency of police officers can be determined generally (e.g., what all officers should know and be able to do) and specifically (e.g., what individuals in specialized positions (bomb expert, homicide investigator) should know and be able to do. Competency expectations of officers vary by law enforcement agency. Often there is a significant gap between the highly and minimally competent (and incompetent)officers. And the number of officers at each level also varies by agency. In some instances, a police organization may have so many officers who are incompetent, or minimally competent, that police performance is pervasively inept. Officers with significant competence problems are a waste of public resources and a threat to public safety. If a reliable and valid body of knowledge (and skills) is available that will reduce the amount of crime in a community, and a police department, or its officers, is unaware of that knowledge or is incapable of utilizing it, public officials, police organizations, and officers are professionally, if not civilly and criminally, negligent.

Productivity

Another persistent problem in police management is **productivity**; that is, the quality and quantity of the work performed. Like competency, there is often a wide range of acceptable productivity levels in police organizations. Many police departments have serious productivity problems because officers are not competent, not motivated, not effectively managed, and/or not engaged in activities that have the greatest potential to accomplish organizational goals and objectives.

The difference between a police department in which a substantial majority of officers are highly competent and productive, and one that has few, if any, of these types of officers, is substantial in terms of organizational effectiveness. As the level of competency and productivity declines in police organizations, the higher the victimization rate and the greater the degree of citizen dissatisfaction. And as noted above, just as incompetent officers are a waste of public resources and a threat to public safety, so are officers who are not as productive as they could be.

The Art and Science of Management

Is management an art or science or both? **Science** involves the systematic study of a subject leading to a general body of knowledge about the subject. There are different types of science. For instance, if we mean the exact sciences, such as chemistry and physics, then management cannot be considered a science. The research controls characteristic of the natural and physical sciences, in which experiments often take place in a laboratory setting, cannot be applied to the study of management and organizational behavior. This does not mean, however, that managers and researchers cannot conduct valuable research on organizational behavior. It does mean that when dealing with the complexity of organizational life, conducting research is more difficult, and therefore the results are not as exact. The inexact sciences, such as psychology and sociology, have been used to systematically study organizational behavior and to develop general concepts and methods.

Art, as it relates to management, involves the systematic application of knowledge and skill in order to achieve an objective. The key word in this definition is application. Accordingly, managers must apply their knowledge and skills to the attainment of goals and objectives. In management, art and science complement each other. Although management has a well-developed scientific basis derived from the inexact sciences, the integrity, experience, intuition, wisdom, and judgment of each individual are also important. It is the wisdom and intuition of the experienced manager that determine how and when scientific data and analysis should be utilized.

Good police management is the blending of art and science in a continuous effort to arrive at a consensus, which may be temporary, among as many interested parties as possible concerning the activities and behavior of police, without alienating those who are not part of the consensus. In making this effort, managers should emphasize the importance of the rule of law, improve their understanding of how the police can become both more effective and more efficient, and strive to improve the quality of the services provided to employees and members of the community. No one said it was an easy job.

Summary

This text on police management is concerned with the scientific study of police organizations in order to improve performance quality and enhance employee satisfaction. Throughout the book, seven major themes provide a foundation for the study of police organizations and management.

Management is the process of working with people in a humane manner in order to achieve objectives and goals. The process of management—organizing, leading, planning, and controlling—provides a framework for the study of management. Such a study must also recognize the differences between private and public organizations. This distinction is particularly important for the study of police organizations, because they are not only substantially different from private businesses but somewhat different from other public organizations. A discussion of integration of expectations is used to explain some of the unique aspects of managing police departments. Two of the most important issues in integrating community and organizational expectations are the output-outcome relationship and police behavior. Three of the most important issues in integrating organizational and individual (employee) expectations are integrity, competency, and productivity.

Discussion Questions

1. Define the concepts of organization and management. How would you define them differently?

2. Discuss the seven major themes of the book.

3. Do you agree or disagree with the authors that integrity is the single most important factor in policing? Why or why not?

4. Discuss the concept of a clinical scientist and how that applies to police management.

5. Do you think police departments can become learning organizations? What do you think this would involve?

6. Discuss the managerial process, or functions, and what happens at each stage.

7. Explain the differences between outputs and outcomes and between efficiency, effectiveness, and productivity.

8. Do you think police managers should focus more on output or on outcome in policing? Which do you believe is more important? Explain your answer.

9. Define the four basic police strategies. Explain how you would use strategies to accomplish organizational goals.

10. When should the police rely on coercion to accomplish their goals?

References

Allison, G. T. 1983. "Public and Private Management." In *Readings in Public Administration*, R. T. Golembiewski and F. Gibson (eds.), pp. 1-19. Boston: Houghton Mifflin.

Berkeley, G. E. 1969. *The Democratic Policeman*. Boston: Beacon.

Brian, S. 1979. "Incorporating Research into Education for Clinical Practice in Social Work: Toward a Clinical Science in Social Work." In *Sourcebook on Research Utilization*, A. Rubin and A. Rosenblatt (eds.), pp. 132-140. New York: Council on Social Work Education.

Davis, K. C. 1969. *Discretionary Justice*. Baton Rouge: Louisiana State University Press.

Funk, C. E. (ed.) 1953. *Funk and Wagnalls New College Standard Dictionary*. New York: Funk and Wagnalls.

Macy, B. A., and Mirvis, P. H. 1976. "A Methodology for Assessment of Quality of Work Life and Organizational Effectiveness in Behavioral-Economic Terms." *Administrative Science Quarterly* 21: 212-226.

McEwen, T. 1995. "National Assessment Program: 1994 Survey Results." In *Research in Brief*, pamphlet. Washington, DC: National Institute of Justice.

National Institute of Justice. 1995. "Community Policing Strategies." *Research Preview*, November.

Royal Commission on the Police. 1962. *Report*. London: Her Majesty's Stationary Store.

Chapter Two

Development of Management Theory

Although this book is primarily concerned with modern management theory and practice, it is necessary to understand the evolution of traditional views and the manner in which they influence current police-management concepts. Management practices can be traced back five thousand years (George, 1968); however, systematic study and general theoretical advances in the field have been relatively recent, beginning in the late nineteenth century. This chapter will provide a basic understanding of the major theoretical advances in management thought and their influence on police managerial theory and practice.

In describing the development of management theory, the chapter will discuss four major approaches: (1) the classical approach, (2) the human relations approach, (3) the behavioral science approach, and (4) contemporary approaches. Figure 2.1 summarizes the primary contributions and evolution of each approach. It should be noted that although each approach differs in its assumptions about individual and organizational behavior, and therefore about how managers should define and attempt to solve organizational problems, managers can benefit from the theoretical advances and lessons learned from each particular viewpoint.

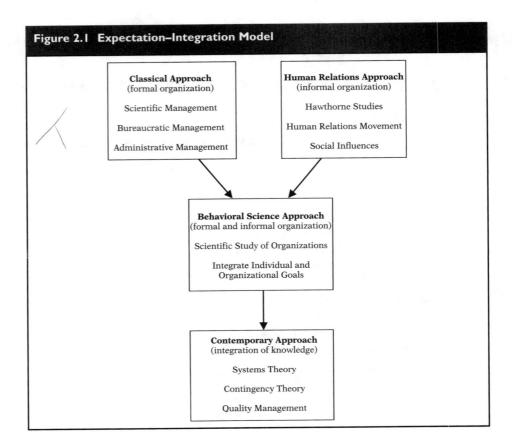

Figure 2.1 Expectation–Integration Model

Classical Approach

The first students of management investigated the anatomy of organizations and subsequently devised certain principles of management that were to be followed if an organization was to operate efficiently. Three primary areas in the development of classical, or traditional, management thought are discussed: (1) scientific management, (2) bureaucratic management, and (3) administrative management (Thompson, 1967).

Scientific Management

The systematic study of complex organizations and their management can be traced to the work of Frederick W. Taylor (1947) and his associates. Taylor began his work in the late nineteenth century and continued into the early twentieth. During this period, inefficiency in large industrial factories was of major concern. Accordingly, Taylor's work focused on methods of increasing worker productivity. He believed that workers were motivated primarily by economic rewards and that organizations should be characterized by a distinct hierarchy of authority comprising highly specialized personnel.

Scientific management sought to discover the best method of performing a specific task. For example, in his studies of the Midvale and Bethlehem Steel companies in Philadelphia, Taylor determined the speed at which workers could load and shovel a certain amount of weight per day. Efforts were then made to find less tiring motions that would allow employees to do more work in a given amount of time with the same degree of fatigue. He believed that if workers were taught the best procedures, with pay tied to output, they would produce the maximum amount of work physically possible, as calculated by *time-and-motion* studies. As a result of this approach, Taylor believed that a worker would acquire a "friendly mental attitude toward his employers and his whole working conditions, whereas before a considerable part of his time was spent in criticism, suspiciousness, watchfulness, and sometimes in open warfare" (Taylor, 1947: 143-144).

With respect to this philosophy, the role of management changed abruptly from the earlier use of a rule of thumb to a more scientific approach, including scientifically selecting, training, and developing workers (in the past, workers trained themselves) and ensuring that all the work would be done in accordance with scientific principles. Thus, scientific management strongly adhered to the formal organization structure and its rules. According to Amitai Etzioni (1964: 20), out of the scientific-management approach came "the characterization of the formal organization as a blueprint according to which organizations are to be constructed and to which they ought to adhere" (1964: 20).

The primary criticism of Taylor's approach stems from his lack of concern for the individual and his over-reliance on economic incentives. Nevertheless, his work added greatly to the knowledge of industrial organizations and set the stage for a more comprehensive view of management theory.

Bureaucratic Management

The concept of bureaucracy is generally associated with the work of Max Weber, who was a major contributor to modern sociology. He studied the effects of social change in Europe at the end of the nineteenth century and coined the term *bureaucracy* to identify complex organizations that operated on a rational basis. Weber believed that such an approach was a means of lessening the cruelty, nepotism, and subjective managerial practices common in the early stages of the Industrial Revolution. For instance, it was standard practice to hire relatives regardless of their competence and to allow only individuals of aristocratic birth to attain high-level positions within government and industry.

It is important to understand that Weber described an ideal type of bureaucracy, intended not to mirror reality but rather to describe how organizations could be structured and managed to become more efficient. Thus, it is not fair to compare Weber's concepts of bureaucratic management with the red-tape syndrome associated with bureaucracy today. His ideal model has the following characteristics:

1. A division of labor based on a "specified sphere of competence."

2. A hierarchy of authority where each lower office is under the control and supervision of a higher one.

3. A specified set of rules applied uniformly throughout the organization.

4. Maintenance of impersonal relationships, because rational decisions can only be made objectively and without emotions.

5. Selection and promotion based on competence, not on irrelevant considerations (Gerth and Mills, 1946: 196-224).

In short, Weber believed that bureaucracy was the most rational means of allowing people to attain private and social goals in a capitalistic society; this approach, however, reflects a highly formalized and impersonal view of management, although it could be considered to be an improvement at the time. It is also not difficult to see similarities with Taylor's theory of scientific management. The major criticism is that employees within the bureaucracy become little more than "cogs in a machine," without much control over their lives.

Administrative Management

While Taylor was concerned with lower-level organizational production and Weber with the structural characteristics of the organization, a third major area of study, known as administrative management, developed during the first half of the twentieth century. It emphasized broad administrative principles applicable to higher levels within the organization. The first major contributor to this area was Henri Fayol, a French businessman, who recognized the need for the development and teaching of management theory and practice: "At present the beginner [manager] has neither management theory nor method, and in this respect some remain beginners all their lives" (1929: 16). In Fayol's most influential work, *Industrial and General Management*, which was published in 1916 (translated into English in 1929 and 1949), he defined fourteen principles of efficient management that he had applied most frequently during his career in the coal and iron industry.

Fayol believed that each of the principles was universal and applicable not only to industrial organizations but also to religious, military, and other types of organizations. He was careful to note that there was no limit to the number of principles that could be developed or to the manner in which they could be applied. Interestingly, he carefully chose the term ***principles*** of management rather than rules or laws in order to avoid any idea of rigidity:

> I shall adopt the term *principles* whilst dissociating it from any suggestion of rigidity, for there is nothing rigid or absolute in management affairs, it is all a question of proportion . . . principles are flexible and capable of adaptation to every need; it is a matter of knowing how to make use of them, which is a difficult art requiring intelligence, experience, decision and proportion. (1949: 19)

Although recent research has found exceptions to his principles under certain conditions, some of which will be discussed in later chapters, in general, these principles are still widely followed today. While such principles cannot be viewed as universal, it is important to understand that Fayol did allow for maximum flexibility in applying them to different organizational circumstances. An adaptation of Fayol's principles is given in Inside Management 2.1.

Inside Management 2.1

Fayol's Principles of Management

1. *Division of Work.* Work specialization can increase efficiency with the same amount of effort. However, there is a limit to how much work should be specialized.

2. *Authority and Responsibility.* Authority includes both the right to command and the power to require obedience; one cannot have authority without responsibility.

3. *Discipline.* Discipline is necessary for an organization to function effectively; however, the state of the disciplinary process depends on the quality of its leaders.

4. *Unity of Command.* An employee should receive orders from one superior only.

5. *Unity of Direction.* There should be one manager and one plan for a group of activities that have the same objective.

6. *Subordination of Individual Interest to General Interest.* The interests of one employee or group of employees should not take precedence over those of the organization as a whole.

7. *Remuneration of Personnel.* Compensation should be fair to both the employee and the employer.

8. *Centralization.* The proper amount of centralization or decentralization depends on the situation. The objective is to pursue the optimum utilization of the capabilities of personnel.

9. *Scalar Chain.* The scalar chain, or hierarchy of authority, is the order of rank from the highest to the lowest levels in the organization; it defines the path of communication. Besides this vertical communication, horizontal communication should also be encouraged, as long as the managers in the chain are kept informed.

10. *Order.* Materials and human resources should be in the right place at the right time; individuals should be in jobs or positions most suited for them.

11. *Equity.* Employees should be treated with kindness and justice.

12. *Stability of Personnel Tenure.* An employee needs time to adjust to a new job and reach a point of satisfactory performance; high turnover should be avoided.

13. *Initiative.* The ability to conceive and execute a plan (through initiative and freedom) should be encouraged and developed throughout all levels of the organization.

14. *Esprit de Corps.* Since "union [unity] is strength," harmony and teamwork are essential to effective organizations.

Adapted from: H. Fayol, 1949. *General and Industrial Management*, translated by C. Storrs. London: Pitman & Sons.

Influential administrative management theorists in the United States included Luther Gulick and Lyndall Urwick, editors of the classic work, *Papers on the Science of Administration* (1937). In this work, Gulick contributed an article that described the major functions of administration by using the acronym POSDCORB—planning, organizing, staffing, directing, coordinating, reporting, and budgeting. In these papers and other works, most notably Urwick's *The Elements of Administration* (1943), the authors expanded the work of Fayol by emphasizing such principles as (1) adhering to the unity of command, (2) making authority commensurate with responsibility, and (3) limiting the span of control.

Administrative theorists believe that by strictly adhering to the *unity of command* principle, which states that an employee should receive orders from one supervisor only (i.e., there should only be one supervisor in charge of each employee), the organization will be under control and operate more efficiently and effectively. In cases where an exception to this principle may occur, the need for written policies is stressed. One example is what is known as *functional control,* in which under certain circumstances (e.g., at the

❖   ❖   ❖   ❖   scene of a homicide) another supervisor, one presumed to have greater expertise in that function (or activity), takes over.

The principle of making ***authority commensurate with responsibility*** simply means that if an employee is assigned the responsibility of accomplishing a given task, he or she must also be given the authority necessary to accomplish the task. For instance, if a detective is given the responsibility of solving a particular crime, authority must be delegated (given) to the individual to make important decisions concerning the direction the investigation will take. As a second example, if officers are given the responsibility of identifying and solving problems on their beats, they must also be given the authority to proceed in a manner they deem the most appropriate, which may include going outside the police or criminal justice system for guidance or solutions.

Span of control is defined as the number of subordinates who report directly to a superior. The classical view has emphasized a small span of control, which allows a supervisor to maintain close contact with and control over all subordinates. Accordingly, Urwick concluded that "no superior can supervise directly the work of more than five or, at the most, six subordinates whose work interlocks" (pp. 52-53).

Classical Police Theory

The early writers of police management theory were heavily influenced by the classical school. This influence is evidenced by the emphasis they placed on Taylor's scientific management stressing increased efficiency, Weber's bureaucracy emphasizing hierarchical authority and control, and the universal principles espoused by the administrative theorists. It is important to understand that in emphasizing classical prescriptions, these early theorists were attempting to create a more professional police organization. The result was a highly bureaucratic structure, managed and organized along classical-military lines in an attempt to insulate the police from partisan politics. This paramilitary model emphasized the law enforcement function and managerial practices intended to control officers' behavior in order to improve crime control and lessen corrupt practices.

Influential writers promoting classical principles as a basis for police management and organizational reform first appeared in the United States in the early 1900s and continued to be influential into the early 1950s. Some editions of the textbooks of these classical writers continued to appear even into the 1990s. Thus, classical ideas, including bureaucratic or paramilitary models and strict authoritarian practices and control, continue to influence police managerial practices and organizational designs to this day.

In general, the classical police theorists differed little in their approaches for improving the police. For example, Fuld's *Police Administration* (1909) emphasized the need to eliminate partisan politics from police management; clearly defined police duties (including the elimination of "nonpolice" functions); and stressed strong supervision and discipline with clear-cut lines of authority, specialization, and improved selection and training of personnel. Fosdick, in his study of 72 American cities, *American Police Systems* (1915), discovered that police departments had not defined their function, had no purpose to their organization, and clearly lacked capable leadership. Smith's

Police Systems in the United States (1940) had a major impact on police reform. It addressed many of the earlier problems of policing, especially partisan politics and the restricted ability of the police to perform their primary function of crime control, but Smith thought that not enough attention had been paid to the administrative structure of police organizations. In later editions, Smith (1960) continued to believe that police organizations could be significantly improved if they were properly designed and supervised according to the "principles of organization," which had won such wide acceptance in military and industrial circles. He paid particular attention to a limited span of control, unity of command, and task specialization.

One significant work is O. W. Wilson's *Police Administration* (1950), followed by later editions with McLaren as coauthor (Wilson and McLaren, 1977). Many of the principles put forth in these texts are still strongly adhered to by police organizations. Like Smith, Wilson and McLaren suggested that an effective crime-control organization should be designed and managed according to "fundamental" organizational principles, including hierarchy of authority, specialization based on need, adherence to the chain of command, a small span of control, and common sense in using the principles (Wilson and McLaren, 1977: 73-86).

V. A. Leonard's highly influential text, *Police Organization and Management* (1951), and subsequent editions with More as coauthor (1993) emphasized the importance of leadership, organization principles, and organization structure. The organizational "principles" of the classical school were compatible with police reformers who felt it necessary to reduce or eliminate the degree of politics and corruption associated with police work. This aim would be accomplished by making police behavior more "objective," or bureaucratic, and thus less "personal" in the political sense.

Human Relations Approach

As the earlier discussion indicates, the classical writers emphasized the formal aspects of organizations while basically ignoring the human aspects. Managers discovered, however, that workers did not always act rationally or follow predicted patterns of behavior. It soon became apparent that the "people part" of management also needed attention. Out of this void grew the **human relations movement,** which emphasized the informal aspects of the organization. Early human relations researchers introduced the scientific method in their studies, which led to a more sophisticated approach to the study of organizational behavior. Later, organizational researchers were more rigorously trained in the behavioral sciences, especially psychology and sociology, and used improved research designs in their studies. This movement toward increased scientific rigor in studying the work environment became known as the behavioral science approach, which is discussed in the following section.

The human relations movement began with the work of Elton Mayo and his colleagues at Harvard University. A series of studies were conducted at the Hawthorne plant of the Western Electric Company from the late 1920s through the early 1930s. The results of these Hawthorne experiments contradicted traditions emphasized by classical theorists and ultimately led to a behavioral approach emphasizing concern for the worker.

The Hawthorne experiments were sparked by an earlier series of studies, known as the ***illumination studies*** (1924-1927), conducted by a group of Hawthorne engineers who were attempting to improve lighting efficiency based on the tradition of scientific management. In one study, an experimental group worked under differing intensities of illumination, while a control group worked under a constant intensity. The researchers believed that the different lighting intensities would significantly affect production; that is, better lighting would lead to increased output. Unexpectedly, it was discovered that as illumination was increased for the test group, both groups increased production. Furthermore, when illumination was decreased, productivity continued to increase. It decreased only after the lighting was dimmed to the extent that the workers could not see properly. This finding suggested that variables other than physical ones, such as lighting, may have had an influence on the increased output.

At this point, Mayo and his colleagues were called in to continue the research. It was hoped that through improved research designs they would be able to determine what variables in the environment were influencing the workers. A second set of experiments took place between 1927 and 1932, the most famous of which was termed the ***relay assembly study,*** in which five women assembling electrical relays were placed in a separate room and observed over a prolonged period. Various working conditions were altered, including increased salaries, shortened workdays, rest periods of varying lengths, and increased participation in decisions. The researchers, who were now acting as alternative supervisors, found that regardless of how they altered the working conditions, productivity increased. They further discovered that productivity continued to increase even after rest breaks were abolished and the original, longer workday was reinstituted. The researchers concluded that increases in productivity were influenced by the complex emotional reaction of the groups and were not related to working conditions.

These results further suggested that when special attention is paid to employees by management, productivity is likely to increase regardless of changes in working conditions. This phenomenon was labeled the ***Hawthorne effect.*** Further research indicated, however, that while the Hawthorne effect had some initial effect, social factors played a more significant role in worker productivity and satisfaction (Roethlisberger and Dickson, 1939: 185-186). Interestingly, it is also likely that the workers viewed the altered supervision (i.e., more attention) as an important positive change in their environment, even though that effect was not intended by the researchers (Adair, 1984).

A final set of studies was conducted between 1931 and 1932; one of these studies is known as the ***bank-wiring room experiment.*** Fourteen workers were observed as a work unit in a separate room for a six-month period. They were paid according to the piece work system, in which their pay depended on the amount of work they produced. Instead of attempting to produce the maximum amount possible, as the classical theorists would have predicted, the group established an output norm for a "proper day's work." In order to be socially accepted by the group, each worker had to stay within the accepted standards set by the group. Workers who overproduced were labeled "rate busters" and those who underproduced were called "chiselers." Throughout the test period, the production averages were surprisingly close to those dictated by the group, suggesting that social acceptance was more important than monetary rewards with respect to productivity.

Although the Hawthorne experiments have been criticized for basic research-design flaws, especially with respect to changing several factors at the same time, they were conducted at a time when behavioral research was just beginning to be applied to organizational behavior. The impact of these studies on the field was enormous; human relationships and informal organization were now considered to be critical factors in properly managing organizations. The major contributions of these studies are summarized below:

1. The level of production is set by social norms, not by physiological capacities.

2. Non-economic rewards and sanctions significantly affect the behavior of the workers and largely limit the effect of economic incentive plans.

3. Often workers do not act or react as individuals but as members of a group.

4. Leadership is important for setting and enforcing group norms, and there is a difference between informal and formal leadership. (Adapted from Etzioni, 1964: 34-38)

Behavioral Science Approach

In order to be classified as a ***behavioral science,*** a field must (1) deal with human behavior and (2) study its subject matter in a scientific manner (Berelson, 1963). The behavioral science approach thus utilizes research according to the scientific method as the foundation for testing and developing theories about human behavior in organizations that can be used to guide and develop managerial policies and practices. The scientific aim is to develop generalizations about human behavior that are supported by data collected in an objective fashion.

As discussed, some of the earliest behavioral science research began with the Hawthorne studies in the mid-1920s. The behavioral science approach did not come into full use, however, until the early 1950s. Behavioral research provided a means for empirically testing earlier theories, as well as increasing scientific knowledge. This research led to the decline of the human relations movement when it was discovered that (1) a satisfied worker was not always the most productive worker, and (2) higher productivity was not necessarily based on work group or managerial relationships but more on the nature of the job itself (Wren, 1979: 475). Consequently, the behavioral sciences were regarded as a more thorough and rigorous approach to the study of human problems in the workplace. According to Wren, the philosophy that replaced human relations "sought to offset the authoritarian tendencies of organizations, to provide for democracy and self-determination at work, to integrate individual and organizational goals, and to restore man's dignity at work" (p. 476).

This philosophy is apparent in the works of such behavioral scientists as Maslow, who developed his hierarchy of human needs in the early 1940s and further extended the theory in *Motivation and Personality* (1954). According to this theory, the needs that motivate people fall into a hierarchy, with lower-

❖ ❖ ❖ ❖   level needs (e.g., physiological and safety needs) at the bottom of the hierarchy and higher-level needs (e.g., for esteem and self-actualization) at the top. Although this hierarchy will be discussed more thoroughly in Chapter 7, it should be pointed out that this work was important because it dramatized to managers that workers have needs other than purely economic ones that are important to them in the workplace. Consequently, if managers want workers who are satisfied and motivated to perform well on the job, they will need to be concerned about more than simply increasing salaries, especially with respect to conditions that relate to higher-level needs. Of course, this concept conflicted with the views of scientific management, which was primarily concerned with pay and lower-level needs.

In *The Human Side of Enterprise* (1960), McGregor defined Theory X and Theory Y assumptions regarding human behavior. Basically, **Theory X** assumes that people have little ambition, dislike work, and must be coerced and threatened with punishment in order to perform satisfactorily. In contrast, **Theory Y** assumes that people do not inherently dislike work and if properly rewarded, especially by satisfying esteem and self-actualization needs, will perform well on the job. These theories are stated as in Inside Management 2.2.

Inside Management 2.2

McGregor's Theory X and Theory Y Assumptions

Theory X Assumptions

1. The average person inherently dislikes work and will try to avoid it.
2. Most people must be coerced, controlled, directed, and threatened with punishment to get them to work toward organizational goals.
3. The average person prefers to be directed, wants to avoid responsibility, has relatively little ambition, and seeks security above all.

Theory Y Assumptions

1. Work, whether physical or mental, is as natural as play or rest, and most people do not inherently dislike it.
2. External control and the threat of punishment are not the only means of bringing about effort toward organizational goals;

people will exercise self-direction and self-control when they are committed.

3. Commitment to goals is a function of the rewards made available (especially rewards that satisfy esteem and self-actualization needs).
4. The average person learns, under proper conditions, not only to accept but to seek responsibility.
5. The ability to exercise a relatively high degree of ingenuity and creativity in the solution of problems is widely, not narrowly, distributed throughout the organization.

Adapted from: D. McGregor, 1960. *The Human Side of Enterprise*, pp. 33-34, 47-48. New York: McGraw-Hill.

McGregor thought that managers who believe in Theory X will set up strict controls and attempt to motivate workers strictly through economic incentives. Consequently, employees are likely to respond in an immature manner that reinforces the manager's assumptions. By contrast, managers who believe in Theory Y will treat employees in a mature way by minimizing controls, encouraging creativity and innovation, and attempting to make work more satisfying with respect to satisfying higher-order needs. Under such conditions, McGregor thought that workers would become committed to organizational goals and perceive them as the most effective way to achieve their own goals, thereby integrating their goals with those of the organization. Although he realized that some workers are relatively immature and dependent and might need greater controls for a while, he believed that if managers switched to Theory Y assumptions, they would improve work environments and performance.

Extensive research on diverse organizations by Likert (1967) has concluded that a managerial system stressing Theory Y assumptions tends to make better use of human resources and enhances both the effectiveness and efficiency of the organization. Both Maslow's needs hierarchy and McGregor's Theory X and Theory Y approach helped managers to develop a broader perspective on workers and the work environment, especially regarding alternative ways of interacting with workers and of recognizing the potential impact of higher-level needs in job performance.

Behavioral Police Theory

Beginning in the early 1970s, police behavioral theorists began to attack the classic police bureaucracy with its emphasis on hierarchical structure, authoritarian managerial practices, and narrow view of the police role. In line with the behavioral research findings of the 1950s and 1960s, which placed a greater emphasis on worker participation and job satisfaction, these theorists stressed a more democratic approach to police management, a more flexible and less hierarchical structure, and recognition of the complex nature of the police role.

By the 1960s, considerable research indicated that the majority of police work was not directly related to law enforcement but rather to maintaining order and providing social services. Although much of this research had methodological problems in defining law enforcement as distinct from maintaining order, it nevertheless provided the impetus for a new perspective on police work by suggesting that strict adherence to a law enforcement and technical approach to the job would not be effective. In short, effective policing required qualified personnel who could ***use discretion wisely*** to deal with a broad range of complex problems and situations.

These findings had serious implications for the ***paramilitary model*** that had become well entrenched in policing. As Bittner noted, "The core of the police mandate is profoundly incompatible with the military posture. On balance, the military bureaucratic organization of the police is a serious handicap" (1970: 51). Bittner viewed the proper use of discretion as central to the professional development of the police role, and he believed that over-reliance on regulations and bureaucratic routine seriously inhibited such development. Furthermore, he suggested that while the paramilitary model helped to secure internal discipline, it continued to hinder the development of the police role, because "recognition is given for doing well in the department, not outside where all the real duties are located" (pp. 54-55). In other words, attention to a neat appearance and conformance to bureaucratic routine is more highly regarded than work methods and performance in the community (i.e., interacting and dealing with the public).

Reiss (1971) also pointed out that bureaucratic structures pose problems for the exercise of professional discretion. These problems are exacerbated for the police, who operate in what he refers to as a command bureaucracy, because they are expected to obey all the bureaucratic rules while exercising professional discretion. As he notes, "A typical line policeman is expected both to adhere to commands and be held responsible for all discretion exercised in the line of duty" (p. 124). In response to these criticisms, Angell (1971) proposed a ***democratic model*** of policing to replace the traditional bureaucratic arrangements. The basic structure of the democratic model is not hierarchical and has no formal ranks or supervisors. Police officers are generalists who work in teams and have considerable flexibility in work assignments; they specialize only when the need arises. The teams are expected to work closely with the communities they serve in solving problems. Such an organizational model emphasizes a broad service role for the police and is concerned about employee job satisfaction.

Along these same lines, Goldstein (1977) suggested that the ***organizational climate*** in police departments must change if the objective is to retain highly qualified (and educated) officers and thus operate properly in a democratic society. Police officers should be more involved in policymaking and in determining methods of operation. They should have greater opportunities to realize their full potential in ways other than promotion. Although Goldstein agrees that a movement toward a more collegial organizational model is in order, he does not believe that a police department should be run as a democracy. He emphasizes that some situations, such as mobilizing a large number of officers to deal with an emergency, will always require authoritarian management practices. Furthermore, he does not think that police administrators should commit themselves to a participatory style of management under all conditions. What is called for, according to Goldstein, "is not a substitution of some radical new style of management but, instead, a gradual movement away from the extremely authoritarian climate that currently pervades police agencies toward a more democratic form of organization" (p. 264).

The "extremely authoritarian climate" noted by Goldstein had become a common characteristic of many police departments by the 1960s. The police were criticized for discriminatory behavior and ineffectiveness in responding to crime, and they were also considered to be using inappropriate management practices. It was suggested that there was even a connection between authoritarian management practices and authoritarian police behavior. Consequently, the human relations and behavioral science bodies of knowledge gradually began to influence the police and help them to understand the importance of increased employee involvement in decision making, of recognizing a broader police role, and of working in partnership with the community. However, this new knowledge and the required managerial skills were not always readily embraced by the police, and in some instances they are still not.

Contemporary Approaches

Influenced by the increased sophistication of behavioral science, theorists have attempted to integrate the knowledge gained from the earlier schools of thought. Such an integrated framework is provided by the relatively recent developments of systems theory and contingency theory and the movement toward quality management. Systems theory provides a broad conceptual base from which to study organizations, whereas contingency theory provides a more specific framework for analyzing organizational behavior. These theories provided a foundation for the quality approach, which attempts to establish a climate of steady progress for organizational systems through continuous improvement. Each of these approaches is briefly described below.

Systems Theory

Systems theory simply means that all parts of a system are interrelated and interdependent to form the whole. According to Luthans (1976):

> A system is composed of elements or subsystems that are related and dependent upon one another. When these subsystems are in interaction with one another, they form a unitary whole. Thus, by definition, almost any phenomenon can be analyzed or presented from a systems viewpoint. There are biological, physical, economic, and sociological systems, and also systems found in organization and management. (p. 16)

Although systems theory is being used to study organizations, it is interesting to note that it was actually developed to study biological and physical systems. From a manager's perspective, it is necessary to utilize systems theory in order to view organizations as a whole and to understand that the actions of one part affect the actions of other parts. In other words, managers must be aware that any changes made in their unit will have a corresponding impact on other units. Thus, managers throughout an organization must continually be in contact with one another to ensure that the activities of their units are in congruence with the overall needs and goals of the organization.

Figure 2.2 illustrates the interrelated and interdependent nature of several subsystems within a police department (depicted by the two-way directional arrows), indicating that the actions of any part of a subsystem affect and, in turn, are affected by the other parts of the system. In this figure, the impacts of the training, communications, and patrol divisions on one another are depicted. For instance, if a department decided—for purposes of increased safety and limited officer liability—to adopt a more restrictive pursuit policy, this decision would have a significant impact not only on how officers are trained but on dispatch and patrol procedures as well. In other words, in order to effectively implement such an important policy change, all three divisions would need to alter their policies, which, in turn, would have an impact on each of the other's operational practices.

Systems can be viewed as either open or closed; a system is *open* if it interacts with its environment and *closed* if it does not. The concept of open and closed, however, is not an absolute but a relative matter. All organizations interact with their environment, but the degree of interaction varies. Essentially, those systems that are more open function more effectively due to their environmental adaptability. For municipal police departments, their environment is the community in which they operate; those departments that are relatively more open (i.e., interact with the environment) are more effective because they are aware of community needs and expectations, and thus can adapt their practices accordingly. An open systems model, represented by the broken lines indicating that the system's boundaries are permeable and thus interactive with the environment, is shown in Figure 2.3.

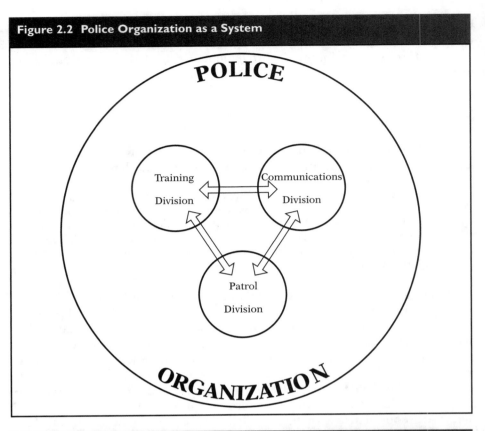

Figure 2.2 Police Organization as a System

Figure 2.3 Police Organization as an Open System

This illustration indicates that an open system interacts with its environment by importing energy (inputs), transforming it into usable products or services (through-puts), then exporting them back into the environment (outputs). In the case of police organizations, the energy inputs from the environment are in the form of money, personnel, material, information, and so on. This environmental input is subsequently transformed and used within the system in the form of hiring and training of officers, purchasing such materials as patrol cars and computers, and processing information such as complaints, calls for service, and communications from neighborhood groups. These outputs, or "products," are then exported back into the environment in the form of police services to the community, such as giving citations and making arrests. And, as noted in Chapter 1, there are also outcomes (results) of police outputs, such as changes in the fear of crime, citizen attitudes, and crime rates.

Figure 2.3 further depicts a feedback loop in which the system processes information inputs from the environment. Open systems maintain a steady state of *homeostasis,* (or internal stability), by processing this information and adapting their behavior accordingly; the information may be either positive or negative. If negative, the system will adapt in order to remain in harmony with its environment and maintain a steady state. Examples of environmental feedback for the police include public opinion, political demands, complaints, and criminal and other statistics. How negative feedback is handled by police departments, through such efforts as policy changes or patrol practices, greatly determines their success (homeostasis) in the community.

Clearly, from this description, open systems theory is significant to management; that is, it provides an analytical approach to the *interactive nature of a system and its environment*. If police organizations are not studied and managed from an open systems perspective, they cannot adapt to changing environmental influences and forces, especially community expectations and needs, thus leading to ineffective or certainly less effective levels of operation. When this happens, the organization will inevitably be forced to change, as external critics make demands that ultimately cannot be ignored. For example, Zhao (1996) indicated that changes in community policing strategies are more likely to be forced on departments by external environmental demands rather than by consciously chosen internal demands (see Chapter 15 for discussion).

Contingency Theory

The systems approach emphasizes the importance of the interrelationships between the parts of the organization and between the organization and its environment. However, because systems theory incorporates natural and biological systems, as well as organizational systems, its concepts are abstract and in general cannot always be applied to specific situations. Contingency theory utilizes this same perspective but attempts to define important relationships—both internal and external to the organization—that affect organization design and managerial practices.

Managers and researchers who discovered that certain methods and practices are effective in one situation but not in others developed what is known as the *contingency approach.* For example, why does a certain leadership style or job design work in one type of organization but not in other types or in one part of an organization but not in other parts? The answer is simply because situations differ, and a managerial method or technique that is effective in one situation may not be effective in other situations. In other words, there are no universal principles that can be applied in all circumstances.

The contingency approach recognizes that many internal and external environmental variables affect organizational behavior. Because these variables differ according to particular situations, there is no one best way for structuring and managing diverse types of organizations. Consequently, the underlying theme of the contingency approach is that *it all depends* on the particular situation. The task for managers then is to determine in which situations and at what times certain methods or techniques are the most effective.

Contingency management attempts to determine relationships between internal and external variables that are relevant to the organization and, based on the findings regarding the nature of the relationships, recommend appropriate managerial practices and organization designs. In this way, contingency theory is more pragmatic with respect to organizational behavior than systems theory, while still incorporating systems concepts. Because the contingency approach allows for the most appropriate managerial practices or methods to be applied according to the situation, it can encompass relevant concepts of both classical and behavioral theories.

Theory Z and Quality Management

Important emerging perspectives in the continual attempt to improve managerial practice include Theory Z and quality management. William Ouchi, in his book *Theory Z* (1981), focused on aspects of Japanese management practices that may be appropriate for adoption in the United States. On the one hand, the success of Japanese companies sparked an interest in this country regarding styles of Japanese management. To this end, Ouchi described the *Theory Z approach* as including job security for workers; participatory decision making, group responsibility, teamwork, and informal controls; increased quality of products and services; slow evaluation and promotion policies and broader career paths; and a greater concern for employees' work and nonwork welfare, including the family. More recently, some of these tenets (especially job security) have been severely challenged by the economic downturn and uncertainties of the Japanese economy.

On the other hand, many American organizations, both private and public, still cling to the classical bureaucratic approach, which emphasizes exactly the opposite types of characteristics as those listed above. Ouchi contends that a movement in the direction of Theory Z characteristics, and a greater commitment to long-term relationships with employees, goals, and quality, can substantially improve organizational effectiveness and worker satisfaction.

Interestingly, the foundation for much of the Theory Z approach started with the ideas of Joseph Juran and W. Edwards Deming, both of whom were invited to teach statistical quality control techniques to the Japanese to help them revitalize their industries following World War II. Juran's research in this area indicated how breakthroughs can be achieved through a process of *continuous improvement,* and that approximately 85 percent of quality problems are under management's control. Deming's work with quality efforts was so highly revered that it was awarded the Deming Prize, the highest honor for Japanese improvement. He later developed the Fourteen Points, listed in Inside Management 2.3, to guide total quality transformation through the continuous improvement of manufacturing, including service, quality, and productivity.

Inside Management 2.3

Deming's Fourteen Points for the Transformation of Management

1. Create constancy of purpose toward improvement of product and service.
2. Adopt the new philosophy of concern for quality.
3. Cease dependence on mass inspection to achieve quality; build quality into the product in the first place.
4. End the practice of awarding business on the basis of price alone. Move toward a single supplier for any one time and build a long-term relationship of loyalty and trust.
5. Constantly improve the system of production and service so that quality and productivity improve and costs decrease.
6. Institute training on the job.
7. Institute leadership. The aim of supervision should be to help people and machines do a better job.
8. Drive out fear, so that everyone may work effectively for the company.
9. Break down barriers between departments so that people work as a team.
10. Eliminate slogans, exhortations, and targets for the work force. Such exhortations only create adversarial relationships, as the major causes of low quality and productivity can be traced to the system and thus lie beyond the power of the work force.
11. Eliminate work standards (quotas) and numerical goals (MBO). Instead, substitute leadership and the processes for improvement.
12. Remove barriers that rob workers of the right to take pride in their work, including abolishment of individual performance appraisals and annual merit or ranking systems. Instead, change the emphasis from sheer numbers to quality.
13. Institute a vigorous program of education and self-improvement.
14. Take action to accomplish the transformation. Put everybody in the organization to work on the transformation.

Adapted from: W. Edwards Deming, 1986. *Out of the Crisis.* Cambridge: M.I.T., Center for Advanced Engineering Study.

Together, the theories of Ouchi, Juran, and Deming form the basis for what has become known in the United States as *quality management* or *total quality management (TQM)* (Milakovich, 1991). First introduced in the private sector, this approach has spread rapidly to the public sector as well—including the police. It is currently estimated that approximately 25 percent of governmental agencies use TQM in at least one functional area of management (West, Berman, and Milakovich, 1994).

Quality management is *customer oriented* and emphasizes the importance of both *human resources* and *quantitative methods* in an attempt to strive toward continuous improvement. In order to maximize the use of human resources, TQM stresses the importance of employee participation, teamwork, and continuous learning and improvement. The quantitative dimension involves the use of the scientific method and statistical techniques to evaluate and improve the processes in an organization and to link those processes to results.

In general, in order to implement TQM, an organization needs to do the following:

1. Create a constancy of purpose and commitment toward the continuous improvement of all processes, products, and services.

2. Use systems and scientific thinking.

3. Develop and use effective leadership instead of management by control.

4. Create an environment where people can be creative, take risks, and experience pride of workmanship, accomplishment, and self-fulfillment.

5. Create an organization of honest and open communication, both vertically and horizontally.

6. Be customer oriented. (Greebler-Schepper, 1990: 7)

Contemporary Police Theory

Police theorists began applying systems theory to the study of police organizations in the early 1970s. Among the first writers to incorporate ***open systems*** theory to policing were Whisenand and Ferguson (1973). They suggested the following reasons for viewing police organizations as open social systems:

> (1) [T]he increased complexity and frequency of change in our society, and (2) the limitations of . . . both the classical and neoclassical [human relations] theories viewed an organization as a *closed* structure. Such nearsightedness produces an inability to recognize that the organization is continually dependent upon its environment for the inflow of materials and human energy. Thinking of an organization as a closed structure, moreover, results in a failure to develop a feedback capability for obtaining adequate information about changes in environmental forces and goal accomplishment. (p. 166)

Whisenand and Ferguson further stated some "specific and compelling" reasons why a police organization should consider itself an open system:

1. A police department can be thought of as either a system (a single agency) or a subsystem. If viewed as a subsystem, it is involved in a complex set of interfaces with other subsystems external to its boundary, such as the district attorney, parole agencies, and the courts. This systems approach effectively helps us to cross boundaries and to identify, establish, and make use of significant interrelationships of various organizations.

2. Police organizations are becoming aware of the limitations of simplistic research. The systems approach allows us to synthesize and utilize research of other relevant fields.

3. A systems approach provides a new perspective on the internal operations and environmental relationships of police organizations.

4. The systems approach relies greatly on empirical data or hard facts. The data include facts not only on a particular police department but also on the processes, interactions, goals, and other characteristics of all organizations (public and private) that exert an influence on it.

5. An important benefit of the systems approach is that it is intended to be action oriented. That is, data are gathered because

they are instrumental in fulfilling a set of objectives or in solving a problem. (p. 167)

Later, Munro (1974) noted that in spite of a substantial amount of money being spent on the police since the mid-1960s, few tangible results could be noticed except in terms of an "escalated police armaments race and an explosion in (largely nonessential) police technology" (p. 9). Munro suggests that this lack of change is due in large part to two factors: (1) refusal by politicians and police to see the law enforcement function in systems terms and (2) the continued employment of an authoritarian and antidemocratic philosophy of management by police departments.

Munro recognized the necessity of viewing the police not only from the perspective of a larger social system but as a part of the **criminal justice system** as well. "The social scientist or managerial analyst," he suggests, "is faced with rather specific consequences resulting from the systematic nature of criminal justice" (p. 12). He notes that it is crucial to view the police in terms of other system elements:

> If the police chief orders a crackdown on drunk drivers, what are the likely consequences for prosecution, the courts and corrections? Very possibly it may result in flooding with work those other components of the criminal justice system so badly that the ends of good administration, let alone justice, cannot be served. It is the responsibility of the analyst to predict such results of policy or management change. The predictions have little chance of accuracy if the implications of system have been ignored. (p. 12)

In the late 1970s, Roberg (1979) applied **contingency theory** to policing. He emphasized contingency concepts and the necessity of identifying both internal and external variables that affect police organizational behavior. Accordingly, such factors as increasing levels of employee education, cultural and gender diversity, and the relatively unstable nature of the environment (e.g., constantly changing laws, multicultural populations, political influences, etc.) must be considered in attempting to determine the most appropriate managerial practices and organization designs. It has become obvious that when such factors are considered, "many of the simplistic classical prescriptions which have been applied to police organization design are clearly inadequate" (p. 190). It was concluded that a less bureaucratic, centralized design was necessary for police to perform effectively.

In the late 1980s, the use of a private-sector process, known as **corporate strategy**, was applied to policing by Moore and Trojanowicz (1988). They suggested that like private-sector managers, police managers should define "the principal financial and social goals the organization will pursue, and the principal products, technologies, and production processes on which it will rely to achieve its goals" (p. 2). A corporate strategy is developed through a process that examines how the organization's capabilities fit the current and future environment; this is accomplished by examining both internal and external environmental demands, then defining the best strategy to meet them. The authors admit that the development of a corporate strategy is a complex matter, but they note that such strategies can be captured in relatively simple phrases or slogans. For example, they cite the mission of the U.S. Environmental Protection Agency (EPA) as "pollution abatement" and the goal of the Federal Trade Commission (FTC) as "the largest public interest law firm in the U.S." Many examples of police departments redefining their corporate strategies through new mission and value statements will be given in the following chapters. Such statements often include terms and phrases dealing with community partnerships, dignity and sensitivity, problem solving, and the provision of quality services.

As noted previously, it has been estimated that about 25 percent of governmental agencies use TQM to some degree (West, Berman, and Milakovich, 1994); with respect to policing, in a survey of approximately 200 Texas police managers, Hoover (1996) indicated that various components of TQM were being utilized. For instance, he measured three primary concepts: (1) culture (i.e., are lower-level employees empowered, is there teamwork and cooperation, are rewards equitable, is there a sense of work ownership?); (2) customers (i.e, are services to the customers measured with respect to what they want, including surveys and complaints?); and (3) counting (i.e., are quality-versus-quantity indicators of police productivity being measured, such as problem solving versus arrests?). He found that the departments were making reasonable application of culture principles, moderate application of customer-orientation techniques, and sparse application of measurement efforts. Thus, although quality-management concepts are being implemented, work remains (especially with respect to implementing quality-performance measures) if police departments are to improve substantially.

Because of its emphasis on quality service to customers (citizens) and attention to continuous improvement, quality management should prove useful to police departments in the transition to community policing. Possibly the first department to utilize quality-management principles for this purpose was in Madison, Wisconsin. In *Quality Policing: The Madison Experience* (Couper and Lobitz, 1991), the police chief of Madison at the time (Couper) and a colleague have written about the experiences of this department's change away from a highly traditional, bureaucratic organization toward a quality-oriented organization. The principles of quality management, or what the authors call "quality leadership," used by this chief in transforming the department are listed below in Inside Management 2.4.

Inside Management 2.4

Principles of Quality Leadership in Madison

1. Believe in, foster, and support teamwork.
2. Make a commitment to the problem-solving process, use it, and let data (not emotions) drive decisions.
3. Seek employees' input before making key decisions.
4. Believe that the best way to improve work quality or service is to ask and listen to employees who are doing the work.
5. Strive to develop mutual respect and trust among employees.
6. Have a customer orientation and focus toward employees and citizens.
7. Manage on the behavior of 95 percent of employees, not on the 5 percent who cause problems; deal with the 5 percent promptly and fairly.
8. Improve systems and examine processes before placing blame on people.
9. Avoid "top down," power-oriented decision making whenever possible.
10. Encourage creativity through risk taking, and to be tolerant of honest mistakes.
11. Be a facilitator and coach; develop an open atmosphere that encourages providing for and accepting feedback.
12. With teamwork, develop with employees agreed-upon goals and a plan to achieve them.

Source: D. C. Couper and S. H. Lobitz, 1991. *Quality Policing: The Madison Experience*, p. 48. Washington, DC: Police Executive Research Forum.

The process that the Madison Police Department went through in chang-ing from a highly traditional police organization toward a quality-oriented organization, emphasizing participation and teamwork, was a very time-consuming and demanding effort. It took approximately nine years from the initial "quality" action (Couper and Lobitz, 1991) and about twenty years from the start of the change process in the department (Wycoff and Skogan, 1993) to reach a state of general implementation of community policing and quality management. If traditional, paramilitary departments are to imple-ment similar significant changes, that is exactly the type of effort they must be willing to put forth. The Madison experience yielded several important themes that can be used as guidelines in this change process: (1) the need for a department to be committed to achieving quality results in a new program; (2) the realization that a department is never a static entity—it must con-stantly measure and respond to the need for change; and (3) the importance of a proactive response to both the department's internal community and its external customers (p. vi).

A national study of police middle managers' receptivity to the principles of reinventing government—that is, improving organizational performance through reorganization, downsizing, and TQM, was undertaken by Vito and Kunselman (2000). As some may remember, *Reinventing Government* (Osborne and Gaebler, 1992) was on the *New York Times* best-seller list and influenced the National Performance Review spearheaded at the federal level by then Vice President Al Gore. The middle managers represented municipal, county and state agencies, including 16 sergeants, 13 lieutenants, three cap-tains, and two corporals.

The top-ranked idea selected from the concept of **reinvention** by the mid-dle managers (66 percent) was **community-owned government**, or empow-ering communities to participate in government agencies and ensure accountability of programs to community-based groups. The second most popular idea (54 percent) was **customer-driven government**, that is, empow-ering citizens as customers to participate in government agencies (e.g., through the use of surveys and other forms of feedback to the department). The third most popular idea was **decentralized government**, or empowering workers to be responsible and accountable in decision-making processes and program procedure. These findings indicate that the elements of reinvention that reflect the ideals of community policing were supported, particularly the empowerment of citizens to establish a partnership with the police to improve service delivery and decentralization of decision making to line per-sonnel in order to improve job satisfaction and organizational efficiency. Whereas additional research is necessary to determine how far-reaching these findings may be, it appears that the ideals of community policing may be reaching police middle management.

The development of policing models and the transition of police organi-zations moving toward community policing strategies is the focus of the fol-lowing chapter. It describes four models of policing, places them in historical context, and explains the reasons for transition from one model to the next.

❖ ❖ ❖ ❖ **Summary**

It is important to understand the development of management thought and its impact on current managerial practices. There are four major approaches: classical, human relations, behavioral science, and contemporary. The classical approach emphasized the formal aspects of organizational behavior. The human relations approach emphasized the informal aspects of the organization. The use of the behavioral sciences to study organizations led to the realization that to manage effectively, both formal and informal aspects of organizational behavior must be understood, including the need to integrate individual and organizational goals. Contemporary theoretical developments have attempted to integrate and utilize the knowledge gained from the earlier approaches, including an understanding of the relative importance of systems theory and contingency theory, Theory Z, and quality management principles, to the study and management of complex organizations. Each of the four major approaches was first discussed from a general managerial perspective, then in relation to the development of police management. Early police theorists were strongly influenced by the classical approach, emphasizing strong hierarchical control, a "professional" orientation, and an emphasis on law enforcement activities. In the human relations and behavioral sciences approaches, police scholars began to stress the need for less authoritarian approaches to management, including the recognition of the complex nature of the police role. Contemporary approaches to police management have taken into consideration both systems theory and contingency theory and have utilized corporate strategies, total quality management (TQM) practices, and reinventing government concepts in order to move toward community-policing concepts.

Discussion Questions

1. Describe the contributions of the scientific, bureaucratic, and administrative areas to the development of classical thought on management.

2. Describe the contributions made by the following classical theorists: Frederick W. Taylor, Max Weber, Henry Fayol, O. W. Wilson, and V. A. Leonard.

3. Discuss the impact of classical police theory on police management practices.

4. Describe the Hawthorne experiments and their contribution to the human relations movement.

5. What effect did behavioral police theory have on traditional police management?

6. Discuss the importance of viewing police departments and their management from an open systems perspective.

7. Discuss how contingency theory might be applied to police management.

8. Briefly describe what is meant by corporate strategy and how it applies to the police.

9. Briefly define Theory Z and quality management approaches.

10. How do you think current police practices have been affected by contemporary police theory?

❖ ❖ ❖ ❖

References

Adair, J. G. 1984. "The Hawthorne Effect: A Reconsideration of the Methodological Artifact." *Journal of Applied Psychology* 69: 334-345.

Angell, J. E. 1971. "Toward an Alternative to the Classic Police Organizational Arrangements: A Democratic Model." *Criminology* 9: 185-206.

Berelson, B. (ed.) 1963. *The Behavioral Sciences Today*. New York: Basic Books.

Berrien, F. K. 1976. "A General Systems Approach to Organizations." In *Handbook of Industrial and Organizational Psychology*, M. D. Dunnette (ed.). Chicago: Rand McNally.

Bittner, E. 1970. *The Function of the Police in Modern Society*. Washington, DC: U.S. Government Printing Office.

Burns, T., and Stalker, G. M. 1961. *The Management of Innovation*. London: Tavistock.

Couper, D. C., and Lobitz, S. H. 1991. *Quality Policing: The Madison Experience*. Washington, DC: Police Executive Research Forum.

Deming, W. E. 1986. *Out of the Crises*. Cambridge, MA: Center for Advanced Engineering Study.

Etzioni, A. 1964. *Modern Organizations*. Englewood Cliffs, NJ: Prentice Hall.

Fayol, H. 1929. *Industrial and General Management*. C. Storrs (trans.). London: Pitman & Sons.

Fosdick, R. 1915. *American Police Systems*. Montclair, NJ: Patterson Smith.

Fuld, L. 1909. *Police Administration*. New York: Putnam's.

George, C. S. 1968. *The History of Management Thought*. Englewood Cliffs, NJ: Prentice Hall.

Gerth, H. H., and Mills, C. W. 1946. *From Max Weber: Essays in Sociology*. New York: Oxford University Press.

Goldstein, H. 1977. *Policing a Free Society*. Cambridge, MA: Ballinger.

Greebler-Schepper, C. 1990. "Total Quality Management: The Road to Continuous Improvement," pamphlet. Lucerne, CA: TQM Plus.

Gulick, L. 1937. "Notes on the Theory of Organization." In *Papers on the Science of Administration*, L. Gulick and L. Urwick (eds.). New York: Institute of Public Administration.

Gulick, L., and Urwick, L. (eds.) 1937. *Papers on the Science of Administration*. New York: Institute of Public Administration.

Hoover, L. T. 1996. "Translating Total Quality Management From the Private Sector to Policing." In L. T. Hoover (ed.), *Quantifying Quality in Policing*. Washington, DC: Police Executive Research Forum.

Kast, F. E., and Rosensweig, J. E. 1985. *Organization and Management: A Systems and Contingency Approach*, 4th ed. New York: McGraw-Hill.

Leonard, V. A. 1951. *Police Organization and Management*. Brooklyn: Foundation Press.

Leonard, V. A., and More, H. 1993. *Police Organization and Management*, 8th ed. Westbury, NY: Foundation Press.

Likert, R. 1967. *The Human Organization*. New York: McGraw-Hill.

Luthans, F. 1976. *Introduction to Management: A Contingency Approach*. New York: McGraw-Hill.

Maslow, A. H. 1954. *Motivation and Personality*. New York: Harper & Row.

McGregor, D. 1960. *The Human Side of Enterprise.* New York: McGraw-Hill.

Milakovich, M. E. 1991. "Total Quality Management in the Public Sector." *National Productivity Review,* Spring: 195-211.

Moore, M. H., and Trojanowicz, R. 1988. "Corporate Strategies for Policing." *Perspectives on Policing.* Washington, DC: Department of Justice.

Munro, J. L. 1974. *Administrative Behavior and Police Organization.* Cincinnati, OH: Anderson.

Osborne, D., and Gaebler, T. 1992. *Reinventing Government: How the Entrepreneurial Spirit Is Transforming the Public Sector from Schoolhouse to State House, City Hall to Pentagon.* Reading, MA: Addison-Wesley.

Ouchi, W. 1981. *Theory Z.* New York: Avon.

Reiss, A. J. 1971. *The Police and the Public.* New Haven, CT: Yale University Press.

Roberg, R. R. 1979. *Police Management and Organizational Behavior: A Contingency Approach.* St. Paul, MN: West.

Roethlisberger, F. J., and Dickson, W. J. 1939. *Management and the Worker.* Cambridge, MA: Harvard University Press.

Smith, B. 1940. *Police Systems in the United States,* 2nd ed. New York: Harper.

Taylor, F. W. 1947. *Scientific Management.* New York: Harper & Row.

Thompson, J. D. 1967. *Organizations in Action: Social Science Bases of Administrative Theory.* New York: McGraw-Hill.

Urwick, L. 1943. *The Elements of Administration.* New York: Harper & Row.

Vito, G. F., and Kunselman, J. 2000. "Reinventing Government: The Views of Police Middle Managers." *Police Quarterly* 3: 315-330.

West, J. P., Berman, E. M., and Milakovich, M. E. 1994. "Implementing TQM in Local Government: The Leadership Challenge." *Public Productivity and Management Review* 17: 175-192.

Whisenand, P. M., and Ferguson, R. F. 1973. *The Managing of Police Organizations.* Englewood Cliffs, NJ: Prentice-Hall.

Wilson, O. W. 1950. *Police Administration.* New York: McGraw-Hill.

Wilson, O. W., and McLaren, R. 1977. *Police Administration,* 4th ed. New York: McGraw-Hill.

Wren, D. A. 1979. *The Evolution of Management Thought,* 2nd ed. New York: Wiley.

Wycoff, M. A., and Skogan, W. G. 1993. "Community Policing in Madison: An Analysis of Implementation and Impact." In *The Challenge of Community Policing,* D. E. Rosenbaum (ed.). Thousand Oaks, CA: Sage.

Zhao, J. 1996. *Why Police Organizations Change: A Study of Community-Oriented Policing.* Washington, DC: Police Executive Research Forum.

Chapter Three

Police Models and Community Policing

CHAPTER OUTLINE

What is the police role in a democratic society? What is the most effective means of implementing this role? What should the police do and how should they do it? The attempts made to answer these and related questions have resulted in four different approaches to, or models of, policing. A police model identifies the characteristics of police management, activities, and practices during a general time period. To be as effective as possible, managers need to understand each model and the reasons for the transition from one model to the next. Although no model is completely applicable to any one police organization, models are a useful device when attempting to communicate important changes in policing. Such significant change is usually the result of the perception that the police are in some type of crisis (e.g., crime increases, corruption, and brutality). As noted in Chapter 1, a failure-reform cycle is a recurring theme in police history. Those reform recommendations that gain the most political, public, and police support gradually change many police departments until another failure-reform cycle begins and a new "model" emerges.

❖ ❖ ❖ ❖   **Models of Policing**

This section briefly traces the historical development of local policing in the United States and identifies four models that have emerged in response to attempts to define the police role in democratic society. The modern era of policing began between the 1830s and the 1850s, when paid daytime police forces were created and integrated with existing forms of law enforcement, notably the nightwatch. The first departments provided a force of officers in one organization, available twenty-four hours a day, to prevent and respond to crime and disorder problems and to provide community services (Lane, 1967; Miller, 1977; Johnson, 1981).

These new police departments, established in Boston (1837), New York (1844), and Philadelphia (1854), were loosely based on the model of the London police that emerged in 1829. This model, designed by Robert Peel, Charles Rowan, and Richard Mayne, emphasized prevention more than apprehension. Prevention was to be accomplished by dispersing police throughout the community so they would be visible in order to keep crime and disorder from occurring and to respond when they did.

The Political Model

In the first stage of the development of modern policing, until the 1920s, policing was dominated by politics. In the political model, politics influenced every aspect of law enforcement, including who was employed, who was promoted, arrest practices, where police worked, and the services they provided. Policing was decentralized and neighborhood oriented, and officers had a great deal of discretion in enforcing the law. Standards of enforcement often varied within cities, and local politicians played a more important role in determining enforcement priorities than did the chief of police. An officer's authority tended to be personal, because officers often had a close relationship with citizens, who expected to be able to influence how officers exercised their discretion (Miller, 1977). In addition to crime prevention and law enforcement, the police also functioned as all-purpose community workers (e.g., health officers, probation officers, and providers of food and shelter to the needy).

By the 1890s, as cities began to grow larger and became more difficult to manage, the politically dominated, often corrupt, police departments (and other local governmental organizations) came under increasing criticism. Over the next several decades, new ideas began to emerge as to how the police role and police departments should be changed. Studies conducted early in the twentieth century (Fuld, 1909: Fosdick, 1915; and Graper, 1921) found that police departments were poorly organized and haphazardly managed. Recommendations made for changing police departments and management practices were based on classical management theory (discussed in Chapter 2).

In 1929, President Herbert Hoover established the National Commission on Law Observance, also known as the Wickersham Commission after the man who headed the investigation. The commission identified the most important problems in law enforcement: excessive political influence, inadequate leadership and management, police lawlessness and brutality, ineffective recruitment and training, and insufficient use of the latest in science and technology. By 1931, it was widely accepted that these were the problems that needed to be addressed in police work (Walker, 1977: 128-134).

After the Wickersham Commission, there was at least the beginning of a national consensus concerning the direction for the professionalization of police. The reform themes that were to characterize law enforcement for the next several decades included (1) organizational centralization, (2) professional standards of behavior and the development of policies and procedures, (3) more education and training, (4) selection and promotion based on merit, (5) commitment to the goal of fighting crime, and (6) the use of the latest in science and technology.

The Reform Model

These reform themes provided the foundation for the professionalization of law enforcement, and a legalistic approach to policing began to dominate thinking about police work. The *reform model* (also called the professional, administrative, bureaucratic, traditional, or legalistic model) was based on the belief that the police should use the standards of the law and organizational policy as a basis for decision making and should not be unduly influenced by politics or personal considerations. Fighting crime (which meant serious crime as defined by the newly created Uniform Crime Reports) was considered to be the most important purpose of the police, and the most meaningful measures of police effectiveness were rapid response to calls, the number of arrests made and citations issued, and the crime rate. Important administrative innovations were introduced during the reform model such as civil service examinations (to eliminate political patronage), routine motor patrol, a quasi-military organizational model, the police academy, and standardized training. Many of these characteristics continue to exist today.

Changes in policing were instituted to make the police more predictable and accountable in their delivery of services. By making policing in America more uniform, police reformers sought to decrease the corruption and scandal that plagued the political model. As such, the police became more reactive than proactive. With the advent of the telephone and car radios, it was easier for citizens to call the police and for police managers to reach officers. Consequently, the "dial a cop" era of policing began. This change also meant that police departments began to concentrate primarily on incidents of crime rather than crime problems (i.e., groups of similar incidents) and their associated conditions.

By the 1960s, however, these reform ideas began to be questioned. Some critics argued that the police were so separated from the political processes in the community that elected officials and community members had little to say about how police functioned in the community. In their desire to overcome historic problems with political corruption and abuses of authority, the police had become isolated and too bureaucratic in their responses to citizen needs. The bureaucratic structures that existed in many departments, as noted above, were the result of the use of classical managerial principles. Criticisms of this approach to management were based on ideas from the human relations school of management and systems theory (see Chapter 2).

The concept of police isolation also became important as a basis for reform. The phrase "we vs. they" became common in characterizing the isolation problem. With the advent of the motor vehicle, police officers did not have to interact with citizens in the same way as they did in the political era. The windshield became a symbolic and actual barrier between the police and the public. Even though there have been few systematic attempts to define and measure this isolation (the extent to which it existed or actually influenced police activities), it remains an important factor in the development of subsequent police models. Police reformers who characterized isolation as a problem were attacking the cornerstone of the reform model—namely, that impersonal and impartial law enforcement is necessary if the police are to be compatible with a democratic society. The character of Joe Friday from the popular television series *Dragnet* provides a good example of the impersonal, "Just the facts, ma'am" relationship between the police and citizens.

Critics also argued that the police emphasis on fighting crime was inappropriate, because they spent little time actually responding to serious crime problems (Fogelson, 1977). There was also some doubt concerning the effectiveness of this approach in reducing the crime rate. The extent to which police engage in fighting crime has long been in dispute because of the controversy surrounding how certain activities should be classified. Certain common police activities, such as patrolling, responding to crimes without making arrests (e.g., incidents of domestic violence), and writing reports about criminal incidents and their investigation, can be placed in either crime-fighting or noncrime-fighting categories. Consequently, it is possible for advocates of reform to argue that the police are not crime fighters, whereas defenders of the status quo can argue just the opposite. Nevertheless, the belief that the police spent a minimal amount of time fighting crime resulted in recommendations that the police adopt more of a social-service orientation.

Even though the reform model sought to make policing on the street-level more predictable, variations remained between police departments regarding priorities. Wilson (1968) notes local police have three core functions: law enforcement, service, and order maintenance (or peacekeeping). He compared the police practices of eight police departments and found variation in how officers exercise discretion. Priorities were a function of the local political culture and the desires of the community. Officers in **legalistic style** departments interact frequently and formally with members of the public, and officers are more likely to make an arrest or issue a citation whenever possible. The priority for officers in these departments is law enforcement. Officers in **service style** departments are likely to intervene frequently with citizens, but avoid invoking the law. As such their priority is providing the community with a variety of service activities. Finally, officers in **watchman style** departments do not interact frequently with citizens, and are least likely to initiate encounters with citizens. The priority of officers in watchman style departments is order maintenance. **Order maintenance** is a tactic used by officers to eliminate disorderly behavior without actually applying the law; the officer may use warnings or counsel instead of arrest. Varieties of police behavior will become more important in the discussion of community policing.

Examples of police activities from the political era (e.g., the friendly, neighborhood foot-patrol officer and social programs) were used to buttress the claims of those who wanted to change the crime-fighting emphasis of the reform model. Unfortunately, many of the friendly neighborhood cops of the political era were lazy, corrupt, brutal, and racist; and there was no real evidence that the police had a close relationship with citizens who trusted and respected them. In addition, public expectations of the police and the definition of and tolerance for inappropriate police behavior were different in the late nineteenth and early twentieth centuries from what they are today.

These and other criticisms of the police were the result of three important historical developments; urban riots, the civil rights movement, and the perception of an increasing crime rate. As minorities, and later women, became increasingly active in trying to raise their status in society, and as people began to be more concerned about crime, the police became one focal point for criticism. By the mid-1960s, this concern was so great that two other national commissions were established, in part, to address problems concerning the police. These were the President's Commission on Law Enforcement and Administration of Justice, established by President Johnson in 1965; and the National Advisory Commission on Civil Disorders, established by Johnson in 1967.

The Service Model: Policing in Transition

Since the late 1960s, attempts to change the police have been a blend of the suggestions that emerged during the reform era and those that are part of what the authors call the ***service model.*** The political era of policing saw the police and the public interacting in a manner that critics considered to be inefficient and corrupt. The reform era produced reforms that critics considered to be too bureaucratic and confrontational, a relationship that was made worse by police isolation from the community. In effect, citizen concerns were subordinated to the desire to professionalize the police. A police officer was supposed to be honest, technically competent, and impartial, although no one knows how many officers actually possessed these characteristics.

Changes took place in the service period in three areas: policy development, selection and training, and organization and management.

Policy Development. In the area of policy, the primary concern was about the way police officers exercised their discretion, particularly the use of force. Gradually, many departments began to develop guidelines for training officers in the use of appropriate methods. Other policy concerns were civil disturbances, crimes in progress, hostage situations, domestic violence, and drug enforcement.

Selection and Training. In the area of selection, attempts were made to make selection (and promotional) procedures more valid and to employ more women and minorities. Accordingly, selection procedures had to become job related. For example, a police department could not require that a prospective officer had to be at least 5 feet 8 inches tall, unless it could be shown that only those or taller individuals could perform required tasks. Likewise, a police department could not require applicants to do pushups or take a certain type of test, unless it was related to the knowledge and skills required to be a police officer (see Chapter 5).

Employment of more women and minorities was based, in part, on the belief that by becoming more diverse, the police would be able to provide better services to women and minorities. It was also hoped that more minority officers would reduce the hostility that existed between police and some minority groups. The police have a long history of attempting to match the persons being policed with officers who, by virtue of similar backgrounds and experiences (e.g., Irish for Irish, blacks for blacks, and so on), may have both greater understanding and more community acceptance. However, it was not until the 1970s that increasing diversity of personnel became a significant reform strategy.

In the area of training, programs for officers became longer and there was more of an emphasis on human relations. In addition, many additional types of training programs for the police were developed (e.g., supervision and management). There was also a rapid increase in the number of college-level criminal justice programs during the 1960s and 1970s; however, many of these programs were oriented toward education (i.e., emphasizing the theoretical and analytical) rather than training (i.e., focusing on skill development).

Organization and Management. In terms of organization and management practices, many changes were attempted, but not all were successful. Three of the most important were community relations programs, crime prevention, and team policing. Although the community relations programs were intended to improve relations between police and citizens, they were often ineffective. Too many police departments used them to explain police policies and practices rather than as means to learn more about community problems and what citizens wanted the police to do about them. In addition, many police officers did not believe that it was their responsibility to be concerned about community relations; rather, it was the responsibility of assigned "specialists."

Team Policing. This was one attempt to apply modern management practices to police departments. It was based on two important principles, decentralization and increased participation. In the reform model, police departments tended to be highly centralized, and neither employees nor citizens were encouraged to become actively involved in determining how police activities should be carried out. The consequence is further isolation of officers from the community. Rather, how police activities should be carried out was considered the responsibility of police executives. Team-policing experiments involved assigning a small group of officers to one area of a community. These officers, as a group (and in consultation with citizens in some experiments), were to identify the most important neighborhood crime and related problems and what to do about those problems. In many ways, modern community policing grew from early experiments with team policing. Team policing and community policing share common components, including a neighborhood focus, decentralized decision making, community input, and a change in the role of the police (Walker, 1993).

Crime prevention also became more important during this period. In many police departments before the 1960s, crime prevention was limited to juvenile delinquency problems. By the late 1960s, police often used crime prevention as a public relations tactic to improve their status in the community. By the mid-1970s, however, police departments began to educate the public about what individuals could do to protect themselves and their property (such as marking their property for identification purposes). Over the next several years, crime prevention began to be more community oriented as police departments began to institute such programs as "block watch," which encouraged residents to become the eyes and ears of the police (Rosenbaum, 1988).

Team-policing experiments in many departments were soon abandoned, primarily because police supervisors and middle managers were not comfortable with decentralized decision making—that is, they did not like to share power with either subordinates or citizens. In addition, some officers not assigned to the experiments were resentful because they either did not understand the program or because team-policing officers appeared to have less work to perform. When police departments create specialized units not dedicated to specific crime issues, the units are usually criticized by other officers, often resulting in conflict and hostility.

The concern about improving community relations, the development of crime prevention programs, and experiments with team policing and other managerial approaches, along with other changes in policy and selection and training, were all part of the service model of policing. These attempts, along with a growing body of research-based knowledge about police activities and behavior, gradually led to the emergence of a new form of policing.

The Community-Policing Model

There is no accurate way to measure the impact of either the reform or service models of policing—that is, how many police departments changed and to what degree. It is clear, however, that many police departments were influenced by the reforms associated with each model. Despite such changes, in the 1970s and 1980s, some police, political leaders, and academics continued to be concerned about the role, effectiveness, and behavior of the police. These concerns tended to focus on (1) how the police should be evaluated, (2) the impact of increased research on the police, (3) how to manage police resources more strategically, (4) how to improve relations with minority groups, and (5) the role of community in responding to crime.

Police Evaluation. In the early 1980s, Wilson and Kelling (1982) argued that the quality of community life should be an important consideration for the police. Their "broken-windows" theory suggests that once a neighborhood is allowed to run down, it can, in a short period of time, become an "inhospitable and frightening jungle." At the same time, research on the fear of crime suggested that citizen fear is more closely associated with neighborhood disorder (e.g., vandalism, graffiti, juvenile gangs, run-down and abandoned buildings, abandoned cars, and so on) than the crime rate (Kelling and Moore, 1988).

One obvious implication was that the police should begin considering not only the crime rate as a measure of their effectiveness but also citizen fear of crime. To do this, however, the police would have to broaden their role to focus on quality-of-life matters, as defined by citizens. According to critics, the police would have to change their crime-fighting orientation, which usually meant emphasizing serious crimes, putting more emphasis on minor violations (e.g., jaywalking, littering, traffic violations, and so on), keeping order, community organizing, and community satisfaction. To that end, they would have to expand both the community relations and crime prevention activities associated with the service model and in some instances, continue or increase strict law enforcement practices (e.g., saturate certain areas, or "hot spots" of crime, with officers, give numerous citations, conduct field interrogations, and make as many arrests as possible).

These aggressive types of law enforcement have long been part of the police response to crime, dating back to the political model. At present, they are variously referred to as proactive policing, saturation, assertive policing, aggressive patrol, and crackdowns. Some critics of police believe that when the police advocate closer ties with the community, while continuing to engage in aggressive enforcement activities, they become the "iron fist in the velvet glove." This characterization is intended to describe what these critics consider to be the implicit deception of strict enforcement cloaked in community concern (Center for Research on Criminal Justice, 1975).

Police Research. Many of the recommendations for changing the police that have been made since the 1970s were the result of the increasing amount of research into policing practices. During the 1960s, the federal government took several steps that created an innovative climate in law enforcement. In addition to the two major national commissions mentioned earlier, the federal government created the Office of Law Enforcement Assistance (OLEA) in 1965 and passed the Omnibus Crime Control and Safe Streets Act in 1968. This act increased funding for OLEA, which became known as the Law Enforcement Assistance Agency (LEAA). From the late 1960s through the 1970s, hundreds of millions of dollars were invested to improve the criminal justice system (Caiden, 1977: 56-59).

The most important impact on the police was the large number of research studies that produced new knowledge about police methods and effectiveness. In addition, LEAA (now called the National Institute of Justice) made grants and loans available to encourage individuals to pursue higher education. With this increase in students came an increase in faculty members, who also contributed to the growing body of knowledge about the criminal justice system.

The body of knowledge about the police during the reform era was based largely on the experience of such police managers as August Vollmer and O. W. Wilson (discussed in Chapter 2). By the 1970s, such knowledge was being challenged by data derived from systematic research. For decades, the reform model of policing relied on three primary tactics for preventing crime (referred to as the 3 R's of policing): ***Routine patrol***, ***rapid response*** to most citizens' request for services, and ***reactive investigations*** by detectives. Studies cast doubts on the effectiveness of each of these tactics. Although many of these studies had flaws, the research raised questions concerning the manner in which police invested their resources and the activities in which they engaged.

Strategic Management. In the 1970s and 1980s, the demand for police services increased. Although the police had modified their responses somewhat as part of the service model, they still emphasized visible police patrol, investigation and apprehension, and rapid response to calls, particularly if a serious crime was involved. However, as demand increased, the police could not keep pace, so they had to search for alternative methods to respond to crime problems and citizen concerns. Not only were the traditional methods being overburdened, but their very effectiveness was being questioned. Concern about the effective and efficient use of police resources, the new

research that questioned traditional police methods, and suggestions that ❖ ❖ ❖ ❖
police consider methods other than law enforcement methods to solve problems resulted in attempts to apply strategic management concepts to the police.

Strategic management involves the identification of organizational goals along with the most effective and efficient manner to achieve them. Police departments are not necessarily required to utilize patrol and investigations as their primarily methods; rather, they should be free to experiment with alternative approaches. Departments that adopt this philosophy have the responsibility to determine the nature of policing in a democracy, alter or modify goals as the environment of policing changes, and determine (through systematic research and analysis) how to best achieve those goals.

As applied to the police, strategic management asks such questions as the following:

1. What are the fundamental purposes of the police?

2. What is the scope of their responsibility?

3. What is the range of possible contributions they can make to society?

4. What are the distinctive competencies of the police?

5. What are the most effective programmatic and technical means for achieving their purposes? (Moore and Trojanowicz, 1988)

Instead of assuming that the police role is essentially predetermined, strategic management is based more on a contingency and systems view of organizations. It adopts the perspective that the police have a distinctive part to play in society, but this part and the manner in which police play it are variable over time and in different communities. As a community resource, the police can do many things in many different ways. Strategic management is simply a flexible approach to determining what those things should be and what ways are most effective and efficient.

Minority-Group Relations. Historically, one of the most persistent and compelling problems confronting the police is their relationship with minority groups. Depending on the time period, "minority group" could mean Irish Americans, Italian Americans, Hispanics or Latinos, African Americans, Asian Americans, Native Americans, gays (and lesbians), and other groups. The police have had a long history of discriminating against members of minority groups, whose communities and neighborhoods have often been plagued by serious crime and disorder. Numerous civil disturbances in the United States have been precipitated by police behavior considered to be inappropriate by minority groups.

The reform model of police saw the relationship with the community as bureaucratic and consequently was not considered to be sufficiently responsive to minority concerns. The service model attempted to be more responsive by diversifying the police force, experimenting with team policing and establishing community relations programs. Although this approach improved police relationships with minorities, minority concerns about police behavior remained high.

In the 1980s, the public became increasingly fearful of crime, especially violence, gang activity, and drug use as alarmingly portrayed by the media.

Many police departments became more legalistic, proactive, and assertive. They tended to rely on aggressive patrol, field interrogations, citations, arrests, and increased undercover activities. These approaches, applauded by many minority leaders, also increased the tension between police and minority citizens, particularly African Americans and Hispanics. The perception that some police officers were brutal racists became widespread. In fact, this perception was often accurate, particularly as it applied to police use of excessive force. However, the degree to which such behavior was racially motivated or willful was much more difficult to determine.

The movement toward community policing has been seen by many law enforcement leaders and academics as a way to reduce tension between minority citizens and the police. Community policing has a broader orientation than community relations programs and is intended to be a department-wide strategy that emphasizes the "co-production of public safety." The police and the public are to become partners in determining the police role and identifying solutions to quality-of-life problems, such as crime and physical and social disorder.

Community and Crime. Community theories concerning crime suggest that social order is more the result of informal social processes in the community than anything the police might do. This idea underscores the importance of involving citizens in responding to disorder, crime, and related problems. It also emphasizes the greater use of informal or neighborhood solutions and other community agencies, such as those for health, recreation, and counseling, to address problems. Because the police have considerable resources and expertise, they should assume a leadership role in motivating citizens to become involved and in coordinating the responses of other agencies. Eck and Rosenbaum (1994) describe this perspective as one of "community engagement" in which the police "help to create self-regulating, self-sufficient communities where levels of crime and disorder are contained by the efforts of local residents and local institutions" (p. 8).

Community Policing

The reform model provided the framework for police professionalism. The service model emphasized well-defined policies to guide officer discretion, a more diverse work force, improving community relations, investing more resources in crime prevention, new approaches in the organization and management of police departments, and a broader role for the police. Taken together, these changes resulted in the police role gradually being directed away from criminal law enforcement toward social service and community problem solving, or simply ***community policing***.

There has been considerable research and discussion concerning community policing. Many police departments have long had what they considered to be a community policing philosophy or programs, but they did not necessarily see their approach as an integral part of the police role, nor did they use it as a basis to reform individual police organizations. There remain a number of complex issues associated with community policing. This section will discuss some of these issues; the next section will provide examples of community policing programs.

Community Policing in Practice ❖ ❖ ❖ ❖

It has been suggested that community policing is the preferred strategy in modern American policing, and police agencies throughout the country report widespread implementation of community policing activities (Office of Community Oriented Policing Services, 1997). This may be partly due to federal support from the 1994 Violent Crime Control and Law Enforcement Act (Cordner 1995; Maguire, Kuhns, Uchida, and Cox, 1997). Hickman and Reaves report in 1999 there were 113,000 community policing officers in state and local agencies, up from 21,000 in 1997. They also state that in 1999 64 percent of local police departments (serving 86 percent of all residents) had full-time officers engaging in community-policing activities, compared to only 34 percent of local police departments (serving 62 percent of all residents) in 1997. Despite this, several fundamental questions remain, namely "What is community policing?" Is it a strategy of policing? Is it a vision of the future for the police? Is it a department-wide orientation or only a specialized programmatic appendage? How does community policing impact officers on the street? How does community influence middle managers (e.g. sergeants, lieutenants, and captains)?

According to Trojanowicz and Bucqueroux (1992: 4-6), community policing (1) is a philosophy, not just an isolated program; (2) involves a permanent commitment to the community, including "average" citizens; (3) broadens the mission of the police beyond crime control; (4) provides full-service, personalized, and decentralized policing; (5) focuses on problem solving; (6) enhances accountability; (7) uses both reactive and proactive policing; and (8) must operate within existing resources. Community policing requires officers to perform new duties and learn new skills. Listed below are some of the possible "duties and activities" of a community officer:

1. Performs law enforcement duties common to police patrol assignments.

2. Attempts to build an "atmosphere of mutual respect and trust" in order to develop a partnership among citizens to identify and prioritize problems related to crime, drugs, disorder, and fear.

3. Shares information with other officers in the department.

4. Identifies and analyzes problems using problem-solving techniques.

5. Educates community members about crime prevention methods and engages in community building by organizing citizens and recruiting volunteers to assist the police in responding to, and solving, problems.

6. Mediates, negotiates, and resolves conflict among citizens and between police and citizens.

7. Visits homes, businesses, and schools to provide information about community policing.

8. Provides assistance to groups with special needs, such as the homeless, battered women, juveniles, elderly, and the disabled.

9. Is concerned not only about crime and fear of crime but about neighborhood decay and the residents' quality of life.

10. Networks with both public- and private-sector organizations to obtain support and cooperation in neighborhood projects.

The Community Policing Consortium described community policing as involving two key components: community partnerships and problem solving. The Community Policing Consortium (1994: vii) indicated

> Community policing is, in essence, a collaboration between the police and the community that identifies and solves community problems. With the police no longer the sole guardians of law and order, all members of the community become active allies in the effort to enhance the safety and quality of neighborhoods.

As will be described below, the two key elements (to a lesser or greater extent) that are present in all forms of community policing include: police-citizen interaction and cooperation, and the use of problem-solving efforts to reduce or alleviate crime-related community problems.

Community policing attempts to build trust between officer and citizen and change each one's perception of the other. The best way to convince citizens that "police are fair and responsive is through personal contacts . . . by plac[ing] police employees in close prolonged contact with the same group of residents . . . to reduce the physical and psychological distance between the police and the community" (Rosenbaum, 1994: 11).

Brown (1989) has also attempted to define community policing by identifying important characteristics of its philosophy and the benefits that, in his opinion, are likely to result for both the community and the police. Inside Management 3.1 identifies and briefly explains the important characteristics of community policing and its possible benefits.

Inside Management 3.1

Characteristics and Possible Benefits of Community Policing

Characteristics

1. The **results** of policing are as important as the process. Police obtain results by emphasizing the identification, analysis, and resolution of problems.

2. Police **values** emphasize citizen involvement in matters that directly affect the safety and quality of neighborhood life.

3. The police must be **accountable** to each neighborhood in a community. Often, neighborhoods have different concerns, desires, and priorities. Officers must routinely interact with residents and keep them informed of police efforts to fight and prevent neighborhood crime.

4. Police departments must be **decentralized.** Police officers must be allowed to participate in important decisions. A police department may also establish a "mini-police station" in certain areas of the city.

5. Police departments **share power** with the community in a partnership to identify and solve problems. Power sharing requires that

citizens take an active rather than a passive role because they have a great deal of information that is useful to the police.

6. The boundaries of **beats** (areas, sectors, or districts) are redesigned to coincide with natural neighborhood boundaries rather than the needs of the police department.

7. Officers are given **permanent assignments** in terms of both their beat and their time shift. An officer should be assigned for at least six months, possibly several years, to the same neighborhood.

8. Beat officers are **empowered** (i.e., given the responsibility and authority) to initiate creative solutions to neighborhood problems.

9. The role of **supervision and management** changes. Patrol officers become "managers" of their beats, while the supervisor becomes responsible for helping the patrol officer to identify and solve problems. Managers are responsible for obtaining the resources and support necessary to solve problems.

10. Police **training programs** change. At the re-

cruit level, officers are provided with information about the complexities and dynamics of the community and how the police fit into the larger picture. New officers are taught organizing skills and leadership skills, as well as how to identify and diagnose problems.

11. ***Performance evaluation*** is based on an officer's ability to solve problems and to involve the community in crime fighting and neighborhood safety.

12. The ***management of calls for service*** changes from only responding to each incident to trying to determine the reasons why such incidents occur and if they are related to a broader problem. Police responses to less serious incidents may change to phone reports instead of going in person, so that officers may spend more time solving problems.

Benefits to the Community

1. The police make a commitment to prevent crime rather than just react to it.
2. Public scrutiny of the police is improved, because more citizens know what police do and why.
3. Police officers are accountable for their behavior not only to the department but also to citizens.

4. Police services will be tailored to the needs of each neighborhood.
5. As citizens become more involved in police activities, the community will become more organized and therefore more effective in responding to problems.

Benefits to the Police

1. The police will receive greater community support.
2. The police will be able to share the responsibility for the control of crime and disorder with citizens.
3. Police officers will have greater job satisfaction because they will be able to see the results of their efforts at problem solving.
4. The communication and cooperation among units (e.g., patrol and investigations) in the police department will be enhanced.
5. Police departments will have to reexamine their organizational structure and managerial practices.

Source: Adapted from Lee P. Brown. 1989. "Community Policing: A Practical Guide for Police Officials." In *Perspective on Policing*, Pamphlet No. 12. Washington, DC: National Institute of Justice.

As a department-wide philosophy that provides the foundation for the strategic use of police resources, community policing answers the three most fundamental questions about the police: Who decides what the police role in a community will be? What is that role? What competencies are required in order to fulfill that role? Who decides this police role is essentially a political question; community policing is based on the assumption that citizens will have substantial input in deciding such a role. Going further, it suggests that the police must act as community leaders in each neighborhood to ensure that a discussion about the police role takes place.

The role the police are to play depends on what the community wants, as long as it is not illegal, based on the citizens' ideas along with the expertise provided by the police. As a practical matter, the police often have more input than do citizens, but at least citizens are given the opportunity to participate. In some situations, citizens may have more information about community crime and disorder problems than do the police. Although the police may be reluctant to listen, that is precisely what they must do. Flexibility in using resources and solving problems is an important part of this community policing.

In practice, there have been at least three community-policing approaches used by police departments. The styles of community policing presented below draw heavily from those described by Greene (2000), though at times the terminology may vary. These styles include neighborhood building, problem-oriented policing, and broken windows policing. These are "pure" types of community policing, and certainly hybrids of these approaches exist within the same police department. Figure 3.1 provides a visual description of the three themes of community policing. Notice that each theme is distinct from one another, but at the same time there exists overlap between the three strategies. Regardless of the dominant approach adopted by the police department, each may be referred to generally as "community policing." Police organizations often emphasize one of these community-policing themes in much the same way police departments in the 1960s identified themselves with one of the core roles of law enforcement, service, and order maintenance (Wilson, 1968).

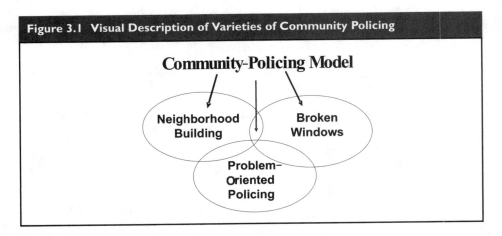

Figure 3.1 Visual Description of Varieties of Community Policing

Neighborhood Building

Neighborhood-building policing involves increasing the rapport between police and citizens, and these groups work together to increase the quality of life within the area. Crime prevention is certainly a key component, but other issues addressed involve victim assistance and reducing fear of crime. The key component of neighborhood building, which differentiates it from other styles of community policing, is the police *empower* community members to take stock in and invest in their community. Citizens are encouraged to take an active role in community development through informal social control. Mastrofski, Worden and Snipes (1995: 540) describe the style in this way:

> The police strengthen citizens' capacity and resolve to resist crime and recover from it. This requires positive relationships with those "invested" in the neighborhood. Crime prevention and victim assistance do not involve law enforcement directly. To the extent that a community policing program concentrates on community building, it deemphasizes law enforcement activities.

Communication regarding policing priorities is horizontal in that police and citizens enjoy equal input. Success is measured through quality-of-life indicators, including fear of crime, livability of the neighborhood, citizen satisfaction with police and other government services, and of course crime rates. Police attempt to contribute to the local neighborhood, which can increase community cohesion. The idea is that as informal social control increases, there is less emphasis on law enforcement or formal social control. Key dimensions of neighborhood building and other policing themes are presented in Table 3.1.

Table 3.1. Comparison of Key Dimensions of Reform-Model Policing and Community Policing

Dimension	Reform-Model Policing	Community Policing Model		
		Neighborhood Building	Problem-Oriented Policing	Broken-Windows Policing
Focus	Law enforcement (primarily)	Crime prevention, victim assistance, rapport building with racial minorities & increasing informal social control	Reducing underlying problems that cause fear, disorder and crime	Aggressive enforcement of public order problems & minor crimes
Activities	Reactive; narrow & crime focused	Proactive; broad & quality-of-life focused	Mixed; broad & criminal, civil remedies through problem solving, SARA	Proactive; narrow & focused on place or behavior
Locus of decision making	Police, minimizes involvement of others	Co-produced between police & citizens	Varies, may involve other government agencies	Police, based on information from community
Communication flow	From police to community	Horizontal; police & community equal partners	Horizontal; police & community equal partners	From police to community
Type of organization and command focus	Centralized command & control	Decentralized in the community	Decentralized with local accountability	Varies, but with internal focus
Implications for organizational change	None	Many, dynamic focusing on community	Varies, focus on problem resolution	Few, limited interventions based on traditional activities
Measurement of success	Arrest and Part I crime rates	Varies, quality of life indicators (fear of crime, calls for service, community cohesion)	Varies, number of problems solved without displacement	Arrests for order crimes, location-specific reductions in target activity, serious crime rates

Adapted from: J. R. Greene, 2000, Community Policing in America: Changing the Nature, Structure and Function of the Police. In Criminal Justice 2000, Volume 3: Policies, Processes and Decisions in the Criminal Justice System, p. 311. National Institute of Justice: Washington, DC. and S. D. Mastrofski, R. E. Worden and J. B. Snipes, 1995, "Law Enforcement in a Time of Community Policing," in *Criminology*, vol. 33, p. 539-540.

The types of activities in which police engage varies, and the decision making is done through a partnership with community residents. Officers may initiate neighborhood clean-ups, eliminating graffiti and other social disorder, "take back the night" initiatives, neighborhood watch programs or block watch programs, which are staffed primarily by residents. Unfortunately there is little empirical evidence that neighborhood watch programs alone have an impact on crime. Rosenbaum (1988: 356), upon conducting an exhaustive analysis of current research on community crime prevention, comments that there is "little evidence that increased social interaction will lead to decreased crime." However, he goes on to comment that such an approach may be effective if initiated as part of a broad-based effort at reducing crime and disorder and not as a single program. Police may work with

Community Based Organizations (CBOs) in formulating these broad-based programs. CBOs are likely to be found in areas that are structurally disorganized and have high levels of violent and property crime (Smith, Novak and Hurley, 1997). Lindsay and McGillis (1986), conducting research in Seattle, found the incidences of some crime (such as burglaries) were reduced in areas where citizens and police participated in broad-based crime prevention programs.

Management in police departments exercising neighborhood building is different than the management of reform era. Both management and officer discretion are decentralized, meaning supervision and activities must vary from neighborhood to neighborhood. This is important, since no two areas may require the same police services. Officers are required to cultivate relationships with local residents. Officers must not only be free from responding to calls for service, but there is also less direct supervision of officers by mid-level managers.

Problem-Oriented Policing

Goldstein (1979) recommended that the police begin to think more in terms of problems than of incidents; they should, in some circumstances, change from an incident-based response strategy to a problem-oriented strategy (e.g., viewing a group of incidents as a potential problem). Goldstein argued that officers should not only try to determine the relationship between incidents that might be occurring in the same family, building, or area but also consider alternatives other than law enforcement to try to solve problems. Such alternatives might include various crime prevention strategies, using civil law to require property owners to improve living conditions, organizing citizens to clean up an area, obtaining services from other governmental agencies (e.g., the street department), or referral of individuals to public and private agencies for assistance (e.g., counseling or mediation). Goldstein's ***problem-oriented policing*** is now more commonly referred to as problem-solving. Although this approach to policing was not new, the fact that Goldstein's ideas were widely disseminated increased their influence.

Greene (2000) notes that problem solving seeks to formalize a methodology to reduce crime, fear, disorder and other neighborhood problems. Officers are encouraged to search for remedies to problems in a systematic fashion. Eck and Spelman (1987) proposed the most popular problem-solving model, which grew from problem-solving in Newport News, Virginia. They suggested officers should address problems by scanning, analyzing, responding and assessing (SARA). The SARA model is described below:

Scanning. Police identify recurring problems within the police and the public. These problems are prioritized and broad goals are developed. After problems are identified, one problem is selected for examination. This is due to the fact that police responses can rarely solve many problems simultaneously, so police should systematically address problems separately. Finally, data are identified that can assist police in understanding the problem.

Analysis. Police identify and understand the conditions that precede and accompany the problem, as well as the consequences the problem has for the police and the public. Police identify the frequency that the problem occurs. Conditions that allow the problem to persist are identified. Creative resources, which can assist the police in understanding the problem, are also distinguished.

Response. Police search for what has been done to reduce the problem. In addition to others in the organization, officers may need to consult with other police departments. Brainstorming for interventions is conducted and one solution is chosen from a range of alternatives. Goals for the response are stated and data requirements are identified. Finally, the police carry out their response.

Assessment. Police determine whether the response was implemented correctly. Then quantitative and qualitative data are collected and used to determine success or failure. If unsuccessful, new plans are to be identified. Unintended consequences (such as crime displacement) are explored. Police conduct an ongoing assessment of the problem to see if the problem arises (from National Institute of Justice, 2000).

Research on the effectiveness of problem-oriented policing is largely based on case studies. This is due to the fact that problem solving is largely a place-oriented task, and since problems vary by place, so too do police responses. Braga, Weisburd, Waring, Mazerolle, Spelman and Gajewski (1999) present one rigorous assessment of the SARA model of problem-oriented policing. They identified 24 high-activity, violent places in Jersey City, New Jersey. These places were randomly assigned to a treatment area (where the SARA model was employed) and a control area where no problem solving occurred. Police did not recruit citizens as partners in problem solving; instead, citizens were used as information sources. Responses to these places varied considerably, but strategies included aggressive maintenance of order, drug enforcement, physical beautification, code enforcement and robbery investigations. They found decreases in violent crime at places where problem solving occurred compared to places where no such activity was employed. They also conducted observations of these places and reported decreases in physical and social disorder. Further, they found the majority of places did not displace crime to adjacent blocks. Although this project was not conducted citywide, these results suggest problem-oriented policing can decrease crime and disorder in the most violent places in urban America.

Management in police departments exercising problem-oriented policing is different from management in either the reform model or neighborhood building. Though officers exercising problem-oriented policing would have more discretion, their discretion is "structured" according to the SARA model of problem-solving. Officers would have more discretion than reform-model policing, but less than in neighborhood building. In order to facilitate structured discretion and lateral communication, officers submit reports to supervisors on the SARA process, and thus make their actions more amenable to supervisory review than neighborhood building.

Broken Windows Policing

A third theme of community policing is based on the writings of Wilson and Kelling (1982) and has become known as ***broken windows policing*** (also known as zero tolerance policing, aggressive order maintenance, or "grime" fighting). Wilson and Kelling indicate crime is indirectly related to social disorder (such as loitering, panhandling, prostitution) and physical disorder (such as dilapidated homes, vacant lots, trash, vandalism and graffiti). Disorder gives the impression the community is unsafe and residents do not care about their neighborhood. This causes residents to be more fearful of crime, which in turn causes residents to become more isolated and to withdraw from the community. Residents become less invested and are less willing to engage in informal social control, and petty crime flourishes. Eventually, more serious criminal behavior occurs and the neighborhood is allowed to decay further. This sequence indicates that if the police can effectively address disorder and petty crime, serious crime will decrease.

Broken windows policing received its greatest endorsement in New York City during the late 1990s under former commissioner William Bratton. In New York, police aggressively enforced crimes previously neglected, including fare jumpers in the subway system and "squeegee men" who lined bridges between the boroughs. Under the Bratton administration, New York City experienced unprecedented reductions in serious crime. While it may be true many factors contribute to reductions in crime (Blumstein and Wallman 2000), and the crime drop in New York reflected national trends, certainly changes in the NYPD contributed to these benefits. Bratton described the impact of broken windows policing in this way (as cited in Kelling and Coles, 1996):

> Reduce disorder and you WILL reduce crime. The strategy is sending a strong message to those who commit minor crimes that they will be held responsible for their acts. The message goes like this: behave in public spaces, or the police will take action. Police will also check you out to make sure that you are not creating chronic problems or wanted for some other more serious crime. Police will also question you about what you know about other neighborhood crime.

Bratton instituted a management tactic known as **Compstat**, which came from the term *Compare Stats* (Silverman, 1999). Compstat involved accurate and timely intelligence, rapid deployment of personnel and resources, effective tactics and relentless follow-up and assessment of tactics (Bratton, 1998). In Compstat meetings, administrators of each division and precinct were held accountable for crime rates and crime prevention initiatives in their area. Using qualitative and quantitative data, administrators were questioned in open forum (though not open to the public) regarding crime trends and patterns, the effectiveness of initiatives, and follow-up to prior problems. Managers were forced to take ownership over their area, which is in contrast to policing in the reform era when leadership was primarily evaluated on their ability to avoid corruption and scandal.

The Compstat process, as described above, is remarkably similar to the SARA problem-solving model. Police departments exercising a broken windows approach to community policing, however, differ from their problem-oriented policing counterparts in that the focus of the response is often aggressive law enforcement. An emphasis of law enforcement is similar to the reform model of policing but with several modifications. Recall that in the reform era police were most concerned with serious crime as described by the UCR, which typically meant violent crimes and serious property crimes. One consequence of this is that petty crime and disorder became defined as "not police business," and officers were less likely to define petty crime and disorder as important. Also in contrast to the reform era, the police are more proactive in enforcement of the law, and do not rely solely on 911 calls for service. Additionally this approach does not mean "full enforce-ment" of all violations of the law. Rather, enforcement is based on "local community standards," coupled with crime analysis. Wilson and Kelling (1982) state that it is important for the community to decide for itself what behavior is acceptable as well as the appropriate level of public order. Thus, it is paramount for officers to understand community norms and expectations based on information from the community itself, and for officers to refrain from using "no discretion" when enforcing the law. Similar to other community policing variations, police-citizen communication is imperative.

Is disorder really related to crime? And can police really decrease serious crime by enforcing order? Research on the ***disorder-crime link***, as well as police interventions is, at best, inconclusive. Skogan (1990) examines the relationship between disorder and crime in 40 urban areas and reports a strong relationship between disorder and robbery victimization even after controlling for population characteristics like poverty rate, instability, and racial heterogeneity. He also states disorder is likely to precede crime, indicating disorder may cause serious crime to occur. However, research conducted by Sampson and Raudenbush (1999) in 196 Chicago neighborhoods calls into question whether there is a direct relationship between disorder and crime. They found the ability of residents with shared expectations for informal social control actually influenced both disorder and crime, indicating there indeed may be a deceptive (or spurious) relationship between disorder and crime. This is important to note because if there is in fact no relationship between disorder and crime, then police efforts to reduce crime through broken-windows enforcement will be minimal.

Research on police efforts to reduce serious crime through ***aggressive policing*** is also mixed. Sampson and Cohen (1988) examined the relationship between aggressive traffic enforcement and rates of robbery. In cities where police aggressively enforced traffic laws, there were corresponding lower rates of robbery. This indicates police can have beneficial effects on less suppressible crimes by engaging in more aggressive behavior. Weiss and McGarrell (1996) examined aggressive traffic enforcement on eight police beats over a six-week period in Indianapolis. On these beats there was a significant decrease in reported burglaries and auto thefts. A control group that received no increase in aggressive police activities did not experience such benefits. Finally, Smith (2001) reported results from a police-directed cleanup in Richmond, Virginia. During a 30-day period, police aggressively enforced minor crime and disorder in a 50-square block in one neighborhood. Activities included numerous field interrogations, summons for traffic and other minor offenses, surveillance of and arresting drug users and buyers, and being highly visible within the area. Smith found a 92 percent reduction in UCR Part I crimes reported to the police during the project, particularly for violent crime, burglaries and larcenies from automobiles. More importantly, he reported serious crime remained low even six months after the "crackdown" concluded. These studies seem to indicate that aggressive policing of relatively minor offenses may have beneficial impacts on serious crimes.

In contrast, some research calls into question the effectiveness of aggressive policing. Sherman, Roschelle, Gartin, Linnell and Coleman (1986) investigated the relationship between aggressive police enforcement of parking regulations and disorderly behavior in a Washington, DC, entertainment district. In addition to enforcement, the local media publicized this "crackdown." Sherman and his colleagues reported only a slight decrease in robberies during the initiative. Weiss and Freels (1996) evaluated the impact of aggressive traffic patrol in Dayton, Ohio. Though the number of arrests for DUI, drugs, and weapons offenses went up, there was no impact on the robbery rate or the number of arrests for Index crimes. Finally, Novak, Hartman, Holsinger and Turner (1999) reported results from aggressive enforcement of disorder in a 10-12 block area of a midwestern city. The enforcement activities arose from meetings between the police and community leaders where citizens voiced their concerns regarding excessive public intoxication and people "cruising" in cars with loud radios late into the night. Though the crackdown resulted in numerous arrests for disorderly offenses, upon examining the rates of robberies and burglaries from the year prior to, and the year after the initiative, no change in serious crime rates was found. These results, taken in totality, indicate there is much to be understood about the disorder-crime link.

There are at least five limitations to the broken windows approach to community policing. First, aggressive order maintenance may require *significant increases in police personnel*. The tactics mentioned in the above paragraph are more reminiscent of crackdowns on illegal behavior, and less of the policing philosophy described by Bratton. Crackdowns are sudden and abrupt increases in police activity in a designated area designed to reduce crime of various types (Sherman 1990). It is unlikely that police departments can sustain a crackdown for an extended period of time without significant increases in police personnel. Because this would involve a significant increase in the police department's budget, many local governments may be unable to allocate such funds to increase police department personnel as was done in New York. For instance, Greene (1999) reports the NYPD increased the number of sworn officers by 39.5 percent between 1990 and 1995.

Second, *civil liberties may be compromised*. Greene goes on to report that since 1995 (approximately the same time Bratton instituted his change in NYPD) civil rights claims against the police for abusive conduct went up by 75 percent. Between 1992 and 1996, the total number of citizen complaints filed with the civilian review board grew by 60 percent. Many of these complaints stemmed from incidents that did not end in arrest or citation, but simply "general patrol incidents" in which the police encounter the public. These complaints were disproportionately concentrated in predominately African American and Latino precincts.

Third, and related to the second, aggressive police tactics *make police more prone to mistakes*. Among the most visible of these mistakes involved the fatal shooting of Amadu Diallo. On February 4, 1999, New York police officers fatally shot Diallo, an unarmed African immigrant, while he was standing in the vestibule of his apartment. Officers confused Diallo with a suspect wanted for an outstanding arrest warrant, and Diallo did not comply with the officers verbal directions (possibly due to language barriers). Diallo reached for an object in his pocket, and officers reported they believed he was reaching for a weapon. It was later discovered Diallo was attempting to grab his wallet. While a jury found the officers not guilty of criminal wrongdoing, it is indisputable that the actions of aggressive law enforcement contributed to a fatal mistake on the part of the police.

Fourth, as Sherman (1997) warned, *police legitimacy* may suffer when officers make arrests for relatively minor offenses. Police may not be seen as fair and equitable, and citizens may feel unnecessarily harassed. Ironically, broken windows policing may actually contribute to an ever-widening gap between the police and the public.

Finally, there is some research that indicates the broken windows approach alone may have **_limited long-term benefits_**. Taylor (2001) examined changes in crime, composition, and decay of Baltimore neighborhoods over several years. He argued that changes in physical disorder, social disorder, and racial composition of the communities had very little influence on crime rates. Instead, he observed local economic conditions were more directly related to crime. In other words, communities that are "weeded" of superficial disorder problems will continue to experience higher crime rates unless the community is "seeded" with economic development. This would require the police to work closely with other public and private agencies in order to develop a more comprehensive, long-term urban revitalization plan if the broken-windows approach is to be successful.

It is not known whether community policing in the long run will prove to be more desirable than other models of policing. The so-called failures of the reform and service models were more the result of political assessments than of objective analysis. Likewise, support for community policing is based more on politics than on systematically acquired data. As Greene (2000:328) observes, "despite billions of federal dollars that were distributed to police departments to further community policing over the past 5 years, there is little systematic linkage between these efforts and community capacity building or crime prevention." It is likely, as more is learned, that community policing will be modified in some manner. Already some cities that have experimented with community policing have de-emphasized it in favor of methods associated with the reform model (e.g., more citations, arrests, field interrogations, and rapid response).

Case Studies

There are many examples of community police programs. The experiences of two cities—San Diego, California, and Tucson, Arizona—are presented in the following case studies. These case studies demonstrate how problem solving and neighborhood building is implemented in different cities. The studies do not describe the problems associated with implementation, which will be addressed in subsequent chapters.

San Diego has been implementing community policing for several years. The police department engages in problem-oriented policing and implements the SARA model of problem solving. Case Study 3.1 describes their effort to reduce graffiti and increase the quality of the life in one community. Tucson began to experiment with community policing in the 1980s. After some initial success, they received a federal grant from the Bureau of Justice Assistance to "demonstrate the importance of crime prevention as a major police activity of equal professional stature to patrol and investigative activities." The programs they developed had three phases: (1) the integration of crime- and drug-prevention activities into all law enforcement operations; (2) the development of working relationships with other governmental agencies and community groups to assess the resources they had available and to develop action plans for specific neighborhoods; and (3) the implementation of the programs. Notice the partnerships and neighborhood building efforts engaged in by the police department and citizens in Case Study 3.2.

Case Study 3.1

Problem-Oriented Policing in San Diego

The San Diego Police Department's (SPPD) Mid-City Division is typical of many urban inner cities. In 1999 it contained a mix of residential and commercial zones, and was populated by lifelong residents as well as new immigrants, and included a large proportion of Section 8 apartments and low-income renters. Despite high rates of serious crimes (including robberies, drugs, prostitution, and auto thefts), the public regarded graffiti as a serious problem in their community.

During the *scanning* phase of problem solving, officers documented over 300 instances of graffiti in the 4-square mile community. Stakeholders (or persons who are concerned with the problem and willing to offer assistance) included residents, merchants, a business association, shoppers, city government, schools and of course the police department.

During the *analysis* phase police sought to understand the complexity of the problem and the consequences graffiti has on the community. The community believed graffiti causes property values to go down, personal safety is jeopardized and the neighborhood decays. The public school district was aware of the problem, and annually spent $500,000 on paint alone to remove graffiti, while the city spent an additional $24,000 to paint walls on other city property. In 1998 and 1999 the police responded to 267 graffiti-oriented calls for service, which amounted to 491 hours of "out of service" time. However, only 34 arrests were made for graffiti offenses (or one arrest for every 14 hours of out of service time). Prior police responses were both ineffective and inefficient. By reducing graffiti, police could significantly increase the amount of time available for responding to other crimes. Police discovered graffiti artists ("taggers") were typically juveniles who resided in the area, and tagging was most likely done between 5 and 8 p.m. Graffiti

was most prevalent on multifamily housing, schools, alleys, dumpsters, telephone poles, and electrical poles and boxes. Motivating factors (or the cause of the problem) were identified as boredom, recognition or popularity, gang membership and personal identification. In focus groups with known taggers, police also learned graffiti was a function of poor self-esteem, impulsivity, need for attention and lack of adult role models. Taggers viewed graffiti as an opportunity for self-expression to be shared with other (and often rival) taggers. Additionally, officers researched tactics used in other places to address graffiti and many were incorporated into the SPPD response.

During the *response* police included multiple tactics. Social workers offered counseling sessions for known taggers. Juveniles on probation would clean up graffiti twice per month. Community stakeholders volunteered to keep their block graffiti-free for 6 months. Officers were assigned as "handlers" to repeat offenders, and officers visited taggers on a regular basis. If the juvenile's graffiti were found in the community, the officer would take the juvenile into custody. Students from a junior high school painted murals on heavily tagged walls.

During the *assessment* officers conducted inspections of the neighborhood. They determined there was a 90 percent decrease in graffiti over a 16-month period. Many chronic taggers stopped painting graffiti, and murals were largely left untouched. Though this is an ongoing project, the SPPD and community residents deemed it a success.

Adapted from: the National Institute of Justice. 2000. "Excellence in Problem-Oriented Policing: The 2000 Herman Goldstein Award Winners," draft. Washington DC, National Institute of Justice.

Management Issues for Community Policing

There are numerous problems associated with moving a police department toward a community policing orientation, because many officers must change their attitude toward police work, learn new skills, and engage in new activities. Total quality management (TQM), first discussed in Chapter 2, may prove useful in this transition because community policing emphasizes the importance of providing personalized service of high quality to customers (Couper and Lobitz, 1991).

Case Study 3.2

Neighborhood Building in Tucson

In phase one of Tucson's program, crime prevention was declared an emphasis for the entire police department. It was to be a part of, rather than apart from, patrols and investigations. No longer would crime prevention be the responsibility of a small, specialized unit. It was to become a goal for all officers, and all were to receive specialized training in this area. The police department even adopted a new mission statement: "The mission of the Tucson Police Department is to serve the public by furthering a partnership with the community to protect life and property, prevent crime, and resolve problems."

In addition to these changes, the department also developed training programs and created a crime-analysis unit. The officers assigned to it received special training and began to develop data for computer analysis. In addition, a process was developed to document the positive contacts officers had with citizens. Such contacts resulted in more citizen input into police activities and, interestingly, citizens tended to desire both more police patrols and a faster response.

In phase two, neighborhood task forces, called community-action teams, were created. In addition, education in crime prevention was emphasized. Police officers were sent to crime-prevention programs and to meet with representatives of other cities. This action resulted in an emphasis on environmental design as a major part of the crime-prevention activities of not only the police department but also other organizations. The department also continued its crime-analysis activities. Twenty-eight neighborhoods were identified, and one was selected for a comprehensive response. A twelve-part plan focused on general neighborhood clean-up, street lighting, street signs and traffic control, clearly marked street names and numbers, speeding vehicles, pedestrian crosswalks, a lack of sidewalks, an underutilized park, an increased police presence, and a response to specific crime problems, such as burglary, gangs, and drugs.

In phase three, the police department began to expand the crime-prevention orientation throughout the community. A massive community education program was undertaken to encourage citizens to volunteer and become involved in neighborhood improvement. A second neighborhood was selected for targeting. The community-action team, along with members of the local school district and leaders of city agencies, joined together to identify problems and to develop strategies. A community survey was conducted to determine the concerns of residents. In order to give the neighborhood a sense of identity and foster pride, a contest was held at a middle school to develop a neighborhood logo, which was placed on signs around the area. Schools were declared drug-free zones, neighborhood clean-up was undertaken, traffic patterns were changed, and anti-graffiti programs were instituted.

Adapted from: Bureau of Justice Assistance.1993. "The Systems Approach to Crime and Drug Prevention: A Path to Community Policing," *Bulletin 1*, September.

TQM, or simply "quality management," emphasizes the importance of continuous improvement, the value of human resources, and the use of quantitative methods (e.g., research and evaluation). Quality management requires well-trained officers who work together, are motivated, and are part of a well-managed system. It also calls for working continuously toward reducing or eliminating system and performance problems.

Deming's 14 principles associated with moving management in general toward a commitment to total quality were presented in Chapter 2. In Inside Management 3.2, these principles are adapted to fit police departments.

Although the principles have been considerably altered, they remain consistent with the quality management philosophy.

Inside Management 3.2

Quality Management's Fourteen Principles
Adapted for Police Departments

1. Develop a constant commitment toward the improvement of officer behavior and the services provided to the community, and to discovering the relationship between what the police do (outputs) and the results (outcomes) obtained.

2. Adopt a philosophy of management that is based on a belief in the desirability of change in order to adapt to the changing community environment in which the police function.

3. Change supervisory and management practices designed to monitor officers whose behavior is inappropriate and to emphasize practices that ensure that officers will not engage in such behavior before they get the opportunity to do so. In other words, prevention is more important than detection. This change requires an in-depth understanding of the organizational and environmental processes that "cause" both good and bad officer behavior.

4. Determine the type of department activities and officer behavior that will result in developing a long-term relationship of loyalty and trust with a substantial majority of members of the community. [The authors do not believe that it is possible for the police, by the very nature of their work, to satisfy or meet the expectations of all members of a community.]

5. Constantly work on police systems and processes in order to improve quality, obtain better results, and sustain a long-term relationship of loyalty and trust with the community.

6. Make a commitment to training of all kinds, particularly on-the-job training to give officers the needed intellectual and technical skills and to show them *exactly* how to do a good job.

7. Emphasize leadership more than management. One purpose of leadership is to help police officers do a better job.

8. Work toward the elimination of fear—fear of the mistakes associated with innovation and fear of punishment for those mistakes—so that everyone can concentrate on doing a good job rather than worrying about the consequences of making a mistake. To a substantial degree this also applies to officer behavior. [The authors believe that both the organization and the community must be more forgiving of officer mistakes that are not intentionally illegal or malicious.]

9. Break down any barriers that exist between departmental functions (e.g., patrol and investigations) so that there will be more team work in problem solving.

10. Do not expect or exhort workers to accomplish things that cannot be accomplished, because this only creates an adversarial relationship between management and workers. Often, the failure to accomplish what managers want is the result of a system failure or is related to something in the police environment, both of which are outside the control of the individual officer.

11. Eliminate quotas, numerical targets, and management by objectives. Instead, substitute leadership to ensure that service—in terms of quality and quantity—will be achieved. In many police departments, it is usually possible for a well-qualified, hard-working officer to accomplish more and do it better than any performance measure might determine.

12. Give back to the worker, supervisor, and manager the right to be proud of their work, and the service they provide. The quality of the service must become more important than the number of services. The police and the community must have a clear understanding of what constitutes quality service.

13. Make a strong commitment to the education and improvement of each employee.

14. Involve everybody in the transformation of the police department because it is everyone's responsibility to ensure that total quality management is implemented.

Source: Adapted from W. E. Deming, 1986. *Out of the Crises* (Cambridge: MIT Center for Advanced Engineering Study.

Although some departments have reported considerable success with quality management practices, some have indicated that TQM's impact was

limited. In order to avoid problems and ensure the most positive results, ❖ ❖ ❖ ❖
departments should be aware of several guidelines:

1. Organizations should not move too rapidly in implementing
   TQM.

2. TQM must be tailored to fit each organization.

3. Training is essential to ensure that all employees understand
   TQM and how it works.

4. Both the organizational processes and the end result, or outputs
   and outcomes, must be considered.

5. Managerial style may be the source of organizational problems
   and an impediment to the use of quality management.

Although quality management may prove useful in the transition to
community policing, departments can be changed without specifically
adopting a quality management approach. Other theories and methods of
departmental change are discussed in Chapter 14 but are closely related to
the ideas of quality management.

Summary

Historically, four models of policing—political, reform, service, and community—have been developed in an attempt to make the police compatible with
a democratic society. The political model, which dominated modern policing
from the 1840s until the 1930s, was characterized by substantial political
influence in all aspects of police work. The reform model, which began to be
influential in the 1930s, was an attempt to overcome problems of excessive
political influence, corruption, and ineffectiveness by adopting classical
organization principles and emphasizing strict law enforcement. The service
model, whose influence began in the 1960s, was based on a broader police
role orientation that stressed community relations, employment of more
women and minorities, and crime prevention. The most recent of these models—community policing—is based on the belief that citizens and police
should work together to identify and solve community problems. Community policing is a philosophy, and is comprised of a number of different programs and methods, including neighborhood building, problem solving, and
aggressive enforcement of disorder. Although community policing has been
adopted in some form by many police departments, there is still uncertainty
over what it actually is and if it is more effective than other approaches to
policing. Quality management has been used in some police departments to
facilitate the transition to community policing. Quality management emphasizes the importance of continuous improvement in all aspects of an organization in order to better serve customers.

Discussion Questions

1. Describe the characteristics of the political model.

2. Describe the characteristics of the reform model and why it developed.

3. Describe the characteristics of the service model and why it developed.

4. Describe the characteristics of community policing and give examples of programs.

5. Discuss the reasons for the development of community policing in the United States.

6. Discuss the challenges facing police managers in the community policing era, and how managing line officers may differ based on how the department defines their community policing mission.

7. What is strategic management and how can it be applied to the police?

8. Discuss the impact that each model of policing has on relations between the police and minority groups.

9. Compare and contrast the development of community policing in San Diego and Tucson.

10. What is quality management and how can it be applied to the police?

11. Discuss how the Madison Police Department used quality management principles.

References

Blumstein, A., and Wallman, J. (eds.) 2000. *The Crime Drop in America.* Cambridge: Cambridge University Press.

Braga, A. A., Weisburd, D. L., Waring, E. J., Mazerolle, L. G., Spelman, W., and Gajewski, F. 1999. "Problem-Oriented Policing in Violent Crime Places: A Randomized Controlled Experiment." *Criminology* 37: 541-580.

Bratton, W. J. 1998. *Turnaround: How America's Top Cop Reversed the Crime Epidemic.* New York: Random House.

Brown, L. P. 1989. "Community Policing: A Practical Guide for Police Officials." *Perspectives on Policing,* Pamphlet No. 12. Washington, DC: National Institute of Justice.

Bureau of Justice Assistance. 1993. "The Systems Approach to Crime and Drug Prevention: A Path to Community Policing." *Bulletin 1,* September.

Caiden, G. E. 1977. *Police Revitalization,* Lexington, MA: Heath.

Center for Research on Criminal Justice. 1975. *Iron Fist in the Velvet Glove.* Berkeley, CA: Center for Research on Criminal Justice.

Community Policing Consortium. 1994. *Understanding Community Policing: A Framework for Action.* Washington, DC: Bureau of Justice Assistance.

Cordner, G.W. 1995. "Community Policing: Elements and Effects." *Police Forum* 5:1-8.

Couper, D. C., and Lobitz, S. H. 1991. *Quality Policing: The Madison Experience.* Washington, DC: Police Executive Research Forum.

Deming, W. E. 1986. *Out of the Crises.* Cambridge: MIT Center for Advanced Engineering Study.

Eck, J. E., and Rosenbaum, D. P. 1994. "The New Police Order." In D. P. Rosenbaum (ed.), *The Challenge of Community Policing: Testing the Promise,* pp. 3-23. Thousand Oaks, CA: Sage.

Eck, J. E. , and W. Spelman. 1987. *Problem-Oriented Policing in Newport News.* Washington, DC: Police Executive Research Forum.

Fogelson, R. M. 1977. *Big-City Police.* Cambridge, MA: Harvard University Press.

Fosdick, R. 1915. *American Police Systems.* Montclair, NJ: Patterson-Smith.

Fuld, L. 1909. *Police Administration.* New York: Putnam.

Goldstein, H. 1979. "Improving Policing: A Problem-Oriented Approach." *Crime and Delinquency* 25: 236-258.

Graper, E. 1921. *American Police Administration.* New York: Macmillan.

Greebler-Schepper, C. 1990. *Total Quality Management: The Road to Continuous Improvement.* Lucerne, CA: Author.

Greene, J. R. 2000. "Community Policing in America: Changing the Nature, Structure and Function of the Police." In *Criminal Justice 2000, Volume 3: Policies, Processes and Decisions in the Criminal Justice System,* pp. 299-370. Washington, DC: National Institute of Justice.

Greene, J. A. 1999. "Zero Tolerance: A Case Study of Police Policies and Practices in New York City." *Crime and Delinquency* 45: 171-187.

Hickman, M. J., and Reaves, B. A. 2001. *Community Policing in Local Police Departments, 1997 and 1999.* Washington, DC: Bureau of Justice Statistics.

Johnson, D. R. 1981. *American Law Enforcement: A History.* St. Louis: Forum Press.

Kelling, G. L., and Coles, C. M. 1996. *Fixing Broken Windows: Restoring Order and Reducing Crime in Our Communities.* New York: Free Press.

Kelling, G. L., and Moore, M. H. 1988. "The Evolving Strategy of Policing." *Perspectives on Policing.* Washington, DC: National Institute of Justice.

Lane, R. 1967. *Policing the City: Boston 1822-1882.* Cambridge, MA: Harvard University Press.

Leibman, M. S. 1992. "Getting Results from TQM." *HR Magazine,* September, pp. 34-38.

Lindsay, B., and McGillis, D. 1986. "Citywide Community Crime Prevention: An Assessment of the Seattle Program." In D. P. Rosenbaum (ed.), *Community Crime Prevention: Does It Work?* pp. 46-67: Thousand Oaks, CA: Sage.

Maguire, E.R., Kuhns, J. B., Uchida, C.D., and Cox, S.M. 1997. "Patterns of Community Policing in Nonurban America." *Journal of Research in Crime and Delinquency* 34(3): 368-394.

Mastrofski, S. D., Worden, R. E., and Snipes, J. B. 1995. "Law Enforcement in a Time of Community Policing," *Criminology* 33: 539-561.

Milakovich, M. E. 1991. "Total Quality Management in the Public Sector." *National Productivity Review,* Spring, pp. 195-211.

Miller, W. 1977. *Cops and Bobbies.* Chicago: University of Chicago Press.

Moore, M. H., and Stephens, D. W. 1991. *The Strategic Management of Police Departments: Beyond Command and Control.* Washington, DC: Police Executive Research Forum.

Moore, M. H., and Trojanowicz, R. 1988. "Corporate Strategies for Policing." *Perspectives on Policing.* Washington, DC: National Institute of Justice.

National Institute of Justice. 2000. "Excellence in Problem-Oriented Policing: The 2000 Herman Goldstein Award Winners." Draft. Washington, DC: National Institute of Justice.

Novak, K. J., Hartman, J. L., Holsinger, A. M., and Turner, M. G. 1999. "The Effects of Aggressive Enforcement of Disorder on Serious Crime." *Policing: An International Journal of Police Strategies and Management* 22: 171-190.

Office of Community-Oriented Policing Services. 1997. *Community Cops.* Washington, DC: U.S. Department of Justice.

Rosenbaum, D. P. 1988. "Community Crime Prevention: A Review and Synthesis of the Literature." *Justice Quarterly* 5: 323-396.

———, ed. 1994. *The Challenge of Community Policing.* Thousand Oaks, CA: Sage.

Sampson, R J., and Cohen, J. 1988. "Deterrent Effects of the Police on Crime: A Replication and Theoretical Extension." *Law and Society Review,* 22: 163-189.

Sampson, R. J., and Raudenbush, S. W. 1999. "Systematic Social Observations of Public Spaces: A New Look at Disorder in Urban Neighborhoods." *American Journal of Sociology* 105: 603-651.

Sherman, L. W. 1997 "Policing for Crime Prevention." In L. W. Sherman, D. Gottfredson, D. MacKenzie, J. Eck, P. Ruter and S. Bushway (eds.), *Preventing Crime: What Works, What Doesn't, What's Promising.* Pp. 8-1 - 8-58. Washington, DC: Officer of Justice Programs.

Sherman, L. W. 1990. "Police Crackdowns: Initial and Residual Deterrence." In M. Tonry and Morris, N. (eds.), *Crime and Justice: A Review of Research,* pp. 1-48. Chicago: University of Chicago Press.

Silverman, E. B. 1999. *NYPD Battles Crime: Innovative Strategies in Policing.* Boston: Northeastern University Press.

Skogan, W. G. 1990. *Disorder and Decline: Crime and the Spiral of Urban Decay in American Neighborhoods.* New York: Free Press.

Smith, B. W., Novak, K. J., and Hurley, D.C. 1997. "Neighborhhod Crime Prevention: The Influences of Community-Based Organizations and Neighborhood Watch." *Journal of Crime and Justice* 20:69-86.

Smith, M. R. 2001. "Police-Led Crackdowns and Cleanups: An Evaluation of a Crime Control Initiative in Richmond, Virginia." *Crime and Delinquency* 47: 60-83.

Stampler, N. H. 1992. *Removing Managerial Barriers to Effective Police Leadership.* Washington, DC: Police Executive Research Forum.

Taylor, R. B. 2001. *Breaking Away from Broken Windows: Baltimore Neighborhoods and the Nationwide Fight Against Crime, Grime, Fear and Decline.* Westview Press: Boulder, CO.

Trojanowicz, R., and Bucqueroux, B. 1992. *Toward Development of Meaningful and Effective Performance Evaluations.* East Lansing: Michigan State University, National Center for Community Policy.

Walker, S. 1977. *A Critical History of Police Reform.* Lexington, MA: Heath.

Walker, S. 1993. "Does Anyone Remember Team Policing? Lessons of the Team Policing Experience for Community Policing." *American Journal of Police* 12: 33-55.

Weiss, A., and Freels, S. 1996. "The Effects of Aggressive Policing: The Dayton Traffic Enforcement Experiment," *American Journal of Police* 15: 45-64.

Weiss, A. and McGarrell, E. F. 1996. "The Impact of Increased Traffic Enforcement on Crime." Paper presented at the annual meetings of the American Society of Criminology, Chicago.

Wilson, J. Q., and Kelling, G. L. 1982. "Police and Neighborhood Safety: Broken Windows." *Atlantic Monthly,* March, pp. 29-38.

Wilson, J. Q. 1968. *Varieties of Police Behavior: Law Enforcement in Eight American Communities.* Cambridge, MA: Harvard University Press.

Wycoff, M. A., and Skogan, W. G. 1993. *Community Policing in Madison: Quality from the Inside Out.* Washington, DC: National Institute of Justice.

Chapter Four

Organization and Group Influence

The first chapter of this text stated that organizations exist for one reason: to accomplish activities that cannot be accomplished individually. Based on this reasoning, an *organization* was defined as social groupings of two or more persons who are interdependent and work in a coordinated manner to achieve common goals. The importance of understanding this definition and its relationship to improving work environments in police organizations will be explored in this chapter. In other words, managers have to realize that in order to improve work environments, and enhance goal achievement, it is necessary to understand (1) what organizations are (their composition or primary characteristics), (2) factors that influence their design, (3) the influence of groups on individuals and work behavior, and (4) managing group behavior and conflict.

Organization Characteristics

At least three characteristics, fundamental to all organizations, are important in understanding police organization behavior: **composition** (individuals and groups), **orientation** (toward goals), and the **methods** used to obtain organizational goals (division of labor and rational coordination). Each characteristic will be described in the following paragraphs.

Composition

Organizations are composed of individuals and groups. Whether or not an individual is a member of any particular group, the influences of others working around that individual, either directly (physically present) or indirectly (psychologically present), are strongly felt. In fact, the organization's social nature is perhaps its primary characteristic.

Individuals

Individuals bring many qualities to an organization, some of them highly beneficial, others not. For instance, every member brings certain physical attributes and abilities, as well as specific attitudes, prejudices, and emotions. The organization, however, never receives the "whole" person. That is, the organization must realize that individual lives are segmented; people play many different roles (e.g., husband or wife, mother or father, or homeowner) and belong to many different groups (religious, political, or social). Accordingly, an individual's total personality is not found in any one particular organization. Allport (1933) developed the concept of **partial inclusion** to refer to this fragmented involvement of individuals in social groupings. This means that organizations must recognize that they will be affected, both in positive and negative ways, by an employee's activities outside of the organization's boundaries, and it must be willing to respond to and to deal with these external influences in a constructive manner.

Groups

A **group** can be defined as two or more individuals who are interdependent and influence one another in the collective pursuit of a common goal. This definition recognizes that group success depends on the interdependence of the group's members and that these members significantly influence one another as they work together. That is precisely why understanding work groups and involving them in the managing process is so critical. Further, a group should be considered a dynamic whole with properties of its own. Thus, it is more than the sum total of individuals who act in their own ways; a system of relationships and expectations holds the members together and gives the group a personality distinct from that of any particular member (Pfiffner and Sherwood, 1960). Groups tend to take on the following characteristics:

1. Group members share one or more goals. These goals may not be the same for every member, but every member has a goal in being a part of the group.

2. Groups develop norms, or informal rules and standards, which mold and guide the behavior of group members.

3. When a group exists for an extended period of time, structure develops that has individual members more or less permanently filling different roles.

4. When a group exists for an extended period of time, the members develop attractions for other group members, the group itself, and the things it stands for. (Adapted from Hare, 1962: 10)

Within organizations there are two primary types of groups: formal, those designated by the organization; and informal, those with membership left to individual discretion. Informal groups occur naturally, often with little regard for the formal organization. Each type of group membership is largely responsible for the attitudes and work behavior developed by its members.

Formal Groups. The organization specifically creates formal groups in an attempt to attain its goals in the most effective manner. An organization's formal groupings (i.e., its formal design) can be depicted by an **organization chart**, which defines the intended functions, relationships, and flow of communication among designated groups. Such charts tell about the relative status of employees, the authority they have, the chain of command, the formal lines of communication, the job activities throughout the organization, and organizational values and priorities (e.g., is it bureaucratic [tall] or more democratic [flat], does it allow for decentralized decision making; is it highly specialized or more generalist?). For example, one can learn much about the Portland (Oregon) Police Department, examining its organization chart in Figure 4.1.

In its transformation toward community policing, the department made some conscious efforts to involve both community and employee participation with respect to "policy issues, public review, and setting priorities for community policing objectives" (Williams, 1995: 159). Thus, both a chief's forum and an advisory committee unit, reporting directly to the chief, were added. There is also an assistant chief, with a support unit, who is responsible for the daily operation of the department. This arrangement allows the chief greater flexibility to interact with the public, as well as to manage internal change. A public information unit also reports to the chief, conveying additional input from the community.

Other organizational values and priorities, with respect to community policing and the public, are readily observable. For instance, under the Services Branch, the Training Division has a specific Community Policing Training unit (in addition to the regular Training Division), and the Personnel Division has a Performance Evaluation Project unit (for developing measurable "quality" community policing-type performance indicators). In addi-

Figure 4.1   Organization Chart, Portland Police Department

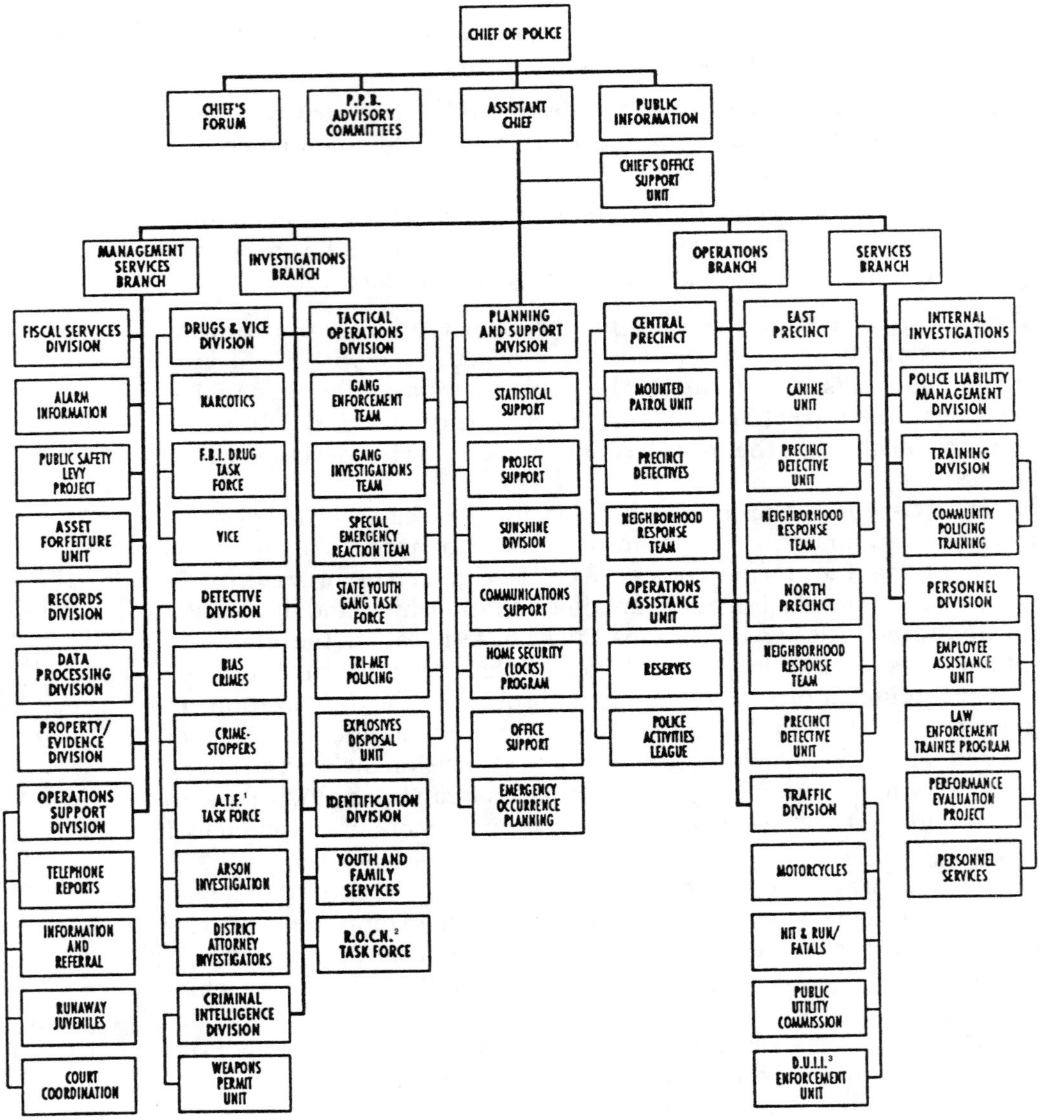

```
                              CHIEF OF POLICE

        CHIEF'S      P.P.B.        ASSISTANT       PUBLIC
        FORUM      ADVISORY          CHIEF      INFORMATION
                  COMMITTEES
                                                CHIEF'S OFFICE
                                                  SUPPORT
                                                    UNIT

    MANAGEMENT      INVESTIGATIONS              OPERATIONS     SERVICES
     SERVICES          BRANCH                     BRANCH        BRANCH
      BRANCH
```

MANAGEMENT SERVICES BRANCH	INVESTIGATIONS BRANCH		PLANNING AND SUPPORT DIVISION	OPERATIONS BRANCH		SERVICES BRANCH
FISCAL SERVICES DIVISION	DRUGS & VICE DIVISION	TACTICAL OPERATIONS DIVISION	PLANNING AND SUPPORT DIVISION	CENTRAL PRECINCT	EAST PRECINCT	INTERNAL INVESTIGATIONS
ALARM INFORMATION	NARCOTICS	GANG ENFORCEMENT TEAM	STATISTICAL SUPPORT	MOUNTED PATROL UNIT	CANINE UNIT	POLICE LIABILITY MANAGEMENT DIVISION
PUBLIC SAFETY LEVY PROJECT	F.B.I. DRUG TASK FORCE	GANG INVESTIGATIONS TEAM	PROJECT SUPPORT	PRECINCT DETECTIVES	PRECINCT DETECTIVE UNIT	TRAINING DIVISION
ASSET FORFEITURE UNIT	VICE	SPECIAL EMERGENCY REACTION TEAM	SUNSHINE DIVISION	NEIGHBORHOOD RESPONSE TEAM	NEIGHBORHOOD RESPONSE TEAM	COMMUNITY POLICING TRAINING
RECORDS DIVISION	DETECTIVE DIVISION	STATE YOUTH GANG TASK FORCE	COMMUNICATIONS SUPPORT	OPERATIONS ASSISTANCE UNIT	NORTH PRECINCT	PERSONNEL DIVISION
DATA PROCESSING DIVISION	BIAS CRIMES	TRI-MET POLICING	HOME SECURITY (LOCKS) PROGRAM	RESERVES	NEIGHBORHOOD RESPONSE TEAM	EMPLOYEE ASSISTANCE UNIT
PROPERTY/ EVIDENCE DIVISION	CRIME-STOPPERS	EXPLOSIVES DISPOSAL UNIT	OFFICE SUPPORT	POLICE ACTIVITIES LEAGUE	PRECINCT DETECTIVE UNIT	LAW ENFORCEMENT TRAINEE PROGRAM
OPERATIONS SUPPORT DIVISION	A.T.F.[1] TASK FORCE	IDENTIFICATION DIVISION	EMERGENCY OCCURRENCE PLANNING		TRAFFIC DIVISION	PERFORMANCE EVALUATION PROJECT
TELEPHONE REPORTS	ARSON INVESTIGATION	YOUTH AND FAMILY SERVICES			MOTORCYCLES	PERSONNEL SERVICES
INFORMATION AND REFERRAL	DISTRICT ATTORNEY INVESTIGATORS	R.O.C.N.[2] TASK FORCE			HIT & RUN/ FATALS	
RUNAWAY JUVENILES	CRIMINAL INTELLIGENCE DIVISION				PUBLIC UTILITY COMMISSION	
COURT COORDINATION	WEAPONS PERMIT UNIT				D.U.I.I.[3] ENFORCEMENT UNIT	

1. Alcohol, Tobacco and Firearms
2. Regional Organized Crime and Narcotics Task Force
3. Driving Under the Influence of Intoxicants

tion, the Internal Investigations unit is under the Services Branch (it is traditionally located under the Investigations Branch), which suggests that the department was concerned about public perception of fair and impartial investigations of its members. Furthermore, a move toward decentralization can be identified by noting that there are detective units at each of the precinct stations (Central, North, and East), rather than one large centralized unit; and through the use of precinct neighborhood-response teams, or teams of officers who "use non-traditional methods to focus on chronic neighborhood problems that are perceived by the residents to interfere with the livability of the neighborhood" (Williams, 1995: 160).

The hierarchical nature of the department—lines of authority and division of responsibilities—is also readily apparent in Figure 4.1. For instance, the chief of police has a span of control of four (i.e., the assistant chief, and the heads of the chief's forum, advisory committees, and public information units), whereas the assistant chief has a span of control of five (i.e., the four branches and the chief's office support unit). In general, the branches (called bureaus in some departments) are headed by captains, while most divisions and precincts are headed by lieutenants, and the units are most likely headed by sergeants. In many medium and large-size police departments however, divisions and units that require certain types of expertise, such as research and development, may be headed by qualified civilians. Furthermore, in many specialized units, such as employee assistance and communications, nonsworn personnel (civilians) may make up the bulk of the work force. Finally, organization charts indicate how a department may group tasks according to function and specialization. For example, while all patrol functions are under the same command (Operations), specialization occurs in mounted and canine patrols, neighborhood response teams, and motorcycle patrol.

It is interesting to observe that although a community-policing approach has been reported in Portland (Williams, 1995), the organization chart indicates that a classic, pyramidal structure is still in place. This is not too surprising, as large police departments may allow for structural "tweaking" (e.g., decentralizing some operational activities), but major structural changes (e.g., flattening the structure by significantly reducing levels and command ranks) are far more difficult and time-consuming. This is not to suggest that Portland has not made some progress toward community policing, but rather to point out that a substantial, long-term effort is required for significant structural changes to occur. For instance, Maguire's study (1997) of the structural characteristics of 236 large municipal departments (with 100 or more sworn members) strongly supports this observation. Maguire found no significant structural differences among those departments that reported that they had adopted community policing (44 percent), those that reported they were in the planning or implementation stages (47 percent), or those that reported having no plans for community policing (9 percent). Zhao and Thurman (1996), in their study of 228 municipal departments in cities with over 25,000 residents in 47 states, found that the core mission (i.e., law enforcement) of American policing has changed very little over the past 50 years, and furthermore, that little substantial structural change has taken place in recent years, despite all of the discussion of community policing.

Findings such as these draw attention to whether departments that claim to be doing community policing really are. For instance, are community policing activities (e.g., problem solving and community meetings): (1) being practiced, (2) being practiced throughout the department, (3) in part of the department, or (4) in a unit made up of volunteers? Or, is the department reporting—perhaps even believing—that it is implementing community policing in order to gain professional status, community support, or even federal funding? (For instance, some departments have used federal money to pay volunteer officers overtime in order to practice "community policing," with little or no additional training.) These are legitimate questions, but there really is no way of knowing for sure until a valid model of community policing is developed and tested on a large sample of departments (Maquire, 1997). However, the research to date on organization structure suggests that at least some, if not the majority of the reports of community policing adoptions are premature or even manipulative. (Further debate on this topic can be found later in this chapter in the section on criticism of classic police design).

Although an organization chart can tell us a great deal about the formal aspects of the organization, it reveals virtually nothing about the informal aspects of organizational behavior. It is likely that the informal relationships and arrangements that inevitably develop will tell us more about how the organization really operates than the formally prescribed arrangements depicted on charts.

Informal Groups. Informal groups develop naturally as a result of nonspecified individual interactions. Because informal groups have such a significant influence on individual behavior in organizations, managers should understand how they work (e.g., identifying leaders and followers) and attempt to work with them to improve work environments. One of the first studies to verify the important differences between formal and informal groups was conducted by Dalton (1959) of the Milo Company. By comparing the Milo formal chart with the informal chart prepared by Dalton (see Figures 4.2 and 4.3), the disparity between the formal and informal power of Milo's major executives can be readily observed.

In the Informal Chart, the managers (except for Forest, who dropped out of the ratings on the Informal Chart) are ranked according to their informal power within the company. Dalton used fifteen "reliable" Milo participants, or "judges," who evaluated the managers based on their perceptions of the managers' actual influence in the company (i.e., the Informal Chart). All the judges were or had been close associates of the managers they were rating. To improve validity, Dalton then challenged the rankings, basing his criticisms on his experiences and conversations with the executives and their subordinates. He discusses his findings as follows:

> In the [Informal Chart's] central vertical, dropping from Hardy and Stevens through Rees, Springer, and Blanke, ranks these officers in that order. Rectangles on the same level and horizontal [Hardy-Stevens, Geiger-Revere, Kirk-Finch] indicate that the officers therein were considered to have equal influence. At the same time each division is ranked according to the estimated power of its leader in plant affairs. That is, Springer is above Blanke, and Revere below (the least influential of the division chiefs). The department heads inside a given division are ranked in the same way but are not compared with those of other divisions.
>
> As shown in [the Formal Chart] Peters was not a department head. But all the judges agreed that he should be put on the informal chart, and thirteen

Figure 4.2   Milo Formal Chart Simplified

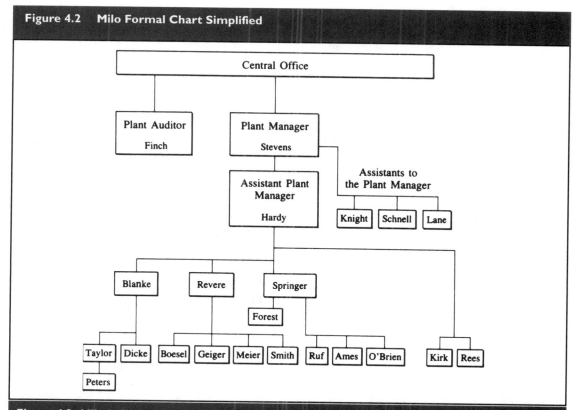

Figure 4.3 Milo Informal Chart of Influence

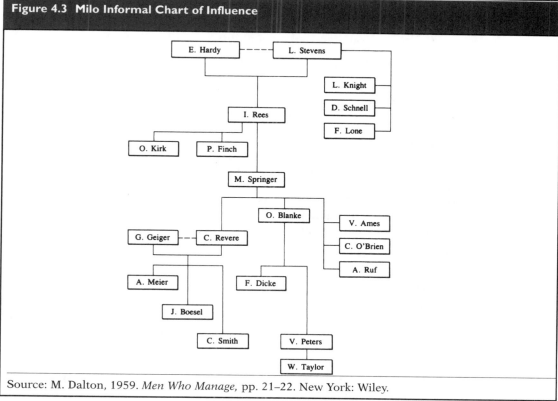

Source: M. Dalton, 1959. *Men Who Manage*, pp. 21–22. New York: Wiley.

ranked him above Taylor. There were minor disagreements on the placement of a few officers. For example . . . [t]wo of the judges placed Peters below Taylor. These dissenters were generally foremen who apparently disliked Peters because he had been brought over from a staff organization by his powerful sponsor, Blanke. The informal chart does not of course measurably show that the executives exercised more or less than their given authority, but it does indicate that formal and actual authority differed. (1959: 22-23)

Although the Dalton study focused on a single organization, it demonstrates that differences between formal and informal arrangements do exist. Of course, such differences also occur in police departments, and much of a manager's success depends on his or her understanding of, and ability to deal with, informal relationships. In this sense, the informal organization can greatly enhance or impede progress toward the organization's goals. As Davis (1981: 332-334) notes, the informal organization brings both problems and benefits to the formal management system. Some problems may arise in dealing with the informal organization: (1) resistance to change, (2) role conflict (i.e., what is good for the employee is not always good for the organization), (3) rumors, and (4) conformity (through group pressure).

Several important benefits may accrue from the informal organization, if dealt with constructively by management:

1. Blending with the formal organization to make a more effective total system (i.e., some requirements in organizations can be better handled through informal relations, which can be more flexible and spontaneous than formal plans and policies).

2. Lightening the work load on management (not every detail needs to be checked).

3. Lending satisfaction and stability to work groups.

4. Providing a useful channel of communication.

5. Acting as a safety valve for employee frustrations and other emotional problems.

Orientation

Organizations are oriented toward the attainment of goals. Many organization theorists feel that this particular characteristic is the most essential to "organized life." Parsons (1960), for example, suggests that the orientation of organizations toward goals is precisely what differentiates them from other social groupings, such as audiences and crowds.

Goals and Objectives

As described in Chapter 1, *goals* were defined as general statements of long-term purpose. Goals are often used to identify the role of the police, for instance, to prevent crime, maintain order, or help solve community problems. They are also often used to identify the primary mission of the police through mission statements. *Objectives* tend to be more specific, time-bounded, quantifiable, and consistent with the organization's goals; the attainment of objectives leads to goal accomplishment.

Both goals and objectives are important because they help to identify the expectations of what the police are doing and how productively they perform.

Unrealistic and unreasonable goals and objectives make the job of managers and employees more difficult and can even ensure failure. When police over-promise, or claim to be able to reduce crime or to solve problems that are largely outside of police control, the public is usually disappointed and critical. When employees fail to behave in accordance with unreasonable managerial expectations, managers are often critical and employees are resentful and may even become less productive. These unreasonable expectations can and often do create an adversarial relationship between the police and the community and between managers and employees (e.g., see the discussion on managers' and street cops' cultures later in this chapter). The problem of an adversarial work environment continues to be one of the most serious impediments to the successful management of police departments.

Police Goals

Three major influences affect the setting of police goals: environmental, organizational, and individual. *Community influences* consist of the legal framework in which police function and the community's input into organizational priorities. As has been stressed, however, there is no such thing as a "single" community constituency to be served by the police. Police managers, therefore, must be aware of the various communities they serve and possibly their differing expectations. Thus, departments within a heterogeneous geographic area, or even precincts or units within the same department, may need to establish different goals or use different methods to attain goals.

Organizational influences are those of powerful members, especially top management, who seek certain goals, primarily for the efficiency and perpetuation of the organization but also to satisfy its members. Finally, *individual influences* generally benefit members (e.g., job security, pay, or fringe benefits). Members often have goals separate from and even conflicting with those of the organization. As Barnard (1938) noted,

> Individual motive is necessarily an internal, personal, subjective thing; common purpose is necessarily an external, impersonal, objective thing even though the individual interpretation of it is subjective. The one exception to this general rule, an important one, is that the accomplishment of an organization purpose becomes itself a source of personal satisfaction and a motive for many individuals in many organizations. (p. 85)

It is clear, as the expectation-integration model discussed in Chapter 1 suggests, that the closer management comes to integrating individual and community goals with those of the organization, the more likely it is that the goal will be accomplished. Integration can be accomplished by continually monitoring individual and community expectations and integrating them with those of the organization.

Identifying and developing goals is one of the most important tasks of police managers in attempting to balance and integrate expectations. Goals provide the frame of reference for more specific performance objectives, and the degree to which objectives are accomplished provides the basis for assessing effectiveness. Such assessment may also provide an opportunity for learning more about police strategies, methods, and activities. Organization improvement is not usually possible without the knowledge acquired through systematic evaluation.

❖ ❖ ❖ ❖   ***Measuring Goals***

As we have noted previously, the products of police departments are more difficult to measure than those of most organizations. For instance, activities such as making quality arrests, maintaining order, solving problems, providing services, and using discretion wisely are difficult to define in a meaningful and valid manner. That is to say, that although it may be relatively easy to count (quantify) the number of arrests that are made by the police, it is much more difficult to get a handle on how "good" the arrests are (quality). For example, was the arrest necessary, was there violence prior to the arrest that could have been prevented, did the arrest lead to a conviction, and so on? To date, the police have made very little effort to develop qualitative measures of performance. Therefore, officers may be performing activities that are supported within the department while incurring the wrath of the community. In addition, because police departments operate in unstable environments, goal priorities are likely to change over time, thus creating new measurement challenges. Nevertheless, if goals are carefully and clearly defined, they can be measured in both a quantitative and qualitative manner.

To properly evaluate a police organization's overall effectiveness, both ***external*** and ***internal goals*** (and objectives) should be assessed. From an external perspective, the organization needs to know the extent to which it is satisfying the community it serves. For instance, are there conflicts between departmental and community goals? If the goals are similar, are the methods used to accomplish the goals acceptable? From an internal perspective, the department needs to know whether its goals are compatible with those of its employees. Is there conflict between what employees think the goals should be and what the department actually stresses, or do goal conflicts exist between operating units in the department. If they are to be meaningful, these goals need to be honest enough to be achievable and specific enough to be measurable. In general, attainable and generally satisfactory evaluation methods for the police include four major areas:

1. ***Crime and Disorder Measures***. Crime and disorder statistics should be compared over time in order to establish reliable trends and patterns. Criminal statistics usually include the Uniform Crime Reports (UCRs) or its replacement, the National Incident-Based Reporting System (NIBRS), and victimization surveys.

2. ***Community Measures***. Community measures may include surveys, interviews, and feedback from community meetings regarding such factors as identifying and solving important problems relating to crime and disorder, fear of crime, and general satisfaction with the police. In addition, representative community boards and police advisory committees that participate in departmental goal setting and performance feedback can be included.

3. ***Employee Measures***. The opinions of employees can be measured by surveys and interviews regarding goal emphases, operating procedures and policies, and concerns with management.

4. ***Performance Measures***. Evaluation of individual employees and group performance should include teamwork and coopera-

tion within the department, as well as with agencies outside of the department and even outside of the criminal justice system.

With respect to crime and disorder, police departments often rely solely on the FBI's ***Uniform Crime Reports*** or UCRs (Part I crimes, also known as the crime index) as their crime-rate measure. This crime index is the rate per 100,000 population of eight common violent and property crimes, including murder and non-negligent manslaughter, forcible rape, robbery, aggravated assault, burglary, larceny or theft, motor vehicle theft, and arson, reported to the police. UCRs, however, are not a very precise measure of actual crime rates, with estimates of less than 50 percent of some criminal acts being reported. The FBI has redesigned the program, called the ***National Incident-Based Reporting System*** (NIBRS), which will help improve the quantity, quality and accuracy of the statistics (Bureau of Justice Statistics, 1997). NIBRS includes 52 data elements on 22 offense categories in the Part A classification. In addition, there are 11 offenses in a Group B category, for which only arrestee data are to be reported; see Figure 4.4.

In addition to providing significantly more crime data, the NIBRS: (1) distinguishes between attempted and completed crimes, (2) provides additional information on victim/offender relationships and characteristics, and (3) includes the location of crimes. Further, it eliminates the "hierarchy rule" of the UCR—which limits reporting to the most serious offense even though multiple offenses were committed within the course of a single criminal incident. For instance, if during the commission of a robbery one person is murdered and another person is assaulted, under the hierarchy rule, only the murder is recorded for the UCRs. Thus, those departments that have adopted NIBRS have a much more sophisticated and accurate understanding of crime and disorder in their community. Unfortunately, only a small percentage of the more than 16,000 police departments submitting crime data have switched to NIBRS; see Inside Management 4.1 for greater detail on the development of NIBRS.

Figure 4.4 National Incident-Based Reporting System

1. Arson
2. Assault Offenses
   Aggravated Assault
   Simple Assault
   Intimidation
3. Bribery
4. Burglary/Breaking and Entering
5. Counterfeiting/Forgery
6. Destruction/Damage/Vandalism of Property
7. Drug/Narcotic Offenses
   Drug/Narcotic Violations
   Drug Equipment Violations
8. Embezzlement
9. Extortion/Blackmail
10. Fraud Offenses
    False Pretenses/Swindle/Confidence Game

Credit Card/Automatic Teller Machine
   Fraud
Impersonation
Welfare Fraud
Wire Fraud
11. Gambling Offenses
    Betting/Wagering
    Operating/Promoting/Assisting Gambling
    Gambling Equipment Violations
    Sports Tampering
12. Homicide Offenses
    Murder and Nonnegligent Manslaughter
    Negligent Manslaughter
    Justifiable Homicide
13. Kidnapping/Abduction
14. Larceny/Theft Offenses
    Pocket-picking

Figure 4.4 National Incident-Based Reporting System (Continued)

Purse-snatching
Shoplifting
Theft from Building
Theft from Coin-operated Machine or Device
Theft from Motor Vehicle
Theft of Motor Vehicle Parts or Accessories
All Other Larceny
15. Motor Vehicle Theft
16. Pornography/Obscene Material
17. Prostitution Offenses
    Prostitution
    Assisting or Promoting Prostitution
18. Robbery
19. Sex Offenses, Forcible
    Forcible Rape
    Forcible Sodomy
    Sexual Assault with an Object
    Forcible Fondling
20. Sex Offenses, Nonforcible
    Incest
    Statutory Rape
21. Stolen Property Offenses (Receiving, etc.)

22. Weapon Law Violations

There are 11 additional offenses which are known as Group B offenses for which only arrestee data are to be reported. Most Group B offenses only come to law enforcement attention when arrests are made.

1. Bad Checks
2. Curfew/Loitering/Vagrancy Violations
3. Disorderly Conduct
4. Driving Under the Influence
5. Drunkeness
6. Family Offenses, Nonviolent
7. Liquor Law Violations
8. Peeping Tom
9. Runaway
10. Trespass of Real Property
11. All Other Offenses

Adapted from: Hoover, L. T. 1999. "Why the Drop in Crime? Part I, Measuring Crime." *Texas Law Enforcement Management and Administrative Statistics Program Bulletin*. Huntsville, Texas: Sam Houston State University, p. 5.

Inside Management 4.1

The New and Improved UCR

For decades, the FBI's Uniform Crime Reporting program has provided law enforcement agencies and other end-users of criminal justice data with the number of violent and property crimes committed in a year, but precious little in the way of details regarding totals. Then along came a highly touted new method for collecting, analyzing, and disseminating crime data, the National Incident-Based Reporting System (NIBRS), which offers a wealth of information for police on each documented incident.

That capability is both a blessing and a curse to a program that to date has been adopted by only a fraction of the more than 16,000 state and local law enforcement agencies submitting data to the Justice Department. Whether it is the considerable cost of converting to a new data-collection system, or uneasiness with the amount of detail it provides in an open forum, NIBRS remains the province of just 2,736 small and midsize departments despite its introduction more than a decade ago. This is just 16 percent of those that submit such data, as compared with the 14,043 that collect data through the UCR program.

Not only does the new program drop the UCR's hierarchy rule, but NIBRS asks more than 50 specific questions about each incident. Queries include information about the race, age, sex, and ethnicity of victims, offenders, and arrestees; the relationship between the victim and offender; and what type of substance the offender may have been using. It also requires details as to the date and hour the offense was committed. Said Ramona Rantala, a statistician with the Bureau of Justice Statistics and author of the study "Effects of NIBRS on Crime Statistics," "I look at summary UCR as two dimensional; it gives you the number of crimes over time. The NIBRS information adds a totally new dimension with all its information."

Adapted from: "The New and Improved UCR—Is Anyone Paying Attention?" 2000. *Law Enforcement News*. Printed with permission from the *Law Enforcement News*, John Jay College of Criminal Justice. September 15: 7.

It has also been suggested that the police should consider having a UCR-like disorder index as a companion to the crime index on major felonies (National

Institute of Justice, 1997). By developing a set of standardized measures for calls for service, over time, the public's perceptions of community disorder could be measured. In reality, such a measure may actually be a better indicator of a city's health and perception of crime problems than the Part I crime index. The UCR is an already established crime measure used by most of the country's police departments and, despite all of its shortcomings, has credibility with the broader community and the media.

Another source of crime data that has become a part of many departments' assessment of crime is the use of *victim surveys*, in which scientifically selected samples of the population are asked about being victims of crime. Victimization data tend to provide a more accurate reflection of a community's incidence of crime. Currently, the most widely used and extensive victim survey is the **National Crime Victimization Survey** (NCVS), which asks a national sample of approximately 120,000 individuals over 12 years of age specific question regarding criminal victimizations. Obviously, by combining UCR data or, better yet, NIBRS data with victimization data, a police department will have an even better understanding of crime and disorder in their community and what to do about it.

Other performance measures that are traditionally used by police departments to record crime levels include arrest rates and the crime clearance rate. *Arrest rates* are calculated as the number of persons arrested for all crimes known to the police. Arrest rates are an extremely poor measure of performance for several reasons. For instance, they rely on UCR measures of crime known and police discretion of when to make arrests (officer levels of quality and quantity of arrests vary significantly). Another problem is that police make substantially more arrests for minor violations than for serious violations, whereas the crime index is essentially based on serious crime. A further problem is the fact that much police work—perhaps the majority—does not even involve law enforcement activities, including arrests. The *crime clearance rate* is calculated as the number of Part I crimes reported to the police divided by the number of crimes for which the police have arrested a suspect. This is another poor measure of police performance for several reasons. For instance, the police usually consider a case to be "solved" even if the suspect is acquitted of the crime charged; furthermore, multiple crimes are often "cleared" by associating them with an arrested suspect who has admitted to similar or other felonies. Additionally, crimes can be solved by *exceptional clearance*, when the police claim to know who committed the crime but cannot make an arrest; for example, when a suspect cannot be found or is no longer alive. In any event, because clearance rates are determined entirely by the police, they are easily subject to manipulation.

With respect to police performance regarding community and problem-solving indicators, although some efforts have been made in this regard, for the most part, the primary measures remain the frequency of serious crime and the number of arrests made by the police. This is unfortunate because as Greene (2000: 359) points out, "most police departments have not linked calls for service to performance measurement, even though these data may more accurately reflect community concerns about crime and disorder or other things that disturb the social fabric" (see preceding discussion on disorder index). Interestingly, this is precisely what was discovered in the beat meetings in Chicago's community policing program known as CAPS (Chicago Alternative Policing Strategy); that is, what the police thought the major neighborhood problems to be (i.e., serious crime) differed significantly from the community's major concerns, which turned out to be quality-of-life problems (Skogan and Hartnett, 1997). Finally, as Greene (2000) further notes, if problem solving is utilized as a performance measure, a system should be developed that allows the police to know if the problem has been resolved or diminished, and whether the level of harm from the problem has been reduced or it takes longer to recur. In either case, the police may have improved their performance, even though it may not be reflected in their traditional measures.

Methods

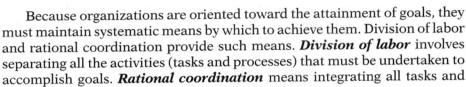

Because organizations are oriented toward the attainment of goals, they must maintain systematic means by which to achieve them. Division of labor and rational coordination provide such means. ***Division of labor*** involves separating all the activities (tasks and processes) that must be undertaken to accomplish goals. ***Rational coordination*** means integrating all tasks and processes so as to maximize efficiency and effectiveness.

Division of Labor

Division of labor or ***task specialization*** is needed throughout most organizations because tasks are too varied and too complex for a single individual to be able to perform them all satisfactorily. Also, it is not possible for a single individual or group to be in the right place at the right time to perform all organizational functions. Thus, the overall organization task is divided among different units responsible for particular activities at particular places and times. Two major types of labor division are vertical, representing the organization's hierarchy of authority, and horizontal, representing different functions performed at approximately equal levels of authority.

Vertical Division. Vertical division is the separate hierarchical levels in an organization and the degree of authority and responsibility within each level. In the formal organization, this hierarchy is known as the ***chain of command.*** As Figure 4.5 depicts, the higher the position in the hierarchy, the greater the power, authority, and rewards; the further down the structure, the greater the number of employees. This vertical division also facilitates the coordination and direction of specialized activities. In general, four separate vertical or hierarchical levels can be found in medium to large police departments; smaller organizations may have only two or perhaps three. Such organizational structures are termed ***pyramids*** because the number of personnel decreases as one goes up the hierarchy; that is, there are fewer personnel at the top.

1. ***Top-level managers*** conduct overall goal formulation and make policy decisions regarding allocation of resources (e.g., chief of police and assistant chiefs).

2. ***Middle-level managers*** formulate objectives and plans for implementing decisions from above and coordinate activities below (e.g., captains and lieutenants).

3. ***Lower-level managers*** implement decisions made at higher levels and coordinate and direct the work of employees at the lowest

level of the organization (e.g., sergeants, corporals, lead officers, and field-training officers).

4. ***Rank-and-file personnel*** carry out specific task activities (e.g., patrol officers, detectives, and other sworn and civilian personnel under the supervision of lower-management personnel).

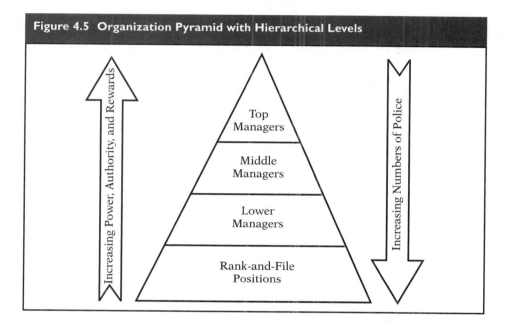

Figure 4.5 Organization Pyramid with Hierarchical Levels

Horizontal Division. Horizontal division is the distribution of activities among groups and individuals who occupy essentially the same level of authority and responsibility. In large organizations, this horizontal specialization is necessary for the effective operation of the organization. However, even in very small departments (e.g., fewer than ten sworn personnel), the horizontal specialization of functions often occurs. For instance, although the primary function of each officer may be patrol, one or two officers may be in charge of investigating major cases and collecting evidence, thus assuming the specialist role of detective. In general, specialization involves grouping similar activities together. Determining such similarity is usually based on the knowledge and skills required to perform them.

Rational Coordination

Rational Coordination. This is the intended integration of activities by management to help organizations run efficiently and accomplish goals. This may not be completely achieved because of poor planning or breakdowns. Rational coordination affects only certain activities; according to the concept of ***partial inclusion*** not all of an individual's behavior can or should be coordinated. Organizations use three methods to attempt to coordinate activities: hierarchical coordination, the organization's administrative system, and voluntary activities (Litterer, 1965).

Hierarchical Coordination. The first method, hierarchical coordination, refers to the degree to which organizations attempt to coordinate their activities through centralization and decentralization. ***Centralization*** is the

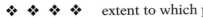extent to which power and authority (decision making) are retained by the top organizational levels.

Decentralization is the extent to which power and authority are delegated to the lower organizational levels. Police organizations may also be centralized or decentralized *geographically;* that is, there may be one central headquarters (centralized) or a headquarters with substations or precincts (decentralized). Police organizations that are centralized in terms of decision making may be either centralized or decentralized geographically. Departments that practice decentralized decision making are most often decentralized geographically as well.

Centralization and decentralization should be viewed as opposite ends of a continuum because it is virtually impossible to find an organization that is completely centralized or decentralized in nature. Both centralization and decentralization provide certain advantages to organizations. For instance, centralization allows for more uniformity of policy and action, lessens the risk of errors by subordinates who lack information or skill, uses the skills of central specialists, allows closer control of operations, and promotes strong leadership because much of the power remains at the top (Flippo, 1970; Carlisle, 1974). Conversely, decentralization allows for lower-level participation in decision making, which leads to job enrichment and potentially increased levels of employee motivation. It also leads to quicker and possibly better decisions because the people making the decisions are closer to the problem and do not have to refer all matters up through the hierarchy. It frees supervisors and upper-level managers to concentrate on broader responsibilities (Stieglitz, 1962).

Inasmuch as both approaches have advantages, managers must take a contingency view in deciding on the degree of centralization versus decentralization. Child (1984) suggests four main factors that indicate when decentralization tends to be more useful: (1) The larger the organization, the more likely decentralization is required because top-level managers have neither the time nor the expertise to make all major decisions; that is, as departments grow, decision making becomes more complex because of increased internal and external demands. (2) Geographic dispersion of operations requires greater decentralization because top-level managers simply cannot keep up with ongoing developments at the various locations. (3) Complex technology also requires greater decentralization because upper-level managers cannot keep abreast of all current technological developments. (4) Environmental uncertainty tends to require greater decentralization because the pace of change is too fast for top-level management to be able to adequately assess situations and make timely decisions.

The Administrative System.   The second method, the administrative system, relies on memoranda and bulletins as two obvious ways to help coordinate work efforts among separate operating units. To the extent that activities and procedures are routine, specific structural means are generally unnecessary. For nonroutine activities, specific units or committees may be established to provide for integration. For example, *ad hoc* committees can be set up for a single purpose, or project managers can be designated to help coordinate or carry out specific activities, such as developing or implementing a new policy. Once the purpose is accomplished, the committee or project manager is no longer necessary and is eliminated.

Voluntary Coordination. The third method, voluntary coordination, refers to the willingness and the ability of individual members and groups to combine their activities with those of other members and groups. Organizations frequently encourage individual members to identify with and commit themselves to the organization. If identification is achieved, individuals will be more likely to coordinate their activities. This, in turn, will help the organization to attain its goals.

Organization Design

Having considered the composition of organizations, this chapter moves on to a discussion of how they should be designed. ***Organization design*** is concerned with the formal patterns of arrangements and relationships developed by management to link individuals and groups together in order to accomplish organizational goals. It was traditionally assumed by the classical school of thought that a pyramidal design was the most appropriate for police departments. Even today, departments that are moving toward community policing, which requires a less bureaucratic approach, steadfastly cling to a pyramidal design.

The classical design, characterized by many hierarchical levels and narrow spans of control (i.e., small number of employees per supervisor) allowing for close supervision and control of employees and operations, is known as a ***tall structure.*** Conversely, a ***flat structure*** is characterized by few hierarchical levels with wide spans of control (i.e., a large number of employees per supervisor), allowing for greater employee autonomy and less control of operations. These differences between tall and flat structures are shown in Figure 4.6. It is easy to see that the tall structure has two extra hierarchical levels and narrower spans of control for closer supervision and control over subordinates.

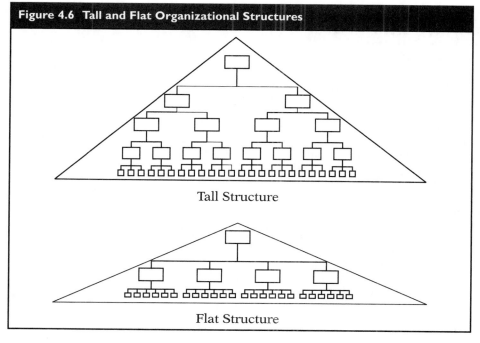

Figure 4.6 Tall and Flat Organizational Structures

Tall Structure

Flat Structure

In general, police departments with tall structures attempt to coordinate their activities through centralization; that is, authority and decision making are retained by the top levels. And, in general, police departments with flat structures tend to use decentralization, where authority and decision making are delegated to lower organizational levels, as a mechanism to control their activities. Tall structures also tend to have a greater degree of specialization with respect to the division of labor of personnel or the number of activities or tasks each individual performs. In other words, the fewer the number of tasks performed, the greater the level of specialization; conversely, the greater the number of tasks performed, the lower the level of specialization. For example, we would classify patrol officers as **generalists** because they perform a wide variety of tasks, whereas we would classify detectives as **specialists** because they perform fewer but more specialized tasks.

In order to make police departments more flexible and to improve decentralized decision making, many departments moving toward community policing are flattening their structures (i.e., reducing hierarchical levels). For example, in Austin, Texas, it was decided to gradually eliminate the rank of deputy chief and one-third of the positions of captain. There were several reasons, but, for the most part, there was a need for more street-level officers to handle calls and be available for the broadened (generalist) role required by community policing (Watson, Stone, and DeLuca, 1998). For reasons similar to those in Austin, the Cedar Rapids, Iowa, police department is reducing the number of ranked officers by eliminating the rank of detective, see Inside Management 4.2. Instead, patrol officers can apply for and qualify to become investigators; they will perform investigative work (the same job as the old detective rank), but, after a period of time, will automatically rotate back into patrol. In this way, the officers gain the experience and understanding of the specialized job of detective and thus have broadened their skill levels to help them better perform their community policing roles.

Inside Management 4.2

Detectives May Be an Endangered Species

In the Cedar Rapids, Iowa, police department, officials said they would be moving forward with the portion of a reorganization plan that calls for the elimination of the agency's detective rank. The proposal, which reduces the number of ranked officers, is in keeping with the department's community policing philosophy. The agency suffered from what some saw as too many chiefs and not enough Indians.

Those who already hold the civil service rank of detective would remain at that level with the same pay, but now other officers would follow them into that rank. In the last five years, the department has not promoted anyone to the rank of detective. Instead, officers will go through a selection process where they apply for a spot in the unit, get a commander's recommendation, and are then interviewed by a functional management team. If they are chosen to come into the detective bureau, they receive the same training as the ranked detectives—interviewing and interrogation, basic crime-scene work and basic investigations.

Under the plan, investigators would be patrol officers who rotate into the division as they would any other specialty, such as narcotics or aviation. The officers would remain in the investigative unit for several months to a year, gaining experience they would then take back with them into the field. "The whole idea," said Public Safety Commissioner David Zahn, "is to move investigation, with community oriented policing, out onto the street."

Adapted from: "Detectives May Be an Endangered Species for One Iowa Department." 2000. *Law Enforcement News*, October, 15, 2000. pps. 1, 8. Printed with permission from *Law Enforcement News*, John Jay College of Criminal Justice.

Criticisms of Classical Design

As police departments move toward community policing, including the decentralization of operations and decision making, becoming less specialized, and flattening the hierarchy, the effectiveness of the classical design, often referred to as a ***paramilitary model,*** is increasingly being questioned. Auten (1981), for instance, suggests that the paramilitary model treats the patrol officer like a soldier and thus is based on inappropriate assumptions about patrol work and democracy. He notes that soldiers are expected to obey orders and to show little, if any, initiative or discretion. They work as part of a larger unit; they perform tasks in a precisely prescribed manner; and they must be uniform in appearance, conduct, and behavior. The nature of the police role is quite different from these expectations. First, strict rules cannot be applied to policing because of the nature of the work. Second, orders are rarely required because most of the work by patrol personnel takes place on the street and out of the purview of supervisors. In addition, if the job is to be performed properly, a great amount of initiative and discretion is required. We might add, because this structure stifles street-level innovation, as discussed in Chapter 3, it may inhibit effective implementation of community policing. It may also eventually lead to officer cynicism that what they are doing has little meaning in the big picture and that they are merely "cogs in the machine."

Auten further explains that patrol officers seldom work in groups; rather, they perform most of their work alone or in pairs (thus, following the "book" cannot be enforced). He also criticizes the uniform appearance of patrol officers (patterned after soldiers), suggesting that it creates a mindset (we-they attitude) and rigidity on the officer's part. Such uniformity is depersonalizing, which may be appropriate for soldiers but is directly contrary to the police service goal. The decreased flexibility perpetuated by this system is also a problem; that is, there is a prescribed way for an officer (like a soldier) to act, even though most situations may be dissimilar. Finally, the managerial philosophy reflected by the paramilitary organization is Theory X oriented; that is, characterized by a philosophy of distrust, control, and punishment. (Theory X and Y philosophies were discussed in Chapter 2.)

Although such criticisms and charges of ineffectiveness are not new and continue to grow, there has been surprisingly little research conducted either supporting or refuting them. However, a study conducted by Franz and Jones (1987) lends empirical support to the critics' charges. In this study, police officers were compared with employees in other city departments that had not been exposed to the paramilitary design. The researchers found that police employees perceived (1) greater problems with communications, (2) greater amounts of distrust, particularly of upper management, (3) lower levels of morale, and (4) lower levels of organizational performance. Franz and Jones concluded that "the data presented—seriously question the capability of the quasi-military police organizational model to meet today's needs" (1987: 161).

Continued Influence of the Paramilitary Design

Auten's critique of the paramilitary model as being based on inappropriate role assumptions about patrol work and the treatment of patrol officers like soldiers is an interesting perspective when combined with some contemporary research on the increasing emphasis on highly specialized **_police paramilitary units_** (PPUs). PPUs are a generic term for units that have traditionally been known as SWAT (special weapons and tactics) teams and more recently referred to as SRTs (special response teams) and ERUs (emergency response units). This section will briefly describe the activities of these units and how an even stronger paramilitary police culture and community presence may be developing.

These units function as military special-operations teams, with their primary function the threat or use of collective force, and not always as a function of last resort. The teams generally wear black or camouflage battle dress uniforms (BDUs) (boots, body armor, and helmets) and are armed with submachine guns, sniper rifles, percussion grenades, tear gas, pepper spray, surveillance equipment, and they sometimes employ armored personnel carriers. Two separate national surveys—one consisting of 473 small departments of under 100 sworn officers (Kraska and Cubellis, 1997) and the other consisting of 548 medium to large departments with over 100 sworn personnel (Kraska and Kappeler, 1997)—provide a developing picture of how these units are increasingly being used. By combining the data from both surveys, the results indicated that over 77 percent of the departments had PPUs, an increase of 48 percent since 1985 (with a continued growth rate expected).

Early formation of SWAT teams in the 1970s and early 1980s was for the primary purpose of reacting to emergency situations beyond the scope of patrol, including civil disturbances, terrorism, hostage situations, and barricaded persons. Today, a much different picture is emerging. The surveys documented 29,962 PPU deployments in 1995, a 939 percent increase over the 2,884 call-outs in 1980 (Kraska and Cubellis, 1997: 620). This significant increase can be attributed to increasing PPU emphasis on executing search and arrest warrants and to their use as a proactive patrol force in high crime areas. These activities consisted almost exclusively of no-knock raids, aggressive field interviews, and car stops and searches—frequently carried out with a great deal of intimidation—leading to increased police-community tensions.

Another study on the use of a PPU in a self-proclaimed community policing department (although it appeared to favor a paramilitary style) in the Southeast found similar results (Kraska and Paulson, 1997) to those described above; that is, the increased use of the PPU was a normal part of routine patrol work. Several themes emerged that are unique to these types of units, including a pronounced military culture, a preoccupation with danger, a high level of pleasure from engaging in paramilitary activities, and viewing of the PPU team as a group of "elite" officers. This integration of PPUs into patrol work appears to delineate a parallel trend with, but in opposition to, community policing: from less militaristic to more militaristic, from generalist to specialist, and from service- and problem-oriented to aggressive crime fighting.

Countering an argument that this buildup and increased use of PPUs reflects a response to crime-rate changes, call-out rates were compared with the rates of violent crimes (homicide, robbery, and rape) from 1980 through 1995 for small-locality jurisdictions, and no significant relationship was found between violent crime and call-outs (Kraska and Cubellis, 1997).

Therefore, changes in the rate of violent crime did not explain the increased   ❖ ❖ ❖ ❖
level of PPU activity; it was concluded that PPUs are thus becoming a normal
part of routine patrol work by moving away from their more traditional
emergency roles and into more routine patrol activities. The authors concluded that:

> . . . we must first recognize that the specter of the military model still haunts
> the real world of contemporary policing, despite the recent rhetoric of demo-
> cratic reforms. . . . [W]e find strong support for the thesis that the military
> model is still a powerful force guiding the ideology and activities of American
> police. This should not be surprising considering the war/military paradigm
> remains an authoritative framework for crime-control thinking and action by
> politicians, bureaucrats, the media, and much of the public. (1997: 622)

It seems clear that the military model still "haunts the real world of contemporary policing," where PPUs may operate in a normalized fashion
alongside a community-policing model. For example, in New York City
(which acknowledges "doing" community policing), a tough anticrime program known as ***Compstat*** (an acronym for compare statistics) has been
adopted where aggressive and sometimes intimidating police tactics may be
used. In general, these include what has become known as ***zero-tolerance***
policing in which officers make many stops and arrests for minor violations
of traffic laws, ordinances and misdemeanors, regardless of public senti-
ment. (This approach is premised on the broken-windows theory, which suggests that strict enforcement of "quality of life" crimes will lead to improved
neighborhood appearance, which in turn, will lead to less disorder.) Such an
approach has undoubtedly played a role in reducing crime; however, questions are being raised as to whether or not it comes at an unacceptable price
(especially in predominately minority neighborhoods). For instance, within
approximately two years after implementation of the program, complaints
of police abuse to the city's civilian review board rose by more than 50 percent (Reibstein, 1997). Clearly, there needs to be a proper balance between
law enforcement, democratic principles, and citizen rights. Law enforcement activities, and even "aggressive" patrols, which under certain conditions can be appropriate, must be carried out without unnecessary intimidation or abuse of civil rights.

It is noteworthy that due to the increased complaints and publicity by the
community over New York's aggressive program, a new police chief (Howard
Safir) implemented a policy directed at improving officer behavior, known as
"***courtesy, professionalism, and respect***," or ***CPR***. This new code of behavior may be working, as citizen complaints filed against officers dropped 21
percent in the first half of 1997, compared with the same period of a year earlier (e.g., brutality from 1,278 to 1,021 and abuse of authority from 1,166 to
829). In addition, charges of discourtesy fell 32 percent, and charges of profanity by police dropped almost 40 percent. It is further important to note
that the department is tracking the number of complaints in order to determine the progress being made. Nevertheless, with complaints numbering in
the thousands in New York, community-police interactions require continuous attention and improvement. Inside Management 4.3 takes a closer look
at the potential problems of this aggressive approach to policing.

According to Sherman (1997), another, and possibly larger concern
about zero-tolerance policing is its long-term effect on people arrested for

minor offenses. Even while massive increases in arrests, like those in New York, may reduce violence in the short run, they may also increase crime in the long run (as arrestees may become more defiant and aggressive). Furthermore, the effects of an arrest experience over minor offenses may permanently lower *police legitimacy*, or the public confidence in the police as fair and equitable—both for the arrested person and for his or her social network of family and friends. Consequently, Sherman points out that zero-tolerance programs should be evaluated in relation to long-term effects on those arrested, in addition to short-term effects on community crime rates. In addition, program development to foster greater police legitimacy in the course of making the arrests is suggested—for example, providing arrested minor offenders an opportunity to meet with a police supervisor who would explain the program to them, answer questions about why they are being arrested, and give them a chance to express their views.

Inside Management 4.3

New York's Aggressive Police Tactics

Dianne Saarinen regularly hosted community forums at which police officials describe how they were fighting drug dealers who had sometimes taken over entire blocks. As crime began to drop, she wrote strong letters of support to the local police, thanking them for their work. Now, however, she is writing a different kind of letter, strongly complaining of police abuse. She says she has heard too many stories of overly rough police conduct, including dragging people out of cars at gunpoint, of abusive tactics, of roughing up people who do not speak English, and of shooting civilians. "In the beginning we all wanted the police to bomb the crack houses," she says, "but now it's backfiring at the cost of the community. I think the cops have been given free rein to intimidate people at large."

Although most experts agree that the NYPD's aggressive zero-tolerance style has played a role in lowering the crime rate, the question remains whether or not this style of policing comes at too high a price. Opinion polls indicate that most New Yorkers approve of the crime strategy (of course, most citizens are not experts in police tactics or civil rights), but in some communities the heavy-handedness is straining already poor relations with young African Americans and Hispanics; for instance, the city's civilian review board has reported a 50 percent increase in complaints over the past two years.

Are increased complaints an appropriate trade-off for reduced crime? William Bratton, the former police commissioner who implemented the aggressive strategy, believes it is not surprising that complaints would increase, as the police are making more arrests and coming into contact with more citizens. He acknowledges that some police go too far, but contends that the reduction in crimes and victimizations is worth it. "In a city of 7.5 million people, 30 million tourists, and 38,000 police, is the level of complaints an appropriate trade-off?" he asked. "I think so, and the people seem satisfied." However, critics wonder if that sort of trade-off is appropriate in a democracy. If there is zero tolerance for lower-level street crimes, why is there not zero tolerance for heavy-handed cops? And the critics are not just from the criminal class or certain neighborhoods. For instance, George Kelling, who coauthored the broken windows theory and helped Bratton implement it, is worried that his ideas are not being implemented appropriately. "There's an enormous potential for abuse," he says. He criticizes departments that demand IDs from residents or conduct neighborhood drug sweeps, indiscriminately stopping and frisking people and often using excessive force.

New York has developed a training program designed to alter excessive behavior, including ethnic-sensitivity lectures and community meetings. The program has been labeled CPR, for "courtesy, professionalism, and respect," and is holding its commanders accountable for citizen complaints in a similar manner that it holds them accountable for the crime rate. It is hoped that through such tactics increased levels of enforcement can be applied but without the excesses of abusive behavior.

Adapted from: L. Reibstein. 1997 "NYPD Black and Blue." *Newsweek*, June 2: 66-68.

Factors Affecting Design

Both external (environmental) and internal (organizational) factors should be taken into consideration prior to determining a specific organization design.

External Influences

One of the most important studies of the effects of environment on organization design was conducted by in the early 1960s by Burns and Stalker (1961). They studied twenty British industrial firms and discovered that the firms had different types of organizational systems, depending on whether they operated in a stable environment with relatively little change over time or in an unstable environment with rapid change and uncertainty.

The firms operating in a stable environment tended to have a ***mechanistic system***, characterized by a rigidly defined organization design with centralized control and decision making, many rules and regulations, and hierarchical channels of communication. Interactions within management tended to be vertical, that is, between superior and subordinate. Such firms were reasonably successful, however, because changes in the environment were relatively gradual, thus allowing upper-level management to stay abreast of them.

In contrast, those firms operating in an unstable, constantly changing environment were more likely to have an ***organic system***, characterized by a flexible organization design with decentralized decision making, few rules and regulations, and both hierarchical and lateral channels of communication. To be successful, these firms required relatively organic systems in order to adapt to their rapidly changing environments. In other words, it was necessary for individuals at many levels to be able to monitor the environment and to help coordinate and make decisions on how to respond to the changing conditions. The major characteristics of mechanistic and organic systems are highlighted in Table 4.1.

Based on the research findings of Burns and Stalker and other organizational theorists (e.g., Woodward, [1958] 1965; Lawrence and Lorsch, 1967; Perrow, 1970), it became evident that organizations operating in different types of environments require different designs if they are to be effective. Consequently, as the contingency approach suggests, the most appropriate design characteristics (mechanistic or organic) should be applied to an organization according to the conditions in which it operates.

The above discussion has important implications for police departments in their attempt to determine a proper organization design; mainly, the department must continually monitor and be willing to adapt to changing environmental conditions. These conditions include such influences as new laws and ordinances (or different interpretations of old ones), crime and disorder, public opinion, political pressures, and special and minority-group interests. Although police/community environments certainly differ from community to community—for instance, large metropolitan communities are likely to be more unstable than small rural communities—the distinction of uncertainty is essentially one of degree. Kuykendall and Roberg, in their discussion regarding the need for police organizations to become more organic, argue that, in general, police work can be characterized as "having a changing and complex work technology in which a variety of nonroutine

Table 4.1 **Characteristics of Mechanistic and Organic Systems**		
Organizational Characteristics	**Mechanistic**	**Organic**
Division of work	Narrow, specialized tasks	General tasks
Performance of tasks	Specific, unless changed by managers	Adjustable, through interaction with others involved in the task
Communication	Mainly vertical	Vertical and horizontal
Communication content	Instructions and decisions issued by superiors	Information and advice
Decision making	Mainly centralized	Mainly decentralized
Span of control	Narrow	Wide
Levels of authority	Many	Few
Quantity of formal rules	Many	Few
Position-based authority	High	Low

Adapted from: T. Burns and G. M. Stalker, 1961. *The Management of Innovation*, pp. 119-122. London: Tavistock; R. M. Howser and J. W. Lorsch, 1967. "Organizational Inputs," p. 168. In J. A. Seiler (ed.), *Systems Analysis in Organizational Behavior.* Homewood, IL: Irwin.

tasks are performed in unstable environmental conditions" (1982: 243). In other words, virtually all police organizations must be aware of, and attempt to adapt to, environmental changes; for some departments, the changes may simply occur more quickly and be more dramatic. Of course, the more organic a department wishes to become, the more difficult and sustained the change effort will have to be (see Chapter 14).

Langworthy (1986), in one of the few studies of environmental influences on police organization design, found that large departments have widely dispersed operations and tend to serve large, usually diverse populations. Accordingly, such departments tend to be decentralized, with authority and decision making widely dispersed. This finding refutes the belief that it is the classical, highly centralized model that has traditionally been used by large police departments. Thus, it appears that the classical model may be an appropriate option only for smaller departments that do not serve wide geographic areas. In a later examination of police design, Langworthy (1992) argued that the type of design depends on the nature of inputs to the police department. For example, if police are viewed as ministers of the law or the local will, then a mechanistic design is most appropriate because it "curbs discretion and insures that either the law or local will is routinely served best" (p. 103). But if police are viewed more as professionals who are expected to use their discretion as well as their collective judgments in solving problems, then organic designs are more appropriate. These findings and logical conclusions support the notion of a contingency approach to police organization design. It is important to recognize, however, that in the increasingly complex and rapidly changing environments in which the police operate, movement toward more organic designs appears not only desirable but necessary if departments are to operate effectively and meet the demands of their communities.

Internal Influences

In addition to external factors, internal factors or the organization's human resources have a significant impact on organization design. Two employee characteristics are most important: (1) skills and abilities and (2) needs (Porter, Lawler, and Hackman, 1975).

Skills and Abilities. Two dimensions of an organization's skills and abilities are most critical: mean level and degree of dispersion throughout the organization. The ***mean or average level*** of skills and abilities refers to the amount of them, including degree of experience and formal education, possessed by an organization's employees. If employees tend to be especially skilled, experienced, and well educated, it is likely that an organization with mechanistic characteristics would perform at levels much lower than its potential, with overt expressions of resentment against the organization (Porter, Lawler, and Hackman, 1975).

In other words, organizations that have highly skilled employees are designed as if their employees were less skilled, underuse their potential human resources, and possibly turn employee efforts against the organization. Of course, it is also possible that employees caught in such a situation will simply resign from the organization and look elsewhere to fully realize their potential. Such a situation has important implications for today's police departments, which are attempting to attract more highly educated personnel, because the traditional paramilitary design does not allow for the level of development desired by many college graduates. There is some evidence to support this notion, because more highly educated officers are more likely to terminate their careers in policing (Cohen and Chaiken, 1972; Levy, 1967, 1973; Marsh, 1962; Stoddard, 1973; Weirman, 1978) and to be less satisfied with their jobs (Griffin, Dunbar, and McGill, 1978; Mottaz, 1983).

The ***degree of dispersion,*** or distribution of the mean level of skills and abilities among employees throughout an organization is a second important dimension for determining its design. For example, two might have employees with the same level of skills and abilities; but one might assign them throughout the organization (i.e., a generalist approach), whereas the other might concentrate them in a few specialized units. In such a situation, it would be inappropriate for both organizations to adopt the same basic designs. The organization with the greater dispersal of experience, skills, and education would be more likely to utilize its employees appropriately in an organic design. Conversely, the organization with the narrow dispersion would most likely be better off adopting an organic design for those units with highly skilled employees and a mechanistic design in the rest of the units.

Needs. Employee needs may also significantly influence the effectiveness of an organization's design. Not all individuals need or desire a flexible, organic design in which they have a great amount of responsibility and decision-making powers. As Porter, Lawler, and Hackman (1975) suggest:

> It is not just a matter of how individuals differ in their needs, say for achievement or affiliation. It is also a matter of how they differ in their characteristic

modes of behaving and in their own views of themselves. . . . We can hypothe-size that if individuals have strong needs for independence and self-actual-ization and have relatively high self-confidence, they will prefer organic-type organizations and will do better in them. Individuals who have less of these traits can be presumed to fare better in a relatively more highly structured or-ganization. (p. 124)

Several comprehensive studies have indicated that college graduates tend to possess a higher degree of the need for responsibility and achieve-ment than noncollege graduates (Astin, 1978; Feldman and Newcomb, 1969; Gaines, Tubergen, and Paiva (1984); Trent and Medsker, 1968). Bowker (1980), for instance, has indicated that because highly educated officers are more likely to be high achievers, managers should try to keep them satisfied by rewarding achievement, not only for motivational purposes but also to avoid turnover. Such research suggests that if the mean level of education continues to increase in police organizations, as about 25 percent of today's officers have graduated from college (Roberg, Crank, and Kuykendall, 2000), there will be less tolerance for departments that are primarily mecha-nistic and a greater need for relatively organic designs if human resources are to be used effectively.

Mechanistic and organic systems appear to be more appropriate under the following conditions:

Organic, low-structured, nonbureaucratic-type designs are most effective when:

1. Individuals have relatively high skills that are widely distributed.
2. Individuals have high self-esteem and strong needs for achieve-ment, autonomy, and self-actualization.
3. The technology is rapidly changing, nonroutine, and involves many nonprogrammable tasks.
4. The environment is relatively dynamic and complex.

Mechanistic, high-structured, more bureaucratic-like designs are most effec-tive when:

1. Individuals are relatively inexperienced and unskilled.
2. Individuals have strong needs for security and stability.
3. The technology is relatively stable and involves standardized ma-terials and programmable tasks.
4. The environment is fairly calm and relatively simple (Porter, Lawler, and Hackman, 1975: 272).

Thus, it is clear that because of the relatively uncertain environments in which they operate, the complex, nonprogrammable, and nonroutine nature of the tasks performed, and the rising level of education of those being employed, organic designs offer more potential for effectiveness to police departments than do mechanistic designs. This conclusion has impli-cations for the development of community policing, which tends to be more organic than traditional approaches. As contingency theory suggests, how-ever, any one type of design may not be effective for the whole organization. Thus, a mix of designs for different parts or units of the organization may be necessary. Understanding the conditions under which organic or mechanistic designs are more favorable should help police managers to determine the most appropriate designs for specific situations.

Group Influence

As already noted, groups greatly affect the attitudes and behavior of individuals in organizations. Groups control many of the stimuli that individuals receive during their organizational activities. ***Discretionary stimuli*** transmitted selectively to individual group members at the discretion of their peers usually have a significant impact on the members' beliefs and attitudes, as well as on job-related knowledge and skills (Porter, Lawler, and Hackman, 1975). Another strong influence in police departments is the police culture, which must also be understood and dealt with by management.

Beliefs, Attitudes, and Relevant Knowledge and Skills

Individuals in organizations do not have a complete or accurate view of their environment unless they obtain information from their work groups. They usually discover the "social reality" of organizational life through direct communication and observation of others. Groups frequently pressure members toward ***uniformity of beliefs and attitudes*** about the work environment, because groups are not usually capable of handling overt disagreements among members. Such pressure is most apparent when new members, whose beliefs and attitudes about the work may be different, join the group. For example, when police recruits report for their first tour of duty, they often hear the veteran officer's advice to rookies: "Forget what you were told in the academy [or college or both], we'll show you how things really are." More experienced officers may also inform the recruits that "divergent" points of view are not appreciated.

Such pressure toward uniformity of beliefs and attitudes can be functional for the group, especially in situations where uniformity of views is essential for completing the work on time. However, such pressure is dysfunctional when the divergent views of group members are intentionally suppressed. Contrary beliefs and attitudes, if explored, can contribute substantially to the problem-solving abilities of the group.

Another type of group-supplied discretionary stimuli helps group members gain the ***relevant knowledge and skills*** needed to perform their jobs. For instance, trial-and-error learning of a new skill or behavior pattern is usually inefficient, and in police work can be dangerous. The help of group members provides shortcuts to the learning process and lessens the risks. Furthermore, many skills and behaviors in police work, such as learning how to handle interpersonal conflicts or define and measure community problems, cannot be effectively learned without the involvement of other people. There are four general ways in which groups can assist members in developing knowledge and skills for use on the job: (1) ***direct instruction***, which is primarily useful in teaching the most simple skills and behaviors; (2) ***feedback*** on appropriate or inappropriate behavior, including the use of positive or negative reinforcements; (3) ***modeling,*** whereby the individual attempts to match the behavior of a model, as in the role playing used by police to train employees how to handle difficult situations; and (4) ***observation,*** where, for example, a recruit is teamed with a veteran officer and acquires on-the-job skills through imitation. In complex jobs like police work, individuals will generally not perform well if left to their own devices. Therefore, the group has a tremendous amount of power and influence over the learning process of police officers.

Police Culture and Socialization

In the field of policing, beliefs, attitudes, and behaviors are also strongly influenced by **police culture**. This culture is primarily developed through a process of **socialization,** or the beliefs, attitudes, values and norms learned in interactions with peers and on-the-job experiences. This socialization process is based on the police work environment, which has generally been characterized by uncertainty, danger, and coercive authority. In turn, the police culture promotes an aggressive, no-nonsense approach to policing and places priority on law enforcement and crime fighting, which, in turn, gives rise to abuses of authority and tension in the community. This culture may impede efforts to detect and investigate corruption and other misconduct, and further, it may resist efforts at reform and change, including the implementation of community policing (Paoline, Myers, and Worden, 2000). Despite this traditional view of the police culture, we do know that police officers' attitudes and values vary more widely than the conventional wisdom may have us believe (e.g., see Worden, 1995).

A study by Paoline, Myers, and Worden (2000) examined the variation in outlooks that are traditionally considered to be part of the police culture as defined above, as well as the relationship between these outlooks and officer characteristics. Data are analyzed from the Project on Policing Neighborhoods (POPN), which surveyed 398 patrol officers in the Indianapolis (IN) Police Department (IPD) and 240 patrol officers in the St. Petersburg (FL) Police Department (SPPD); both departments had begun to implement community policing. Interestingly, while the findings did not imply that the police culture does not exist, they indicated that the outlook did not encompass all of the attitudes and values traditionally associated with that culture. However, this variation is not patterned strongly by their characteristics. Only modest differences were found with respect to officers' race and length of service, and weak or no differences associated with their sex, education, and training in community-policing topics (although it should be noted that very little, if any, training on these topics occurred). Finally, some differences were associated with community-policing specialists in both departments, but these differences most likely reflect the self-selection of officers into community policing assignments.

Overall, while a divergence from traditional police culture was found, these differences were not patterned by the officers' characteristics; the findings further indicated that just as white men with working-class backgrounds formed varying occupational outlooks in managing the strains of police work, so do women, minorities, and college-educated officers. Thus, it appears that the fractures in the police culture may afford better prospects for the implementation of community policing than conventional wisdom allows. In other words, because culture is apparently not determined by the nature of the work, it may be more malleable and subject to organizational influences than originally anticipated.

This research may have important implications with respect to the nature of the police culture and its impact on organizational change in general, and community policing in particular. It would appear that it is more important to "facilitate the practice of community policing than [to put forth] efforts to win officers' hearts and minds more directly" (p. 602). In other words, it is critical for managers to change the working environment to support the practice of community policing; that is, to ensure performance appraisal and rewards, supervision and leadership, and training in necessary skills and concepts. Concerted efforts by police managers to allow officers to engage in community-policing activities, rather than concerted efforts to change their attitudes, most likely holds more promise for successful reform (also, see Crank, 1997). Thus, managers should do all in their power to change operating policies and procedures toward the new system (community policing), and employee behavior will likely adapt.

As noted previously, socialization in policing occurs when recruits inculcate the attitudes, beliefs, values, and behavioral patterns of experienced officers. From this early socialization, police officers tend to develop a view of their job different from that of their managers. For example, Reuss-Ianni (1983) in her study of New York police, observed that these divergent views may result in two distinct cultures within the same organization, namely a **manager's culture** and a **street cop's culture**.

This differing perspective of the patrol officer's job developed because the manager's view is often shaped by experiences that remove him or her from the street reality of officers. One example common to police work is the **ends-means dilemma**. Police managers must be concerned with both ends (i.e., results) and means (i.e., how the result are achieved). Managers are concerned with departmental priorities, policies, and procedures, whereas officers are concerned with doing the job "according to the street," often acquired not from the department's view of reality but from the officer's perspective, determined by trying to "survive." These differing perspectives can result in an adversarial relationship, where street cops maintain their own "code," which can include the following maxims:

1. Take care of your partner first, then the other officers.

2. Don't "give up" [inform on] another cop; be secretive about the behavior of other officers.

3. "Show balls"; take control of a situation and don't back down.

4. Be aggressive when necessary, but don't go looking for trouble.

5. Don't interfere in another officer's sector or work area.

6. Do your fair share of work and don't leave work for the next "shift"; however, don't do too much work.

7. If you get caught making a mistake, don't implicate anybody else.

8. Other cops, but not necessarily managers, should be told if another officer is dangerous or "crazy."

9. Don't trust new officers until they have been checked out.

10. Don't volunteer information; tell others only what they need to know.

11. Avoid talking too much or too little; both are suspicious.

12. Protect your "ass"; don't give managers or the system an opportunity to "get you."

13. Don't "make waves"; don't make problems for the system or managers.

14. Don't "suck up" to supervisors.

15. Know what your supervisor and other managers expect.

16. Don't trust managers; they may not look out for your interests. (Adapted from Reuss-Ianni, 1983: 13-16.)

Because both the manager's and the street cop's cultures must relate to the expectations of the communities they serve, there is both a public and a private world of policing. The **public world** of policing is characterized as the essence of police work—that is, dedicated public servants performing dangerous work for our safety. Although the managers' and officers' perspectives of police work may differ, neither group tends to be completely candid because both have a vested interest in maintaining an image that avoids controversy. For example, if officers use excessive force to make an arrest, they will probably not admit it because of the street culture norms to be secretive about illegal or inappropriate behavior. Managers may attempt to uncover the inappropriate behavior, but they may not disclose it, or disclose only parts of it. There may be potentially serious adverse consequences to the department, or they may be willing to disregard illegal tactics if a desirable result is obtained. Police managers, if they are to be effective leaders, must be willing to deal with such situations, both formally and informally, as the need arises.

In general, the **private world** of policing has been characterized as politically conservative, closed, or secretive, with a high degree of cynicism and an emphasis on loyalty, solidarity, and respect for authority (Doyle, 1980). Undoubtedly, this private world of the street cop's culture has the strongest influence on the socialization process throughout the department and most likely the greatest impact on police behavior. A significant problem for managers arises when the behavior dictated by the street culture conflicts with both organizational and community interests. This conflict is most apparent when a certain degree of deviant behavior (e.g., excessive force, racism, sexism, free meals, or gratuities) becomes acceptable, or at least tolerated, at the street level. Police managers must be willing to deal with such behavior from both ethical and legal perspectives. Accordingly, they need to be aware of group pressures, especially with respect to the street cop's culture, and how they influence, either positively or negatively, officer behavior. And, as the research by Paoline, Myers, and Worden (2000) clearly suggests, the police culture is malleable to organizational influences; that is, if strong policies regarding deviant and excessive behavior are developed and enforced by management, it is likely that they will have the desired effect.

Managing Group Behavior and Conflict   ❖ ❖ ❖ ❖

Police managers need to be well informed about managing group behavior and possible conflict between and among groups. Because today's police departments tend to be relatively diverse in cultural background and level of skills, it is natural that different groups will have different—and often conflicting—demands on management. The remainder of this chapter will discuss the varied nature of an increasingly influential type of group in police departments: employee organizations and group-communication networks. It will also discuss how group conflict may be constructively resolved.

Employee Organizations

Historically, the best-known police employee organization has been the ***police union*** or ***association***, which is made up of police officers and is their official representative in collective bargaining with the employer. Because police departments operate on a local level, there is no single national police union. Instead, local departments may belong to one of many national unions. The largest include the Fraternal Order of Police (FOP) and the International Union of Police Associations (IUPA), which is affiliated with the AFL-CIO. Other local police unions are affiliated with the Teamsters, the American Federation of State, County, and Municipal Employees (AFSCME), and other smaller national unions.

Although a union is an employee organization, not all employee organizations are unions. As Walker (1992) notes, police officers have historically belonged to ***fraternal organizations.*** These groups are generally organized along ethnic lines. Nationally, for example, African-American officers are represented by the National Organization of Black Law Enforcement Officers (NOBLE), Latino officers by the Latino Police Officers Association, and Asian officers by the Asian Police Officers Association. Employee groups may also form their own local organizations. In San Francisco, for example, the black officers association is known as Officers for Justice; in San Jose, California, it is known as the South Bay Association of Black Law Enforcement Officers (SABLE).

As departments become more diverse in their make-up, additional employee organizations develop. For instance, many departments have women's organizations (e.g., the Women's Police Officer Association); gay and lesbian officers are represented in California by the Golden State Peace Officers Association. Furthermore, police officers and supervisors are often represented by their own associations. It is apparent that if departments are to maintain high-quality work environments, police managers must be able to deal effectively with the diverse needs, expectations, and conflicts of these employee organizations. In general, it is best to establish a working relationship with each group and to share with them the department's expectations. Then, if there are conflicts, they can be dealt with in an open and honest manner.

Police Unions

The police labor movement has gone through several stages. Police associations were evident as early as the 1890s but did not establish themselves until the mid-1960s. Two previous attempts were made to unionize police employees but failed. The first attempt failed after the Boston police strike of 1919, which created a backlash against police unions throughout the country. The second, between 1943 and 1947, failed because of unfavorable court decisions and strong resistance by police chiefs.

Since the mid-1960s, however, police unionization has had a great deal of success. Several developments contributed toward this success, including the following:

1. ***Lagging Salaries and Benefits.*** Officers were angry over the fact that their salaries and benefits had fallen behind those available in other jobs that they might consider.

2. ***Poor Police Management.*** Officers were angry and alienated over the way their departments were managed. At the time, police chiefs had virtually unlimited power in managing their departments, and many operated in an arbitrary and vindictive manner. Officers who were critical of management were often punished with frequent transfers and assignments to low-status jobs. Officer participation in any form of decision making was virtually nonexistent.

3. ***Social and Political Alienation.*** During the social unrest of the 1960s and 1970s, police officers felt that they were being attacked from all sides; for example, they resented accusations of discrimination from civil rights groups, and felt that Supreme Court decisions were "handcuffing" them in fighting crime.

4. ***A New Generation of Officers.*** The movement toward unionization was led by a new generation of officers; they were generally younger and more assertive than the established leaders of police fraternal groups.

5. ***The Law-and-Order Mood.*** Unionization succeeded, in part, because unlike the earlier two periods, there was little opposition to them. Because there was great concern over "law and order," mayors and council members did not want to appear hostile toward the police; thus, they were less likely to become involved in matters of unionization.

6. ***A New Legal Climate.*** Unions also succeeded because the attitudes of the courts changed dramatically. Previously, they held that police and public employees had no right to unionize, but by the 1960s, they had adopted the position that employees did have the right to form unions. (Adapted from Walker, 1992: 371)

The early development of police unionization was controversial and often shrouded in conflict, especially with police management. Once established, unions demanded higher salaries; better fringe benefits; more participation in how, when, and where officers worked; and more elaborate disciplinary procedures to protect employees. They also tended to fight back against the charges of critics. In many police departments, employee organizations have become a major obstacle in effecting change. What began as an attempt to improve the lot of the working police officer has often become a barrier to improving standards and performance. Of course, members of police unions do not always agree with this perspective. From their point of view, they may be acting to preserve "hard-won" gains and prevent a decline in "professionalism." In addition, some unions are vocal proponents of organizational change that will improve performance. In some cases, police unions may be more progressive than police managers.

The issues that are negotiated between police unions and management tend to fall into one of three categories: salaries and benefits, conditions of work, and grievance procedures. ***Salaries and benefits*** are influenced by a number of factors, including the economic health of a community, the inflation rate, salaries in comparable police departments (or salaries of comparable positions in other occupations), management's resistance, the militancy of the police union, and the amount of public support for either labor or management.

Conditions of work include a broad range of possible issues, many of which have traditionally been considered management prerogatives, such as the procedures for evaluation, reassignment, and promotions; equipment and uniforms; the number of persons assigned to a car or section of the community; the use of civilian employees; how seniority and education will be used in assignments and promotions; hours worked and off-duty employment; and training and professional development. Critics argue that this kind of union activity is detrimental to the effective management of the department and the provision of quality services to the community (e.g., see Bouza, 1985). Others, however, blame the poor management and treatment of employees as promoting such union activity; they view employee influence over management prerogatives in positive terms, potentially leading to improved managerial practices (e.g, see Kleismet, 1985).

Grievance procedures are concerned with the process to be used in accusing an officer of a violation of departmental policies and procedures of law. Usually, this process involves an identification of officer rights (which may even be codified in state law), how the complaints must be filed, how evidence is obtained and processed, who will make disciplinary decisions, and what appeals, if any, will be allowed. Quite often, police unions, in an effort to protect employees from arbitrary treatment by managers, will demand elaborate grievance mechanisms that frustrate attempts to respond to almost any type of inappropriate police behavior. However, grievance procedures may also be a useful way of clarifying work rules or, said another way, of understanding and agreeing on performance expectations.

Labor-management relations in the police department involve the recognition of shared governance. To achieve this, police managers must keep lines of communication open with union leaders and treat them with respect; it is important to keep in mind that these leaders often have a strong informal influence over organizational members. Accordingly, they should be kept abreast of managerial decisions in order that they can share this information with the membership. To facilitate this process, union representatives should also be encouraged to serve on task forces and participate in management meetings. In this way, union membership can be assured that there are no hidden agendas concerning the union or the negotiating process. An open and participative relationship with the union may help to avoid the costly and unpleasant effects that often result from strikes, job actions (i.e., work slowdowns or speedups), refusals to negotiate, and media attention.

Viewed positively, labor-management relations are a way to improve communication, clarify performance expectations, and ensure responsible employee behavior. Along with understanding how groups may affect individual behavior, managers must also understand how groups communicate in order to solve problems or complete task assignments.

Group Communication Networks

Group communication networks, or the pattern of information flow among group members, significantly affect group performance, satisfaction, and morale. Although countless communication networks exist for small groups, the five major structures in which most of the research has been conducted are shown in Figure 4.7.

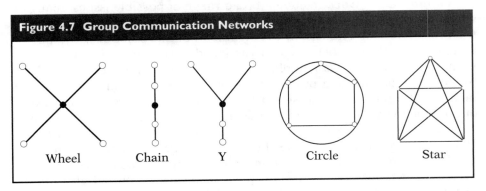

Figure 4.7 Group Communication Networks

Each network represents a five-member group, with the dots depicting individual members and the connecting lines to indicate two-way communication channels. The first three networks depicted in Figure 4.7 are generally centralized in that most messages must flow through a key person in the network. The **wheel network** is the most centralized, in that all communications must flow through and are controlled by the individual in the center of the wheel. In the **chain network,** the members at both ends can communicate with one another, but the individual at the center still tends to control the communication process. In the **Y network,** only two members can communicate directly with each other; the individual at the fork usually becomes the controller of messages. The last two networks are more decentralized, in that communication is less restricted among the members and no one individual controls the messages. In the **circle network**, each member can communicate with the person on either side; in the **star network** which is the most decentralized, each member can communicate with any other member.

Research on the effects of these networks suggests that for relatively simple problems and tasks, the centralized networks are the most effective—the wheel, followed by the Y, the chain, the circle, and the star. The reason is that in solving simple problems and completing simple tasks, shared communication among members is not necessary, so group members are more likely to accept the decisions and work efforts of others in the network. By contrast, complex problems and tasks tend to be completed more effectively with the decentralized networks—the star, followed by the circle, the chain, the Y, and the wheel—because a more complete sharing of information and weighing of alternatives among network members is helpful (Applewhite, 1965).

In those networks with the least restrictive communication channels, group members tend to have the highest degree of satisfaction—the star, followed by the circle, the chain, the Y, and the wheel. In the centralized networks, the members who are located in the center positions (represented by the black dots in Figure 4.7) become the recognized leaders of the group and are very satisfied, while those members farthest from the center are the least satisfied. Finally, some research has indicated that group morale in the decentralized networks was higher, regardless of the complexity of the task (Shaw, 1981). Consequently, any time that centralized networks are used, there may be a morale problem among group members. However, using a decentralized network to work on simple problems or tasks may result in no recognized leader, poorer performance, and longer time toward completion. This is a dilemma for managers, who may need to develop ways in which to improve morale if centralized networks are used for long periods of time by any one group.

From these findings, it is clear that, depending on the situation, there are trade-offs in using any particular type of group communication network. Therefore, police managers need to apply contingency theory and attempt to determine under which conditions a specific network should be used. Three useful propositions to keep in mind when considering group communication networks include the following:

1. Specific communication networks can either increase or decrease performance, satisfaction, and morale levels of group members.

2. Certain communication networks are beneficial to some group members while detrimental to others.

3. The choice of an appropriate communication network depends on the specific situation and involves such matters as the complexity of the problem or task, the need for a team leader, and the amount of time available.

Managing Group Conflict

Police managers must recognize that conflicts both within and between groups are common. Robbins (1974) defines ***conflict*** as a perceived difference between two or more parties that results in mutual opposition. Traditionally, police management has viewed conflict as dysfunctional and has attempted to ignore it, even when clearly present. According to contemporary theory, however, conflict is not only inevitable but is a vital element for change and, if properly managed, is potentially beneficial for the organization.

Some of the negative aspects of conflict include hostility between and among individuals and groups, the withholding of information and resources, and interference with one another's efforts. Some of the positive aspects include defining problem areas and the need for change, increased morale as group members deal with areas of concern and frustration, and creativity and innovation by encouraging new ideas (Tjosvold, 1984). Thus, some conflict is beneficial, although too much can be detrimental. For instance, low conflict levels may be an indication that problems are being hidden and creativity stifled. Too much conflict, however, may indicate that an excessive amount of effort is being directed at dissension. Accordingly, police managers need to balance the positive with the negative aspects of conflict and, when necessary, be able to resolve intergroup conflict.

One type of conflict, which is generally dysfunctional and should be avoided, is **competition.** According to quality management principles, teamwork and group efforts should be encouraged and rewarded because they tend to lead to higher levels of performance. Competition, by contrast, frequently leads to a lack of coordination and communication among groups, which, if not resolved, may create a hostile environment and low performance levels. One of the most common types of competition in police departments has to do with performance levels. For example, detective and patrol units may compete for information in an attempt to solve criminal cases; in some instances, patrol officers and detectives have not communicated with each other on a case for fear that the other would gain an advantage in solving the case and thus receive the credit. Such a situation may also develop between police organizations (e.g., local, state, or federal) who are attempting to solve an important case and wish to receive the credit, even though the solution might be reached faster by cooperating with the other organization.

A second example is the competition among patrol units to produce the greatest number of arrests. Generally, such a situation develops when competition is encouraged (or required) by management, who, in turn, may be evaluated in terms of its unit's "productivity." As noted previously, the productivity levels of police departments are often more difficult to assess than those of private-sector organizations, where bottom line figures may be more appropriate. Simply using quantitative measures (e.g., the number of arrests made), while ignoring qualitative measures (e.g., the number of prosecutions and/or convictions resulting from arrests) is likely to produce negative results. Such tactics may lead to the increased use of technical arrests, which may also be bad arrests in that they may disregard procedural or civil rights of citizens. Such competitive managerial practices, rather than leading to increased levels of performance, may instead lead to internal strife and community hostility.

Resolving and Reducing Intergroup Conflict

Because police managers must live with intergroup conflict, they will need to be aware of the types of methods that can be used to resolve or reduce dysfunctional levels of conflict. There are several such methods (Robbins, 1974; Rahim, 1989).

Problem Solving. One way to reduce tensions is to hold face-to-face meetings with the conflicting groups in order to identify the conflict(s) and resolve them. The groups openly debate the issues and share all relevant information until a decision is reached. This method has been effective in conflicts resulting from misunderstandings or language barriers. For solving more complex problems, such as conflicts in which groups have different value systems, this method has been less successful.

Superordinate Goals. Another way to reduce conflict is to develop a common set of goals and objectives that cannot be attained without the cooperation of the groups involved. Such goals would supersede all other goals of any of the individual groups. For instance, if a serial murderer or rapist were stalking a community, the safety of the community would be more important than which unit (detective or patrol) or police department received credit for an arrest.

Compromise.   Some conflicts may be resolved by having each of the groups agree on a decision in which there is no distinct winner or loser. Compromise is very effective when the goal sought (e.g., money or recognition) can be divided equitably. If such division is not possible, an attempt is made to have each group give up something of value in order to obtain other desired outcomes. Compromise may involve a facilitator, as well as the total group or its representative for negotiating and voting. The aim is to offer both groups the chance to be in a better position, or at least in no worse position, after the conflict is resolved.

Altering the Human Variable.   Sometimes, conflict can be reduced by focusing on the cause of the conflict and the attitudes of the individuals involved and by trying to change them. This method is time-consuming and costly but can be beneficial in the long run. Chapter 14 discusses methods that can be used to change behavior.

Altering the Design Variables.   Still another method is changing the formal design of the department, especially with respect to jobs, units, and reporting relationships. Some of the methods include rotating members among groups, transferring or exchanging certain members, or assigning a coordinator or liaison among groups in order to keep them communicating with one another. Alarid (1999) suggests change can be facilitated and conflict reduced by using small groups of people who are not members of the same subculture group (e.g., mixing officers from different shifts/divisions or mixing sworn officers with civilian personnel, different departments and/or various ranks). This is advantageous because people who are less familiar with each another have less reputation to protect. If management attempts to break the subculture apart, officers will be likely to resist the change effort even more strongly.

The above methods are generally the most effective for long-term solutions to resolving and reducing conflicts; however, there may be a need for more temporary solutions. In such cases, avoidance and authoritative command may be useful methods. ***Avoidance*** simply means that some way is found to avoid the conflict for the short term, although eventually it must be confronted. ***Authoritative command*** is still the most frequently used method for resolving intergroup conflict in police departments. Management simply resolves the conflict as it deems appropriate and communicates this decision to the parties involved. Subordinates normally abide by such a decision, at least in the short run, whether or not they agree with it. Of course, if the cause of the conflict remains, the problems will most likely recur, and possibly at a higher level. Police managers, for the most part, should view authoritative command as a short-term solution to buy time to work on more long-lasting results. Finally, the authors believe that most, if not all, of the above methods could also benefit through a mutual sharing of expectations by the parties involved. If managers and groups can honestly and openly share their expectations, the groundwork for mutual understanding and cooperation will be in place.

❖ ❖ ❖ ❖   ## Summary

The fundamental characteristics of organizations include their composition (individuals and groups), orientation (toward goals), and methods used to obtain goals (division of labor and rational coordination). In regard to organization design, police managers need to be concerned with the formal pattern of arrangements that link individuals and groups together in order to accomplish organizational goals. External influences include the type of environment in which an organization operates; specifically, a turbulent, constantly changing environment is better suited to an organic design; a relatively stable, unchanging environment is better suited to a mechanistic design. Because police departments have relatively unstable environments, and especially for those moving to community policing, the classical/paramilitary design may no longer be appropriate. Internal influences include the department's human resources; namely, employee skills and abilities and how they are distributed throughout the department, as well as employee needs.

Because formal and informal groups control many of the stimuli to which their members are exposed, they significantly affect the beliefs and attitudes, as well as the job-relevant skills and abilities, of these members. Accordingly, managers must understand how groups work and how to effectively deal with group behavior. Police culture is also an important influence on employee behavior. Thus, the socialization process that leads to both a street cop's and a manager's culture should be recognized. Because of the diverse cultural and ethnic make-up of many police departments, managers must be able to effectively deal with different types of employee organizations, including police unions. Groups tend to develop certain communication networks that also have an impact on performance and satisfaction. Thus, managers need to understand how these networks work in order to be able to use the most effective network in the circumstances. Finally, although intergroup conflict may be positive and a vital element for change, dysfunctional conflict, such as too much competition among groups, needs to be effectively controlled. Several constructive methods used to resolve or reduce conflict include problem solving, setting superordinate goals, compromise, altering the human variable, and changing the design variables.

Discussion Questions

1. Discuss three fundamental characteristics of organizations that are important to understanding organizational behavior.

2. Differentiate between formal and informal groups in organizations. Describe the Dalton study and its importance.

3. What influences must be considered when establishing the goals of a police department? How do these relate to community policing?

4. Discuss why measuring police goals is difficult. Describe several methods that can be used to assess the achievement of those goals.

5. Discuss how both division of labor and rational coordination help police departments to reach their goals.

6. Describe the classical organization design. Discuss several criticisms of this design as it applies to police departments; why is police legitimacy important?

7. Describe the major characteristics of mechanistic and organic models. Under what conditions does each model appear to be more appropriate?

8. Discuss the impact of group influences on individual behavior in organizations. What is police culture and what influence does it appear to have on individual behavior in police departments?

9. Provide examples of those communication networks that are the most appropriate for simple and complex problems and tasks.

10. Discuss potential positive and negative aspects associated with group conflict. Describe at least four methods that can be used by police managers to resolve and reduce intergroup conflict.

❖ ❖ ❖ ❖

References

Alarid, L. F. 1999. "Law Enforcement Departments as Learning Organizations: Argyris's Theory as a Framework for Implementing Community-Oriented Policing." *Police Quarterly* 2: 321-337.

Allport, F. H. 1933. *Industrial Behavior.* Chapel Hill: University of North Carolina Press.

Applewhite, P. B. 1965. *Organizational Behavior.* Englewood Cliffs, NJ: Prentice-Hall.

Astin, A. W. 1978. *Four Critical Years: Effects of College on Beliefs, Attitudes, and Knowledge.* San Francisco: Jossey-Bass.

Auten, J. H. 1981. "The Paramilitary Model of Police and Police Professionalism." *Police Studies* 4: 67-78.

Barnard, C. I. 1938. *The Functions of the Executive.* Cambridge, MA: Harvard University Press.

Bouza, A. V. 1985. "Police Unions: Paper Tigers or Roaring Lions?" In W. A. Geller (ed.), *Police Leadership in America: Crisis and Opportunity,* pp. 241-280. New York: Praeger.

Bowker, L. 1980. "A Theory of Educational Needs of Law Enforcement Officers." *Journal of Contemporary Criminal Justice* 1: 17-24.

Bureau of Justice Statistics. 1997. *Implementing the National Incident-Based Reporting System: A Project Status Report.* Washington, DC: Department of Justice.

Burns, T., and Stalker, G. M. 1961. *The Management of Innovation.* London: Tavistock.

Carlisle, H. A. 1974. "A Contingency Approach to Decentralization." *Advanced Management Journal,* July: 9-18.

Child, J. 1984. *Organization: A Guide to Problems and Practice.* London: Harper & Row.

Cohen, B., and Chaiken, J. 1972. *Police Characteristics and Performance.* New York: Rand Institute.

Couper, D. C., and Lobitz, S. H. 1991. *Quality Policing: The Madison Experience.* Washington, DC: Police Executive Research Forum.

Crank, J. P. 1997. "Celebrating Agency Culture: Engaging a Traditional Cop's Heart in Organizational Change." In Q. C. Thurmann and E. F. McGarrell (eds.), *Community Policing in a Rural Setting,* pp. 49–57. Cincinnati: Anderson.

Cronkhite, C. 1988. "Santa Ana's Reorganization—Matrix Community Oriented Policing." *Journal of California Law Enforcement* 22: 94-99.

Dalton, M. 1959. *Men Who Manage.* New York: Wiley.

Davis, K. 1981. *Human Behavior at Work: Organizational Behavior,* 6th ed. New York: McGraw-Hill.

Doyle, M. A. 1980. "Police Culture: Open or Closed?" In V.A. Leonard (ed.), *Fundamentals of Law Enforcement: Problems and Issues,* pp. 61–83. St. Paul, MN: West.

Feldman, K. A., and Newcomb, T. M. 1969. *The Impact of College on Students.* San Francisco: Jossey-Bass.

Flippo, E. B. 1970. *Management: A Behavioral Approach,* 2nd ed. Boston: Allyn & Bacon.

Franz, V., and Jones, D. M. 1987. "Perceptions of Organizational Performance in Suburban Police Departments: A Critique of the Military Model." *Journal of Police Science and Administration* 15: 153-161.

Gaines, L., Tubergen, N., and Paiva, M. 1984. "Police Officer Perceptions of Promotion as a Source of Motivation." *Journal of Criminal Justice* 12: 265–275.

Greene, J. R. 2000. "Community Policing in America: Changing Nature, Structure and Function of the Police." In *Criminal Justice 2000,* Volume 3: *Policies, Processes, and Decisions in the Criminal Justice System,* pp. 299-370. Washington, DC: National Institute of Justice.

Griffin, G. R., Dunbar, R. L. M., and McGill, M. E. 1978. "Factors Associated with Job Satisfaction Among Police Personnel." *Journal of Police Science and Administration* 6: 77-85.

Hare, A. P. 1962. *Handbook of Small Group Research.* New York: Free Press.

Howser, R. M., and Lorsch, J. W. 1967. "Organizational Inputs." In J. M. Seiler (ed.), *Systems Analysis in Organizational Behavior.* Homewood, IL: Irwin.

Kast, F. E., and Rosenzweig, J. E. 1974. *Organization and Management: A Systems Approach,* 2nd ed. New York: McGraw-Hill.

Kleismet, R. B. 1985. "The Chief and the Union: May the Force Be With You." In W. A. Geller (ed.), *Police Leadership in America: Crisis and Opportunity,* pp. 281-285. New York: Praeger.

Kraska, P. B., and Cubellis, L. J. 1997. "Militarizing Mayberry and Beyond: Making Sense of American Paramilitary Policing." *Justice Quarterly* 14: 607-629.

Kraska, P. B., and Kappeler, V. E. 1997. "Militarizing American Police: The Rise and Normalization of Paramilitary Units." *Social Problems* 44: 1-18.

Kraska, P. B., and Paulson, D. J. 1997. "Grounded Research Into U. S. Paramilitary Policing: Forging the Iron Fist Inside the Velvet Glove." *Policing and Society* 7: 253-270.

Kuykendall, J., and Roberg, R. R. 1982. "Mapping Police Organizational Change: From a Mechanistic Toward an Organic Model." *Criminology* 20: 241-256.

Langworthy, R. H. 1986. *The Structure of Police Organizations.* New York: Praeger.

——. 1992. "Organizational Structure." In G. W. Cordner and D. C. Hale (eds.), *What Works in Policing?* pp. 87-105. Cincinnati, OH: Anderson.

Law Enforcement News. 2000. "Detectives May Be an Endangered Species for One Iowa Department." October 15: 1,8.

Law Enforcement News. 2000. "The New & Improved UCR—Is Anyone Paying Attention?" September 15: 1.

Lawrence, P. R., and Lorsch, J. W. 1967. *Organization and Environment: Managing Differentiation and Integration.* Homewood, IL: Irwin.

Levy, R. J. 1967. "Predicting Police Failures." *Journal of Criminal Law, Criminology, and Police Science* 58: 265-275.

——. 1973. "A Method for the Identification of the Higher Risk Police Applicant." In J. R. Snibbe and H. M. Snibbe (eds.), *The Urban Policeman in Transition,* pp. 25-52. Springfield, IL: C. C. Thomas.

Litterer, J. A. 1965. *The Analysis of Organizations.* New York: Wiley.

Maguire, E. R. 1997. "Structural Change in Large Municipal Police Organizations During the Community Policing Era." *Justice Quarterly* 14: 547-576.

Marsh, S. H. 1962. "Validating the Selection of Deputy Sheriffs." *Public Personnel Review* 23: 41-44.

Mottaz, C. 1983. "Alienation Among Police Officers." *Journal of Police Science and Administration* 11: 23-30.

National Institute of Justice. 1997. *Measuring What Matters. Part Two: Developing Measures of What the Police Do.* Washington, DC: Department of Justice.

Paoline, E. A., Myers, S. M., and Worden, R. E. 2000. "Police Culture, Individualism, and Community Policing: Evidence From Two Police Departments." *Justice Quarterly* 17: 575-605.

Parsons, T. 1960. *Structure and Process in Modern Societies.* Glencoe, IL: Free Press.

Perrow, C. 1970. *Organizational Analysis: A Sociological View.* Belmont, CA: Wadsworth.

Pfiffner, J. M., and Sherwood, F. P. 1960. *Administrative Organization.* Englewood Cliffs, NJ: Prentice-Hall.

Porter, L. W., Lawler, E. E., and Hackman, J. R. 1975. *Behavior in Organizations.* New York: McGraw-Hill.

Rahim, M. A., ed. 1989. *Managing Conflict: An Interdisciplinary Approach.* New York: Praeger.

Reibstein, L. 1997. "NYPD Black and Blue." *Newsweek,* June 2: 66, 68.

Reuss-Ianni, E. 1983. *Two Cultures of Policing: Street Cops and Management Cops.* New Brunswick, CT: Transaction Books.

Robbins, S. P. 1974. *Managing Organizational Conflict: A Nontraditional Approach.* Englewood Cliffs, NJ: Prentice-Hall.

Roberg, R., Crank, J. and Kuykendall, J. 2000. *Police & Society,* 2nd ed. Los Angeles, CA: Roxbury Publishing Company.

Sayles, L. R., and Strauss, G. 1966. *Human Behavior in Organizations.* Englewood Cliffs, NJ: Prentice-Hall.

Shaw, M. E. 1981. *Group Dynamics: The Psychology of Small Group Behavior.* New York: McGraw-Hill.

Sherman, L. W. 1997. "Policing for Crime Prevention." In L. W. Sherman, D. Gottfredson, D. MacKenzie, J. Eck, P. Reuter, and S. Bushway (eds.), *Preventing Crime: What Works, What Doesn't, What's Promising,* pp. 8/1-8/58. Washington, DC: Office of Justice Programs.

Skogan, W. G. and Hartnett, S. M. 1997. *Community Policing, Chicago Style.* New York: Oxford University Press.

Stieglitz, H. 1962. *Organizational Planning.* New York: National Industrial Conference Board.

Stoddard, K. B. 1973. "Characteristics of Policemen of a County Sheriff's Office." In J. R. Snibbe and H. M. Snibbe (eds.), *The Urban Policeman in Transition,* pp. 281-297. Springfield, IL: C. C. Thomas.

Tjosvold, D. 1984. "Making Conflict Productive." *Personnel Administrator,* June: 121-130.

Trent, J. W., and Medsker, L. L. 1968. *Beyond High School.* San Francisco: Jossey-Bass.

Walker, S. 1992. *The Police in America: An Introduction,* 2nd ed. New York: McGraw-Hill.

Watson, E. M, Stone, A. R., and DeLuca, S. T. 1998. *Strategies for Community Policing.* Upper Saddle River, NJ: Prentice-Hall.

Weirman, C. L. 1978. "Variances of Ability Measurement Scores Obtained by College and Non-College-Educated Troopers." *Police Chief,* August: 34-36.

Williams, E. J. 1995. *Implementing Community Policing: A Documentation and Assessment Organizational Change.* Ph.D. dissertation. Portland, OR: Portland State University.

Woodward, J. [1958] 1965. *Management and Technology.* London: H. M. Stationery Office.

Worden, R. E. 1995. "Police Officers' Belief Systems: A Framework for Analysis." *American Journal of Policing* 14: 49–81.

Zhao, J., and Thurman, Q. 1996. *The Nature of Community Policing Innovations: Do the Ends Justify the Means?* Washington, DC: Police Executive Research Forum.

Selection and Diversity

As noted in the previous chapters, the nature of policing and police organizations is changing—becoming more complex and challenging—necessitating the importance of hiring and retaining the highest-quality personnel available. Although the quality of police personnel has always been important, with the increased complexity of the police role and the movement toward community policing, the quality of personnel has perhaps become the key element in the effective operation of the police.

The debate over the meaning of "quality," however, is not easy to resolve. For instance, does a person need a certain level of intelligence, and how is that measured? Are certain physical characteristics important? Should higher education be required? What about moral and ethical values? Quality considerations also suggest that departments should select personnel, including women, who are representative of the communities they serve because they help provide a greater understanding of issues related to gender, race, and ethnicity. Cultural diversity in policing is discussed in the final section of this chapter.

Any discussion of police selection and police development (the topic of Chapter 6) requires an understanding of the community's social, political, administrative, and economic character. To what degree is the population homogeneous or heterogeneous? To what degree do elected, appointed, or influential citizens attempt to involve themselves in personnel matters? How much money is available to support personnel? What salaries and benefits are to be given to employees? What is the available labor pool? Who is responsible for the selection and development process? Is it the police department itself or an organization that may serve more than one police department? The answers to these questions determine the approach to, and limitations in, the design and implementation of policies for managing police human resources.

Police selection and development are also heavily influenced by a city or county civil service system. For instance, civil service requirements may affect a department's criteria for selection, promotion, and discipline. Civil service provisions were enacted in 1883 in the Pendleton Civil Service Act, which tried to eliminate the political influence of selecting police officers (as discussed in Chapter 3). But civil service also had a number of negative side effects. For instance, Wilson and McLaren (1977: 248), who were early critics of civil service, believed that civil service rules provided too much security for "incompetent and untrustworthy" officers, who are virtually impossible to "weed out." Today, although it is possible to terminate incompetent or dishonest police employees, as a result of civil service, it is an onerous, expensive, and time-consuming effort.

Critics further argue that because of the protections provided by the law of equal employment opportunity, civil service regulations are not only unnecessary but generally impede the effective management of police departments. Suffice it to say that regardless of which side one argues, police managers are heavily influenced by civil service regulations and must take them into account. If a police manager believes that, for instance, underqualified applicants are getting through the selection phase, it would be prudent to make sure that recruit training is rigorous enough to either improve or eliminate such applicants. Or, if management believes that effective control is being compromised, then management should make sure that investigations into wrongdoing are fully documented and the action taken is thoroughly explained. Managers must not use civil service regulations as an excuse to overlook performance problems.

A police department makes essentially three selection decisions: ***entry, reassignment,*** and ***promotion.*** Police entrance selection usually applies to the lowest-level position (patrol), though entrance to supervisory and managerial levels is possible. A few departments recruit for lower and middle-level managers (e.g., sergeants, lieutenants, and captains) from outside the organization. Some, but not many, select a chief of police from the outside. Because most sheriffs are elected, potential candidates may include people outside the sheriff's department or even outside the law enforcement field.

All states have created statewide standards for parts of the personnel process (e.g., selection, training, promotion, and some aspects of evaluation). For example, many states now have a Peace Officer Standards and Training

(handwritten margin note: also termination)

Commission (POST). There is still considerable variation among states, how- ❖ ❖ ❖ ❖
ever, and some departments do not adhere to the established personnel standards because they are not obligated by law to do so.

Hiring recruits who can become effective patrol officers is the primary
purpose of the selection process. It is vitally important because recruitment,
selection and training is an extremely expensive process. Furthermore, once
candidates are selected and are employed for a minimum amount of time,
they essentially receive tenure and may be with the department for twenty
years or longer. Although incompetent or dishonest officers can be disciplined, reassigned, or in some cases terminated, each process consumes a
great deal of managerial time and effort. Therefore, it is important to attract
and hire high-quality personnel who will be contributing members of the
department throughout their careers.

If high-quality police recruits are to be chosen, the selection process
should be designed to **screen in,** rather than **screen out,** applicants.
Screening out identifies applicants who are unqualified and removes them
from consideration, while leaving all those who are minimally qualified in
the applicant pool. Recruits are then selected from this pool who may not be
well qualified for police work. In contrast, screening in identifies the best-
qualified candidates for the applicant pool. The department will select its
recruits from these applicants, thus ensuring a relatively high-quality candidate. Interestingly, many police departments still rely on screening out applicants, but the process has been under attack since at least 1973, when the
National Advisory Commission on Criminal Justice Standards and Goals
noted:

> The selection of police personnel should be approached positively; police de-
> partments should seek to identify and employ the best candidates available
> rather than being content with disqualifying the unfit. The policy of merely
> eliminating the least qualified results in mediocrity because it allows mar-
> ginal applicants to be employed along with the most qualified. (1973: 20)

Recruitment

The initial step in the recruitment process is attracting well-qualified candidates. The relationship of the number of applicants to those who qualify for
positions affects the quality of the personnel employed. The most common
recruitment methods in policing include (1) advertisement, through bro-
chures, newspapers, television, radio, mass mailings, and journals; (2)
requests to special-interest groups, such as neighborhood, social, political,
and minority groups; (3) public-service announcements on television and
radio; (4) requests to university career planning and placement offices (cam-
pus recruiting is essential if educational requirements are to be increased);
and (5) referrals from current employees (Chapman, 1982; International City
Management Association, 1986; Langworthy, Hughes, and Sanders, 1995).
Some larger police departments have expanded their recruitment efforts to a
national level, and many departments (of all sizes) now announce position
openings on the department's website. In some police departments, officers
are given such incentives as extra days off or a pay bonus if they recruit someone into the organization. Some departments send their recruiters to other
cities and states in an attempt to enlarge the applicant pool.

One of the major problems with advertising has been the **police image** that has been portrayed. Police departments have always had difficulty portraying the reality of police work. They often present only the most favorable image of both the department and the police role, especially highlighting an ethnically and sexually diverse organization that continually performs adventurous and exciting work. Although this image may be effective from a recruitment perspective, it may also be deceitful. The recruits' perception of reality in the organization after employment rarely matches the advertised image. There is a strong possibility that such discrepancies lead to employee disenchantment and frustration. Consequently, although the organization needs to present an effective image for recruitment purposes, that image should be accurate and realistic. In other words, as the expectation-integration model suggests, such an initial sharing of expectations could lead to a more productive long-term relationship between employer and employee.

In attempting to recruit the best-qualified applicants, departments should recognize that different **recruitment strategies** may be necessary. For example, Meagher and Yentes (1986) found a high degree of consensus between male and female officers regarding their personal reasons for entering policing; women, however, were substantially less interested in "fighting crime" than were men. These findings suggest that although recruitment strategies for both men and women can be essentially the same, to attract women, recruiters should emphasize the helping nature of the role, including community service and problem-solving activities. In a national study of recruitment, selection, and training practices (Langworthy, Hughes, and Sanders, 1995), based on 60 departments with more than 500 sworn personnel, 52.5 percent responded that they use recruiting strategies to target women.

In another study, Slater and Reiser (1988) found ethnic groups differed in their reasons for entering policing. The three main reasons selected by each group in diminishing order of importance were as follows: blacks—variety, public service, and responsibility; Hispanic—variety, responsibility, pay, and public service; Asian—responsibility, public service, and variety; caucasian—variety, adventure, and responsibility. These findings suggest that departments may need to vary their recruitment efforts somewhat, depending on the particular group. The study by Langworthy, Hughes, and Sanders (1995) indicated that 90 percent of the surveyed departments use recruiting strategies to attract minorities.

In order to improve recruitment in today's competitive market, departments may need to consider nontraditional methods. For example, in New York, the use of a **police cadet corps,** designed to increase applicants with college degrees, may also increase women and minority applicants as well. The New York cadet corps, in operation since 1986, is used to recruit college seniors who are interested in joining the force after graduation; they receive scholarship money and agree to serve as police officers for two years. While attending college, the students work part time as police cadets, thus gaining valuable field experience (*Law Enforcement News,* 1989: 13). After completing the program, the cadet is promoted to the rank of police officer while completing their degree (Zecca, 1993).

Another innovative recruitment program is the Sacramento, California, **community service officer** (CSO) program. The department, which requires 60 units of college credit, attributes much of its success in minority employment to its CSO program. CSOs are recruited out of high school at age 18 to join the department in paid positions; they must meet the same qualifications (except for age and education) as sworn officers and attend the same police academy. Following graduation from the academy, CSOs are assigned support duties that do not require sworn authority or a weapon. While working as CSOs, they are required to attend college (with tuition assistance from the department). After earning at least 60 college credits and attaining age 21, the CSO is eligible to become a sworn officer (Carter, Sapp, and Stephens, 1989: 89).

Another recruitment strategy that departments are using to attract women, minorities, and college graduates is to grant **special entry conditions** for these groups. Such conditions include lower education and fitness standards, exemptions from examinations, quotas, faster promotion, higher pay, and waiting list preferences. Langworthy, Hughes, and Sanders (1995) reported that approximately 40 percent of the surveyed departments have special entry conditions for minorities, 32 percent for women, and 28 percent for college graduates.

Selection

The selection process determines which candidates are best suited to the needs of the organization. The process must decide whether candidates have the requisite skills and abilities to perform effectively. In order to make such judgments, various selection criteria are used, including pre-employment standards and pre-employment testing to establish a ranking system from which candidates are hired. It is crucial that these standards and tests be valid and reliable indicators of job performance. **Validity** is the degree to which a measure actually assesses the attribute it is designed to measure. For example, is the physical-strength and agility criterion traditionally used for selection related to the ability to satisfactorily perform the job? If not, then it is not a valid criterion for selection. **Reliability** refers to a measure's ability to yield consistent results over time. In the physical-strength and agility example, the measure would be reliable if a candidate taking the test on more than one occasion received the same or similar score. Departments attempt to use criteria that are both valid and reliable; of course, it is possible to have criteria that are valid but not reliable or reliable but not valid. For instance, although a physical-strength score may be reliable, it may not be valid if it cannot be shown to be job related.

In addition, validity is important because invalid criteria may have an adverse impact on groups that are protected by equal employment opportunity (EEO) laws and regulations. The Equal Employment Opportunity Act of 1972 extended to public departments the "anti-discrimination in employment" provisions of Title VII of the 1964 Civil Rights Act. Title VII prohibits any discrimination in the workplace based on race, color, religion, national origin, or sex, even if the discrimination is unintentional. In *Griggs v. Duke Power Company* (1971), the Supreme Court held that an employer's requirement of a high school diploma and two standardized written tests for a position disqualified a higher percentage of blacks than whites and could not be shown to be related to job performance. Consequently, the standards had a ***disparate impact*** on Griggs specifically and on blacks in general. A selection method can be considered to have a legally disparate impact when the selection rate of a group is less than 80 percent of the most successful group; this is also known as the ***four-fifths rule*** (see Biddle, 1993). Prior to *Griggs*, selection standards could be used as long as they did not intentionally discriminate; after *Griggs*, standards could not be used that were intended to be impartial but in fact were discriminatory in practice.

In another important decision, *Albemarle Paper Company v. Moody* (1975), the Supreme Court found that selection and promotion tests or standards must be shown to be related to job performance; that is, the standard must be ***job related.*** This decision had far-reaching implications for police selection, because all selection criteria must be shown to be related to on-the-job performance. It is important to note, however, that departments can require a standard, even though it may have a disparate impact, if the standard can be shown to be a valid predictor of job performance. For example, in *Davis v. City of Dallas* (1985), the Supreme Court upheld the Dallas Police Department's forty-five-college-hour requirement, even though it discriminated against minorities, because of the professional and complex nature of police work. Legal precedent for higher educational requirements had previously been established by other professions. Such a job-related standard, known as a ***bona fide occupational qualification*** (BFOQ), is permissible under Title VII, even though it may exclude members of a protected group.

Police departments, of course, should attempt to use selection methods that not only are valid but also do not have an adverse impact. This means that departments must commit resources to validating their selection and testing methods through a job analysis. A ***job analysis*** identifies the behaviors necessary for adequate job performance. Based on such identification, the ***knowledge, skills, and attitudes*** (KSAs) required for the on-the-job behaviors are formulated; procedures (e.g., tests and interviews) are then developed to identify candidates who meet these requirements. The procedures are tested relative to their effectiveness of predicting job performance (Schneider and Schmitt, 1986). Because job analysis can be quite complex, it is often conducted by an industrial or organizational psychologist or someone with similar qualifications. Although the job-validation process is a rigorous undertaking for any department, it should not be looked upon merely as a legal obligation; selection systems that can be scientifically shown to produce high-quality candidates in a fair manner will withstand legal scrutiny and produce candidates most likely to serve the community effectively (Sauls, 1985: 31).

Pre-Employment Standards

Candidates are measured against a department's view of what is required to become an effective police officer. A number of minimum standards are established that must be met prior to employment. These standards are usually quite rigid and establish certain finite qualifications, which, if not met, will most likely eliminate the candidate from further consideration. Such standards may apply to age, vision, height and weight, physical agility, residency, education, background, psychological condition, and medical condition. Although not all departments have all of these requirements, they are common to many. The standards themselves, however, vary considerably.

Physical and Demographic Standards

Age. Traditionally, police departments allowed applicants to be between the ages of 21 and 32 to 38, with some accepting applicants as young as 18. Many managers believe that 18- to 21-year-olds may not be mature enough to perform police work satisfactorily, and if hired, should be assigned service duties only, much like the police corps and CSO program described above. There have been legal challenges to age requirements, primarily at the upper limits. The Age Discrimination in Employment Act (ADEA) of 1967 and the amendment of 1974 have extended equal employment opportunity to apply to age, specifically to people 40 or older. Police departments have traditionally set maximum age limits for hiring because they also had mandatory retirement ages; many departments were temporarily exempt from the ADEA and were allowed to retain minimum-maximum age policies for a period of time (March 3, 1983, to December 31, 1993). Since January 1, 1994, however, this exemption has not applied, and today departments must be in compliance with the ADEA. Any recruiting or hiring practices that tend to discourage persons over forty from applying might be deemed discriminatory. Without a BFOQ, for example, terms such as "recent graduate" or "young" cannot be used in advertising for police officer positions (Rubin, 1995: 7). In compliance with the ADEA, departments are now hiring recruits over 40 and even 50; for example, the Los Angeles Police Department hired a 59-year-old recruit as a probationary police officer (*San Jose Mercury News*, 1994).

Height and Weight. Stringent minimum and maximum height-and-weight requirements were standards for most departments in the past. As with age requirements, however, these requirements have been changing over the past several decades due to legal challenges. For instance, minimum-height requirements have been challenged successfully as being discriminatory against both women and minority groups, especially Asians and Hispanics. For example, in *Vanguard Justice Society v. Hughes* (1979), the court noted that a five-foot-seven-inch height requirement excluded 95 percent of the female population but only 32 percent of the male population and was therefore evidence of sex discrimination. Because of such rulings, the general standard has now become weight in proportion to height. According to one national survey, fewer than 4 percent of municipal departments still maintain minimum-height or minimum-weight requirements (Fyfe, 1987).

Vision Requirements. Another BFOQ may be adequate vision. Vision requirements were also traditionally very stringent, ranging from 20/20 to 20/70 uncorrected in both eyes. Further, departments used to require vision to be 20/20 once corrected with contacts or eyeglasses. This standard too has been relaxed over the years, because such a requirement cannot be job validated and eliminates otherwise strong candidates. Virtually all police departments, however, still maintain certain corrected and uncorrected vision requirements.

Physical Agility and Strength. Testing of physical agility and strength has been related to an assumed need for physical strength and endurance. For example, candidates would be required to perform a number of sit-ups, push-ups, and chin-ups, possibly perform a rope climb, and run a certain timed distance (a half-mile to two miles); if they fell below a certain minimum, they would be eliminated. Again, because many of these standards could not be shown to be job related, they were found to be discriminatory. Accordingly, some departments have changed their physical requirements to meet job-related criteria, such as climbing a fence or dragging a body (using a weighted dummy or a sack of sand); due to the difficulty of distinguishing between who can and cannot perform the job, physical testing is moving toward health-based testing rather than meeting specific physical standards (Gaines and Kappeler, 1992). A number of departments examine applicants' cardiovascular capacity, body fat composition, flexibility, and dynamic and absolute strength (Schofield, 1989). Tests are developed to measure these attributes, and a passing cut-off score is determined based on population norms, generally at the fiftieth percentile in one's age and sex groups.

Residency

Most large police departments do not have a residency requirement and recruit throughout their state or nationwide. Whether or not a department has such a requirement has a strong impact on those who may be recruited. There are essentially two types of requirements: (1) an applicant must reside within a geographic area (state, county, or city) for a specific period of time (one year is common) prior to application (pre-employment), and (2) an applicant must relocate after he or she is selected (post-employment). Reaves and Goldberg (1999) reported in their national survey of local departments with at least 100 sworn officers that approximately 60 percent required some type of residence requirement for new officers. This proportion was higher for law enforcement personnel employed at the state level. Proponents of such requirements argue that it is important for people to have an understanding of the community in which they work and that those who live in the community have a greater stake in and concern for the community. Pre-employment requirements are often supported by politicians, especially during times of high unemployment, because special-interest groups demand their fair share of public-service jobs.

Opponents of residency requirements argue that they unnecessarily restrict the applicant pool because the best candidates simply may not live within the geographic limits; it can also have a negative impact on minority recruitment. It seems clear, however, that if departments wish to hire the best available personnel, then it makes little sense to establish policies that severely restrict the applicant pool; thus, departments should not have pre-employment residency requirements. If a residency requirement is necessary for political or other reasons, then a post-employment policy that allows the recruit a reasonable period of time to relocate seems reasonable.

Education

Desires for increased education of the police can be traced back to 1917, when August Vollmer made the effort to recruit college-educated officers. Proponents of better-educated officers argue that education is a key component of police professionalism and that education can positively affect individual officer performance. This is achieved by having an increased tolerance of people, the ability to effectively analyze complex problems, and applying more effective verbal skills in attaining solutions (Goldstein, 1977; Worden, 1994). As Worden (1990:576) stated, "Because college education is supposed to provide insights into human behavior and to foster a spirit of experimentation, college-educated officers are (hypothetically) less inclined to invoke the law to resolve problems, and correspondingly are inclined more strongly to develop extralegal solutions." However, advances in raising educational requirements for police have been slow and sporadic. Until the 1980s, in many police departments, an officer with a college degree was often viewed with contempt or resentment; it was not understood why anyone with a degree would want to enter policing. Although times have changed considerably, college requirements for the job have not. A national study conducted in 1997 by the Bureau of Justice Statistics (Reaves and Goldberg, 2000) of more than 3,000 state and local police departments, serving communities of all sizes, indicates that overall only 1 percent of departments requires a college degree for employment (see Table 5.1).

Table 5.1   Minimum Educational Requirements for Local Police Departments by Size of Population Served, 1997

Population Served	Total with Requirement	Percent of Agencies Requiring a Minimum of:			
		High School Diploma	2-Year Some College*	4-Year College Degree	College Degree
All sizes	97%	83%	5%	8%	1%
1,000,000 or more	100%	63%	31%	6%	0%
500,000–999,999	100	63	25	12	0
250,000–499,999	100	74	15	6	4
100,000–249,000	100	72	17	10	1
50,000–99,999	100	71	14	13	3
25,000–49,999	100	76	9	11	3
10,000–24,999	99	79	6	11	2
2,500–9,999	98	85	4	8	1
Under 2,500	95	84	4	6	1

Note: Detail may not add to total because of rounding.
*Non-degree requirements

Reaves, B. A. and Goldberg, A. L. 2000. *Local Police Departments, 1997*. Washington, DC: Bureau of Justice Statistics, p5.

Table 5.1 also indicates that in some jurisdictions the figure is higher than 1 percent; for example, 13 percent of departments in jurisdictions having more than 50,000 residents but less than 100,000 require a two-year degree, and 31 percent of departments in jurisdictions of more than 1,000,000 population require some college. Two other national studies have reported that although college-degree requirements for initial selection are low, many officers later obtained degrees. A 1988 study of almost 500 departments (Carter, Sapp, and Stephens, 1989) found that approximately 23 percent of the officers had obtained a college degree. A 1994 study on departments with more than 500 sworn officers (Sanders, Hughes, and Langworthy, 1995) reported that approximately 28 percent of the officers were college graduates. These results are noteworthy because they suggest that although college degree requirements remain low, in general, approximately only 25 percent of today's officers have graduated from college.

Given the increasing numbers of college-educated officers in the field, such slow progress in developing higher educational standards is perplexing, especially in view of the fact that the preponderance of evidence indicates that, in general, college education has a positive effect on officer attitudes, behavior, and performance (e.g., see Roberg, Crank, and Kuykendall, 2000, Chapter 11). The Carter, Sapp, and Stephens (1989: xxii–xxiii) study of nearly 500 departments indicated that the chief executives had strong beliefs regarding the advantages possessed by officers with higher levels of education. With such support for higher education, the question may be posed: Why have educational standards not been raised by most police departments? The Carter et al. study found that the two most common reasons cited were (1) fear of being sued because college could not be quantitatively validated to show job relatedness and (2) fear that such requirements would be discriminatory toward minorities.

As noted earlier, the courts have upheld higher educational requirements in policing to be job related (e.g., see *Davis v. City of Dallas*, 1985). With respect to discrimination, the courts must strike a balance between requirements that are necessary for effective job performance and discriminatory practices. In *Davis*, the city of Dallas conceded that the college requirements did have a "significant disparate impact on blacks" (1985: 207). However, the court held that the complex requirements of police work took precedence over the discriminatory effects. Furthermore, Carter, Sapp, and Stephens discovered that the average educational levels of the various racial and ethnic groups and overall minority representation are not significantly different from the majority (see Table 5.2).

Table 5.2	Mean Years of Education by Race/Ethnicity and Minority Representation in Police Organizations		
Group	**Mean Years**	**Percentage in Police**	**National Percentage**
Black	13.6	12.3	12.1
Hispanic	13.3	6.4	8.0
White	13.7	80.3	76.9
Other	13.8	1.0	3.0

Adapted from: D. L. Carter, A. D. Sapp, and D. W. Stephens, 1988. "Higher Education as a Bona Fide Occupational Qualification (BFOQ) for Police: A Blueprint," *American Journal of Police* 7: 20. MCB University Press, Ltd. Reprinted by permission: MBC University Press, Ltd.

These data indicate that higher education does not appear to have the negative impact on minority-officer recruitment that was initially feared. If departments are willing to employ aggressive or nontraditional recruitment methods in order to hire qualified minority candidates, higher educational standards should not have a disparate impact. Consequently, it is time for departments to campaign actively for the adoption of a four-year college requirement for initial selection, especially for those departments that are attempting to adopt community policing. An added benefit of requiring a college degree is that it will not only substantially reduce the pool of applicants (an important consideration in some large police departments) but also allow departments to continue to screen in only the best available candidates.

Furthermore, it could be persuasively argued that if the field is to become more professional and police departments are to become more organic and adaptable, then a **college degree** will have to become more than just a nicety for upwardly mobile (i.e., promotion-seeking) officers; it must become a **minimum standard for entry.** Results from empirical research support the need for higher education by outlining differences between attitudes and performance. First, research has demonstrated that officers with higher levels of education are less authoritative than their counterparts (Parker, Donnelly, Gerwitz, Marcus and Kowalewski, 1976; Roberg, 1978; Smith and Aamodt, 1997), and had a greater acceptance of minorities (Weiner, 1976). Both of these attitudes may be helpful for organizations attempting to make a transition toward community policing. Second, college-educated officers often perform differently when encountering citizens. For example, college-educated officers were less likely to receive complaints about their performance from citizens (Cascio, 1977; Cohen and Chaiken, 1972; Finnegan, 1976; Sanderson, 1978; Trojanowicz and Nicholson, 1976), less likely to use deadly force (Fyfe 1988), and less likely to use unreasonable or excessive force (Worden 1994). These decisions, as will be discussed later in Chapter 11, may result in less exposure to civil liability for both the officer and the police department (Carter and Sapp, 1989).

Third, research has demonstrated that it is beneficial for the individual seeking a career in policing to pursue higher education. Polk and Armstrong (2001) examined the influence of education on career paths of Texas police officers. Their research indicated officers with higher levels of education were more likely to move to other specialized positions within the department as well receive promotions to higher ranks. Furthermore, officers with higher levels of education also received a new assignment or promotion quicker than their counterparts. They concluded it was to a police department's advantage to use this information in their selection process, and also to encourage advanced education for existing officers (by offering tuition remittance, preferential shifts to coincide with classes, and other educational incentives).

In reality, this may be easier said than done. Police departments are but one of many organizations competing for and retaining educated, qualified individuals. Private industries can offer compensation that police departments cannot, including higher pay, flexible working hours, upward mobility, annual bonuses or additional compensation, additional vacation time, and preferential retirement packages. This has forced some police departments to relax their educational standards. Inside Management 5.1 focuses on one department's reaction to this problem.

Background

Departments usually conduct an extensive investigation of an applicant's past experience, behavior, and work history in an attempt to assess character

---

Inside Management 5.1

Police Departments Ease Education Requirement

Faced with a declining number of applications, the Portland Police Department (PPD) and the New York Police Department (NYPD) have relaxed their education requirements for new recruits.

In 1996 the PPD implemented a four-year degree for police recruits. This policy, however, is being rescinded due to the fact the number of qualified applicants has diminished over time. Between 1993 and 1995, PPD received an average of 2,500 applications per year. After the policy was implemented, the number of applicants plummeted to around 550 per year. Thus, the department is having trouble filling vacant positions, and with over 200 new expected vacancies over the next several years, the department risks abnormally low personnel levels. Instead of a bachelor's degree the PPD will require an associate's degree (or the equivalent number of credit hours without a degree). However, officers seeking promotion to the rank of sergeant will still be required to hold a bachelor's degree.

In 1995, the NYPD instituted a policy requiring applicants to possess two years of college credit. Commissioner Bernard Kerik has waived this requirement due to declining applicant pools. At the same time he also lowered the age requirement from 22 to 21 years old. Many support this decision. Patrick J. Lynch, president of the Patrolmen's Benevolent Association, stated, "I have always disagreed with requiring college education for police officers. We have a major recruitment problem as it is, and then you disqualify a huge number of people. It's a mistake." Not everyone agrees. Rev. Jesse Jackson indicated, "An educated police officer is a better police officer. The fact is that the chin bar of justice must be kept high—academically, morally, and emotionally. One does not have to dumb down recruits to make better police."

Time will tell if these policies will have a significant effect on policing in Portland or New York.

Adapted from: "Pressed for Applicants, NYPD Waives Two-Year College Standard." 2000. *Law Enforcement News*, October 31: 1-10. "Strapped for Personnel, Portland Kills Four-Year Degree Requirement for Recruits." 2001. *Law Enforcement News*, January 15/31: 1. Printed with permission from the *Law Enforcement News*, John Jay College of Criminal Justice.

---

and general suitability for police work. In general, this investigation is composed of a background investigation and a polygraph examination.

Background Investigation. A thorough background investigation is one of the most important aspects of the selection process. It is based on the extensive personal history provided by the candidate; the investigator attempts to determine if the person is honest and reliable and would make a contribution to the department. Family background, employment and credit history, employment and personal references, friends and neighbors, education records, criminal and possibly juvenile records, drug use, and when appropriate, military records are all checked to develop a general assessment of the person's lifestyle prior to applying for police work. Cohen and Chaiken (1972), in their study of New York police applicants, found that applicants who were rated as excellent by the background investigators had the lowest incidence of misconduct (some 36 percent had personal complaints filed), whereas the applicants rated as poor had the highest incidence of misconduct (some 68 percent had complaints filed). Because these investigations are time-consuming and expensive, some police departments, especially smaller ones with limited resources, may not be very thorough. Nevertheless, because the background investigation appears to be a good predictor of future police behavior, no shortcuts should be taken at this stage.

Two important aspects of the background investigation relate to a candidate's criminal record and history of drug use. In general, a criminal record does not automatically disqualify one from police service. For example, one

survey found that 96 percent of departments would reject an applicant with a
felony conviction and that 90 percent would reject an applicant with a juvenile felony conviction (Eisenberg, Kent, and Wall, 1973). With respect to misdemeanor convictions, departments vary widely, but the trend is to examine
the type and extent of violations and make a determination based on the candidate's overall record. Some research suggests that pre-employment use of
illegal drugs is one of the best indicators of post-employment drug use by
police officers (Kraska and Kappeler, 1988). Several court cases have laid the
foundation for a permissible drug-use standard for police employment. For
instance, a Dallas Police Department standard requiring police applicants to
not have recent or excessive histories of marijuana use was upheld (*Davis v.
City of Dallas*, 1985). In *Shield v. City of Cleveland* (1986), the court upheld
drug-testing requirements and the rejection of applicants who tested positive
for narcotics, amphetamines, or hallucinogens. In both these rulings, the
courts indicated that such requirements were job related and therefore not
discriminatory. It is also important to note that each of the departments used
an objective testing system that prevented any form of individual discrimination. Thus, it would appear that stringent drug-use standards can be used as a
selection criteria, as long as that standard is applied objectively to all police
candidates.

Polygraph Examination. The polygraph, or lie detector, is used to
check the accuracy of background information and to determine if there has
been any inappropriate behavior, past or present, on the applicant's part (e.g.,
criminal acts and illegal drug use). Although the polygraph has been touted
by some as an effective tool in discovering problems with applicants, some
research has suggested that it is not a reliable method to determine truth or
falsehood of an individual's statements (e.g., see Hodes, Hunt, and Raskin,
1985; Kleinmuntz and Szucko, 1982; Rafky and Sussman, 1985). One problem with the polygraph is the amount of stress it puts on a candidate and the
false positives that result—that is, when a candidate is falsely accused of
lying. Therefore, some jurisdictions have made such testing illegal. Furthermore, some departments still ask unethical or discriminatory questions
about an applicant's lifestyle or sexual practices that are private matters. If a
polygraph examination is administered, then all questions relating to the
applicant's background should be job related. Finally, the polygraph should
never be used as a substitute for the background investigation, only as a sup-
plement to it.

Psychological Condition

Psychological screening to determine a candidate's suitability for police
work has become more common in recent years; it may be written, oral, or
both. After the tests are administered, they are usually scored by a psychologist, who is looking for serious emotional problems that would disqualify a
candidate or for a profile of a person who would make a "good" police officer.
This process is known as the "screening out" model, where undesirable candidates are eliminated. However this process has received a considerable
amount of controversy. For example, research has indicated that some tests
are racially biased (Winters, 1989) and not job related (Dwyer, Prien, and Bernard, 1990). After reviewing the literature, Burbeck and Furnham (1985) suggested that such tests may be useful for sifting out people suffering from
some mental abnormality but not for predicting job performance. Metchik

(1999) also cautioned that the screening out model has questionable validity and reliability, it does not differentiate individuals who will become mediocre officers from those who will become superior officers, and the potential for false positives (i.e., incorrectly eliminating good candidates) is high.

Because of these problems with psychological testing, it has been argued by some critics (e.g., see Dwyer, Prien, and Bernard, 1990) that until such time that predictors for job relatedness are developed, clinical assessments for screening police candidates should be eliminated. In the interim, it is suggested that because the best predictor of future behavior is past behavior, the background investigation should be more thorough in scope in order to identify candidates with tendencies toward morally unacceptable or violent behavior. Police departments should consider increasing their utilization and scope of background investigation for screening purposes and rely less on the use of clinical judgments.

Part of the problem of selection revolves around the changing nature of policing (i.e., toward community policing and away from reform policing) and the perception of what is a good officer (Grant and Grant, 1995). For instance, the Independent Commission on the Los Angeles Police Department (1991) found that prior violent behavior of applicants appeared not to be a negative factor in selection in the Los Angeles Police Department. Such a finding suggests, at least at that time, that a "rough and aggressive" demeanor was perceived to be an asset to police performance rather than a warning signal for potential abusive or violent behavior. Metchik (1999) indicated that among the primary goals of community policing is the ability of officers and citizens to work in partnership to improve neighborhood quality of life. As such, the "thin blue line" between the police and the public is vanishing, and the role of the officer is changing. Therefore, the traditional screening model may not be suitable in that it may eliminate individuals who would in reality be very good officers in the era of community policing.

Nevertheless, psychological testing has become an emerging tool for police managers during the screening practice. Recently the Milwaukee Police Department has implemented the Minnesota Multiphasic Personality Inventory (MMPI) as part of their selection process, although it is unclear whether (or how much) the department will rely on the results to determine the suitability of recruits (Testing 1,2,3, 2001).

Medical Condition

Virtually all police departments have certain medical requirements that must be met before an individual can be hired. A medical examination is given by a physician either designated by the department or chosen by the candidate. The exam attempts to determine the general health of the candidate and identify specific conditions, such as heart, back, or knee problems. In general, any "weaknesses" that may be aggravated by the requirements of police work will eliminate the candidate from further consideration. The reason is that the costs of losing an officer to injury or illness, often with long-term disability compensation or a lawsuit, are too great. If a department requires some form of drug testing, it usually takes place during this phase of the process.

Pre-Employment Testing

❖ ❖ ❖ ❖

The pre-employment standards for police organizations, and the legal justifications, change periodically. This is an area in which managers need specific, and the most current, information in order to select the "best" qualified candidates. Although pre-employment standards are usually scored on a pass-fail basis and are used to eliminate candidates, pre-employment tests are generally used to place candidates in order of rank. The two most commonly used selection tests are some form of written test and an oral interview. Some departments use the written test simply as a qualifier (i.e., on a pass-fail basis) and the oral interview as the only criterion for rank order.

Written or Cognitive Tests

Traditionally, departments have used some type of written or cognitive test, usually a form of standardized intelligence test or jurisdictionally specific knowledge test for screening purposes and to rank order candidates. Few attempts were made, however, to determine if these tests had any impact on the applicant's ability to be a successful police officer. Although it is easy to argue that police officers should be intelligent and knowledgeable, it is difficult to determine what kind of intelligence or knowledge is being measured and what level should be required. In addition, it has also been found that minorities tend to score lower on police-entry exams; for example, Sproule (1984) and Gaines, Costello, and Crabtree (1989) found that minorities score on average at least one standard deviation below other applicants. If a simple rank ordering of candidates is used, it will generally create an adverse impact. These problems have led to attempts to validate police written tests empirically since at least the late 1970s (e.g., see Crosby, Rosenfield, and Thornton, 1979), and for departments to seek exams that are more objective and job related (Law Enforcement Assistance Administration, 1973).

Gaines and Falkenberg (1998) examined the written exams for 419 police-officer applicants in one jurisdiction. While they found males and females did not score differently, they did find African Americans had significantly lower scores than whites. Exam scores were primarily a function of educational level of the applicant, and the exam was unrelated to how well they fared during the oral board. They found the exam had questionable validity in that it did not discriminate between highly qualified and less qualified applicants. They concluded the exam "is not particularly effective in selecting a pool of qualified applicants for policing" (Gaines and Falkenberg, 1998: 182). Since the exam primarily measured educational level, they recommended simple adoption of a minimum educational requirement. In fact, they argued that the pool of candidates would be more racially diverse if a two-year college requirement been used in lieu of the exam. Alternatively, it would make sense for police departments to institute a written examination aimed at the level of a two-year college student.

This validation process is critical, because the practice known as ***race norming,*** or using different cutoff scores on employment-related tests on the basis of race, color, religion, sex, or national origin, has been prohibited by the Civil Rights Act of 1991 (Public Law 102–166). Section 703(1) of the act bans setting differential standards or test scores designed to benefit protected class members by equalizing work opportunities (Pynes, 1994). This provision would appear to invalidate the Equal Employment Opportunity

❖ ❖ ❖ ❖ Commission's testing guidelines, which have permitted employers to use different cutoff scores for both minorities and nonminorities, when lower scores for one group are just as predictive of job ability as higher scores are for the other group. Setting differential test scores to benefit protected classes is permitted, however, for programs that were in accordance with affirmative-action laws prior to the passage of the 1991 Act (Pynes, 1994).

Although written tests have limitations, departments must have a way of distinguishing among a large pool of candidates and therefore will continue to use such testing. A primary concern is that the tests be objective. Objective testing standards can be defined as measures of relevant knowledge, skills, and abilities used in a neutral manner without regard to the individual's membership in any group (Pynes, 1994). There also appears to be a consensus building in that *cognitive employment tests* (i.e. the ability to synthesize and analyze material) are an important selection criterion and are equally valid for virtually all jobs (Schmidt, 1988). Hunter (1986), for instance, found the following with respect to cognitive ability tests: (1) general cognitive ability predicts performance ratings in all lines of work, although validity is higher for complex jobs than for simple jobs; (2) general cognitive ability predicts training success at a uniformly high level for all jobs; (3) data on job knowledge show that cognitive ability determines how much and how quickly a person learns; and (4) cognitive ability predicts the ability to react in innovative ways to situations in which knowledge does not specify exactly what to do.

Oral Interview

Almost all police departments use some form of oral interview, usually at the end of the selection process. The interview allows police representatives (and sometimes community members), to observe the candidates directly with respect to their suitability for the department and to clear up any inconsistencies that may have developed in the earlier stages of the process. Candidates are measured on attributes that generally are not measured elsewhere, including communication skills, confidence, interpersonal style, decision-making skills, and overall demeanor. The interview is not usually substantive, that is, with specific questions about police policy or the department, but it can be. Typical questions might include these: Why do you want to be a police officer? How have you prepared yourself for a career in law enforcement? What types of books or magazines do you read? Why do you want to work for this department? There will usually be a few questions about hypothetical situations and how the person would respond (i.e., make decisions) to them. Often, there is an interview board that includes at least three persons: a departmental representative (e.g., a police officer with the rank of sergeant or above), a civil-service representative, and a representative from the community. In many departments, the interview is highly structured, using specific questions and evaluation forms in an attempt to make the interview job valid. A score is assigned to each candidate, which when combined with the written score, provides a total score; candidates are then rank ordered with respect to hiring priority (though some departments may assign more weight to either the written test or the oral interview).

Some departments use only the oral interview to rank order candidates. This method has been useful in helping to overcome the potential adverse impact of other selection criteria and to increase the employment of women and minorities. Although an interview is more flexible, it is more subjective, and there is no strong evidence that it is a useful predictor of future police performance (Burbeck and Furnham, 1985). Other research indicates that the validity, or reliability, of the oral interview is also suspect and that the characteristics of the raters influence the ratings and ultimately the rankings of the candidates (Falkenberg, Gaines, and Cox, 1990; Doerner, 1997). Methods that help to improve the validity of the oral interview include using only those rating factors that are critical components of the job; training the raters so that they clearly understand the process and how responses should be graded; and using set standards that raters can compare with candidate responses (Gaines and Kappeler, 1992).

Table 5.3 presents a summary of the general steps of the police selection process and the most important concerns at each step.

Table 5.3 Process Summary of Police Selection	
Steps	**Related Issues**
Recruitment	Advertising, requests, and referrals
Selection Criteria	Age, height, weight, vision, criminal record, and possible residency requirement
Written Examination	General intelligence or job content
Physical Examination	Agility and endurance
Oral Interview	Communication skill, interpersonal style, and decision-making ability
Psychological Testing	Emotional stability and psychological profiles
Background Investigation	Character, employment or credit history, education, references, and criminal record
Polygraph Examination	Character and background information
Medical Examination	General health and specific problems

Table 5.4 represents the findings of the national survey of police recruitment, selection, and training practices (Langworthy, Hughes, and Sanders, 1995), comparing a 1994 sample of 59 departments with a similar sample of 71 departments surveyed in 1990. The sample departments were given a list of 13 possible selection procedures and asked to identify which they used. As expected, 90 percent of the departments required a written test, oral interview, background check, and medical exam. Significant increases were reported for intelligence tests, psychological interviews, written references, and practical tests (e.g., assessment centers, discussed in Chapter 6). Such changes are not surprising in light of legislation regarding fair hiring practices. With an increased use of practical tests, "these departments appear to be moving toward selection methods which have been shown to test the skills which are necessary in performing the police job" (Langworthy, Hughes, and Sanders, 1995: 29).

The selection of police candidates is time-consuming and expensive. Given the costs, the steps of the process are normally arranged from the least costly and most likely to eliminate the most candidates to the most expensive. Accordingly, the written and physical agility tests are usually given at the

Table 5.4	Percent of Departments Using Various Selection Steps		
	1990 (N=71)	1994 (N=59)	Change (N=58)
Background Check	98.6	96.6	-1.7
Medical Exam	95.9	98.3	3.4
Written Test	94.3	96.6	1.7
Oral Interview	94.3	98.3	3.4
Physical Agility Test	80.3	84.7	5.2
Psychological Interview	83.1	91.5	12.0*
Intelligence Test	76.1	94.5	15.5*
Polygraph	69.0	69.5	3.4
Written References	57.7	71.2	17.2*
Psychometric Tests	56.4	55.9	-6.9
Drug Test	23.9	22.2	-7.1
Handwriting Analysis	11.2	10.2	-3.4
Practical Tests	7.0	28.8	22.4*

*Significant Increase ($p < .05$)

Adapted from: R. Langworthy, T. Hughes, and B. Sanders, 1995. *Law Enforcement Recruitment, Selection and Training: A Survey of Major Police Departments in the U. S.*, p. 26. Highland Heights, KY: Academy of Criminal Justice Sciences, Police Section. Reprinted by permission.

beginning, followed by the medical exam, polygraph examination (if used), psychological testing (if used), background investigation, and finally the oral interview. The passage of the Americans with Disabilities Act (ADA) in 1990 will have a substantial impact on this traditional sequence.

The Americans with Disabilities Act

The purpose of the ADA is to eliminate barriers to equal employment opportunity and to provide equal access to individuals with disabilities to the programs, services, and activities delivered by government entities (Rubin, 1994). Thus, the ADA prohibits discrimination against *qualified* individuals with a disability; it does not mean that by having a disability, one is entitled to protection under the law, but if a person meets the selection criteria for a job and has a disability, he or she cannot be discriminated against for the job. Generally, blanket exclusions of individuals with a particular disability are not permissible. For instance, to exclude all persons with diabetes would ignore the varying degrees of severity and the ability to control the symptoms (Rubin, 1994). Also, standards that tend to screen out individuals or groups of individuals on the basis of disability must be related to functions that are essential to the job.

The ADA requires that applicants be given a conditional offer of employment prior to taking a medical exam or any other test that may be disability related. A good rule of thumb is that questions that would disclose information regarding a disability, whether asked on an application or during an interview, may be construed as a disability-related inquiry. That holds true for any selection procedure that would disclose information regarding a disability. Therefore, police "agencies that customarily use psychological exams, polygraph tests, background checks, and medical exams will need to evaluate their hiring process in light of ADA" (Rubin, 1994:

3). If any of these tests are to be administered prior to a conditional offer of employment, then no questions may be asked relating to medical or other types of disabilities unless they are essential to police performance. Although the full impact of the ADA on police selection is complicated and ongoing, departments will need to change many of their current procedures to ensure that selection criteria that screen out persons with disabilities are job related and that questions relating to disabilities (unless job related) are asked only after a conditional offer of employment has been made.

Once candidates are selected, they are usually rank ordered and employed based on departmental needs. This ranking lasts for a given period, usually from six months to two years, before candidates are retested. Once selected, candidates attend a recruit-training program, discussed in Chapter 6.

Cultural Diversity in Policing

One of the more critical issues of police selection is the diversity—especially in terms of race, ethnicity, and gender—of the force that is ultimately hired. Diversity in policing has been considered important since the mid-1800s, when modern policing began in the United States. There have always been proponents of matching the cultural types of people being policed with the same cultural types of police officers. In the last several decades, the diversity of a police department has again become important for both political and performance reasons. Although it is clear that diversity has widespread political support in many communities, the actual difference that diversification makes in police effectiveness is less clear.

Many people in and outside law enforcement believe that a diverse police organization is more effective than one that is not. In fact, diversity has become so important that it is often considered to be a significant strategy to reform those departments that are considered to have performance problems, particularly as they relate to police use of force and community fear and distrust of the police. The evidence regarding the impact of diversity on police effectiveness can be categorized as either testimonial or empirical. **Testimonial evidence** is based on the opinions of individuals who have strong political beliefs about the importance of diversity and the opinions of individuals whose experience (e.g., as citizens or police officers) has led them to believe that a diverse organization is either more or less effective. In general, testimonial evidence is usually favorable. The *empirical* (data-based) *evidence* regarding the effectiveness of diversity is derived from systematic study of one or more effectiveness criteria (e.g., crime rates; arrest rates; citizen trust of police; or fewer complaints, civil suits, and confrontations). There is no empirical evidence that, in the long term, diversity makes a measurable, sustained increase in the effectiveness of the police. Similarly, there is no empirical evidence that diversity decreases the effectiveness of the police either.

Given all the possible factors that can influence the relationship between police and citizens, it is unlikely that a police department that is a "perfect cultural match" for a community will necessarily be more effective for that reason alone. In the long term, the integrity, competence, and style of the individual, and the philosophy, strategies, and methods of the organization, have the greatest impact on effectiveness. However, diversity continues to have substantial political support because many people believe that women and minorities, for reasons of equity, should be employed given the discrimination they have experienced in the past.

Policing remains a predominately white male occupation. Historically, police departments have systematically discriminated against women and minorities in employment, assignments, promotions, and social acceptance. In addition, many white men have not, and do not, consider women and minorities to be their equals in terms of either capabilities or competencies. Beginning in the 1960s, governmental intervention was required in order to ensure that discrimination in employment and promotion was eliminated. Legally, and in terms of government policy, this intervention became known as affirmative action. An ***affirmative action plan*** requires that an affirmative, or positive, effort be made to redress past discriminatory practices and assure equal employment opportunity. Such plans have been developed ***voluntarily,*** though often with political pressure or by ***court-ordered consent decree*** following legal action.

Many departments, at least initially, vigorously resisted the attempt to change employment practices, but they usually failed because of their poor records of employing women and minorities. In other words, departments are bound by law to adhere to equal employment opportunity provisions. Indeed, it appears that affirmative actions plans make a difference; for example, one study (Police Foundation, 1990) found that in those departments under court order to increase the representation of women and minorities, women represented 10.1 percent of all sworn officers. In those departments with voluntary affirmative action plans, the figure was 8.3 percent. Finally, in those departments with no affirmative action plans, women made up only 6.1 percent of the officers. There can be little question that without affirmative action, there would be substantially fewer women and minorities working in police departments.

Changing Diversity in Police Organizations

The number of women and minorities in police departments has consistently increased since the 1960s, even though this increase has been uneven. For instance, a survey of municipal police departments serving cities of 50,000 or more (Martin, 1989) indicated that in 1978 women made up 4.2 percent of sworn personnel and by 1986 they made up 8.8 percent. In local departments with 100 or more officers, about 99 percent had women officers, but fewer than 1 percent had 20 percent or more female representation. Most of these organizations are sheriff's departments where many women officers work in the jails (Carter, Sapp, and Stephens, 1989). With respect to minorities, Walker (1989) reported that in the nation's fifty largest cities, between 1983 and 1988, nearly half (45 percent) made significant progress in the employment of black officers; however, 17 percent reported a decline in their percentage of African Americans. Of these departments, 42 percent reported significant increases in the percentage of Hispanic officers employed; approximately 11 percent indicated a decline and 17 percent reported no change.

The 1997 survey of more than 3,000 police departments by the Bureau of Justice Statistics (Reaves and Goldberg, 2000) provides the most comprehensive look at the cultural changes taking place in policing to date. The increasing percentages of women and minorities can be readily observed in Figure 5.1. Women comprised 10.0 percent of all full-time local police officers in 1997, compared to 8.8 percent in 1993, 8.1 percent in 1990 and 7.6 percent in 1987. Black officers accounted for 11.7 percent of the total in 1997, compared to 11.3 percent in 1993, 10.5 percent in 1990 and 9.3 percent in 1987. Police departments experienced the greatest increase in Hispanic officers, who made up 7.8 percent of the total in 1997, compared to 6.2 percent in 1993, 5.2 percent in 1990 and 4.5 percent in 1987. All minorities made up about 21.5 percent of the total in 1997, with an estimated 48,950 officers. This represents a 26 percent increase from 1993. In 1993, there were an estimated 71,244 minority officers, which was larger than the 61,710 in 1990 and the 51,872 in 1987.

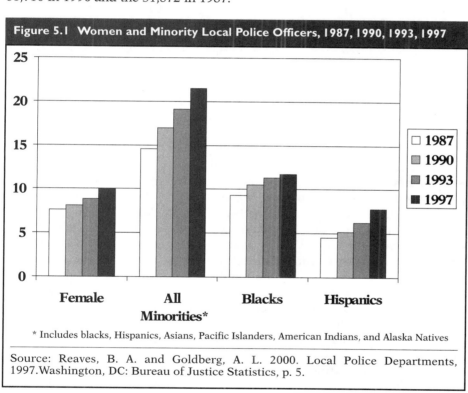

Figure 5.1 Women and Minority Local Police Officers, 1987, 1990, 1993, 1997

* Includes blacks, Hispanics, Asians, Pacific Islanders, American Indians, and Alaska Natives

Source: Reaves, B. A. and Goldberg, A. L. 2000. Local Police Departments, 1997. Washington, DC: Bureau of Justice Statistics, p. 5.

The uneven increase of both women and minority officers in departments is represented in Table 5.5. Although women comprised 10 percent of all local police officers in 1997, their percentages were highest in large jurisdictions, with 15.9 percent of officers in jurisdictions of 1,000,000 or more in population and 14.1 percent in jurisdictions with at least 250,000 residents but fewer than 1,000,000 (see Table 5.5). Similarly, minority officers made up approximately 21.5 percent of the total, but their percentages were also the highest in large jurisdictions, with black officers making up approximately 19.1 to 23.4 percent in jurisdictions over 250,000 residents; Hispanic officers were also the most represented in jurisdictions with populations above 250,000, making up 9 to 15.6 percent. Each of these groups had the highest percentage of officers in jurisdictions with more than

1,000,000 population (i.e., blacks with 21 percent and Hispanics with 12 percent). Other minorities, including Asians, Pacific Islanders, American Indians, and Alaska Natives, represented 1.5 percent of the total, with 1.2 percent in jurisdictions with more than 1,000,000 population; all other jurisdictions had under 6.6 percent representation.

Table 5.5   Gender and Race of Full-Time Sworn Personnel In Local Police Departments, by Size of Population Served, 1997

Population served	Total			White			Black			Hispanic			Other*		
	Total	Male	Female	Total	Male	Female	Total	Male	Female	Total	Male	Female	Total	Male	Female
All sizes	100%	90.0%	10.0%	78.5%	72.2%	6.3%	11.7%	9.1%	2.5%	7.8%	6.8%	1.0%	2.1%	1.9%	0.2%
1,000,000 or more	100%	84.1%	15.9%	64.7%	57.1%	7.6%	17.8%	12.5%	5.4%	15.6%	12.9%	2.7%	1.9%	1.6%	0.2%
500,000-999,999	100	86.0	14.0	63.1	56.2	7.0	23.4	17.7	5.7	7.0	6.1	0.8	6.6	6.1	0.5
250,000-499,999	100	85.9	14.1	69.6	60.6	9.0	19.1	15.2	3.9	9.3	8.3	1.0	1.9	1.7	0.2
100,000-249,999	100	90.1	9.9	78.9	71.7	7.2	11.6	9.7	1.9	7.2	6.6	0.6	2.3	2.2	0.1
50,000-99,999	100	92.3	7.7	85.4	79.3	6.1	7.5	6.5	1.0	5.4	4.9	0.5	1.6	1.5	0.1
25,000-49,999	100	93.4	6.6	88.5	83.1	5.4	6.0	5.2	0.8	4.6	4.3	0.3	0.8	0.8	--
10,000-24,999	100	94.7	5.3	91.9	87.3	4.6	4.3	3.9	0.4	2.7	2.6	0.1	1.1	1.0	0.2
2,500-9,999	100	94.9	5.1	89.1	84.8	4.3	4.8	4.3	0.4	4.1	3.9	0.2	2.0	1.8	0.2
Under 2,500	100	96.9	3.1	89.3	86.8	2.5	5.3	5.0	0.2	3.2	3.1	0.1	2.3	2.0	0.2

Note: Detail may not add to total because of rounding.
*Includes Asians, Pacific Islanders, American Indians, and Alaska Natives.
--Less than 0.05%.

Source: Reaves, B. A. and Goldberg, A. L. 2000. *Local Police Departments, 1997*. Washington, DC: Bureau of Justice Statistics, p 5.

It is interesting to take a look at how the nation's largest jurisdictions and departments are progressing with respect to diversity, because they tend to set the trends in policing. In 1993, full-time sworn officers in these departments, sometimes referred to as the Big Six—New York, Los Angeles, Chicago, Houston, Detroit, and Philadelphia—employed approximately 42 percent female and minority officers, up from 37 percent in 1990 (Reaves and Smith, 1996). In other words, about 58 percent of the officers in these departments were white males. Another way to view the progress of diversity is to look at those departments that have the largest percentage of women and minority representation. Table 5.6 presents the top five local police departments, with 100 or more officers, which have respectively the largest percent of women, blacks, Hispanics, Asians/Pacific Islanders, and American Indian/Alaska Natives.

Finally, it is interesting to identify cultural diversity among police administrators. Although data is limited, it appears the proportion of females and minorities in positions of policy making in American police departments are equally dismal, and many indicators point toward less representation at the top of the organization than at the bottom. In 1999, 21.9 percent of all sworn officers were female in the Chicago Police Department. Females comprised 22.8 percent of all line officers, but only 16 percent of all supervisory positions (i.e., lieutenants and sergeants) and only 8 percent of all top command positions (i.e., chiefs, deputy chiefs, commanders and captains). Similarly, females made up 12 percent of the sworn officers in the Houston Police Department, but only 7.7 percent of commanders and 3.7 percent of the top command (Sourcebook of Criminal Justice Statistics, 1999).

Cultural diversity (or the lack thereof) can have several consequences of which police managers need to be aware. First, females and minorities may

Table 5.6 "Top Five" Local Police Departments with Percentage of Women and Minority Officers		
Department	**Number of Officers**	**Percent Women**
Pittsburgh, PA	1,122	29
Madison, WI	327	28
Washington, DC	3,618	25
Boulder, CO	137	24
Bossier, LA	176	23
Black		
Washington, DC	3,618	69
East Orange, NJ	285	66
Gary, IN	243	63
Jackson, MS	417	62
Atlanta, GA	1,612	58
Hispanic		
Laredo, TX	269	100
McAllen, TX	195	90
Brownsville, TX	180	82
El Paso, TX	1,013	66
Sante Fe, NM	117	56
Asian/Pacific Islanders		
Honolulu, HI	1,619	76
San Francisco, CA	2,006	14
Berkeley, CA	199	19
Vallejo, CA	141	11
Oakland, CA	617	10
Culver City, CA	119	10
San Jose, CA	1,336	10
American Indian/Alaskan Natives		
Modesto, CA	248	10
Tulsa, OK	800	6
Long Beach, CA	838	5
Duluth, MN	141	4
Lawrence, KS	110	4

Source: Reaves, B. A. and Goldberg, A. L. 2000. *Local Police Departments, 1997.* Washington, DC: Bureau of Justice Statistics, p 5.

feel like "tokens" within the police organization, and this may place undue pressure on them to succeed. As Belknap observed,

> The pressure of being a token within one's profession is heightened by responsibility borne of representing every other person of one's token group. For instance, a police department or law firm hiring its first woman may consciously or unconsciously base further hiring of women on this token's performance. In addition to standing out and being watched, this is a huge responsibility for a new token employee. The lack of logic should also be evident. Just as some white males are incompetent workers, so will some women and people of color be incompetent workers. However, most people do not use incompetent white male workers as a basis to form opinions on whether to hire other white males. It is recognized that even with affirmative action, some incompetent workers have been hired, but it is also necessary to recognize that incompetent white males have been hired before and since affirmative action policies. Regardless of which hiring measures are used, some incompetent people of every racial, ethnic, sex, and class category will be

hired. Unfortunately, there is a tendency to focus on the less competent employees of the outsider groups to "justify" discrimination in hiring. (2001: 363–364)

Second, females and minorities may be privy to inappropriate comments from dominant groups. This often includes overt sexism or racism (to be discussed below). Research has reported females and racial minorities were often subjected to different types of inappropriate comments, including racist or sexist jokes or racial or sexual stereotyping (Haarr, 1997; Morash and Haarr, 1995; Martin, 1994). The obvious fact is this behavior is illegal and creates a hostile work environment. In an extreme case, behavior could be qualified as *quid pro quo harassment*, where the employee is forced to choose between employment and sexual demands (Rubin 1995). However, negative effects can occur even in situations that are not so blatant. Not only can tokenism lead to feelings of animosity, but this could also lead to unequal socialization into the "thin blue line" of policing and reduced feelings of solidarity and "brotherhood" by allowing diversity in the "fraternity" of policing (notice the masculine terms). Tokenism may also lead to a high attrition rate and low retention rate of female and minority officers.

The data presented in this chapter indicate that many police departments are already culturally diverse and are becoming more so all the time. Even though growth in cultural diversity is uneven throughout the country, it is probable that within the next two or three decades, half or more of local police officers in many departments will be women and minorities. It is apparent that if police organizations now and in the future are to operate effectively, then racial, ethnic, and gender-based conflict must be reduced to a minimum. Management must make every effort to have officers understand one another, realize that differences can be beneficial, and view the organization as an integrated system working toward similar goals in the community.

Understanding Diversity

If an organizational culture is to accommodate the changing levels of diversity discussed above, management must attempt to deal with the problems that may exist or develop with respect to diversity. It must first attempt to understand the types of issues that have typically caused misunderstanding and animosity between groups of police employees. To this end, racism, sexism, and discrimination will be discussed. These terms can be defined in general or within the context of a society's historical experience. In general, *racism* and *sexism* refer to the differential attitudes about and/or treatment of individuals, based on such factors as race, ethnicity, gender, sexual orientation, and religion. *Discrimination,* or differential treatment, can be either beneficial or harmful; for example, an individual could be either given or denied a job or admission to college based on one or more of the above factors.

When racism, sexism, and discrimination are defined in terms of a society's historical experience, victims of discrimination may believe that the dominant, and therefore repressive, members of society cannot be discriminated against. In the United States, many women and minorities rightfully believe that white men, as the dominant group, have engaged in pervasive and systematic discrimination. And because white men continue to be the most powerful group in society, it is not possible to discriminate against them. When a woman or minority person is given a job, promotion, or another opportunity instead of a white male, even when the white man may be better qualified, this treatment is not seen as a form of discrimination or "reverse racism" or "reverse sexism." Rather, it is considered a morally justifiable response to the historical experience of women and people of color. Of course, the other side of this issue is that white males often feel that as a result of some affirmative action practices, they are being unfairly discriminated against, even though they are not personally racist or sexist and have not been discriminatory in their actions.

It is vitally important for managers to attempt to develop, with members of the organization, definitions for sexism, racism, and discrimination. This task will undoubtedly prove difficult, but without a consensus as to what these terms in practice actually mean, it may not be possible to respond effectively to conflict. Where significant differences do exist, managers must make sure that the parties involved understand each other's points of view and try to reach a compromise. Once the definitions are determined, the organization should go through a ***diversity self-study*** in which department practices and individual language and behavior are scrutinized. The goal of the self-study is to identify those aspects of organizational life that contribute to diversity conflict and to develop realistic plans to respond. Police managers may consider some of the following issues:

1. How diverse is the police department?

2. Does the makeup of the department reflect the qualified representation of the city it serves?

3. Are females and people of color given equal opportunity for (a) promotion, (b) preferred assignments, (c) preferred shifts, and (d) assisting in the construction of policy?

4. Are females and people of color over represented in certain positions (e.g., are females assigned to positions that may be construed as "not real police work," like public relations officers? Are minorities disproportionately assigned to beats that are predominately populated by minorities?)

5. Are there any conditions that currently exist within the organization that may inadvertently foster feelings of "tokenism"?

Some of the methods for reducing resistance to change and implementing innovation discussed in Chapter 14 may be useful prior to and following the self-study process.

Summary

With the increasing complexity of the police role and the movement toward community policing, the quality of police personnel has become perhaps the key factor to the effective operation of police organizations. Thus, screening in, as opposed to screening out, candidates should be used in order that only the best qualified are selected for the applicant pool. In this way, departments are assured of selecting relatively high-quality candidates, who may be with the organization for a period of twenty years or longer. When attempting to recruit the best-qualified applicants, departments will need to recognize that different recruitment strategies may be necessary in order to attract a culturally diverse pool. Candidates must meet a number of pre-employment standards, which attempt to depict a department's view of what is required to become an effective officer—for example, physical agility, educational, psychological, background, and polygraph examinations. Pre-employment selection tests are also used and usually include written tests, oral interviews, or both. Some departments, however, also require reading exams because the reading ability of applicants has declined in recent years.

The Americans with Disabilities Act prohibits discrimination against qualified individuals with a disability. This act will have a substantial impact on the traditional sequencing of selection steps because applicants must be given a conditional offer of employment prior to taking any tests or exams that may be disability related. The increasing cultural diversity of police departments is probably the most profound change that has taken place in policing in the last three decades. Because of this change, it is management's responsibility to attempt to establish an organizational culture that promotes the benefits of diversity. A diversity self-study, including all organizational members, may prove beneficial in this regard.

Discussion Questions

1. Describe the meaning of "quality" with respect to police personnel. Explain what you consider to be the most important criteria with respect to quality in police recruits.

2. What is the Pendleton Civil Service Act? What are its positive and negative benefits?

3. What impact have civil service systems had on the selection and development process in police organizations?

4. Explain the concept of screening in applicants versus screening out applicants.

5. Discuss how recruitment and selection processes may differ in the community policing era.

6. Describe several different recruitment strategies and nontraditional methods of recruitment. Explain why such practices might be necessary in police recruitment.

7. Describe five pre-employment standards that you consider to be the most important in the selection process and explain why.

8. Explain the relevance of validity and reliability to selection criteria in the hiring process.

9. Explain the concept of disparate impact and equal employment opportunity with respect to selection.

10. Briefly describe the changing cultural diversity of police personnel. Why is it important for police managers to understand diversity?

References

Albermarle Paper v. Moody. 1975. 10 FEP 1181.

Belknap, J. 2001. *The Invisible Woman: Gender, Crime, and Justice*, 2nd edition. Stamford, CT: Wadsworth.

Biddle, R. E. 1993. "How to Set Cutoff Scores for Knowledge Tests Used in Promotion, Training, Certification and Licensing." *Public Personnel Management* 22: 63–70.

Burbeck, E., and Furnham, A. 1985. "Police Officer Selection: A Critical Review of the Literature." *Journal of Police Science and Administration* 13: 58–69.

Carter, D. L., and Sapp, A. D. 1989. "The Effect of Higher Education on Police Liability: Implications for Police Personnel Policy." *American Journal of Police* 8: 153–166.

Carter, D. L., Sapp, A. D., and Stephens, D. W. 1989. *The State of Police Education: Policy Direction for the 21st Century.* Washington, DC: Police Executive Research Forum.

Cascio, W. F. 1977. "Formal Education and Police Officer Performance." *Journal of Police Science and Administration* 5: 89–96.

Chapman, S. G. 1982. "Personnel Management." In B. L. Garmire (ed.), *Local Government Police Management*, 2nd ed., pp. 241–273. Washington, DC: International City Management Association.

Cohen, B., and Chaiken, J. M. 1972. *Police Background Characteristics and Performance.* New York: Rand Institute.

Crosby, A., Rosenfield, M., and Thornton, R. F. 1979. "The Development of a Written Test for Police Applicant Selection." In C. D. Spielberger (ed.), *Police Selection and Evaluation*, pp. 143–153. New York: Praeger.

Davis v. City of Dallas. 1985. 777 F.2d 205 (5th Cir.).

Doerner, W. G. 1997. "The Utility of the Oral Interview Board in Selecting Police Academy Admissions." *Policing: An International Journal of Police Strategies and Management* 20: 777–785.

Dwyer, W. O., Prien, E. P., and Bernard, J. L. 1990. "Psychological Screening of Law Enforcement Officers: A Case for Job Relatedness." *Journal of Police Science and Administration* 17: 176–182.

Eisenberg, S. Kent, D. A., and Wall, C. 1973. *Police Personnel Practices in State and Local Government.* Washington, DC: Police Foundation.

Falkenberg, S., Gaines, L. K., and Cox, T. C. 1990. "The Oral Interview Board: What Does It Measure?" *Journal of Police Science and Administration* 17: 32–39.

Finnegan, J. C. 1976. "A Study of Relationships Between College Education and Police Performance in Baltimore, Maryland." *The Police Chief* 34: 60–62.

Fyfe, J. J. 1987. *Police Personnel Practices.* Washington, DC: International City Management Association.

Fyfe, J. J. 1988. "Police Use of Deadly Force: Research and Reform." *Justice Quarterly* 5: 165–205.

Gaines, L. K., and Kappeler, V. E. 1992. "Selection and Testing." In G. W. Cordner and D. C. Hale (eds.), *What Works in Policing: Operations and Administration Examined*, pp. 107–123. Cincinnati, OH: Anderson.

Gaines, L. K., Costello, P., and Crabtree, A. 1989. "Police Selection Testing: Balancing Legal Requirements and Employer Needs." *American Journal of Police* 8: 137–152.

Gaines, L. K., and Falkenberg, S. 1998. "An Evaluation of the Written Selection Test: Effectiveness and Alternatives." *Journal of Criminal Justice* 26: 175–183.

Goldstein, H. 1977. *Policing a Free Society.* Cambridge, MA: Ballinger Publishing Co.

Grant, J. D., and Grant, J. 1995. "Officer Selection and the Prevention of Abuse of Force." In W. A. Geller and H. Toch (eds.), *And Justice For All: Understanding and Controlling Police Abuse of Force*, pp. 151–162. Washington, DC: Police Executive Research Forum.

Griggs v. Duke Power Company. 1971. 401 U.S. 424.

Haarr, R. N. 1997. "Patterns of Interaction in a Police Patrol Bureau: Race and Gender Barriers to Integration." *Justice Quarterly* 14: 53–85.

Hodes, C. R., Hunt, R. L., and Raskin, D. C. 1985. "Effects of Physical Countermeasures on the Physiological Detection of Deception." *Journal of Applied Psychology* 70: 177–187.

Hunter, J. 1986. "Cognitive Ability, Cognitive Aptitude, Job Knowledge, and Job Performance." *Journal of Vocational Behavior* 29: 340–362.

Independent Commission on the Los Angeles Police Department. 1991. *Report of the Independent Commission on the Los Angeles Police Department.* Los Angeles: Independent Commission on the LAPD.

International City Management Association. 1986. *Municipal Yearbook.* Washington, DC: International City Management Association.

Kleinmuntz, B., and Szucko, J. J. 1982. "Is the Lie Detector Valid?" *Law and Society Review* 16: 105–125.

Kraska, P. B., and Kappeler, V. E. 1988. "Police On-Duty Drug Use: A Theoretical and Descriptive Examination." *American Journal of Police* 7: 1–28.

Langworthy, R., Hughes, T., and Sanders, B. 1995. *Law Enforcement Recruitment, Selection and Training: A Survey of Major Police Departments in the U.S.* Highland Heights, KY: Academy of Criminal Justice Sciences—Police Section.

Law Enforcement Assistance Administration. 1973. *Equal Employment Opportunity Program Development Manual.* Washington, DC: Government Printing Office.

Law Enforcement News. 1989. "Police Corps Ride Again." *Law Enforcement News* Sept: 1,13,14.

Martin, S. E. 1989. "Women in Policing: The Eighties and Beyond." In D. J. Kenney (ed.), *Police and Policing: Contemporary Issues,* pp. 3–16. New York: Praeger.

Martin, S. E. 1994. " 'Outsider Within' the Station House: The Impact of Race and Gender on Black Women Police." *Social Problems* 41: 383–400.

Meagher, M. S., and Yentes, N. A. 1986. "Choosing a Career in Policing: A Comparison of Male and Female Police." *Journal of Police Science and Administration* 14, issue 4:320–327.

Metchik, E. 1999. "An Analysis of the 'Screening Out' Model of Police Officer Selection." *Police Quarterly* 2: 79–95.

Morash, M., and Haarr, R. N. 1995. "Gender, Workplace Problems, and Stress in Policing." *Justice Quarterly* 12: 113–140.

Parker, L., Donnelly, J., Gerwitz, J., Marcus, J., and Kowalewski, V. 1976. "Higher Education: Its Impact on Police Attitudes." *The Police Chief* 43: 33–35.

Police Foundation. 1990. *Community Policing: A Binding Thread Throught the Fabric of Our Society* Washington, DC: Author.

Polk, O. E., and Armstrong, D. A. 2001. "Higher Education and Law Enforcement Career Paths: Is the Road to Success Paved by Degree?" *Journal of Criminal Justice Education* 12: 77–99.

Pynes, J. E. 1994. " Police Officer Selection Procedures: Speculations on the Future." *American Journal of Police* 13: 103–112.

Rafky, J., and Sussman, F. 1985. "An Evaluation of Field Techniques in Detection of Deception." *Psychophysiology* 12: 121–130.

Reaves, B. A. 1996. *Local Police Departments, 1993.* Washington, DC: Bureau of Justice Statistics.

Reaves, B. A., and Smith, P. Z. 1996. *Law Enforcement Management and Administrative Statistics, 1993.* Washington, DC: Bureau of Justice Statistics.

Reaves, B. A., and Goldberg, A. L. 2000. *Law Enforcement Management and Administrative Statistics, 1997.* Washington, DC: Bureau of Justice Statistics.

Roberg, R. R. 1978. "An Analysis of the Relationships Among Higher Education, Belief Systems, and Job Performance of Patrol Officers." *Journal of Police Science and Administration* 6: 336–344.

Rubin, P. N. 1995. *Civil Rights and Criminal Justice: Employment Discrimination Overview.* Washington, DC: National Institute of Justice.

Rubin, P. N. 1994. *The Americans With Disabilities Act and Criminal Justice: Hiring New Employees*. Washington, DC: National Institute of Justice.

San Jose Mercury News. 1994. "Rookie Cop, 59, Can't Escape Media." November 29, p. 3B.

Sanders, B., Hughes, T., and Langworthy, R. 1995. "Police Officer Recruitment and Selection: A Survey of Major Departments in the U. S." In *Police Forum*. Richmond, KY: Academy of Criminal Justice Sciences.

Sanderson, B. B. 1978. "Police Officers: The Relationship of College Education to Job Performance." *The Police Chief* 44: 62.

Sauls, John G. 1985. "Establishing the Validity of Employment Standards." *FBI Law Enforcement Bulletin* August: 27–32.

Schmidt, F. 1988. "The Problem of Group Differences in Ability Test Scores in Employment Selection." *Journal of Vocational Behavior* 33: 272–292.

Schneider, B., and Schmitt, N. 1986. *Staffing Organizations*, 2nd ed. Glenview, IL: Scott, Foresman.

Schofield, D. L. 1989. "Establishing Health and Fitness Standards: Legal Considerations." *FBI Law Enforcement Bulletin*, June, pp. 25–31.

Shield Club v. City of Cleveland. 1986. 647 F. Supp. 274 (N.D. Ohio).

Slater, H. R., and Reiser, M. 1988. "A Comparative Study of Factors Influencing Police Recruitment." *Journal of Police Science and Administration* 16: 168–176.

Smith, S. M., and Aamodt, M. G. 1997. "The Relationship Between Education, Experience and Police Performance." *Journal of Police and Criminal Psychology* 12: 7–14.

Sourcebook of Criminal Justice Statistics. 1999. Washington, DC. Bureau of Justice Statistics.

Sproule, C. F. 1984. "Should Personnel Selection Tests Be Used on a Pass-Fail, Grouping, or Ranking Basis?" *Public Personnel Management Journal* 13: 375-394.

Testing 1,2,3. (2001). *Law Enforcement News*, February 14: 1–11.

Trojanowicz, R. and Nicholson, T. 1976. "A Comparison of Behavioral Styles of College Graduate Police Officers v. Non-college-Going Police Officers." *The Police Chief* 43: 57–58.

Vanguard Justice Society v. Hughes. 1979. 471 F. Supp. 670.

Walker, S. 1989. *Employment of Black and Hispanic Police Officers, 1983–1988: A Follow-up Study*. Omaha: University of Nebraska-Omaha, Center for Applied Urban Research.

Weiner, N. L. 1976. "The Educated Policeman." *Journal of Police Science and Administration* 4: 450–457.

Wilson, O. W., and McLaren, R. C. 1977. *Police Administration*, 4th ed. New York: McGraw-Hill.

Winters, C. A. 1989. "Psychology Tests, Suits, and Minority Applicants." *Police Journal* 62: 22–30.

Worden, R.E. 1990. "A Badge and a Baccalaureate: Policies, Hypotheses and Further Evidence." *Justice Quarterly* 7:565–592.

Worden, R. E. 1994. "The 'Causes' of Police Brutality: Theory and Evidence on Police Use of Force." pp 31–60 in *And Justice for All: Understanding and Controlling Police Abuse of Force*, edited by W. A. Geller and H. Toch. Washington, DC: Police Executive Research Forum.

Zecca, J. M. 1993. "The CUNY/NYPD Cadet Corps." *ACJS Today*, May/June: 5.

Chapter Six

Human Resource Development

Developing an organization's human resources for a successful career in police work commences shortly after the selection process ends. Development begins with the training of the newly hired recruits, moves to a second phase that includes performance and evaluation, and continues into a third phase of long-term development, or career growth.

Recruit Training

The initial training of the recruit is generally conducted through a police-training academy where the program is determined by a state standards organization, for instance, in California where this approach was developed, it is known as POST for Peace Officer Standards and Training Commission.

Although all police departments must meet minimum standards, some departments provide substantially more training. Larger organizations often maintain their own academies, whereas smaller departments tend to send their recruits to regional or county academies.

Some states now require that people complete one of these basic training programs prior to being considered for employment. As a result, the department hires an already trained employee and does not have to pay for the training, including the recruit's salary while attending the academy. Another recent development in pre-employment screening is testing for literacy. Because literacy skills in police applicants have been markedly declining, and written civil service tests do not adequately screen for literacy, some states (e.g., Michigan and California) require all candidates to pass one of any number of tests designed to measure reading and writing skills before they enter the academy (Clark, 1992). Since 1988, for example, the regional training center for Miami-area police departments has required participants in its preservice program to take a test to make sure that they can read at a tenth-grade level. The requirement was imposed because, according to the training center, earning a high school degree does not guarantee that the graduate can read beyond the junior high school level (Clark, 1992). Such a low-level reading standard reflects a limited role concept, suggesting that police work is essentially a low-status, low-skill occupation. Most likely, such low standards produce many marginal employees who later have a difficult time adjusting to the rigors of police work and thus become incompetent and troublesome employees. Because the Miami example undoubtedly reflects a national concern, the arguments for moving toward a college-degree hiring standard become even stronger.

Until the late 1950s, training was primarily the responsibility of cities and counties and a few colleges and universities; curriculum and amount of training, if any, varied widely. From 1984 to 1997, the average nationwide basic recruit-training requirement increased from about 350 hours (IADLEST, 1997) to about 600 hours (Reaves and Goldberg, 2000). This increased time for recruit training has been the result of the increased knowledge about the police role, which in turn has led to a greater diversity in subject matter and training methods utilized in the academy.

Recruit training is influenced by program design and delivery. Some of the more important considerations in the design and delivery of a recruit-training program include program orientation, teaching philosophy and instructional methods, course content and evaluation, and field training.

Program Orientation

One of the important issues in police training is whether the orientation should be stressful or nonstressful. **Stressful training** is like a military boot camp or basic training; **nonstressful training** has a more academic environment. Many recruit programs continue to use a stressful orientation, expecting recruits to be obedient and subjecting them to both intellectual and physical demands in a highly structured environment. Discipline and even harassment have been an integral part of many of these programs. For in-service training (i.e., training after employment) with more experienced officers, a more academic environment is the norm.

Although stressful police training has a long tradition, no evidence exists
that this approach is a valid way to train recruits (Berg, 1990) or that it is any
more or less effective than a nonstressful approach. Probably the most comprehensive study in this area (Earle, 1973) indicates that nonstressful training produced officers who received higher performance evaluations, liked
their work more, and got along better with the public. Given the trend toward
community policing, problem solving, and higher educational requirements,
a stress-oriented approach is likely to be counterproductive and should be
replaced by a more academic approach. •

Program Philosophy and Instructional Methods

The philosophy of a program revolves around two primary approaches:
training and education. ***Training*** can be defined as the process of instructing
the individual how to do a job by providing relevant information about the
job; ***education*** can be defined as the process of providing a general body of
knowledge on which decisions can be based as to why something is being
done while performing the job. Training deals with specific facts and procedures, whereas education is broader in scope and is concerned with theories,
concepts, issues, and alternatives. Many police training programs are heavily
oriented toward teaching facts and procedures to the exclusion of theories,
concepts, and analytical reasoning. A strict reliance on this approach is problematic, because so much police work requires analysis and reasoning
instead of application of specific procedures that supposedly fit all circumstances. Therefore, many academies are attempting to increase the percentage of time spent on an educational approach by employing professionals in
the social sciences, especially criminal justice and criminology, psychology,
and sociology, as instructors. With the ever-increasing recognition of the
complexity of the police role and hence the necessity to utilize both training
and education to prepare police recruits adequately, the traditional distinction between the two approaches has become less significant.

Another important aspect of program development is the type of instructional methods to be used. In large part, this is determined by assumptions
regarding how learning takes place; that is, how do adults learn? Although this
phase of development is often explicitly overlooked, it is vitally important
because developing instructional methods incorporates assumptions about
learning. There are two schools of thought in this area: behavioral and Gestalt.
Behavioral theorists believe that learning is a function of ***stimulus and
response*** (S-R), or trial and error. Desired behavior, or the learning of knowledge
and skills, is rewarded; undesired behavior, or the failure to learn, is punished or
ignored. Trainees are given points or some form of credit for desirable behavior,
such as attendance, promptness, or performance. ***Gestalt theorists*** do not support the stimulus-response approach; they maintain that learning is more ***cognitive***. It involves gaining or changing insights, points of view, or thought patterns. More emphasis is placed on the analytical processes of reasoning and
problem solving (Roberg, 1979a). The two theories can be differentiated in that
behaviorist teachers want to change the behaviors of students in a significant way,
whereas Gestalt-oriented teachers want to help students change their understandings of significant problems and situations (Bigge, 1971).

Instructional methods are influenced by teaching philosophies, which in turn are influenced by learning assumptions. Two contrasting philosophies are pedagogy and andragogy. **Pedagogy** involves a one-way transfer of knowledge, usually by lecturing on facts, in which absolute solutions are expected to be memorized. **Andragogy** stresses analytical and conceptual skills and promotes the mutual involvement of instructor and student. Knowles (1970) describes pedagogy as the art and science of teaching children and andragogy as the art and science of helping adults learn. Although he does not necessarily suggest any fundamental differences between the way adults and children learn, he believes that there are significant differences that emerge in the learning process as maturation takes place. Accordingly, the **andragogical learning model** is based on four assumptions about the characteristics of adult learners: (1) the learner's self-concept moves from that of a dependent personality toward that of a self-directing human being; (2) the learner accumulates a growing reservoir of experience, which becomes an increasing resource for learning; (3) the learner's readiness to learn becomes oriented increasingly toward the developmental tasks of his or her social roles; and (4) the learner's time perspective changes from one of postponed application of knowledge to immediate application and, accordingly, his or her orientation toward learning shifts from subject-centeredness to problem-centeredness (pp. 38–39).

These four andragogical assumptions, quite different from pedagogical assumptions, have strong implications for program design. First, the learning climate (psychological as well as social) should be **cooperative and nonthreatening**; students and teachers should view themselves as **joint inquirers** (this would suggest that a nonstressful environment is more conducive to learning). Second, the teaching-learning transaction is seen as a **mutual responsibility** of both the teacher and the learners. The teacher's role is that of resource person and facilitator, who is more a catalyst to learning than an instructor. Mutual planning, self-diagnosis of needs, and mutual assessment of the learning experience are emphasized, because adults are more motivated to learn those things that they need to learn. Third, there is a shift away from transmittal techniques (such as pure lectures, assigned readings, and audio-visual presentations) toward more **participatory techniques,** which can tap the experiences of the learners (such as group discussion, simulation exercises, role playing, field projects, seminars, and counseling). Finally, the orientation to learning is problem centered and focuses on the **practical concerns** of the learners.

Because insight, analysis, and problem solving are or should be important aspects of police training, instructors should consider using andragogical methods for a good part of their training program (Roberg, 1979b). At the same time, pedagogical teaching methods are also necessary in police training, especially for those activities that require memorization (e.g., laws and policies) and behavioral techniques (e.g., traffic stops or approaching a suspect). The type of instructional methods used in the academy are also critical to the development of community policing. Although many training programs currently use more role playing, simulations, and problem analysis than they used to, they rarely emphasize conceptual understanding and insight development. Even though the importance of the andragogical learning model and methods of instruction in police training has been recognized since at least the late 1970s (see Roberg, 1979b), programs still tend to emphasize how to do a job rather than why the job is necessary or why one method is more effective than another. In contemporary training, officers would most likely benefit from an andragogical approach in many of the skills of policing, including public speaking, interpersonal communications, problem solving, and cultural diversity. For example, small group discussions and the sharing of life experiences would allow recruits to resolve issues pertaining to race, sex, ethnicity, and the whole concept of diversity (Birzer, 1999; Birzer and Tannehill, 2001).

Course Content and Evaluation

Police training programs and curricula should be based on two common assumptions: first, the programs should incorporate the ***mission statement*** of the department and ***ethical considerations*** second, training should be based on what an officer actually does every day (Alpert and Smith, 1990; Bayley and Bittner, 1989). The subject matter to be taught in the academy should be based on a task analysis of the jobs to be performed by the recruits. Such task analysis still tends to be more the exception than the rule, with training based more on legal requirements and experience. Nevertheless, some departments have tried to identify police tasks that are important to the job and to base their training on them. Some states have conducted comprehensive task-analysis studies of several police positions (e.g., entry-level and managerial positions).

The importance of basing training on what an officer actually does cannot be overstated; that is, to what degree is reality presented and discussed? What image of the police is presented? Traditionally, training has underrepresented order maintenance and social-service aspects of the police role while overrepresenting law enforcement activities; such an emphasis has undoubtedly contributed toward a "macho" view of policing that is still prevalent. Of course, the particular image presented can have a significant impact on the way recruits view their role as police officers. Because the training program is seen as representing the department's view of police work, an unrealistic presentation of policing will not only send the wrong message to recruits but most likely make initial adjustments to the job more difficult as well.

As the complex nature of the police role has become recognized (see Roberg, 1976), training requirements, including the number of hours trained and the number of subjects covered, have increased significantly. According to the Bureau of Justice Statistics national survey (Reaves and Goldberg, 2000), of 3,412 local and state agencies nearly all departments serving a population of 2,500 or more had a training requirement for new officer recruits, as did four-fifths of those serving fewer than 2,500 residents. The average number of training hours required ranged from more than 1,300 hours in those serving 250,000 to 999,999 residents to 422 hours in those serving fewer than 2,500 residents(see Table 6.1). As can be seen, the overall departmental average was approximately 600 hours, with about two-thirds in the classroom and one-third in the field. When departments are weighted according to the number of officers, Reaves and Goldberg (2000) estimate that the average new local police recruit in 1997 was required to take more than 1,000 hours of training, with about two-thirds of it in the classroom.

Table 6.1	Training Requirements for New Officer Recruits in Local Police Departments, by Size of Population Served, 1997		
	Average Number of Hours Required		
Population Served	**Total**	**Classroom**	**Field**
All Sizes	599	395	204
1,000,000 or more	1,252	875	374
500,000–999,999	1,357	822	535
250,000–499,999	1,356	782	574
100,000–249,999	1,145	649	496
50,000–99,999	938	537	501
25,000–49,999	919	518	401
10,000–24,999	780	470	310
2,500–9,999	602	399	203
Under 2,500	422	321	101

Note: Average number of training hours excludes departments not requiring training.
Source: Reaves, B. A., and Goldberg, A. L. 2000. *Local Police Departments 1997*.
Washington, DC: Bureau of Justice Statistics: p. 5 .

Interestingly, only 3 percent of all local police departments operated a training academy. However, over 80 percent of those serving a population of 250,000 or more had their own academy, while only 5 percent or less of those serving a population of under 100,000 had their own (see Table 6.2). Nationwide, almost half (44 percent) of all officers were employed by a department that operated an academy; put another way, almost half of the nation's local police officers are employed by a department that serves a population of 250,000 or more.

Table 6.2	Percentage of Local Police Departments with Training Academies, by Population Served, 1997
Population Served	**Percent with Training Academy**
All Sizes	3
1,000,000 or more	94
500,000–999,999	96
250,000–499,999	82
100,000–249,999	45
50,000–99,999	5
25,000–49,999	2
10,000–24,999	2
2,500–9,999	1
Under 2,500	2

Source: Reaves, B. A., and Goldberg, A. L. 2000, p. 5 Local Police Departments 1997.
Washington, DC: Bureau of Justice Statistics.

Another national survey of some 700 state and local agencies with over 100 sworn officers, again using 1997 data (Reaves and Goldberg, 1999), found that the median number of hours of classroom training required of new officers was highest in state police agencies, with 823 hours, followed by county law enforcement, with 760 hours; municipal police, with 640 hours, and lastly, sheriff's departments, with 448 hours. The median number of hours required for field training was 480 for county and municipal police, 436 for sheriff's departments, and 360 for state police. This survey is important because it describes differences among types of departments; for example, training requirements were highest for county police, with 1,240 total hours, followed by state police, with 1,183; municipal police, with 1,120, and sheriff's departments with 884. On average, the nation's larger police departments required 1,107 training hours for new recruits, including 668 in the classroom and 449 in the field.

An example of the diverse topics covered in present-day recruit training can be seen in California's curriculum (mandated by POST), which includes 41 topics (domains). These are to be covered in a minimum of 599 hours of training—larger departments require more hours—with an additional 65 hours of testing. The testing includes both scenarios (in which simulated field situations are presented and recruits respond to them) and written exams. In addition, once a recruit becomes a sworn officer, he or she must also complete a minimum of 24 hours of POST-certified training once every two years. Table 6.3 provides a list of the topics covered and the minimum number of hours required on each topic.

Whether recruit training is based on task analysis or experience, the department must determine what subject matter is most important because most (if not all) programs are constrained by time and resources. The amount of time devoted to any particular subject emphasizes to recruits the importance attached to that subject by the department. Table 6.3 shows the POST certified California Police Training Curriculum that is used throughout the state, and the varying amount of hours devoted to certain subjects, with a low of 4 hours to a high of 72 hours. It should be noted that in police training, there will always be debate regarding what topics should be covered and how much time should be devoted to each. For example, given its importance to effective and just policing, should the area of professionalism and ethics receive more time? What about the use of force? And, there are no topics on community policing and/or problem solving (crucial to departments transitioning to community policing). If such topics were added or expanded, however, would other topics then need to be dropped or cut back? Answering such questions is the reason why it is so important that the training for any particular job be based on task analysis; the importance attached to the subject matter is then based on scientific evidence rather than on a few individuals' experience, intuition, or guesswork as to what is important.

For instance, in one national survey on ***police ethics*** of 874 members of the International Association of Chiefs of Police (IACP), it was found that while 83 percent of the departments provided some form of ethics training for their recruits, 71 percent provided four classroom hours or less of programming. Only 17 percent provided eight hours of training for ethics. For supervisors, although 65 percent of the departments provided some kind of ethics training, it was generally for four hours or less. The report concluded that although most saw a high need for ethics training, the amount of time earmarked for it was far less than might be expected. Clearly, the implications of ethical behavior in policing a democratic society should make ethics a primary topic in training. It is important to understand that while the behavior of police officers may not violate any laws or departmental policies, it may still be unethical. However, if officers are trained and socialized to perform

Table 6.3	California Police Academy Training Curriculum Content and Minimum Hourly Requirements	
Domain Number	**Domain Description**	**Minimum Hours**
01	History, Professionalism, and Ethics	8
02	Criminal Justice System	4
03	Community Relations	2
04	Victimology/Crisis Interventions	6
05	Introduction to Criminal Law	6
06	Crimes Against Property	10
07	Crimes Against Persons	10
08	General Crimes Statutes	4
09	Crimes Against Children	6
10	Sex Crimes	6
11	Juvenile Law and Procedure	6
12	Controlled Substances	12
13	ABC (Alcohol, Beverage Code) Law	4
14	Laws of Arrest	12
15	Search & Seizure	12
16	Presentation of Evidence	8
17	Investigative Report Writing	40
18	Vehicle Operations	24
19	Use of Force	12
20	Patrol Techniques	12
21	Vehicle Pullovers	14
22	Crimes in Progress	16
23	Handling Disputes/Crowd Control	12
24	Domestic Violence	8
25	Unusual Occurrences	4
26	Missing Persons	4
27	Traffic Enforcement	22
28	Traffic Accident Investigation	2
29	Preliminary Investigation	42
30	Custody	4
31	Physical Fitness/Officer Stress	40
32	Person Searches/Baton, etc.	60
33	First Aid and CPR	21
34	Firearms/Chemical Agents	72
35	Information Systems	4
36	Persons with Disabilities	6
37	Gang Awareness	8
38	Crimes Against the Justice System	4
39	Weapons Violations	4
40	Hazardous Materials	4
41	Cultural Diversity/Discrimination	24
	Minimum Instructional Hours	599
	Types of Testing	**Hours**
	Scenario Tests	40
	POST-Constructed Knowledge Tests	25
	Total Minimum Required Hours	664

Adapted from: Commission on Peace Officer Standards and Training, 1995 (May 12). *Bulletin 95–9: Regular Basic Course Required Minimum Hours Increases from 560 to 664*. Sacramento, CA: POST.

their jobs in an ethical manner, they will be more likely to observe the law and departmental policies. This is why, as discussed in Inside Management 6.1, ethics must be incorporated into all academy and field training.

Inside Management 6.1

An Interview with Professor Edwin Delattre, Author of *Character & Cops*

Question: When it comes to training and ethics, what kind of program would you recommend? Do you think a special course in ethics is the way to go in police academy training?

Delattre: It's perfectly all right to have a course devoted to constitutional heritage and the obligations of police under the Constitution, and what an oath of allegiance to the Constitution means in daily life. You can explain the principle of human dignity and how the idea of minimum necessary force follows from it, and so on. But if such a course is expected to stand all by itself, it's doomed to failure because the newcomers get the impression that it has nothing really to do with the rest of their training and the responsibilities they'll have on a daily basis. They will treat the ethics sessions as irrelevant to what they really know to be policing. There has to be a resonance between what you did in any course on ethics and what's done in all the other courses in programs of education. So, for example, when you explain to people that you're trying to make them competent with respect to policy and practice as it relates, say, to traffic chases, it's worth making the point that when you voluntarily accept responsibilities that affect the lives of others, you also accept the duty to become good at the fulfillment of those responsibilities. This is something you need to know, you need to be competent at it in order to be good at your duties, so that becoming competent in these matters has ethical consequences. That kind of resonance is essential to affecting the culture of the institution and the expectations of the people who work in it in the right way.

The other thing is that ethics has to be seen to be believed. You can talk about ethics till doomsday; there's no evidence that any course on ethics ever taught in human history made anybody a better person. I know lots of philosophers who are very good in all sorts of reasoning about ethical problems and dilemmas, but I wouldn't trust them as far as I could throw them. And it's not just a conceptual matter, it's a matter of disposition, or respect for persons, of not being so focused on your own self-gratification that you're willing to manipulate others and deceive them.

In practice, people are most affected by considerations of ethics when they see people who are just quietly and unassumingly decent, and that matters more than any course in ethics that was ever taught.

Question: What about the role of supervisory officers when it comes to making sure that there isn't any corruption and that the officers under them are kept at a pretty high level of ethics and integrity?

Delattre: Clarity and open ears are the most important things. That is to say, you have to listen to others. You have to be explicit about your expectations, rooted in the policies of the department, nothing tongue in cheek. I've seen people beat up suspects in custody when there was no chance that their supervisors didn't know it. You stop and say, "Wait a minute, what do you think you're doing; this is against the law; it's against policy. Stop right now." They don't care whether it's illegal; they just want the results. Given the slightest impression that that's true is a license for wrongdoing and exceeding one's authority. This doesn't mean fulminating about standards and all that. It means forging a department in which the voice of recruitment, the voice of academy training, the voice of field training, the voice of supervision all the way to the top is one voice, and the ways of behaving are one way of behaving with respect to matters of character and integrity. This is how we do things here; this is how I do things here in the interest of justice and public service that can be trusted. You can't self-righteously set an example; you have to be a particular kind of person and hope that others will look to you and say, "Yeah this person really rings true when he says, 'We don't take, we don't beat up on suspects in custody, we don't falsify reports.' That's just exactly the way the person really is." There's no other way to achieve that that I've ever heard of.

Adapted from: Simonetti Rosen, M. 1997. "A LEN Interview with Prof. Edwin J. Delattre of Boston University." *Law Enforcement News* May 15: 11–12. Printed with permission from the *Law Enforcement News*, John Jay College of Criminal Justice.

Another topic that appears in need of expansion is the ***deescalation of force to reduce violence between police and citizens*** (Alpert and Moore, 1993). While some academies may cover this area briefly under a Use of Force topic, Alpert and Moore (1993) propose that nonaggressive behavior that reduces violence should be reinforced and established as the model for other officers to copy. Such training would need to recognize and emphasize the use of nonaggressive behavior that, when appropriate, does not lead to an arrest. This understanding would in turn lead to the recognition that many problems in the community can be solved without the use of force. In this vein, officers need to develop skills in ***anger management*** and ***dispute resolution***, so when faced with verbal challenges they can deescalate the situation without risking First Amendment liability of free expression rights (see Vaughn, 1996; Vaughn and Kappeler, 1999). As new developments occur in policing, they must be added to the curriculum. For example, such areas as cultural diversity, victimology, crisis intervention, crimes against children, domestic violence, persons with disabilities, and gang awareness were not adequately addressed or even discussed a decade ago, and still are not in some recruit training programs. For instance, a study of a regional training academy in Ohio (Marion, 1998) found that ethics and helping the elderly or victims of crime were not included in the curriculum. In addition, the author discovered that the academy was lacking in its ability to transmit the proper attitudes for new officers; an obvious element of sexism, elitism, and the portrayal of policing as a "macho" profession by some instructors was apparent. As the author notes, such attitudes will likely be adopted by the recruits, who may begin to act and think in a similar fashion. In addition, as laws become more complex in certain areas, officers will need additional training. For example, the scope of the Americans with Disabilities Act has expanded as a result of legal rulings that municipalities must train police to differentiate between persons who are drugged or drunk and those who are disabled (Clark, 1994).

A topic that has long been neglected in recruit training is ***policing and teenagers***, who may need to be dealt with differently than adults (see Inside Management 6.2). One study, for example, on the perceptions of inner-city children and teenagers in Athens, Georgia, found that officers need to be trained to be aware of the potential impact of their "unnecessarily negative, threatening, and impersonal contacts with children and teenagers" (Williams, 1999: 167). In another study of juveniles' attitudes toward the police, Hurst and Frank (2000) found juveniles generally had less favorable perceptions of the police than adults. This was particularly true for nonwhite juveniles. Juveniles who reported having officer-initiated contacts in which they perceived the officer treated them poorly had significantly lower overall ratings of police. On the other hand, when juveniles initiated the encounter and reported the officer treated them favorably, they were more likely to have positive attitudes toward the police.

Finally, one interesting breakthrough that may have implications for policing is the developing area of ***virtual reality training***. Although this type of training is essentially untapped, it appears to have great potential as far as providing a safe training experience. It works by programming data into computers to generate three-dimensional images to create virtual (lifelike) environments. These are usually viewed through a head-mounted device

---

Inside Management 6.2

Teens to Write Section of Department's Manual in Effort to Improve Relations

---

In what may be the first program of its kind in the state, Pleasanton (CA) police have invited teens to help write a new section of the department's police training manual. The section will be "teen specific," said Officer Michael Tryphonas, who helped write the department's inch-and-a-half-thick training manual. Although the new section is still in the early draft stage, new regulations will likely help guide officers on how teens should be approached differently on the street than adults. For example, teens may need more explanation than an adult of what law may have been violated.

Teens voiced concerns about their relationship with police last year at a "Youth Speak Out" event hosted by the Pleasanton Youth Commission. They said they often feel harassed and unfairly singled out by police. Teens say they want officers to be firm but not condescending, and they want explanations of what they did wrong and of the consequences. "This will help promote awareness and bridge gaps," said Eddie Richardson, 16, vice chairman of the Pleasanton Youth Commission, whose members are helping write the new regulations. The police manual's new sections will be required training for new officers, and will be part of the annual recertification training for current officers.

Adapted from: Mendoza, M. 2000. "A New Program Calls on Teens to Help Write a Section of the *Pleasanton Department's Manual in an Effort to Improve Relations.*" *The Valley Times* February 6: pp. A3, A34.

(goggles or a helmet), providing users with a sense of depth. Users remain stationary and use a joystick or track ball to move through the environment; they may wear a special glove to manipulate objects or employ virtual weapons to confront virtual aggressors (Hormann, 1995). Another method is to use a training simulator, similar to those used to train pilots; see Inside Management 6.3 for an example of pursuit driving. Recruits can make decisions and act on them without risk to themselves or others; these actions can then be critiqued, allowing trainees to learn from their mistakes. It appears that virtual reality can offer law enforcement benefits in a number of areas, including pursuit driving, firearms training, high-risk-incident management, incident re-creation, and processing crime scenes (Hormann, 1995).

How effective is the training provided to the recruits? One means of evaluating training is to follow up on field performance to determine the areas in which recruits are having the most difficulty; methods used can include the observation of recruits, the evaluation of recruit performance, and surveys of recruits, trainers, and supervisors. In general, the validity of the measurement will be higher if more than one of these methods is used. Once problems are identified, a determination can be made as to how to improve the program. In addition, as new knowledge and skills become available, they should be incorporated into the program. In addition, police managers must monitor instructors and the types of attitudes that are being imparted at the academy. Recruits need to leave the academy with attitudes that are appropriate for a culturally and sexually diverse society. Instructors who convey sexist, racist, or macho attitudes should be removed as trainers and given counseling to determine whether they should remain on the force.

Community-Policing Training

As community policing becomes more widespread, it will become necessary to significantly expand or even develop an entire training curriculum to

---

Inside Management 6.3

Pursuit Simulation Training

While it is no substitute for actual driving experience, a driving simulator used by the Medina County, Ohio, Sheriff's Department has proven to be an effective means of determining how and when a pursuit should be called off. "The training simulator not only provided training, but it stimulated interest in our pursuit policy and caused a review of that policy through a committee which made some recommendations," said Chief Deputy Tom Miller.

Over 70 officers were trained when the department leased the simulator for a week in October. Deputy Dave Swinehart swerved around a computerized image of a transit bus, past a produce truck and a minivan as a BMW pulled ahead of him, roaring through two red lights. Swinehart, a 10-year veteran who has been involved in actual high-speed pursuits, pulled left, dodging a pickup truck that had pulled over, then right, to avoid a child on a skateboard. When the BMW whipped left into a school zone, however, Swinehart tapped his brakes, ending the simulated pursuit. "It was the right decision," said driving instructor Daryll Rocklin. "Good recognition. You're not going to chase through a school zone."

Miller recalled that when he started in law enforcement 25-years ago, a pursuit policy was about a paragraph long. The Medina County department's now runs approximately two pages, due mainly to the addition of examples and instances of when a chase should be cut off. By using the simulator, Miller said, police saw how frequently unexpected obstacles appear on the road.

According to 1998 statistics, 15 people died in Ohio as a result of police chases, including 10 who were not being pursued "You always want to catch the bad guy," said Geoffrey Alpert, an expert on police pursuits, "but there's a growing awareness that high-speed chases can create risks that run counter to the basic police mission of protecting the public."

Adapted from: "Pursuit Simulation Training is No Ordinary Crash Course." 2000. *Law Enforcement News* November, 15: 6. Printed with permission from the *Law Enforcement News*, John Jay College of Criminal Justice.

---

adequately train recruits into its philosophy and practices. According to the Bureau of Justice Statistics national survey (Hickman and Reaves, 2001), just over half of local police departments offered eight or more hours of training in community policing to some or all new officer recruits in both 1999 and 1997 (see Table 6.4). About two-fifths of all departments provided community policing training for new recruits.

Although Table 6.4 does not indicate the types of community policing training offered, Reaves and Goldberg (2000) indicate that such training "helps officers develop skills in areas integral to successful community policing such as problem-solving, SARA (scanning, analysis, response, assessment), and community partnerships" (p. 4).

Table 6.4 further indicates that in 1999, at least 94 percent of the departments serving 500,000 or more residents trained all new recruits in community policing, as did more than 80 percent of those serving 150,000 to 499,999 residents. For those departments at the lower end of the population scale, approximately half of those serving 2,500 to 9,999 residents, and a fourth of those serving fewer than 2,500 residents trained all recruits in community policing.

While the Bureau of Justice Statistics data provides evidence regarding how many departments provide eight hours of community policing training, it gives us no information with respect to what topics are being taught or whether eight hours is sufficient to allow officers to do community policing. Since community policing is a paradigm shift for the field, it would seem that eight hours of training can provide little more than a brief introduction to the concept. While there is little doubt that additional training is necessary in order to allow officers to properly implement community policing, the obvious question of how much additional training remains. As we have discussed previously, it is difficult to decide how much time and what topics are necessary for any area of police training; however, there has been some debate and suggestions put forth regarding a training curriculum for community policing.

Table 6.4	Community-Policing Training for New Officer Recruits in Local Police Departments, by Size of Population Served, 1997 and 1999			
Percent of Agencies Providing 8 or More Hours of Community Policing Training for:				
Population Served	**At Least Some Recruits**		**All Recruits**	
	1997	**1999**	**1997**	**1999**
All sizes	53%	54%	40%	41%
1,000,000 or more	94	100	94	94
500,000–999,999	87	100	87	96
250,000–499,999	91	89	82	85
150,000–249,999	83	90	75	81
50,0009,999	87	89	75	75
25,000–49,999	82	87	65	69
10,000–24,999	69	76	53	61
2,500–9,999	58	63	45	46
under 2,500	37	35	25	24

Source: Hickman, M. J., and Reaves, B. A. 2001. p.4. *Community Policing in Local Police Departments, 1997 and 1999*. Washington, DC: Bureau of Justice Statistics.

Palmiotto, Birzer, and Unnithan (2000) have developed a training curriculum for those departments that are implementing community policing. For these departments, knowledge regarding the philosophy and practice of community policing should be incorporated throughout the training curriculum; however, there are a number of specific classes that should be included. Of course, some of these topics may already be covered in the academy, and they should be retained and possibly expanded. Table 6.5 provides a list of the topics, some learning objectives, approximate sequence, and recommended number of hours.

Palmiotto, Birzer, and Unnithan (2000) further suggest that the method of training used should emphasize self-directed learning on the recruit's part; if community policing is to be successful, officers will have to be self-starters. The authors suggest that recruits would benefit from an environment that incorporates the assumptions from the andragogical model of learning, described earlier. In this context, recruits would be allowed to bring life experiences into the training session, and to meet in small groups to discuss issues pertaining to race and gender with persons other than their own race or gender. Further, self-directed group discussions and active debate within the context of training issues would help recruits to develop personal understandings of individual differences. This in turn would allow recruits to better understand community policing, with its emphasis on police-community interaction.

Community-policing training should also include "nontraditional" instructors who have particular knowledge about the community and com-

Table 6.5	Recruit Training Curriculum for Community Policing	
Subject	**Class Content Highlights**	**Number of Hours**
WEEK 1		
Departmental philosophy	Community partnerships	4
	Democratic values/customer based	
Organizational structure	Departmental structure/communication	8
	Organizational change/strategies of	
Community structure	Demographic/social/political make-up	4
	Quality of life issues	
Cultural diversity	Definition/value of understanding/bias crimes	
	Cultural organizations and leaders	16
Police history	Development of police/in America	
	Modern policing/major research findings	8
WEEK 2		
Police operations	Patrol/investigation/support units	
	Police-community relations	8
Police mission	Mission/values and professionalism	
	Goals and objectives	8
Police culture	Understanding police culture/myths	
	Evolving police culture	8
Police discretion	Definition/importance/complexity of role	
	Legal/departmental police to police discretion	8
Police misconduct	Definition/types of internal affairs	8
WEEK 3		
Police ethics	Definition/morality and law/behavior	
	Analyzing ethical dilemmas	20
Problem solving	Defining problems/SARA model	
	Identification of resources	20
WEEK 4		
Crime prevention	Definition/environmental design	
	Crime prevention programs	40
Community policing	Definition/philosophy/strategies	
	Future and long-range implementation	40

Adapted from: M. J. Palmiotto, M. L. Birzer, and N. Prabha Unnithan. 2000. *Policing: An International Journal of Police Strategies and Management* 23, pp. 15–16.

munity agencies that may assist the police in identifying and solving problems. For example, in Greensboro, North Carolina, a planner with the Department of Housing and Community Development routinely participates in the recruit training program. She teaches a session on the responsibilities and functions of other city departments and how they can help in solving community problems. In addition, she familiarizes the recruits with the neighborhoods in which they will be working, where they can get information that may be helpful, and explains that her department will assist in conducting citizen surveys (Roche, Adams and Arcury, 2001).

Field Training

After successfully completing the academy, recruits generally go through a field training program to prepare them for the real world of policing. This on-the-job, or apprentice, training has been an integral aspect of the recruit training process for some time, but it has become much more sophisticated since the mid-1970s. The traditional assignment of new officers being broken in by experienced old timers is giving way to highly structured programs using *field training officers* (FTOs), that is, well-qualified, experienced officers especially trained to act as mentors for new recruits. In a national survey of 588 police departments of all sizes, McCampbell (1986) found that 64 percent of those responding had a formal field training program, but 36 percent still do not use such programs. Major advantages of such programs include a reduced number of civil liability suits, standardization of the training process, and better documentation of recruit performance, thus improving the department's ability to make informed decisions about recruit retention (McCampbell, 1986) and, it might be added, a method for helping it to determine the effectiveness of academy training. Interestingly, however, a national study of recruitment, selection, and training practices in 60 departments with more than 500 sworn officers (Langworthy, Hughes, and Sanders, 1995) found that only 56 percent expected FTOs to communicate training needs to the academy. Police managers should develop a policy that requires periodic communication between the FTO program and the academy to update training needs.

The importance of FTOs cannot be overstated because they will have a significant impact not only on the training of the recruit but on imparting the organization's culture and socialization as well. This is the first opportunity officers have to get a taste of the street. To this point, recruits have learned in the academy how to behave like police officers, but under the guidance of the FTO, the officer is exposed to actually acting like an officer. This particular stage of socialization was referred to as the "encounter" by Van Maanen, 1973). However, the FTO has the opportunity to subvert what has been taught by advising the rookie to "Forget what you learned in the academy . . . I'll show you how to be a 'real street cop.' " Very often the recruit learns demeanor and values from the FTOs, making this position an incredibly important component in the development of young police officers.

The national study by Langworthy, Hughes, and Sanders (1995) observed that the mean number of years required to become an FTO in those departments surveyed had decreased significantly from 1990 to 1994 (from 2.6 to 1.9 years). The authors suggested that this decrease "may be because departments are having difficulty recruiting officers for the FTO assignment and have lessened their standards to fill training slots" (1995, p. 39). Much can be learned about the importance of maintaining high standards in the selection of FTOs from the Christopher Commission's report on the Los Angeles Police Department in the wake of the Rodney King beating. Case Study 6.1 is an excerpt from the Commission's report regarding the process then in use by the Los Angeles Police Department to select and train FTOs. As the Commission notes, not only should rigorous selection standards be established, but officers with an aptitude for and interest in training junior officers should be encouraged to apply.

With FTO programs, the probationary period is usually a highly structured experience in which new officers must demonstrate specific knowledge and skills. Frequent evaluations are made of the recruits' performance, usually by several FTOs who supervise their work in different areas and different shifts. In general, there are three phases in an FTO program (McCampbell, 1986: 4–5):

Case Study 6.1

Los Angeles Police Department: Selection and Training of FTOs

Upon graduation [from the academy] the new officer works as a "probationary officer" assigned to various field training officers. The FTOs guide new officers' first contacts with citizens and have primary responsibility for introducing the probationers to the culture and traditions of the Department. The Commission's interviews of FTOs in four representative divisions revealed that many FTOs openly perpetuate the siege mentality that alienates patrol officers from the community and pass on to their trainees confrontational attitudes of hostility and disrespect for the public. This problem is in part the result of flaws in the way FTOs are selected and trained. The hiring of a very large number of new officers in 1989, which required the use of less experienced FTOs, greatly exacerbated the problem.

Any officer promoted to Police Officer III by passing a written examination covering Department policies and procedures is eligible to serve as an FTO. At present there are no formal eligibility or disqualification criteria for the FTO position based on an applicant's disciplinary records. Fourteen of the FTOs in the four divisions the Commission studied had been disciplined for use of excessive force or use of improper tactics. There also appears to be little emphasis on selecting FTOs who have an interest in training junior officers, and an FTO,s training ability is given little weight in his or her evaluation.

The most influential training received by a probationer comes from the example set by his or her FTO. Virtually all of the FTOs interviewed stated that their primary objective in training probationers was to instill good "officer safety skills." Although the Commission recognizes the importance of such skills in police work, the probationers' world is quickly divided into "we/they" categories, which is exacerbated by the failure to integrate any cultural awareness or sensitivity training into field training.

The Commission believes that, to become FTOs, officers should be required to pass written and oral tests designed to measure communication skills, teaching aptitude, and knowledge of Departmental policies regarding appropriate use of force, cultural sensitivity, community relations, and nondiscrimination. Officers with an aptitude for and interest in training junior officers should be encouraged by effective incentives to apply for FTO positions. In addition, the training program for FTOs should be modified to place greater emphasis on communication skills and the appropriate use of force. Successful completion of FTO School should be required before an FTO begins teaching probationers.

Adapted from: Independent [Christopher] Commission on the Los Angeles Police Department, 1991. *Report*, pp. xvi-xvii. Los Angeles: California Public Management Institute.

Phase 1: The first weeks (eight to 20 or more) are for regional academy training; if the recruit passes, there may be additional weeks of classroom training provided by the department.

Phase 2: In the second phase (12 or more weeks), the recruit is assigned to the first FTO for several weeks, followed by a second FTO on a different shift, and then to a third FTO on another shift. The officer then returns to the original FTO. During each tour, there are daily observation reports by the FTOs and weekly evaluation reports by supervisors (usually sergeants). At the end of this phase, the recruit moves on to Phase 3, is given remedial training, or is dismissed. Figure 6.1 is an example of the San Jose (California) Police Department's Daily Observation Report Form, which is used to rate the daily performance of recruits. Extensive training is provided to FTOs in how to evaluate and provide guidance to police officer recruits.

Phase 3: In the third phase (16 or more weeks), the recruit is assigned a solo beat outside the training district and is evaluated every couple of weeks by the supervisor. After about ten months, a review board determines whether the recruit is certified to continue Phase 3; if so, he or she continues to work the solo beat (with monthly evaluations); if not, he or she returns for

Figure 6.1 San Jose Police Department's Daily Observation Report Form

The daily observation report form lists thirty areas of performance in which recruits are expected to be able to perform in a satisfactory manner while on patrol. The rating scale ranges from not acceptable (1) to superior (7), with the midrange acceptance level (4). FTOs must provide written comments on the most and least acceptable performance areas of the day on all ranges of 2 or less and 6 or more.

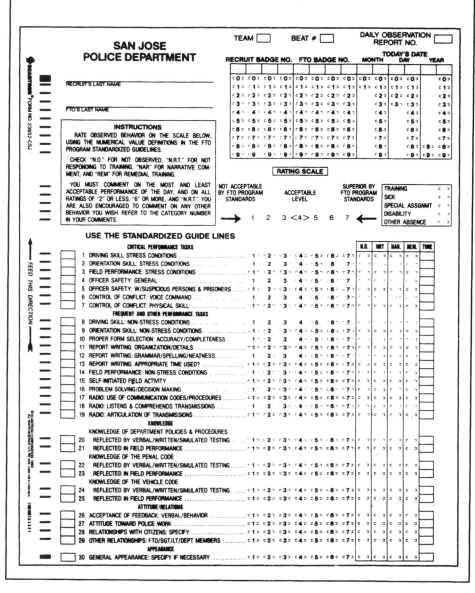

remedial training. In the final two weeks, an FTO in plain clothes rides along and observes the recruit. At the end of this phase, the recruit is either certified as a permanent employee, Phase 3 is extended, or he or she is dismissed.

FTO programs have not always been as effective as was hoped. Although some monetary incentive and special training is generally provided, many officers believe that being an FTO is both burdensome and stressful. Evalua-

Figure 6.1   San Jose Police Department's Daily Observation Report Form (Continued)

THE MOST ACCEPTABLE AREA OF PERFORMANCE TODAY WAS RATING CATEGORY NUMBER _____
A SPECIFIC INCIDENT WHICH DEMONSTRATES TODAY'S PERFORMANCE IN THIS AREA IS: _____

THE LEAST ACCEPTABLE AREA OF PERFORMANCE TODAY WAS RATING CATEGORY NUMBER _____
A SPECIFIC INCIDENT WHICH DEMONSTRATES TODAY'S PERFORMANCE IN THIS AREA IS: _____

DOCUMENTATION OF PERFORMANCE AND COMMENTS:
CAT. NO.

RECRUIT OFFICER SIGNATURE   TRAINING OFFICER SIGNATURE

Source: Reprinted by permission of San Jose Police Department, San Jose, California and Scantron Corporation, Tustin, California.

tion is undoubtedly one of the most difficult managerial tasks to perform, and many managers do not do it well. FTOs frequently engage in evaluation activity on a daily basis. Their evaluations may be challenged, and if a trainee is terminated, the FTO may be sued. Unless the stress of being an FTO is lessened substantially, it may be difficult to encourage the best officers to participate. In order for high-quality officers to apply for the FTO position, it is necessary to increase both the status and pay of the position; with the position considered to be a promotion with pay perhaps equaling that of a first-level supervisor. In addition, evaluations should be conducted less frequently and, for the most part, determined by a group of FTOs rather than by an individual. In other words, a recruit should work with several FTOs over a period of several weeks or months, and a group evaluation of each recruit's performance should be used instead of the daily evaluations by individual FTOs. Of course, each FTO should still give daily advice and guidance to the recruit, while keeping a daily evaluation log that would be used in determining group FTO evaluations of the recruit. Such a procedure should not only increase the validity of the evaluation but help to reduce FTO stress as well.

After the recruit has passed the FTO program, he or she may become a permanent, sworn police officer or work for an additional period in the field on probationary status. During this time, officers are evaluated several more times, and if their performance is acceptable, they become permanent employees.

Performance and Evaluation

Once employees are adequately trained, it is the department's responsibility to make sure that they perform effectively. This performance and its evaluation comprise the second phase in the development process. *Evaluation* involves comparing employees' activity and behavior with *standards of performance* set forth by the department. Several important questions regarding this process emerge: Who has expectations about police behavior that formally or informally become standards? What are the standards of performance? Are these standards valid and reliable? Who does the evaluation? How often is it done? How are evaluations used? What are the problems in performance evaluation?

The expectation-integration model provides a useful means of looking at sources of expectations that may become standards of police performance. For example, diverse community groups have expectations, there are legal expectations, and there are individual and organizational expectations. Each of these expectations, to some degree, may have an impact on policies and procedures that provide officers with guidance and requirements for their performance. Historically, performance evaluation has gone through several identifiable trends: (1) from subjective to more objective criteria, (2) from an emphasis on quantity to an emphasis on both quality and quantity, and (3) from a critical checklist approach to using goals and objectives.

Trends in Evaluation

The first trend in evaluation, as in selection, has been a tendency toward the development of *valid and reliable evaluation measures.* The assessment of personnel, particularly since the 1960s, has gradually become more concerned with specific performance requirements other than indirect or nonessential measures, for example, a fixation on one's appearance (e.g., well groomed and well dressed). Although an officer's appearance is rarely discounted (nor should it be), it is essentially an indirect measure of performance and not necessarily directly linked to effectiveness. In community policing, valid and reliable measures will need to be expanded to include problem solving and community organizing skills (see discussion below).

The second trend has been a ***decline in an emphasis on quantity*** and an increase in an emphasis on quality, although quantity is still important. The reform model emphasizes production as measured by quantifiable activities, such as the number of investigations, arrests, citizen contacts, and rapid response times. This concern for quantity emphasizes law enforcement activities while overlooking many other police activities (Wycoff, 1982). Because it is more difficult to assess the other, more qualitative, police functions (i.e., order maintenance, community service, and problem-solving activities), law enforcement activities have become the most important, prestigious, and rewarded. Since the 1970s, a concern for quantity has begun to be balanced with a concern for quality; for instance, in addition to the number of investigations or citizen contacts made, the quality of the investigation (e.g., process or result) or contact with the citizen (e.g., satisfaction level) has been recognized in performance evaluation.

The third trend is a movement away from listing evaluative criteria to identifying and evaluating ***performance based on goals and objectives.*** Prior to the 1970s, and even now in many police departments, evaluation procedures at most levels have involved developing a list of criteria to use as a basis for evaluating performance. These criteria include a mix of qualitative and quantitative factors, often including attitude and appearance. Officers are rated by category, either a general one or in comparison to other officers. For example, on appearance, an officer might be rated "excellent," "good," "average," or "below average" or perhaps in the "highest 10 percent," "next highest 20 percent," and so on. The former is a general classification scheme, whereas the latter requires a comparison with other officers. The major types of performance evaluation methods are shown in Table 6.6.

In a goals-and-objectives approach, which may incorporate aspects of a management-by-objects (MBO) system, performance is measured by the accomplishment of specific purposes. As noted previously, goals are usually broad statements of purpose that identify an organization's mission—for example, to prevent, reduce, or control crime. Objectives are quantifiable, measurable, and time bounded, if possible. A patrol unit might have as an objective a 10 percent reduction in the citizen's fear of crime in the next six months; an individual patrol officer might have an objective of closing down a "crack" house in three months. Each of these objectives is measurable, or quantifiable—one with citizen surveys, the other with the elimination of a drug problem. Each individual's objectives are related to the unit's objectives, which in turn are related to the organization's goals, to provide a unity of purpose. Although this system is not without flaws (because of the difficulty of quantifying many police activities), it does change the basis for performance evaluation from subjective checklists to specific accomplishments.

Changing Measures of Police Performance

Each of the three trends discussed in the preceding section has played an important role in helping to reform the performance evaluation process—traditionally based on quantitative factors discussed above—by recognizing an expanded police role and the need for community input. For instance, Alpert and Moore (1993: 123) suggest that existing measures of individual performance could be improved by (1) auditing clearance and arrest rates

Table 6.6 Performance Evaluation Methods

Method	Definition
1. Discrete category scale	Identification of personal or job traits that are evaluated in terms of a series of categories such as:
2. Graphic scale	

Needs Improvement	Standard Performance	Outstanding Performance

The number of categories usually ranges from two to five, but there can be more.

Identification of traits, but evaluated on the following type of scale.

Unsatisfactory	Poor	Good	Superior	Excellent

This is a more flexible version of the discrete category scale. Responses can be placed anywhere on the continuum.

3. Adjective scale	Identification of traits that are more complete in evaluative response. An example is:

Handles situations clumsily; ignores policy, etc.	Judgment often illogical; tends to overlook policy, etc.	Acts judiciously under most circumstances, etc.	Judgments impartial and logical, etc.	Thinks soundly and logically, etc.

Method	Definition
4. Simple ranking: a. Simple order	Ranking of "best" to "worst" employee.
b. Alternative ranking	Employees halved into "highest" and "lowest" performing groups. Highest half ranked from top down, lowest half from bottom up.
c. Group ranking	Criterion groups established to represent specific levels of performance. Employees being evaluated are placed in a group appropriate to their level of performance.
5. Paired comparison	Every employee compared with all others being evaluated. Employee receiving highest number of favorable comparisons is ranked highest; conversely, fewer favorable comparisons results in lowest ranking.
6. Forced distribution	The bell-shaped curve or normal frequency distribution is employed; an example would be allocating 10% for highest and lowest rankings, 20% for next highest and lowest groups, and 40% for the middle group.
7. Free response	Evaluation of employee in "rater's own words."
8. Performance checklists	Checklist of desirable traits, behavior provided. Rater checks those that apply to employee. Items checked can be given different weights to determine total rating.
9. Forced choice	Sets of descriptive statements concerning performance are used, and the rater selects those that best describe the employee's performance.

and (2) developing statistical evidence on the use of force and brutality and also on (3) the incidence of discourtesy and corruption. They suggest the following additional measures:

- Police-related and intergovernmental activities that improve the social fabric of the community

- Projects with the assistance of private industry that improve informal and formal social control in the community

- Changes in fear of crime

- Victimization and police service programs that help promote community spirit in those neighborhoods where none existed

Table 6.7   Community-Policing Tasks and Activities

Activities are listed beneath the tasks they are intended to accomplish. Several activities could be used to accomplish a number of different tasks.

1. *Learn characteristics of area, residents, businesses*
   a. Study beat books
   b. Analyze crime and call-for-service data
   c. Drive, walk area and make notes
   d. Talk with community representatives
   e. Conduct area surveys
   f. Maintain area/suspect logs
   g. Read area papers("shopper" papers)
   h. Discuss area with citizens when answering calls
   i. Talk with private security personnel in area
   j. Talk with area business owners/managers

2. *Become acquainted with leaders in area*
   a. Attend community meetings, including service club meetings
   b. Ask questions in survey about who formal and informal area leaders are
   c. Ask area leaders for names of other leaders

3. *Make residents aware of who officer is and what s/he is trying to accomplish in area*
   a. Initiate citizen contacts
   b. Distribute business cards
   c. Discuss purpose at community meeting
   d. Discuss purpose when answering calls
   e. Write article for local paper
   f. Contact home-bound elderly
   g. Encourage citizens to contact officer directly

4. *Identify area problems*
   a. Attend community meetings
   b. Analyze crime and calls-for-service data
   c. Contact citizens and businesses
   d. Conduct business and residential surveys
   e. Ask about other problems when answering calls

5. *Communicate with supervisors, other officers and citizens about the nature of the area and its problems*
   a. Maintain beat bulletin board in station
   b. Leave notes in boxes of other officers
   c. Discuss area with supervisor

6. *Investigate/do research to determine sources of problems*
   a. Talk to people involved
   b. Analyze crime data
   c. Observe situation if possible (stakeout)

7. *Plan ways of dealing with problems*
   a. Analyze resources
   b. Discuss with supervisor/other officers
   c. Write patrol management plan, review with supervisor

8. *Provide citizens with information about ways they can handle problems (educate/ empower)*
   a. Distribute crime prevention information
   b. Provide names and number of other responsible agencies; tell citizens how to approach these agencies

9. *Help citizens develop appropriate expectations about what police can do and teach them how to interact effectively with police*
   a. Attend community meeting/make presentations
   b. Present school programs
   c. Write article for area paper
   d. Hold discussions with community leaders

10. *Develop resources for responding to problems*
    a. Talk with other officers, detectives, supervisors
    b. Talk with other agencies or individuals who could help

11. *Implement problem solution*
    a. Take whatever actions are called for

12. *Assess effectiveness of solution*
    a. Use data, feedback from persons who experienced the problem, and/or personal observation to determine whether problem has been solved

13. *Keep citizens informed*
    a. Officers tell citizens what steps have been taken to address a problem and with what results
    b. Detectives tell citizens what is happening with their cases

Adapted from: Oettmeier, T. N., and Wycoff, M. A. 1997. "Personnel Performance Evaluations in the Community Policing Context." Washington DC: Community Policing Consortium.

Based on research within the Houston Police Department on performance evaluation relating to community policing, a task force identified new performance criteria on tasks and activities officers performed within their neighborhoods (Wycoff and Oettmeier, 1994). These tasks and activities, discussed in a later report relating to community policing (Oettmeier and Wycoff, 1997), are depicted in Table 6.7.

Because problem solving is such an integral part of community policing, being able to adequately respond to community problems becomes a critical criteria for adequate performance. According to Goldstein (1990), evaluating police response to problems requires the following:

- A clear understanding of the problem

- Agreement on the interest(s) to be served in dealing with the problem, and their order of interest

- Agreement on the method used to determine the extent to which these interests (goals) are reached

- A realistic assessment of what might be expected of the police (e.g., solving the problem versus improving the quality of the management of it)

- Determination of the relative importance of short-term versus long-term impact

- A clear understanding of the legality and fairness of the response (i.e., recognizing that reducing a problem through improper use of authority is not only wrong, but likely to be counterproductive)

Goldstein cautions against defining success as the literal solving of a problem, since many police and community problems, by their very nature, are unmanageable due to their magnitude. Instead, he suggests that officers should be involved in identifying the measurable conditions they would like to see change and should attempt to improve the condition. For instance, Spelman and Eck (1987) have developed five degrees of effectiveness of outcomes that officers might achieve in problem solving:

- Total elimination of the problem

- Reducing the number of incidents it creates

- Reducing the seriousness of the incidents it creates

- Designing methods for a better handling of the incidents

- Removing the problem from police consideration, assuming it can be handled more effectively by another agency

In addition to these "new" performance criteria, Trojanowicz and Bucqeroux (1992) suggest that quantitative measures for ***innovation*** (i.e., an imaginative approach toward problem solving) and ***teamwork*** (i.e., working as a team with other officers and/or other social service agents to solve problems) should be considered when evaluating the performance of a community policing officer.

If these or similar changes are made in the evaluation of performance, a reward system emphasizing these activities must be developed and implemented. As Alpert and Moore (1993) suggest, because most departments provide incentives, such as promotions, merit increases, and officer-of-the-month recognition, they must start to reward their officers for behavior other than aggressive actions that lead to an arrest or heroic actions. Although rewards for these actions are important, other types of behavior deserve recognition, lest they remain lost and hidden behind more visible and aggressive police actions. Activities that should receive more attention include exemplary service to a neighborhood and the defusing of a potentially violent situation (e.g., avoiding a shooting or physical confrontation). As discussed previously, Alpert and Moore propose that **nonaggressive behavior that reduces violence needs to be reinforced, rewarded, and established as the model for other officers to copy**. Officers should be recognized and rewarded for nonaggressive behavior that, when appropriate, does not lead to an arrest. This in turn leads to the recognition that many problems in the community can be solved without the use of force.

Problems and Issues in Evaluation

In rating performance, a number of problems must be addressed. One is the tendency for some raters to be either too strict or too lenient, usually when performance standards are vague and not valid. The more general the standard, the more it is open to a number of interpretations; consequently, the rater's values, priorities, and expectations may become more important than the actual performance.

Other rating problems are central tendency and the halo effect. Problems of *central tendency* are those in which a rater tends to give everyone average ratings that do not distinguish each individual's performance. The *halo effect* occurs when the same rating is given to an employee on all performance standards, based on knowledge of the employee's performance in only one area. Other problems include *disagreements between raters* (i.e., different supervisors give substantially different ratings to the same employee), and *disagreements over time* (i.e., an employee receives substantially different ratings at different points in time). Although some change in performance is to be expected and even desired, significant variations suggest that there may be some problem with the measure.

Such problems can be overcome by using only evaluators who are directly familiar with an employee's performance; the use of several raters will further add to the validity of the evaluation. Evaluations should be based on specific, valid standards of performance and should be used only by raters who have been trained in what the standards mean and who is responsible for applying them (e.g., direct supervisors or peers). Most performance evaluation problems can be resolved if standards are precise, valid, and applied by well-trained raters. The evaluator's motivation to do a good job is probably the most important factor in obtaining valid evaluations. Therefore, police departments must attach proper importance to performance evaluation while giving special consideration to the manner in which evaluators are chosen. Accurate performance evaluations should be an important factor in assignment and promotion decisions.

Several issues in performance evaluation include how often evaluations are performed, how they are used, and who conducts them. In most departments, evaluations tend to be more frequent during the officer's probationary period, perhaps even daily in some FTO programs. However, once an officer is off probation (generally after one year but up to two years in some depart-ments), evaluations occur much less frequently, usually every six months or once a year.

How Evaluations Are Used

Some departments use evaluations to chart changes over time and to help in decisions about reassignment and promotion. Evaluations may also be useful in promoting organizational change. In Houston, for instance, when its police department was attempting to move toward community policing, its managers viewed performance evaluation as a critical support system that could be used to communicate and reinforce expectations about the new philosophy (Wycoff and Oettmeier, 1994). Some departments, how-ever, treat evaluations as little more than a necessary activity (e.g., a civil ser-vice requirement), taking action only when serious problems are docu-mented. In such departments, because of the lack of commitment to the evaluation process, its validity, and therefore its usefulness, are suspect. Some departments do not use individual performance evaluations. Usually, such a department believes that the process is too time-consuming, political, or invalid; or that the department is too disorganized to run the process effec-tively. For example, the Madison (Wisconsin) Police Department, in its change to community policing, decided to abandon individual evaluations because of recognized shortcomings until a more appropriate process could be developed. In the interim, the department emphasized teamwork among officers and managers and the improvement of organizational systems (Wycoff and Oettmeier, 1994).

Who Conducts Evaluations?

In most police departments, the performer's ***immediate supervisor*** is responsible for carrying out evaluations (e.g., sergeants evaluate officers, and lieutenants evaluate sergeants). This arrangement is rarely questioned, and evaluation is perceived as an important part of a supervisor's job. However, performance evaluations should not necessarily be limited to one's immedi-ate supervisor. While the supervisor should have the major say in how an offi-cer has performed, input from investigators, self, peers, and citizens could all be beneficial. ***Investigators***, for instance, can provide another source of input for supervisors; those working in the same neighborhoods frequently conduct follow-up investigations based on an officer's preliminary investiga-tion. Investigators can therefore provide information regarding the officer's writing skills, procedural and legal knowledge, and, if they worked a case together, feedback on their ability to get along and initiative to pursue a case to its logical conclusion (Oettmeier and Wycoff, 1997).

Oettmeier and Wycoff suggest that officers should have the opportunity for ***self-evaluation***; that is, their input should not be limited to just agreeing or disagreeing with the supervisor's observations. They should be able to pro-vide supervisors with examples of successful work projects, and to identify efforts that may not have been known to the supervisor. Further, they should be allowed to discuss any perceived failure, why it occurred and what was learned from the experience. Although few police departments use ***peer eval-uations***, they could be helpful in certain situations—for example, when offi-cers are working as a team or where the supervisor is unable to directly observe officer behavior. Peer evaluations can help in the discovery of communication and coordination problems among team members and in the sharing of mutual expectations. In Houston, however, many officers felt that they should not be allowed to assess each other because officers will "snitch off" other officers; it will cause conflicts among officers; officers are not competent to evaluate others; and it will create role confusion (Oettmeier and Wycoff, 1997: 25).

In some departments, ***officers evaluate their supervisor***. Although officers are familiar with only a part of a supervisor's responsibilities, they can provide feedback on the nature of officer/supervisor relationships, how responsive supervisors are, whether they act as a leader or coach, how they communicate, and so on. The evaluation should be constructive in order that sergeants will be responsive to the feedback. The process could be designed as anonymous in order that officers will not fear retaliation (Oettmeier and Wycoff, 1997). In Houston, officers were required to complete a form assessing their sergeant but had the option of signing their names to the document (Wycoff and Oettmeier, 1994). In Madison, these evaluations took the form of questions about the changes the manager needed to make in order for the officer to perform more effectively. These assessments or critiques are for gathering information rather than for grading and are used by managers for self-diagnosis (Wycoff and Oettmeier, 1994).

An integral aspect of community policing is the importance of ***citizen feedback*** with respect to the perceived needs of the community and their level of satisfaction with the police. Because officers will increase the amount of time they spend working directly with citizens, citizens will form opinions about different aspects of their performance. Community leaders, civic club personnel, business association personnel, and apartment managers can all provide input to a sergeant about an officer's performance. They may have knowledge regarding communication skills, the nature of their relationship, and collaborative problem-solving efforts (Oettmeier and Wycoff, 1997). A number of departments have used ***community meetings*** for obtaining such feedback, others have employed ***door-to-door surveys*** conducted by officers, and a few with adequate resources and knowledge have conducted ***scientific community surveys***. In Madison, for example, surveys are routinely mailed to a sample of all citizens who have received service from the department in an effort to measure satisfaction and to improve service. Officers in Madison's Experimental Police District (EPD) receive evaluations directly from citizens; although the identity of the citizen is not known, the officer receives general information about the type of situation on which the evaluation is based. After reading the evaluation, the officer removes his or her identification from it and gives it to the supervisor. The individual responses are then pooled to examine whether the district as a whole is meeting citizen expectations (Wycoff and Oettmeier, 1994).

From the research presented, it is clear that properly designed and conducted performance evaluations can be an important management tool for the development of community policing for at least two reasons. First, performance evaluations can enhance the attitudes and knowledge of officers to provide a broader role perspective emphasizing quality services, and second, they can be used to help shape behavior and promote organizational change. If a department decides to revise its current performance evaluation system, the following points are worth considering:

1. Officers want feedback and a permanent record of their accomplishments and performance.

2. Officers often feel they are doing more than they are receiving credit for, given the typical narrow design of their evaluation instruments and performance criteria.

3. The goals and structure of the organization should be decided before new performance measurement is developed.

4. There should be different forms for different assignments (unless law prohibits).

5. Any significant alteration of past practices is likely to cause some dissatisfaction among supervisors. It is likely that this shall pass as the new process becomes familiar and has practical value to the supervisor.

6. Performance evaluation should be given priority as a critical supervisory responsibility. Removing meaningless administrative duties from sergeants allows them to spend more time verifying officer performance.

7. Citizen involvement is central to performance evaluation; citizens are a good source of information about an officer's style and adequacy of effort and community satisfaction with results. They should not, however, be put in a position of judging the appropriateness of an officer's decisions.

8. The process should be as simple as reasonably possible. This will increase both acceptance and the probability that the information will actually be utilized. (Oettmeier and Wycoff, 1997: 27)

Career Growth

Once a person is recruited, selected, and trained and completes probation in a police department, his or her career begins, and career growth becomes important. *Career growth* can be for individual development as well as for a specific position within the department; it can involve training within or outside the department; and it attempts to match the needs of the individual with those of the department.

Research has identified three career stages that employees pass through during their working life: establishment, maintenance, and decline. From their twenties to their forties, employees are usually getting established in their careers. The degree to which they will be successful is largely determined during this period. From about 40 to 55, many individuals reassess their lives and careers. In the process, they may change their lifestyles and even their values. Finally, from the mid-fifties through retirement and beyond, individuals prepare to adjust to a different type of life without work or with reduced work. Effective *career planning* takes into consideration all phases of the employee's career (Schultz and Schultz, 1986).

Managers must not only be concerned with upgrading the knowledge and skills of officers in their current positions, but they must plan to incorporate officers' interests with *career paths* that involve position enhancement, new assignments, and promotion. For instance, assume Officer Nancy

❖ ❖ ❖ ❖   Brown has worked in a medium to large police department for 25 years and has the following career path:

- Assigned to patrol for five years

- Transferred to traffic unit for two years, where she worked as an enforcement specialist

- Promoted to sergeant and transferred back to patrol for two years

- Transferred to detective unit for three years, where she worked as a robbery and homicide investigator

- Promoted to lieutenant and transferred to a training unit, which she supervised for three years

- Promoted to captain and supervised the patrol division for three years

- Transferred to the detective unit again and placed in charge for three years

- Promoted to assistant chief and served for four years prior to retirement

An effective career-path program must be able to provide for the improvement of officers' knowledge and skills in each area of assignment. In addition, managers need to be alert to officers' declining interest in their current assignment in order to take action, if possible, before morale and performance are adversely affected. Managers need to develop career-path programs that will financially reward officers for staying in patrol and performing well. In many departments, the only way to obtain a pay increase after five or six years of service (other than cost-of-living adjustments) is to be promoted or transferred to a specialized position. This is not an effective system because good performers, even though they may wish to stay in patrol, think that they need to be promoted or become specialists to receive adequate compensation.

Since the 1970s, the Los Angeles Police Department, for example, has had a *career-path program* that builds in several career-path levels below the rank of lieutenant, each with its own pay scale. This program allows officers to pursue careers below the command level. All police departments should have overlapping pay scales in which patrol officers and investigators, if highly competent, could be paid at levels equal to those of management. Such a system would encourage many excellent officers to stay in patrol and investigations. This is the system in academe, for example, where the most highly regarded professors are often paid more than their managers (e.g., chairs and deans) and possibly even more than the college president. The Mesa, Arizona, Police Department has a different type of program to reward patrol officers and promote career growth. The *career enhancement program* compensates officers for various skills the department deems important. As Inside Management 6.4 indicates, this program is based on a four-level system, where pay is increased at each succeeding level.

It should further be emphasized that highly regarded and influential specialists, such as an FTO officer, must also be compensated at levels appropriate to their position. If, for instance, FTOs are not adequately rewarded for their time and effort, the best available officers will not aspire to become training officers (see Case Study 6.1). This is a common situation in many departments today and suggests that recruits may not be receiving the best possible training. With respect to rewarding managers who perform well, some cities, such as Sunnyvale, California, offer bonuses and salary increases for their managers under a pay-for-performance program. Under this system, a ***management achievement plan*** is established for departmental managers, who, based on their performance set forth in the achievement plan, can earn a salary bonus (Candelaria, 1993).

Inside Management 6.4

Special Skills Are Worth More in Mesa

The Career Enhancement Program is intended to keep skilled personnel on the force by promoting job satisfaction and professional growth. Open to all officers below the rank of sergeant and Master Police Officer, it assigns point values to a variety of categories, including fluency in Spanish, driving accident-free for a period of two years, and being a certified paramedic or a field training officer. Compensation ranges from $40 to $160 a month for the most experienced officers. "The concept of the program is to allow officers to stay at the front-line levels, and as they attain skills and abilities throughout their careers, we're going to compensate them for it," said Commander Dan Saban, who chaired the committee that developed the program.

In this four-level phased program, officers must earn 15 points and have served three years since graduating from the academy to be eligible for the first level. To progress, they must stay at the current level for two years and earn more points. To reach level 4, they must attain 65 points and have served two years at level 3. The highest level can be attained in eight years. In addition to the numerous skills and certifications that are being assigned point values, full-time specializations are also part of the program—for example, the aviation section, bike unit, traffic section, crime scene officer, DARE/GREAT programs, and special investigations division. Any officer who returns to patrol for at least one year from a specialized assignment will receive 10 points.

Officers must also have an overall performance rating of "meets standards" or better on the last two years' performance ratings and be approved by the Professional Enhancement Committee, a team composed of a lieutenant, a sergeant, and an officer appointed by the chief. Should a permanent promotion be made to sergeant, participation in the program ends.

Adapted from: Law Enforcement News. 2001. "Special Skills Are Worth More in Mesa." *Law Enforcement News* February 28: 6. Printed with permission from the *Law Enforcement News*, John Jay College of Criminal Justice.

Advanced Training

Police officers and managers must be kept up to date on changing laws, community needs and expectations, and police methods and technologies, and must be prepared for reassignment or promotion. Large departments often have resources sufficient to allow them to develop and maintain their own advanced training programs. Midsized and smaller departments usually must find outside programs. Many states, as a result of statewide training and standards commissions, have developed extensive career growth programs for the police. Departments can often send their officers to such programs to prepare them for almost any assignment or promotion. Many departments also use private trainers or consultants, as well as university programs to upgrade their personnel, and many allow for flexible schedules or provide incentives for officers to attend college. In general, experienced older officers and managers want to be treated as peers rather than students and usually prefer a more academic approach to a stress-related one. This fact suggests that experienced officers would most likely prefer and benefit from an andragogical approach to training.

In-Service Training

The primary purpose of *in-service training* is the regular updating of all members of the department in a wide variety of subjects. It usually involves subject matter that all department members must know in order to function well. For example, officers must continually be aware of changing laws and ordinances, newly developed techniques, operating policies and procedures, and departmental changes and expectations. The Bureau of Justice Statistics national survey (Reaves and Goldberg, 2000) of over 3,400 local and state agencies found that 87 percent of local police departments required officers to complete in-service training. On average, officers were required to complete 29 hours of such training during the year. Departments moving toward community policing must incorporate the above concepts into their in-service training. The San Diego Police Department, for example, has developed an eight-hour training program in problem solving called problem-oriented policing (POP). The training emphasizes the history and methods of community policing and problem solving, a problem-solving model with case studies and scenarios, barriers and benefits from adopting POP, peer support and guidance to promote POP, and the examination of expectations and concerns about implementing POP (San Diego PD, 1993: 17). As Table 6.8 indicates, in 1999, 63 percent of local police departments provided at least some community policing training to their in-service sworn personnel. And 28 percent trained all in-service officers in community policing; interestingly, at least 40 percent of those departments serving populations over 50,000 and less than a million trained all of their sworn officers.

Table 6.8   **Community-Policing Training for In-Service Sworn Personnel in Local Police Departments, by Size of Population Served, 1997 and 1999.**

Population Served	Percent of Agencies Providing 8 or More Hours of Community Policing Training for			
	At Least Some Officers		All Officers	
	1997	1999	1997	1999
All sizes	62%	63%	27%	28%
1,000,000 or more	81	81	37	31
500,000–999,999	83	83	33	54
250,000–499,999	93	85	43	43
150,000–249,999	88	93	48	45
50,000–149,999	89	91	42	40
25,000–49,999	88	88	35	34
10,000–24,999	75	82	25	27
2,500–9,999	70	69	26	26

Note: Table includes community-policing training of 8 or more hours that occurred during the 2-year period ending June 30, 1999 or the 3-year period ending June 30, 1997.

Source: Hickman, M. J., and Reaves, B. A. 2001. p.4. *Community Policing in Local Police Departments, 1997 and 1999*. Washington, DC: Bureau of Justice Statistics

Specialized Training

Specialized training attempts to prepare officers for specific tasks (e.g., stakeouts or decoy work) or for different jobs throughout the department (e.g., homicide investigator or supervisor). Specialized training is essential if officers are to perform effectively outside the role of patrol officer.

Officers promoted to first-line supervisory positions (i.e., sergeant) should be provided with some form of **supervisory training.** Such training may be in-house or external and usually covers leadership behavior, specific job requirements, and policies and procedures. Once an officer is promoted to a managerial or executive position (e.g., lieutenant or higher), additional **management training** is necessary. The role of the police manager is even more complex than that of first-level supervisor and requires not only increased knowledge of management's role in the department but also long-range planning, policy development, and resource allocation. In California, for example, each of these types of training is required: Police chiefs must complete an 80-hour executive development course within two years of appointment; captains must complete an 80-hour management course within 12 months; lieutenants must complete an 80-hour management course (different in content from the captain's course) within 12 months; and sergeants must complete an 80-hour supervisory course within 12 months.

In addition, in those departments using community policing, some training relating to the concepts, processes, and new role requirements for managers is necessary. In San Diego, for example, a sixteen-hour POP training program for supervisors has been implemented. The course includes the basic course in POP (eight hours), issues and concerns for supervisors regarding the analysis of problems, supervision of problem solving, and performance evaluations. The department also has an executive-level POP orientation course (four hours), which emphasizes the history and methods of community policing and problem solving and discusses the issues and concerns of implementation and operational strategies. Finally, the department has developed training courses in POP for investigators (eight hours) and for trainers (40 hours) (San Diego PD, 1993: 17–18).

One national survey of 144 police departments, including the two largest departments in each state, found that 97 percent provided in-house first-line supervisory training and 78 percent made the training mandatory (Armstrong and Longenecker, 1992). This training was conducted prior to, or at the time of, promotion by 51 percent of the departments; 49 percent were provided the training following the promotion. The subjects most frequently taught included supervisory techniques (95 percent), use of the disciplinary process (92 percent), counseling techniques (80 percent), employee evaluation and review (79 percent), and motivational techniques (73 percent). Other topics included management theory (68 percent), handling employee grievances and complaints (64 percent), EEOC guidelines and affirmative action (62 percent), and department personal-harassment policy (52 percent).

Management training was provided by 81 percent of the departments. Of those, 37 percent offered the training in-house, and the remaining 63 percent sent their managers outside the department (e.g., to state agencies, contract agencies, or the FBI). The most common subject areas included management strategy (77 percent), budgeting (70 percent), management by objectives (63 percent), labor negotiations and contract administration (63 percent), administration of discipline (58 percent), police planning (52 percent), and workforce allocation and patrol strategy (45 percent). Finally, the departments reported that fully 90 percent of the police managers receiving advanced management training considered it to be a worthwhile experience.

One of the most troublesome aspects of supervisory and management training for police is the evaluation procedure, or lack thereof. Although recruit training is often rigorously evaluated, training for experienced officers and managers rarely includes any meaningful evaluation of performance. Thus, it is unlikely that an experienced officer will ever be "washed out" or required to improve, regardless of how inadequate his or her performance might be. This can be a serious problem in supervisory and management training programs because many of the participants may not take the training seriously and thus will not attain the skills and knowledge necessary to be effective. Consequently, departments should require all supervisory and managerial training programs to include a ***meaningful performance evaluation*** because only in this way can they be sure that their future managers are effectively trained for their new roles.

Promotion and Assessment Centers

Promotion in police departments is usually based on one or more of several evaluative criteria, including an officer's (1) time on the job (seniority) or time in rank, (2) past performance, (3) written examination, (4) oral interview, and (5) college hours or degrees. In general, a percentage weight is assigned to each evaluative criterion used and an overall promotional score is given. As openings at the next level of rank occur, individuals are promoted according to their score. Which criteria are used and what weight is assigned varies by department, according to what the department or civil-service commission regards as the most important. Often, police departments use only one or two criteria, even though they may have little, if any, relationship to the supervisory or managerial position for which the candidate is applying. Such a process can easily lead to the selection of the wrong candidate, which may have a long-term negative impact on the department and the officers being supervised.

In one of the few studies in this area, Roberg and Laramy (1980) analyzed the promotional results of a large police department that used a written exam (70 percent), performance evaluation (11.25 percent), seniority (10 percent), and college hours (8.75 percent) as criteria for promotion to sergeant. In general, the results indicated that seniority (above the minimum requirement) should not be used as a criterion, and that those with college hours scored higher on the written exam. The study found that the department needed to carefully assess and validate the content of its promotional program through analysis of the type of behavior required for effective job performance (e.g., supervisory ability), instead of relying on possibly outdated departmental values (e.g., seniority). Because it is difficult to measure supervisory or managerial potential based on these criteria alone, many departments are now using an assessment center, which is perhaps the most promising method for selecting officers for promotion.

An ***assessment center*** is a process that attempts to measure a candidate's potential for a particular managerial position. It uses multiple assessment strategies, typically spread over a two- or three-day period, which include different types of job-related simulations and possibly the use of interviews and psychological tests. Common forms of job simulations include in-basket exercises (e.g., carrying out simulated supervisory or managerial assignments such as writing memos or reports or responding to letters or personnel matters), simulations of interviews with subordinates, oral presentations, group discussions, and fact-finding exercises (Filer, 1977). The candidate's behavior on all relevant criteria is evaluated by trained assessors who reach a consensus on each participant. The primary advantage of this approach is that it evaluates all candidates in a simulated environment under standardized conditions, thus adding significantly to the validity and reliability of the selection process. Case Study 6.2 describes the essential elements and procedures of an assessment center.

Case Study 6.2

Essential Elements of an Assessment Center

The Task Force on Assessment Center Guidelines identifies ten essential elements for a process to be considered an assessment center: job analysis, behavioral classification, assessment techniques, multiple assessments, simulations, assessors, assessor training, recording behavior, reports, and data integration.

A properly conducted job analysis is a cornerstone of the assessment center. Planning an assessment center should be influenced by the results of the job analysis, which will identify the type of tasks to be conducted by job holders, along with the various knowledge, skills, and abilities needed to perform those tasks successfully.

Behavioral classifications will be identified for the position, based on information obtained through the job analysis. These classifications will serve as a basis upon which the assessors will evaluate. Each evaluation should be limited to approximately ten different behavior classifications, as testing for too many classifications may confuse the assessors.

Specific behavioral observations should be recorded systematically. In many cases, the assessors will use handwritten notes, observation scales, behavioral checklists, or preprinted scoring forms. Assessors must also keep record of their observations during an exercise in preparation for the integration discussion. Integration of behaviors is essential, whether based on pooled information from assessors and from techniques used at a meeting of the assessors, or through a statistical integration process validated in accordance with professionally accepted standards. Information may be successfully integrated by consensus or some other method of arriving at a joint decision. It is imperative, however, that the assessors' methodology be supported by research evidence showing reliable and valid aggregations of the observations.

Adapted from: F. M. McLaurin, 1994 (October 31). "Is It Truly An Assessment Center?" *Law Enforcement News*, p. 7. Reprinted with permission from *Law Enforcement News*, John Jay College of Criminal Justice, N.Y.C.

The major disadvantage of assessment centers is that they are relatively costly. However, the increased validity and reliability in selecting the best personnel for managerial positions suggests that they are likely to save the department money in the long run. It certainly makes sense to spend more money up front in the promotion process than to have to deal with problematic managers after it becomes apparent that they are not qualified for the position.

Lateral Entry

Lateral entry refers to the ability of a police officer, at the patrol or supervisory level, to transfer from one department to another, usually without losing seniority. This concept is viewed by many as an important step toward increased professionalism through the improvement of career growth. Lateral entry is not a new concept, having been strongly endorsed by the 1967 President's Commission Task Force on Police:

> To improve police service, competition for all advanced positions should be opened to qualified persons from both within and outside of the department. This would enable a department to obtain the best available talent for positions of leadership. . . .If candidates from within an agency are unable to meet the competition from other applicants, it should be recognized that the influx of more highly qualified personnel would greatly improve the quality of the services. (1967, p. 142)

Implicitly, this recommendation increases the competition for leadership positions; if those already within the department are not as well qualified, they will need to upgrade their skills and educational levels. Of course, this need is one of the primary obstacles to implementing lateral entry; older officers within the department feel that they should be provided the opportunity for advancement, not an "outsider." Although this resistance can be a problem, probably of greater significance are the restrictions of civil service limitations, including retirement systems, which generally are not transferable. Because of these restrictions, and lack of departmental support, lateral entry is still used sparingly today. Some legislative reforms that contribute to its implementation have been made; before lateral entry can become widely adopted, however, individual departments will need to openly, and perhaps aggressively, become its proponent. Undoubtedly, the expanded use of lateral entry would increase the quality of the applicant pool for most police departments, thus improving the selection of police supervisors and managers.

Summary

The purpose of human resource development is to prepare officers for a successful career in all aspects of police work. The development of programs should be based on job analysis of the types of tasks employees perform and should integrate task requirements with employee skills and expectations. The developmental process includes three major phases: recruit training, performance and its evaluation, and the career growth of employees throughout their work life.

In preparing recruits for the job, decisions must be made about program orientation, philosophy, instructional methods, course content, and program evaluation. Those departments transitioning to community policing will need to substantially broaden their training curriculums and place increased emphasis on the andragogical learning model. Following academy training, recruits generally go through an on-the-job field-training program prior to job assignment; many departments use a field-training officer (FTO) program for this purpose. Once trained, officers need to be evaluated on their performance by valid and reliable job measures, including goals and objectives and qualitative as well as quantitative measures of police functions. Community-policing departments are beginning to emphasize a broader perspective of the police role and to use community input in the evaluation process. The career growth of officers is important because they must be prepared for changes not only in their current jobs but also for changes in job assignments and promotions. The department should establish career paths that allow for employees at all levels to remain motivated throughout their careers. Finally, because promotions have long-term implications for the organization, departments should carefully analyze the process and criteria used. Assessment centers may offer the greatest potential in this area.

Discussion Questions

1. Identify the three phases associated with the human resource development process. In general, what happens in each phase?

2. Discuss several important implications of the program philosophy and instructural methods used in recruit and community-policing training.

3. Discuss what you believe to be the most important topics in recruit training curriculums. What impact does community policing have on recruit training curriculums?

4. Discuss what you believe to be the most important criteria in the selection of FTOs. How would you ensure that those selected meet these criteria?

5. Discuss the major trends that have developed with respect to performance evaluation. How might existing measures of performance be improved?

6. Describe at least three problems that may arise with respect to performance evaluation.

7. Identify the three career stages that employees pass through during their working life. Why is it important to recognize that such stages exist?

8. Discuss the concept of career growth. Why is it important for departments to be concerned with the development of career paths?

9. Describe several types of advanced-training programs and why departments must make such training available.

10. Discuss why assessment centers are perhaps the most promising method for selecting officers for promotion.

References

Alpert, G. P., and Moore, M. H. 1993. "Measuring Police Performance in the New Paradigm of Policing." In *Performance Measures for the Criminal Justice System*, pp. 109–140. Washington, DC: Bureau of Justice Statistics.

Alpert, G., and Smith, W. 1990. "Defensibility of Law Enforcement Training." *Criminal Law Bulletin* 26: 452–458.

Armstrong, L. D., and Longenecker, C. O. 1992. "Police Management Training: A National Survey." *FBI Law Enforcement Bulletin* 61: 22–26.

Ash, P., Slora, K., and Britton, C. F. 1990. "Police Agency Selection Practices." *Journal of Police Science and Administration* 17: 258–269.

Bayley, D., and Bittner, E. 1989. "Learning the Skills of Policing." In R. Dunham and G. Alpert (eds.), *Critical Issues in Policing: Contemporary Readings*, pp. 87–110. Prospect Heights, IL: Waveland Press.

Berg, B. L. 1990. "First Day at the Police Academy: Stress-Reaction-Training as a Screening-out Technique." *Journal of Contemporary Criminal Justice* 6: 89–105.

Bigge, M. L. 1971. *Learning Theories for Teachers.* New York: Harper and Row.

Birzer, M. L. 1999. "Police Training in the 21st Century." *FBI Law Enforcement Bulletin* July: 16–19.

Birzer, M. L., and Tannehill, R. 2001. "A More Effective Training Approach for Contemporary Policing." *Police Quarterly* 4: 233–252.

Candelaria, G. 1993. "Pay for Performance." *FBI Law Enforcement Bulletin* 62: 19–23.

Clark, J. R. 1992. "Why Officer Johnny Can't Read." *Law Enforcement News,* May 15: 1, 16–17.

———. 1994. "Sweep of Disabilities Act Widens as Court Mandates More Police Training." *Law Enforcement News,* November 30: 1, 6.

Commission on Peace Officer Standards and Training. 1995 (May 12). *Bulletin 95–9: Regular Basic Course Required Minimum Hours Increases from 560 to 664.* Sacramento, CA: POST.

Dunnette, M. D., and Motowidlo, S. J. 1982. *Police Selection and Career Development,* pp. 241–273. National Institute of Law Enforcement and Criminal Justice. Washington, DC: International City Management Association.

Earle, H. H. 1973. *Police Recruit Training: Stress vs. Non-Stress.* Springfield, IL: C. C. Thomas.

Feldman, P., and Lopez, R. J. 1995. "Fuhrman Case: How the City Kept Troubled Cop." *Los Angeles Times,* October 2: 1A, 18A.

Filer, R. J. 1977. "Assessment Centers in Police Selection." In C. D. Spielberger and H. C. Spaulding (eds.), *Proceedings of the National Working Conference on the Selection of Law Enforcement Officers.* Tampa: University of South Florida.

Goldstein, H. 1990. *Problem-oriented Policing.* Philadelphia: Temple University Press.

Guardian Association of the New York City Police Department v. Civil Service Commission of New York. 1980. 23 FEP 909.

Hickman, M. J., and Reaves, B. A. 2001. *Community Policing in Local Police Departments,* 1997 and 1999. Washington, DC: Bureau of Justice Statistics.

Hormann, J. S. 1995. "Virtual Reality: The Future of Law Enforcement Training." *Police Chief* July: 7–12.

Hurst, Y. G., and Frank, J. 2000. "How Kids View Cops: The Nature of Juvenile Attitudes Toward the Police." *Journal of Criminal Justice* 28: 189–202.

International Association of Chiefs of Police. 1998. "Ethics Training in Law Enforcement." *Police Chief* January: 14–24.

International Association of Directors of Law Enforcement Standards and Training. 1997. *IADLEST: 1997 Executive Summary of the Sourcebook.* Richmond, VA: CJ Data/Flink & Associates.

Knowles, M. S. 1970. *The Modern Practice of Adult Education: Andragogy Versus Pedagogy.* New York: Association Press.

Langworthy, R., Hughes, T., and Sanders, B. 1995. *Law Enforcement Recruitment, Selection and Training: A Survey of Major Police Departments in the U.S.* Academy of Criminal Justice Sciences—Police Section: Highland Hts., KY.

Law Enforcement News. 2001. "Special Skills Are Worth More in Mesa." *Law Enforcement News* February 28: 6.

Law Enforcement News. 2000. "Pursuit Simulation Training Is No Ordinary Crash Course." *Law Enforcement News* November 15: 6.

Law Enforcement News. 1989. "Police Corps Rides Again." *Law Enforcement News,* September: 1, 13, 14.

Marion, N. 1998. "Police Academy Training: Are We Teaching Recruits What They Need to Know?" *Policing: An International Journal of Police Strategies & Management* 21: 54–79.

McCampbell, M. S. 1986. *Field Training for Police Officers: State of the Art.* Washington, DC: National Institute of Justice.

McLaurin, F. M. 1994. "Is It Truly an Assessment Center?" *Law Enforcement News,* October 31: 7.

Mendoza, M. 2000. "A New Program Calls on Teens to Help Write a Section of the Pleasanton Department's Manual in an Effort to Improve Relations." *The Valley Times* February 6: pp. A3, A34.

Oettmeier, T. N., and Wycoff, M. A. 1997. *Personnel Performance Evaluations in the Community Policing Context.* Washington, DC: Community Policing Consortium.

Palmiotto, M. J., Birzer, M. L., and Unnithan, N. P. 2000. "Training in Community Policing: A Suggested Curriculum." *Policing: An International Journal of Police Strategies and Management* 23: 8–21.

President's Commission on Law Enforcement and Administration of Justice. 1967. *Task Force Report: The Police.* Washington, DC: U.S. Government Printing Office.

Reaves, B. A., and Goldberg, A. L. 1999. *Law Enforcement Management and Administrative Statistics, 1997: Data for Individual and Local Agencies with 100 or More Officers.* Washington, DC: Bureau of Justice Statistics.

——. 2000. *Local Police Departments 1997.* Washington, DC: Bureau of Justice Statistics.

Roberg, R. R., ed. 1976. *The Changing Police Role: New Dimensions and New Perspectives.* San Jose, CA: Justice Systems Development.

—— 1979a. *Police Management and Organizational Behavior: A Contingency Approach.* St. Paul, MN: West.

——. 1979b. "Police Training and Andragogy: A New Perspective." *Police Chief* 46: 32–34.

Roberg, R. R., and Laramy, J. E. 1980. "An Empirical Assessment of the Criteria Utilized for Promoting Police Personnel: A Secondary Analysis." *Journal of Police Science and Administration* 8: 183–187.

Roche, W. M., Adams, R. E., and Arcury, T. A. 2001. "Community Policing and Planning." *Journal of the American Planning Association.* Winter: 78–90.

San Diego Police Department. 1993. *Neighborhood Policing.* San Diego, CA: Author.

Schultz, D. P., and Schultz, S. E. 1986. *Psychology and Industry Today,* 4th ed. New York: Macmillan.

Simonetti Rosen, M. 1997. "A LEN Interview with Prof. Edwin J. Delattre of Boston University." *Law Enforcement News* May 15: 11–12.

Spelman, W., and Eck, J. E. 1987. "Newport News Tests Problem-oriented Policing." *NIJ Reports* January–February: 2–8.

Trojanowicz, R., and Bucqueroux, B. 1992. *Toward Development of Meaningful and Effective Performance Evaluations.* East Lansing, MI: Michigan State University, National Center for Community Policing.

U.S. Civil Rights Commission. 1981. *Who's Guarding the Guardians?* Washington, DC: Government Printing Office.

Van Maanen, J. 1973. "Observations on the Making of Policemen." *Human Organization* 32: 407–418.

Vaughn, M. S. 1996. "Police Civil Liability and the First Amendment: Retaliation Against Citizens Who Criticize and Challenge the Police." *Crime & Delinquency* 42: 50–67.

Vaughn, M. S., and Kappeler, V. E. 1999. "Law Enforcement: Pissing Off the Police—Civil Liability Under the First Amendment and the Fighting Words Doctrine." *Criminal Law Bulletin* 35: 594–624.

Williams, B. N. 1999. "Perceptions of Children and Teenagers on Community Policing: Implications for Law Enforcement Leadership, Training, and Citizen Evaluations." *Police Quarterly* 2: 151–173.

Wycoff, M. A. 1982. *The Role of Municipal Police: Research as Prelude to Changing It.* Washington, DC: Police Foundation.

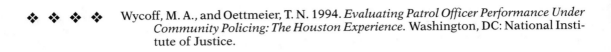

Wycoff, M. A., and Oettmeier, T. N. 1994. *Evaluating Patrol Officer Performance Under Community Policing: The Houston Experience.* Washington, DC: National Institute of Justice.

Motivation and Job Design

Chapter 4 described the fundamental characteristics of police organizations, the factors that influence their design, and the relevance of group behavior in determining the success of an organization. This chapter turns attention to the individuals working in police departments. If policies and practices that lead to the attainment of both organizational and individual goals and objectives are to be implemented, managers must have a basic understanding of how people are motivated and how job design affects their motivation and behavior.

Motivation

One useful definition of motivation suggests that it has to do with (1) the direction of behavior, (2) the strength of the effort put forth once an individual chooses to follow a course of action, and (3) the persistence of the

185

behavior, or how long the person continues to behave in a particular manner (Campbell, Dunnette, Lawler, and Weick, 1970: 340). ***Motivation,*** then, is the force within an individual that initiates, directs, and sustains a particular behavior. Because motivation is an internal force, we cannot measure the motivation of others directly. Instead, we generally infer their motivation by observing their behavior. For instance, we might conclude that the rookie officer who works late and volunteers for extra assignments is highly motivated to do well. Of course, managers prefer motivated employees because they are more likely to be productive.

Motivation, therefore, is an important factor in individual performance. Performance, however, is also influenced by the ability of the individual. A key principle of motivation states that a person's performance is a function (f) of ability and motivation, as expressed by the following formula:

$$\text{Performance} = f (\text{ability} \times \text{motivation})$$

According to this principle, tasks cannot be performed successfully unless the person has the necessary ability. ***Ability*** can be defined as an individual's talent for accomplishing work-related tasks. Keeping in mind individual differences, it is important to understand that although motivation leads to the degree of effort exerted, it has no relationship to ability. If a person has low ability levels, he or she may be highly motivated and put forth a great deal of effort but still not perform well. Conversely, if ability levels are high, even relatively low levels of motivation and effort may produce satisfactory performance. Without a high degree of motivation and effort, however, even employees with considerable ability will perform at a level below their capability.

Because employees will not perform to their ability levels unless they are sufficiently motivated, managers must have at least a rudimentary understanding of what motivates people to perform or behave in certain ways on the job. The more a manager understands about individual behavior, the easier it will be to predict how employees will react to certain organizational stimuli and consequently which stimuli can be used most effectively to motivate them. Thus, good management entails knowing how to motivate individuals to perform well. To that end, a basic knowledge of the theories of motivation is necessary.

Theories of Motivation

Motivational theories can be grouped into two general categories: content and process. ***Content theories*** attempt to identify ***what*** in the work environment motivates behavior (such as money, social interaction, or growth needs). ***Process theories*** describe ***how*** motivation is translated, or energized, into behavior. Although content and process theories are not mutually exclusive, most research has focused on one approach or the other.

Content Theories

Traditionally, management study of motivation has focused on separate human drives that motivate people to work. For instance, Taylor and other classical theorists viewed economic rewards as the primary motivating factors; human relations theorists emphasized the importance of social factors and informal relationships. These approaches, however, tended to be simplistic and did not provide managers with an adequate understanding of the complex nature of the motivational process in work environments. Three major contributions that have led to a better understanding of the content of work motivation are discussed below.

Need Hierarchy Theory

In 1943, Maslow postulated a hierarchy of human needs that incorporated five distinct levels; Figure 7.1 depicts this hierarchy along with several examples of related work needs. Basic to this theory is the concept that the satisfaction of lower-level physiological needs activates higher-level social and psychological needs (Maslow, 1943). This does not mean that the two levels of need could not operate concurrently but that lower-level needs must be fulfilled first. Once a given level of need is satisfied, it is no longer a motivating factor, and the next level of need must be activated in order to motivate the individual. Maslow identified the needs as follows, from the lowest to the highest:

Physiological needs, such as hunger, thirst, sleep, and sex

Safety needs for security from danger and deprivation

Social needs for friendship, affection, affiliation, and love; the need to belong

Esteem needs for self-respect and the respect of others; ego or status needs

Self-actualization needs for developing one's capabilities; the need for self-fulfillment or the realization of one's full potential

Although Maslow's need hierarchy is not specifically directed at work motivation, it has become popular with managers over the years, probably

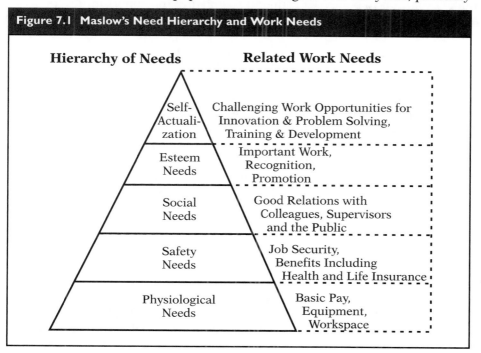

Figure 7.1 Maslow's Need Hierarchy and Work Needs

Hierarchy of Needs   **Related Work Needs**

Self-Actualization	Challenging Work Opportunities for Innovation & Problem Solving, Training & Development
Esteem Needs	Important Work, Recognition, Promotion
Social Needs	Good Relations with Colleagues, Supervisors and the Public
Safety Needs	Job Security, Benefits Including Health and Life Insurance
Physiological Needs	Basic Pay, Equipment, Workspace

because of its simplicity and appeal to common sense: Managers only need to learn five needs and their sequence. Although Maslow's hierarchy has stimulated thinking about a person's differing needs, it has some shortcomings. Research suggests that needs cannot be neatly separated into five distinct levels; instead, they tend to cluster into two primary categories, namely, **higher level** (e.g., esteem and self-actualization) and **lower level** (e.g. physiological and safety). The hierarchy of needs may also not be the same for everyone; people can have overlapping needs and work on satisfying several at the same time, even though some needs may be more important than others at a certain period in time (Mitchell and Moudgill, 1976; Wahba and Bridwell, 1976). This finding further suggests that needs may change during an individual's psychological development. For instance, lower-level needs appear to be more important early in life, and higher-level needs tend to become more important as the individual matures. Although some generalizations can be made about higher-level needs increasing with maturity, significant individual differences in motivation exist in the work environment, and managers must be aware of them.

Early research on the police suggests that lower-level needs tend to be reasonably well fulfilled by officers' jobs, but higher-level needs are not. For example, Lefkowitz (1973, 1974) found that the police appear to attach a great deal of importance to the potential gratification of personal needs through their jobs. He discovered that upper-level needs (self-actualization, esteem, and autonomy) tend not to be satisfied through the job, but lower-level needs (security and social) are relatively well satisfied. Another study by Cacioppe and Mock (1985), directly testing the self-actualization needs of Australian police officers, supports Lefkowitz's findings. This study noted that self-actualization needs were not often met in traditional police work. Cacioppe and Mock suggested the development of "personal and organizational programs in police departments to enhance the opportunities for self-actualization" (p. 181). These findings are not surprising when the traditional paramilitary design of police departments is taken into account. With such a design and job structure, there simply was no attempt to build into the job the potential growth needs of individual employees. In another study, with contradictory results, Van Maanen (1975) found that police obtain the greatest satisfaction of their self-actualization and social needs and the least satisfaction of their esteem, autonomy, and safety needs. Although Van Maanen's findings clearly contradict Maslow's hierarchy, especially with respect to safety needs (as pointed out above), the needs hierarchy is not necessarily the same for everyone and can change over time. And because low pay was often a significant problem for police during the 1970s, low fulfillment of safety needs for officers of this time period is not necessarily surprising.

Two-Factor Theory

In the late 1950s, Frederick Herzberg and his colleagues (1959) conducted extensive interviews with 200 accountants and engineers and discovered that job satisfaction and job dissatisfaction come from two separate sets of factors, which he termed **satisfiers,** or motivating factors, and **dissatisfiers,** or "hygiene factors." Satisfiers related to the nature of the work, or **job content,** and to the rewards that result directly from performing job-related tasks. The major satisfiers included achievement, recognition, the work itself, responsibility, advancement, and growth. Dissatisfiers arose from the individual's relationship to the organizational environment, or to the ***job context*** in which the work was being performed. The major dissatisfiers included company policy and administration, supervision, salary, status, and working conditions. These factors were called dissatisfiers because they did not lead to job satisfaction; that is, they did not motivate employees to put forth extra effort on the job. Figure 7.2 graphically displays Herzberg's two-factor, or motivation-hygiene, theory. Several of these hygiene factors, including administrative policies and procedures, supervision, and working conditions have been shown to contribute significantly to stress in police officers (Crank and Caldero, 1991; Kroes, Margolis, and Hurrell, 1974).

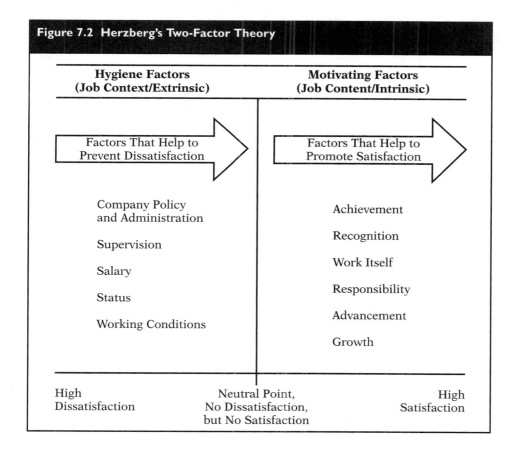

Figure 7.2 Herzberg's Two-Factor Theory

Hygiene Factors (Job Context/Extrinsic)	Motivating Factors (Job Content/Intrinsic)
Factors That Help to Prevent Dissatisfaction	Factors That Help to Promote Satisfaction
Company Policy and Administration	Achievement
Supervision	Recognition
Salary	Work Itself
Status	Responsibility
Working Conditions	Advancement
	Growth

High Dissatisfaction — Neutral Point, No Dissatisfaction, but No Satisfaction — High Satisfaction

It is also interesting to note that present-day thought suggests that one of the better ways to improve satisfaction, thus increasing employee motivation, is for managers to praise or recognize employees for good work. Of course, recognition is one of Herzberg's intrinsic motivating factors, and as described in Inside Management 7.1, it is easy to use and costs little. Undoubtedly, praise or recognition could be used more successfully in policing, especially with respect to community policing, in which creativity and efforts to try new approaches, although not always successful, should be recognized.

Inside Management 7.1

Best Motivational Tool Costs Nothing: Managers, Don't Be Stingy with Praise

In an age of workplace anxiety, thanking an employee for a job well done can mean more than cash, and yet most managers are stingy with their praise.

"Thanking employees is not a common practice in most work environments," said author and management specialist Bob Nelson, who is vice president at Blanchard Training & Development in San Diego. "It doesn't take a lot of money. It takes a little time, a little thoughtfulness, and a little creativity to turn any employee into a highly motivated individual. Today, the best managers are like coaches, counselors, colleagues, and cheerleaders all rolled into one."

Indeed, in one study conducted in a variety of work settings of 1,500 employees, Gerald Graham concluded that the most powerful employee motivator is personal thanks from a manager for a job well done.

Nelson listed some compelling reasons for praise:

It provides "an effective low-cost way of encouraging higher levels of performance."

It reinforces employees' sense of security about their position.

It supports employees as they are being asked "to do more and to do it more autonomously."

The new, smaller pool of employees coming into the work force "expects work to be both purposeful and reinforcing."

Praise makes employees feel good about themselves and their jobs, and this spirit translates into better customer service.

In his book, *1,001 Ways to Reward Employees,* Nelson reels off numerous examples of companies that recognize employees without spending a dime. "A sincere word of thanks from the right person at the right time can mean more to an employee than a raise, a formal award, or a whole wall of certificates or plaques." Some successful examples of what Nelson terms "no-cost recognition" are as follows:

The city of Philadelphia put the name of an outstanding worker in lights, using an electronic message board on a downtown skyscraper.

Whenever Federal Express buys a new airplane, it inscribes the name of an employee's child in large letters on the nose. The employee's family is flown to the plant for the launch.

At Xerox Corporation, a bell is rung to recognize good performance. At Pacific Gas & Electric, a ship's bell is rung to herald good work.

"When people do things right," Nelson concluded, "acknowledge it!"

Adapted from: S. Ross, 1995. "Best Motivational Tool Costs Nothing." *San Jose Mercury News,* February 17: pp. 1G, 2G.

Herzberg's two-factor theory of motivation can be related to Maslow's need hierarchy in that *hygiene factors* correspond to *lower-level needs,* whereas *motivators* correspond to *higher-level needs.* According to Herzberg, such lower-level needs as working conditions and salary are not effective motivators; as such, their fulfillment should not be expected to improve job performance. By contrast, the two-factor theory suggests that, assuming that the organizational environmental conditions are acceptable (e.g., working conditions and salary), higher-level needs, such as recognition, responsibility, and growth should be emphasized in order to improve motivation and work performance. Finally, it is important to recognize that Herzberg's two-factor theory applies and extends Maslow's need hierarchy specifically to work motivation. As will be discussed later in this chapter, the work of Herzberg and his colleagues has had a significant impact on job-enrichment programs.

Research on the police showing that job satisfaction can be separated into "extrinsic" (job content) and "intrinsic" (job context) factors received support in an early study of work satisfaction and municipal police officers (Slovak, 1978). More recent research further lends support to the two-factor theory of motivation in policing. For example, a study of the Madison (Wisconsin) Police Department's experimental police district (EPD) found that officers in the EPD were somewhat more satisfied with their work than were non-EPD officers (Wycoff and Skogan, 1993). The former had more responsibility and latitude in their jobs to make decisions about their work (including scheduling) and how they would go about doing it (including problem solving). It should be noted that these results could have been influenced by the fact that the EPD officers were volunteers who may have initially been more highly motivated.

A study in an urban county sheriff's office where all officers throughout the agency practiced community-policing activities found similar results (Halsted, Bromley, and Cochran, 2000). In general, the results suggested that those officers with a service orientation also demonstrated a significant positive relationship to job satisfaction (e.g., personal growth and development), while no relationship was found between a crime control orientation and job satisfaction. In another study, Hoath, Schneider, and Starr (1998) examined the relationship between career orientation and job satisfaction among 239 members of a municipal police department. The authors found job satisfaction is highest among officers identified as "careerists," or those motivated by extrinsic rewards and who place a high value on prestige, recognition, advancement, and financial security. Officers identified as careerists may be most suitable for traditional policing roles; the implications for community policing will be discussed in the final section of this chapter.

Achievement Motivation Theory

David McClelland has been studying the need for achievement and its motivational implications for more than three decades. The **need for achievement** (indicated as "n Ach") is the desire to accomplish challenging tasks and to achieve a high standard of performance in one's work. According to McClelland (1985), individuals with a **high n Ach** prefer situations in which they can (1) take responsibility for problem solving, (2) set challenging yet achievable goals and take calculated risks, and (3) receive identifiable and recurring feedback on how they are performing. Interestingly, and often contrary to popular belief, people with high "n Ach" typically avoid extremely difficult goals because of the increased risk of failure. It would appear that because such people like to solve problems, which often require innovative solutions, they can be a valuable source of creativity in organizations. The implications for the problem-oriented aspects of community policing are obvious; therefore, police managers should attempt to select for, and instill, at least a moderately high level of "n Ach" among their employees, as suggested below.

In order to motivate high achievers, managers must make sure that such individuals have challenging yet reachable goals and must provide relatively quick feedback regarding achievement. Based primarily on his own theory and research on need achievement, McClelland has made several suggestions about how managers may develop a positive high "n Ach" among employees—that is, a high "n Ach" where there is no fear of failure (Gibson, Ivancevich, and Donnelly, 1991: 16). Thus, managers would attempt to do the following:

1. Arrange tasks so that employees receive periodic feedback on their performance, providing information that enables them to make modifications or corrections.

2. Point out to employees role models of achievement, identify and publicize the accomplishments of achievement "heroes" (the winners).

3. Work with employees to improve their self-image by giving them moderate challenges and responsibilities.

4. Encourage employees to think realistically, that is, about setting realistic goals and the ways that they can accomplish them.

There is some police research that tends to support n Ach theory, at least in part. For instance, Gaines, Tubergen, and Paiva (1984) discovered that promotion was an important factor in meeting the need to achieve for some officers. In general, they found that older, more experienced, and more highly educated officers were more likely to view promotion as helping them realize their potential and develop more satisfying interests. These authors point out that managers should realize that these officers desire departmental rewards and that if only limited number of positions are open for promotion, then other departmental rewards (e.g., commendations, praise, and special assignments) can be used to help satisfy their needs. Bowker (1980) has indicated that because highly educated officers are more likely to be high achievers, managers should try to keep them satisfied by rewarding achievement, not only in order to maintain high levels of motivation but also to avoid turnover. He noted several avenues that the department could use to maintain their satisfaction, including promotion, job enrichment, job transfers, leaves of absence, and in-service training.

Content theories have made an important contribution to the practice of management by allowing managers to reevaluate the classical prescription that only lower-level needs (hygiene factors) are important to motivate people. Clearly, employees are motivated by more than these needs.

Process Theories

In contrast to content theories, concerned with attempting to identify specifically what motivates behavior, process theories attempt to explain how behavior is motivated—that is, how it is energized, how it is directed and sustained, and how it is stopped. These theories are concerned with the cognitive (thought) processes that people use in deciding how to behave in a certain way. They attempt to define the major variables that lead to motivation and explain how these variables interact to produce certain behavior patterns. The most influential process theories include expectancy theory, equity theory, and goal-setting theory.

Expectancy Theory

The most widely acknowledged expectancy theory of work motivation, developed by Victor Vroom (1964), views individual motivation as rational choices that people make about the rewards they expect to receive before they perform their jobs. The theory rests on two basic assumptions:

1. Individuals have cognitive expectations about what outcomes are likely to result from their behavior.

2. Individuals have preferences among these outcomes.

According to Vroom, the process can be represented as follows:

$$\text{Motivation} = \text{Valence} \times \text{Expectancy}$$

In other words, motivation is equal to the summation of valence times expectancy. The model has several important variables that must be defined and understood before it can be useful to managers. Each is described below.

Expectancy refers to the individual's belief that a particular behavior will be followed by a particular outcome (e.g., "If I work hard, I will receive a pay increase or a promotion"). The degree of belief ranges from a certainty that the outcome will follow to a certainty that it will not. The individual's perception of what is likely to occur is important, not the objective reality of the situation.

Valence involves the strength of an individual's preference for a particular outcome (e.g., a person may value a transfer in job assignments over a small merit increase). Depending on their level of desire for the outcome, individuals have a positive, neutral, or negative preference. The more positive the valence, the greater the amount of effort put forth to obtain the outcome. Again, the perceived value of an outcome, not its objective value, is important.

Instrumentality involves the relationship as perceived by the individual between a first-level outcome and a second-level outcome, each with its own valence attached. **First-level,** or **performance outcomes** resulting from behavior are associated with doing the work itself and include such factors as productivity, turnover, and absenteeism. **Second-level,** or **result outcomes** are those consequences that first-level outcomes are likely to produce, including pay increases, promotion, praise, transfer, and group acceptance. Thus, individual preferences for first-level outcomes are dictated by the extent to which people believe that attainment of second-level outcomes will occur. It follows that if one perceives that one's effort is not instrumental in producing a desired outcome, then there will be little motivation to perform well. Figure 7.3 presents an example of the general model of expectancy theory.

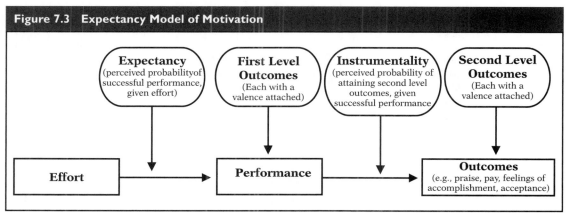

Figure 7.3 Expectancy Model of Motivation

According to the expectancy model, first-level outcomes result from an individual's perceived probability of performing successfully on the job, given the effort exerted. Performance usually involves factors relating to productivity, including both quantity and quality. For example, in police work, quantity factors might include number of arrests made, calls handled, or investigations completed; quality factors might include problem-solving efforts and community interactions, number of convictions obtained or number of cases solved, and so on. Second-level outcomes are those consequences that first-level outcomes are likely to produce, given successful performance, including pay, praise, acceptance, and so on. It is important for managers to understand that the higher the value attached to a second-level outcome, the greater the amount of effort will be exerted to accomplish a first-level outcome (i.e., to perform well). Consequently, not only are individual preferences important to understand, but the types of second-level outcomes (or rewards placed on performance factors by the organization) will go a long way in determining police performance in the community.

Based on the above discussion, expectancy theory has at least three clear implications for police managers. The ***first implication*** is to ***clarify expectancies that employee effort will lead to task accomplishment.*** If employees are to be motivated to perform well, they must understand what is expected of them and that it is possible for them to attain a desired level of performance. Thus, if a department expects its officers to be innovative and to use problem-solving techniques in their work, they must communicate this expectation throughout the department, as well as develop specific methods (e.g., training programs and reward structures) that will help lead to the accomplishment of such activities.

The ***second implication*** is to ***link valued second-level outcomes to performance goals of the organization.*** Showing through example that there is a link between performance goals and desired second-level outcomes increases the employees' belief that hard work and good performance result in outcomes they prefer. For example, establishing a relationship between accomplishing department goals and second-level outcomes, such as promotions, merit pay increases, or specialized assignments (e.g., field-training officer, school-resource officer, etc.), should lead to increased levels of motivation.

The ***third implication*** is to ***determine which second-level outcomes are important to individual employees.*** If employees are to remain motivated, they must be able to attain rewards that are positively valiant, or desirable, to them personally. Some police officers, for example, may be more highly motivated by job satisfaction, others by peer-group influences or by departmental recognition through improved pay, promotion, or specialized assignments. By taking individual differences into account, police managers can attempt to make highly valued rewards available to their officers and thus strengthen motivation.

Expectancy theory has been applied to numerous studies on policing. In the earliest study, Van Maanen (1975) measured whether perceptions of "working especially hard" on a particular activity would lead to favorable rewards within the organization. The study measured the motivational levels of recruits during their first thirty months of employment and found that at the end of this period, their motivational levels had decreased significantly.

Their levels of motivation were found to be almost as low as those of a control group of veteran officers, suggesting that the recruits believed that "working especially hard" was linked to few, if any, of the organization's rewards.

Similar findings by Guyot (1991) indicated that the department under study did not provide incentives to work hard, and therefore only a very low percentage of officers had any extrinsic reasons to do so. On the one hand, extrinsic reasons included such factors as seeking promotion (controlled by civil service tests), being chewed out (supervisors rarely expect more than a minimal job), making money (salaries are fixed by rank, with increments for longevity), and keeping their job (civil service protection makes firing difficult). On the other hand, several internal factors provided motivation for many officers to work hard; for instance, 33 percent felt that the public needed the services of the police, and 57 percent worked hard for the satisfaction of a job well done.

These studies suggest that although police managers need to pay attention to all three of the implications of expectancy theory, they should give special attention to implication number two—***establishing a link between organizational goals and second-level outcomes.*** The officers in the studies were not being rewarded for the types of activities that lead to organizational goal accomplishment, and consequently, their motivational levels to perform well significantly declined. Similar results were found in a study of nineteen Pennsylvania police departments that attempted to measure the effects of expectancy theory on making driving under the influence (DUI) arrests (Mastrofski, Ritti, and Snipes, 1994). The authors found that an officer's capability and opportunity for DUI arrests were the most significant predictors, and that instrumentality factors (e.g., manager's priorities, advancement, and recognition of good work) were not important indicators of officer productivity. This finding suggests the possibility that departments did not link organizational rewards to DUI arrest productivity.

In a recent study of expectancy theory of patrol officers and problem solving in two departments, DeJong, Mastrofski, and Parks (2001) compared community policing officers(CPOs) with general patrol ("beat") officers in each department and concluded that CPO officers were primarily affected by instrumentality variables (e.g., perception of departmental rewards for problem solving and managerial priorities). In general, it was found that the desire for promotion significantly increases problem-solving time for CPOs but has no effect on beat officers, and that CPOs are influenced by their perception of the district managers' priority placed on problem solving. Differences in implementing community policing between the two departments had an effect on the amount of time spent on problem solving. CPO specialists in St. Petersburg worked in a team with beat officers and were freed from responding to calls-for-service, were relatively autonomous and defined neighborhood problems themselves, and were found to be more active problem solvers than their counterparts in Indianapolis. In contrast, CPOs in Indianapolis who worked in specialist units were not freed from calls-for-service and had problems defined for them by upper management were no more likely than beat officers to engage in problem solving. However, CPOs in Indianapolis also spent more time in problem solving if they thought it was a management priority.

While instrumentality variables were the most influential in predicting an officer's motivation to perform problem-solving activities, interestingly,

❖ ❖ ❖ ❖   opportunity and ability variables had only a modest impact, while an officer's personal view of what police work should be, and the view of his or her peers, had practically no significance. The importance of these findings may be substantial to a department's quest to increase problem solving and movement toward community policing; first, by establishing that managers should utilize expectancy theory for purposes of motivation, and second, in order to increase problem solving, managers need to assign more officers to specialist CPO jobs. The authors note that despite reformers' efforts to change police work environments by solving problems proactively, the police remain the principal means of responding to randomly distributed social problems. Only through specialized assignments can they be freed, or free others (e.g., detectives) from responding to fluctuating calls-for-service.

The implications of these findings for job design, community policing, and problem solving may be far reaching, especially with respect to the need for CPO specialists. For instance, even if departments link rewards to problem-solving activities, if there is not enough free time to engage in such activities, there is little likelihood that problem solving can take place. On the other hand, even if departments have specialist CPOs who are provided substantial amounts of free time for problem-solving activities, upper management must still make it clear that problem solving will be linked to organizational rewards, and supervisors must reinforce this message.

Equity Theory

The essence of equity theory as developed by Adams (1963) is that employees compare their efforts and rewards with those of others in similar work situations. This theory is based on the premise that individuals who work for an organization in exchange for rewards wish to be treated equitably by the organization. Accordingly, individuals compare their own *job inputs* (e.g., skills, experience, training, race, or gender) and *job outcomes* (e.g., pay, benefits, recognition, or promotion) with others in similar work situations. *Equity* exists when the employee perceives that the ratio of his or her inputs (efforts) to outcomes (rewards) is equivalent to the ratio of others. *Inequity* exists whenever an individual's inputs-outcomes ratio is either less than or greater than the inputs-outcomes ratio of the other person.

In essence, equity is a relative term (i.e., compared to another) rather than an absolute (i.e., compared to a set standard). Although the theory predicts that an individual will feel inequitably treated when he or she perceives that his or her inputs-outcomes ratio is greater than that of the other person (e.g., receiving a higher pay raise than a colleague, even though it is perceived that one's inputs have been the same), research suggests that the individual adjusts to such conditions of over-reward relatively quickly. In other words, employees adjust to the over-reward (e.g., higher pay), considering that it is merited; although they may work harder for a while, they rather quickly drop back to a normal level of performance.

Equity theory has two major premises regarding individual motivation: (1) the perception of inequity creates tension, and (2) this tension makes people want to reduce or eliminate it. The greater the perceived inequity, the greater the level of tension and thus the motivation to reduce it. The theory suggests that individuals may pursue a number of alternatives in order to reduce the tension and attempt to restore a sense of equity:

1. ***Changing inputs.*** Employees may increase or decrease their efforts on the job in order to make their inputs more equitable with outcomes or rewards.

2. ***Rationalizing perceptions.*** Employees may rationalize their perceptions by deciding that inputs or outcomes are really greater or smaller than originally perceived or that the outcomes being received are really of more or less value than previously thought.

3. ***Changing the comparison other.*** Employees may change their comparison person by making comparisons with input-outcome ratios of some other individual. Such a change can restore feelings of equity.

4. ***Changing inputs or outcomes of the comparison other.*** If the comparison other is in one's work group, then it may be possible to change his or her inputs, for example, by asking a colleague to decrease or increase his or her effort or responsibility.

5. ***Changing the situation.*** If the perceived inequity is strong enough, and none of the above alternatives has worked, the individual may quit the job or transfer to another unit or location.

In police work, there are many areas where perceived inequities can arise. For instance, inequities are frequently perceived between and among work units, especially comparisons between specialist (e.g., detective, traffic, or juvenile) and generalist (e.g., patrol) units. In other words, patrol officers may feel that their treatment by the organization is inferior to the treatment received by those in the specialized units in terms of pay, prestige, work load, and job content. Also, organizations moving toward community policing must be careful when experimental units are used in the transition process, because "regular" patrol officers may perceive such units as elite and therefore will not cooperate with them or will actively work against them.

Although police officers may use any of the alternatives noted above to reduce tensions and restore feelings of equity to their particular situations, equity theory suggests that managers need to maintain a two-way communication with their employees regarding equity perceptions and to take steps to remedy legitimate inequities. One of the advantages of implementing community policing throughout the organization, is that officer roles become more generalized or enriched and thus may be perceived more equitably. In fact, in community policing, the patrol officer becomes perhaps the most important position in the organization, and working in cooperation with other officers and specialists to improve community livability becomes an essential byproduct.

Furthermore, police managers should be sure that employees understand the rules and procedures that govern the allocation of outcomes relative to inputs; that is, they must make clear ***what type of performance will receive what type of reward***. This issue is similar to expectancy theory with respect to the importance of linking rewards to performance outcomes. The key here is that by communicating truthfully with each employee and ***clarifying expectations***, managers should be able to reduce feelings of tension and inequity. Accordingly, managers should base rewards as much as possible on ***objective and tangible***, as opposed to subjective, ***criteria***. It follows that employees should be able to participate in but not dictate the setting of their own goals (see the following section). As a result, individuals who fail to meet expectations will be more likely to understand why their rewards are less than those of higher-level performers.

Equity theory also has important implications for police-department and civil-service reward systems. In order for motivational levels to remain high, it is necessary that the highest-level performers receive the greatest rewards. Usually, salary increases and promotions are based more on seniority (time spent with the organization) than on actual job performance. Employees often receive yearly across-the-board salary or step increases regardless of their performance, or they are promoted on the basis of their seniority or loyalty to the organization, not because of their knowledge or leadership abilities. Such practices reduce motivation to be a high-level performer (i.e., why should anyone work so hard when everyone, regardless of performance level, receives the same reward?). Although police managers are generally required to follow these strict salary structures, a possible solution would be to withhold yearly step increases from employees who did not meet performance standards while granting salary increases to those who exceeded standards of expected performance. In this way, higher-level performers would be motivated to continue to excel, and lower-level performers would have role models to emulate if they wished to receive similar rewards.

Goal-Setting Theory

Goal setting, as originally proposed by Locke (1968), suggests that a person's goals and intentions are the primary determinants of behavior. In other words, once a person intends to do something (e.g., a project or task), he or she will push forward until the goal is achieved. Locke proposes that more difficult goals result in higher levels of performance if these goals are accepted by the individual.

Locke and Latham (1984) suggest that goal setting works by directing attention toward a goal, providing effort, increasing persistence, and developing strategies to achieve the goals. Feedback with respect to results is also an important element in motivating through goal setting. The success of goal setting depends on determining goals that have certain characteristics. For instance, goals should be: (1) measurable, (2) challenging yet attainable (similar to n Ach theory), (3) relevant to the work of the organization, and (4) time-limited in the sense of when the goal must be accomplished. It is likely that individuals will be committed to attaining goals when they have a high likelihood of reaching the goal, have a strong connection between goal accomplishment and rewards, and highly value the rewards.

Although, in general, research supports goal setting and increased performance, there can also be some problems attached to the process if it is not applied appropriately. For instance, some managers and researchers (Gibson, Ivancevich, and Donnelly, 1991) have found the following:

Goal setting is complex and hard to sustain.

Goal setting works well for simple jobs but less well for complex jobs, that is, jobs in which goals are not easily measured (this would include community policing).

❖ ❖ ❖ ❖

Goal setting can encourage game playing, such as setting low, easily achievable goals in order to look good.

Goal setting can be used as a check on employees , a control device to monitor performance.

Goal accomplishment can become an obsession; in some situations, it has become so important that employees have neglected other important aspects of their jobs.

It appears that under the right conditions and used correctly, goal setting can be a highly motivating method of improving police performance. For it to be effective, managers must carefully monitor the process and be sure that the goals are readily accepted by employees and are moderately difficult to achieve. In congruence with equity theory, employees should be allowed to participate in setting their own or team goals and have input regarding their measurement. Managers must also be sure that an appropriate amount of *feedback* on performance is provided, as well as allowing enough *autonomy* to be able to successfully accomplish the goal(s). A study by Zhao, Thurman, and He (1999) supports the importance of feedback and autonomy to satisfaction and motivation. Approximately 200 officers of the Spokane Police Department (Washington) completed surveys designed to measure sources of job satisfaction with respect to their work environment. Regarding officer satisfaction with supervisors, the only variables found to be significantly correlated were job autonomy and feedback from supervisors, underscoring the importance of allowing officers the leeway to do their jobs and of the need to communicate regarding how well they are doing their jobs.

The discussion of content and process theories of motivation indicates that managers can influence employee motivational levels. To do so, however, requires some knowledge of individual needs, expectations, achievements, comparison with others, and goal setting. One of the best vehicles managers have to improve motivation is through job design

Job Design

Job design is concerned with appropriately developing and structuring work activities in order to meet individual and organizational needs. Jobs that are designed in order to reward and motivate employees leads to increased work effort and productivity, which, in turn, leads to increased organizational performance. Some of the initial work on job design can be traced to the work of Frederick Taylor (1947), who attempted to improve worker productivity by "scientifically" designing jobs. As may be recalled, Taylor designed jobs to be highly efficient by simplifying them and tying productivity to pay. This approach, however, ignored the impact of the individual worker. Subsequently, the Hawthorne studies indicated the importance of considering the human aspects of organizational behavior and management. By ignoring the human element in work design, scientific managers failed to consider that some employees are dissatisfied with jobs that are boring, provide little challenge, and over which they have little or no control. Such job dissatisfaction can lead to behavior that is counterproductive to the organization's effectiveness because it can contribute to low levels of morale and performance and high levels of absenteeism and turnover. Consequently, it is important for managers to attempt to design jobs that are both stimulating and rewarding to the employees who must perform them.

Although scientific management concentrated on extrinsic rewards of the job (e.g., pay and fringe benefits), more recent approaches, known as ***job redesign,*** have attempted to change jobs in order to increase intrinsic rewards that can be obtained from the work itself, such as feelings of growth, esteem, and self-actualization. Accordingly, it is believed that as internal levels of motivation increase, negative work behaviors decrease, thus leading to improved performance. This section discusses job expansion, or how jobs can be redesigned to improve intrinsic rewards. A job characteristics model is also presented as a tool to help managers diagnose which aspects of a job should be expanded. Finally, traditional police jobs and efforts to enrich them, especially through community policing, will be explored.

Expanding Jobs

Attempts to redesign, or expand, jobs to fit individual employee needs in order to improve satisfaction and motivation can take one of two forms: job enlargement or job enrichment. ***Job enlargement*** is expanding the content of a job by increasing the number or variety of tasks of similar difficulty. It is known as ***horizontal job loading*** because employees perform a greater number of tasks at approximately the same level of difficulty. ***Job enrichment*** increases both the variety and control of some tasks normally assigned to those holding a higher (vertical) position in the organization. It is known as ***vertical job loading*** because employees perform more difficult work. Efforts to expand, or "load," jobs both horizontally and vertically are generally also referred to as job enrichment.

The impetus for loading jobs vertically was provided by Herzberg's (1966) two-factor theory. As discussed previously, this theory states that only factors, labeled as "motivators," intrinsic to the work itself (i.e., job-content factors, such as achievement, recognition, and responsibility) can increase employee motivation to perform. Dissatisfiers, or "hygiene factors" (i.e., job-context factors, such as company policies, supervision, and salary), are extrinsic to the work and therefore not capable of improving employee motivation.

As early as the mid-1970s, it was suggested that patrol officer motivation and levels of performance could be improved through job redesign by emphasizing "motivators" (Baker, 1976). Such an emphasis became part of a concept known as team policing (discussed in Chapter 3). In general, team policing attempted to enrich traditional policing by allowing for increased flexibility in decision making, by combining patrol and investigative functions (i.e., officers performed some investigations on their own), by increasing interaction among team members, and by increasing interaction with the community.

Individual Differences

Although job redesign can be a very effective motivator, managers should be aware that this will not always be the case. Job-expansion programs may not account for ***individual differences*** and consequently may not be satisfying to all employees. In other words, the same motivating factors included in a job's redesign will usually not motivate all employees in that job. This potential dilemma was alluded to earlier by suggesting that officers with higher-level needs would probably be more satisfied with a community-policing role than would officers with lower-level needs. In other words, some officers may not feel comfortable with increased levels of decision making and problem-solving authority or increased interaction with the community. A study of Philadelphia police officers who participated in a Community Oriented Police Education (COPE) program lends support to the need for managers to pay attention to individual differences (Greene, 1989).

The COPE program involved both police and citizens in the areas that the officers patroled, and it included aspects of race relations, problem solving, use of power and authority, interactions with the community, community resources, and crime prevention. The study compared groups of officers who completed the COPE program with a group that did not participate. In general, it was found that those officers who were more positively motivated were more satisfied with their work and more supportive of police and community contact. By contrast, officers who were more concerned with job security (including their ability to control and direct their own behaviors without community interference), were more likely to resist community contact and to perceive less support for the police. This finding suggests that officers who are seeking to protect the security of their job are the least likely to be satisfied with community policing, because they may seek to minimize their contacts with the public.

A more recent study echoes the findings of Greene and further emphasizes the importance of individual differences. In their study of a medium-sized police department transitioning toward community policing, Russel and MacLachlan (1999) found that while levels of job satisfaction improved for officers who supported such a change, for many others, the reverse was true. For those officers who were initially unsupportive of community-policing activities, increases in decision-making authority and personal discretion served to further isolate these officers from those who were supportive of community policing. Thus, the community-policing innovations implemented within this department appeared to produce lower levels of employee satisfaction in many of these more traditional officers.

Another consideration with respect to job redesign and individual differences relates to the increasing level of higher education among today's police officers. Some research indicates that higher education has an impact on officer attitudes toward their jobs. For instance, Griffin, Dunbar, and McGill (1978) found that as officers' educational levels increase, their feelings of job satisfaction are related more to internal factors, such as being in control. The researchers suggested that unless steps are taken to allow for more control for these officers, there is a likelihood of "increasing job dissatisfaction, frustration, and ultimately resignation" (p. 181). Another study by Mottaz (1983) on work alienation and the police found that more-educated officers tend to place greater importance on self-fulfillment in work and are therefore more sensitive to alienating conditions, such as powerlessness and meaninglessness. To reduce alienation on the job, Mottaz suggested that it will be necessary to focus on the officer's tasks and provide greater opportunities for autonomy and achievement.

In a large-scale reanalysis of police officers in three metropolitan areas, Worden (1990) found that although higher education was not significantly related to attitudes or certain types of performance, college-educated officers did have a greater preference for autonomy. In addition, citizens found these officers to be exceptional in their problem-solving capabilities. In another study of over 500 officers in five police departments, Dantzker (1992) found that patrol officers with a college degree were more satisfied with their jobs than were their colleagues with less education. However, this was only true for officers with up to five years of experience; after that, satisfaction levels dropped. If these officers are to remain in patrol after five or so years, managers will need to develop ways to maintain their levels of satisfaction with the job. Possibilities cited by Dantzker include job enrichment, promotion, job transfers, leaves of absence, and in-service training.

Interestingly, although it seems that officers with higher education would be more supportive of community policing, results from research remain far from conclusive. Lewis, Rosenberg, and Sigler (1999) indicate no relationship between education and support for community policing among officers and administrators. Similarly, Lamm Weisel and Eck (1994), using surveys of officers in six cities, found no relationship between educational attainment and support for community policing. Finally, Winfree, Bartku, and Seibel (1996) conducted research in four municipal departments in New Mexico, and report officers with higher levels of education had less support for community-policing activities. Thus, while higher education may contribute to a preference for job enrichment among officers, educational attainment does not automatically indicate greater support for community policing. While these findings appear contradictory in nature, since community policing is generally associated with job enrichment, it is possible that the manner in which the various departments were attempting to "implement" community policing could have had an impact; that is, were the jobs actually being enriched or simply paid "lip service" with little or no increase in autonomy and decision making? Certainly, additional research is needed in this area to further understand the implications of these findings.

Based on the research findings just discussed, the challenge for police managers attempting to redesign jobs for community policing will be to attempt to match, at least initially, those officers who are the most enthusiastic and challenged by such jobs, while gradually expanding the movement throughout the organization. Officers with more traditional job orientations, who may be negatively affected by such changes, will need to be dealt with constructively in order to maintain their performance at acceptable levels. It is even possible that these officers can benefit their organizations by remaining in traditional police jobs; this issue will be further discussed in the final section.

Job Characteristics Model

An important approach to job redesign that attempts to integrate aspects of both job enlargement and job enrichment is the ***job characteristics model (JCM)***. This model, developed by Hackman and Oldham (1976, 1980), specifies the conditions under which people become psychologically motivated to perform more effectively on the job. The model, shown in Figure 7.4, identifies ***five core job dimensions*** that stimulate ***three critical psychological states,*** which in turn lead to several beneficial ***personal and work outcomes.***

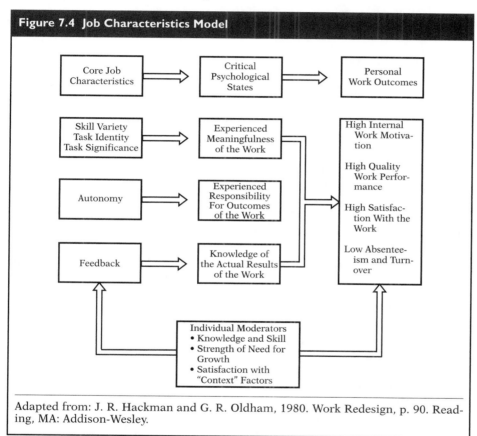

Figure 7.4 Job Characteristics Model

Adapted from: J. R. Hackman and G. R. Oldham, 1980. Work Redesign, p. 90. Reading, MA: Addison-Wesley.

The model indicates three job dimensions—skill variety, task identity, and task significance—that result in a person's experiencing the job as meaningful. ***Skill variety*** refers to the different activities (i.e., skills and tasks) involved in carrying out the work. ***Task identity*** refers to the degree to which the job requires completion of a whole piece of work from beginning to end. ***Task significance*** refers to the degree to which the job affects the lives or work of other people.

A fourth job dimension, ***autonomy,*** refers to the degree to which a job allows the worker independence and discretion in scheduling the work and in determining the procedures to carry it out. Autonomous jobs help a worker experience responsibility for work outcomes. The fifth job dimension, ***feedback,*** refers to the degree to which a worker obtains direct and clear information about the effectiveness of his or her job performance. Jobs that are designed to provide a high level of feedback to the employee lead to increased knowledge of the results of the work.

According to the job characteristics model, a job is most likely to increase internal work motivation when all of the following are true: (1) the job is high on at least one or more of the three job dimensions that lead to experienced meaningfulness of the work, (2) the job is high on autonomy, and (3) the job is high on feedback. A ***motivating potential score (MPS)*** is a measure of the degree to which these three conditions are met. In other words, MPS is computed by combining the scores of jobs on the five dimensions:

$$\text{MPS} = \left[\frac{\text{Skill Variety} + \text{Task Identity} + \text{Task Significance}}{3} \right] \times \text{Autonomy} \times \text{Feedback}$$

As the formula indicates, a low score on either autonomy or feedback will significantly reduce the overall MPS of a job; on the other hand, a low score on one of the three job dimensions that contribute to experienced meaningfulness will not by itself reduce the MPS as dramatically. Consequently, the job characteristics model specifies that by redesigning jobs to increase variety, identity, significance, autonomy, and feedback, the employees' psychological attitudes toward the work will change and should result in improved work outcomes, including greater internal motivation, higher-quality work performance, greater satisfaction, and lower absenteeism and turnover.

It is also important to point out that the model predicts that employees who have a high need for growth (i.e., for personal achievement and development) will respond more favorably to a job high in motivating potential (i.e., the core job dimensions) than will employees with a low need for growth (i.e., who emphasize lower-level needs). In fact, the model suggests that negative consequences are likely if employees have a low need for growth and jobs are relatively high on the core job dimensions. Of course, this supports both the Greene (1989) and Russell and MacLachlan (1999) findings discussed in the last section, and reiterates the importance of recognizing individual differences.

Hackman and Oldham (1975) have developed an instrument, the ***Job Diagnostic Survey (JDS)***, that can be used to measure each of the core job characteristics, as well as to assess both jobs and employees with respect to the potential for job enrichment. Research has found that employees may differ in their reactions to increases in the core job characteristics; for example, they are more likely to feel motivated by such job changes if they have the necessary knowledge and skills to perform the redesigned job, and if they have a high need for growth. Inside Management 7.2 provides a brief overview of the process used for assessing jobs for their motivating potential through the JDS, helping managers to determine whether or not they should attempt to enrich jobs with respect to their employees' needs.

Jobs can be enriched in a number of ways. Five distinct steps to enrich different core job dimensions (Hackman, Oldham, Janson, and Purdy, 1975) are identified in Table 7.1. Interestingly, a community-policing approach to job redesign may use all of the methods specified in Table 7.1 to enrich the core job dimensions defined in the job characteristics model. For example, with respect to problem solving, responsibility for planning, implementation, and control are paramount (see Table 7.1, number 4), which should lead to increased autonomy. In addition, various tasks may be combined (see

Inside Management 7.2

Using the Job Diagnostic Survey

Diagnosing the Job

The Job Diagnostic Survey is used to assess the target job and employees' reaction to it. The instruments measure the following:

1. ***The objective characteristics of the job itself.*** These include both an overall indication of the "motivating potential" (i.e., Motivating Potential Score) of the job as it exists and the score of the job on each of the five core dimensions.

2. ***The motivation, satisfaction, and work performance of employees on the job.*** In addition to satisfaction with the work itself, the JDS measures how people feel about other aspects of the work setting, such as pay, supervision, and relationships with coworkers.

3. ***The employees' need for growth.*** Because research indicates that employees who have a strong need for growth are more likely to respond to job enrichment than employees with a weak need, it is important to know at the outset just what kinds of satisfactions motivate employees. Then it is possible to identify where changes should begin and which persons need help in adapting to the enriched job.

Job Enrichment Implementation

Once the job has been diagnosed using the JDS, what approach to job enrichment should be used? Four important questions, to be addressed in sequence, provide the answer:

1. ***Are motivation and satisfaction central to the problem?*** Sometimes organizations undertake job enrichment to improve the work motivation and satisfaction of employees when the real problem lies elsewhere. For example, work performance of the patrol unit is highly dependent on the communications unit; if dispatching and other vital functions provided to patrol are faulty, low performance could result. Under such circumstances, it would be more appropriate to focus attention on improving the operations of the communications unit than to implement job enrichment techniques. Consequently, the first step is to determine whether or not employee motivation and satisfaction are problematic by examining employee scores in these areas on the Job Diagnostic Survey. If employee motivation and satisfaction are low, the change agent (or manager) should continue on to question 2; if motivation and satisfaction are already high, then the change agent should attempt to identify the real problem.

2. ***Is the job low in motivating potential?*** The manager should compare the Motivating Potential Score of the target job with the MPS scores of other jobs (MPS scores on many different types of jobs have been published by Hackman and Oldham) to determine whether or not the job itself is a probable cause of the motivational problems discovered in question 1.

3. ***What specific aspects of the job are causing the difficulty?*** At this point, the manager should examine the job in each of the five core dimensions to determine the specific strengths and weaknesses of the job as currently structured; that is, which dimensions score low on MPS. Plans are then made for improving those dimensions. For example, if a job scores reasonably high in autonomy and feedback but one or more of the core dimensions that contribute to experienced meaningfulness (i.e., skill variety, task identity, or task significance) score low, then these latter three dimensions should be strengthened.

4. ***How ready are the employees for change?*** Once a need for improvement in the job is established and the troublesome aspects of the job have been identified, then the manager should consider the specific steps to take to enrich the job (see Table 7.1). The needs of the employees for growth should be considered because those with strong needs for growth tend to respond more readily to job enrichment than those with weak needs for growth. The JDS provides a direct measure of the need for growth and can be helpful in planning how to introduce the changes (i.e., slowly or more rapidly) and in deciding whose jobs should be redesigned first.

Adapted from: J. R. Hackman and G. R Oldham, 1976. "Motivation Through the Design of Work: Test of a Theory," *Organizational Behavior and Human Performance*, 16: 251-279; J. R. Hackman, G. R. Oldham, R. Janson and K. Purdy, 1975. "A New Strategy for Job Enrichment," *California Management Review* 27: 57-71.

number 2), which should lead to increased skill and task variety; new work groups may be formed (see number 1), which should lead to increased task identity and significance; client or community relationships may be enhanced (see number 3), which should lead to increased skill variety, autonomy, and feedback; and finally, opening feedback channels (see number 5) will provide more direct information about performance, which should lead to improved relationships with the community.

Table 7.1   Steps to Enrich Core Job Dimensions

Job Enrichment Method	Description of Method	Core Job Dimension
1. Forming work units	Distributing work in a logical way so that workers have "ownership" and a sense of responsibility	Task identity Task significance
2. Combining tasks	Combining tasks that have been functionalized or specialized into new, larger modules of work	Skill variety Task variety
3. Establishing client relationships	Providing the worker contact with the user of his or her product or service	Skill variety Autonomy Feedback
4. Vertical loading	Increased worker responsibility for planning, doing, and controlling the work	Autonomy
5. Opening feedback channels	Providing the worker with as much direct information as possible about his or her performance	Feedback

Adapted from: J. R. Hackman, G. R. Oldham, R. Janson, and K. Purdy, 1975. "A New Strategy for Job Enrichment," *California Management Review* 27: 57-71.

One of the more extensive tests to date of the effect of the job characteristics model on police job redesign has been in the Madison (Wisconsin) Police Department through their quality policing (QP) program. As part of a larger study on the change process to QP in Madison, Wycoff and Skogan (1993) surveyed officers working in the Experimental Police District (EPD), where quality policing was first implemented and compared them with a non-EPD control group. In general, officers implementing, quality policing in the EPD had greater freedom to make decisions about the work they did and how they did it, more flexibility in scheduling their time to accomplish specific tasks, smaller work groups, and a closer working relationship between officers and supervisors; comparisons between the two groups generally used measures taken prior to the implementation of QP and after approximately two years of operation.

Measures primarily associated with the job characteristics model included (1) satisfaction with job growth potential, (2) perceived significance of work, (3) strength of task identity, and (4) perceived initiative or autonomy. Other job-related measures of the study included perceived officer satisfaction with the kind of work done, with the organization itself, and with supervision. Group comparisons indicated that with respect to the first four measures associated with the job characteristics model, EPD officers experienced larger increases in all four areas and significant increases in personal growth and task identity. EPD officers were also significantly more satisfied with their work as well as with supervision and the organization itself by the end of the study.

These findings suggest that job enrichment for policing can significantly increase job and organization satisfaction and levels of personal growth. It should be noted, however, that individual differences may have accounted for some of the differences in Madison; the members of the EPD were volunteers for the program and thus may have been more motivated toward a quality or community-policing job design to begin with. Nevertheless, it appears that a job redesign toward community policing can be successful in improving job satisfaction and performance, if properly matched to individual needs.

In an effort to identify those variables that most significantly contribute to officer job satisfaction, Zhao, Thurman, and He (1999) examined the influences of demographic variables and work environment on police officer job satisfaction. From the Spokane Police Department in Washington state, 199 of the department's 257 sworn employees completed the Job Descriptive Index (JDI) to measure multiple dimensions of job satisfaction and the Diagnostic Job Survey (JDS), which measures the five core job dimensions of the Job Characteristics Model. It was discovered that the officers' satisfaction with work is primarily associated with their perceptions about skill variety, task identity, and autonomy, the recognition they receive, and the capability to do the work. Years of service and rank were associated negatively with officers' satisfaction with work, which supports previous findings.

The results further indicated that ethnicity, gender, and level of education did not predict officers' satisfaction with work, which suggests that all officers would benefit from job enrichment, regardless of their personal characteristics. While these findings appear to be contradictory to the general research, the authors pointed out that the SPD has been implementing community policing very aggressively since 1992. Therefore, the work environment may contribute differently, and more positively, to job satisfaction than in other agencies. Such results, if they can be replicated elsewhere, may have significant implications for those departments committed to organization-wide community policing.

Job Redesign and Community Policing

Just as police departments have been criticized for overreliance on the paramilitary, classical organization design, so too has the traditional design of police jobs. Historically, many police departments, particularly those emphasizing a reform style, have tended to stress a narrow perspective of the police role and the community, and have consequently designed their jobs from a narrow, primarily law enforcement perspective. However, as the complexity of the police role has become recognized, as police have become better educated, and as community policing has developed, it is clear that traditional job designs are often not meeting the needs of police personnel, the organization, or the community.

In attempting to enhance community livability through problem solving and crime prevention efforts, community-policing jobs are substantially redesigned by increasing the use of officer discretion and power, especially with respect to utilizing alternatives other than those available primarily through the criminal justice system. In attempting to identify and solve community problems, officers may need to use counseling, mediation, referral to social agencies, or services from other public and private agencies. Community policing also emphasizes teamwork while attempting to find solutions to problems. Although "working with others" frequently means other departmental members (e.g., other patrol officers, specialists, or detectives), it may also include members of agencies outside the department (e.g., health, welfare, fire, transportation, animal control, housing, and counseling) or with individuals or groups within the community. The enriched nature of a community police officer's day is depicted below.

A Community Police Officer's Day

In addition to traditional law enforcement activities, such as patrol and responding to calls for service, the day might include the following:

Operating neighborhood substations.
Meeting with community groups.
Analyzing and solving neighborhood problems.
Working with citizens on crime prevention programs.
Conducting door-to-door surveys of residents.
Talking with students in school.
Meeting with local merchants.
Making security checks of businesses.
Dealing with disorderly people.

Source: S. D. Mastrofski, 1992. "What Does Community Policing Mean for Daily Police Work?" *National Institute of Justice Journal*, August, p. 24.

The research on the impact of community policing activities on officer attitudes and performance is mixed. On the one hand, it does appear that in programs or units that are relatively well developed, such activities can significantly increase levels of personal growth and job satisfaction, as well as improving attitudes toward the department itself, supervision, and the community (see Hayeslip and Cordner, 1987; Hornick, Burrows, and Phillips, 1989; Wycoff and Skogan, 1993; Skogan and Hartnett, 1997; and Zhao, Thurman, and He, 1999). On the other hand, in programs that were either partially or poorly implemented, officers' attitudes and job satisfaction levels were not so positive, usually with no discernible differences between experimental and comparison groups (see Weisburd and McElroy, 1988; McElroy, Cosgrove, and Sadd, 1993; Rosenbaum, Yeh, and Wilkinson, 1994; and Wilson and Bennett, 1994).

Although we must be cautious with interpreting results from programs that were different with respect to implementation, assignment of personnel (especially with the use of volunteers who may be more motivated to begin with), and internal and external conditions, some encouraging results have been reported. The early results appear to be threefold: (1) officers who value internal needs for personal growth and job satisfaction—both characteristics associated with higher education—benefit from a community policing-enriched job design; (2) more traditionally oriented officers (Greene, 1989) or "careerists" who value extrinsic rewards such as recognition and security, likely will not benefit from job enrichment; and (3) less clearly, it seems that in some departments with organization-wide community policing, all officers appeared to benefit from job enrichment.

Clearly, these results suggest that individual differences (between both departments and individual officers) need to be taken into consideration by management when planning for job enrichment. As Greene has noted:

> Community policing for some officers may represent a personal growth challenge, the chance to meaningfully participate in work decisions, and the enlightened work environment suggested by these programs. But for other officers community policing can be something completely different; it can be more work to be done at the same pay, it can be added responsibility without commensurate authority or autonomy, and it can mean that officer autonomy is actually restricted by an observant and activated community. For officers who may value these concerns, community policing may be perceived as more detrimental than beneficial. (1989, p. 181)

Greene further adds that because innovative programs in policing have been criticized for "creaming" off the "better" officers, it is not clear that community policing will "work with all or even the majority of officers currently policing American communities" (p. 180). Although this topic may have important long-term implications for the field, and whether or not community policing programs can, or should, be implemented throughout an organization, the initial challenge for police managers moving toward community policing will be to place those officers who desire change and personal growth into community-oriented jobs.

Job Fit, Satisfaction, and Patrol Work

Since the research suggests that many police officers are not satisfied in a community policing-oriented job, a more specialized approach may be appropriate. In a study with potentially significant results in this area, Lawton, Hickman, Piquero, and Greene (2000) examined the interrelationships between officers' perceptions of job impact (i.e., levels of crime, quality of life, and police-community interaction) and job satisfaction. In a random survey, 168 community-oriented and 117 motorized (traditional) patrol officers in the Philadelphia Police Department were compared, and both groups appeared to attain job satisfaction similarly. The findings indicated that perceived job impact is largely determined by job satisfaction (i.e., what the officers think they should be doing). In other words, officers who were more satisfied with their jobs were more likely to perceive that they had an impact on their work environment, regardless of their work assignment.

The implications of these findings could be important in the current trend toward the adoption of community policing. Since it appears that officers can be *equally satisfied* in either traditional or community-policing roles, *matching* officers appropriately to these jobs may prove beneficial. "Job-fit," or how well a job suits the needs and strengths of an employee, could then become an important factor in the placement of officers into traditional or community policing roles. Because of potential conflicts between the two roles, it is generally preferable to assign officers performing both roles to the same unit, where they can work together. This was the approach taken by the Chicago Police Department in the development of their community policing approach, known as CAPS (Chicago Alternative Policing Strategy). See Case Study 7.1 for a description of how jobs were changed in implementing this program.

Case Study 7.1

Job Redesign and CAPS

Jobs were changed for the officers who served in each prototype or experimental district by dividing them into beat teams (community policing) and rapid-response teams (traditional) who primarily responded to calls-for-service. The department took this approach rather than forming what is known as a split force of community policing officers and regular ("real") policing officers; such an approach has been shown to create tension between the two units and ultimately to undermine community policing.

By using beat teams, a majority of a team's time could be spent within its assigned geographical area. This new beat integrity, including the freedom from responding to 911 calls, was accomplished by increasing the number of officers who served in the experimental districts by about 13 percent. Beat officers were to work with schools, businesses, and residents to identify and solve problems and to serve as coordinators for service requests to other city agencies. They attended various neighborhood meetings to work with existing community organizations, as well as regularly held public beat meetings, to increase communications between residents and beat officers.

Adapted from: W. G. Skogan and S. M. Hartnett. 1997. *Community Policing, Chicago Style*. New York: Oxford University Press, pp. 89–90.

The Chicago Alternative Policing Strategy (CAPS) offers one of the more practical and innovative models of job design for departments transitioning to community policing. The program began in 1993 and was implemented in five out of Chicago's 25 police districts. Jobs were changed for those officers who served in each of the five experimental districts by dividing officers into beat teams and rapid-response teams. Beat team officers were primarily responsible for community collaboration and problem-solving activities within the experimental district, while rapid-response officers focused on responding to calls-for-service. Over time, officers would alternate between beat and rapid-response cars in order to ensure that community policing did not become confined to special units (Skogan and Hartnett, 1997).

The CAPS program was expanded to encompass the remainder of the city by the end of 1995. External evaluations of the program with respect to citizen attitudes have been impressive. Yearly surveys of city residents conducted throughout most of the 1990s indicate increasing satisfaction with CAPS regarding police demeanor, responsiveness, and performance (Chicago Community Policing Evaluation Consortium, 2000). Nationwide deployment of such beat teams (community policing) and rapid-response teams (traditional) could serve to maximize public satisfaction with police service while permitting varied police roles that could help to increase officer job satisfaction and, presumably, officer performance.

For the near term, this specialist approach appears promising with respect to community-policing implementation, while at the same time satisfying individual officer needs and expectations regarding job content. It also provides a solution to the need for community policing officers to be freed from routine calls-for-service in order to have time to practice community- and problem-oriented activities (DeJong, Mastrofski, and Parks, 2001). While both types of officers in Chicago (i.e., beat and rapid-response) were divided into separate teams in the same district, another approach, similar to team policing, would be to have both sets of officers working on the *same teams*. This would further increase the interdependence and cooperation between work-team members, which, as we have seen, can have a significant motivating potential (VanderVegt, Emans, and VandeVliert, 1998). Such a *dual-role team policing* approach could be useful in implementing a change toward organization-wide community policing (or any degree in between) by gradually moving additional officers into community policing roles.

Interestingly, as it becomes increasingly clear that community policing officers need additional time off from responding to calls in order to adequately perform their jobs, it would also appear that there may always be a need for traditional policing roles to handle calls-for-service. If this assumption is accurate, officers would then either need to be "matched" to each particular role or rotated between roles, as in Chicago. Additional research is warranted on the viability of such approaches, as well as on the criteria to be used in the placement of officers into traditional and community policing roles.

Summary

If organizational and individual goals are to be accomplished, police managers will need to have a basic knowledge of motivation and job design. Without an adequate understanding of these concepts, it is not possible to understand what motivates individuals to perform and how to design jobs to improve performance. Both motivation and ability are important aspects of performance. The two major approaches to the study of motivation include content theories, which attempt to identify what motivates behavior, and process theories, which attempt to describe how motivation is energized into behavior. The most influential content theories are need hierarchy, two-factor, and achievement motivation; critical process theories include expectancy, equity, and goal setting. The discussion of these theories indicates that managers can influence employee levels of motivation and thus improve their work performance.

Job design is a potentially significant method of enhancing motivation and job performance. Expanding jobs to better fit employee needs has taken two general approaches: job enlargement, which increases the number or variety of tasks at the same organizational level; and job enrichment, which expands not only the variety of tasks but also the level at which they are performed. One promising approach to job redesign that attempts to integrate aspects of both job enlargement and job enrichment is the job characteristics model. In general, it appeared that police job redesign for community policing can be beneficial for some officers, especially those with strong growth needs and higher levels of education.

Although it is still too early to tell what the effects of community policing may be on the majority of the nation's police officers, it appears that, at least initially, departments may want to consider assigning teams of officers performing both traditional and community policing roles. In this way, officers can be matched to "fit" the job based on their needs, thus improving levels of satisfaction, while at the same time, providing community-oriented officers more time for problem solving.

Discussion Questions

1. Define motivation and provide a work-related example of how it might be applied to policing.

2. Explain how content theories of motivation work and how they have made an important contribution to the practice of management.

3. Discuss Herzberg's two-factor theory of motivation and compare this theory with Maslow's need hierarchy theory.

4. Describe the three general implications of Vroom's expectancy model of motivation. What does the research on expectancy theory and police performance suggest?

5. In what ways can equity theory and goal-setting theory be useful to police managers?

6. Differentiate between job enlargement and job enrichment. Provide an example of how each could be applied to policing.

7. Describe how the job characteristics model attempts to improve personal and work outcomes. What steps might be taken to enrich the core job dimensions of traditional police job designs?

8. Provide an example of how the Job Diagnostic Survey might be used to evaluate the motivational potential of police work.

9. Briefly describe the results of several studies that tested the effects of the job characteristics model on police job redesign. What is the significance of these results?

10. Briefly review the conflicting results of the research on police job redesign for community policing. With respect to these results, discuss several implications for implementing community policing.

References

Adams, J. S. 1963. "Toward an Understanding of Equity." *Journal of Abnormal and Social Psychology* 67: 422–436.

Baker, T. J. 1976. "Designing the Job to Motivate." *FBI Law Enforcement Bulletin* 45: 3–7.

Bennett, R. R., and Greenstein, T. 1975. "The Police Personality." *Journal of Police and Administration* 3: 439–445.

Bowker, L. 1980. "A Theory of Educational Needs of Law Enforcement Officers." *Journal of Contemporary Criminal Justice* 1: 17–24.

Cacioppe, R. L., and Mock, P. 1985. "The Relationship of Self-Actualization, Stress and Quality of Work Experience in Senior Level Australian Police Officers." *Police Studies* 8: 173–186.

Campbell, J. P., Dunnette, M. D., Lawler, E. E., and Weick, K. E. 1970. *Managerial Behavior, Performance and Effectiveness.* New York: McGraw-Hill.

Chicago Community Policing Evaluation Consortium (2000). *Community Policing in Chicago, Year Seven: An Interim Report.* Chicago: Illinois Criminal Justice Information Authority.

Crank, J. P., and Caldero, M. 1991. "The Production of Occupational Stress in Medium-sized Police Agencies: A Survey of Line Officers in Eight Municipal Departments." *Journal of Criminal Justice* 19: 339–349.

Dantzker, M. L. 1992. "An Issue for Policing—Educational Level and Job Satisfaction: A Research Note." *American Journal of Police* 12: 101–118.

DeJong, C., Mastrofski, S. D., and Parks, R. B. 2001. " Patrol Officers and Problem Solving: An Application of Expectancy Theory." *Justice Quarterly* 18: 31–61.

Dunham, R. B., Smith, F. J., and Blackburn, R. S. 1977. "Validation of the Index of Organizational Reactions with the JDI, the MSQ, and the Faces Scale." *Academy of Management Journal* 20: 420–432.

Farrell, M. J. 1984. "The Development of the Community Patrol Officer Program: Community-Oriented Policing in the New York City Police Department." In J. R. Greene and S. D. Mastrofski (eds.), *Community Policing: Rhetoric or Reality?*, pp. 75–88. New York: Praeger.

Gaines, L. K., Van Tubergen, N., and Paiva, M. A. 1984. "Police Officer Perceptions of Promotion as a Source of Motivation." *Journal of Criminal Justice* 12: 265–275.

Gibson, J. L., Ivancevich, J. M., and Donnelly, J. H. Jr., 1991. *Organizations,* 7th ed. Homewood, IL: Irwin.

Greene, J. R. 1989. "Police Officer Job Satisfaction and Community Perceptions: Implications for Community-Oriented Policing." *Journal of Research in Crime and Delinquency* 26: 168–183.

Griffin, G. R., Dunbar, R. L. M., and McGill, M. E. 1978. "Factors Associated with Job Satisfaction Among Police Personnel." *Journal of Police Science and Administration* 6: 77–85.

Guyot, D. 1991. *Policing as Though People Matter.* Philadelphia, PA: Temple University Press.

Hackman, J. R., and Oldham, G. R. 1975. "Development of the Job Diagnostic Survey." *Journal of Applied Psychology* 60: 159–170.

———. 1976. "Motivation Through the Design of Work: Test of a Theory." *Organizational Behavior and Human Performance* 16: 250–259.

———. 1980. *Work Redesign.* Reading, MA: Addison-Wesley, 1980.

Hackman, J. R., Oldham, G. R., Janson, R., and Purdy, K. 1975. "A New Strategy for Job Enrichment." *California Management Review* 27: 57–71.

Halsted, A. J., Bromley, M. L., and Cochran, J. K. 2000. "The Effects of Work Orientations on Job Satisfaction Among Sheriff's Deputies Practicing Community-Oriented Policing." *Policing: An International Journal of Police Strategies & Management,* 23: 82–104.

Harris, R. 1973. *The Police Academy: An Inside View.* New York: Wiley.

Hayeslip, P. W., and Cordner, G. W. 1987. "The Effects of Community-Oriented Patrol on Police Officer Attitudes." *American Journal of Police* 6: 95–119.

Herzberg, F. 1966. *Work and the Nature of Man.* Cleveland, OH: World.

Herzberg, F., Mausner, B., and Snyderman, B. 1959. *The Motivation to Work.* New York: Wiley.

Hoath, D. R., Schneider, F. W., and Starr, M. W. 1998. "Police Job Satisfaction as a Function of Career Orientation and Position Tenure: Implications for Selection and Community Policing." *Journal of Criminal Justice* 26: 337–347.

Hornick, J. P., Burrows, B. A., and Phillips, D. M. 1989. *An Impact Evaluation of the Edmonton Neighborhood Foot Patrol Program*, November. Paper presented at the annual meeting of the American Society of Criminology, Reno, NV.

Kroes, W. H., Margolis, B. L., and Hurrell, J. Jr. 1974. "Job Stress in Policemen." *Journal of Police Science and Administration* 2: 145–155.

Lamm Weisel, D.L., and Eck, J. E. 1994. "Toward a Practical Approach to Organizational Change: Community Policing in Six Cities." In D. P. Rosenbaum (ed.), *The Challenges of Community Policing: Testing the Promises*, pp. 53–74. Thousand Oaks, CA.: Sage.

Lawton, B. A., Hickman, M. J., Piquero, A. R., and Greene, J. R. 2000. "Assessing the Interrelationships Between Perceptions of Impact and Job Satisfaction: A Comparison of Traditional and Community-oriented Officers." *Justice Research and Policy* 2: 47–72.

Leavitt, H. J. 1978. *Managerial Psychology*, 4th ed. Chicago: University of Chicago Press.

Lefkowitz, J. 1973. "Attitudes of Police Toward Their Job." In J. R. Snibbe and H. M. Snibbe (eds.), *The Urban Policeman in Transition*, pp. 203–232. Springfield, IL: C. C. Thomas.

———. 1974. "Job Attitudes of Police: Overall Description and Demographic Correlates." *Journal of Vocational Behavior* 5: 221–230.

Lewis, S., Rosenberg, H., and Sigler, R. T. 1999. "Acceptance of Community Policing Among Police Officers and Police Administrators." *Policing: An International Journal of Police Strategies and Management* 22: 567–588.

Locke, E. A. 1968. "Toward a Theory of Task Motivation and Incentives." *Organizational Performance and Human Performance*, May: 157–189.

Locke, E. A., and Latham, G. P. 1984. *Goal Setting: A Motivational Technique That Works!* Englewood Cliffs, NJ: Prentice-Hall.

Lundman, R. J. 1980. *Police and Policing: An Introduction*. New York: Holt, Rinehart & Winston.

Maslow, A. H. 1943. "A Theory of Human Motivation." *Psychological Review* 50: 370–396.

Mastrofski, S. D. 1992. "What Does Community Policing Mean for Daily Police Work?" *National Institute of Justice Journal*, August: 23–27.

Mastrofski, S. D., Ritti, R. R., and Snipes, J. B. 1994. "Expectancy Theory and Police Productivity in DUI Enforcement." *Law and Society Review* 28: 113–148.

McClelland, D. 1985. *Human Motivation*. Glenview, IL: Scott, Foresman.

McElroy, J. E., Cosgrove, C. A., and Sadd, S. 1993. *Community Policing: The CPOP in New York*. Newbury Park, CA: Sage.

Mitchell, V. F., and Moudgill, P. 1976. "Measurement of Maslow's Hierarchy." *Organizational Behavior and Human Performance* 16: 334–349.

Mottaz, C. 1983. "Alienation Among Police Officers." 1983. *Journal of Police Science and Administration* 11: 23–30.

Muir, W. K. 1977. *Police: Streetcorner Politicians*. Chicago: University of Chicago Press.

National Advisory Commission on Criminal Justice Standards and Goals. 1973. *Police*. Washington, DC: Government Printing Office.

Neiderhoffer, A. E. 1969. *Behind the Shield*. Garden City, NY: Doubleday.

Rosenbaum, D. P., Yeh, S., and Wilkinson, D. L. 1994. "Impact of Community Policing on Police Personnel: A Quasi-Experimental Test." *Crime & Delinquency* 40: 331–353.

Ross, S. 1995. "Best Motivational Tool Costs Nothing." *San Jose Mercury News*, February 17, pp. 1G, 2G.

Russel, G. P., and MacLachlan, S. 1999. "Community Policing, Decentralized Decision Making and Employee Satisfaction." *Journal of Crime & Delinquency* 22: 31–54.

Skogan, W. G., and Hartnett, S. M. 1997. *Community Policing, Chicago Style*. New York: Oxford, University Press.

Skolnick, J. H. 1966. *Justice Without Trial.* New York: Wiley.

Slovak, J. S. 1978. "Work Satisfaction and Municipal Police Officers." *Journal of Police Science and Administration* 6: 462–470.

Taylor, F. W. 1947. "The Principles of Scientific Management." In *Scientific Management.* New York: Harper & Row.

Van Maanen, J. 1972. *Pledging the Police.* Ph.D. dissertation, University of California, Irvine.

——. 1975. "Police Socialization: A Longitudinal Examination of Job Attitudes in an Urban Police Department." *Administrative Science Quarterly* 20: 208–228.

VanderVegt, G., Emans, B., and VandeVliert, E. 1998. "Motivating Effects of Task and Outcome Interdependence." *Group & Organization Management* 23: 124–143.

Vroom, V. 1964. *Work and Motivation.* New York: Wiley.

Wahba, M. A., and Bridwell, L. G. 1976. "Maslow Reconsidered: A Review of the Research on the Need Hierarchy Theory." *Organizational Behavior and Human Performance* 16: 212–240.

Weisburd, D., and McElroy, J. E. 1988. "Enacting the CPO Role: Findings from the New York City Pilot Program in Community Policing." In J. R. Greene and S. D. Mastrofski (eds.), *Community Policing: Rhetoric or Reality?*, pp. 89–102. New York: Praeger.

Wilson, D. G., and Bennett S. F. 1994. "Officers' Response to Community Policing: Variations on a Theme." *Crime & Delinquency* 40: 354–370.

Winfree, L. T., Bartku, G. M., and Seibel, G. 1996. "Support for Community Policing Versus Traditional Policing Among Nonmetropolitan Police Officers: A Survey of Four New Mexico Police Departments." *American Journal of Police.* 15: 23–50.

Worden, R. E. 1990. "A Badge and a Baccalaureate: Policies, Hypotheses, and Further Evidence." *Justice Quarterly* 7: 565–592.

Wycoff, M. A., and Skogan, W. K. 1993. *Community Policing in Madison: Quality from the Inside Out.* Washington, DC: National Institute of Justice.

——. 1994. "The Effect of a Community Policing Management Style on Officers' Attitudes." *Crime & Delinquency* 40: 371–383.

Zhao, J., Thurman, Q., and He, N. 1999. "Sources of Job Satisfaction Among Police Officers: A Test of Demographic and Work Environment Models." *Justice Quarterly* 16: 153–172.

❖ ❖ ❖ ❖

Leadership and Management

Leadership is a crucial managerial activity. Police officers of all ranks function as leaders when they attempt to obtain compliance, or cooperation, from other persons in performing a task, solving a problem, or accomplishing a goal or objective. Patrol officers, investigators, and other operational personnel act as leaders when dealing with victims, suspects, informers, witnesses and often when they are involved in community policing and problem solving. Supervisors, managers, and executives function as leaders when organizing, planning, and evaluating police activities and motivating employees. This chapter describes some of the more important studies that have been conducted about leadership and managerial styles. Leadership and managerial style are often used interchangeably, although they can be defined differently. As used here, they have the same meaning until the last section of this chapter, when possible differences are discussed.

Leadership and Related Concepts

Stodgill (1974) identifies eleven perspectives on, or definitions of, leadership; including **leadership** as a function of group processes, the art of inducing compliance, a form of persuasion, the exercise of influence, a power relationship, and an instrument of goal achievement. Davis (1972: 100) suggests that leadership is "the ability to persuade others to seek defined objectives enthusiastically." Hunsaker and Cook (1986: 303) define leadership as "a process that involves actions taken by one person to influence the behavior of one or more others toward goals desired by the leader." The most important concepts in these definitions are "ability and actions," "process and persuasion," "enthusiastic others," and "goals and objectives." Leaders act to convince other persons to work hard to accomplish a specific purpose. Other important concepts related to leadership are influence, authority, power, and politics, each of which is briefly addressed below.

Influence and Authority

Influence is more general than either power or authority, but it is closely related. Influence is the process of altering, affecting, or changing attitudes, behaviors, values, or beliefs. The process involves the person who attempts to change the behavior and the person, group, or target of the influence process. **Authority** is the right to lead. In police departments, the right to lead is granted by departmental rank and status. The designation of sergeant, lieutenant, or captain indicates the person is a manager in an official leadership position. The department assumes that it has the right to designate leaders and that employees will accept the authority of those leaders. But acceptance of such authority does not always occur because employees may not perform as the leader expects. In this sense, authority is limited to the degree to which managers can obtain cooperation from employees. The formal authority granted to managers is only one dimension of effective leadership.

Power

Power is the ability to manage rather than the right to manage, as in the case of authority. When one person is influenced by another person, he or she is subject to the power of the influential person. Any personal characteristic or ability or practice that allows one person to influence another is related to power. Authority gives some power, but there are a number of other ways to influence people even when an individual is not in a position of authority (Kuykendall and Unsinger, 1979). Such a person can use one or more of five different types or sources of power—reward, coercive, legitimate, referent, and expert (French and Raven, 1959).

Reward power requires giving something of value to others. By virtue of their formal authority, managers have reward power, which varies considerably by rank and type of organization. Public managers, including the police, usually have less reward power than managers in the private sector because public managers have only limited influence in determining employees' salaries, fringe benefits, and at times even job assignments and promotions. But police managers can reward officers through performance evaluations and positive feedback.

Coercive power, the reverse of reward power, is taking away or threatening to take away something valued; e.g., money, job, promotion, status, acceptance, love. The disciplinary system of organizations is implicitly coercive because the possibility of disciplinary action (e.g., reprimand, suspension, termination) is based on the assumption that employees will behave themselves in order to avoid unwanted consequences. In general, in police departments the more coercion (threats of and actual punishment) is relied upon by managers, the more that both the quality and quantity of employee performance will decline. On the other hand, if there is a widespread consensus in the organization concerning what is considered to be inappropriate behavior, and what should be done about it, a failure to discipline may result in morale problems.

Legitimate power is similar to the concept of authority because people grant to others the right to influence them. Managers have legitimate power because employees, to a certain degree, give them the right to direct their behavior. They do so primarily because the manager is in a position to reward and punish the employee but also because of the manager's personality, ability, or knowledge. Police officers are excellent examples of individuals with legitimate power because they represent the legitimate force of government. They, in effect, are community-disorder managers.

Referent power is given to another by people who desire to associate, or identify, with that person, usually because of that person's personality, attractiveness, resources, or accomplishments. Officers who are admired for whatever reason may have considerable influence in a police department. Managers who are not admired or respected have little referent power. Historically, this has been a significant problem in police organizations. Individuals placed in leadership positions who are not respected by their peers and subordinates have great difficulty in becoming effective.

Expert power is granted to those people who have knowledge or expertise. To the degree that an individual is influenced by the ideas, advice, or guidance of another as to how to function as a police officer or perform some specific task, expert power is at work. Leaders who are perceived to lack a thorough understanding of what it is like to "work the streets" are more likely to be distrusted by officers.

Numerous studies have attempted to analyze the impact of using French and Raven's types of power. Selected results of this research are presented in Inside Management 8.1.

Organizational Politics

Politics involves the acquisition and use of power. At times the concepts of politics and power have negative connotations; however, it is not power itself that is negative but how it is used. Organizational politics involves the use of power and formal authority either to facilitate the accomplishment of goals and objectives or to enhance or protect a person, a career, a work unit, or the entire department. Power and authority can also be used to make the accomplishment of goals and objectives more difficult and to harm a person, a career, or a work unit.

Inside Management 8.1

Research Findings Concerning the Use of Power

1. A decrease in reward power may result in an increase in the use of coercive power. [Authors' note: The limits on the reward power available to police managers may be one reason they often rely on coercive power].

2. The use of coercive power results in greater resistance than does the use of reward power, and individuals using coercive power are not as well liked as those using reward power.

3. The more legitimate the use of coercion, the greater the conformity; the greater the strength of the threatened coercive act, the greater the conformity. [Authors' note: This means that persons conform their behavior to organizational rules; it does not necessarily mean they are productive employees.]

4. Coercive power is effective in the short run in securing conformity and compliance, but it may also produce fear, frustration, alienation, and a desire for revenge among employees. The negative impact on performance may result in greater reliance on coercion by managers, setting up the vicious cycle of "blame and punish" management.

5. The more expert a person is perceived to be in one area, the more likely he or she is capable of exerting influence in other areas.

6. The use of expert power has the strongest correlation with employee performance because it is closely related to a climate of organizational trust. [Authors' note: Police leaders who are also police experts are probably the most competent managers, providing they possess the necessary managerial knowledge and skills].

7. Referent power has an impact similar to expert power if it is essentially emotional, but the influence may be short-lived and is easily manipulated for selfish gain.

8. Legitimate power, or the authority of position, is usually the initial basis for managerial action but continued and sole utilization of this type of power creates dissatisfaction, resistance, and frustration among employees.

9. Reward power is probably the most influential in determining employee behavior; however, tangible rewards like pay and promotion may be limited by factors outside the manager's control. In addition, the rewards available to the manager may not be valued by the employee or employees; if they are not valued, then employees may believe that they are being manipulated.

Adapted from: F. Luthans, 1985. *Organizational Behavior Modification and Beyond*, pp. 445-460. Glenview, IL: Scott Foresman.

Playing politics in an organization is facilitated by knowing the right people, forming coalitions, and co-opting those whose support is needed to accomplish some purpose. Knowing the right people involves networking. Individuals who, regardless of their rank or position, know influential people often have an advantage. Individuals can also advance their interest by obtaining the support of others and forming a coalition. Unions and associations are examples of this approach. Co-opting others to gain their support often involves bargaining, which results in a deal (White and Bednar, 1986: 449–545).

Managers must continually decide how they will use their power and for what purpose. They cannot always depend on the rational processes of the organization to obtain a successful outcome. Being political is the reality of organizational life in many police departments. But when authority or power is used illegally, unethically, or to advance personal or work-group interests to the detriment of the organization, playing politics becomes destructive.

Leadership Styles

Leaders' or managers' styles have been discussed from three major theoretical perspectives: trait, behavioral, and situational or contingency. ***Trait theories*** attempt to identify the characteristics associated with effective leadership. ***Behavioral theories*** are concerned with identifying and defining the different styles managers use. ***Situational theories*** are concerned with which managerial styles are most appropriate, given a particular situation. Trait and behavioral theories often overlap because leadership traits may include both desirable characteristics (e.g., honesty) and behavior (e.g., takes risks). In this section, some of the more important research for each theory is discussed, followed by an analysis of police-related studies.

Trait Theories

Effective leaders may be studied to determine their traits. Often, these leaders are considered to be great women or men who were born with the necessary traits or abilities to be successful. Research in this area has produced little agreement on qualities of outstanding leaders or how they could be identified (White and Bednar, 1986: 491–492). In addition to the "great man or woman" approach, trait theory also includes intuitive and research components. The intuitive component is based on general observation and judgment in which the traits identified are subjective and difficult to define; for example, honesty, industriousness, sincerity, and dependability. The research component is more systematic, in that careful consideration is given to definitions and measurements of traits. Table 8.1 presents some of the leadership characteristics associated with both the intuitive and research components of trait identification.

Table 8.1 Traits Associated with Leadership	
Integrity	Intelligence
Supportiveness	Responsibility
Self-confidence	Vision
Sincerity	Emotional Control
Industriousness	Motivation
Flexibility	Persistence
Interpersonal Skills	Decisiveness
Intuition	Communication Skills

Adapted from: R. M. Stodgill, 1974. *Handbook of Leadership*. New York: Free Press.

Stampler (1992) reviewed numerous books and articles on general leadership and identified several important traits, or characteristics, of leaders. (1) Effective leaders tend to structure expectations, which involves communicating their beliefs and performance expectations to others. (2) Good leaders have integrity and tell the truth; that is, they present the facts as they believe them to be. (3) They are also aware of their own strengths and weaknesses and are open to others' opinions and critiques. (4) Leaders must also become a "living emblem" or role model for the principles and beliefs of the organization. (5) Finally, they possess leadership intuition, which means they are empathetic yet objective in dealing with people because they tend to understand why people behave as they do.

In his research concerning desirable leadership traits, Bass (1981) found that the best leaders are self-confident, have the ability to influence others' behavior, and tend to take the initiative in social situations. Effective leaders also have a strong drive for responsibility and task completion, demonstrate originality in problem solving, have good organizing skills, pursue goals with vigor and persistence, and are willing to accept the consequences of their actions. Bass (1981) also noted that good leaders are able to deal effectively with interpersonal stress and to tolerate frustration.

Kouzes and Posner (1987) surveyed 2,615 managers in the United States and found that four leadership characteristics or traits were identified by more that 50 percent of them: honesty (83 percent), competency (67 percent), being forward looking (62 percent), and being inspiring (58 percent). Combining both traits and behavioral perspectives, Kouzes and Posner suggest that the most effective leaders make the following "behavioral commitments":

1. Look for opportunities to change and improve.

2. Take risks, experiment and learn from mistakes.

3. Advocate an uplifting vision of the future that motivates others.

4. Appeal to followers' values, hopes, and interests.

5. Encourage participation.

6. Foster trust and collaboration among followers.

7. Share information and power.

8. Increase the visibility and discretion of subordinates.

9. Become a role model by living by articulated values.

10. Reward small victories that show progress and commitment.

11. Recognize individual contributions to the organization.

12. Reward team accomplishments on a regular basis.

Police-Trait Research

Police management literature is replete with intuitive observations on what makes an effective leader. Generally, the desirable traits for police managers are similar to those discussed in the previous section. Research on desirable traits has been limited; consequently, only two studies are described in this section.

Price (1974) examined women in police leadership roles. She found that, compared with men, women tended to have more of the traits associated with effective leadership. Female supervisors and managers tended to be more emotionally independent, intellectually aggressive, flexible, and self-confident than their male counterparts. Female leaders were also more liberal and creative.

The National Advisory Commission on Criminal Justice Standards and Goals (1977) conducted a study of 1,665 police chiefs to discover the most important characteristics of effective leadership and the most desirable management skills. The traits and skills identified by the chiefs of police included the ability to (1) maintain morale, (2) develop subordinates so they will be effective team members, (3) be able to relate to the community, (4) organize personnel and maintain effective review and control of operations, (5) communicate effectively, and (6) establish priorities and objectives.

Couper and Lobitz (1993), in discussing quality management, report that the employees of the Madison, Wisconsin police department believe that quality leaders are competent, visible, involved, and respectful of their employees. In addition, the behavior of quality managers includes being in touch with their employees, providing them with the necessary information, being able to "fix" problems and "improve" the organization, and have a willingness to take risks. Finally, quality managers must be "champions"; that is, they must be able to "walk what they talk." The leaders beliefs and behavior must be consistent with the beliefs and behavior they advocate for the organization and its employees.

The criticisms of trait theories include inconsistent research findings and the inability to distinguish between successful and unsuccessful leaders or between leaders and nonleaders. Also, as noted earlier, the definition and measurement of traits is problematic. In addition, effectiveness may be the result of what leaders have learned and how they behave rather than a character or personality trait. Situational demands may be more important than traits in determining desirable leadership qualities (White and Bednar, 1986: 491–493).

Behavioral Theories

Behavioral theories focus on the activities or behavioral styles of managers and on patterns of behavior that can be observed and measured. What leaders do is considered to be more important than their individual traits (Roberg, 1979: 160–161). Initial research established the groundwork for future inquiries by describing three basic leadership patterns or styles: authoritarian, democratic, and laissez-faire. The **authoritarian manager** directs employees, allowing minimal participation. The **democratic manager** encourages the employees to participate. The **laissez-faire manager** essentially allows complete freedom, providing little or no direction (Lewin and Lippit, 1938; Luthans, 1985: 476). These patterns are important because they identify a major recurring theme in behavioral theories—namely, the degree to which leaders allow subordinates to participate in deciding what will be done and how it will be done in the work environment.

When considering the studies of behavior theories described below, one should remember that although the terms used to describe leadership styles are different, they are related to two elements: the individual employee or work group and the task to be performed or goal to be achieved. Managerial behavior can vary in the degree of interest and concern shown to either of these elements.

❖ ❖ ❖ ❖   **Ohio State and University of Michigan Studies**

In the 1940s and 1950s, researchers at Ohio State University analyzed more than 1,700 descriptors of behavior that could be related to leadership. They found two primary characteristics related to effectiveness: initiating structure and consideration. *Initiating structure* refers to the degree to which a leader attempts to define and organize tasks for subordinates or followers. Leaders who tend to emphasize a high degree of structure are task oriented. *Consideration* refers to the degree to which the manager is aware of and sensitive to employee needs. A high degree of consideration is reflected in an emphasis on friendship, mutual trust, respect, interest in an employee's ideas, and sensitivity to the feelings of others. At about the same time, University of Michigan researchers conducted studies using similar variables. These were the degree to which leaders were either *employee-centered* or *production-centered*.

Perhaps the most important result of the Michigan research was presented in Likert's *New Patterns of Management* (1961). Likert believed that there were four styles or systems of management, briefly described below. He advocated a System 4 approach to management because his research indicated that it was the most effective.

> *System 1: Exploitative authoritative*, in which managers are autocratic and subordinates are exploited.

> *System 2: Benevolent authoritative*, in which managers have both authoritarian and paternalistic traits.

> *System 3: Consultative*, in which managers solicit input from subordinates but make all the important decisions.

> *System 4: Participative*, in which managers allow total participation, providing guidance or structure but allowing decisions to be made by consensus or the majority.

Based on the Ohio State and Michigan studies, four individual leadership styles, depicted in Figure 8.1, can be identified:

1. High concern for both structure (production or task or goal) and consideration for the employee

2. Low concern for both structure and consideration

3. High concern for structure, low concern for consideration

4. Low concern for structure, high concern for consideration

The research on these four styles has been mixed. Some effective leaders tend to emphasize either a high degree of structure or a high degree of consideration. Often subordinates tend to prefer a leader who is primarily concerned with consideration, but the leader's superiors may tend to prefer one who is more concerned with initiating structure. Although the Ohio State research did not identify one style as being consistently most effective, other researchers have found that a high concern for *both* structure and consideration is often related to greater employee satisfaction and productivity (e.g., see White and Bednar, 1986: 494–496; Hunsaker and Cook, 1986: 308–310; Roberg, 1979: 160–165).

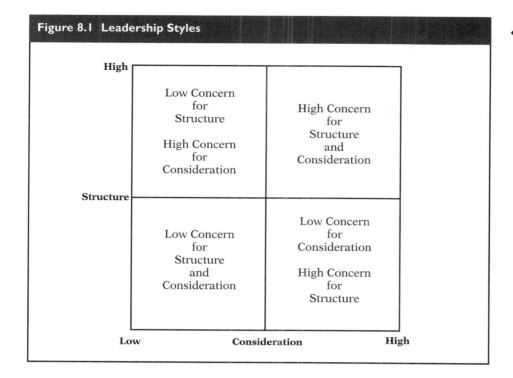

Figure 8.1 Leadership Styles

❖ ❖ ❖ ❖

The Managerial Grid

One of the best-known leadership models based on the Ohio State and Michigan research is Blake and Mouton's managerial grid (1964, 1968,1978,1986). They used the variables of ***production*** (similar to initiating structure and emphasizing tasks and organization needs and goals) and ***people*** (similar to considerations and emphasizing relationships and individual needs and goals) to construct a grid that identifies five managerial styles. The grid identifies five styles, as depicted in Figure 8.2, by both number and name.

1. ***The 1/1, or impoverished manager***, has a low concern for both production and people, is generally indifferent to both organizational and employee needs, and emphasizes the importance of organizational rules and regulations.

2. ***The 1/9, or country club manager***, characterized by a high concern for people but a low concern for production, tries to avoid conflict and maintain good fellowship by being nice to people even when they have performance problems.

3. ***The 9/1, or authority-obedience manager*** (originally called the task style), characterized by a low concern for people but a high concern for production, tends to concentrate on production or tasks with little regard for employee needs.

4. ***The 5/5, or the organization-man manager*** (originally called the middle-of-the-road style), characterized by a moderate concern for both production and people, tends to stress production but with an awareness that morale cannot be ignored.

5. ***The 9/9, or team manager***, characterized by a high concern for both production and people, emphasizes the integration of task and human requirements in realizing goals and objectives.

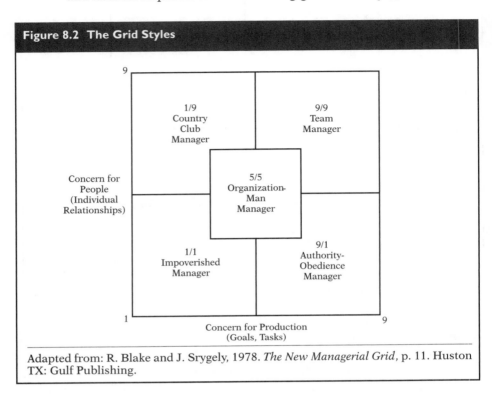

Figure 8.2 The Grid Styles

Adapted from: R. Blake and J. Srygely, 1978. *The New Managerial Grid*, p. 11. Huston TX: Gulf Publishing.

Blake and Mouton considered the 9/9 style to be the most effective followed by the 5/5, 9/1, 1/9 and 1/1. After the managerial grid was developed, they added to their study of managerial styles by identifying behaviors, or what they call elements, to further clarify what is required for effective leadership. They believe that managers should take the initiative, inquire into the background and substance of problems, and express their opinions while encouraging others to do likewise. Managers must also be adept at resolving conflict, making decisions, and critiquing or evaluating organizational activities.

Transactional and Transformational Leaders

Burns' (1978) contribution to the study of leadership combines elements of both trait and behavioral theories. He describes two types of leaders—transactional and transformational—based on how leaders and followers influence each other. ***Transactional leaders*** tend to engage in bargaining with employees, telling them what they need to do to gain rewards (pay, status, promotion) and take corrective action when performance goals or standards are not met. In effect, the organizational bargain is that managers will trade jobs, pay, promotion, and so on for good performance.

Transformational leaders tend to do more than just bargain with employees. They attempt to induce employees to accept the group or organization mission or purpose, tend to be concerned about individual needs and problems, and provide intellectual stimulation. Often, transformational leaders are both inspirational and charismatic. This type of leader tries to persuade followers to commit themselves to a cause or worthwhile purpose.

The characteristics and behavior of transactional and transformational leaders have been elaborated upon by Bass (1985, 1990, 1995) and Bass and Avolio (1991, 1993). Transactional leaders tend to clarify the responsibilities and tasks for followers and the benefits to be derived if they perform well. This type of leader develops a positive and rewarding interaction with followers and tends to "manage by exception" (e.g., only gets involved when there are problems).Otherwise, there is an absence of leadership.

Transformational leaders attempt to develop trust and an emotional connection with followers. Leaders perceived to be "charismatic" tend to be the most effective in this regard. This type of leader motivates employees by fostering a climate of trust, inspiring followers to transcend self-interest with emotional appeals to accomplish goals, and provides a stimulating intellectual environment in which followers are encouraged to question organizational processes (i.e., the way work is done). Bass and Avolio (1993) argue that the most effective leaders are both transactional and transformational.

The importance of charisma as a component of effective leadership has received increasing attention in recent years. When initially identified as an important trait of effective leadership, it suffered from problems of definition and measurement. More recently, ***charismatic leadership*** has been associated with being a "strategic thinker" and "inspirational." Some students of management also associate it with being a "visionary." As the definition of charisma has become more specific, attempts have also been made to link it to such organizational characteristics as employee group cohesion and empowerment; however, it has not been linked to improved effectiveness in organizational outcomes because there are important factors, other than leadership, that determine organizational effectiveness (Conger and Kanungo, 1998). Waldman, Ramirez, House and Puranam (2001) found that the perception of a leader being charismatic results in that leader being more effective during periods of environmental uncertainty and during the organizational adaptations that may be required (e.g., moving from traditional to community-oriented policing).

In addition to continuing problems of definition and measurement, charisma is also a function of follower perception—that is, the perception of who is and is not charismatic varies widely. And charisma without integrity may result in a decline in organizational effectiveness. In this regard, Trevino, Hartman and Brown (2000) address ***ethical leadership*** by discussing the relationship between a moral person and a moral leader. Both are important "pillars" in the development of a reputation for ethical leadership. A moral person is honest and trustworthy, "does the right thing," behaves morally in their personal life, and has a concern for people. A moral manager communicates their ethical expectations, rewards and disciplines on the basis of these expectations and becomes a role model whose actions reflect the ethical principles they advocate for the organization.

Transformational leadership and employee performance have also been linked to the employees' perception that the leader is "fair." Fairness is determined by the degree to which the employee trusts their immediate supervisor and the perception that performance will be evaluated using "just procedures." This is particularly important if employees are to become more committed to the organization and engage in the types of behavior (e.g., conscientious, courteous, altruistic) that benefit the organization (Pillai, Schiesheim and Williams,1999). In police organizations, officer productivity is closely linked to the perception that they are treated fairly by the organization. Also, police officers often believe that "management"is a major, if the not the most important, source of stress in their work. Building trust between officers and management, and the perception that they will be treated fairly, is a significant managerial challenge.

Police Behavioral Research

Pursley (1974) studied what he called traditional and nontraditional chiefs of police. He found that nontraditional chiefs were characterized by a willingness to delegate and involve subordinates in decision making. In contrast, the more traditional chiefs tended to emphasize structure (or organization goals) and wanted to control the work of subordinates.

Reams, Kuykendall, and Burns (1975) used Likert's classification of management systems (exploitative authoritative, benevolent authoritative, consultative, and participative) to determine the system of management of a model police department—that is, a department that had the attributes associated with progressive policing in the 1970s. The results indicated that such a department was operating under a consultative style (System 3), which department members agreed was the most appropriate system. Officers did not believe true participative management (System 4) was either possible or desirable in policing because authoritative leadership is necessary in some situations (e.g., crises) and to obtain acceptable levels of performance from some employees.

Auten's (1985) study of police administrators in Illinois found that about 66 percent considered themselves to be consultative managers, but about 45 percent of lower-ranking personnel thought that administrators had a more autocratic style. This difference is important because it is not uncommon for the perceptions of a manager's style to vary—that is, managers may believe they tend to use one style, but subordinates may have a different perception.

The managerial grid of Blake and Mouton has also been used to study the styles of police managers (Kuykendall, 1977: 89–102; and Kuykendall, 1985: 38–70). Although all five grid styles were used by the police managers participating in the research, the preferred styles were 9/9, 5/5, and 9/1. The styles of police managers tended to change as the managerial activity changed, and few managers maintained the same style in all managerial activities. When thinking about how to manage or planning activities, most police managers considered themselves to have a 9/9 or 5/5 style; however, when engaged in implementation or evaluation activities, their styles tended to be more varied, and many of the managers who had a 9/9 or 5/5 style changed to a 9/1 or 1/9 style. Based on the research instrument (i.e., a leadership assessment survey) that was used, police managers were "very effective or effective" when planning (primarily using 9/9 and 5/5 styles) but "less effective" when engaged in implementation and evaluation activities (tending to change to a 9/1 or 1/9 style). There was more style variation in the evaluation component of management than in other areas. This suggests that the evaluation, or control, function may be the most difficult for managers.

Stampler (1992) studied chiefs of police and their immediate subordinates in fifty-one cities. His analysis is based on elements of both trait and behavioral theories of effective leadership. This research was in part intended to determine differences between executive leadership and executive management. According to Stampler, management tends to be more associated with the technical aspects of planning, organizing, and controlling. Leadership is more associated with vision and greatness, including a commitment to organizational values, such as integrity, fairness, and concern for others. Leaders tend to make clear the expectations they have for the organization and subordinates, have a vision of the future, be honest, be aware of the needs of others, as well as being self-aware, and possess intuition.

Stampler developed a typology based on the distinction between management and leadership. A person primarily concerned with managing attempts to control the organization's resources, generates substantial paperwork, and spends most of his or her time in the office, which is in effect a command center. A leader does little if any hands-on or detailed work and is oriented toward the future rather than the present. Leaders develop a common and inspiring vision concerning the future of the organization. Based on the distinction between leadership and management, Stampler developed four types:

> *Type 1*: high leader, low manager
>
> *Type 2*: high leader, high manager
>
> *Type 3*: low leader, high manager
>
> *Type 4*: low leader, low manager

Of the 51 chiefs of police in Stampler's study, 8 were Type 1, eighteen were Type 2, 8 were Type 3, and 18 were Type 4. Interestingly, immediate subordinates did not tend to agree with the chief's perception of themselves as leaders. In general, subordinates did not believe that the chiefs emphasized leadership as often as the chiefs thought they did. In other words, when the chiefs completed the survey instrument, the style that emerged was not always the same one that resulted when subordinates were asked about the chief's leader-manager orientation. Such findings are not uncommon in leadership research. Leaders or managers often see themselves differently from the way their subordinates do.

As a result of his research, Stampler identified nine key dimensions of big-city executive leadership and executive management: four leadership dimensions and five management dimensions. The leadership dimensions apply primarily to the chief of police (or any chief executive of a law enforcement organization), and the management dimensions apply primarily to the organizational levels immediately below the chief. These dimensions are presented as in Inside Management 8.2.

Denstein (1999)studied the leadership styles of 480 Australian police executives using the transactional and transformational leadership questionnaire developed by Bass and Avolio (1991). The results indicated that police executives tend to engage in transformational leadership significantly less than other types of managers. Police leaders were more likely to engage in transactional leadership and practiced "management by exception"(i.e., do not get involved unless there is a problem) significantly more than did other managers.

Inside Management 8.2

Stampler's Leadership and Management Dimensions

Leadership Dimensions

Modeling Expected Behavior Should be an activist who inspires a shared vision of the future and who has integrity and credibility.

Exhibiting Interest and Concern: Should take the time to show interest and support for subordinates, to show that they care about others.

Serving the Community: Should spend a substantial amount of time meeting with citizens and groups, and this should be done in the company of other police personnel so that they can observe the leader's behavior. By doing this the executive "models" the type of behavior expected of all personnel when interacting with the community.

Valuing Openness and Diversity: Should be open to different points of view and value other person's opinions, and should welcome questions and criticisms about department policies and practices.

Management Dimensions

Setting Standards: Should identify expected behavior and performance in all areas of police operations. These standards should, in effect, answer the ques-

tion: "How good is good enough." Standards (goals, objectives, policies, procedures) should be nondiscriminatory, reasonable, and job related.

Keeping Promises: Should ensure that the organizational performance and officer behavior that is promised to the community is delivered as promised.

Maintaining Technical Competence: Should have a high level of technical competence in areas such as planning, budgeting, organizing, monitoring, controlling, telecommunications, and other technologies.

Thinking and Behaving Rationally: Should possess strong analytical skills and have an analytical temperament; should develop accurate and thoroughly analyzed information; should avoid emotional reactions to situations and problems.

Demonstrating Fiscal Responsibility: Should be the budget director of the organization and should be responsible for long-range planning as it relates to the budget.

Source: N. H. Stampler, 1992. *Removing Managerial Barriers to Effective Police Leadership*. Washington, DC: Police Executive Research Forum.

Engel (2000) studied the effects of supervisory style on police behavior in two cities. Four styles were identified; traditional, innovative, supportive, and active. ***Traditional supervisors*** are task oriented, expect aggressive law enforcement, are more likely to take over situations and are more likely to punish than reward subordinates. ***Innovative supervisors*** are more relationship than task oriented. They expect community-oriented activity, are receptive to change in the organization and attempt to develop the problem-solving skills of subordinates. ***Supportive supervisors*** are both relationship-oriented and protective of subordinates. This type of supervisor acts as a buffer between management and the officer. They try to inspire subordinates, encourage creativity and emphasize teamwork. The ***active supervisor*** engages in high levels of both supervisory and patrol activities. They are decisive, tend to take over situations, and, although not inspirational, have positive views of subordinates, and function as both supervisor and street officer.

The active style was found to have the most influence on patrol officers behavior (e.g., citations, use of force, police-initiated activities and community and problem-oriented activity). Engel (2000) believes this may be the result of the productivity of supervisors as they work with subordinates and "lead by example." Active supervisors are often admired by their subordinates, who may also fear this type of supervisor because they are active in holding subordinates accountable for both the quality and quantity of their work. Active supervisors also tend to clarify the expectations of subordinates, which is important for the unpredictable situations in which police officers become involved; that is, the supervisor "takes charge" when there is doubt concerning what should be done. In addition, this type of supervisor may be perceived to be charismatic.

Engel (2001), in a subsequent analysis, notes that all four styles were equally represented (about 25 percent for each type) among the 86 supervisors and managers studied. However, females are more likely to use the traditional style than are males, and non-white supervisors are more likely to use the innovative style and less likely to use the supportive style than are whites. One possible explanation for the greater use of the traditional style by females is their tendency to rely more on "rules and regulations" to control their subordinates, particularly if the female supervisors perceive their legitimacy (i.e., they deserve to be supervisors) is questioned by subordinates.

The relative effectiveness of the traditional, innovative, supportive and active supervisory styles cannot be determined outside the context of each police department, organizational goals, and community expectations. In addition, we believe that it may be more important for the manager to be able to adjust styles based on assignment, problems, and types of subordinates than it is to adopt one style.

Behavioral theories of leadership have been criticized on several grounds. The Ohio State and Michigan studies, for example, could not identify a most effective style. Increasingly, researchers found that effectiveness could not be separated from the specific circumstances (e.g., the type of group being lead or type of organization) in which the leader functioned. In the 1960s, situational or contingency theories began to emerge in an attempt to explain the complex interaction of traits, behavior, and situational variables. However, as recent research indicates, both trait and behavioral theories of leadership continue to be important.

Situational or Contingency Theories

By the 1960s and 1970s, a third major set of variables, those concerned with the managerial problem or situation, began to be influential. Research to determine which leadership styles were most effective in different types of situations resulted in the development of contingency theory.

Continuum Model

Tannenbaum and Schmidt (1973) developed one of the better-known approaches to contingency leadership, often referred to as the "authoritarian-democratic continuum." The two styles they identify are based on the degree of managerial authority and the amount of freedom exercised by subordinates. At one extreme is *boss-centered* or authoritarian, leadership style; at the other is the *subordinate-centered* or democratic style. The more managers emphasize their authority, the more likely they will be considered to have an autocratic style. The more they emphasize participation by subordinates in decision making, the more likely they will be considered to have a democratic style. At the midpoint of the continuum is the manager who makes tentative decisions but may change them in the light of feedback from subordinates. Figure 8.3 depicts the authoritarian-democratic continuum and the different stages between authoritarian and democratic leadership styles.

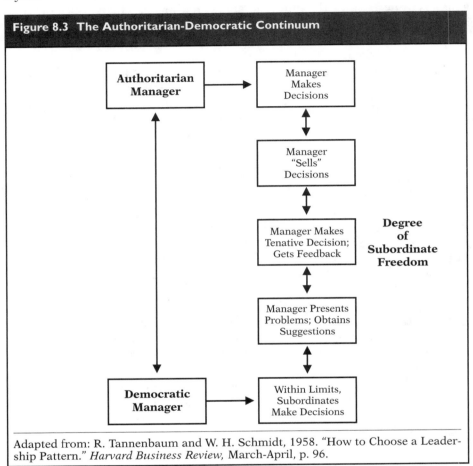

Figure 8.3 The Authoritarian-Democratic Continuum

Adapted from: R. Tannenbaum and W. H. Schmidt, 1958. "How to Choose a Leader-ship Pattern." *Harvard Business Review*, March-April, p. 96.

In determining which leadership style to employ, three important forces, or influential factors, should be considered: forces in the manager, forces in the subordinates, and forces in the situation (Roberg, 1979: 169).

Forces in the manager include his or her value system, confidence and trust in subordinates, managerial inclinations, and feelings of security. What are the basic assumptions that managers make about employees? How much participation should they allow? How much does the manager trust subordi-nates? How knowledgeable and competent are they? Is one style of manage-ment more comfortable than another style? To what degree is a manager comfortable with letting go when it comes to supervising subordinates? Is the manager secure in his or her job? Is he or she secure in terms of abilities?

Forces in the subordinate are the degree of their:

1. need for independence

2. readiness to assume responsibility for participation in decision making

3. tolerance for ambiguity

4. perceived importance of the decision or problem

5. understanding of and commitment to organizational goals

6. possession of the required knowledge, skills, and experience

7. expectation of being asked to participate in decisions

The more a subordinate possesses these characteristics, the more likely a democratic style of management would be appropriate. The more a subordinate does not possess these characteristics, the more likely that an autocratic managerial approach will be necessary.

Forces in the situation include community or environmental demands, type of organization, demands from upper levels of the organization, group effectiveness, type of problem, and time constraints. Some communities or groups external to an organization may demand or expect that the organization solve a problem or perform a service in a certain way. The community or superiors may prefer one style over another. Managers must also decide how effectively groups work together, because excessive conflict detracts from participatory problem solving. Also, if the problem is outside the knowledge, skills, and experience of subordinates, their participation in solving the problem may not be meaningful. Lastly, the manager may not have time to allow subordinates to participate.

Fiedler's Contingency Theory

Another major contributor to the situational approach is Fiedler (1967). His approach is unique because it suggests that a leader's effectiveness can be improved by structuring the job to fit his or her style. Fiedler argues that it is easier to change a leader's work environment than to change his or her style or personality. Not only does leadership performance depend on the manager, it also depends, perhaps to a greater degree, on the organization. There are a number of ways in which the working environment in an organization can be changed. Managers can be (1) given more or less authority, (2) given different types of tasks to perform, or (3) reassigned to other activities in the organization.

The basis for Fiedler's ideas is a twofold leadership style that emphasizes tasks (production, organization structure, and goals) and human relations (individual needs and goals, as well as relationships among people). Fiedler characterizes the situations facing managers by the strength of the leader-employee relationship, the degree to which the work or task is structured or spelled out, and the degree to which the leader has not only authority but also power.

A leader's style can be determined by using a questionnaire to identify his or her least preferred coworker (LPC). If the LPC is described favorably, then the manager tends to be considerate, and employee or relationship centered. If the LPC is characterized in unfavorable terms, then the manager tends to be controlling, is task or job-centered, and emphasizes structure.

When the leader-employee relationship is strong, when the work is structured, and when the leader has authority, the style should be task-oriented. In this type of situation, the leader is accepted and liked, and employees need and want direction. The leader should also use the task-directed style when situational conditions are unfavorable because employees are not motivated and need firm direction. When the tasks or activities are not highly structured, or the leader's relationship with the employees is not well established and accepted, he or she should use a relationship-oriented approach. Showing more concern for relationships and the people involved, and emphasizing cooperation in determining tasks and activities, is most effective in this type of situation. Figure 8.4 indicates the relationships between situational conditions and the appropriate leadership style of managers. There are four combinations of conditions (1-4) in which the leader should be task oriented, and four other combinations (5-8) when the leader should emphasize a relationship-oriented approach.

Figure 8.4 Fiedler's Leadership Theory

Situational Conditions	Task-Oriented				Relationship-Oriented			
	T	T	T	T	H	H	H	H
Task Structure (Structured/Unstructured)	S	S	U	U	U	S	S	U
Leader-Member Relationship (Good/Poor)	G	G	G	P	G	P	P	P
Position Power/Authority (Strong/Weak)	S	W	S	W	W	S	W	S

Adapted from: F.E. Field Fielder, 1965. "Engineer the Job to the Manager," *Harvard Business Review*. Sept–Oct., p. 118.

In 1986, Fiedler and a colleague elaborated on Fiedler's original leadership model by developing a ***cognitive resource theory***. They suggest that intellectual abilities, technical competence, and knowledge of the job are all important to successful leadership. These cognitive abilities result in the leader being able to perform managerial functions more effectively. Cognitive resources are particularly important in the task or directed leadership style, because the leader is better able to specify employee expectations, instructions, and performance standards.

Path-Goal Theory

House and Mitchell's (1975) ***path-goal*** approach is another important contingency theory of leadership. A leader's effectiveness is determined by the motivation of subordinates, ability to perform, and job satisfaction. Leaders use one or more of four types of leadership to ***clarify the paths*** by which subordinates can accomplish goals. In order to do this, leaders must take into consideration the expectations of subordinates and create the belief that performance will lead to desired results or rewards.

  ❖ ❖ ❖ ❖

  The four types of leadership are directed, supportive, participative, and achievement oriented. ***Directed leadership*** lets subordinates know what is expected of them, maintains standards of performance, and expects compliance with these standards. This style is most effective when subordinates work on ambiguous (as opposed to clear and easily understood) tasks. When expectations are unclear, the leader's role is to ensure that subordinates understand how they are to perform.

  Supportive leadership is characterized by friendliness, approachability, and concern for the needs of subordinates. This type is most effective when tasks are stressful, frustrating, or unsatisfying, because employees need psychological and emotional support more than any clarification of expectations, although that continues to be important.

  Participative leadership involves consulting with employees, asking for suggestions, and using employee input in decision making. This approach to leadership results in helping employees understand what is expected of them. It also tends to create a greater commitment to goals, a greater feeling of control, more ego involvement, and a sense of ownership.

  Achievement-oriented leadership involves setting challenging goals for subordinates and expecting them to strive hard to realize those goals. This style is based on the assumption that subordinates are responsible, work hard, and can be successful. This leadership style usually results in subordinates' striving for higher standards and having more confidence in their ability to perform effectively. This style is appropriate when employees are performing ambiguous, nonroutine tasks.

Employee-Maturity Theory

  Hershey and Blanchard (1977) argue that effective leadership is the result of the emphasis given to task and relationship behavior as they relate to different types of situations. ***Task behavior*** is defined as the degree to which leaders engage in one-way communication by explaining when, where, and how tasks are to be accomplished. ***Relationship behavior*** is defined as the extent to which a leader provides emotional support and engages in two-way communication. These two variables can be used to create four possible leadership styles: telling, selling, participating, and delegating. The types of situations can be analyzed by the degree of maturity of the employee, which is defined as the degree to which they are competent and willing to work.

  The ***telling style*** (high task, low relationship) is characterized by one-way communication, in which the manager defines the subordinates roles and tells them what, how, when, and where to perform. The ***selling style*** (high task, high relationship) uses two-way communication and emotional support to persuade subordinates to psychologically buy into decisions. The ***participating style*** (low task, high relationship) involves two-way communication and facilitating behavior to encourage shared decision making. The ***delegating style*** (low task, low relationship) lets followers run their own show. Delegating is considered to be the most effective style with employees of high maturity; participating should be used with somewhat less mature workers. For employees with low to moderate maturity, the selling style is considered most effective. When employees are organizationally immature, a telling orientation is most appropriate. The Hershey and Blanchard situational leadership model is depicted in Figure 8.5.

Figure 8.5 Situational Leadership

High	Employee Maturity: High to Moderate Style: Participating High Relationship Low Task	Employee Maturity: Low to Moderate Style: Selling High Relationship High Task
Relationship Behavior	Employee Maturity: High Style: Delegating Low Relationship Low Task	Employee Maturity: Low Style: Telling Low Relationship High Task
	Low **Task** **High** **Behavior**	

Adapted from: P. Hershey and K. H. Blanchard, 1977, *Managing Organizational Behavior*, p. 113, Englewood Cliffs, NJ: Prentice-Hall.

The original Hershey and Blanchard leadership model was revised somewhat in the 1980s by Blanchard, Zigarmi, and Zigarmi (1985). The dimensions of leadership were changed from task to directive and from relationship to supportive. Styles were determined by the degree to which leaders were both directive and supportive in dealing with subordinates. The leadership-style names were also changed from telling, selling, participating, and delegating to directing, coaching, supporting, and delegating. These new titles were thought to be more descriptive of actual leader behavior.

The new model is applied based on the degree of competence and commitment of the employee. Employees that are high in both areas are most effectively managed using the ***delegating style***. Employees with some competence but low commitment should be managed using the ***coaching style***. The ***directing style*** is considered appropriate if an employee is committed but lacks competence, and the ***supporting style*** should be used for employees with high competence but a changing level of commitment.

Police Contingency Research

Jermier and Berkes (1979) used the path-goal theory as the basis for a study of 158 police officers randomly selected from a midwestern police department of about 800 personnel. Two important factors associated with job satisfaction were (1) the degree to which leaders allowed officers to participate in decision making and (2) task variability, which means that officers enjoyed having a variety of tasks to perform. In those situations where officers were unclear as to how to perform tasks, they wanted their supervisors or managers to explain exactly what was expected (i.e., directed leadership). They also appreciated leaders who were supportive during periods of stress.

Weisburd, McElroy, and Hardyman (1988) studied the style of supervisors in the community patrol officer program in the New York City Police Department. Although these supervisors may not have been representative of the entire department, the ones in the program tended to use a form of situational or contingency leadership. As the person was being supervised or as the task was changed, the styles of the supervisors also tended to change.

Southerland's (1989, 1990) research assessed supervisor styles in one police department using the situational leadership model—called Situational Leadership II—developed by Blanchard, Zigarmi, and Zigarmi (1985). She found that, according to the model, those supervisors who tended to use the most appropriate styles were perceived by subordinates to be the best sergeants. The worst sergeants tended to use the most ineffective styles. However, Southerland also discovered that officers wanted both more direction and support than the model would indicate. In other words, many officers wanted direction and support even when the leadership model indicated that it was not really necessary.

In a survey of members of several police departments, Witte, Travis, and Langworthy (1990) found that many officers believed that participative management would improve police operations in their departments, but only those individuals in positions of power indicated they were satisfied with the level of participation in the organization. The importance of participation is underscored by the research of Wycoff and Skogan (1994), who examined how employee participation changed between 1987 and 1989 in the Madison (Wisconsin) Police Department. During this period, as previously discussed, Madison adopted the principles of quality management. As a result, participative management practices were increasingly used. Employees responded favorably to these changes as they become more satisfied with their work, the organization, and their supervisors. As employees were given more autonomy, they tended to enjoy police work more and to consider their work to be important. These changes in attitude also made the officers more receptive to suggestions for additional changes in the department.

The original contingency model of Hershey and Blanchard has also been used to study police managers. One study of 155 managers found that although they used all four styles, they were most comfortable using the telling and selling styles and reluctant to use either the participating or delegating style. Both the telling and selling styles require a high-task emphasis, and the participating and delegating styles require a low-task style. This research found that many police managers, regardless of the situation, are reluctant to give subordinates a wide latitude in how to perform their job (Kuykendall and Unsinger, 1979).

The Hershey and Blanchard contingency model has also been used to identify the most appropriate managerial style for five types of police employees (Kuykendall and Roberg, 1988). This typology, and the most appropriate managerial style for each type, was developed in discussions with approximately 400 police managers. The results are presented in Case Study 8.1.

Case Study 8.1

Police Employee Typology and Managerial Styles

Rookies are concerned with proving themselves as police officers; therefore, they are primarily interested in organizational expectations. Rookies tend to have positive work-related attitudes, are usually highly motivated, but are not very competent, in an organizational sense. From the perspective of the Hershey and Blanchard model, this type of employee is considered to be of low maturity and the most effective managerial style would be *telling*, which has a high-task emphasis. However, as the rookie proves he or she can perform the job, a selling style should be adopted.

Workers tend to be moderately motivated, have generally positive work-related attitudes, and are either moderately or highly competent. The *participating* managerial style is most effective for this type of police employee.

Stars are motivated and highly competent but may have only moderately positive work-related attitudes. Sometimes this type of employee is openly critical of organizational practices. Although the most effective managerial style for stars is *delegating*, there may be times when selling or even telling is more appropriate.

Cynics are competent, but their motivation and attitudes tend to be a function of the specific task they are performing; they think some aspects of police work are more important than others (e.g., serious crime vs. social service work). In general, they are pessimistic, suspicious and often distrustful. When an employee's cynicism gets in the way of performing his or his job, the most appropriate style is *selling*, but it may be necessary to use a telling approach if the cynic does not cooperate. There may be more cynics in police organizations than any other employee type.

Retirees and *depleted* employees may be competent but have little or no motivation, but for different reasons. Retirees are disenchanted with their jobs for personal reasons, have a lack of interest in the nature of police work, and may be close to retirement, or a combination of these. The most appropriate style for the retiree is the telling style. Depleted employees cannot be effectively managed because for emotional or psychological reasons they cannot perform effectively. Employees that are "burnt out" or "stressed out" fit into this category, and managers need to provide them with expert assistance (e.g., a psychologist) because few managers are capable of effectively dealing with such problems.

Adapted from: J. Kuykendall and R. Roberg, 1988. "Types of Police Employees: A Managerial Analysis." *Journal of Criminal Justice* 16(2): 131-138.

Police Leadership and Management

Leading police officers and departments is not an easy task. The discussion of the policing models in Chapter 3 indicates both the controversy and complexity surrounding the police role and the management of police departments. Leadership is perhaps the most important factor in the successful transition of police departments from one model to another. Although the terms leadership and management can be used interchangeably, as noted earlier, they can also be defined differently. When *leadership* is distinguished from management, leaders tend to be viewed as *inspirational role models* who identify desirable values and a vision of the future to which members of a department and the community will hopefully subscribe. Leaders are the individuals who possess the desirable values and traits others want to emulate. *Management* tends to be identified with the *more immediate and pragmatic concerns* of administering an organization, program, or work unit—that is, planning, organizing, and controlling activities.

The next two sections provide a separate discussion of leadership and management. The discussion of leadership emphasizes the role of police executives and, to a lesser degree, all officers in those departments that practice community policing. Some of the concepts discussed are also applicable to the internal management of police departments. Police executives function not only as leaders in the community but also as leaders and managers of their departments.

Police Leadership

The organizational and community activities of the police leader have historically been considered primarily the responsibility of executives (the top two or three levels) in the department. At the executive level, the leadership role is that of ***philosopher***, in which police executives engage in an intellectual discourse about the rule of law in society, the police role, police integrity, the rights and responsibilities of citizens, the appropriate policing model for a community, and solutions to crime problems, among other issues. Executives also encourage others in the community to take part in this discourse, not only because it is both their right and responsibility to participate but because by doing so both the police and citizens will become better informed.

As police departments experiment and undergo changes, the most successful police leaders will be like the ***transformational*** leader described by Burns (1978) and Bass (1985, 1990, and 1995) and Bass and Avolio (1993). Perhaps the most important characteristic of this type of leader is the ability to understand the relationship between the department and the complex environment in which police function. Based on this understanding, transformational leaders are able to develop a vision of the future for the department. They are responsible for developing and articulating a vision for improving the quality of police services. This vision must be easily understood and clearly explained to all who are affected.

A leader's vision can be professional or political or both. A ***professional vision*** is one that identifies the responsibilities of individual police officers and the most appropriate strategies and methods to accomplish goals. A ***political vision*** is one in which the leader defines the most appropriate fit for police in a democratic society that is specific to a particular time period or community. How should the police relate to the community? Should the police have an intimate or detached relationship with citizens? Which laws should be enforced and which ignored?

It is crucial that police leaders involve both the community and employees in the development of a vision, particularly if the vision requires significant changes in the behavior of employees or alters the type and frequency of services available to citizens. If there is no involvement, there is likely to be strong resistance to, and even outright rejection of, the leader's ideas. A leader's vision may be so different from that of rank-and-file police officers that substantial conflict may result.

When a vision is ordered and resistance develops, the tendency is to rely on coercion to obtain cooperation and commitment. Although this practice may result in some immediate changes, any long-term, significant changes in the department will be minimal, and more than likely, the leader's vision will be abandoned in practice even though it will persist for a time as the "official" vision of the organization. This problem continues to be serious, because any actual changes that take place do not match the rhetoric of reform of departmental and community leaders. The authors believe that it may prove to be the most serious problem in determining the effectiveness of community policing; that is, many departments will advocate community policing while making only limited attempts to actually change their organizations.

Although the political aspects of the leader's role in policing have long been recognized, community policing requires that police leaders become political activists in attempting to bring about both departmental and community change. As a political activist, a police executive can engage in both "good" and "bad" politics. Good politics is the ***politics of responsiveness***, in which the police are open, share information, and are sensitive to governmental and community inputs in planning and policy formulation. Bad politics is the ***politics of preference,*** in which community representatives and elected officials are allowed to intrude (often based on self-interest) in a nonpublic, often secretive, manner in an attempt to influence the decision making processes in the police department (Farmer, 1984).

One of the most important political and professional responsibilities of a leader is to build and maintain an alliance between police and community. Police leaders must do this while at the same time emphasizing the importance of the rule of law and impartial law enforcement in a democratic society. Of particular importance is the police relationship to minority groups. As noted previously, the police and minority groups have had recurring problems developing mutual trust and respect. The police need to make a conscious effort to understand the culture, problems, and aspirations of all identifiable groups in the community. Often, minority-group neighborhoods have serious crime and disorder problems, and if the police are not very careful about how they function in such areas, the relationship between the police and minority citizens can become adversarial, characterized by conflict, violence, complaints, fear, and distrust.

Being involved in the political processes of a community, particularly in relation to changing police departments is not without risk. Case Study 8.2 illustrates the potential political risks associated with being a chief of police.

Police Management

This section suggests some guidelines for effective management within the police department. As many of the studies in this chapter indicate, it is common for social scientists and management scientists to use typologies to identify and describe different managerial styles. Once styles are developed, the next step is to determine which style is most effective. Although numerous studies have identified the styles of police managers, there is no research that relates organizational and employee effectiveness or ineffectiveness to a particular style or styles. Despite the lack of evidence in this area, this section will provide some basic guidelines that the authors believe are consistent with the most valid and reliable research in the management area.

Police managers may be able to initially obtain effective performance by virtue of their position (legitimate power), but eventually expert and even referent power become important if higher levels of effectiveness are to be realized and sustained. Although reward and coercive power are important, both can be overused, and dependence on coercive methods can be, and often is, counterproductive. To be effective, police officers need to become capable

---

Case Study 8.2

Chief of Police Elizabeth Watson

In 1990, Elizabeth Watson was appointed chief of police in Houston, Texas. She replaced Lee Brown, who was leaving to become police commissioner of the New York City Police Department. In 1992, after approximately two years, she was terminated by a newly elected mayor. The new mayor, when explaining the reason for the termination, indicated that the new administration would be better off with a new chief so that there would be a clean break with problems of the past, even if the problems might not be Chief Watson's fault.

What problems was the new mayor talking about? When Lee Brown was chief of police in Houston he had introduced community policing to the department. This attempt at significant change had numerous critics, including many police officers and community members who believed that this community strategy resulted in slower response times and made the police less effective. Watson was Brown's protégé, had risen rapidly through the ranks of the Houston Police Department, and was a strong advocate of community policing.

Her appointment as chief of police was somewhat controversial and, coupled with her support of community policing, resulted in political problems for the mayor and city council. In fact, her appointment performance and community policing became campaign issues that in part resulted in the election of a new mayor, the one who fired Watson. Watson was attempting to carry on with the community strategy of Brown, and she did not have the support of many officers who preferred a more traditional crime-fighting approach. When Watson became a political issue that affected the mayoral race, it was almost inevitable she would be terminated.

Attempting to implement significant change in a police department may create considerable political turmoil in a community. Often, some (possibly the majority) police officers do not like the change, and some citizens and groups may also be critical if they think police effectiveness or services will be changed. Police represent a valuable resource to the community. How that resource is to be used is an important political issue. When a chief of police advocates a use of that resource that creates substantial controversy, his or her tenure in office may be short-lived.

Author's Note: After she left Houston, Elizabeth Watson became chief of police in Austin, Texas. Her successor in Houston was a male officer who held the "politically correct" views about the "appropriate" role of the police in that city. Under the new chief, Houston deemphasized its community strategy in favor of a return to increased patrolling and rapid response to calls for service; that is, an emphasis on the traditional approach to crime fighting. Interestingly, neither Brown, Watson, nor the new chief of police had any reliable and valid knowledge as to the likely long-term results of community, as compared with this policing strategy. When community policing was first introduced in Houston, evaluations indicated that it was more effective than traditionally oriented policing. When Houston returned to the old strategy, an increase in arrests and a decline in the crime rate were reported. Depending upon how the research is conducted, the measures of effectiveness that are used, and the time frame of the evaluation, it is conceivable that any one police model or strategy can be shown to be either more or less effective than another model or strategy. This is one reason why the correct use of the research process in policing is so important.

Adapted from: R. G. Hunt and J. M. Magenau, 1993. *Power and the Police Chief*, pp. 24-29. Newbury Park, CA: Sage Publications.

---

and respected, even admired, task performers before they can become effective managers.

Managers who combine legitimate with referent or expert power are often the most influential persons in a police department. Often, however, officers and managers may disagree on who has the real *expertise* in policing. The authors believe that being task competent is critical in police work. Police managers (and leaders), at all levels, must be knowledgeable about the work that their subordinates perform. One of the most frequent complaints voiced by patrol officers about managers is that managers lose their understanding of street reality and become more concerned with their political and organizational survival. From the point of view of many street cops, the

❖ ❖ ❖ ❖ higher in the organization a manager goes, the less expert power he or she possesses.

Perhaps the most desirable of the managerial styles for the police is the *team-manager* style of the managerial grid, or the ***selling (or coaching) style*** of Hershey and Blanchard, both of which reflect a high degree of concern for both the task or goal and the person or the relationships among individuals. Either style should be the basic style of the police manager but with a readiness to adjust to a more ***directed,*** or ***telling approach*** if the employee or group continues to have performance problems. It should be the style of preference when dealing with crises, or critical field situations, because employees usually want and need specific guidance. Managers should also be willing to allow subordinates almost complete freedom if they are competent, responsible, and motivated.

The work of Stampler (1992), summarized in Inside Management 8.2, also provides some important guidelines both for leadership and as a basis to assess managerial effectiveness. The authors believe that leaders or managers in a police department should adhere to the leadership and managerial dimensions developed by Stampler and have the ***capacity to use several managerial styles*** based on an assessment of the employee and situation. Given the state of the research on police leadership, more than likely this approach will result in reasonably or highly effective performance in a leadership role within a department.

The following are characteristics of management that are used in two private-sector companies, Federal Express and Levi Strauss, that provide a valuable summary of what it means to be an effective manager in police departments. Although many of the ideas have been previously discussed, it is useful to restate them because they are important to the successful operation of police departments.

1. ***Charisma and Courage (or role model):*** Behaves in such a manner that others respect and trust him or her. Believes in personal accountability for both self and others. Transmits a sense of excitement and importance about the mission of the organization and work group. Has the ability to focus on what is really important and is direct, open, and dedicated to the success of others. Coaches others to adopt these types of behavior. Stands up for his or her ideas even when others disagree. Believes that it is important for the manager or leader to do what he or she thinks is right. Does not avoid confrontation when it is necessary.

2. ***Individual Consideration:*** Regards each member of the organization as important, independent of rank or function. Treats each employee as an individual and coaches and teaches those who need assistance, particularly newcomers. Provides feedback and shows respect and appreciation (emotional support, positive feedback, and other rewards) for good work to both those who are innovative and those who support the routine activities of the organization. Uses delegation to provide learning opportunities for employees.

3. ***Communication:*** Listens to employees and makes it clear that what they have said has been heard. Continually clarifies the performance expectations of the organization, including goals and objectives. Provides clear

feedback, both positive and negative, about how employees are performing.

4. ***Intellectual Stimulation:*** Emphasizes the importance of using evidence and reasoning, rather than only personal opinion, in making decisions. Communicates new ideas to employees and encourages them to think about problems and organizational processes in new ways.

5. ***Empowerment:*** Believes that those individuals closest to the important organizational problems should have both increased responsibility and authority. Trusts employee's and delegate's problem-solving and decision making to the lowest possible level in the organization.

6. ***Diversity:*** Values the different backgrounds and ideas that are present when the organization has a diverse (e.g., diverse in gender, ethnicity, race, experience, and perspective) workforce. Encourages the expression of different points of view.

7. ***Dependability:*** Behaves in a responsible manner, including following through on assignments and keeping commitments. Not afraid to admit mistakes and accepts responsibility for his or her own actions. Can work effectively with minimal contact with his or her boss.

8. ***Flexibility:*** Provides stability when the organization is changing or there are changes in the organization's environment. Remains calm and objective even when confronted with several problems at the same time. Has the ability to remember what is important, and to make changes as new circumstances may dictate.

9. ***Judgment:*** Makes decisions based on objective evaluations of alternative courses of action. Is aware of the important assumptions, is knowledgeable about important facts, and takes human factors into consideration in arriving at logical decisions.

10. ***Integrity:*** Adheres to a formal code of ethics. Has a strong sense of professional responsibility, including a commitment to honesty, competence, and productive work. Believes in creating an organizational culture that values integrity. Personifies the ethical and moral standards of the individual and the organizational culture.

Adapted from: R. H. Waterman, 1994. *What America Does Right*, pp. 299-302. New York: W.W. Norton and Co.

Summary

The role of police managers is to balance and integrate the expectations of the community, organization, and employees. Awareness of the different types of power, the varying styles for managing subordinates, and the broader responsibility of police leaders should help managers become more effective. The stylistic tendencies of leaders can be discussed from three theoretical perspectives: trait, behavior, and situation, or contingency. Each theory has made an important contribution to the understanding of leadership effectiveness; however, the situational approach has probably been the most influential.

Research on police managers has been somewhat limited. Attempts have been made to identify traits of police leaders and also to use behavioral and situational models to describe their styles and how their styles are used. There is no conclusive research, however, that indicates which particular style or styles are most effective. Guidelines for effective police management can be developed using suggestions from all three leadership theories. However, one must be careful not to overgeneralize about effective leadership because definitions of effectiveness can vary somewhat over time and from community to community.

Discussion Questions

1. Identify and discuss at least two possible definitions of leadership.

2. Discuss the five different types of power and give examples of each one.

3. Define the trait theory of leadership and explain two examples of trait leadership research.

4. Define the behavioral theory of leadership and explain two examples of behavioral leadership research.

5. Discuss the results of the research that has used the managerial grid to study police leadership styles.

6. Define the situational, or contingency, theory of leadership and explain two examples of research on this theory.

7. Discuss the results of the research that has used Hershey and Blanchard's employee maturity theory to study police leadership styles.

8. Discuss in detail the section "Police Leadership and Management."

9. What is the appropriate professional and political vision for police in a democracy?

10. Which theory of leadership is the most appropriate for police managers to use? Explain your answer.

References

Auten, J. H. 1985. "Police Management in Illinois." *Journal of Police Science and Administration* 13: 325-337.

Bass, B. M. 1981. *Stogdill's Handbook of Leadership*. New York: Free Press.

Bass, B. M. 1985. *Leadership and Performance Beyond Expectations*. New York: Free Press.

——. 1990. *Bass and Stodgill's Book of Leadership*. New York: Free Press.

——. 1995. "Transformation Leadership Redux" *Leadership Quarterly* 6: 463–478.

Bass, B. M., and Avolio, B. J. 1991. *The Multi-factor Leadership Questionnaire*. Palo Alto, CA: Consulting Psychologists Press.

Bass, B. M., and Avolio, B. J. 1993. "Transformational Leadership." In M. M. Chemers and R. Ayman (eds.), *Leadership Theory and Research:* 49–80. San Diego: Academic Press.

Blake, R. R., and Mouton, J. S. 1964. *The Managerial Grid*. Houston, TX: Gulf Publishing Co.

——. 1968. *Grid Organization Development*. Houston, TX: Gulf Publishing.

——. 1978. *The New Managerial Grid*. Houston, TX: Gulf Publishing.

——. 1986. *Executive Achievement*. Houston, TX: Gulf Publishing.

Blanchard, K., Zigarmi, P., and Zigarmi, D. 1985. *Leadership and the One Minute Manager*. New York: William Morrow and Company.

Burns, J. M. 1978. *Leadership*. New York: Harper and Row.

Conger, J. A., and Kanungo, R. N. 1998. *Charismatic Leadership in Organization*. Thousand Oaks, CA: Sage.

Couper, D. C., and Lobitz, S. H. 1991. *Quality Policing: The Madison Experience*. Washington, DC: Police Executive Research Forum.

Davis, K. 1972. *Human Behavior at Work*, 4th ed. New York: McGraw-Hill.

Denstein, I. L. 1999. "Senior Australian Law Enforcement Leadership Under Examination." *Policing: An International Journal of Police Strategies and Management* 22:45–57.

Engel, R. S. 2000. "The Effects of Supervisory Styles on Patrol Officer Behavior." *Police Quarterly* 3: 262–293.

Engel, R. S. 2001. "Supervisor Styles of Patrol Sergeants and Lieutenants." *Journal of Criminal Justice* 29:341–355.

Farmer, D. J. 1984. *Crime Control: The Use and Misuse of Police Resources*. New York: Plenum Press.

Fiedler, F. E. 1965. "Engineer the Job to the Manager." *Harvard Business Review* Sept–Oct., p.118.

——. 1967. *A Theory of Leadership Effectiveness*. New York: McGraw-Hill.

——. 1986. "The Contribution of Cognitive Resources to Leadership Performance." *Journal of Applied Social Psychology* 16: 532–548.

French, P. Jr., and Raven, B. 1959. "The Bases of Social Power." In *Studies in Social Power*, ed. D. Cartwright. Ann Arbor, MI: Institute for Social Research. Cited in Luthans (see below), pp. 449–457.

Hershey, P., and Blanchard, K. 1977. *Managing Organizational Behavior*. Englewood Cliffs, NJ: Prentice-Hall.

House, R. J., and Mitchell, T. R. 1975. "Path-Goal Theory of Leadership." In *Organizational Behavior and Industrial Psychology*, eds. K. N. Wexley and G. A. Yurkl, pp. 177–186. New York: Oxford University Press.

Hunsaker, P., and Cook, C. W. 1986. *Managing Organizational Behavior*. Menlo Park, CA: Addison Wesley.

Hunt, R. G., and Magenau, J. M. 1993. *Power and the Police Chief*. Newbury Park, CA: Sage.

Jermier, J. M., and Berkes, L. J. 1979. "Leader Behavior in a Police Command Bureaucracy." *Administrative Science Quarterly* 24: 1–23.

Kouzes, J. M., and Posner, B. Z. 1967. *The Leadership Challenge: How to Get Extraordinary Things Done in Organizations*. San Francisco: Jossey-Bass.

Kuykendall, J. 1977. "Police Leadership: An Analysis of Executive Styles." *Criminal Justice Review* 2: 89–102.

——. 1982. "The Leadership Styles of Police Managers." *Journal of Criminal Justice* 10: 311–322.

——. 1985. "The Grid Styles of Police Managers." *American Journal of Police* 4: 38–70.

Kuykendall, J., and Roberg, R. R. 1988. "Types of Police Employees: A Managerial Analysis." *Journal of Criminal Justice* 16: 131–138.

Kuykendall, J., and Unsinger, P. C. 1979. *Community Police Administration*. Chicago: Nelson-Hall.

Lewin, K., and Lippit, K. 1938. "An Experimental Approach to the Study of Autocracy and Democracy." *Sociometry* 1: 292–300.

Likert, R. 1961. *New Patterns of Management*. New York: McGraw-Hill.

Luthans, F. 1985. *Organizational Behavior Modification and Beyond*. Glenview, IL: Scott Foresman.

National Advisory Commission on Criminal Justice Standards and Goals. 1977. *Police Chief Executive.* Washington, DC: Government Printing Office.

Pillai, R., Schiesheim, C. A., and Williams, E. R. 1999. "Fairness Perceptions and Trust as Mediators for Transformational and Transactional Leadership." *Journal of Management* 25: 897–930.

Price, B. R. 1974. "A Study of Leadership Strength of Female Police Executives." *Journal of Police Science and Administration* 2: 219–226.

Pursley, R. D. 1974. "Leadership and Community Identification: Attitudes Among Two Categories of Police Chiefs." *Journal of Police Science and Administration* 2: 414–422.

Reams, R., Kuykendall, J. and Burns, D. 1975. "Police Management Systems: What Is an Appropriate Model?" *Journal of Police Science and Administration* 3: 475–481.

Roberg, R. R. 1979. *Police Management and Organizational Behavior: A Contingency Approach.* New York: West.

Southerland, M. D. 1989. "First-Line Police Supervision: Assessing Leadership Styles." Paper presented at the Annual Meeting of Southern Criminal Justice Association, Jacksonville, Florida.

——. 1990. "First-line Supervision: Organizational Performance and Officer Satisfaction." Paper presented at the Annual Meeting of the Academy of Criminal Justice Sciences, Denver, Colorado.

Stampler, N. H. 1992. *Removing Managerial Barriers to Effective Police Leadership.* Washington, DC: Police Executive Research Forum.

Stephens, D. W. 1992. "Executive Responsibility." In *Police Management: Issues and Perspectives*, L. T. Hoover, ed., pp. 305–322. Washington, DC: Police Executive Research Forum.

Stodgill, R. M. 1974. *Handbook of Leadership: A Survey of Theory and Research.* New York: Free Press.

Tannenbaum. R., and Schmidt, W. H. 1973. "How to Choose a Leadership Pattern." *Harvard Business Review*, May–June: 162–180.

Trevino, L. K., Hartman, L. P. and Brown, M. 2000. "Moral Person and Moral Manager: How Executives Develop a Reputation for Ethical Leadership." *California Management Review* 42: 128–144.

Waldman, D. A., Ramirez, G. A. House, R. J., and Puranam, P. 2001. "Does Leadership Matter?" *The Academy of Management Journal* 44: 134–143.

Waterman, R. H. 1994. *What America Does Right.* New York: W. W. Norton and Co.

Weisburd, D., McElroy, J., and Hardyman, P. 1988. "Challenges to Supervision in Community Policing." *American Journal of Police* 7: 29–50.

White, D. B., and Bednar, D. A. 1986. *Organizational Behavior.* Boston: Allyn and Bacon.

Witte, J. J., Travis, L. G., and Langworthy, R. H. 1990. "Participatory Management in Law Enforcement." *American Journal of Police* 9: 1–24.

Wycoff, M. A., and Skogan, W. G. 1994. "The Effect of a Community Policing Management Style on Officers' Attitudes." *Crime and Delinquency* 40: 371–383.

Chapter Nine

Planning and Research

Police departments need to stay abreast of employee and community concerns and expectations, and those of other organizations and criminal justice agencies, to be able to adapt to changing conditions. Accordingly, planning and research are of vital importance in police departments. This chapter addresses important aspects of planning, the research process, and two approaches to planning. Controlling, another important managerial function, also discussed in Chapter 10, is closely associated with planning. The controlling process in management includes evaluation of the plans, identification of any performance problems, and taking corrective action, if necessary. The corrective action hopefully occurs prior to the development of frequent or serious problems. It is important to remember that although planning and controlling are discussed in separate chapters, they are closely related.

Planning and Plans

Planning is the process of deciding in advance what is to be done and how it is to be done (Kast and Rosenzweig, 1985: 478). Instead of accepting the future, managers, by planning, may be able to affect that future. Planning is essentially an intellectual process that is strongly influenced by how a manager thinks about his or her organization. One way of thinking is based on a systems theory perspective, in which the organization is considered to be a system made up of "interdependent components that work together to accomplish the aim of the system" (Dobyns and Crawford-Mason, 1994: 34).

There are at least two approaches to thinking in attempting to understand a system, analytical and synthetical. An ***analytical*** approach involves taking the system apart, trying to understand each part, then using this knowledge to understand the whole system. A ***synthetical*** approach considers all the organizational processes together to try to understand how they relate to one another and to the environment in which the system functions. Analysis will tell a manager how something is done—for example, how cars are assembled or the steps police officers go through to investigate a crime. Synthesis is more concerned with why cars are assembled in a certain manner or why police investigate crimes the way they do. Analysis asks, how does each part work? Synthesis asks, how do the parts work together?

When planning for police departments, it is important to adopt a systems thinking perspective. The police department is made up of a series of organizational processes (e.g., patrol, investigations, and communications) that interact to produce the behavior of officers, the services or outputs they provide, and the outcomes (e.g., changes in crime) that result. All these have an impact on other organizations, including criminal justice and other public and private organizations, and on individual citizens. These organizations and individuals in turn have an impact on the police department. Police leaders and planners need to understand this whole and how each part and process contributes to or detracts from what the department is trying to accomplish. Such systems thinking requires that understanding come before action (Dobyns and Crawford-Mason, 1994).

Creativity is an important part of planning. There are several different types of creativity, including imitation, inductive and deductive reasoning, and idea linking through free association. ***Imitation*** involves using plans, programs, methods, and so on developed by others; for example, one police department adopts the patrol allocation system developed by another department. If this approach is used, managers must make sure the circumstances that resulted in the development of the plan are similar. ***Inductive reasoning*** moves from the specific to the more general; for example, an increase in the number of citizen complaints may mean there are problems in police training and supervision. ***Deductive reasoning*** is just the reverse; that is, it moves from the general to the specific. For example, if an organization assumes that the primary role of the police is to maintain order, then it specifies the policies and procedures that are necessary to implement this assumption.

Idea linking is often done through free association. Individuals participating in planning are encouraged to identify any ideas, without limitations or inhibition, that might relate to the problem or plan at hand. This may result in important, innovative solutions, particularly when those involved come from different organizational levels (e.g., officer, supervisor, middle manager) and different backgrounds in terms of experience and education (Kuykendall and Unsinger, 1979). That is one reason why planning should involve as many people as possible, because it not only improves the quality of the plans but also results in a better understanding of them and often better services to the community (Rue and Byars, 1992). Figure 9.1 depicts the relationship between creativity and the different types of plans discussed below.

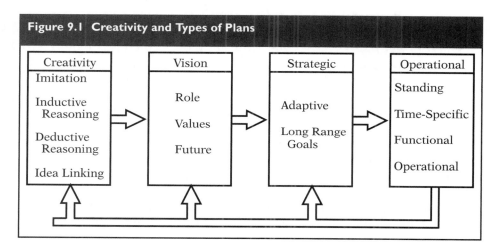

Figure 9.1 **Creativity and Types of Plans**

Types of Plans

There are numerous ways to categorize the types of plans used by police departments. *Reactive plans* are developed as the result of a crisis. A particular problem may occur for which the department has no plan and must quickly develop one, sometimes without careful preparation. *Proactive* plans are developed in anticipation of problems. Although not all police problems are predictable, many are, and it is possible for a police department to prepare a response in advance. For example, civil disorders have been common in the history of the United States; therefore, police departments, particularly in large cities, need to have a plan as to how to respond to them.

Plans can also be categorized as (1) visionary, (2) strategic, or (3) operational. *Visionary plans* are essentially statements that identify the role or mission of the police in the community and a future condition or state to which the department can aspire. A vision may also include a statement of values to be used to guide the decision-making processes in the department; however, values can also be developed later in the planning process. The concept of vision is discussed in more detail later in this chapter and, as noted in Chapter 8, is an important part of leadership.

Strategic planning for organizations includes the identification of existing and future problems in the community, the determination of the resources needed to address those problems, and the management and personnel adjustments that may be required. Strategic planning also includes identifying the internal strengths and weaknesses of the organization. In Chapter 1, four police operational strategies were identified, that is, presence, law enforcement, education, and community building. These four strategies differ from the organizational strategy because they are concerned with how to accomplish organizational goals and objectives that are the result of a strategic planning process. One of the most important aspects of strategic planning is to focus on external environmental factors that affect the goals and objectives of the department and how they will be achieved. Important environmental factors include personnel needs, population trends, technological innovations, business trends and demands, crime problems, and community attitudes. Strategic planning is important to police managers because it allows them to prepare for and deal with the changing community conditions in which their departments operate.

Operational plans are designed to meet the specific tasks required to implement strategic plans. There are four types of operational plans: (1) standing; (2) functional; (3) operational-efficiency, effectiveness, and productivity; and (4) time-specific.

Standing plans provide the basic framework for responding to organizational problems. The organizational vision and values, strategic statement, policies, procedures, and rules and regulations are examples of standing plans. Standing plans also include guidelines for responding to different types of incidents, for example, a civil disturbance, hostage situation, crime in progress, and felony car stops.

Functional plans include the framework for the operation of the major functional units in the organization, such as patrol and investigations. Functional plans include the design of the structure, how different functions and units are to relate and coordinate activities, and how resources are to be allocated (Kuykendall and Unsinger, 1979).

Operational-efficiency, effectiveness, and productivity plans are essentially the measures or comparisons to be used to assess police activities and behavior (outputs) and results (outcomes). If one of the goals of the police department is to reduce the crime rate, any change that occurs can be compared to past crime rates in the same community or crime in other communities, a state, or the nation. If the crime rate was reduced while holding or reducing costs, that would reflect an improvement not only in effectiveness but also in departmental productivity.

Time-specific plans are concerned with a specific purpose and conclude when an objective is accomplished or a problem is solved. Specific police programs or projects—such as a drug crackdown, crime prevention program, or neighborhood clean-up campaign—are good examples of time-specific plans. Another example is the budget, which represents the financial plan of a police department for a specified time period, usually one year or more.

Initially, the *budget* is an estimate of the financial costs of successfully managing the police department. After it is approved, a budget becomes a guide for the expenditure of funds and identifies the monetary constraints for the manager. The budget includes not only the available funds but also the procedures for spending the money and the methods for auditing spending. Usually, there is a budgetary plan for the entire department, each major departmental function, and each unit and program.

As one of several departments in municipal and county government, the police must compete in a political decision-making process in which each department is allocated a share of the available financial resources. The amount given to a police department is based on the funds available, the persuasiveness of police leaders and their ability to obtain political support, and an assessment of police performance. Although police budgets can be reduced or remain stable, in many communities they increase in almost every budgetary cycle because of inflation or a concern about crime and related problems.

The planning associated with budget development may only identify the costs of what already exists in and is desired by the organization. Or it may include an on-going assessment of the quantity and quality of services provided and the results of those services. The budgeting process often requires that a police department assess itself in relation to its mission in the community. It asks: What do the police do? How much does it cost? What benefits are derived? How could it be done better? How much would it cost to add or delete activities and programs? The more comprehensive the budgeting process and the more persons involved, the more useful the budget is as a planning and controlling tool to manage and improve the organization (Kuykendall and Unsinger, 1979; Sheehan and Cordner, 1995).

Planning Responsibilities

Executive managers (e.g., chief, deputy chief, sheriff, or undersheriff) are concerned about the vision of the organization, strategic planning, and long-range and general plans. They tend to spend more time on planning than those at other levels in the organization because of the need to prepare the organization to adapt to changing environmental conditions and to balance and integrate diverse expectations about police activities and behavior.

Middle managers (e.g., captains and lieutenants) participate in all types of plans and provide both general and specific plan implementation. They are particularly concerned with operational plans. Middle managers are probably the most critical persons in determining the success or failure of a plan. They need to make any adjustments that become necessary when the plan is implemented. Because it is difficult to anticipate all possible contingencies, it is common for plans to be adjusted. Making adjustments can be an important learning process because in effect an experiment is taking place. When the police decide that one approach to solving a problem is less effective than is desired and develop another approach, they are in effect developing a hypothesis based on a theory. These terms are discussed in detail in the next section.

Supervisors oversee the day-to-day activities of officers as they implement plans. Supervisors can also play a key role in gathering data concerning plan efficiency and effectiveness and in making suggestions as to how plans can be changed. In fact, supervisors, as a result of their daily interaction with operational personnel and firsthand observation of community problems, may be the most important persons in the organization in proposing new theories and hypotheses concerning police activities and behavior. In fact, the authors are inclined to believe that the success or failure of a police organiza-

tion is determined more by what supervisors (usually sergeants) do or do not
do than any other person or position in the organization.

In police departments in which there is widespread employee participation, patrol officers and investigators not only participate in the planning but
also provide feedback concerning plan efficiency and effectiveness. In some
community-policing programs, officers have the responsibility for managing
members of the community, and even employees of other organizations, in
responding to problems. This managerial role requires that officers engage in
all four functions of management: developing plans, organizing community
members, providing leadership by motivating and supervising citizens, and
evaluating and controlling.

Planning in Perspective

In an ideal world, the plans developed would always be followed and
would always produce the desired outputs and outcomes. In the real world,
this rarely happens. Police departments do not function in a stable political
and community environment, and problems and expectations are ever
changing. Although it is prudent and necessary to plan rationally, the basic
attitude toward planning should be one of flexibility. Any effective plan is
intended to anticipate or solve departmental problems. The results of the
plan are always viewed as only a temporary solution that requires periodic
reexamination. Managers and employees need to establish a mindset that
planning leads to temporary solutions to problems and that planning solutions will include problems that also require adjustments. And the problems
for which the solutions are proposed are likely to change. Thus, planning is a
continual process and an integral part of the department's and employee's
work life.

Although all planning is temporary, some plans, such as the vision, values, and strategy, basic organization structure, and standing plans, including
some policies, procedures, and regulations, are altered less often than others.
The success of planning is directly related to how much the planner knows
and how effective he or she is in communicating ideas to others. The people
primarily responsible for planning should be selected based on their education, intellectual prowess, and skills in research, analysis, and communication.

Scientific Method and the Research Process

Chapter 1 noted the importance of the scientific method and research process in police management. In many police departments, officers are increasingly being asked to participate in research projects or interpret and use data
from research studies. Community policing requires that police officers
understand and often use the scientific method to systematically acquire and
analyze data. In using the scientific method, it is necessary to (1) be knowledgeable about the problems and relationships under study, (2) understand
and be able to develop theories, and (3) be aware of and use different methods
for conducting research.

Body of Knowledge

Quality management stresses the importance of having profound knowledge about important subjects in a particular field, especially the research process, systems theory, and statistical methods and their applications. In policing, all fields of knowledge, at some point, may be useful. It is, of course, impossible for police officers to be well informed in all areas, but it is possible for them to be reasonably well informed about police research, research methods, and how statistics are used in general.

By reading important books, journals, magazines, and newspapers and attending college courses, training programs, and seminars, police officers can become and remain well informed. Recommended materials to be read on a regular basis are listed and briefly discussed in Inside Management 9.1. There are, of course, many other journals and magazines that could be listed for example, *Justice Quarterly, Criminology, Journal of Criminal Justice, Criminal Law Bulletin,* and various regional or state journals and magazines. Realistically, however, police officers are unlikely to read material from a large number of magazines and journals, and the ones listed in Inside Management 9.1 below will provide both officers and managers a substantial amount of useful information.

Inside Management 9.1

Important Sources of Information About the Police

Police Chief, published by the International Association of Chiefs of Police (IACP), is designed primarily for police practitioners. Many of the articles are written by police officers and often describe the programs and practices of police departments in the United States and sometimes in other countries.

FBI Law Enforcement Bulletin, published by the United States Department of Justice, is similar to *Police Chief* in orientation and content.

Policing: An International Journal of Police Strategies and Management (formerly known as the *American Journal of Police* and *Police Studies*) is published by MCB Press and focuses on domestic as well as international issues related to the police. *Police Quarterly,* published by the Police Section of the Academy of Criminal Justice Sciences (ACJS), is a more academic journal. Most of the articles present the results from research studies, and it also includes book reviews.

Law Enforcement News, a police newspaper published by the John Jay College of Criminal Justice in New York City, has many interesting articles, book reviews, and interviews with police concerning contemporary police issues.

Police- and criminal justice-related studies and reports are published by the National Institute of Justice (NIJ), Bureau of Justice Statistics (BJS), Bureau of Justice Assistance (BJA), Police Foundation, Police Executive Research Forum (PERF), International Association of Chiefs of Police (IACP), and the International City Manager's Association (ICMA). Information about all these organizations and their publications can be found in most public libraries.

In addition to reading these materials, police officers and managers can also become members of professional and academic organizations that hold meetings to discuss police- and criminal justice-related matters. In addition to IACP and PERF (noted in Inside Management 9.1), there are more specialized organizations, such as the International Association of Auto Theft Investigators (IAATI). All states have police professional organizations, such as the California Peace Officers Association (CPOA). There are also more academically oriented organizations, such as the American Society of Criminology (ASC) and the Academy of Criminal Justice Sciences (ACJS).

When police officers and leaders are well informed about the body of knowledge that exists in policing, they are better able to understand problems and develop and implement new or improved plans. This understanding, which includes various theories, provides the basis for explaining problems and relationships and for further expanding the body of knowledge in the field. The department becomes a learning organization whose members are engaged in a process of continual improvement of activities and behavior.

Theories and Hypotheses

How many times have you heard someone say, "It's a good theory, but it doesn't work in practice?" How many times do students in criminal justice courses say, "It's too theoretical?" In fact, there is probably nothing more practical than a good theory because the most accurate and concise statements about reality are based on sound theories.

A *theory* can be defined as a statement or a set of interrelated statements that attempt to explain and predict a phenomenon by specifying relationships between or among variables. *Variables* are concepts that can take on different values, such as different age groups or different types of crime. When these variables are converted from concept (e.g., age) to measurable form (e.g., age ranges from one to five years, six to ten, eleven to fifteen, and so on), we move from the conceptual to the empirical. In other words, the concept becomes a variable that can be measured empirically; for example, one can discover how many people there are in each age group.

In order for a theory to predict or explain a phenomenon, it must state *relationships* between variables and have measurable variables (i.e., concepts that can be quantified or operationalized). When we say that two variables are related, we mean that a change in one variable is accompanied by some degree of change in the other. An *independent variable* is the assumed cause or determining factor; a *dependent variable* is the assumed effect or result. In order to test, or confirm through research, whether a relationship exists between variables, it is first necessary to form a *hypothesis,* which can also be called a theory in testable form. A hypothesis, or hypotheses if more than one relationship is being tested, is simply a suggested explanation of the predicted relationship between the variables.

What are called hypotheses in research are often similar to statements made by police officers; for example, "If we question the suspect in a certain manner, he or she will confess." This statement predicts a relationship between an independent variable (the method of questioning) and a dependent variable (a confession). Such a statement may be based on something the officer has learned in college, in training courses, from reading, or from experience. Without proper testing, however, this predicted relationship may be true less often than the officer believes, and unless other "methods" are tried and the results systematically recorded and analyzed, the number of confessions secured may not increase or may actually decrease.

In the early 1970s, a now famous experiment was conducted in Kansas City concerning the relationship between police patrol (independent variable) and certain types of crime (dependent variable), among other variables (Kelling, Pate, Dieckman, and Brown, 1974). Prior to this study, the police had developed a theory that "visible police patrol prevents crime." Police patrol was considered to be the "backbone of policing." This theory had some limited empirical support, that is, conclusions drawn from an analysis of data gathered from a few studies that used a systematic research process.

The researchers in Kansas City formulated hypotheses concerning the relationship between different levels of police patrol and certain types of crime (and attitudes of citizens). An experiment was conducted to determine the validity of these hypotheses. It was found that different levels of police patrol had no apparent influence on the number of reported crimes. As a result of this and subsequent research, the theory that visible police patrol prevents crime began to be modified to a theory that in some situations visible police patrol may prevent certain types of crime for a certain period of time. To test this theory, it would be necessary to state it as a testable hypothesis so that the variables could be measured empirically: "In low-income areas (some situations), twice the normal levels of police patrol (a quantifiable level of visible police) will reduce the number of aggravated assaults and robberies (a quantifiable level of violent crimes) during the period that the higher levels of patrol are maintained (a certain period of time)."

Or research could be conducted that would test various levels (e.g., from normal to five times normal) of different types of patrol (e.g., proactive vs. reactive) on a specific crime (e.g., residential burglaries). Assume that this research was conducted and found that in order to have a measurable impact on the residential burglary rate, police departments would have to use proactive patrol at a level three times or more that of normal patrol. Such a finding would then become part of the body of knowledge concerning the relationship between the independent variable, patrol, and the dependent variable residential burglary. However, it would be necessary to replicate the research in different communities and areas before an acceptable theory that predicts the relationship between levels and types of police patrol and specific types of crime could be formulated and reliably used.

In the case of the patrol-crime relationship, such replications are essential, because the size and population density of patrol areas (or beats or sectors or districts) vary considerably among communities. In a large patrol area, doubling or tripling the level of patrol would increase police visibility somewhat; in a substantially smaller area, it would increase police visibility much more.

Police departments should never alter policies or practices based only on a single study conducted in one community. Instead, they should wait until the research has been replicated to ensure that any changes that are made will produce the desired result. Or a police department may elect to conduct its own experiment on a small scale to determine what changes, if any, it wants to make.

With respect to police management, there are three types of research: archival, analytical, and experimental. ***Archival research*** is another term for ***review of the literature.*** The body of knowledge about policing has grown enormously since the 1960s. Numerous articles, books, and monographs provide important insights about policing. Not all police officers and managers are knowledgeable about (not just familiar with) the research on police and important related subjects. Instead of an intellectual discourse on theories, concepts and methodologies, the police have tended to emphasize the political and technical aspects of the work. This lack of an intellectual tradi-

❖ ❖ ❖ ❖   tion has resulted in both effectiveness and efficiency problems that were, and are, avoidable.

Analytical research is concerned with "collecting and analyzing data about a condition, problem, situation, or relationship" (Cordner, Fraser, and Wexler, 1991: 335). Examples include a survey to determine the salaries and benefits of other police departments or a survey of citizen attitudes concerning a particular police activity or program or policing in general. Archival and analytical research may or may not involve the use of theories or hypotheses. They can be directed at describing something (e.g., the type of computers used in selected police departments) or answering a question; for example, how many police departments allow their officers to use their marked patrol vehicles when they are off duty? Answers can be obtained by reviewing the literature in this area or by developing a questionnaire to use in a survey of other police departments.

Experimental research is the most effective approach for convincingly demonstrating any relationship that might exist between variables. In fact, this type of research is necessary if the cause-and-effect relationship between two or more variables has either not yet been determined or is insufficiently known. For some relationships, like that between police patrol and crime, there exists a considerable body of useful knowledge, but for many other relationships in policing (e.g., does a certain policing style reduce the incidence of citizen complaints) there is less, or no, useful knowledge other than the experience of officers. Experimental research begins with a review of the literature on a given subject. Based on what is known, the researcher designs the experiment so that the results will add to the body of knowledge in that area (Cordner, Fraser, and Wexler, 1991). Inside Management 9.2 provides a list of important considerations in the design of experiments.

Inside Management 9.2

Critical Issues in the Design of Experiments

1. Choose a design and methods of investigation that are appropriate for both the problem or policy being studied and the available data. Not all problems are suitable for field experiments. The research method must fit the particular type of problem. In some cases, surveys or participant observation may be more appropriate.

2. Choose a problem or policy that employees or citizens care about or that needs improvement. Because experiments can be complicated, time-consuming, and expensive, any experiment should emphasize the more important problems in the department.

3. Consider the legal and ethical issues that may arise, including the possible consequences of the research. The research process and design should impose the fewest possible problems for those in the experiment. Unless the experiment is likely to identify less expensive or more effective alternatives, it should not be conducted.

4. Maintain the random assignment of persons, cases, or other units into treatment and control groups during the experiment because random assignment is not biased or arbitrary.

5. When researchers are used who are not part of the police department, the researcher and the practitioner should cooperate from the outset of the experiment.

6. The researcher needs to have a thorough understanding of the problem before beginning. It is important to involve all persons in the department and community who may have knowledge about the problem.

7. Experiments should be used to inform policy but not necessarily to make policy. The results of research assist the manager in deciding what course of action to follow, but there are often other considerations that may be important; for example, the action may be too expensive or unacceptable to the community. In some instances, experimental research may

result in persons being treated differently. Assume it is discovered through research that the effectiveness of the police response to domestic violence problems is influenced by the socioeconomic status of those involved. Should the police treat wealthy people differently from poor people?

8. Attempt to replicate the experiment in different settings before encouraging the adoption of more "effective" alternatives. Assume that an experiment was conducted that evaluated three different police-officer styles when giving traffic tickets, and that it was discovered that one style was more effective in terms of ensuring the cooperation of citizens. Before a policy requiring a particular style is adopted, the original experiment should be replicated several times to ensure that the style identified is in fact more effective in a wide variety of settings.

Adapted from: J. H. Garner and C. A. Visher, 1988. "Police Experiments Come of Age." *National Institute of Justice Reports*, September/October, pp. 2-8.

The remainder of this chapter discusses two approaches to planning in police departments—systematic planning and the SARA process, which is associated with community policing. Both involve the use of the scientific method and research.

Systematic Planning

The systematic planning process described in this section is sometimes called traditional planning. It identifies a step-by-step process that can be used to develop all types of plans. The authors prefer the term *systematic planning,* because "traditional" may suggest to some students that the process is outdated, which is untrue. The six steps are listed below:

1. Development of an organizational vision and strategy.
2. Identification of organizational values.
3. Formulation of structural design and operational plans.
4. Forecasting, scanning, data gathering, and analysis.
5. Identification and selection of alternatives.
6. Plan execution and control.

Some of these steps are undertaken less often than others. The first four steps would be important if a new police department were being established or if an existing department was undergoing substantial changes. The first four steps in effect provide the basic blueprint of the department; although there may be slight modifications from time to time (e.g., an arrest policy is changed), substantial changes are less frequent. The last three steps apply not only to significant changes in the organization but also to the ongoing planning process that addresses more immediate concerns and problems.

The Organizational Vision and Strategy

What is the ideal role of police in a free society? Toward what end or purpose should the police aspire? These questions are answered through the development of an organizational vision or aim. The vision is the basis for all other plans in the organization and in effect becomes the frame of reference for police decision making.

A vision should describe the role of police in the community, the basic principles that guide police behavior, the role of management, the broad standards for evaluating police behavior and performance, and the role of leadership in striving toward the realization of the vision. The Madison (Wisconsin) Police Department went through several revisions before developing a vision statement for the department. The final vision noted that the police organization was devoted to improvement, excellence, maintaining customer satisfaction, and operating by the principles of quality leadership. To do this the organization will emphasize being creative, using a systems orientation, encouraging employee participation, teamwork, data-based decision-making and being part of the community (Couper and Lobitz, 1991).

The Madison vision is primarily concerned with the management goals of the department and how it should relate to the community. It does not describe a role, or mission, for the police. This is important because the concepts of vision and strategy, and even values, can overlap. Managers should be less concerned about this overlap than about making sure that all the important areas are covered in the planning process. The development of the vision in Madison was also assumed to be the responsibility of the chief executive. The authors believe, however, that the entire organization, and the community, should be involved in vision development; otherwise, it may not be widely accepted.

After the vision is developed, a strategic plan is necessary to provide a framework for fitting the organization into the environment in which it functions. What overall approach is the most appropriate for integrating community, employee, and organizational expectations? The organization's strategy would include a consideration of a policing model, such as the reform service, and community models discussed in Chapter 3, and a managerial model. Inside Management 9.3 describes the strategy of community policing.

Inside Management 9.3
Organizational Strategy

The foundation of a successful community-policing strategy is the beneficial ties between police and community members that result in a productive relationship based on mutual trust. Community policing consists of two complementary components, community partnership and problem solving. To develop a community partnership, police must develop positive relationships with the community, must involve the community in the quest for better crime control and prevention, and must pool their resources with those of the community to address the most urgent concerns of community members. Problem solving is the process through which the specific concerns of communities are identified and the most appropriate remedies are found.

Community policing does not imply that police are no longer in authority or that the primary duty of preserving law and order is subordinated. However, using the expertise and resources that exist within communities will relieve police of some of their burdens. Local government officials, social agencies, schools, church groups, business people—all those who work and live in the community and have a stake in its development—will share responsibility for finding workable solutions to problems that detract from the safety and security of the community.

The community for which a patrol officer is given responsibility should be a small, well-defined area based on the unique geographical and social characteristics of neighborhoods. Patrol officers are the primary providers of police services and have the most extensive contact with community members. Effective community policing depends on optimizing positive contact between patrol officers and community members. Patrol officers will be assisted by immediate supervisors, other police units, and other government and social agencies. Upper-level managers are responsible for ensuring that the entire organization backs the efforts of patrol officers.

The police organization will be equally concerned about the needs and expectations of both its employees and citizens. It will create a responsive working environment that is conducive to a free and candid expression of ideas and that emphasizes preventing problems rather than blaming employees for mistakes and punishing them. The organization will continuously improve its system and processes to ensure that employee and citizen expectations are met and

to ensure that:

1. the probability of each citizen becoming a crime victim will be reduced

2. citizens will feel only minimal concern for their personal safety

3. citizens will believe they are receiving the highest quality of police services

Adapted from: Bureau of Justice Assistance, 1994. *Understanding Community Policing: A Framework for Action*, pp. 13-14. Washington, DC: U.S. Government Printing Office.

Organizational Values

The next step of the planning process identifies the fundamental beliefs of the organization. This step may be unnecessary if the values have been identified in the organizational vision or strategy statement. However, even if they are listed in earlier steps, it may be appropriate to list them separately to underscore their importance to both citizens and police employees. Inside Management 9.4 identifies the values associated with the reform and community models of policing. The New York City Police Department, as part of their strategic planning, identified basic values, listed below, that they pledged to follow when working in partnership with the community (Brown, 1991):

1. Protect the lives and property of citizens.

2. Enforce the law in an impartial manner.

3. Fight crime through prevention.

4. Aggressively pursue violators of the law.

5. Maintain a higher standard of integrity than other citizens.

6. Value human life.

7. Respect the dignity of each individual.

Inside Management 9.4

Values in Policing

Values of the Reform Model of Policing:

1. Police authority is based solely on the law. Professional police departments are committed to enforcement of laws as their primary objective.

2. Communities can provide police with assistance in enforcing the law, and helpful citizens will provide police with information to assist them in carrying out their mission.

3. Responding to citizen calls for service is the highest police priority, and all calls must receive the fastest response possible.

4. Social problems and other neighborhood is-

sues are not the concern of the police unless they threaten the breakdown of public order.

5. Police, as experts in crime control, are best suited to develop police priorities and strategies.

Values of the Community-Policing Model:

1. The police department is committed to the positive evolution, growth, and livability of the community.

2. In attempting to maintain a peaceful community, the police role involves cooperating with others in the creation and maintenance of a way of life which strikes the optimum

balance between the collective interests of all citizens and the personal rights of all individuals.

3. The police derive their authority not only from the law but also from community norms and expectations.

4. The community will be involved in all policing activities that directly affect the quality of community life.

5. The police will work with other public and private agencies to foster crime prevention and problem solving.

6. The police will be sensitive to, and show respect for, all citizens and their problems and will emphasize positive social interaction rather than just the technical application of procedures when interacting with citizens.

7. Policing strategies must preserve and ad-

vance democratic values and the constitutional rights and personal freedom of all citizens.

8. The delivery of police services should be decentralized to the neighborhood level.

9. The public should have input into the development of policies that directly affect the quality of neighborhood life.

10. The department should seek the input of employees into matters that affect employee job satisfaction and effectiveness.

Adapted from: R. Wasserman and M. H. Moore, 1988. "Values in Policing." Pamphlet, National Institute of Justice. Washington, DC: Government Printing Office. Along with other changes, the term *traditional model* was changed to *reform model*.

The importance of the values of a police department began to be recognized in the 1960s, when social science research identified the significance of the informal police organization, the socialization process in the development of officers, and the exercise of discretion. When making discretionary decisions, what values guide police officers? Research in this area suggested that many police officers held values that were in conflict with those of the department and those reflected in professional codes of ethics and legal requirements for police behavior. An example of this is the officer's values concerning how to resolve "ends–means conflicts" in policing. When is it appropriate (based on the officer's values) to ignore law and organizational policy in order to "get the job done"?

Organization Design and Operational Plans

After the vision, strategy, and values of the organization are determined—which often overlap—the organization design or structure must be determined as well as the basic guidelines for how the department is to function. This design includes an organization chart that identifies the relationships between individuals, programs, and basic functions, as well as basic guidelines for police activities and behavior (policies); the step-by-step process for carrying out tasks (procedures); and specific requirements for officers (rules or regulations).

Another activity that is often considered to be part of this stage is the development of goals and objectives (which may also be part of the vision or strategic phase of planning). As previously noted, a goal is a broad, qualitative statement of purpose; an objective is more specific, usually quantifiable, and has a time frame. Objectives are, in effect, steps toward goals that identify a direction and provide a basis for evaluation. Criteria for the development of objectives are presented in Inside Management 9.5.

Inside Management 9.5

Criteria for Developing Objectives

1. Objectives should be compatible with and supportive of goals.

2. Objectives should be expressed in terms of numbers, ratios, or percentages in order to provide a basis for evaluating results.

3. The objective should lead to improved performance. The goal of setting objectives is to obtain a high level of performance. It is always more desirable to have high expectations of employees that can be adjusted downward than to have expectations that can easily be exceeded.

4. Objectives should also be compatible and integrated. For example, a qualitative patrol objective to be more aggressive in enforcing laws in some neighborhoods may be incompatible with a community policing objective to improve relations with citizens. The problem of incompatible objectives may be one of

the most serious for police departments. It is particularly crucial when a police department is moving from one model, such as the reform model of policing, to another, such as community policing.

5. Managers must take into consideration any constraints that may exist. Are adequate resources available? Are objectives compatible with the expectations of citizens and officers?

6. Objectives are not rigid performance requirements; rather, they are adjustable targets toward which employees can strive. If objectives are not realized, it is more important to understand why than it is to "punish" the employee.

Adapted from: J. Kuykendall and P. Unsinger, 1979. *Community Police Administration*, p. 88. Chicago: Nelson-Hall.

Scanning, Data Gathering, and Analysis

While strategic planning involves preparing for anticipated changes in the community that may require police attention, *scanning* is a process in which planners and managers look for existing problems in the department and in the community. How can police managers and planners identify problems in the department and the community? One way is to assume that every process and person is less effective than is possible and that both can be continuously improved. Another way is to develop indicators of potential problems. For example, the inability to achieve an objective might be indicative that something is wrong with the objective, the person or persons charged with accomplishing it, the resources available, or the procedures used.

In scanning, *data gathering* and *data analysis* are crucial. The research process discussed earlier in the chapter is of vital importance in this step. The better the data and the analysis, the more likely the police will understand a trend or problem and be able to develop an effective response. Although all steps in the planning process are important, data gathering and analysis are probably the most important because they provide the basis for changes that may take place. One way to gather data is to conduct a survey. An example of a limited, "short form," citizen survey used by police departments is presented in Table 9.1.

Another way to gather data—called a community-needs assessment—uses a variety of research approaches. The results of a needs assessment are used to assist the police and any other relevant agency in developing a plan to respond to crime and disorder in the most effective and efficient manner. A community-needs assessment, if conducted properly, will accomplish the following:

Table 9.1   Short Form Citizen Survey

Answer the questions by circling the responses that fit your opinions.

	Strongly Disagree	Disagree	Uncertain	Strongly Agree	Agree
1. I avoid going out during the daytime because I am afraid of crime.	1	2	3	4	5
2. The police do the best job they can against crime in this neighborhood.	1	2	3	4	5
3. (Name of neighborhood) is a better place to live now than it was a year ago.	1	2	3	4	5
4. My fear of crime is very high.	1	2	3	4	5
5. Most of the crime problems in this area are caused by drugs.	1	2	3	4	5
6. There is a good chance that I will be the victim of a theft or burglary this year.	1	2	3	4	5
7. The police officers who patrol really know what's going on.	1	2	3	4	5
8. I avoid going out after dark because I am afraid of crime.	1	2	3	4	5
9. Fear of crime is very high in this area.	1	2	3	4	5
10. There is a good chance that I will be the victim of a rape or assault this year.	1	2	3	4	5
11. Most of the crime problems around here are caused by gangs.	1	2	3	4	5
12. I regularly see police officers on patrol in this neighborhood.	1	2	3	4	5
13. I am more afraid of crime than I have ever been.	1	2	3	4	5
14. Police officers hassle people too much in this neighborhood.	1	2	3	4	5
15. Most of the crime problems are caused by unsupervised kids.	1	2	3	4	5
16. The police are doing a better job in this area than they were a year ago.	1	2	3	4	5
17. The crime problem in this area is not as bad as it was a year ago.	1	2	3	4	5
18. Most of the crime in this area is caused by people who don't live here.	1	2	3	4	5
19. The police should organize sports and other programs for kids.	1	2	3	4	5

Please provide the following information as indicated.

20. What is your age ____(years).
21. Sex?   ❑ Male   ❑ Female
22. How many years have you lived in this city? ____years.
23. In the area? ____years
24. How many persons are there in your household? ____persons
25. During the last year, have you

a. been the victim of a property crime	yes	no
b. been the victim of a violet crime	yes	no
c. had a positive contact with police	yes	no
d. had a negative contact with police	yes	no
e. took steps to protect against a crime	yes	no

Adapted from: the Bureau of Justice Assistance, 1994. *Neighborhood-Oriented Policing in Rural Communities: A Program Planning Guide*, pp. 79–80. Washington, DC: U.S. Government Printing Office.

1. Document and clarify the existing crime and disorder problems in the community or a specific area or neighborhood.

2. Document citizens' perceptions concerning crime, their fear of crime, and how crime has affected their lives.

3. Assist in the identification of the conditions that are associated with crime and disorder problems and citizen concerns and attitudes.

4. Involve both citizens and the police in the process of identifying and hopefully solving problems.

5. Provide baseline data for reducing or solving problems because the extent of the problem must be known before changes can be measured.

Identifying and Selecting an Alternative

After the data have been gathered and analyzed, the possible solutions or alternatives for solving a problem must be considered. Conceptually, this includes the identification of one or more of the four operational police strategies identified in Chapter 1. Also, planners must decide if the operational strategies selected will be implemented within the existing organizational structure or if a new program or unit should be established. This step is probably the most creative part of the planning process. After alternatives are proposed, one or more must be selected. In quality management, the alternative selected is tested before it is used throughout the department. Such testing involves the use of the research process described previously.

Alternatives must also be assessed in terms of available resources, the capabilities of those expected to implement them, and general acceptance in the department and the community. An alternative solution will probably fail if there are inadequate resources to implement it, if those charged with its implementation do not have the knowledge and skills to do so, or if a substantial number of citizens or police employees are opposed.

One of the most important considerations in selecting an alternative is any political implications that may be involved. Of course, the nature of the problem makes a difference. There are few if any political implications for changing the types of report forms used by a police department, but there may be serious political implications if a change in a major police policy (e.g., use of force) is being considered.

Community policing is a good example of the importance of politics in selecting alternatives; for example, what is the best strategy for policing? Community policing has become so well accepted that it may be politically unwise to criticize it or to advocate another model or strategy for local police. This means that a certain police plan, whether it might be a particular vision, strategy, value, or policy, may gain so much support that it would be politically unacceptable to oppose it. For many politicians and police leaders, community policing is the current politically correct approach to law enforcement.

❖ ❖ ❖ ❖   **Plan Execution and Control**

In the last step, the plan is put into place. A successful plan is directly related to the process that precedes this step. Those persons charged with implementation must be committed to the plan or at least be willing to give it a try; they must be knowledgeable about the plan; be competent to carry it out; have the support of superiors and those that are affected by the changes; have adequate resources; and evaluate the plan. Evaluation is part of the control function of management. What happened when the plan was executed? Did it succeed or fail? Why? What changes should be made, if any? When police departments engage in evaluation, they become learning organizations and broaden their understanding of what works in policing. The controlling function of management is more fully addressed in Chapter 10.

Community Policing: The SARA Process

As indicated previously, community policing includes problem solving. There is a specific planning process associated with problem solving. This process, referred to as SARA, has four steps: scanning, analysis, response, and assessment. The SARA process is not unique; rather, it is an abbreviated version of the systematic planning process and is used to address specific problems in the community. Each of the four steps in this planning process is explained below.

Scanning to Identify Problems

Scanning to identify specific problems is easier if a needs assessment has been completed. Although a needs assessment does more than attempt to identify problems, it is likely that an analysis of the data obtained will indicate problems that the community would like the police to address. Scanning involves a more specific and detailed examination to provide additional information about a particular area, neighborhood, patrol beat, or a series of crimes.

A problem is not the same as an isolated incident. An ***incident-based response*** by the police focuses on a particular incident, such as a robbery or assault, without any specific attempt to connect it to other similar incidents or to those in a particular area that may be indicative of a larger problem. A ***problem*** can be defined as two or more incidents that are related to criminal conduct, that may have the potential to cause harm, or that citizens are concerned about (Spelman and Eck, 1987).

It is important to be as specific as possible in defining problems; for example, a "robbery problem" becomes "robberies committed at convenience stores at night in the Willow Glen area by what appear to be members of a certain type of gang." The more details the police have about the problem, the more likely they will be able to develop an effective response. Once a problem is identified, an effort is made to determine the underlying patterns and conditions associated with it (Bureau of Justice Assistance 1994b; Spelman and Eck, 1987).

There are a number of methods that the police can use to identify problems in the community. Inside Management 9.6 provides an example of several different approaches to problem identification.

Inside Management 9.6
Methods of Problem Identification

Calls for Service

The police can undertake an analysis of all calls to determine patterns; in particular, the police should look for repeat calls from a particular location (e.g., an area, apartment complex, bar, or person.)

Officer Observation and Experience

Experienced patrol officers are often able to identify problems. Officers know about repeat domestic calls, repeat false alarms, areas overtaken by drug activities, and other types of problems. They may also be able to identify opportunities to prevent crimes or accidents. Patrol officers, particularly foot patrol officers, who frequently interact with citizens may also learn about the problems that members of the community consider to be important.

Citizen Complaints

Problems can often be identified based on the number and types of complaints that the police receive. Complaints are made in person, by phone, and through the mail. Meetings between police and citizens are also an important source of information about possible problems. This approach is particular important in identifying the types of problems not formally reported to the police or that the police did not think are particularly important.

Crime Analysis

The analysis of crime includes a consideration of police reports and calls for service. Police reports include information about the suspect and victim, time and location, and other persons or unique circumstances. An analysis of calls for service will permit the police to identify particular types of crimes or locations ("hot spots") that may require a problem-solving response. The "hot spot" analysis is particularly important because it is quite common for many calls for service to come from a small percentage of citizens and places. For example, in one study, it was found that 50 percent of all calls came from 3 percent of the locations in the community. Another part of crime analysis is "crime mapping." which is a technique that permits to police to determine crime patterns by time and area. Larger police departments use computers for this purpose.

Community Groups

Many communities have organizations (e.g., Loyal Order of the Moose, Veterans of Foreign Wars, neighborhood associations) that the police can work with to identify and solve problems.

Surveys

There are a number of different types of surveys that the police can conduct to identify problems and to find out more about citizen opinions and concerns. Questionnaires can be used to survey the entire community or only one area or neighborhood.

Other Information Sources

Other possible sources that may prove useful in identifying problems include television, radio, and newspapers. Talk-radio shows and the editorial pages in newspapers, which include letter from citizens, may also prove useful.

Adapted from: Bureau of Justice Assistance, 1994. *Neighborhood-Oriented Policing in Rural Communities.* Washington, DC: U.S. Government Printing Office; B. Webster and E. F. Connors, 1993. "Police Methods for Identifying Community Problems," *American Journal of Police,* XII: 75-102.

Analysis

Once a problem has been identified, additional data about that problem are gathered and analyzed. In addition to the methods discussed previously, information can be obtained from victims or complainants, personal observations, discussions with other officers, interviews (with individuals and at community meetings), and existing departmental records, including arrest reports and any previous crime analysis that has been conducted (California Department of Justice, 1993: 96).

One of the first steps in the analysis is to group the data into relevant categories. Data are obtained about the victim, the offender, and the circumstances (e.g., crime scene) or environment in which the problem occurred. The behavior of victims and when, where, and why they were victimized are all important in problem analysis. The questions of importance for offender behavior include (1) the type of crime committed and the possible or actual suspects; (2) when the crime was committed; and (3) the method of operation (Bureau of Justice Assistance, 1994a). The information to be obtained about and from offenders is sometimes called an offender profile. Table 9.2 identifies the type of data that needs to be obtained to develop this profile.

Table 9.2 Offender Profile Characteristics	
Age, sex, and race	Residence/work relative to crime scene
Level of intelligence	Evaluation/analysis of the crime(s)
Sexual interests	Sequence of events during crime(s)
Social/emotional problems	Personality characteristics
Marital/relationship problems	Mood before, during, after crime(s)
Appearance and grooming	Lifestyle
Clothing style	Prior criminal history
Employment history/problems	Motive for the crime(s)
Work habits	Friends and family members

Adapted from: Federal Bureau of Investigation, 1991. "Criminal Investigative Analysis Profiling and Consultation Program." Cited in S. Gottlieb, S. Arenberg, and R. Singh, 1994. *Crime Analysis*, p. 59. Montclair, CA: Alpha Publishing.

    Another useful tool in problem analysis is ***mapping*** which involves the identification (and time)of the location of crime and related problems (e.g., number of ambulance calls). In addition to location and type of crime, a map may also include information like the percent of unemployed in an area, income levels, number of single-parent households, number of abandoned buildings, location of liquor stores, and so on. This information allows the police to relate crime trends with community characteristics that may be associated with those crimes. The map is then used to select police strategies to respond and the resources to be allocated. The more information about related conditions, the more likely the police will be able to design a response that will reduce crime and disorder and maintain that reduction (Rich, 1999).

    Mapping has become so important in police planning that the National Institute of Justice has established a Crime Mapping Research Center to conduct research and provide information about the mapping process. While essential, gathering data is a technical problem easily solved with sufficient resources. Determining what data should be collected, what the data mean, and what should be done is more difficult. Both the vision and organization strategy provide guidance on this point. The value or importance placed on each individual operational police strategy—presence, law enforcement, education, and community building—will determine how the police will respond. The more the police know about the output-outcome relationship, the more likely that the effectiveness of the organization will improve.

    Understanding the circumstances, area, and characteristics that may invite criminal activity is particularly important in the analysis of many problems. What is it about the residents, transients, traffic patterns, houses, buildings, streets, shrubbery, lighting, appearance, and so on, of an area or location that may invite criminal activity? What characteristics of an area or location make it less likely, or more difficult, to engage in criminal activity?

For each incident that is part of the larger problem under consideration it is important to understand the sequence of each incident, including what preceded the act, the act itself, and what followed. In addition, information is needed about the day, time, and location, and any crime prevention measures that had been taken. Finally, it is important to determine the apparent attitude of residents in the area and the likelihood that witnesses, if any, will cooperate (Bureau of Justice Assistance, 1994b).

Table 9.3 provides an example of the type of analytical model that is used by some police departments in problem analysis. Although this model does not include all the variables discussed in this section, it does present not only a framework for the types of data needed but also the manner it which these data can be organized.

Table 9.3	Analytical Model for Problem-Oriented Policing	
Actors	**Incidents**	**Current Responses**
Victims	*Sequence of Events*	*Community*
Lifestyle	Events prior to the act	Area affected by problem
Security measures used	Event itself	Community as a whole
Victimization history	Events after the act	Commuters and visitors
Offenders	*Physical Context*	*Public Agencies*
Physical description	Time of day	week
Identity (if possible)	Access control	if any
Lifestyle	Surveillance	if any
Third Parties	*Social Context*	*Private Organizations*
Relationship to incident	Likely cooperation of witnesses	Business and industry Personal data
		Media

Source: Adapted from California Department of Justice, 1993. "Systematic Inquiry Through S.A.R.A." In *Community Oriented Policing and Problem Solving*, p. 98. Sacramento, CA: Attorney General's Office.

Response

Deciding how to solve the problem is the most creative step in the problem-solving process. It requires a thorough analysis and an adequate understanding of the problem. Often the response may involve other public agencies. In fact, in community policing, other governmental agencies and private organizations and business are often involved. The response is limited only by the imagination and the resources of those involved and the willingness to experiment and take risks.

The response can focus on the offender, the victim, the environment, or all three. Offenders can be arrested and prosecuted, or discouraged in other ways from committing crimes (e.g., by increasing patrol or organizing a citizen's patrol). Potential victims can be encouraged to change their behavior and response to criminal incidents through education programs and training in self-defense. The characteristics of a particular area or building can also be altered to make criminal incidents less likely. Abandoned cars can be towed away, grass and weeds and shrubbery can be trimmed or removed, buildings can be painted, lighting can be improved, and residents can be encouraged to be more alert.

Assessment

Discovering the impact of the response is the evaluation phase of the SARA process. Were the goals and objectives achieved? What went right and what went wrong? What was the reaction of the citizens and the officers involved? The assessment process often involves the following:

1. comparing statistics relative to the problem before, during, and after the response

2. comparing attitudes of those involved before and after the response

3. checking with complainants to determine their changing attitudes

4. maintaining contact with other groups that are involved to determine their reaction

5. continuing to monitor the area and its problems

The use of the SARA process is ongoing in community policing. Many, if not all, communities have the kind of problems that lend themselves to this type of response. The third step, developing the response, is perhaps the most important because it is strongly influenced by the vision and strategy of the department. To be most effective in designing responses, police leaders need to think of the police role as including any lawful activity that has a positive impact on problems and that is acceptable to citizens in the community. Their role may mean organizing day-care centers for children, mobilizing citizens to clean up their neighborhoods, trying to help a citizen get a bank loan to refurbish his or her home, providing advice about personal problems, or engaging in aggressive law enforcement activities.

As stated several times in this chapter, once plans are made and implemented, they are usually evaluated to determine their impact. Evaluation is an ongoing process and is part of the controlling function in management. In police management, the term ***accountability*** is often used in addition to, or in lieu of, ***control***. The next chapter addresses the issues of control and accountability in policing.

Summary

Planning is an important managerial function and is closely related to control. Numerous types of plans are useful in police departments. Although planning is the primary responsibility of managers, all police officers may be involved in the planning process, particularly in community policing, because they may have to work with citizens to develop the plans needed to respond to a particular problem.

Two approaches to planning are discussed in this chapter. The first approach—systematic planning—identifies the stages that a planner goes through in developing, implementing, and evaluating a plan. The second approach is the SARA process that is associated with community policing. The steps in this process include scanning for problems, analyzing those problems, developing a response, and assessing the results.

Discussion Questions

1. Define and give examples of visionary and strategic plans.

2. Define and give examples of each type of operational plan.

3. Discuss the responsibilities of managers, supervisors, and officers in the planning process.

4. Discuss how managers can keep abreast of the body of knowledge in law enforcement and related fields.

5. Explain how a hypothesis is used in research and give an example.

6. Define and give examples of the different types of research.

7. Discuss the critical issues in the design of experiments.

8. Identify and explain each stage of the systematic planning process.

9. What is a needs assessment? Why is it important to community policing?

10. What is SARA? Explain its use in problem-oriented policing.

References

Brown, L. P. 1991. "Policing New York City in the 1990s." New York: New York City Police Department.

Bureau of Justice Assistance. 1994a. *Understanding Community Policing: A Framework for Action.* Washington, DC: U.S. Government Printing Office.

——. 1994b. *Neighborhood-Oriented Policing in Rural Communities: A Program Planning Guide.* Washington, DC: U.S. Government Printing Office.

——. 1993. *Problem-oriented Drug Enforcement: A Community-based Approach for Effective Policing.* Washington, DC: U.S. Government Printing Office.

California Department of Justice. 1993. "Systematic Inquiry Through S.A.R.A.," *Community Oriented Policing and Problem Solving,* pp. 97–100. Sacramento, CA: Attorney General's Office.

Cordner, G. W., Fraser, C. B., and Wexler, C. 1991. "Research, Planning and Implementation," pp. 333–362. In W. Geller (ed.), *Local Government Police Management,* 3rd ed., pp. 333–362. Washington, DC: International City Management Association.

Couper, D. C., and Lobitz, S. H. 1991. *Quality Policing: The Madison Experience.* Washington, DC: Police Executive Research Forum.

Dobyns, I., and Crawford-Mason, C. 1994. *Thinking About Quality.* New York: Times Books.

Federal Bureau of Investigation. 1991. "Criminal Investigative Analysis Criminal Profiling and Consultation Program." Cited in S. Gottlieb, S. Arenberg, and R. Singh, *Crime Analysis*. Montclair, CA: Alpha Publishing.

Garner, J. H., and Visher, C. A. 1988. "Police Experiments Come of Age." *NIJ Reports,* September/October.

Kast, F. E., and Rosenzweig, J. E. 1985. *Organization and Management: A Systems and Contingency Approach,* 4th ed. New York: McGraw-Hill.

Kelling, G. L., Pate, T., Dieckman, D., and Brown, C. E. 1974. *The Kansas City Preventive Patrol Experiment: A Summary Report.* Washington, DC: The Police Foundation.

Kuykendall, J., and Unsinger, P. 1979. *Community Police Administration.* Chicago: Nelson-Hall.

Rich, T. 1999. "Problem Solving With Maps."*National Institute of Justice Journal* Oct.: 3–8.

Rue, L. W., and Byars, L. L. 1992. *Management: Skills and Application,* 6th ed. Boston: Irwin.

Sheehan, R., and Cordner, G. W. 1995. *Police Administration,* 3rd ed. Cincinnati: Anderson.

Spelman, W., and Eck, J. 1987. "Problem-Oriented Policing." *Research in Brief,* January. Washington, DC: National Institute of Justice.

Wasserman, R., and Moore, M. H. 1988. "Values in Policing," Pamphlet. Washington, DC: National Institute of Justice.

Webster, B., and Connors, E. F. 1993. "Police Methods for Identifying Community Policing." *American Journal of Police* 12: 73–101.

Chapter Ten

Control and Accountability

Once an organization is formed and a plan is developed and implemented, control becomes important. The controlling function is the last step in the managerial process, but when a problem is identified, the three other functions—organizing, leading, and planning—are often used in an attempt to solve it. In policing, the term *accountability* is often used instead of *control*; therefore, the terms are used interchangeably in this chapter.

Control is concerned with both the police department and the individual officer. The organization is held accountable relative to both the activities and behavior of employees (outputs) and the results achieved (outcomes). The individual officer is held accountable for his or her behavior and the quality and quantity of work performed. This chapter addresses the control process for both the department and the individual officer, with the exception of personnel evaluation, which was discussed in Chapter 6, and civil liability, which is discussed in Chapter 13.

Managerial Control

One of the most important premises of an organization is that it will function smoothly; yet, it rarely does so. One of the manager's responsibilities is to engage in any reasonable process that will guide activity and behavior toward some predetermined purpose. Control means knowing what is actually happening relative to what the organization wants to happen (Rue and Byars, 1992: 458). The manager performs the function of controlling by "checking to determine whether or not plans are being adhered to, [and] whether or not proper progress is being made, [and] acting, if necessary, to correct any deviations" (Halmann, 1962: 485).

When controlling, a manager makes a comparison between a standard and the activities, behavior, and outcomes that actually occur. If it is discovered that there is a gap, deviation, or what is called a problem, the manager must analyze it to determine the causes. That done, the manager develops a solution, a plan of action, or an experiment that will hopefully solve the problem, that is, result in more appropriate or effective or efficient performance in the future.

The assumptions made about individual employees are critical in determining the managerial controlling process. At one extreme is the assumption that employees are essentially irresponsible and will take every opportunity to deviate from organizational standards. At the other extreme is the assumption that employees are basically responsible and "self-correcting" and need only proper training, supervision, and leadership to become highly effective and productive. For purposes of managerial controlling, and in the absence of compelling evidence to the contrary, managers should make positive assumptions about employees. On the other hand, it is important to remember that police organizations often have employees—from a few to a substantial number—who must be strictly supervised.

Related Concepts

To better understand the control function of management it is necessary to review related concepts, some of which were discussed in previous chapters. The *inputs* in a police department are the resources—money and time—given to it to carry out its mission. These are processed—organizational design, training, policies, and so on—and converted into the *outputs* of a police department. Outputs can be grouped into two broad categories—activities and behavior. Police *activities* are those things officers spend their time doing: writing reports, giving citations, making arrests, patrolling, conducting investigations, engaging in crime prevention, solving problems, community organizing, and so on. Police *behavior* includes the style of officers, how quickly they change styles as situations or problems change, the language they use, their tone of voice, the decisions they make (i.e., discretion), how aggressive or passive they are, how motivated, how proactive, and so on. What happens as a consequence of these outputs are called ***outcomes,*** for example, crime rates, the degree of citizen fear of crime, and citizen attitudes toward the police in general and toward specific police activities (e.g., a crime prevention program) and individual officers.

A ***standard*** is a statement or belief that identifies that which is expected or considered to be desirable. Standards may be either general or specific. The more general the standard, the more it requires interpretation by employees and managers. Standards may be written or unwritten; that is, they may be formal or informal. ***Written standards*** are usually a goal, objective, policy, procedure, rule, or regulation. ***Unwritten standards*** are often called norms or values, although formal standards may also be a reflection of the values and norms of the department. ***Norms*** provide one possible basis for decision making—for example, when officers should issue a citation. ***Values*** are fundamental beliefs about what is appropriate and inappropriate activity and behavior. Norms and values are an important part of the culture of an organization.

A ***performance indicator*** is either a direct or an indirect measure of the extent to which activity and behavior, or outcomes, conform to what is expected or desired. The number or type of citizen complaints can be used as a performance indicator (an indirect measure) of how well officers follow certain types of policies and procedures. Or the number of arrests or citations or reports written can all be used as indirect performance indicators to assess officer productivity, that is, how hard officers are working. A performance indicator can also be a direct measure of a standard. For example, if a police department had an objective of trying to respond to all crimes in progress within five minutes, the frequency with which they did or did not do so would be the performance indicator of the effectiveness of police emergency response time. Figure 10.1 depicts the relationship of the concepts described above.

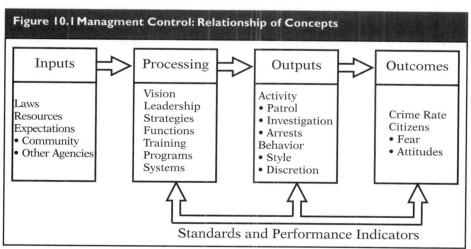

Figure 10.1 Managment Control: Relationship of Concepts

Performance indicators can be expressed either quantitatively or qualitatively. ***Quantity*** is the amount of something—money, time, percentages, rates. In general, ***quality*** is related to that which the department, peers, or members of the community consider to be desirable and effective. Qualitative standards are expressed in many policies, procedures, methods, and rules. In addition, some departments have developed specific definitions for the types of behavior, or the appropriate style, expected of officers in certain situations—for example, how to treat a citizen who does not cooperate when being given a traffic ticket.

In policing, making quality assessments often involves some degree of subjectivity. What is the appropriate style for police officers? When two officers confronted with a similar problem respond differently, which one is qualitatively superior? What is a quality police-citizen encounter? Quality assessments in police work are also based on whether or not activity and behavior conform to the unwritten values and norms of the police culture. In some departments, an officer who showed restraint in dealing with an unruly suspect would be complimented by fellow officers or superiors, although in other departments such behavior would be criticized. Differences between the managerial and street cop culture in police departments was discussed in Chapter 4.

Methods of Control

Managerial control can occur prior to, during, or after activity and behavior. **Preliminary controls** attempt to prevent a problem; for example, officers must obtain approval before conducting a search. **Concurrent controls** involve the direct observation or measure of activity or behavior as it is taking place; for example, a supervisor may oversee the investigation of a crime. **Postaction controls** involve the identification of problems after they occur (Rue and Byars, 1992).

Some of the more common methods of control include budgets, direct observation, written reports, audits, time-related analysis, and management by objectives. A **budget** is the financial plan of an organization and is used to identify how much money can be spent, and actually is spent, by the organization. **Direct observation** is built into the organizational hierarchy. Supervisors and managers at all levels should directly observe employees on a regular basis.

The use of **written reports** is quite common in police departments. Such reports can be required periodically (e.g., weekly, monthly) or as they may be needed. Reports can be analytical or informational. An **analytical report** analyzes changes such as those in the number of arrests or traffic citations as this relates to changes in the crime rate or citizen attitudes toward the police. What do the data mean and how can they be used? An **informational report** includes only information or data without analysis—for example, the number of calls for service, crimes reported, arrests and citations, and complaints.

Many organizations also use **audit** procedures in the controlling process. An audit can be conducted by an individual or group within the organization or by an outside agency. The purpose of an audit is to evaluate the entire organization or a unit or program (e.g., patrol or investigations). Some large police departments have an audit unit, which may be called a staff inspection or inspection unit, to conduct internal audits periodically or as needed.

Time-related charts are used in both planning and controlling. They identify (1) each task required to complete an activity or to accomplish a goal or objective, (2) the sequence of those tasks, and (3) the estimated time it takes to complete each one. An example of this is a program evaluation and review technique (PERT) chart. After a PERT chart has been developed and the activity is underway, the chart can be used to determine if tasks are being done in the appropriate sequence and in a timely manner.

Management by objectives, discussed in previous chapters, is another potentially useful method of control because objectives identify outputs and outcomes that are measured. Assuming the objectives are reasonable and achievable, any failure to achieve an objective indicates a possible performance problem (Rue and Byars, 1992: 466–471).

The police culture discussed in previous chapters is an important method of control because it has substantial influence on police activity and behavior. The ***culture*** of an organization "communicates how people in the organization should behave by establishing a value system conveyed through rites, rituals, myths, legends, and actions." (Rue and Byars, 1992: 438). The culture of an organization is similar to the personality of an individual. Both individuals and organizations can be characterized as aggressive, friendly, innovative, conservative, and so on. In policing, the culture of a department has become increasingly important in managerial control. Theoretically, if the culture can be changed, different values and norms will result, which in turn will produce changes in officer activity and behavior (and possibly different outcomes). Making such a significant change in a department is difficult and takes a sustained effort for many years. An organization's culture is made up of at least seven characteristics:

1. *Individual Autonomy*
How much independence and responsibility is given to employees?
What are the opportunities for exercising initiative?
How much discretion do they have?

2. *Structure*
How many policies, procedures and rules are there?
To what degree are these standards followed?
To what extent is direct supervision used to control employees?

3. *Support*
Is employee training adequate?
Do managers and supervisors assist employees?
Do managers demonstrate compassion and understanding?

4. *Identification*
Do employees identify with the organization?
Do employees identify with a particular unit or shift or group?
What are the different policing styles of employees?

5. *Performance Rewards*
Are rewards based on actual performance?
What types of rewards are utilized?
Do employees expect to be rewarded if they perform effectively?

6. *Conflict Tolerance*
What is the extent, and type, of conflict between employees?
Between employees and managers?
Between employees and citizens?
Are conflict discussions open and candid?

7. Risk Tolerance
Are employees encouraged to take risks?
To be innovative?

Police Accountability

The police are a very powerful force in society and have the potential to use that power in both constructive and destructive ways. The police are accountable to elected and appointed officials, the general public, those individuals who receive police service (e.g., victims and suspects), and other parts of the criminal justice system (e.g., prosecuting attorneys and judges). The political processes of a community, the governmental or administrative structure, and the law function to control the police department by determining the police role. The officer is controlled primarily through the structure of the department.

The methods of accountability used in police departments have the potential to improve effectiveness and efficiency and to reduce inappropriate activity and behavior. They also have the potential to reduce the productivity of officers. This is more likely to occur if the accountability methods are punishment-oriented. Only those mistakes or behaviors that are knowingly willful should be punished. Other types of inappropriate activity or behavior are more likely the result of managerial and system inadequacy than of individual failure, for example, inadequate selection, training, supervision, tools, equipment, and so on.

Another important accountability problem in policing results from the lack of knowledge about the output-outcome relationship. If the combination of operational strategies and resources invested in each strategy selected by the organization is not the most effective, then accountability becomes a process in which the resulting activity is "managed" to be more efficient. In this regard, police management may become a process in which the goal is "efficient ineffectiveness."

Police Role

The discussion of changing police models in Chapter 3 identifies different perspectives about the police role. The transition from the reform to the community model has resulted in a broader conception of the police role. The police role is developed during the initial stages of the planning process (i.e., organization vision, strategy, values, and goals). Police goals (and objectives) for the organization can be developed for both police outputs and outcomes. Output measures in the Reform Model included response time (i.e., how rapidly police respond to calls for service in general and/or to emergency situations), number of arrests and citations, percent of arrests or clearance rate (i.e., cases "solved" divided by total cases), proportional allocation of resources (i.e., resources are divided based on time and location of problems or calls for service). Outcome measures were primarily concerned with the number and type of citizen complaints and the crime rate in general, by category (property and violent) and individual crime (e.g., robbery, burglary, larceny theft). Using ***Crime in the United States***, also known as the ***Uniform***

Crime Reports, the police could compare their crime rate nationally, region-   ❖ ❖ ❖ ❖
ally, and with cities and counties of similar size.

As the Community Model of policing became more important, additional measures of accountability began to be suggested. These included the fear of crime, citizen attitudes about both the police organization and the activities and behavior of officers. Both fear of crime and citizen attitudes, discussed in Chapter 9, are measured primarily by the use of surveys conducted by the police organization or other public or private organization—for example, a university. Fear of crime is related to crime rate, the type of crime, and signs of disorder (e.g., graffiti, "run-down" buildings, abandoned cars, evidence of drug use, gang activity, and so on). Often, citizens are more concerned with minor crimes and disorder than with what police consider to be more serious crimes—for example, murder, rape, robbery. The public are not unconcerned about more serious crimes; rather, when asked, they tend to voice more concern about visible signs (e.g., graffiti) and events (e.g., drug sales or use) that affect their daily lives.

Other measures of police effectiveness have also been suggested. These measures are related to the "quality of life" in an area or neighborhood—for example, amount of graffiti, improved property values, fewer rental unit vacancies, less truancy, more businesses, new jobs, increase in citizens who use public transportation and public parks (Langworthy, 1999). Assessing the police relative to the quality of citizens' lives is based on a role conception that broadens the police mandate in the community.

As the police role has become more complicated, both the expectations of the police and the measures, or standards, used to determine their effectiveness and to hold them accountable have also increased. This results in the likelihood that both the organization and the manager will be required to invest more resources in the controlling process. Consequently, managers must determine those measures of accountability that are most meaningful. In general these include the integrity, style, competency and productivity of officers, the crime rate, and public opinions (based on systematic surveys) of the police. Future measures, especially with regard to community policing, remain to be determined.

Political Control

Public, and consequently political, concern about the police usually results from public perceptions that are shaped by opinions of community leaders, media coverage, and the experiences citizens have with officers. Although public criticism and political concern and suggested police reforms may be warranted, criticism and concern are also a consequence of the inherent role conflict of the police in a democratic society. No matter what the police do or do not do, it is not possible to exercise the police power of government in a racially diverse, economically stratified society with differing views about the causes of crime without some and often substantial criticism of the police and demands for change. This is one reason that police reform recommendations are not always based on a thorough understanding of the nature and extent of the "police problem." Rather, reformers recommend changes that are compatible with their political views about how best to police a community. The "best way" is the one that is most likely to satisfy the public, whose criticism of the police is, at times, based on unreasonable, if not irrational, expectations (e.g., shooting to wound dangerous suspects rather than shooting to kill), and prejudices (e.g., only a minority officer can effectively police a minority community).

In local law enforcement, the primary means of political control are **selection of the chief executive** (chief of police or sheriff), the **budgetary process,** and **policy.** Chiefs of police are usually appointed; sheriffs are usually elected. Whether appointed or elected, the professional competency of a prospective chief or sheriff may be less important than his or her political opinions about the role of the police. Usually, a person cannot become a police executive, no matter how competent, unless his or her views about the police role are compatible with those of political and community leaders. At the same time, it is not uncommon for a marginally qualified or unqualified person to become an executive if he or she has the politically correct perspective.

Police activities can also be controlled by reducing or increasing the budget; for example, to obtain more money a police department is told they must develop a community-policing program. Significant policies are a striking example of political control; for example, many police departments have a more restrictive use-of-force policy than is required by law. Almost all major policies about how police should exercise their discretion are the result of police self-assessment, public criticism, and, in some circumstances, political pressure to change or develop a policy to guide the police. There are numerous policies in police organizations pertaining to selection, training, and management of police that are the result of the changing political context of policing. The experiences of Houston and Los Angeles are useful to illustrate the political control of the police. In Houston, community policing was introduced in the 1980s, partly in response to public concern about inappropriate police behavior. However, community policing was not widely supported by employees in the department. In the early 1990s, the chief of police (see Case Study 10.1), who supported community policing, lost her job and was replaced with an advocate of what became known as crime-specific policing, which emphasized the presence and law enforcement police strategies. In Los Angeles, public concern about the use of these strategies, and the aggressive behavior of some officers when enforcing the law, was heightened after the Rodney King incident and subsequent civil disorder.

In other words, at approximately the same time that Houston was rejecting community policing for a crime-specific (or crime-control) approach, Los Angeles was rejecting a crime-control approach in favor of community policing. And in both cities, the supporters were able to provide "evidence" that their approach was most effective. Case Study 10.1 briefly describes the development of crime-specific policing in Houston. Case Study 10.2 discusses the Christopher Commission's assessment of the Los Angeles Police Department's crime-control departmental culture.

Case Study 10.1

From Community to Crime-Specific Policing (CSP) in Houston

Houston became a showcase for community policing in the 1980s, even though there was widespread resistance in the police department.

Numerous community-policing programs were introduced and positive results were reported. The cornerstone of the community policing initiative was neighborhood-oriented policing, which was a decentralized and personalized approach to providing a broad range of law enforcement, crime prevention, and social services to residents. Critics exhibited their disdain for neighborhood-oriented policing by referring to it as the "nobody on patrol" program. This label was intended to communicate what critics considered to be the most serious problem of community policing; that is, too few officers were patrolling and available to respond to calls for service because too much time was spent in community-policing activities, which were not considered to be "real police work."

In the early 1990s, some but not all community policing activities were abandoned in favor of CSP. Philosophically, the assumption of community policing is that law enforcement cannot make a significant difference in the crime problem because crime and disorder are a product of social and economic forces in the community. CSP is based on the assumption that law enforcement can have an impact on the crime problem and that the mission of the police is primarily related to crime and not quality-of-life issues, including social and physical disorder in the community.

Strategically, CSP includes proactive, aggressive patrol, and proactive crime specific investigation efforts. For the police, neighborhood security, not the quality of life, is the primary police mission. Examples of CSP activities include parole-violator apprehension programs, saturation patrol in certain areas, and zero-tolerance patrol, which means that even minor violations of the law are not tolerated. Saturation patrol involved increases of four to six times the usual patrol levels.

After initiating CSP, Houston experienced dramatic reductions in the crime rate: however, crime rates also declined nationally and in other Texas cities during the same period. There is evidence to suggest, however, that the drop in crime was even more dramatic in Houston. Although there are numerous factors that can explain a significant drop in crime (e.g., the prison population increased rapidly in Texas and some other states during this period), one possible explanation is that CSP is more effective than community policing. [Authors' Note: Any dramatic decline in the crime rate may be the result of changes in police reporting or arrest practices. Evidently, this was not the case in Houston, where special efforts were made to ensure that reporting practices were not changed.]

Source: "Crime Specific Policing in Houston," 1994. *Telemasp Bulletin*, Texas Law Enforcement Management and Administrative Statistics Program, Vol. 1 (December). Huntsville, Texas.

Case Study 10.2

The Organization Culture of the Los Angeles Police Department

According to the Christopher Commission, the LAPD has an organizational culture that emphasizes crime control over crime prevention. This crime control approach (similar to the reform model) includes an emphasis on the aggressive detection of major crimes and a rapid response to calls for service. Patrol officers are rewarded for the number of calls and arrests and for being "hard-nosed." Individuals whom officers consider to be "suspicious" are frequently stopped and questioned.

This approach to policing results in numerous situations in which citizens and the police are in conflict. Citizens will often complain of officers being rude and disrespectful, and when citizens question the police about being stopped, officers may become even more aggressive and use some form of verbal or physical coercion. One possible consequence of increased police-citizen conflict is that the police become more isolated from the communities and the people they serve.

The commission recommended that the police department adopt a community policing orientation to replace the crime control approach. The values of community policing, most fundamentally restraint and mutual respect, are most difficult to incorporate into the behavior of officers . . . [operating in a crime control] system. [Officers] . . . are trained to command and to confront, not to communicate . . . and are expected to produce high citation and arrest statistics and low response times. . . . [Consequently, officers] do not . . . also have the time to explain their actions, to apologize when they make a mistake, or even to ask about problems in a neighborhood. Community policing concepts, if successfully implemented, offer the prospect of effective crime prevention and substantially improved community relations. "[To be successful] community-based policing . . . must be an attitude, a culture . . . that has its threads going through the whole fabric of the organization. Community-based policing . . . should have the effect of 'humanizing' officers' perceptions of those whom they police . . . increase the effectiveness of the police and diminish the tension between the public . . . [and officers]."

Source: Independent Commission on the Los Angeles Police Department, 1991. *Report*, pp. 104-105. Los Angeles: California Public Management Institute.

In both Houston and Los Angeles, these two approaches to policing (i.e., community and crime-specific) were cast as being at odds in order to provide a standard against which to measure that which existed—that is, a department that critics claimed had serious problems. As a rule, the most important factor in determining a reformer's political ideology relative to the role of the police is the assumptions made about the causes of crime. In Houston, critics argued that community policing had failed and needed to be replaced with crime-specific policing. In Los Angeles, critics argued just the reverse. The reforms recommended in both cities were based more on the political ideology and biases of reformers than on systematic analysis and objective and substantial evidence that one approach is more effective than the other. In general, conservatives prefer "criminals" to be cited, arrested, and punished, whereas liberals do not want the police to enforce laws except for the most serious crimes, preferring instead prevention, community policing, and other more "humane" solutions.

Professional Control

What is a profession? To be considered a profession, an occupation must have a rigorous selection process, a body of knowledge developed primarily from the use of the scientific method (i.e., systematic, reliable, and valid research), extensive education and training, and a code of ethics that identifies, for members, their responsibilities and also provides guidelines for ethical behavior.

The professional process attempts to control behavior by teaching members how to perform their jobs—that is, how to be most effective. Also, the code of ethics of the profession provides an important frame of reference for the exercise of discretion. Ideally, in a profession the members *internalize* the skills and values of that profession; that is, they are both competent and believe in the values reflected in the code of ethics. A personal commitment to competency and a professional code of ethics are probably the most effective control mechanisms in policing.

Administrative Control

Police departments are only one of several organizations in local government. The police are supervised by either elected or appointed officials. Sometimes there will be a police commission that supervises the police. Administrative control includes an evaluation of both the police department and employees. The specific measures of control are concerned with both the outputs (activity and behavior) and outcomes (crime rates, fear levels, and attitudes of citizens).

Internal Administrative Control

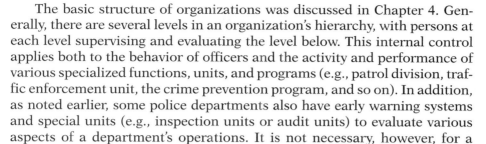

The basic structure of organizations was discussed in Chapter 4. Generally, there are several levels in an organization's hierarchy, with persons at each level supervising and evaluating the level below. This internal control applies both to the behavior of officers and the activity and performance of various specialized functions, units, and programs (e.g., patrol division, traffic enforcement unit, the crime prevention program, and so on). In addition, as noted earlier, some police departments also have early warning systems and special units (e.g., inspection units or audit units) to evaluate various aspects of a department's operations. It is not necessary, however, for a department to have a specialized group to conduct audits; in smaller police departments they can be conducted by one supervisor or manager on a part-time basis.

Early warning systems, or *"EWS"* are data-driven programs designed to identify officers whose behavior appears to be problematic and to attempt to get those officers some kind of intervention, usually in the form of counseling or training (Walker, Alpert, and Kenney, 2001: 199). The basis for the development of EWS is research that found that a relatively small percentage of officers (2 to 11 percent) are responsible for a substantial percentage (about 40 to 60 percent) of the behavioral problems of officers (e.g., incivility, excessive force, incompetence). Most often, the number of complaints, by both citizens and other officers, and the frequency of the use of force, are used as indicators to identify *"problem" officers*; that is, officers who have an unusual or disproportionate (i.e., compared to the average or norm of all officers) number of indicators within a certain time period (e.g., month, year) are targeted for intervention (Walker, Alpert, and Kenney, 2001).

Departments that employ an EWS tend to report a reduction in the number of complaints; that is, the "problem" officer adjusts his or her activity and behavior in such a manner that the number of problem indicators declines. Whether this reduction is related to a decline in productivity (i.e., less activity) or an improvement in behavior is unknown. There are several factors other than the inappropriate or incompetent behavior of the officer that determine the number of indicators of problem behavior. The area in which the officer works and the shift (time of day) and work rate are all important. These three factors often determine the level of activity, the types of strategies employed by the police, and the frequency of conflict with citizens. Even the racial and ethnic mix of an area when compared with the race or ethnicity of the officer may be influential. Do white officers who work in African American areas get more complaints? Do Hispanic officers who work in white areas get more complaints?

If a police organization is effectively managed, does it need an EWS? It can be argued that in a well-managed organization, supervisors should know when and how often their officers are engaging in inappropriate activity and behavior. EWS proponents argue, however, that no management system is perfect, that an EWS provides another, and important, accountability mechanism. And further, that an EWS has a positive impact on public opinion and may result in a reduction in the number of civil suits.

An *audit* involves assessing a representative sample of a particular type of police activity or program. For example, a department may elect to utilize undercover decoys to arrest muggers or rapists. Yet, these types of programs often result in police abuse of force and an increased risk to officers. An audit of this program would involve taking a representative sample of the arrests made by officers and interviewing witnesses, defendants, officers, and other interested parties to check on officer behavior. This type of audit can be used for any police activity and may identify problems that need to be addressed.

Research and development units can also become involved in the controlling process. They are concerned not only with the development of budgets, policies, procedures, methods, and rules but also with the evaluation of particular programs, functions, or units. Depending on the size of the department, the number of specializations or functions (e.g., patrol, investigations, or traffic) can be few or numerous. In addition, many police departments have programs, such as a crime prevention program or a community-policing activity, in a particular area. Whether it is a function, unit, or program, the process of evaluation is similar. In conducting evaluations, there are several important considerations:

1. Is the activity ***reaching the intended audience***? For a major departmental function like patrol, the concern here is how patrol resources are used. It is important for police departments to be able to analyze the problems in the community and allocate their resources so that those problems are addressed in the most effective possible manner.

2. Is the activity being ***properly delivered***? This question relates to the competency, motivation, and integrity of personnel. Are they knowledgeable and skilled? Do officers need to be retrained? How motivated are they? Do they believe in what they are doing? Do they make an honest effort to do the work they are expected to do?

3. Is the activity ***efficient***? Is the department getting the optimum return for the money invested? What is the relationship between the outputs (or outcomes) and the money it cost to achieve them? How does the cost compare with other police departments? How does the cost compare with past costs in the department? How can the activity be made more efficient?

4. Is the activity ***effective***? To what degree are goals and objectives accomplished? This may be the most important part of the evaluation process. The significance of the relationship between what police do and what happens as a result has been previously discussed. If goals and objectives are related to police outputs, then effectiveness is more easily determined because the police have more control over what they do. If they are stated in the form of outcomes, there must be an understanding of the relationship between what police do and what happens as a result; otherwise, measures of effectiveness are less significant (Berk and Rossi, 1990: 66–78).

Employee Control

The managerial basis for controlling individual officers is related to changing ideas about how to organize and manage police departments; how-

ever, most management schools of thought have essentially the same control process:

1. Both the exclusion and inclusion, or selection, of certain "types" of individuals for the department

2. Training programs to provide the methods and skills to perform according to existing standards (e.g., ethics, law, policy, and so on) through an officer's career

3. Supervision of officer behavior to guide, motivate, evaluate, and ensure compliance with standards

4. Some form of counseling, retraining, or discipline for individuals who deviate from those standards

The primary differences in managerial control systems are the nature of the selection and training process, the extent and specificity of the standards provided, the degree to which employees participate in establishing standards, and the reaction of supervisors and managers to deviations. All police departments are obligated to follow the laws that are applicable to their jurisdiction; however, the type, nature, and extent of other types of standards, like policies, vary among departments. Theoretically, the more officer participation is allowed in setting standards, the more likely it is that officers will follow those standards.

Productivity. Another important issue in the control of individual employees is their productivity. The variations in arrest practices of officers in New York City provide a useful illustration. During the first seven months of 1994, it was discovered that:

1. About 25 percent, or 7,900 officers, made no arrests.

2. About 47 percent, or 14,852 officers, made one or two arrests.

3. About 18 percent, or 5,900 officers, made between 2 and 13 arrests.

4. About 9 percent, or 2,948 officers, made 14 or more arrests (*Law Enforcement News*, September 30, 1994). Printed with permission from the *Law Enforcement News*, John Jay College of Criminal Justice.

There are at least four possible reasons for officer differences in arrest productivity: (1) the career aspirations of each officer, (2) the officer's assignment relative to the opportunity to make arrests, (3) officer indifference or incompetency, and (4) supervision and management. In addition, few or no arrests can be indicative of an officer's perception that they have been or will be unfairly criticized by the public or managers. This fear may result in a belief that is not uncommon in some police departments—that is, "many arrests, many problems; few arrests, few problems; no arrests, no problems".

Of course, the degree to which the arrest data in New York City are considered to be indicative of a productivity problem is influenced by the philosophy of the department (e.g., crime-specific vs community policing). In community policing, few arrests would probably be considered a positive indication that many officers were using more educational and community-

❖ ❖ ❖ ❖   building strategies, rather than the law-enforcement strategy alternatives in problem solving.

This argument was used by police leaders in Los Angeles to explain the sharp decline in arrests and traffic citations between fiscal year 1990–91 and 1994–95. The number of arrests (from 290,000 to 189,000) decreased by 35 percent, and the number of traffic citations (from 617,621 to 385,210) dropped by 37 percent (*San Jose Mercury News*, 1996). This decline probably had less to do with community policing than it did with the unwillingness of officers to enforce the law, particularly in the aftermath of the Rodney King incident and public demands that more officers be punished for their real and imagined misdeeds. More than likely, many officers were afraid that if they continued to enforce the law and write frequent traffic citations and if citizens complained, they would be made an example of by the new chief in order to appease the public. In other words, the police *culture* was changed but not by community policing; instead, the employees adopted the "few arrests, few problems; no arrests, no problems" attitude.

Appropriate Behavior. Another important issue in the control of individual officers is the appropriateness of police behavior. There are essentially six methods that managers can use to ensure appropriate behavior: selection and training; proscriptive and prescriptive standards; effective supervision and management; changing the culture; leadership modeling; and adoption of an explicit ethical frame of reference. The selection process and training, the police culture, and effective supervision and management have already been discussed. Ethical issues are addressed in Chapter 11.

Police departments need both proscriptive (what not to do) and prescriptive (what to do) standards. An example of a ***proscriptive standard*** is a policy in which the police can use deadly force only when their life or someone else's life is in immediate danger. An example of a ***prescriptive standard*** is a policy in which police officers are required to make arrests in certain situations (e.g., domestic violence). Usually, there are more proscriptive than prescriptive standards in police departments, but increasingly departments are training officers how to intervene in a variety of situations.

The leaders in a department may become ***role models,*** and employees may adopt their values, behavior, and approach to problem solving. However, there are many considerations in the selection of police leaders other than whether they are the types of individuals that police officers will admire, respect, and emulate. It is quite common for a substantial number of officers in a department to hold some police managers in low regard because they are considered to be immoral, incompetent, autocratic, not supportive, or "politicians" more concerned about their survival than the interests of the department and subordinates. If police managers are to become role models, they must be selected for their integrity, competency, communications skill, and ability to inspire confidence and trust.

Managerial Responses to Problems

The reaction of managers to an officer's deviation from standards varies. They may (1) ignore it, (2) act formally or informally, or (3) protect the officer. Just as some officers are incompetent or indifferent to their responsibilities, so are some managers. Such a manager often does not look for or ignores deviations because they require him or her to evaluate and respond to the performance of an individual or group. Because a response is often difficult and may involve considerable conflict and controversy, a manager may elect to ignore the problem unless forced to respond.

A manager's ***formal responses*** include counseling or training (e.g., advising or teaching the person how to improve) or some type of disciplinary action (e.g., reprimand, suspension, demotion, or termination). As noted above, the political climate of a community (e.g., its concern over excessive use of force) can also influence the reaction of police managers to officer deviations. The more public criticism there is of certain types of police behavior, the more likely managers are to use some form of punitive discipline. Some managers like to make an example of an employee in order to send a signal to other officers that certain types of behavior will not be tolerated. However, employees may consider this type of managerial response to be politically motivated and unfair. From the employees' point of view, they are being made scapegoats to satisfy political interests.

If a manager believes a deviation exists but has insufficient evidence to act formally, an ***informal response*** might be employed. Most commonly, it involves transferring an employee to a new work or area assignment. Certain types of assignments can be used so often in a department that they may become known as punitive assignments (e.g., foot patrol on a beat with the least interesting activities). In some instances, if the problem is related to the behavior of the officer when interacting with the public, the officer may be assigned to a job with minimal public contact. In addition, the manager may hope that this type of informal, punitive control will result in a resignation or retirement. Although often used by police managers, we do not recommend this type of "informal" response.

Managers may be aware of a deviation but elect to protect the individual involved for at least five reasons: The manager may (1) approve of the "deviant" activity or behavior; (2) believe that the most likely department response will be too punitive; (3) be influenced by the so-called code of silence in policing; (4) believe that acknowledging the deviation will result in criticism of the manager; or (5) simply want to avoid dealing with a problem by denying that it exists.

Review of Police Behavior

The response of the police department to complaints is another important method of management control. All departments have some way of responding to citizen complaints about methods and officer behavior. In many small and moderate-sized departments, their response may be the part-time responsibility of only one officer, probably a supervisor or manager. In larger departments, it has been the practice to establish a unit, often called ***internal affairs*** or ***professional standards,*** to respond to complaints.

The exclusive reliance upon the police to investigate themselves has long been controversial. Those who advocate that the "police should police the police" believe that it is a management prerogative to do so and that it can be done effectively. Critics of this approach believe that the police are often inclined to cover up and protect brother and sister officers accused of wrongdoing. As a result of this type of criticism, some communities have created methods to review police activities and behavior externally.

External review is usually called either civilian review or civilian oversight, although the actual name used in a specific city may be different. Some communities have a police commission or board that is responsible for overseeing the police department. A commission usually consists of prominent members of the community who are appointed for a specified term. In some instances, the police commission is responsible for the external review of at least some citizen complaints, although in some communities there is both a police commission and another organization for civilian review.

Arguments for external review include beliefs that police misconduct is widespread or frequent enough to be a problem; that more thorough and fair investigation of complaints against officers is needed; and that it will deter officer misconduct, improve public attitudes toward the police, and promote police professionalism. Arguments against external review include the beliefs that police misconduct is not a serious problem; it will deter effective police action, which will result in a decline in public satisfaction; and that it will undermine police professionalism (Walker, 2001:55).

There are basically four approaches to external review:

1. A civilian review board employs civilians to investigate complaints filed against officers. Findings of the investigation, and recommendations about possible courses of action, are made to the police chief or sheriff. However, the police are usually not required to follow the recommendations.

2. Police officers investigate complaints against officers and make recommendations to the chief executive. The results of the investigations are given to the civilian review board, which then reviews the investigations and may make additional recommendations.

3. Police officers investigate complaints and make recommendations, but if the complaining party is not satisfied, then he or she may appeal to a civilian group or board.

4. A civilian monitor is appointed to evaluate the investigations of complaints conducted by police officers and to make recommendations about the appropriateness of those investigations. In addition, this auditor or monitor makes recommendations concerning how the investigations of complaints can be improved. (Walker and Wright, 1995: 1–3)

Since the 1970s, the number of police agencies that have established some type of external review has increased; however, the percentage of agencies with external review is very small and is limited primarily to the largest police agencies (Walker, 2001: 6). The extent to which external review has resulted in actual reductions in inappropriate police activity and behavior, or improved police performance, is difficult to determine. Although external review may change the public's perception of the police, it is uncertain whether it reduces the extent to which the police abuse their authority. If officer morale is affected in a negative way, and officer productivity declines, external review may contribute to both a less effective and less efficient organization.

Legal Control

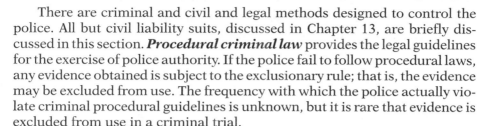

There are criminal and civil and legal methods designed to control the police. All but civil liability suits, discussed in Chapter 13, are briefly discussed in this section. ***Procedural criminal law*** provides the legal guidelines for the exercise of police authority. If the police fail to follow procedural laws, any evidence obtained is subject to the exclusionary rule; that is, the evidence may be excluded from use. The frequency with which the police actually violate criminal procedural guidelines is unknown, but it is rare that evidence is excluded from use in a criminal trial.

If a police officer's inappropriate behavior is illegal, he or she may be ***criminally prosecuted*** for violation of one or more ***substantive laws***, which define criminal conduct at both the state and federal levels. In addition to being prosecuted for a specific crime, officers may also be prosecuted by the federal government if the criminal act was associated with, or motivated by, a desire to violate the ***civil rights*** of the suspect. Civil liability is discussed more fully in Chapter 13.

In some states, officers may also be ***decertified*** by the state agency that certifies them to practice policing in that state. All states have some type of state standards organization that identifies the requirements (e.g., selection, training, performance during a probationary period) that an individual must meet before becoming a sworn police officer. If the inappropriate behavior of an officer is serious enough, the officer may be decertified; that is, he or she can no longer be a police officer anywhere in that state.

Control in Community Policing

All the control processes and methods discussed so far are important for community policing. One planning and control process suggested for community policing identifies a series of questions to be answered. They are listed below.

1. To what degree has the police department engaged community residents, businesses, and other organizations in a discussion about the ***identification*** of important crime and disorder problems?

2. Have those persons and organizations affected by the problem been ***involved*** in a problem-solving process?

3. Have those persons and organizations affected by the problem been involved in ***solutions*** to solve the problem?

4. Have the police identified the ***roles*** to be played by individuals and organizations—both public and private—in the problem-solving process?

5. What is the ***frequency and quality*** of the interaction of the police with citizens and organizations in the problem-solving process?

6. How are the solutions to problems to be ***monitored*** and ***who*** is to do this monitoring?

7. Are the **roles** of the police, citizens, and organizations in the monitoring process clearly **defined** and **understood?**

8. If the monitoring process identified **problems,** what, if anything, was done about those problems?

9. What **impact** was there on the problem?

10. How is **satisfaction** with the results or **effectiveness** of the problem-solving effort to be determined?

11. If the results are not considered to be "satisfactory" or "effective," what are the **reasons?**

12. What was **learned** from the problem-solving activity and how could it be improved?

13. What was the overall impression of the extent of **cooperation** between police and citizens in the problem-solving process? How could the interaction be **improved?** Did the process contribute to **mutual respect** and **understanding** between the police and the community? (Adapted from California Department of Justice, 1992: 87–91)

To successfully incorporate problem solving into the department, there must be a standard by which to compare what exists with what is desired. This comparison allows the manager to make changes prior to (preliminary controls) and during (concurrent controls) the solution to the problem. After the solution has taken place, postaction control becomes important.

Problem Analysis in Controlling

One of the most difficult and important aspects of management involves the determination of the reasons for an unacceptable deviation from an organizational standard and what to do about it. In quality management, it is assumed that some variation in performance is inevitable, and as long as it is within an acceptable range, there is no cause for concern. Deviation analysis asks the following types of questions: What is the problem? Why does it exist? What should be done about it? The search for the answers to these questions often results in the manager becoming more knowledgeable about both his or her organization and management. It also gives the managers and employees the opportunity to be creative. The remainder of this chapter identifies and discusses four steps that can be used in defining and analyzing problems in controlling.

Step 1: Pre-Problem Solving

The first step is to ask, does a deviation really exist? Deviation is an unacceptable gap between that which is expected and that which occurs. There are, in general, six possible "deviation gaps" that managers may have to address:

1. **The Citizen Expectation—Organizational Performance Gap.** For example, citizens expect the police to provide a given level of patrol in their area and that level of patrol is not provided.

2. ***The Citizen Expectation—Officer Performance Gap.*** For example, residents of a particular area believe that one or more officers harass them too much.

3. ***The Organizational Standard (policy or procedure)—Officer Activity Gap.*** For example, a police department requires its officers to patrol their beats in a certain manner, but one or more officers do not do so.

4. ***The Organizational Standard (policy or procedure)—Officer Behavior Gap.*** For example, the police department requires that officers explain to citizens the reason(s) why they are being detained or arrested, but one or more officers does not do so.

5. ***The Organizational Standard (objective)—Output Gap.*** For example, the department requires officers to give a certain number of citations, and one or more officers does not do so.

6. ***The Organizational Standard (objective)—Outcome Gap.*** For example, the police hope to be able to reduce the crime rate a certain amount, but that does not happen.

Does an important and significant gap exist, one that requires attention and that can justify the resources (money and time) necessary to identify the reasons for the problem and attempt to solve it? It is important at this step to attempt to quantitatively measure the gap if possible. If the problem is qualitative, it may be more difficult to measure the gap, because the definition of the problem will be more subjective and more open to debate and disagreement. It is possible that after appropriate consideration and analysis, managers may decide that little, if any, action is necessary (Van Gundy, 1981: 18–21).

Step 2: Definition and Analysis

The second step in deviation analysis is the definition of the problem. The more information the definition includes, the more structured the problem is and the more likely that the causes can be determined and solutions found. Examples of increasingly structured problem statements are provided below:

1. Some of the officers in our department are not very productive.

2. Several officers on the evening shift are not adequately patrolling their beats.

3. Officers Smith, Jones, and Austin, who work on the evening shift in beats 10, 11, and 12, are not patrolling the new construction sites in their area.

As the problem becomes increasingly well defined, some of the reasons for it may become apparent. For example, in example three given above, it may be known that Officer Smith has personal problems, that new construction sites have security guards, or that beat 10 is very large. However, even if the problem is well structured, all the information needed to determine the causes of the problem will probably not be known. To obtain further information, numerous problem-analysis methods can be employed. Two of these are discussed below.

❖ ❖ ❖ ❖   ### Dimensional Analysis

Problems can be analyzed in terms of five possible dimensions: substantive, spatial, temporal, quantitative, and qualitative. The **substantive dimension** is concerned with whether something being done should be stopped or changed, or whether something that is not being done should be. Dimensional analysis addresses substantive problems by asking four questions:

1. To what degree is it a problem of attitudes or actual behavior?

2. Is the problem one of cause or effect? Is the present problem the cause of a more serious problem or is it the actual problem?

3. How serious is the problem? Is it threatening to the well-being of employees or the effectiveness and efficiency of the organization or is it a relatively minor problem?

4. How visible or invisible is the problem? Is the extent of the problem known or is some or all of it hidden?

The **spatial dimension** of a problem is related to its actual location. Is the problem close by or far away? Exactly where does the problem exist? Is it isolated or widespread? The **temporal dimension** is related to "time" aspects. Is the problem about to happen, or has it already happened. Has the problem been in existence a long time, or is it only recent? Is the problem constant, or does it come and go? If it comes and goes, how often and when does it occur?

The **quantitative dimension** of the problem is concerned with identifying the number of times the problem occurs or if it is a single problem or more than one problem. How many people are involved? Can the problem be expressed in amounts; that is, frequency, percentages, size, and so on. How complex is the problem and can the complexity be measured? The **qualitative dimension** is related to the importance of the problem when compared to the values of the organization or to its survival (Van Gundy, 1981). Major brutality and corruption scandals threaten a department's survival in the sense that some police officers may lose their jobs and may actually be sent to prison if convicted of a crime.

Kepner-Tregoe Problem Analysis

One of the more interesting approaches to analyzing problems was developed by Kepner and Tregoe (1976). This process involves not only the analysis of the problem but also the selection of one or more solutions. However, only that part of the process related to problem analysis will be presented here. Kepner and Tregoe identify seven steps in the analysis process, which have been consolidated into five steps:

1. Compare what managers hope will happen with what is actually happening.

2. It is quite common for managers to be confronted with more than one problem to analyze and solve. It is, therefore, necessary to establish priorities and then select the problem to be addressed. First, the manager must determine which deviations in performance are acceptable and which are more serious. Then, he or she must determine if some problems are similar and can be grouped together. Finally, for all the problems requiring atten-

tion, the manager establishes priorities in terms of each problem's seriousness, urgency, and growth potential (i.e., is it likely
to increase or get worse).

3. Now that the problem for analysis and action has been identified, the manager must develop a specific definition of the problem, when and where it occurs, how extensive it is, and who is involved. The more specific the definition of the problem, the more
likely that limits can be determined.

4. Once the problem is specified, the manager attempts to distinguish between what the problem is and what the problem is not.
This distinction assists the manager in his or her search for clues
as to the causes of the problem. Just as one asks questions about
time, frequency, and location, one also determines who is not involved and when and where and under what circumstances the
problem does not happen.

5. The manager uses the characteristics in the previous step to begin to identify the possible causes of the problem. For example, it
may happen only on the evening patrol shift in one part of town
during the weekend, and it does not happen on other shifts, in
any other part of town, or during other times during the week.
What is unique about these differences? Could it be the personnel? Could it be that the problem is specific to that time and area?
At this stage the manager makes deductions from the available
evidence and begins to formulate a hypothesis that may explain
the cause-and-effect relationship.

Step 3: Generating Ideas

The third step in defining and analyzing the problem is the generation of
ideas about the solution. The planning phase of the planning-control cycle
begins with this step. There are two basic approaches to the generation of
ideas about how to solve the problem or problems that have been analyzed.
Managers may choose either to use ready-made solutions, if they are available, or to develop new solutions, using, for example, the brainstorming techniques described in Chapter 9. If a ready-made solution is used, the manager
must be certain that it will fit the particular problem. For example, if a police
department believed that they were having an inadequate impact on the
crime rate (an unacceptable deviation), they might elect to adopt the patrol
practices of another department that claimed they had a significant impact
on crime. If, however, the two communities were substantially different in
important ways, then it is likely that the results would be different. It is not
always necessary to completely adopt the methods of one or more police
departments to solve problems. If a manager is knowledgeable about a variety of approaches, then several different methods could be combined (Van
Gundy, 1981).

❖ ❖ ❖ ❖   **Step 4: Selection and Implementation**

After identifying the possible solutions for a problem comes the fourth step, selecting one or more of these solutions. Solutions should be evaluated in terms of (1) their acceptance by those involved; (2) the availability of the money, personnel, and information required; (3) the time available to choose a solution relative to the time required for carrying it out; (4) the difficulty of the solution relative to the knowledge and skills of those responsible for its implementation; and (5) the possible results of using a solution compared with the desired result. In other words, when is the problem "solved" (Van Gundy, 1981)?

Once the solution has been selected, the implementation and control phase begins. It is important to remember that the proposed solution is really one or more hypotheses that state what is likely to happen to the problem if that solution is implemented. For example, "A 50 percent increase in the number of one-person patrol units will improve the response time to emergency calls by an average of two minutes or more." The evaluation of the results of increasing the number of one-person units will determine if the hypothesis would be accepted or rejected. If rejected, then a search for solutions to the response time "deviation" would have to continue, or the department would have to decide that the problem no longer required attention.

Summary

Control and planning are two of the major managerial functions and are closely related. Control involves comparing that which exists with that which is desired. If the comparison indicates a significant "deviation," then a managerial response is necessary. Managers should be aware of several important concepts relative to control, particularly efficiency and effectiveness and outputs and outcomes. Police managers need to know how these concepts apply to police departments. One of the most interesting aspects of the control process is the analysis of the deviations that occur. There are numerous approaches that managers can use to analyze problems.

Control in police departments is concerned with both the department and the individual officer. Departments are evaluated in terms of the degree to which they accomplish goals and objectives; officers are assessed in terms of their activities and behavior. The political processes and the administrative structure of the community, as well as legal methods and the police department's structure and management practices, and professionalism, are all part of the control process. Within the department, the extent to which officers subscribe to professional values and the departmental culture is also important. When a department is engaged in community policing, a number of unique evaluation issues need to be considered.

Discussion Questions

1. Define managerial control and give an example of its use.

2. Define and give examples of police activities, behavior, outputs, and outcomes. Discuss all four in terms of both efficiency and effectiveness.

3. Distinguish between preliminary, concurrent, and postaction controls and give examples of each one.

4. What is an organization's culture? Why is it important to police departments? Give examples of the values that might exist in a police department's culture.

5. Explain how administrative and political processes in a community interact to control a police department.

6. What is an early warning system and how does it work?

7. Discuss what you consider to be the most important aspects of controlling relative to community policing.

8. Should police departments have some type of external review? Explain your answer.

9. What is deviation analysis and how does it apply to the managerial function of control?

10. Compare and contrast dimensional analysis and the Kepner-Tregoe methods of problem analysis.

References

"Arresting Statistics." 1994. *Law Enforcement News*, September 30: 3, 10.

Berk R. A., and Rossi, P. H. 1990. *Thinking About Evaluation.* Newbury Park, CA: Sage Publications.

Bureau of Justice Assistance. 1993. *Problem-Oriented Drug Enforcement.* Washington, DC: U.S. Government Printing Office.

———. 1994. *A Policy Guide to Surveying Citizens and Their Environment.* Washington, DC: U.S. Government Printing Office.

California Department of Justice. 1992. *Community Oriented Policing and Problem Solving.* Sacramento, CA: California Department of Justice.

Crime-Specific Policing in Houston. 1994. *Telemasp Bulletin.* Texas Law Enforcement Management and Administrative Statistics Program. Vol. 1 (December). Huntsville, Texas.

Halmann, T. 1962. *Professional Management: Theory and Practice.* Boston: Houghton Mifflin.

Independent Commission on the Los Angeles Police Department. 1991. *Report.* Los Angeles: California Public Management Institute. Also known as the Christopher Commission.

Interview with Police Chief Robert Ford. 1996. *Law Enforcement News*, September 15: 11.

Kepner, C. H., and Tregoe, B. B. 1976. *The Rational Manager.* Princeton, NJ: Kepner-Tregoe, Inc.

"L.A. Arrests Plunge Since King Beating." 1996. *San Jose Mercury News*, March 14: 3B.

Langworthy, R. H. ed. 1999. *Measuring What Matters: Proceedings from the Policing Research Institute Meetings.* Washington, DC: National Institute of Justice.

Robbins, S. P. 1984. *Essentials of Organizational Behavior.* Englewood Cliffs, NJ: Prentice Hall.

Rue, L. W., and Byars, L. L. 1992. *Management: Skills and Application*, 6th edition. Boston: Irwin.

San Jose Mercury News. 1996. April 20: 3.

Van Gundy, A. B. 1981. *Techniques of Structured Problem Solving.* New York: Van Nostrand.

Walker, S., and Wright, B. 1995. "Citizen Review of the Police, 1994: A National Survey." *Fresh Perspectives,* Pamphlet. Washington, DC: Police Executive Research Forum.

Walker, S., Alpert, G.P., and Kenney, D. J. 2001. "Early Warning Systems For Police." Pp. 199–215 in R. G. Dunham and G.P. Alpert eds. *Critical Issues in Law Enforcement.* 4th ed. Prospect Heights, IL: Waveland.

Walker, S. 2001. *Police Accountability: The Role of Citizen Oversight.* Belmont, CA.: Wadsworth.

Wasserman, R., and Moore, M. H. 1988, "Values in Policing." *Perspectives on Policing,* Pamphlet. Washington, DC: National Institute of Justice.

Chapter Eleven

Behavior, Safety, and Stress

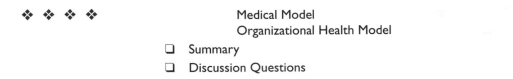

The most important issue in policing is the behavior of officers. Although the frequency of behavioral problems varies over time and between communities, there have always been numerous officers who engage in illegal and unethical conduct, use unnecessary and excessive force, and do little work. Concern about police behavior is the major reason why police organizations are criticized. If police managers are to be effective, they must have a thorough understanding of police behavior. The first section discusses theories of police behavior, variables that influence the exercise of discretion, and the use of force. This is followed by discussions of officer safety and officer stress, which are important factors in police behavior.

Police Behavior

Worden (1995) identifies three theoretical approaches to explaining police behavior: sociological, psychological, and organizational. *Sociological theory* tends to emphasize the dynamics of police-citizen interaction. Police officers, as a result of their training and experience, tend to view situations in a certain manner and act accordingly. Most of the research in this area has attempted to identify external factors that influence an officer's discretion. *Psychological theory* is primarily concerned with the "police personality." Officers may have a certain type of personality prior to employment, or their personalities may change as a result of their police experience. One of the most interesting approaches that is used to describe the police personality can be found in the considerable research that has attempted to identify the different styles of officers. A "style" is a description of an officer in terms of his or her attitudes, outlook, and approach to police work. *Organizational theory* suggests that it is the police department and the organizational culture that are the most important considerations in police behavior. Police work has both an occupational and an organizational culture. Not only are there occupational beliefs shared by many officers (e.g., many criminals are "assholes"), each department also has its own culture (e.g., how hard to work) (Worden, 1995).

Theories of police behavior can also be grouped into four other categories: predispositional, socialization, attitudinal, and situational. The *predispositional theory* is based on the importance of the officer's experiences prior to employment. If an officer is dishonest or honest, or brutal or temperate in the use of force, he or she was probably predisposed to engage in this type of behavior before joining the police. The *socialization theory* is based on the officer's experiences after employment. This theory suggests that the police experience is so influential that behavior is determined primarily by training, organizational experiences, and peers, rather than by pre-employment personality. *Attitudinal theory* is concerned with an individual's motives for becoming a police officer and with attitudes and personality traits of individuals both prior to and after employment. ***Situational theory*** ❖ ❖ ❖ ❖ attempts to explain police behavior in terms of the characteristics of the situations in which police become involved, such as the behavior of suspects (Lester, 1995).

In general, research on police behavior indicates that police officers, contrary to conventional wisdom, are not psychologically homogeneous, intensely loyal to one another, or preoccupied with order; nor are they necessarily suspicious, secretive, cynical, conservative, or authoritarian. Their attitudes tend to be diverse relative to both their functions and their means of performance. The police socialization process does not necessarily result in officers having the same outlook; rather, it results in divergent attitudes (i.e., sentiments and behavioral tendencies) and values (i.e., fundamental beliefs) (Worden, 1995).

Perhaps the most common type of research on the outlook of police officers has been attempts to identify a typology of police styles. A style characterization indicates the officer's beliefs about the role of the police, the most important police tasks, and how to interact with citizens. Muir (1977) identified distinct styles adopted by police officers, and these styles varied by their passion and perspective. Passion was defined as how comfortable the officer was with the use of authority and coercion, and perspective was the degree of compassion the officer had for citizens (including offenders). Officers were identified as being the ***professional***, the ***enforcer***, the ***reciprocator***, or the ***avoider***. Professionals had a high level of passion and perspective, meaning they had compassion for citizens and were comfortable with the exercise of authority. Professionals understood that coercion was part of policing but when possible attempted other means of persuasion rather than the exercise of authority. Muir felt these officers were the ideal types. Enforcers had a high level of passion but a low level of perspective. Enforcers were quick to exercise authority and use force during encounters with citizens and did not care to understand the human perspective of the job. Reciprocators had a high level of perspective but a low level of passion. In other words, these officers were uncomfortable with the exercise of authority. In order to reduce the opportunity to use coercion, the reciprocator attempted to gain cooperation from citizens through negotiation. In this regard, reciprocators may be very similar to social workers. Finally, avoiders had a low level of both passion and perspective. Not only were they uncomfortable with the exercise of authority and coercion, but they also failed to have compassion for citizens. Like their label implies, they attempted to avoid situations that may have required them to interact with citizens.

This simplistic effort to group police behavior using two or more variables is often applied by social scientists to subdivide a problem; for example, the behavior of officers. Rarely does any one officer's behavior completely fit a style. Rather, styles tend to overlap and vary, depending on the type of work and the resulting adjustment, education, years of experience, personal problems, and the nature of the situation. Police styles will be further discussed later in this chapter.

❖ ❖ ❖ ❖ **Research on Police Behavior**

Worden (1995) classifies the perspectives of police behavior into nine categories. These categories, except for coercion, which is addressed later, are consolidated into five categories and discussed below.

Perspective on Human Nature

Research on human nature has tended to focus on the degree to which officers are cynical. Cynicism may be generalized (i.e., one's world view may be cynical) or focused (i.e., directed at the criminal justice system, some part of the system, or a problem). Cynical police officers tend to be pessimistic, suspicious, and distrustful, believing that individual choice (not circumstances) determines whether a person is good or bad or deserving or undeserving. The important issues here are the degree to which a person is cynical prior to employment; the extent to which the police experience determines the extent of cynicism; how cynicism changes over time; and how it influences officer style, discretion, integrity, and productivity.

Role Orientation

Opinions of police officers about their role vary. Some see themselves as crime fighters who deter crime by making arrests and issuing citations. Others believe that the police role involves not only fighting crime but also problem solving, crime prevention, and community service. It is not clear, however, exactly what experiences determine a particular officer's role orientation. More than likely, prior to employment, it is the media and the views of family and friends, some of whom may already be police officers. After employment, it is both the organization's approach to policing and the influence of peers. In addition, some officers tend to develop their own perspective about the police role, irrespective of the organization and peers.

Legal and Departmental Restrictions

What are the beliefs of police officers concerning the violation of legal or departmental restrictions? Some officers believe that the ends justify the means in policing, often because they think that legal and policy guidelines are too restrictive, resulting in criminals going free and thereby increasing crime and victim suffering. In addition, some officers believe that the criminal justice system is not punitive enough, so if there is to be "any justice," they must "punish" the criminal, even if it involves inappropriate officer behavior.

Clientele and Selective Enforcement

The opinions of citizens and representatives of other organizations (e.g., courts and prison) influence beliefs and behavior. Generally, when citizens are hostile and critical of police, it is because they believe that the police are engaging in inappropriate behavior. However, hostility and criticism also result when the police either increase the frequency with which they enforce one or more laws or fail to enforce certain laws.

Many police departments and officers prioritize criminal offenses. Those considered to be the most serious receive the most attention. Those considered to be a low priority (such as traffic offenses) receive little, if any, attention. Ignoring low-priority crimes creates a climate of expected toleration among citizens, which often results in increased frequency of low-priority crimes. If the police begin to enforce previously unenforced laws, violators may consider this to be an abuse of authority and criticize the police, especially when police crack down on a certain type of crime or in a certain area.

Police also tend to receive criticism in communities that have high rates of offending, particularly when police "aggressively" enforce the law. Although some criticism is valid, it may also be a product of violators who want to keep the police from enforcing the law and who wish to direct the focus of the community away from their criminal activity to police abuse of authority. Whatever the reason for public criticism, it often has a substantial influence on police behavior. When officers consider others to be hostile or critical, the officers' in-group solidarity may be strengthened. That in turn may result in increased police secrecy and possibly increased use of force.

Management, Job Satisfaction, and Peer Groups

The organization structure and management are also important considerations in police behavior. Organizations and managers both reward desired behavior and punish undesired behavior. Theoretically, officers will be more likely to engage in desired behavior if it is rewarded and avoid behavior that is likely to be punished (see Chapter 7). However, if an officer can depend on the "silence" of fellow officers, he or she may be less concerned about engaging in inappropriate behavior. The *peer group* is very influential in policing. Police officers depend upon one another for both physical and emotional support, especially in dangerous situations. Loyalty to peers can result in increased secrecy in the organization, particularly when that loyalty is valued more highly than ethical, legal, and organizational guidelines.

The nature of the work is also important in police behavior. Officers who like their work and the way they are treated in the organization are more likely to be motivated and productive. Officers who do not like their work may do as little as possible. The enjoyment of work is a function of the intrinsic nature of the work, the rewards provided by the organization, the manner in which employees are treated by managers, peer group relationships, and the response of "customers." Managers can either increase or decrease enjoyment through job design (see Chapter 7) and the way they treat employees (see Chapters 7 and 8). Being motivated and productive, however, does not necessarily mean that the activity and behavior of an officer would necessarily be appropriate or that the work would be performed competently. The goal of managers is to produce motivated, productive, and competent officers who engage in appropriate activities and behavior.

Police Skills

Bayley and Bittner (1989) believe that job experience contributes to officers' learning in three areas: goals, tactics, and presence. Patrol officer goals include meeting departmental expectations, maintaining order, avoiding injury, preventing crime, and keeping the public from being upset enough to complain. In departments with a community-policing orientation, these goals would also include the identification, analysis, and solution of problems.

Patrol officer tactics are concerned with all phases of police-citizen interaction—the initial contact, what happens during the interaction, and the solution of the problem. The presence of a police officer means not only that an officer has to do something, he or she must be something. The most important characteristics of an effective presence are external calm and internal alertness. Generally, police believe that it is important to be nonprovocative when interacting with citizens. To be so, officers need a demeanor that pacifies and placates individuals. At the same time, however, they must be alert to possible danger to themselves and others.

The learning that takes place in police work, as noted, is both formal and informal. Goals and tactics are acquired from both the organization, through training, policies, and procedures, and from other officers. Presence is basically acquired through experience as officers struggle to integrate demeanor and action while controlling their emotions. The failure to do so may result in unnecessary violence, injury, and even death to both officer and citizen.

Police Discretion

It was not until the 1950s that discretion among officers was "discovered" by researchers and administrators. But what exactly is "discretion"? Davis (1969: 4) commented: "A public officer has discretion whenever the effective limits on his power leave him free to make a choice among courses of action or inaction." Discretion can be demonstrated by the relatively infrequent use of arrest powers during encounters. For example, in an early field observation of police officers, Reiss (1971) reported that officers rarely made arrests of citizens, even when there were legal grounds to do so. By choosing not to arrest a citizen in encounters, the officers were exercising their discretion to not "invoke the law." It is impossible, impractical, and perhaps inefficient to eliminate discretion from policing. However, admitting that officers have the ability to make discretionary choices in how to interact with citizens implies that police managers cannot control officers. Therefore, police decision making, or discretion, involves three important and separate choices: (1) whether to get involved in an event (this is not a choice if the officer is sent by the department); (2) how to behave in an event or how to interact with citizens; and (3) which alternative to select to solve the problem.

A police officer can observe a violation of the law and, using discretion, do nothing, treat the person harshly, or let the person off. Different officers in the same situation may make different choices. Many police decisions have *low visibility*; that is, they are known only to one or two other individuals (e.g., a suspect, victim, or fellow police officer) (Goldstein, 1960). Low visibility is an important consideration in trying to manage police officers. They work by themselves, or with only one other officer, for long periods of time and often with minimal supervision. As Lundman (1979: 160) observed, "To a large extent, the work of the police officer is unsupervised, and to a lesser extent, it is unsupervisable."

There has been considerable research on variables that influence police decision making. They must be assessed relative to the police role. For example, it has been found that highly bureaucratic departments often produce officers who see their role as primarily that of crime fighters who should be somewhat distant from citizens. Advocates of community policing believe that such views are inappropriate for the police. Proponents of a more legalistic approach to policing would argue just the opposite.

The research on police discretion can generally be grouped into four categories of variables: organizational, neighborhood (or community), officer, and situational. Some of the most important variables in each category are discussed below. This discussion is based on research summaries of Brooks (1989), Riksheim and Chermak (1993), and Sherman (1985).

Organizational Variables

Highly bureaucratic departments have rigid rules and regulations and tend to have many different levels (e.g., chief of police, deputy chief, captains, lieutenants, sergeants, corporals, detectives, patrol officers) and specializations. They emphasize crime fighting more than service, tend to be impersonal, and may overemphasize punitive discipline in an attempt to control officer behavior. Officers from large departments tend to have a more distant relationship with citizens and are less likely to be sympathetic. Those in smaller departments tend to be involved in less aggressive anticrime activities and to be less enforcement oriented. In addition, the more frequently officers change work periods (or shift or tour of duty) and the areas (beat, district, or sector) in which they work, the less communication they will have with citizens.

Neighborhood Variables

There is a hypothesized relationship between neighborhood characteristics and behavior by police officers: Neighborhoods characterized as socially disorganized are said to have more crime because residents are not able or willing to control crime themselves and thus rely on more police intervention (Shaw and McKay, 1942). Therefore, characteristics of disorganized neighborhoods (such as residential mobility, racial heterogeneity, and poverty) may affect officer behavior. In these areas, officers are more prone to be aggressive and punitive. Furthermore, the extent of reported crime in an area influences the officer's perception of danger. The more the perceived danger, the greater the likelihood an officer will respond with a legalistic (make an arrest) or coercive response (verbal threats or physical abuse). Police also tend to be more aggressive and proactive in high-crime areas. The opinions of the citizens in a particular neighborhood or area are also influential in police behavior. In general, when citizens in an area are hostile and uncooperative, the police are more likely to be repressive and abusive.

Officer Variables

Three important individual factors that influence police behavior are age and experience, race or ethnicity, and education. It is difficult to separate age and experience, because most individuals entering police work are young (i.e., in their twenties) and grow older as they gain experience. In general, younger officers often work harder and are more aggressive and more punitive than older officers. This may reflect the fact that younger officers want to engage in "real police work," which often translates into making arrests, issuing citations, and engaging in many self-initiated contacts with citizens. Older officers may be more cynical and thus make fewer arrests, citations, and contacts with citizens. For example, Crank (1993) found that as length of service increases, officers are less likely to make arrests. However, the quality of the older officers' work may be superior.

The race of the officer is also important. There is some evidence that black officers are more respected by the black community, but they may also be stricter than whites in dealing with black citizens. Black officers tend to be more aggressive than white officers and to make more arrests in black neighborhoods. However, when controlling for other factors, there are few differences between white and black officers in deciding whether to arrest citizens or in exercising force.

The education of the officer is important because college-educated officers communicate better with the public, perform more effectively, make better decisions, receive fewer complaints, and show more sensitivity to racial and ethnic groups. As Worden (1990: 576) stated, "Because college education is supposed to provide insights into human behavior and to foster a spirit of experimentation, college-educated officers are (hypothetically) less inclined to invoke the law to resolve problems, and correspondingly are inclined more strongly to develop extralegal solutions."

Situational Variables

Among the variables that explain officer discretion, situational variables have consistently been shown to have the greatest impact. Though these variables are described in greater detail elsewhere (Roberg, Crank, and Kuykendall, 2000), a brief discussion here is warranted in order to assist police managers in understanding officer behavior. Generally, situational variables can be separated into three distinct categories: legal variables, extralegal variables, and social variables.

Legal variables are factors based on the rule of law that influence behavior. Examples of legal factors include (1) the type of offense or activity that is performed by the citizen, and (2) physical evidence or testimony that this activity occurred. It makes sense that legal variables should influence officer discretion. Two legal variables in particular are related to officer discretion;. namely, seriousness of the offense and level of evidence implicating a citizen in a crime. The more serious the crime, the greater the possibility of a formal police response (e.g., written report, investigation, or arrest) or a harsh one (e.g., verbal abuse, threats, or the use of physical force). Similarly, where there is greater and more prohibitive evidence, there is an increased likelihood of arrest.

Extralegal variables are characteristics of the citizen involved in the encounter or the citizen's behavior. Extralegal variables include citizens' class, race, gender, and age. The category also includes attitude displayed by the citizen (also known as demeanor). Indeed, few topics stir emotions regarding the criminal justice system process more than discriminatory behavior by those in the criminal justice system. Yet the influence of extralegal factors remains unclear.

Suspects in a lower socioeconomic status are more likely to be treated harshly and arrested. The majority of research on race in police behavior supports the contention that blacks are treated more harshly than whites and are more likely to be arrested. This finding may be the result of the fact that blacks and possibly other minorities are more likely to resist police authority or display a "bad" attitude. Recently, differential targeting of black motorists has become a significant topic of debate, and this phenomenon is discussed further in Inside Management 11.1.

The majority of the existing literature reported citizen gender did not influence the likelihood of arrest by an officer. However, Visher (1983) found females were less likely to be arrested than males who engage in similar behavior, especially when females act in an appropriate, "ladylike," fashion. However, the opposite could be true as well. When females act outside of their

Inside Management 11.1

Driving While Black and Racial Profiling

Racial profiling involves police-initiated actions that rely on the race, ethnicity, or national origin rather than the behavior of an individual or information that leads the police to a particular individual who has been identified as being, or having been, engaged in criminal activity (Ramirez, McDevitt, and Farrell 2000: 3). In other words, racial profiling occurs when race is used as the sole (or primary) influential factor guiding officers' discretionary activities. There are two key components of this working definition. First, encounters must be police-initiated, or proactive. Officers often have great discretion to choose with whom they interact, but at other times the decisions are beyond their control. Obvious examples of encounters beyond the officers' control are calls for service and responding to the scene of an accident. In order to discover any bias in decision making, it is important to examine only officer-initiated encounters.

Second, police officers must use the race of the citizen and not the citizen's behavior as the factor that influences their decisions. Although research consistently shows racial and ethnic minorities are overrepresented throughout the criminal justice system, explaining this overrepresentation proves exceedingly difficult. If factors other than race have more explanatory value when determining the activities of officers, the claim that officers are engaging in racial profiling becomes weak. Race and other extralegal characteristics must offer greater explanatory value only after controlling for legally relevant factors.

Discovering racial profiling among American police organizations has become an important policy issue. Five years ago only a select few police organizations identified this phenomena as being so problematic that they felt it was necessary to monitor police–citizen encounters. Today, over 100 police organizations currently monitor their officers for signs of racial profiling. Although several have done so pursuant to a federal consent decree, most agencies voluntarily conduct such research. There is both anecdotal and empirical evidence that such disparity occurs (Harris, 1999). Data collected that led to several consent decrees (Wilkins v. Maryland State Police 1993, U.S. v. New Jersey State Police 1999) reveal some startling estimates:

- Although 17.5 percent of speeders on Maryland highways were black, 79.2 percent of all vehicle searches were of black motorists,

- Although blacks accounted for 13.5 percent of motorists on New Jersey highways, blacks represented 35 percent of all motorists who were stopped and 73.2 of those who were searched,

- Blacks were six times more likely than whites to be stopped, and Latinos were four times more likely.

Although these figures clearly suggest some type of racial or ethnic bias, it is likely that most American police organizations do not systematically engage in racial profiling. Whether or not a particular organization is engaging in such activities is at its core an empirical question.

Surprisingly few empirical studies have been conducted addressing this issue. Smith and Petrocelli (2001) examined traffic stops in Richmond, Virginia, during a six-week period. They discovered that indeed minority drivers were more likely to be stopped by officers, compared to the racial composition of the city. However, they also found that blacks were less likely to be subject to consent searches, and were less likely to receive a ticket or be arrested.

Police managers must be cognizant of these issues and be held accountable for the identification and monitoring of the traffic enforcement practices of their officers. This requires managers to examine the racial and ethnic characteristics of citizens who receive tickets, as well as those who receive warnings. Further, managers may need to monitor specific officers in order to detect patterns of improper behavior. This will require managers to take into consideration issues related to several specific areas:

- Do officers stop minorities more often than whites?

- Do officers give citations/arrests to minorities more often than to whites?

- Do officers search minorities more often than whites?

- What are the parameters associated with the search (e.g., consent search, incident to arrest, inventory)?

- Do officers stop minorities more often than whites for a greater length of time (indicating possible harassment)?

- Do officers stop minorities more often than whites when certain characteristics are present (e.g., more often at night? more often when multiple people are in the vehicle? more often for subjective traffic offenses, such as "Following too close")?

Adapted from: Harris, D. A. 1999. "The Stories, the Statistics, and the Law: Why 'Driving While Black' Matters." *Minnesota Law Review.* 84: 265–326; Ramirez, D., McDevitt, J., and Farrell, A. 2000. *A Resource Guide on Racial Profiling Data Collection Systems: Promising Practices and Lessons Learned.* Bureau of Justice Assistance: Washington DC.; *United States v. New Jersey*, 1999, Civil Action No. MLC-99–5970; *Wilkins v. Maryland State Police*, 1993, Civil Action No. CCB; Smith, M. R., and Petrocelli, M. 2001. "Racial Profiling? A Multivariate Analysis of Police Traffic Stop Data," *Police Quarterly* 4: 4–27.

gender role, they may be more likely to be sanctioned by the police because they are more deserving of arrest. As Visher (1983: 6) clarified, ". . . if women fail to conform to traditional female roles, then the assumed bargain is broken and chivalrous treatment is not extended." Furthermore, some research has found officers are more likely to act aggressively and punitively during encounters with disrespectful juveniles.

One of the most important factors in police discretion is the ***attitude of the suspect***. Disrespectful or uncooperative suspects—that is, those who, according to the police, "flunk the attitude or personality test," are more likely to be cited, arrested, and verbally and physically abused than suspects who do not have "bad" attitudes. Almost without exception, researchers have revealed that failure to show deference and respect to police officers substantially increases citizens' chances of being arrested. In other words, "Hostility toward the implementers of the law begets the sanctions of the law" (Friedrich 1977: 372). When citizens fail to display respect for officers or to defer to their authority, the officers perceive this action as a threat and are more inclined to respond with application of the law, such as arrests.

Social variables include characteristics of how the officer and citizen engaged in an encounter, including whether the encounter was initiated by the officer (i.e., proactive), relationships between the victim and the offender, and the presence or absence of other citizens or officers. In proactive encounters, officers are more likely to face antagonism from citizens because proactive police behavior is more intrusive and less likely to be supported by citizens. As a result of the increased likelihood of a negative response, police are more likely to make arrests and treat citizens harshly, particularly suspects. If the relationship between the offender and the victim is close, the police may be reluctant to make an arrest because they believe it will create problems between the parties in the future. It is also clear that the presence of other police officers and bystanders influences what police do. If an officer thinks other officers expect him or her to be harsh or punitive, write a report, or make an arrest, then the officer is likely to do so. Further, officers who work alone tend to behave differently from officers who work in pairs. Single officers are more likely to make arrests because they are concerned about taking control of a situation. Two-person units may be less likely to make arrests but are more likely to treat suspects harshly, possibly because each officer is concerned about what his or her partner will think, particularly if a suspect challenges police authority. Furthermore, police are more likely to respond harshly in public settings (e.g., on the street or in a bar) than they are in private settings (e.g., in a home).

A great deal of the empirical research has focused on situational and social variables that influence an officer's decision to arrest. Generally, research has found citizens were more likely to be arrested:

1. For serious offenses

2. Where there was more evidence that the citizen commited the crime

3. When the citizen displayed hostile demeanor toward the officer

4. When a victim or witness requests the officer to make an arrest

5. The victim and the offender were strangers (versus acquaintances)

6. The encounter was officer initiated

7. The citizen was intoxicated

8. When there were other officers or bystanders observing the encounter

Discretion and Community Policing

Given the foregoing discussion on variables that influence police behavior, it is reasonable to ask: Will these variables have the same influence on behavior in the era of community policing? Ten years ago, Mastrofski (1992: 23) remarked, "Although interest in community policing has grown rapidly in the last decade, we know remarkably little about what it means to the work of the street-level officer." This observation is largely true today. Under community policing, the general goals of policing broaden to include more non-law enforcement tasks (Cordner, 1995). Officers are encouraged to use differential enforcement based on community values and norms. The types of interactions and encounters between the police and the public would also most likely change. Additionally, police are encouraged to utilize community residents in order to set crime prevention priorities. It is plausible to infer that there will therefore be an increase in the quantity and quality of police–citizen interactions, and thus a change in the relationship between the police and the public.

Mastrofski, Worden, and Snipes (1995) examined officers' decisions to arrest citizens in Richmond, Virginia. They spent nearly 1,300 hours observing officers during the course of the officers' day. They were able to identify officers who had favorable attitudes toward community policing as well as officers who had negative attitudes toward community policing. They found that officers with more favorable attitudes toward community policing were more "selective" in making arrests than those officers with less favorable attitudes. They reported that arrest decisions for officers with less favorable views toward community policing were more strongly influenced by legal variables compared to those with positive views. Neither group was strongly influenced by extralegal variables. They contended that officers who support community policing tend to make different discretionary choices than traditional officers. However, they were unable to thoroughly describe the arrest patterns for officers with positive views of community policing, commenting, "community-oriented officers 'march to the beat of a different drummer'. . . but our model gives a poor account of that 'beat'" (1995:556).

These results indicate that while researchers have a good understanding of decision making in the reform era of policing, factors influencing discretion in the community-policing era remain unclear. Clearly, additional research and understanding is needed in this area. Similar research was conducted by Novak et al. (2002), who conducted 442 ride-a-longs and observed how officers acted during encounters with citizens in Cincinnati, Ohio. They examined the decision-making processes of traditional beat officers as well as officers assigned to community-policing assignments. They found that while these officers by and large used similar variables when deciding whether to make an arrest, several interesting differences were observed. For example, community-policing officers were more likely to take victim preferences into account than their counterparts, indicating that community-policing officers may be more responsive to citizens' demands. They also found community-policing officers were not more likely to arrest disrespectful citizens. Further, traditional officers were significantly more likely to arrest intoxicated citizens. These finding indicate community-policing officers may be more tolerant of nonconforming behavior than their counterparts.

Democratic Context of Police Discretion

In a democratic society, the use of certain variables by police officers (including race, ethnicity, national origin, and religion; socioeconomic, political, and celebrity status; gender and sexual orientation; appearance; and relationships, such as a family member, fellow police officer, or friend) is problematic and controversial. The previous section noted some of these effects.

When police interact with citizens, it is usually for a law enforcement or educational purpose. Law enforcement encounters, which include field interrogations, issuing citations, and making arrests, are more controversial because they may involve police behavior that citizens find unwelcome (e.g., an intrusion, abuse, citation, or arrest). Although any police decision based on controversial variables is important (e.g., when to cite or arrest or to use force), perhaps the most important decisions involve **proactive** law enforcement.

Law enforcement encounters are usually initiated by an officer who (1) observes illegal behavior; (2) observes "suspicious behavior" (e.g., a person who sees a police officer, looks away, begins to walk faster, and tosses an object into a trash container); (3) has or is given knowledge about a person's illegal or suspicious behavior; or (4) uses a combination of other variables (e.g., gender, appearance, age, race, area, or time of day) to decide whether to intervene. Should a police officer intervene in a group of teenage males of the same ethnic group who are wearing gang colors? If an intervention takes place, the officer is predicting that individuals with these characteristics—which are also stereotypes—are more likely to engage in inappropriate behavior. Although the predictive capability of the police is unknown, many officers consider it to be accurate because they have developed a "street sense," that is, an **intuitive judgment** based on experience.

When intuitive decisions are based on sensitive variables, such as race and gender, the potential for controversy is high. One method used by the police to avoid allegations of, say, racism or sexism is to "get pc" (probable cause) before they intervene. In other words, they attempt to find a legal basis for the intervention, which is usually not difficult to do given the number of community ordinances (e.g., a curfew) and traffic and criminal laws that exist. Police consider such efforts to be "creative" police work, but citizens often consider them an attempt to "mask" the actual intent of police, which is to intervene based on the variables that are controversial in a democratic society.

Managers must address these issues in training programs, the development of policies and procedures, and the selection of supervisors. One of the most difficult problems for the police to overcome is the perception that they are racist or sexist, that they target particular groups for selective enforcement of the law, or that they give preferential treatment to some groups (e.g., the wealthy or other police officers). Although it is unrealistic to believe that controversial variables will not continue to be used in police discretion, the burden is properly placed on the police to explain and justify their reliance on them.

Performance Categories

❦ For managerial purposes, police behavior can be grouped into four performance categories: competence, productivity, integrity, and style. An understanding of some of the important considerations in each category will assist the manager in understanding behavioral problems.

Competence

What does it mean to be a good police officer? Who is highly competent, who is average, and who is marginal or incompetent? What values, attitudes, knowledge, skills, and style are necessary for an officer to be considered competent? Although knowledge and skill are important, they are applied within the social and political context of both the police organization and the community. Therefore, values, attitudes, and style also become part of his or her competency. A knowledgeable and skilled patrol officer who is too aggressive would not be considered competent in many communities, but in others he or she would be a "good cop." The authors believe that before an officer's behavior can be characterized as competent, he or she must possess the necessary knowledge and skills to perform assigned tasks with the attitude and style deemed appropriate by the department and the community.

The most important component of competency is cognitive ability (i.e., the ability to read, write, synthesize, and analyze). Although well-managed police departments can have substantial influence on the other aspects of competency through training and supervision, cognitive ability is controlled primarily through the selection process. The less demanding a police department is relative to cognitive ability, the more likely it is to have competency problems.

Productivity

The productivity of officers is also an important behavioral issue. How hard do officers work? What is a reasonable day's work? Who are the highly productive officers? Productivity varies widely in police departments; in many departments, there are some and often many officers who do not work very hard. All the information presented in this book can be used to improve productivity in police work; however, to obtain greater productivity, managers must be careful not to overuse punishment or the threat of it. Those who do often have the most productivity problems. As noted previously, one of the beliefs in punitive police departments is that the less the effort or work, the fewer the problems and the lower the risk for the officer. Or stated another way, "a sure way to get into trouble is to do your job."

Integrity

Integrity is concerned with police violations of organizational guidelines (e.g., policies and procedures), lying, acceptance of gratuities, corruption (e.g., accepting money to allow illegal gambling, drug sales, or drug distribution), other criminal acts on and off duty (e.g., theft, using or selling illegal drugs, spousal abuse, murder). Another possible integrity problem that requires managerial attention is the private purchase of governmental authority—that is, police officers who are paid to work as security officers for a private business, such as a mall or a club. The decisions made by officers working in a private capacity may be different from those made when working as a public police officer; that is, the officer may do what the employer wants rather than what the police department would expect. Also, officers may be reimbursed in cash to avoid the payment of taxes, which is illegal.

Many, if not most, police departments have a serious integrity problem in one or more of these areas. Responding to integrity problems basically involves a willingness to seek out and confront the behavior. Managers must develop clear guidelines concerning appropriate and inappropriate behavior and hold accountable officers who violate them. Managers must stress that a commitment to integrity is more important than any other value in the department. Officers who report integrity problems should be celebrated in the department and the community. Police departments should provide incentives (e.g., favorable consideration in the promotional process) for any officer who exposes a brutal, dishonest, or corrupt police officer. Any officer who criticizes another officer for reporting an integrity problem should be terminated.

Managers must also be aggressive in seeking out officers who are dishonest and corrupt. Police departments need "integrity control" units, which are responsible for searching for officers who may have integrity problems. Such units should not only investigate complaints but also stage undercover operations in which suspicious or randomly selected police officers are placed under surveillance. The arguments against this proactive approach to integrity control are that (1) it assumes that a substantial number of officers have integrity problems and (2) it will result in a decline in morale and productivity. Unfortunately, there is ample evidence that many police officers in the past and today have integrity problems. A temporary decline in morale and productivity is insignificant compared to the havoc wrought by dishonest and corrupt police officers.

Police departments must do everything possible to create an organizational culture in which each officer places integrity above loyalty to peers. The message must be clear and unequivocal: no matter how competent, popular, or productive they are, ***officers with integrity problems cannot be "good cops."*** Until the vast majority of police officers *and* managers believe this truth, the 150-year-old integrity crisis in modern policing in the United States will not be resolved.

Style

What should the officer's style be? Friendly (sociable)? Formal (businesslike)? Assertive (forceful)? When an officer detains a citizen, should the officer explain why? What are the different styles of policing that exist in the organization? Which style or styles are most effective relative to the mission of the organization? Which ones are questionable or unacceptable?

There has been considerable research concerning the style of both organizations and officers (e.g., see Wilson, 1968; Muir, 1977). As noted previously, styles are discerned by noting differences in certain characteristics, like compassion and assertiveness, among officers. Managers may find it useful to identify the most important characteristics associated with appropriate police behavior. This process will result in categorizing officers into different groups, each of which will represent a different style of policing. It is important to remember that they are only a simple analytical tool. It is rare that any one person fits completely into a style category. However, if a manager is aware that in some situations some officers use a style considered to be undesirable, given the organization's mission, corrective action can be taken. If a manager can identify an appropriate style for certain situations, then it can be taught to officers.

The Use of Force

Although estimates vary, police kill about 600 citizens each year, shoot and wound about 1,200, and shoot at but miss about 1,800. The number of citizens injured while resisting police authority is unknown, but estimates vary from about .1 percent to 1 percent of all police–citizen encounters (Geller and Scott, 1992). Assuming that approximately 90 percent of police officers (estimated at 600,000) have at least one citizen encounter per hour worked (estimated at 1,800 hours per year), this is a total of approximately 1,080,000,000 police–citizen encounters per year. Based on the estimates of Geller and Scott, between 108,000 and 1,080,000 citizens are injured by the police each year.

When police officers interact with citizens, they can attempt to control the encounter **verbally** by (1) asking questions; (2) using persuasion (e.g., using logic, humor, or appeals to conscience or civic responsibility); (3) issuing instructions (which are a milder form of orders); (4) giving orders (formal, perhaps even forceful, commands); and (5) making threats concerning the possible consequences (e.g., imminent arrest) if there is a failure to comply. Officers may also be tempted to verbally abuse citizens, that is, insult and denigrate them, but that type of police behavior is always inappropriate. The possible **physical** responses by the police include physical restraint (e.g., restricting use of the body, hands, or feet), nonlethal or less-than-lethal (LTL) weapons (e.g., baton, pepper spray, Oleoresin Capsicum (OC) spray, taser, rubber bullets, beanbag guns), and lethal force (e.g., carotid or bar arm control, or the use of a firearm).

The citizen response to a police intervention ranges from cooperation to varying degrees of verbal and physical resistance; ultimately, the resistance may involve a threat to the officer's, or another person's, life. Citizens may question, criticize, verbally abuse, or threaten officers. Physical resistance to the police may be passive, token or mild, aggressive and vigorous, or lethal. Aggressive and lethal (deadly) resistance can be incompetent or competent. **Incompetent resistance** denotes threat or attack by a person who cannot carry out the threat (e.g., many children, some disabled or elderly persons, or some intoxicated individuals). **Competent resistance** includes threats by individuals who appear to have both the capacity and the willingness to cause significant bodily injury or death.

Determining whether a threat is competent or incompetent is controversial and problematic. Often, the police and community and the officer and the police organization may disagree. Most often, disagreements are related to the type of weapon used by the citizen; the age, size, and physical capability of the person; and the proximity of the threat. To illustrate the difficulty in determining the competency of a threat, a police officer might answer the following questions. Is a baseball bat a deadly weapon when used by an adult male? An adult female? An adult male who is threatening to use the bat but is twenty feet away? A ten-year-old boy? A person under five-feet tall? Any person who is extremely intoxicated? What is the threat posed by an elderly intoxicated woman who is trying to throw a knife at officers standing 25 feet from her? What is the threat of a man who fires all the bullets from his weapon at an officer, misses, then drops his firearm?

Officers often use force when citizens resist arrest. Therefore, in order to reduce the incidence of resisting arrest, it is important for officers and police managers to understand the circumstances in which citizens resist. Kavanagh (1997) examined 1,108 arrests made at the Port Authority Bus Terminal in Manhattan over a one-year period. He found citizens were more likely to resist an arrest when

1. the citizen was intoxicated.

2. the citizen displayed disrespectful behavior to the officer.

3. there was violence associated with the crime.

4. the citizen was being arrested for a serious crime.

5. the arrest occurred during the daytime.

6. other citizens were also being arrested at the scene.

7. the officer initiated the encounter (proactive).

Additionally, other factors were unrelated to citizen resistance. These included characteristics of the officer (e.g. race, age, height, weight, education, attitudes), characteristics of the citizen (e.g. race, age, gender, height, weight) and inter-race encounters (e.g., white officer, black suspect; black officer, white suspect). Based on these factors, managers should focus additional training on making officers more aware of situations where there is an increased likelihood of resistance and promote methods or strategies for reducing the need to use force—or excessive force—under these conditions.

Assessing the Use of Physical Force

The use of physical, less-than-lethal, and ***lethal force*** can be characterized relative to its timeliness, necessity, proportionality, excessiveness, and brutality. ***Timeliness*** is related to the amount of time officers should wait before using some type of force when confronted with resistance. In general, unless there is an immediate and serious threat or possibility of escape, officers should be encouraged to be patient and to spend a substantial amount of time attempting to use verbal skills to secure compliance. If a police department demands that officers spend a minimum amount of time responding to certain types of problems, the officers may have to use force more frequently.

Necessity is the state in which force is justified, given the situation. It refers to both the timeliness and the type of force used relative to the threat posed or the intensity and persistence of the resistance. ***Proportionality*** means that the force used was necessary and appropriate for the situation in question, which is determined by the threat presented. Proportional force should be no greater than what is sufficient to overcome the resistance or confront the threat. Deciding if the force used was disproportionate to the situation is at times difficult, and opinions can and do vary widely.

Excessiveness is the condition wherein force is disproportionate to the   ❖ ❖ ❖ ❖
situation or problem. Excessive force is determined by the type of force used,
the intensity of the force, its duration, and possibly the results of its use. If a
person who questioned a police officer about a traffic citation was maced,
such force was clearly excessive. When a suspect offers mild resistance but
the police response is particularly vigorous, the intensity of the response is
excessive. If a suspect is under control but the officer continues to use force,
then the unnecessary duration of force renders it excessive. When a person
receives either a moderate or serious injury, unless the resistance to police
was vigorous, the use of force may be considered excessive.

Brutality is the intentional use of either unnecessary or excessive force
by an officer, who may also be committing a crime. Although brutality is difficult to determine, there are several useful indicators: (1) statements of intent
before, during, or after the use of force; (2) force that is obviously disproportionate to the situation; (3) force at an intensity level that was clearly uncalled
for; and (4) the continued use of force after it is obvious that it is no longer
necessary.

The standards that are used to determine if the force used was unnecessary, excessive, or brutal are (1) *legal* (What is the current statutory and case
law?); (2) *policy* (What are the organization's guidelines?); (3) *training*
(What are officers trained to do?); (4) *community* (What does the community think and expect?); and (5) the *highly skilled officer*. Legal standards,
policy, and training standards are discussed briefly below, as well as elsewhere in this book. The community and highly-skilled-officer standards are
discussed below.

The community assessment of the use of force is often important to both
the community and the police. Unfortunately for both, public expectations of
the police are at times unreasonable. Some citizens expect police officers to
do things they cannot do, or not to do things that those same citizens would
do if they were in similar situations. For example, in a national survey conducted in 1994, 26 percent of the respondents and 46 percent of "blacks/
other" indicated that they could not think of "any situations" in which they
"would approve" of a police officer "striking an adult male citizen." When
asked this question about specific situations, 6 percent and 9 percent among
"blacks/other" said they would not approve of a police officer striking a citizen even if the citizen was using his or her fists to attack the officer. Further,
21 percent and 35 percent among "blacks/others" said they would not
approve a police officer striking a person even to keep that person from
escaping from custody (Maguire and Pastore, 1995: 152–153).

The higher percentages among blacks and other minorities are based on
historical, and in some communities present-day, problems involving unnecessary and excessive, if not brutal, use of force. Often, minorities assume that
police use of force is unjustified in the absence of substantial proof to the contrary. Unfortunately, this belief may increase rather than decrease hostility
between police and minority groups. If the police perceive the minority
response to be unreasonable, and if it becomes an important factor in how an
officer is treated by the organization or the criminal justice system, police
resentment of, and hostility toward, the minority group may increase.

There is some evidence that citizens who observe police use of force that
they perceive to be excessive have lower overall ratings of police performance, regardless of whether the force was actually excessive. Of the 992 citi-

zens surveyed by Soo Son et al. (1997), 13.7 percent had observed police use force within the past 12 months which they perceived as excessive. These citizens reported significantly lower levels of satisfaction with the police than citizens who did not observe excessive use of force. Further, nonwhite citizens harbored significantly lower levels of satisfaction than whites.

Similar results seem to occur when citizens are asked about a specific, well-publicized encounter between the police and the public. Jefferis et al. (1997) reported results from a survey conducted in Cincinnati, Ohio. On April 25, 1995, a television reporter filmed a violent encounter between a young black male and several police officers. Officers were summoned to a bus stop in the downtown area to disperse a crowd. An encounter occurred in which the youth refused to comply with officers' requests to leave the area. The situation escalated to the point where the youth was thrown to the ground and sprayed with Oleoresin Capsicum spray, and finally handcuffed. The video was repeatedly shown on the evening news, and much media publicity was dedicated to this incident. A survey of citizens was conducted and the authors found that the videotaped use of force incident not only had "a negative impact on citizens' perceptions of police use of force during arrest situations, but that the effect was substantially greater for non-Caucasians. Furthermore over a ten-year period, non-Caucasians were consistently more likely than Caucasians to believe police used force excessively" (Jefferis et al. 1997: 381). They recommended police take additional steps (perhaps through community-policing efforts) to enhance the image of the police and improve police–citizen relations. They also recommended police should continue to reduce the use of non-lethal and excessive force.

The highly-skilled-officer standard is based on the belief that each police department has some highly skilled officers who are more likely than others to make appropriate decisions concerning the use of force. Any force that would not be used by a highly skilled officer would be either unnecessary or excessive, if not brutal (Klockars, 1995).

Although the identification of highly skilled officers could prove useful, there are several possible problems. Both managers and working officers (e.g., patrol, investigators, and so on) would have to agree on who is "highly skilled." Does "highly skilled" apply to those officers who use force the least or to those who use it most effectively? Are officers who fail to use force in certain situations just as much of a problem as those who use it unnecessarily or excessively? In addition, it might also prove difficult to identify the values, attitudes, and skills of the most highly skilled officers and to incorporate them in selection, training, and evaluation of other officers. Moreover, if the talents of the highly skilled become the organizational standard, may be considered by other officers to be unreasonable. The assumption that all police employees, or even a majority, can become as "good" as the "best" is questionable.

Violence-Prone Officers

Just as it may be possible to identify those highly skilled officers who minimize the use of violence, it may also be possible to identify those who are most prone to use violence. Scrivner (1994) identifies the characteristics of police officers who are prone to use unnecessary or excessive force and uses the characteristics to develop five profiles of violence-prone officers, which are discussed below.

Officers with Personality Disorders

Police who have disordered personalities have pervasive and enduring traits that are manifested in antisocial, narcissistic, paranoid, or abusive tendencies. These conditions impair judgment and interaction with other individuals, in particular those who challenge the officer's authority. These officers tend to lack empathy for others. The characteristics tend to be present prior to employment but may be intensified by the police experience. Individuals with this type of personality pattern do not usually learn from experience or accept responsibility for their behavior. They often receive numerous citizen complaints. There is little that can be done to alter their behavior.

Officers with Traumatic Job-Related Experiences

Traumatic situations, such as justifiable police shootings, put some officers at risk. These officers are not unsocialized, egocentric, or violent. Personality factors appear to have less to do with their vulnerability to excessive force than the emotional baggage they have accumulated from previous incidents. The officers are often burned out, have become isolated from their work group, and may attempt to conceal their symptoms. It may be some time before these officers are discovered, and this may not occur until the officer loses control and uses excessive force. Officers in this category can be helped by critical debriefing, particularly if it is done immediately after the traumatic incident. There should also be follow-up counseling to minimize the development of symptoms.

Officers with Early-Stage Career Problems

Young and inexperienced officers who are immature (e.g., "hotdogs," "badge happy," or "macho") are impressionable and impulsive, with low tolerance for frustration. However, they bring positive attributes to their work and can outgrow these tendencies with experience. They need strong supervision and a highly structured field-training program under the guidance of an officer with extensive "street" experience. These officers must be shown what it means to be professional as defined by the organization.

Officers with Inappropriate Patrol Styles

These officers tend to combine a dominant command presence with heavy-handedness. They also tend to be particularly sensitive to challenges to their authority. They use some type of force to show they are in charge. This type of behavior is acquired on the job and can often be changed. The longer this pattern continues, however, the more difficult it is to change. Such officers need strong supervision and training early in their career. Once the style is developed, they may respond to peer feedback, situation-based interventions, and individual assistance.

Officers with Personal Problems

Officers who are most frequently seen by a psychologist because of excessive use of force have personal problems. Some have specific problems, such as marital separation, divorce, loss of status, and so on, that may affect their job performance. Others have a more tenuous sense of self-worth and higher levels of general anxiety, which may be masked under normal conditions. A change in the personal life of such officers may make it difficult for them to deal with fear, animosity, or emotionally charged situations. The first indication of such a problem is erratic behavior. Supervisors who have been properly trained can often determine who these officers are and respond accordingly. In fact, police departments should develop an early-warning system to help identify them.

Managing the Use of Force

One of the goals of police departments should be to use force of all types as a last resort and only when there is clear and compelling evidence that no other alternative is likely to be effective, given the situation, the resources available, and the competency of those involved. Departments must recognize, however, that in some situations, force is not only necessary but required if serious injury or death to police or other persons is to be avoided. If the police become too concerned about avoiding the use of force, they may avoid risky situations or incur increased injuries and deaths to both themselves and citizens.

Managing the use of force situations is not unlike managing any other behavior in a police organization. The important concerns are leadership, legal and policy guidance, training, tactics, and tools. *Leaders* must clarify the organizational values concerning the use of force and ensure that they are understood throughout the organization. *Policy guidelines* must be compatible with state and federal laws and may be even be more restrictive. It is not uncommon, for example, for state law to allow officers to use deadly force in situations where it is prohibited by a police department. The policy trend in the last several decades has been to provide more explicit guidance as to when and under what circumstances the use of force is appropriate. Inside Management 11.2 provides a description of the use of force policy guidelines as used in Kansas City, Missouri.

Training should not only provide the self-confidence, skills, and judgment required to make decisions about force; it should also be replicated often enough to ensure that high levels of proficiency are maintained. *Tactics* involve the methods to be used to respond to problems with the potential for the police use of force. Tactics include basic officer-safety procedures, the number of officers to be used, how they are to be positioned, who is to make the critical decision, and the intervention philosophy to be followed (e.g., rapid and forceful or patient and restrained). The *tools* that can used by police include the physical ability of officers, such protective devices as body armor, shields, and helmets, various restraining devices (on arms and legs), nonlethal or less-than-lethal weapons (e.g., pepper spray, taser, vehicle interdiction devices, nets), and deadly force. Marion (1998) examined the curriculum of a police academy in Ohio and found recruits were required to complete 543 hours of training prior to hitting the streets. Within the academy, recruits completed 134 hours (24.7 percent) of training directly related to how and when to use force. Nearly half of these hours were devoted to firearms training. However, officers were also trained in less-than-lethal force tactics, including OC spray, defensive weapons (e.g., PR-24 or "night stick"), unarmed self-defense, and "verbal judo" (effective communication, used to defuse potentially dangerous situations). Training curriculums vary greatly from state to state, as well as from department to department, but the level of

Inside Management 11.2

Use of Force Policy—Kansas City (MO) Police Department

The KCPD instituted a policy to guide officers in their decisions to use lethal and nonlethal force. Officers may use force in order to control the subject or for personal defense. Officers may use physical force in order to:

1. Make an arrest
2. Protect themselves and others from physical injury
3. Restrain or subdue a resistant individual
4. Bring an unlawful situation safely and effectively under control

In addition, lethal force is only authorized in order to:

1. Protect an officer or other from what is reasonably believed to be an imminent threat of death or serious bodily harm.
2. To prevent the escape of a person:

- from the scene of a violent crime where it is reasonably believed he or she caused or attempted to cause death or serious bodily injury

- who is reasonably believed to be armed and to have committed an offense in which he/she caused or attempted to cause death or serious bodily injury

- who may otherwise endanger life or inflict serious physical injury unless arrested without delay

To further guide officers' decisions, a situational force model is used throughout the department. This model recommends specific responses based on the level of resistance used by citizens.

This model requires some additional explanation. First, traditionally, police departments have referred to similar models as a "use of force continuum." However the term *continuum* is somewhat misleading in that it implies officers must begin with the lowest level response and then proceed to higher levels. In reality officers are not

Level	Citizen Resistance	Description of Resistance	Officer Response
I	Compliant	Citizen is cooperative but must be given verbal instructions for compliance.	• Mere presence • Verbal instructions / directions
II	Passive Resistance	Citizen is not controlled by verbal instructions but does not prevent officer from taking control.	• Options available at Level I • Empty-hand restraints (wrist locks, escort techniques) • Nerve receptor manipulation (pressure points on elbows, shoulder, mandible) • PR-24 (pressure but not striking) • Oleoresin Capsicum Spray
III	Active Resistance, Nonassaultive	Citizen actively resists arrest but does not assault officer (e.g., pulling away, fleeing, pushing).	• Options available at Level II • Lateral vascular neck restraint
IV	Actively Assaultive, Non Life Threatening	Citizen is aggressively offensive without possesing a weapon.	• Options available at Level III • Strongarm takedown or other takedown techniques • PR-24 strikes or jabs (to legs, arms) • Empty-hand strikes (knee strikes, forearm strikes, open-palm strikes) • Multiple officer control • Less than lethal munitions (beanbag gun)
V	Actively Assaultive, Life Threatening	Citizen is aggressively offensive with or without weapons, and intends to assault officer in life-threatening manner.	• All options at Level IV • Firearm-retention techniques • Firearm (handgun or shotgun)

obligated to exhaust all (or any) lower level responses instead their response must be appropriate based on the level of resistance encountered. Second, in Level II resistance, a "PR-24" is a long stick-like object typically carried by officers. Though the PR-24 can be used for striking (at Level III) it is only to be used to administer pressure to induce compliance at Level II. Third, at level III, "Lateral vascular neck restraint" is similar to a chokehold. Due to the fact that chokeholds may inadvertently cause death, many departments do not permit officers to administer them to induce compliance. However, officers in the KCPD receive additional training in the proper use of this technique and continue to use it today.

Upon first glance this model provides for a great deal of officer discretion. Officers encountering similar levels of resistance may choose very different responses. The reason for this is that officers are to evaluate the situation in order to determine the most appropriate technique to be used, and are taught to evaluate variables related to the incident. Among these variables are the size of the officer and citizen, number of suspects and officers at the encounter, current injuries sustained by suspects and officers, skill level of the officer and the emotional state of the suspect (e.g., impaired by drugs or alcohol). Therefore, there may be some variation in officer response given the totality of the circumstances.

Adapted from: The Kansas City (MO) Police Department, Procedural Instruction Policy 01-3, effective March 14, 2001, and personal communication with Officer Chip Huth, Instructor, Kansas City (MO) Police Department, May 29, 2001.

emphasis on the use of force described above is probably pretty typical. Similarly, ongoing officer training (or what is commonly known as "in-service" training) will also vary, but it is not clear how much ongoing officer training is devoted to honing use-of-force techniques.

The use of force should also be **monitored.** Departments should "collect information on every occasion in which force of any kind or degree is used" (Klockars, 1995: 23). The **use-of-force report** should be as carefully written as any crime report and should provide a detailed account of what led to the use of force, the type and degree of force used, the resistance or threat posed, the impact of its use, and subsequent events. Statements of all witnesses should be included, as well as a listing of any relevant physical evidence. After the report is prepared, the use of force should be evaluated as to whether it was (1) timely and necessary; (2) acceptable but unnecessary in the presence of other alternatives; and (3) a violation of organizational policy or criminal law. As reports accumulate and are evaluated, the body of knowledge increases concerning effective techniques in avoiding or minimizing the use of force, and officers can be trained how to respond more effectively to verbal and physical resistance.

Officer Safety

In 1999, 42 police officers were feloniously killed in the United States. Of these, 41 (97.6 percent) were killed with a firearm, and 25 (59.5 percent) were killed with a handgun. Of handgun deaths, nearly half (12) were killed with a 9mm. Twenty-seven (65.8 percent) of the officers killed with firearms were slain while wearing body armor (meaning body armor is not a foolproof method of defense), and five (12.2 percent) were killed with their own handgun. The majority of these officers were white (88.1 percent), male (92.8 percent) with an average age of 36. According the FBI, 49 assailants were identified in connection to the deaths of police officers in 1999. The typical offender was male (95.9 percent), white (55.1 percent) with an average age of 27. This is, however, somewhat misleading, because over half of the offenders were below age 24. There are indications these offenders had a history of encounters with police, along with a history of violence and drug use. For example, 41 (83.6 percent) had a prior arrest for any crime, 11 (22.4 percent) had been arrested for a violent crime, and 14 (28.5 percent) were on probation or parole at the time of the killing). Twenty-one (42.9 percent) had prior arrests for a drug law violation, 19 (38.7 percent) had prior arrests for assaulting an officer or resisting arrest, and 19 (38.7 percent) had prior arrests for weapons violations. Even with these figures, in 1999 fewer officers were feloniously killed than in the previous 23 years (Federal Bureau of Investigation, 1997, 2000). To personalize this problem, Inside Management 11.3 presents detailed information on five officers feloniously killed in the line of duty in 1999.

Inside Management 11.3

Detailed Description of Selected Felonious Killings of Law Enforcement Officers, 1999

January 10: Oakland (CA) Police Department. A sniper shot a 41-year-old officer on a highway overpass as he searched the roadside for a weapon discarded during a vehicle pursuit. The sniper, using a 7.62 mm semiautomatic rifle, shot the victim and another officer. The other officer was struck in the handcuff case, and was unharmed. Reportedly, the sniper believed the shootings would cause officers still in pursuit of his friends' vehicle to terminate the chase and return to the fallen officers. The sniper was 19 years old.

January 20: Villa Rica (GA) Police Department. A 35-year-old captain with 12 years of experience was shot during a routine traffic stop. After issuing a warning to the suspect, the captain became suspicious that the motorist was transporting drugs. As the captain prepared to conduct a search of the vehicle, the motorist allegedly shot the officer in the right wrist and in the back of the head with a .25-caliber handgun, subsequently fleeing the scene. A passing motorist discovered the victim officer. The 32-year-old suspect was later apprehended in Canada, charged with murder, and extradited to the United States for trial.

January 23: East Hartford (CT) Police Department. A 26-year-old officer was shot while responding to a noise complaint. The two-year veteran arrived at the scene and questioned a 23-year-old male suspect. The suspect allegedly produced a .38-caliber handgun and shot the officer in the front of the head. The noise complaint was related to a robbery in progress by the suspect and a 29-year-old female accomplice. Reportedly, two other accomplices were also

waiting at the scene, and the four drove away after the officer was shot. All four suspects were arrested within a week of the shooting.

October 6: Missouri State Highway Patrol, St. Joseph (MO). A 43-year-old sergeant was shot while investigating a suspicious person. The officer observed a vehicle matching the description of one driven by a man who had allegedly left a truck stop without paying for gas. Witnesses reported the suspect was stopped on the side of the road and, upon seeing the officer, the suspect obtained a handgun from inside the vehicle. The officer chased the suspect and attempted to subdue him by jumping on his back. The suspect shot the officer twice in the chest and once in each arm. The officer was able to shoot the suspect in the leg. The suspect then shot and killed himself.

December 12: National Parks Service, Kailua-Kona (HI). A 47-year-old ranger, while conducting foot patrol on an isolated beach, was killed while investigating a suspicious person. The officer was investigating a suspicious homeless man and his three dogs, which were allegedly harassing park visitors. During the encounter an altercation ensued and the dogs attacked the officer. During the struggle the suspect gained possession of the officer's 9mm handgun and shot the officer in the chest and head. The suspect was caught two days later.

Adapted from: Federal Bureau of Investigation, 2000. " Law Enforcement Officers Killed and Assaulted, 1999." Washington, DC: Department of Justice.

Felonious killings of police officers are only part of the big picture regarding officer safety. In 1999, in addition to the 42 officers feloniously killed, another 65 officers were killed accidentally in the line of duty. Of these, 51

(78.5 percent) were killed in an automobile, motorcycle, or aircraft accident and 9 (13.8 percent) were killed when struck by another vehicle. In other words, officers are more likely to be killed in a traffic-related accident than by an assailant. But these figures pale in comparison to the number of officers injured while on duty. In the same year, 55,026 officers were assaulted during encounters with citizens. Of these, 16,193 (29.4 percent) were assaulted while responding to a disturbance call (Federal Bureau of Investigation, 2000). The aggregate number of officers injured and killed is important in understanding the problem of police danger and officer safety, but it does not adequately communicate the seriousness and the emotional impact of those deaths and injuries.

How dangerous is police work? Danger can be considered from three perspectives: perceived, potential, and actual. *Perceived* danger relates to the individual's or public's belief about danger in police work. It is influenced by a variety of factors, including media coverage, television, movies, books, and the actual and reported experiences of officers. In general, many people, including police officers, believe that police work is an extremely dangerous job. *Potential* danger relates to those situations that *could* become dangerous for the officer—for example, a felony car stop. Potentially dangerous encounters are often characterized by behavior that adds to the officer's concern (e.g., threats, shouting, challenges to police authority, name calling, and so on). *Actual* danger involves the number and rates of injury and death that result from accidents and attacks by citizens. The data presented above indicate the extent to which officers are confronted with dangerous persons and situations. It appears officers perceive police work to be more dangerous than it actually is; however, it is important to understand these perceptions because "officer safety" issues permeate every encounter between the police and the public. The perception of danger is always present, and officers are trained and socialized to accept this belief. The underlying presence of danger may influence behavior in that officers may be constantly looking for danger in every encounter with citizens, even with citizens who mean no harm to the officer. It is possible the move toward community policing may mitigate this problem. As officers and citizens become more acquainted with each other and these groups work more closely in crime prevention partnerships, officers may begin to view encounters with citizens differently, with presumably less fear of danger.

Another useful way to analyze danger in police work is to categorize it in terms of how it is precipitated; that is, is it initiated by a person or is it a function of the situation? Few occupations include both the possibility and reality of *person-initiated danger*—that is, an attack against the worker by another person. *Situational danger* is a function of a particular problem, for example, a high-speed chase in policing, the frequency with which a taxi driver is at risk of a traffic accident, the use of certain equipment, or the height at which a person has to work.

One of the most interesting aspects of danger is that officers *initiate* a substantial number of the encounters in which they are injured or killed, and they often know that many of these situations are potentially dangerous. In one study on officer fatalities, Konstantin (1984) discovered that contrary to popular belief, most police are not killed in citizen-initiated contacts. He found that approximately 73 percent of incidents resulting in officer deaths were initiated by the officers, the remaining 27 percent initiated by citizens. In addition, most officers are killed in the types of situations that they know are the most dangerous (e.g., making arrests, robberies in progress, car stops and pursuits, assaults on officers, domestic violence and disturbance calls, and investigating suspicious persons). Even with this knowledge, they may fail to follow the training and procedures that would reduce the likelihood of injury or death. In a study of 31 officers feloniously killed in California between 1990 and 1994, it was discovered that an estimated 80 percent of the deaths were preventable and primarily the result of "poor tactics, poor judgment, overconfidence, complacency, and rushing in without a plan." Poor positions, such as not having adequate cover or leaving cover too soon, were a significant factor in 84 percent of the deaths (California Commission on Peace Officers Standards and Training, 1996: xii).

Under what circumstances are officers injured during assaults? Kaminski and Sorensen (1995) examined 1,550 nonlethal police assaults in Baltimore County over a two-year period. They found the odds that an officer was injured during the assault increased when certain situational characteristics were present. Specifically, officers were more likely to be injured during an assault when (1) more than one officer was assaulted, (2) suspects used bodily force rather than a weapon, (3) there was a single assailant, (4) suspects were under arrest, attempting to escape, or fighting upon arrival (rather than approaching or conversing with the officer), (5) the assailant was not intoxicated, and (6) officers were responding to disturbances or other legal situations (rather than domestic disputes). The authors suggested that these final two findings may reflect the fact that officers perceive encounters with intoxicated citizens and domestic disputes to be dangerous and thus exercise greater caution when encountering these citizens. They found that officers were more likely to be injured during encounters with nonwhite suspects, indicating these encounters were characterized by greater hostility. They also reported characteristics of the officers that were related to injury, in that short and tall officers were more likely to sustain injury than "medium"-sized officers. Further, younger officers and officers without a college education were more likely to be injured than seasoned veterans or officers with a college education. Finally, they found that some individual officers sustained injuries on multiple occasions. Based on their findings, they outline several policies police managers could initiate to reduce officer injuries:

1. Greater proficiency with unarmed defensive tactics

2. Additional in-service training for officers with less than five or six years of service

3. Tailor-made defensive tactics for officers who are either short or tall

4. Identification of officers who are at risk for multiple injuries, and work with these officers to reduce the number of use-of-force encounter.

5. Training to assist officers in identification of high-risk assailants (e.g., hostile suspects who attempt to escape during arrest situations)

6. Community relations and awareness programs to reduce tension and hostility between police and nonwhite suspects

7. Continuation of hiring officers with higher education levels

8. Greater caution when responding to nondomestic disturbance calls

The California Commission on Peace Officers Standards and Training (1996) suggest that managers—with effective supervision, appropriate training programs, and policies—can further reduce the number of injuries or deaths. Managers must have as a goal the total elimination of job-related deaths and injuries. The most important persons in this regard are the immediate supervisor and middle manager. They must be ever vigilant to make sure that officers follow safety and response guidelines. In addition, all incidents involving the use of force and citizen resistance of any type, including verbal, should be reported and used not only to assess the officer's style and discretion but also as a basis for improving future police responses. Any time a police officer or citizen is injured or killed, the department should view such an event as a ***critical management failure,*** which requires an immediate and comprehensive reassessment of all related programs, policies, and personnel.

This type of response is necessary because managers need to reduce the fear level of officers if they hope to modify some of the behavioral consequences associated with irrational fear, including hypervigilance, unwillingness to take risks, verbal abuse of citizens, overreliance on the use of force, unnecessary and excessive force, and brutality. Managers must convince officers that ***officer safety, next to integrity***, is the most important priority in the department.

Managers must also undertake a massive ***community education program,*** in which citizens are instructed how to behave when interacting with officers. Citizens must be told that they have an absolute obligation to cooperate with the police and to follow police orders. Citizen grievances cannot and should not be resolved "in the streets." Unfortunately, some individuals believe that it is their right to challenge police authority at the very moment that authority is being exercised. The police have far more problems with such individuals, and will continue to have them, until there is a change in citizen attitudes and behavior. Just as the police must modify their behavior in some situations in order to secure public respect and cooperation, citizens must also modify their behavior in order to reduce the fear level of officers.

Stress

Whether health problems are inherited or related to personal lifestyle, it is clear that a person's health has a significant influence on behavior and productivity. One of the most important considerations in the health of police officers is stress.

Selye defines ***stress*** as "the body's non-specific response to any demand placed on it" (1974: 60). A person is under stress when he or she is required to adapt to a particular situation. ***Physiological stress*** deals with the biological effects on the individual, including such problems as heart disease, high blood pressure, and ulcers. ***Psychological stress*** is more difficult to define, and its consequences are more difficult to determine. Psychologists often use the term ***anxiety*** to express the psychological effects of stress.

There are two main types of stress: ***eustress***, which is positive, and ***distress***, which is negative. Negative stress can be either acute, which includes such emergencies as the use of deadly force, incidents of violence, and high-speed pursuits. Chronic, which is low level and more gradual (Farmer, 1990) includes persistently troublesome problems such as concern about court decisions or managerial support. Each type of stress is present in police work, but events that are acutely stressful require immediate and substantial physical and psychological adaptation; chronic stress does not. Chronic stress tends to be cumulative. Minor stress may accumulate to produce major stress with such consequences as a heart attack or actual physical or mental breakdown. Prolonged emotional stress—the kind that may be part of the everyday work environment—can produce wear and tear on the body, with effects that may prove irreversible if not treated in time (Territo and Vetter, 1981).

Stress, like beauty, is a subjective matter; one person's experiences with stress may have little in common with another person's. Distress for some is eustress for others. Although perceptions of distress and levels of tolerance for stress vary from person to person, everyone is susceptible to the ravages of stress. Nevertheless, it is important not to overdramatize the problem. Policing is probably more stressful than many other occupations, but, in general, it is not an extremely stressful job (French, 1975; Pendleton et al., 1989; Terry, 1981, 1983).

Some Sources of Stress

There are four possible person-centered categories of police stressors: those within the organization, those external to the organization, those inherent in police work, and individual. These stressors are listed in Table 11.1.

Violanti and Aron (1995) examined 60 police stressors in a large New York police department. They categorized sources of stress into two general categories. First, ***departmental stressors*** were those related to the bureaucratic nature of the police organization. These factors included lack of administrative support, authoritative discipline structures, and minimal influence on decision making. Second, they found ***police work itself*** to be a source of stress. These factors included shift work, boredom, danger, apathy, and exposure to human misery. Violanti and Aron reported many of the most significant stressors to be related to the task environment of policing, including killing someone in the line of duty, fellow officer killed, physical attacks, battered children, and high-speed chases. These characteristics are inherent in policing, and will likely be experienced by many police officers (to a lesser or greater degree). However, they also reported that the ***organizational environment*** (or departmental stressors) contributes to stress, including shift work, inadequate department support, incompatible partners, insufficient personnel, and excessive discipline. Similarly, Crank and Caldero (1991) examined police officers in medium-sized police departments in Illinois. They divided stressors into five categories: department, task environment,

Table 11.1 Stressors in Police Work

External Stressors
Frustration with the criminal justice system 　Lack of consideration in scheduling officers for court appearances 　The perception of inadequate public support and negative public attitudes 　Negative, biased, and inaccurate media coverage
Internal Stressors
Policies and procedures that officers do not support 　Inadequate training and career development opportunities 　Inadequate recognition and rewards for good work 　Inadequate salary, benefits, and working conditions 　Excessive paperwork 　Inconsistent discipline 　Favoritism regarding promotions and assignments 　Politically motivated administrative decisions
Police Stressors
The unhealthy consequences of shift work 　The potential role conflict between law enforcement and serving the public 　Frequent exposure to human suffering 　Boredom interrupted by the need for sudden alertness 　Fear and danger involved in certain situations 　Being responsible for protecting other people 　Too much work to do in time allotted
Officer Stressors
Fears regarding job competence and success 　Fears regarding safety 　The possible need to take other jobs to support family or to pursue education 　Altered social status in the community

Adapted from: R. M. Ayres and G. S. Flanagan, 1992. Preventing Law Enforcement Stress; *The Organization's Role*, pp. 4–5. Washington, DC: Bureau of Justice Assistance.

judiciary, personal or family concerns, and city government. They reported that more than two-thirds of officers identified the police department itself as their principal source of stress. Officers cited problems related to management and shift changes among their chief concerns (42 percent). Task environment was a distant second (only 16 percent). These studies appear to indicate that whereas police managers can have a limited influence on the task environment of policing, they may be able to affect officer stress by management directives.

If the police organization itself is a source of individual officer stress, there is reason to believe that the size of the department may influence officers' experience with stress. Brooks and Piquero (1998) suggested that officers in larger organizations may be more prone to stress because (1) large organizations promote impersonal relationships; (2) there may be more pressure for advancement within the department; and (3) officers may have more contact with crime and other criminal justice system agencies. Indeed, their research indicated that officers from large organizations reported more stress from administrative factors, stress from the criminal justice system, and personal stress than officers in small or medium-sized departments.

As discussed in Chapter 3, community policing is a new model for policing. However, community policing may actually contribute to stress experienced by line officers by making their role more ambiguous. Lord (1996) notes that in addition to stressors related to the police occupation, officers in departments implementing community policing may encounter other stressors related to organizational change. These include a lack of recognition (from the public, administration, and other officers), lack of communication between officers and supervisors, lack of participation in decision making, and role changes related to community- policing philosophies and practices. Her research indicated that many of these components related to change caused officers to experience physiological responses (e.g., responses to anxiety), lack of job involvement, and a propensity to leave the department. These findings suggest that managers must pay careful attention to the change process in implementing community policing (see Chapter 14).

Some Consequences of Stress

There is no question that stress contributes to or causes a number of serious problems for individual officers, though the extent and frequency of reactions stemming from stress is somewhat unclear. These problems include physical and emotional health, drug and alcohol abuse, suicides, and family problems, including divorce (see Table 11.2). Such problems are important for managers in terms of the consequences for the individual as well as for the effectiveness and efficiency of the organization. An officer with a problem is rarely as productive as he or she could be, and in some cases, there may be serious performance deficiencies or excesses, such as unnecessary use of force. While it is not possible to adequately address all consequences of occupational stress in policing, several consequences are highlighted below. These include suicides, substance abuse, and post-traumatic stress disorder.

Suicides are a problem of critical concern in police departments. In a study in Buffalo, New York, police officer suicides were found to be 53 percent higher than those of other city workers. Further, it was discovered that "police officers are eight times more likely to commit suicide than to be killed in a homicide, and are three times more likely to commit suicide than to die in job-related accidents" (Law Enforcement News (LEN), November 15, 1996: 1). Violanti, Vena, and Marshall (1996) found that male police officers had a suicide rate that was 8.3 times higher than the homicide rate. Male officers also had a suicide rate that was 3 times higher than that of other male municipal government employees. Guralnick (1963) reported the suicide rate of male officers to be 1.8 times higher than that of the general population, and that said suicides accounted for 13 percent of all police deaths (compared to only 3 percent of all deaths in other occupations). Some of the stress-related reasons given for police suicides include shift work, social strain, exposure to human suffering, physical illness, and a perceived loss of control on the job and in the officer's personal life. ***Stress management programs*** appear to be useful in reducing the number of these suicides. After the development of a suicide awareness program, which included a

Table 11.2 Reactions to Stress in Policing

Physical Reactions	Emotional Reactions	Cognitive Reactions	Behavior / Coping Reactions
• Headaches • Muscle aches • Sleep disturbances • Changes in appetite • Decreased interest in sexual activity & impotence • Heart disease • Ulcers	• Anxiety • Fear • Guilt • Sadness • Anger • Irritability • Feeling lost or unappreciated • Withdrawal	• Flashbacks • Nightmares • Slowed thinking • Difficulty making decisions & problem solving • Disorientation • Lack of concentration • Memory lapses • Post Traumatic Stress Disorder	• Reduced motivation • Reduced job satisfaction • Lack of job involvement • Absenteeism • Premature retirement • Poor relationships with non-police friends • Divorce • Substance abuse • Suicide

Adapted from: Kureczka, A. W. 1996. "Critical Incident Stress in Law Enforcement." *FBI Law Enforcement Bulletin*, Feb./March: p. 15.; Lord, V. B. 1996. "An Impact of Community Policing: Reported Stressors, Social Support, and Strain Among Police Officers in a Changing Police Department." *Journal of Criminal Justice* 24(6): 503-522.; Lord, V. B., Gray, D. O., and Pond, S. B. 1991. "The Police Stress Inventory: Does it Measure Stress?" *Journal of Criminal Justice* 19: 139-150..

discussion of the signs of impending suicide, the number of suicides in the New York City Police Department dropped between 1994 and 1995 (LEN, November 15, 1996: 1).

The relationship between suicide and policing, however, is far from consistent. For example, Stack and Kelley (1999) observed inconsistencies in the empirical research, and also noted that most research on police suicide was limited to samples drawn from a few local police departments. To combat this apparent shortcoming, their analysis used the 1985 National Mortality Detail File and included data from 12,000 local police departments, 3,000 sheriff's offices, 49 state police agencies, and various federal law enforcement agencies. Suicide rates for police officers were compared to that of other males in the population. Their analysis indicated that suicide rates for police officers (25.6 per 100,000) were only slightly higher than the suicide rate of nonpolice (23.8 per 100,000). Further, after controlling for socioeconomic status and other variables, being a police officer was not a significant factor in odds of death by suicide. This appears to indicate that whereas the policing occupation may be inherently stressful, occupational stress may not truly be related to suicide.

Drug and alcohol abuse are also particularly serious problems because they play a major role in health, suicides, and family difficulties. Many police officers in the United States have a serious drinking or drug problem or both. In some departments, the problem is so severe that it can be called an epidemic. Hurrell and Kroes (1975) noted that police administrators had informally reported that as many as 25 percent of the officers in their departments abused alcohol. In their survey of 852 police officers, Richmond et al. (1998) reported a relatively high rate of unhealthy lifestyles. Specifically, they found almost half of the respondents reported excessive consumption of alcohol, and younger officers were particularly more likely to consume a lot. In fact, they reported that about two-fifths of male officers and about one-third of female officers reported binge drinking. They warned that excessive consumption of alcohol could have detrimental effects on officer performance, including slower reaction time, impaired performance, absenteeism, and liver problems. They reported other research that found alcoholic liver disease deaths among officers (1.2 percent) to be twice as high as those of the general public (0.6 percent). They also noted a high level of other unhealthy behavior, including smoking, being overweight, and absence of exercise. Finally, they noted that 12 percent of male officers and 15 percent of female officers reported moderate or severe stress-related symptoms. Unfortunately, they failed to examine the relationship between stress and alcohol consumption; however, they inferred that these life-style choices and stress were related.

Davey, Obst, and Sheehan (2000) conducted a survey of 4,193 Australian police officers regarding their alcohol use. They found the frequency with which officers consumed alcohol was similar to national averages; however, they did report that officers were more likely to engage in binge drinking. Thirty percent of their sample were classified as at risk for harmful levels of consumption, while 3 percent were classified as alcohol dependent. Consumption and substance abuse may not be limited to off-duty behavior. Perhaps most startling was the fact 25 percent of their sample reported drinking alcohol while on duty. Kraska and Kappeler (1988) found similar patterns of substance abuse in a medium-sized police department. Twenty percent of officers used marijuana while on duty at least twice per month.

There is some evidence that officers who are frequently exposed to crises or traumatic events may suffer from ***post-traumatic stress disorder (PTSD)***. Stressors leading to PTSD include shooting someone, being shot at, instances of child abuse, spouse abuse and rape cases, being threatened or having family members threatened, and observing death (of victims or colleagues) through homicide, suicide, or natural disaster. Martin, McKean, and Veltkamp (1986) found that of the 53 officers studied, 14 reported symptoms of post-traumatic stress. Although little is known about the extent, or effect, of PTSD among police officers, it may lead to an increase in the use of excessive force (Kellogg and Harrison, 1991).

Recently, Stephens and Miller (1998) examined the prevalence of PTSD among 527 police officers in New Zealand, and further examined whether PTSD was related to on-the-job traumatic experiences or experiences off the job. They that found the incidence of PTSD among police officers was similar to that in the civilian population of those who had experienced traumatic events. They also reported that as the number of traumatic events experienced by the individual officer increases, so too does the likelihood and frequency of PTSD symptoms. Traumatic events experienced on duty were more strongly related to PTSD. Among the most traumatic events were knowing of a police officer's death, a robbery/mugging or holdup encounter, and chronic distress.

Of course, caring for officers at risk for PTSD is desired from the humane and human relations position, but the influence of PTSD has other direct implications for the police organization and police managers. Vaughn (1991) estimated that approximately 70 percent of officers involved in deadly force incidents leave the department within five years, and this attrition can lead to large expenditures to replace officers. First, police managers should be aware of officers at high risk for traumatic events, as these cumulative events may eventually lead to more serious problems. Second, after traumatic events occur, the police organization should be prepared to assist the officers involved to reduce the likelihood of long-term debilitating experiences. In their study of suburban officers, Robinson, Sigman and Wilson (1997) found that the majority of officers said a ***critical-incident debriefing or counseling sessions*** would be beneficial in reducing the reaction to stressful events. Third, police managers should consider establishing a ***long-term maintenance program*** designed to reduce chronic stress from these events. For example, in Fort Worth (Texas) the Psychological Services Unit facilitates peer counseling in the wake of traumatic events (Greenstone, Dunn and Leviton, 1995).

Stress-Intervention Models

There are two perspectives, or models, for dealing with stress: the medical model and the organizational health model. According to the medical model, the individual is assumed to be vulnerable to the effects of police stress, and selection and training are required to reduce the potential effects of stress-related factors. In training, the emphasis is on the officer's stress-coping abilities and on treatment for stress-related problems. This individual approach to stress is also referred to as person centered. Until recently, this person-centered approach has been the most influential in attempting to understand and respond to stress-related problems. The medical model does not take into consideration that, from an officer's perspective, most of the significant stressors are related to the organization and management, and not the inherent nature of police work.

Medical Model

The clinical responses to these stressors fall into three categories: elimination, coping, and counseling. Officers and managers can work together to identify and try to eliminate stressors. The individual, with the support of family, peers, and the organization, can attempt to improve his or her stress-coping capacity. In addition, psychologists may be used to assess this capacity of individuals prior to, and after, employment. Finally, an officer can seek the assistance of a professional counselor.

Organizational Health Model

Although individual stress-related problems are not discounted, and clinical intervention may be necessary, in the organizational health model it is the manager's responsibility to develop and maintain a healthy work force by improving the work environment, particularly as it relates to stress. This approach is based on the assumption that (1) personal stress may be and often is the symptom of an unhealthy workplace, and (2) the most effective means of dealing with stress is to develop a healthy working environment (Ayres and Flanagan, 1992).

This model emphasizes the importance of identifying management practices and organizational characteristics that contribute to police stress. These characteristics have been addressed in other chapters so they will not be discussed again. As emphasized throughout this book, the organizational environment that results from job design, organizational structure, and management style determines in large part the morale and productivity of employees.

What is a "good place to work"? Levering (1985) found that in the "100 best companies" he studied, five phrases were repeatedly used to describe the organization and management:

1. This is a "friendly place."

2. "There isn't much politicking around here."

3. "You get a fair shake" in this organization.

4. This is "more than a job."

5. "It's just like a family" around here.

All the information presented in this book can be used in an attempt to create police organizations that could be characterized by these five phrases. Realistically, however, it is difficult to create a police department to which all these characteristics would apply. Police departments are inherently bureaucratic and political because major policy decisions and the selection, promotion, and evaluation of employees are strongly influenced by prevailing political ideologies, both nationally and in each community. Consequently, it is unlikely that police managers can create an organization in which there will be no "politicking."

The organizational health perspective also includes the consideration of social support. An individual may be more or less insulated against the effects of stress depending on whether he or she has a social-support network (of friends, coworkers, and family members). **Social supports** may help people to cope with stressful circumstances and thus lessen their potentially negative effects (Cullen et al. 1985). Indeed, Stephens and Long (2000) indicated that social support through communication with supervisor and peers may reduce moderate levels of stress. Officers who were able to communicate with these groups had correspondingly lower levels of stress. It is clear that supervisory support can reduce work-related stress, and family support is helpful in lessening personal life stress.

Other activities that can become part of the organization's response to stress are listed below:

1. Establish quality-of-work-life activities designed to improve communication and increase participation in decision making throughout the organization.

2. Address workplace environmental issues including quality of equipment, work space, compensation packages, and related aspects.

3. Develop training programs in stress awareness. Police should consider stress management as simply another skill to be learned, like criminal law or police procedure.

4. Establish specific police-stress programs. They can be part of larger departmental psychological services, an organizational health program, or a general employee-assistance program.

5. Establish operational policies that reduce stress. Consider the effects of shift assignments and scheduling, report writing, and so forth.

6. Improve management skills overall, especially in people-oriented aspects of supervision and management; include stress-management skills in supervisory practice.

7. Utilize peer-counseling programs. Because peers may have already experienced many of the same problems, they can be invaluable sources of help to fellow officers.

8. Develop support groups by taking advantage of the natural groups that already exist informally and formally within the organization.

9. Establish physical-fitness programs that can help the individual to withstand occupational stress. Such programs should also address stress-related dietary issues.

10. Family activities can be an important source of assistance to the officer. In particular, as spouses have more knowledge about the nature of police work and its stressors, they are in a better position to provide support. (adapted from Farmer, 1990: 214–215)

Ultimately, in policing, it is the behavior of officers that determines organizational effectiveness and the extent to which the community cooperates with, and supports, the police. If officers are honest, competent, responsible, not abusive or excessive in the use of force, and treat citizens with courtesy and respect, they will have few problems in the community. It is the manager's responsibility to ensure that all officers meet these requirements.

Summary

An understanding of the theories of police behavior and the variables that influence discretion is crucial for the effective management of police departments. For managerial purposes, the behavior of officers falls into four categories: competence, productivity, integrity, and style. One of the most important aspects of police behavior is the decision to use some kind of force. Such use should be evaluated in terms of timeliness, necessity, excessiveness, and whether or not it was intentional.

Police concern about safety is a major factor in police behavior. Although the actual risk of death is lower for police than for many other occupations, the perceived risk is high. If police managers can reduce officer concern about personal safety, officers may use less force and are less aggressive. Stress in policing is also an important factor in police behavior. Police officers tend to believe that the department and managers create more stress for them than do the problems inherent in the occupation. Effective managers can have a significant impact on stress in the organization.

Discussion Questions

1. Theories of police behavior were grouped into seven possible categories. Identify and explain each one.

2. How are police goals, tactics, and presence related to police behavior?

3. Define police discretion. Identify the categories of variables that influence police discretion and give examples for each category. How might discretion differ in the community-policing era?

4. Identify and explain the four categories of police behavior that are important in the management of police departments.

5. Distinguish between a competent and an incompetent threat to police officers. Give examples of each one.

6. Discuss the following terms as they relate to the use of force by police: timeliness, necessity, excessiveness, and brutality.

7. Identify and discuss the five types of violence-prone officers.

8. Discuss how perceived danger may influence (a) officer behavior, (b) officer use of force, and (c) officer stress.

9. Explain the following terms: physiological stress, psychological stress, eustress, distress, acute stress, and chronic stress.

10. Discuss ways police managers can reduce officer stress.

References

Ayres, R. M., and Flanagan, G. S. 1992. *Prevention Law Enforcement Stress: The Organization's Role.* Washington, DC: Bureau of Justice Statistics.

Bayley, D. H., and Bittner, E. 1989. "Learning the Skills of Policing." In R. G. Dunham and G. P. Alpert (eds.), *Critical Issues in Policing,* pp. 121–145. Prospect Heights, IL: Waveland Press.

Brooks, L. W. 1989. "Police Discretionary Behavior." In R. G. Dunham and G. P. Alpert (eds.), *Critical Issues in Policing,* pp. 87–110. Prospect Heights, IL: Waveland Press.

Brooks, L. W., and Piquero, N. L. 1998. "Police Stress: Does Department Size Matter?" *Policing: An International Journal of Police Strategies and Management* 21: 600–617.

California Commission on Peace Officers Standards and Training (POST), 1996. *California Law Enforcement Officers Killed and Assaulted in the Line of Duty, 1990–1994 Report.* Sacramento, CA: Author.

Cordner, G.W. 1995. "Community Policing: Elements and Effects." *Police Forum* 5:1–8.

Crank, J.P. 1993. "Legalistic and Order-Maintenance Behavior Among Police Patrol Officers: A Survey of Eight Municipal Police Agencies." *American Journal of Police* 12(1): 103–126.

Crank, J. P., and Caldero, M. 1991. "The Production of Occupational Stress in Medium-Sized Police Agencies: A Survey of Line Officers in Eight Municipal Departments." *Journal of Criminal Justice* 19: 339–349.

Cullen, F. T., Lemming, T., Link, B. G., and Wozniak, J. F. 1985. "The Impact of Social Supports on Police Stress." *Criminology* 23: 503–522.

Davey, J. D., Obst, P. L., and Sheehan, M. C. 2000. "Developing a Profile of Alcohol Consumption Patterns of Police Officers in a Large Scale Sample of an Australian Police Service." *European Addiction Studies* 6: 205–212.

Davis, K.C. 1969. *Discretionary Justice*. Baton Rouge, LA: Louisiana State University Press

Farmer, R. E. 1990. "Clinical and Managerial Implications of Stress Research on the Police." *Journal of Police Science and Administration* 17: 205–218.

Federal Bureau of Investigation. 1997. "In the Line of Fire: A Study of Selected Felonious Assaults on Law Enforcement Officers." Washington, DC: Department of Justice.

Federal Bureau of Investigation, 2000. " Law Enforcement Officers Killed and Assaulted, 1999." Washington, DC: Department of Justice.

French, P. Jr. 1975. "A Comparative Look at Stress and Strain in Policemen." In W. H. Kroes and J. J. Jurrell, Jr. (eds.), *Job Stress and the Police Officer*, pp. 60–72. Washington, DC: Department of Health, Education and Welfare.

Friedrich, R. 1977. "The Impact of Organizational, Individual and Situational Factors on Police Behavior." Unpublished Ph.D. dissertation, University of Michigan.

Geller, W. A., and Scott, M. S. 1992. *Deadly Force: What We Know*. Washington, DC: Police Executive Research Forum.

Goldstein, J. 1960. "Police Discretion Not to Invoke the Criminal Process." *Yale Law Journal* 60: 593–594.

Greenstone, J. L., Dunn, J. M., and Leviton, S. C. 1995. "Police Peer Counseling and Crisis Intervention Services Into the 21st Century." *Crisis Intervention and Time-Limited Treatment* 2: 167–187.

Guralnick, L. 1963. "Mortality by Occupation and Cause of Death Among Men 20-64 Years of Age." *Vital Statistics Special Reports* 53:3. Bethesda, MD: U.S. Department of Health, Education and Welfare.

Harris, D. A. 1999. "The Stories, the Statistics, and the Law: Why 'Driving While Black' Matters." *Minnesota Law Review* 84: 265–326.

Hurrell, J. J., Jr., and Kroes, W. H. 1975. "Stress Awareness." In W. H. Kroes and J.J. Hurrell, Jr. (eds.), *Job Stress and the Police Officer*, pp. 234–246. Washington, DC: Department of Health, Education and Welfare.

Huth, C. Personal communication, May 29, 2001.

Jefferis, E. S., Kaminski, R. J., Holmes, S., and Hanley, D. E. 1997. "The Effect of a Videotaped Arrest on Public Perceptions of Police Use of Force." *Journal of Criminal Justice* 25: 381–395.

Kaminski, R. J., and Sorensen, D. W. M. 1995. "A Multivariate Analysis of Individual, Situational and Environmental Factors Associated with Police Assault Injuries." *American Journal of Police* 14: 3–48.

Kansas City Police Department. 2001. "Procedural Instruction Policy 01–3, effective March 14, 2001." Unpublished document. Kansas City, Missouri.

Kavanagh, J. 1997. "The Occurrence of Resisting Arrest in Arrest Encounters: A Study of Police-Citizen Violence." *Criminal Justice Review* 22: 16–33.

Kellogg, T., and Harrison, M. 1991. "Post-Traumatic Stress Plays a Part in Police Brutality." *Law Enforcement News*, April: 1, 12.

Klockars, C. B. 1995. "A Theory of Excessive Force and Its Control." In W. A. Geller and H. Toch, *And Justice for All: Understanding and Controlling Police Abuse of Force*, pp. 11–30. Washington, DC: Police Executive Research Forum.

Konstantin, D. N. 1984. "Law Enforcement Officers Feloniously Killed in the Line of Duty: An Exploratory Study." *Justice Quarterly* 1: 29–45.

Kraska, P. B., and Kappeler, V. E. 1988. "Police On-Duty Drug Use: A Theoretical and Descriptive Examination." *American Journal of Police* 7: 1–28.

Kroes, W. H., Margalis, B. L., and Hurrell, J. J. 1974. "Job Stress in Policemen." *Journal of Police Science and Administration* 2: 145–155.

Lester, D. 1995. "Officer Attitudes Toward Police Use of Force." In W. Geller and H. Toch (eds.), *And Justice for All: Understanding and Controlling Police Abuse of Force*, pp. 177–186. Washington, DC: Police Executive Research Forum.

Levering, R. 1988. *A Great Place to Work*. New York: Random House.

Levering, R., Moskovitz, M., and Katz, M. 1985. *The 100 Best Companies to Work for in America*. New York: New American Library.

Lord, V. B. 1996. "An Impact of Community Policing: Reported Stressors, Social Support, and Strain Among Police Officers in a Changing Police Department." *Journal of Criminal Justice* 23: 503–522.

Lundman, R.J. 1979. "Organizational Norms and Police Discretion: An Observational Study of Police Work with Traffic Law Violators." *Criminology* 17: 159–171.

Maguire, K., and Pastore, A. L. 1995. *Source of Criminal Justice Statistics, 1994*. Bureau of Justice Statistics. Washington, DC: U.S. Government Printing Office.

Marion, N. 1998. "Police Academy Training: Are We Teaching Recruits What They Need to Know?" *Policing: An International Journal of Police Strategies and Management* 21:54–79.

Martin, C. A., McKean, H. E., and Veltkamp, L. J. 1986. "Post-Traumatic Stress Disorder in Police and Working with Victims." *Journal of Police Science and Administration* 14: 98–101.

Mastrofski, S.D. 1992. "What Does Community Policing Mean for Daily Police Work?" *National Institute of Justice Journal* 225. Washington, DC: National Institute of Justice.

Mastrofski, S. D., Worden, R. E., and Snipes, J. B. 1995. "Law Enforcement in a Time of Community Policing." *Criminology* 33: 539–563.

Muir, W. K. 1977. *Police: Streetcorner Politicians*. Chicago: University of Chicago Press.

Novak, K. J., Frank, J., Smith, B. W., and Engel, R. S. 2002. "Revisiting the Decision to Arrest: Comparing Beat and Community Officers." *Crime and Delinquency* 48:70-98.

Pendleton, M., Stotland, E., Spiers, P., and Kirach, E. 1989. "Stress and Strain Among Police, Firefighters and Government Workers: A Comparative Analysis." *Criminal Justice and Behavior* 16: 196–210.

Ramirez, D., McDevitt, J., and Farrell, A. 2000. *A Resource Guide on Racial Profiling Data Collection Systems: Promising Practices and Lessons Learned*. Washington, DC: Bureau of Justice Assistance.

Reiss, A.J. 1971. *The Police and the Public*. New Haven: Yale University.

Richmond, R.L., Wodak, A., Kehoe, L., and Heather, N. 1998. "How Healthy Are the Police? A Survey of Life-Style Factors." *Addiction* 93: 1729–1737.

Riksheim, E. C., and Chermak, S. M. 1993. "Causes of Police Behavior Revisited." *Journal of Criminal Justice* 21:353–382.

Roberg, R., Crank, J., and Kuykendall, J. 2000. *Police and Society*, 2d ed. Los Angeles: Roxbury Publishing.

Robinson, H. M., Sigman, M. R., and Wilson, J. R. 1997. "Duty-Related Stressors and PTSD Symptoms in Suburban Police Officers." *Psychological Reports* 81: 835–845.

Schmidt, A. K. 1985. "Deaths in the Line of Duty." *NIJ Reports*, pp. 6–8. Washington, DC: National Institute of Justice.

Scrivner, E. M. 1994. "Controlling Police Use of Excessive Force: The Role of the Police Psychologist." *Research in Brief*. Pamphlet. Washington, DC: National Institute of Justice.

Selye, H. 1974. *Stress Without Distress*. Philadelphia: Lippincott.

Shaw, C.R., and McKay, H. D. 1942. *Juvenile Delinquency and Urban Areas*. Chicago: University of Chicago Press.

Sherman, L. W. 1985. "Causes of Police Behavior." In A. S. Blumberg and E. Niederhoffer (eds.), *The Ambivalent Force*, 3rd ed., pp. 183–189. New York: Holt, Rinehart and Winston.

Smith, M. R., and Petrocelli, M. 2001. "Racial Profiling? A Multivariate Analysis of Police Traffic Stop Data." *Police Quarterly* 4: 4–27.

Soo Son, I., Tsang, C. W., Rome, D. M., and Davis, M. S. 1997. "Citizens' Observations of Police Use of Excessive Force and Their Evaluation of Police Performance." *Policing: An International Journal of Police Strategies and Management* 20: 149–159.

Stack, S., and Kelley, T. 1999. "Police Suicide" In D. J. Kenney and R. P. McNamara (eds.), *Police and Policing: Contemporary Issues*, 2nd Edition, pp. 94–107. Westport, CT: Praeger.

Stephens, C., and Long, N. 2000. "Communication with Police Supervisors and Peers as a Buffer of Work-Related Traumatic Stress." *Journal of Organizational Behavior* 21: 407–424.

Stephens, C., and Miller, I. 1998. "Traumatic Experiences and Post-Traumatic Stress Disorder in the New Zealand Police." *Policing: An International Journal of Police Strategies and Management* 21: 178–191.

Territo, L., and Vetter, H. J. (eds.). 1981. *Stress and Police Personnel*. Boston: Allyn and Bacon.

Terry, W. C., III. 1981. "Police Stress: The Empirical Evidence." *Journal of Police Science and Administration* 9: 61–75.

——. 1983. "Police Stress as an Individual and Administrative Problem." *Journal of Police Science and Administration* 11: 156–165.

Terry, W. C. 1985. "Police Stress as a Professional Self-Image." *Journal of Criminal Justice* 13: 501–512.

United States v. New Jersey, 1999, Civil Action No. MLC-99-5970.

Vaughn, J. 1991. "Critical Incidents for Law Enforcement Officers," in J. Reese, J., Horn, J., and Dunning, C. (eds.) *Critical Incidents in Policing*," pp. 143–148. Washington, DC: U.S. Government Printing Office.

Villa, B. J., and Morrison, G. B. 1994. "Biological Limits to Police Combat Handgun Shooting Accuracy." *American Journal of Police* 13: 1–31.

Violanti, J. M., and Aron, F. 1995. "Police Stressors: Variations in Perception Among Police Personnel." *Journal of Criminal Justice* 23: 287–294.

Violanti, J. M., Vena, J. E., and Marshall, J. R. 1996. "Suicide, Homicides, and Accidental Death: A Comparative Risk Assessment of Police Officers and Municipal Workers." *American Journal of Industrial Medicine* 30: 99–104.

Visher, C.A. 1983. "Gender, Police Arrest Decisions and Notions of Chivalry." *Criminology* 21: 5–28.

"What's Killing America's Cops?" 1996. *Law Enforcement News*, November 15: 1.

Wilkins v. Maryland State Police, 1993. Civil Action No. CCB-93-483.

Wilson, J. Q. 1968. *Varieties of Police Behavior*. Cambridge, MA: Harvard University Press.

Worden, R. E. 1990. "A Badge and a Baccalaureate: Policies, Hypotheses and Further Evidence." *Justice Quarterly* 7: 565–792.

——. 1995. "The 'Causes' of Police Brutality." In W. A. Geller and H. Toch (eds.), *And Justice for All*, pp. 31–60. Washington, DC: Police Executive Research Forum.

Chapter Twelve

Use of Resources

The resources of a police department consist primarily of its employees, plus the technology used that enhances and extends the human potential. The "resource" provided by each person varies somewhat relative to interpersonal skills, cognitive abilities, job-related knowledge and commitment. Advocates of diversity also argue that gender, sexual orientation, and cultural background are resources that have the potential to enhance an individual's and therefore the organization's effectiveness. In this chapter, the emphasis is on human resources in general, not the resource potential of each officer. A substantial majority of resources are invested in the patrol or investigations, or operational, function of policing; consequently, the focus will be on these areas.

❖ ❖ ❖ ❖   **Police Resources**

In police departments, there are both "sworn" and "civilian" employees. A *sworn* employee is one who takes an oath to uphold the constitution and to follow the law and the police code of ethics. By taking this oath, officers become an extension of the police power of government and therefore function as the legal representatives of that government. All other employees are in the *civilian* category and usually do not have police powers. The proportion varies among departments, from 60 to 90 percent sworn officers and 10 to 40 percent civilians. The emphasis in this chapter is on sworn police officers who are assigned to patrol or some type of investigative or specialized crime-related work. The chapter provides an overview of the issues in resource determination and allocation and a summary of the best available research concerning police effectiveness.

Resource Determination

Are police resources sufficient to accomplish the organization's goals? There are three methods used by police departments to determine the resources needed. The *intuitive* approach is essentially an educated guess based on the experience and judgment of police managers. The *workload* approach requires an elaborate information system, standards of expected performance, well-defined community expectations, and prioritization of police activities. To determine workload, the department must be able to identify precisely what the community expects the police to do, which calls must be processed, which calls can be ignored or given only a minimum response, and an expected level of service. Although the workload approach is rarely used for an entire department, it is sometimes used internally to determine the needed resources for functions (e.g., traffic unit) or programs (e.g., crime prevention).

Perhaps the most frequently used is the *comparative* approach, based on the ratio of police officers per 1,000, or 10,000, inhabitants. Among cities with 100 or more officers the ratio per 10,000 ranges from approximately 13:10,000 to over 100:10,000. The national average is about 23:10,000 (Reaves, 1999). The variation between ratios is so great that this approach to determining resource needs can easily be manipulated; consequently, comparisons should be made only between communities that are similar in size (e.g., population, population density and square miles) crime problems, public expectations, and political and historical context.

Whether or not adding more police reduces the crime rate or improves public satisfaction with the police continues to be debated. At some point, additional police resources would probably have an impact on crime and public opinion, but exactly the amount of additional resources that would be required would vary, based on conditions that contribute to, or detract from, the frequency and type of police problems, how the resources were used and how effectively the police are managed. On the other hand, there would undoubtedly be a point at which a reduction in police resources would result in an increase in crime and a decrease in public satisfaction, but this would also depend on the unique characteristics of each community and how the police department was managed. It is possible that 100 well-managed, "good" police officers are more effective than 200 less capable and motivated officers.

When police departments are given additional resources, it is important to distinguish between the total increase in personnel and the number of officers who are working at any given time. Unlike many organizations, police departments are always "open." Officers work only about 40 hours a week, they take vacations, are ill sometimes, go to court, participate in training programs, and so on. In addition, when departments employ more officers, they may create new supervisory and management positions, which would result in some experienced officers being promoted. It is important to distinguish between the number of new personnel and the ***operational impact*** of those personnel. In general, the operational impact of new personnel is about 20 percent (or less) of the total personnel added to the organization; that is, only about one in five are actually "working" at any given time.

There are at least three ways that managers can improve resources without adding additional personnel: (1) improving motivation; (2) higher levels of competency; and (3) improving efficiency (e.g., changing reporting systems, adding technology). As previously noted, most, if not all, police organizations have officers who are not as productive or competent as they should be. It is the managers' responsibility to ensure that motivation, competence, and efficiency are high before asking for more personnel; otherwise, not only will existing resources be underutilized, so will the new personnel.

Resource Allocation

Police resources are invested in the operational strategies—presence (police visibility), law enforcement (field interrogations, investigations, citations, arrests), education (knowledge and skills to reduce both victimization and to influence potential offenders) and community building (strengthen the positive socialization processes of the community), discussed in Chapter 1 that are believed to be the most effective in accomplishing the goals of the organization. The department's specializations or functions and programs (e.g., patrol, investigation, and traffic enforcement) use the strategy or strategies that are considered to be the most appropriate for that particular function. The design or structure of the organization—that is, its positions, functions, or specializations and programs—are a reflection of the managers' view as how to best allocate resources by purpose, process, time, and area.

Purpose

Although citizen fear of crime and attitudes toward the police, and the extent and nature of disorder, are measures of police effectiveness, the ***primary purpose*** of the police is to ***prevent crime.*** Prevention is used to describe both a strategy and a result. As a ***strategy***, it refers to the non-law enforcement activities of the police that are intended to reduce crime (e.g., programs for juveniles, victims and targets of crime, and community organizing and some problem-solving activities). We use prevention to describe a ***result***; a prevented crime is one that does not occur because of either the existence or activity of the police. The relationship between police and crime is difficult to assess, but in general there are at least three possible crime levels in the relationship: (1) the crime that would exist if there were no police force, (2) the crime that exists with an "average" police department, and (3) the crime that exists with an "excellent" police department. An "excellent" department is effectively managed and is adequately staffed with productive and competent officers whose activities are based on the best available knowledge concerning police effectiveness. Although it is not known what the actual differences in the crime rate would be at each level, the authors believe that the crime rate would be lower at each level, possibly substantially lower, ***regardless*** of other factors (e.g., the age structure of the population, poverty, and unemployment) that contribute to the crime problem. Research concerning the effectiveness of the police is discussed at the end of this chapter.

Not only can police prevent some crimes, they can also contribute to the crime problem by engaging in criminal activity (e.g., corruption), by being unproductive or incompetent, or by not using the most effective strategies. Inside Management 12.1 provides an example of how productivity and competence problems almost certainly resulted in a higher crime rate, and more victims, in two cities.

Inside Management 12.1

Productivity, Competence, and Crime in Two Cities

New York City provides an example of the possible relationship between inadequate police productivity and crime. In 1996, for the third year, New York City reported sharp declines in the crime rate. Although numerous factors may account for this decline (e.g., changing age structure of the population, more persons in prison for longer periods, more stable, and less violent, drug-distribution networks, using federal racketeering statutes to break up gangs), the police attribute it primarily to improved allocation of officers to "hot spots" of crime, more citations and arrests for quality-of-life crimes (e.g., drinking in public, urinating on the street), and crackdowns on drug dealers, gangs, and auto chop shops. Basically, beginning in mid-1994, police leaders in New York City increased police presence (more visible patrol officers) in some areas and required officers to become more productive, particularly by increasing the number of citations and arrests.

Prior to this time, the poor productivity of New York City officers was reported in a study which found that in the first seven months of 1994, 25 percent made no arrests and 47 percent made only one or two arrests. Although the opportunity to make misdemeanor and felony arrests varies by the extent of the crime problem in an area, a competent and motivated police officer can make in almost any area, many more arrests in seven months than did 72 percent of New York City officers. There are various reasons why officers make few if any arrests (e.g., type of assignment, community policing, and too many calls for service), but the two most important reasons are lack of motivation and poor management. In New York, if as suggested by police leaders, increases in the strategies of both presence and law enforcement resulted in a de-

crease in the crime rate, then the failure to make these changes earlier resulted in a higher crime rate, particularly as evidence supporting the effectiveness of combining these two strategies in New York has existed for more than 40 years.

A lack of police competence may also contribute to the crime problem. For instance, in Washington, D.C., in 1996, the chief of police indicated that 2,700 officers (about three quarters of the police force) needed to be retrained, in part because patrol officers and supervisors had an inadequate knowledge of the law and police procedure. The lack of legal and procedural competence (which also results in a lack of investigative competence) was probably one reason why the department had a 30 percent "clearance by arrest" rate for homicides, which is well below the 65 to 70 percent (or higher) clearance rate for many other police departments. In other words, over 50 percent of the homicides that would have resulted in an arrest in other cities went unsolved in Washington D.C. Although it is not certain that the murderers who were not arrested committed additional crimes, it is likely that some of them did.

Sources: "Arresting Statistics," 1994. *Law Enforcement News*, September 30: 3, 10; "Massive retraining effort due for DC cops," 1996. *Law Enforcement News*, February 14: 7; "DC's Metro police keep searching for some light at the end of a long tunnel," 1996. *Law Enforcement News*, June 30: 1, 6; C. Krauss, 1995. "New York Sees Steep Drop in Rate of Violent Crime," 1995. *The New York Times*, December 31: sec. Y, p. 13; E. Polley, 1996. "One Good Apple," *Time*, January 15: 54-56; F. Adams, 1964. "Operation 25." In S. Chapman (ed.), *Police Patrol Readings*, pp. 206-214. Springfield, IL: Charles C. Thomas.

Process

❂ Police processes are oriented to incident, person, problem, or place (location). The ***incident-oriented*** process involves the steps that police go through to respond to a specific crime or related event. The crime is reported or observed, the police respond and conduct an inquiry, and they attempt to identify a suspect and make an arrest.

The ***person-oriented*** process involves finding and arresting individuals wanted for one or more crimes and the identification of individuals believed to be recurringly involved in criminal activity, who may be monitored by the police in hopes of obtaining sufficient information to make an arrest. The person category refers to both criminals and victims. To what degree can the police predict who will become involved in criminal activity? To what degree can they predict who will become a victim of a crime? Persons wanted for crimes or suspected of criminal activity or who are on probation or parole can become the focus of police activity. Individuals who are more likely to be victimized (e.g., senior citizens, children, and persons who have repeatedly been victimized) can also receive attention.

The ***problem-oriented*** process involves the police response either to a "group of similar incidents" (e.g., domestic violence, drunk driving, and auto theft) that occur throughout the community or to all the incidents in a certain "location" (e.g., a neighborhood or apartment complex). The problem refers to a particular type of crime, or related problem like gun possession, and what may be unique about that crime. How serious is the crime as determined by the law? The community? Is it more likely to be committed in a public or private place? Does the crime have a victim or does it involve the buying and selling of illegal goods and services? Is the criminal more likely to be a stranger or someone the victim knows? Are more serious crimes likely to result from less serious crimes (e.g., do domestic disturbances lead to murder)? To what degree can the crime be predicted in terms of time and location? How difficult is the crime to solve? If arrests are rarely made, should the police focus more on an educational than a law enforcement response? To what degree is the crime preventable by the police or by the police and community working together?

Crimes can be grouped into any number of general categories: felonies or misdemeanors, property crimes or violent crimes, crimes with a victim or victimless crimes, or crimes committed by a stranger or by an intimate (i.e., the victim knows the suspect). Crimes can also be grouped by a specific crime—for example, homicide, robbery, or auto theft. Or they can be grouped according to a problem that includes different types of crimes like the drug problem or the gang problem or the domestic violence problem.

When considering the problem approach for police intervention, the circumstances that give rise to the problem must be known, as well as the person or persons who are or might be involved and the location and time in which the problem is likely to occur.

The ***place-oriented*** process refers to both the specific location (e.g., address) or area in which crimes occur. Are there addresses and areas in the community in which a substantially greater number of crimes are committed? What types of crimes occur at these locations, and when do they occur? Can the address or area be changed in ways that crimes can be prevented? Can the police respond in a way that will increase the number of arrests?

Recently, what has become known as ***hot-spot*** research has found that a large number of calls for service and crime come from a few areas in a community. Sherman, Gartin and Buerger (1989) found that only 3 percent of places (addresses) in Minneapolis accounted for 50 percent of the calls that police received. When repeat occurrences are considered, an even smaller number of places are involved. For example, second robberies occurred at only 2.2 percent of the places. One of the most startling findings was that 161 addresses in Minneapolis had 15 or more calls for police service during the period of the study. The places that have a disproportionately large share of police calls are often apartment complexes or a block with a tavern or bar.

Historically, this same information was discovered by many police departments through the use of pin maps—that is, placing on a map different colored pins for different types of crimes or problems. More recently, it is part of the crime mapping process discussed in Chapters 9 and 10.

This type of ***place analysis*** is useful for the police and has the potential for reducing both the number of calls for service and the number of crimes. Such reductions are not always certain, however, because the combination of strategies and methods to be employed is not necessarily clear. Problem-solving policing may be useful for some areas (e.g., trying to close down a tavern or getting an apartment owner to take steps to reduce crime); whereas in other areas, police crackdowns may be more useful. Police ***crackdowns*** involve an increased use of the strategies of presence and usually law enforcement. Inside Management 12.2 describes police crackdowns that have been used to respond to places of crime and to target specific problems.

Inside Management 12.2

Police Crackdowns

An important development in proactive police work is the use of what has become known as a crackdown. Although this approach, under different names (e.g., police descents), dates back over 100 years, the term ***crackdown*** began to be used in the 1980s and 1990s. Crackdowns can be defined as sudden increases in officer presence and law enforcement (e.g., field interrogations, citations, and arrests), either for specific types of offenses or for all offenses in specific areas. Drunk driving, public drug markets, streetwalking prostitutes, domestic violence, illegal parking, and even unsafe bicycle riding have all been targets for publicly announced crackdowns. The theory behind this approach is that crackdowns make the risk of apprehension far more uncertain than in any fixed level of normal police patrol activity in which the law is selectively enforced. One type of crackdown involves policy changes about how to handle a specific type of offense or offender (e.g., make arrests in domestic violence situations, target high-risk couples). Another type involves full enforcement of the law in a particular area (e.g., citations for all traffic violations or full enforcement of curfew ordinance). Often, in crackdowns, some people applaud the police action while others condemn it for being too intrusive and an abuse of police authority.

The evaluation of crackdowns indicates that there is an initial deterrent effect on some offenses. There is also some residual deterrence; that is, the crime reduction continues for a time even after the crackdown is over. Short-term crackdowns appear to have less deterrence decay, which is the time frame for, and the extent of, the lessening of the deterrent effect associated with the crackdown. Research has also indicated that an announcement effect may have some influence on crime. This term refers to any publicity associated with a police crackdown. Simply announcing that the police are going to crack down in a certain area or for a certain type of crime may have a deterrent effect.

When using crackdowns, it is important to determine what combination of police activities (e.g., increased presence, more field interrogations, more traffic citations, and more undercover activity) influences what crimes and for how long. Plus, it is important to know how long the crackdown should last to obtain the maximum effect. How many officers are needed? What exactly should they do? How long should

they do it? When should they return to the area? It may be that the random selection of areas, or crimes, as targets for short-term crackdowns (possibly only an hour or less) may be the most effective and efficient use of police resources.	Adapted from: L. W. Sherman, 1990. "Police Crackdowns," *NIJ Reports*. Washington, DC: National Institute of Justice; and authors' commentary.

Another tactic police organizations have used is to pool their resources. For example, over the past decade police organizations have engaged in collaborative efforts to disrupt drug trafficking in their communities. Recognizing drug dealing and trafficking as a regional problem, these departments began to form ***multi-jurisdictional drug task forces***, in order to combine their resources and information. The premise of these drug task forces is that by pooling resources police organizations can (a) avoid overlapping investigations, (b) increase the efficiency of drug investigations, and (c) increase the effectiveness of drug investigations. Police departments typically assign officers to a single regional unit dedicated to reducing drug trafficking by making more arrests in the participating agencies' jurisdictions. Yet despite the creation of thousands of task forces (supplemented by millions of dollars from the federal government) the impact of these cooperative ventures has not been adequately evaluated (Sherman et al., 1997). Further, little is known regarding what type of organizational arrangement between participating agencies is most efficient.

Results from a series of research efforts have begun to shed some insight on these issues. Research on drug task forces in Ohio indicate that police departments participating in drug task forces report higher drug-case quality than those not participating in these joint ventures. Similarly, these agencies report significantly more communication and cooperation among police departments in reducing the availability of drugs. However, the actual number of arrests for drugs was not related to participation in drug task forces (Jefferis et al., 1998; Smith et al., 2000). Furthermore, task forces with more agencies participating, and who report high levels of participatory management, report correspondingly higher levels of perceived effectiveness (Pratt et al., 2000). In short, while participating in drug task forces achieves some goals associated with the process of reducing crime (e.g., communication, perceptions of police managers), it is unclear whether these collaborative ventures actually reduce drug trafficking, or whether it is an efficient use of police resources.

Time and Area

Because police departments are open all the time, they must decide how to distribute resources twenty-four hours a day throughout the year. Most often, they do so by determining the changing workload and allocating personnel accordingly. If half or more of the problems occur at night, then half of more of the officers should be assigned to work at night. The number of problems also determines the allocation of resources by area. Generally, there is an attempt to equalize workload for officers. The size of the area to which officers are assigned is primarily determined by the level of activity; the higher the level of activity, the smaller the area.

The time and area analysis of calls to police and crime results in the "beat," or "district," structure of the organization and the time frame for different "shifts" or "watches. " Almost all police departments follow a 4-10 or a 5-8 plan; that is, 10 hours a day, four days a week or 8 hours per day, 5 days a week. Usually, there are three shifts in each 24-hour period, but there may also be 4 or 5 shifts that overlap to accommodate the uneven workload. Calls for the police and police problems are not evenly distributed during a day, week, month, or year; consequently, there are usually more officers working at some time periods than others. The allocation of police resources by time and area, particularly in large departments, is a complex issue that would require more detail than is appropriate for this chapter (Patrol Allocation, 1995). One example of a useful aid in resource allocation—computerized mapping—is discussed in Inside Management 12.3.

Inside Management 12.3

Computerized Mapping

Computerized mapping has been used in policing since the 1960s; however, it became more common with the recent development of PC-based software. This software has many crime control and crime prevention applications, including identifying the location of a crime, the location of the person reporting the crime, and if the perpetrator is known, his or her last known address, known associates, and location of any recovered property. Other useful planning data that can be incorporated into the mapping process include the location of abandoned dwellings and cars and incidents of vandalism.

Perhaps the most useful feature of crime mapping involves overlaying different types of maps; for example, one map showing the location of crimes for a certain period with another map showing the unemployment rates of residents, the location of abandoned buildings, or citizen reports of drug activity. In other words, maps can not only be developed for the type and location of crime but also for many "explanatory" variables—that is, a characteristic that may be associated with the crime problem in that area.

Police departments have long used "pin maps" for identifying places and types of crime throughout a jurisdiction. Although such maps are useful, computerized mapping provides for a more sophisticated, flexible, and analytical approach. There are a number of departments (e.g., San Diego, Los Angeles, Dallas) that use mapping in their crime analysis units. The Chicago Police Department's crime-mapping system is titled Information Collection for Automated Mapping (ICAM). With this system, officers can find data concerning current crime and community conditions in an area by simply using a mouse to click an incident type, a location, and a time period. ICAM is considered to be an important part of Chicago's Alternative Police Strategy (CAPS), or community-policing, program.

In Hartford, Connecticut, community organizations and other city agencies are working with the police department to incorporate the use of computer mapping that will provide data for all the groups involved. The type of data to be collected includes but is not limited to crime, calls for service, number of complaints, arson and fire-inspection reports, building-inspection reports, and tax-delinquency reports.

In Savannah, Georgia, computerized mapping was used to address the violent crime problem. The mapping process included data on serious felonies, public disorder, and other disturbances, with map overlays depicting neighborhood blight and deterioration (e.g., substandard and vacant housing or unmaintained private property), and social and economic data such as teenage pregnancy, child abuse, juvenile unrest, and per capita income. In all, 29 different factors were assessed, including data from the Health and the Children's Services departments. The study found a marked association between crime and violence, dilapidated housing, fires, unmaintained properties, derelict vehicles, sewerage and drainage problems, unemployment, female-headed households, child abuse, child neglect, teenage pregnancy, drug abuse, and juvenile delinquency.

Adapted from: T. R. Rich, 1995. "The Use of Computerized Mapping in Crime Control and Prevention Programs," *Research in Action*. Washington, DC: National Institute of Justice.

Community Policing and Crime ❖ ❖ ❖ ❖

As discussed, the community-policing approach to crime is more broadly based than police-specific responses (e.g., presence and law enforcement). Other approaches include not only the educational strategy and community organizing but partnerships with other public, private, and community organizations. Police responses to crime will be more effective if both managers and officers have an understanding of the substantial research on crime prevention. Some of the more important research is briefly summarized below. Police managers are encouraged to explore each of these areas in greater depth, as well as the research on the prevention of specific crimes (e.g., substance abuse and retail-sector crimes).

Community Crime Prevention

Community crime prevention is based on the assumption that if a community can be changed, so can the behavior of those who live there; this is the basic premise behind the neighborhood-building approach to community policing. Attempts to change communities include the following: (1) organizing the community to improve and strengthen relationships between residents to encourage residents to take preventive precautions, and to obtain more political and financial resources; (2) changing building and neighborhood design to improve both public and police surveillance, which improves guardianship; (3) improving the appearance of an area to decrease the perception that it is a receptive target for crime; and (4) developing activities and programs that provide a more structured and supervised environment (e.g., recreation programs).

Although community crime prevention is closely associated with the community-policing movement, the evidence of its effectiveness is limited, in part, because of the lack of understanding of social relationships within neighborhoods and how crime is influenced by both the broader community and societal trends. Perhaps the most promising approach to responding to high-crime areas is to focus on the relationship between the poverty of youth and crime. High-crime areas have a disproportionately large number of criminals and victims; consequently, while developing programs to support, socialize, and supervise youth, it is also important to protect the "fearful, vulnerable and victimized" (Hope, 1995).

Situational Crime Prevention

The *situational approach* to crime prevention attempts to reduce opportunity for crime by making it more difficult to commit, increasing the risk of the perpetrator's arrest, and reducing the possible rewards. This approach is based on opportunity theories of crime and the identification of specific methods for addressing a specific crime problem. There is considerable evidence that situational crime prevention is effective, even when the displacement of crime is taken into consideration (Clarke, 1995).

Examples of some of the methods used in this approach include target hardening; access control; entry and exit screening; target removal; and formal, employee, and natural surveillance. *Target hardening* involves the use of barriers, reinforced materials, locks, safes, and protective (even bullet-proof) screens. ***Access control*** attempts to exclude potential offenders from buildings and other areas by using personal identification numbers, entry phones, fencing, reception desks in apartments and public buildings, and barriers to interrupt the flow of vehicular and pedestrian traffic. Entry and exit ***screening*** includes screening of baggage and passenger at airports, book-detection screens in libraries, designing tickets to make them easier to check for accuracy, and the use of automated ticket gates. ***Target removal*** involves taking away objects of crime—for example, requiring phone cards instead of money to make calls and persuading hospital inpatients or hotel guests to turn in their valuables for safekeeping.

Formal and employee surveillance involves public and private police (security guards, store detectives) and business employees. Surveillance can be conducted by individuals or by alarms, video cameras, and radar or a combination thereof. The presence of employees at key locations (e.g., doorman at apartments, conductors on buses, and parking lot attendants), and the number of employees (two or more working at night) may also reduce crime. ***Natural surveillance*** occurs as individuals go about their daily routine. This type of surveillance can be improved by making it easier to observe possible crime targets and offender activities, which may require removing or trimming shrubbery, improving lighting, creating unobstructed views, and placing businesses in areas with more public activity (Clarke, 1995).

Developmental Crime Prevention

Certain childhood factors are indicative of the probability of delinquent behavior. Three of the most important factors are disruptive behavior at an early age, cognitive deficits, and inadequate or poor parenting. Those preadolescence prevention programs that address all three factors and last for a prolonged period tend to have the most positive effects (Trembley and Craig, 1995). Although it is not normally the police responsibility to become involved in such activities, they should provide support for the investment of resources in these areas. When communities do not have such programs, the police can take the ***initiative*** to see that they are developed.

Public Health and Crime Prevention

Where the criminal justice system tends to view violent crime as a problem of public order, public health officials consider violent crime to be intentional injuries that are part of the health problems in a community. Other differences between the criminal justice and public health perspectives include the following: (1) the criminal justice response tends to focus on the offender, the public health response on the victim; and (2) the criminal justice system tends to emphasize violence among strangers, the public health perspective emphasizes the importance of healing victims and the community.

Public health officials are less concerned about the intentions (the moral culpability) of the offender than they are about identifying risk factors indicative of violence, including "persons at greater risk of disease or injury and the places, times, and other circumstances that are associated with increased risk" (Moore, 1995: 244). Risk factors can be grouped into three categories;

structural or cultural, criminogenic commodities, and situational. ***Structural or cultural risk factors*** include poverty and violence on television. ***Criminogenic commodities*** include when and under what circumstances guns, alcohol, and drugs are available. ***Situational risk factors*** include "festering, unsolved disputes" between couples, spouses, tenants and landlords, and gangs (Moore, 1995). Gradually, the police are learning more about the strategies or combination of strategies that are the most effective in responding to crime, citizen fear of crime, and citizen attitudes. As this body of knowledge grows, and as more police managers become aware of and apply this knowledge, the authors believe that the police will be able to substantially improve their impact on crime.

Patrol and Investigations

In local law enforcement, the substantial majority of police resources are invested in patrol and investigations. In general, as police departments increase in size, they tend to become more specialized. Patrol and investigative specialists are connected by a crime response process that includes an initial gathering of information followed by a subsequent investigation and case development, if an arrest is made. As a rule, departments with 25 to 30 or more officers divide this process between the initial and subsequent investigation. Patrol officers conduct the preliminary investigation for most crimes, and investigative specialists (sometimes called detectives) do the follow-up investigation. Although patrol officers engage in numerous activities not related to responding to specific crimes, it is the dividing of the crime response process that has resulted in the creation of investigative specialists.

Some officers may become traffic specialists, emergency response officers (e.g., responding to crimes in progress or hostage situations), crime prevention officers, and investigative specialists for each type of crime (e.g., arson, auto theft, and sexual assault). The advantages and disadvantages of specialization will not be discussed here except to say that, aside from instances in which a high degree of expertise is necessary, specialization does not necessarily improve effectiveness and efficiency. In fact, it may result in both officers and the organization being less productive than is possible.

Using Police Strategies

Not only do managers have a choice in the resources to be invested in each police strategy, they must make other important decisions. Strategic responses can be either reactive or proactive or both. ***Reactive responses*** occur as the result of a request for police services. The majority of incidents in which police become involved are reactive because they are the result of a citizen who calls the police. ***Proactive responses*** involves any activity initiated by the police. When police conduct field interrogations, issue citations, or initiate a crime-prevention program or community-policing program, they are making a proactive response.

One of the important issues in determining the degree to which the police should be proactive or reactive is related to the role of the police in a democratic society. Although it is inevitable that the police will be somewhat proactive (e.g., issue traffic citations), the more proactive they are, the more they intrude in the community because they decide what areas or persons or problems to target. There are certain variables (e.g., race and gender) used in police decision making that are potentially controversial. In reactive policing, the citizen requests police services and, in effect, gives permission to intrude into his or her life. Nevertheless, many citizens who could benefit from police assistance do not request it and therefore are not served unless the police initiate contact.

In general, citizens are more likely to resent and criticize police proactivity when the police emphasize the law enforcement strategy (which may be accompanied with higher levels of police presence) than when they engage primarily in the education or community building strategies. To some degree, the style of an officer when conducting field interrogations, issuing citations, and making arrests can offset citizen resentment and criticism, but in reality, many citizens not only resent the message (law enforcement), they also resent the messenger (the officer).

Covert, or invisible police activity, involves officers patrolling in unmarked vehicles, with or without a uniform, surveillance of suspected criminals or locations, and clandestine (undercover) investigations. Covert police activity not only places officers at greater risk (e.g., more danger and stress), it is often resented by both criminals and citizens. However, covert police activity is a necessary part of law enforcement because it is one of the most effective and efficient ways to respond to some crimes (i.e., those involving the buying and selling of illegal goods and services) and criminals (e.g., some professional criminals).

Overt, or visible, police activity involves an officer being visible (e.g., in uniform or marked patrol car) or acknowledging that they are police officers (e.g., detectives in plainclothes conducting a follow-up investigation). The substantial majority of police officers are overt when working. For patrol officers, their frequency of visibility at any given point establishes the extent of police presence in an area. They may engage in discretionary, random, or directed patrol.

- *Discretionary patrol* occurs when officers decide where to patrol when not otherwise occupied. Generally, what is referred to as discretionary patrol is usually called *random patrol*; but that term is inappropriate, because officers usually do not randomly select where they patrol. In addition, some police departments have used randomly assigned patrol units in areas or streets within a jurisdiction to increase the probability of being present or close by when a crime occurs (Nelson, 1964; Elliott, 1973). Consequently, discretionary and random patrol are distinctly different.

- *Directed patrol* occurs when officers are told where to go to patrol when they are not busy doing other things. Usually, they are directed to locations in their area that are believed to have the type of problems (i.e., occurring in public rather than in private) that patrol will deter. A determination as to where to send officers to patrol is usually based on crime analysis conducted by the department or the patrol officer. Crime analysis was addressed in Chapter 9 when planning was discussed. An additional example of crime analysis and "innovative" management, called Compstat, is presented in Inside Management 12.4, and was also discussed in Chapter 3.

The Compstat process is based on the assumption that an organization should have timely and up-to-date information about the problems the organization was created to address; that managers should be held accountable for the behavior and productivity of their subordinates; that employees who are allowed more participation in analyzing problems and developing solutions will be happier and more motivated; that communication between various organizational functions is important; and that decentralized organizations are better able to adapt to changing environmental conditions.

Inside Management 12.4

The Compstat Process in New York City

The New York City Police Department, described as an aircraft-sized police department, is being given credit for changing from an "often Byzantine bureaucracy" to a "reinvented" and "reengineered" organization that has become a "highly maneuverable task force of dozens of smaller ships." This change is primarily the result of the introduction of the Compstat process, in which timely information about crime patterns and associated factors (crime analysis) is gathered and used as a basis for the rapid deployment of resources to "attack" crime. The methods used to respond to crime are evaluated, and managers (precinct commanders in New York) are held accountable for reductions in the crime rate. As part of the "reengineering" of the department, employees are "empowered," communication between the various functions is stressed (e.g., patrol and investigations), and authority and responsibility are decentralized to the precinct level (or identifiable neighborhoods or areas in smaller communities).

This process, and associated organizational and management changes, were borrowed, in part, from the private sector. "Crime reduction" became the department's "bottom line" or "profit and loss statement." The precints (or substations or neighborhoods) are "profit cen-

ters." The department was "reengineered" to move from a reactive organization, which measured success by rapid response to emergency calls and arrest rates, to a more proactive organization, which believed the police can do something about the crime rate.

Comstat is described as "revolutionary" in nature. Police leaders in New York City believe that it provides a new perspective on community policing; that community policing is not incompatible with aggressive law enforcement activities. The process, and the decline in crime, has resulted in interest from numerous other police departments. Individuals familiar with the process believe that it may become the "dominant mode of policing" in the United States. One person described Compstat as "a many splendored thing" in which it has expanded from an "informational need about crime statistics" and "command accountability" to "a vehicle for planning, evaluation and coordination."

Adapted from: P.C. Dodenhoff, 1996."...the NYPD and its Compstat process," *Law Enforcement News*, December 31, pp. 1, 4-5. Printed with permission from the *Law Enforcement News*, John Jay College of Criminal Justice.

Mobility

The mobility of the police, particularly patrol officers, is concerned with the manner in which the actual patrol takes place. Officers may be assigned to "fixed posts"; walk; ride horses, bicycles, motor scooters, or motorcycles; drive automobiles; fly in planes and helicopters; use boats, snowmobiles, dog sleds, or, on occasion, roller skates. Each form of mobility has both advantages and disadvantages; the choice of which form of mobility is not only related to effectiveness but is also determined by cost, access, population density, visibility, and community preferences.

Walking, or foot-patrol beats usually cover very small areas compared with the beats of a motorized patrol; therefore, walking tends to be the most expensive form of mobility. For mechanically mobilized officers, the cost of mobility varies considerably. As a rule, costs increase with size and technology (e.g., a bicycle is less expensive than a helicopter). The type of mobility is particularly important in densely populated areas congested with traffic. Patrol officers on foot, on bicycles, or on motorcycles have easier access to some areas (e.g., where there is no automobile access or the area is too small or congested) than do officers in automobiles. The form of mobility also largely determines visibility—that is, what the police officer can "see." For example, officers in helicopters can see things that officers on foot or in automobiles cannot see. This difference is important because watching is an important part of the patrol officer's function. Lastly, community preferences may be influential; for example, a community may prefer foot patrol or believe that the use of helicopters is too intrusive.

Police Effectiveness: Research Findings

How effective are the police in preventing crime? What is known about the output-outcome relationship in policing? Sherman, Gottfredson, Mac-Kenzie, Eck, Reuter and Bushway (1997) reviewed hundreds of studies, conducted between 1966 and 1996, concerning the effectiveness of a variety of programs and methods on crime (selected studies of police effectiveness since 1997 are discussed in Chapter 3). These studies were rated based on the quality of their research design using a scale of 1 to 5; the higher the score, the more reliable and valid the results. Sherman and colleagues (1997) grouped crime-related research into seven areas: community, family, school, labor-markets, "place" crime prevention, policing, and criminal justice. What follows is a brief summary of the findings of the highest rated studies.

What Works or Is Promising

Deciding which studies are relevant to the police requires a judgment concerning the police role. For purposes of this section, the police role is broadly defined, consistent with the community-policing model. As discussed in Chapter 1, the police accomplish their objectives using four major strategies. In which operational strategies, or combination of strategies, should police managers invest their resources? The research highlighted below is organized around these four strategies; the fifth strategy is developed by combining the themes from the other four.

Strategy 1: Presence Strategy (Patrol)

- Increasing directed patrol in high crime or "hot spot" areas

Strategy 2: Law Enforcement Strategy

- Orders of protection, and women's shelters (to reduce victimization)

- Nuisance abatement ordinances and enforcement in residential areas

- Proactive arrests of repeat offenders

- Proactive drunk driving arrests

- Arrest of employed suspects in domestic violence incidents

- Increased levels of traffic enforcement to discover illegally carried handguns

- Issuing arrest warrants for absent suspects in domestic violence cases

- Zero-tolerance of disorder is accomplished by enforcing minor violations of the law and use of civil abatement ordinances (if done in a manner that does not alienate the public).

Strategies 3 and 4: Education and Community Building Strategies

- Mentoring programs for at-risk teenagers (to reduce truancy, drug use, and violence)

- After-school recreation programs (to reduce juvenile arrests, drug use, and vandalism)

- Gang prevention programs that provide support and encouragement to leave gangs

- Target hardening—Prevention may occur if the places at which crimes take place are altered or changed in the following ways: increase number of employees present; use of metal detectors; use of guards; construct street closures (to reduce entry and exit points in an area); and increasing the security of homes and businesses (e.g., locks, barriers, lighting).

- Community-policing activities in which the community is involved in setting priorities

- Community-policing activities directed at improving police legitimacy (to build acceptance and trust)

Strategy 5: Combined Operational Strategies

The following combines the above four strategies in an attempt to prevent crime (Sherman, Shaw and Rogan, 1995; Kennedy, Piehl, and Braga 1996). Although the use of combined strategies appears promising, no rigorous evaluation has been conducted.

- Problem-oriented policing in general

- Adding more police in communities regardless of assignment (recent research supports this but earlier research does not)

- Interagency response to gang members, who focus on the use of firearms, to use nonviolent means to resolve conflicts (police, prosecutors, probation and parole, clergy, community groups, and social services)

What Does Not Work

The research by Sherman et al., (1997) further indicates that the following approaches are not effective in crime prevention, therefore police managers should not invest their resources in them.

- Mobilizing the community to fight crime in inner-city areas

- Gun buyback programs

- Neighborhood block-watch programs

- Arrest of juveniles for minor offenses

- Drug market arrests

- Community-policing activities that do not have a specific crime focus

Many of the evaluation studies reviewed by Sherman and colleagues (1997) did not provide reliable and valid evidence that a particular activity or program did or did not work because the research design was inadequate. Of course, this does not mean that they were necessarily effective or ineffective; rather, that effectiveness could not be determined. And, of course, there are police activities and programs that have not even been evaluated. Moreover, there are always problems with social science research that attempts to determine "cause and effect" relationships. It is difficult to conduct evaluation research in the "real world" because it is rarely possible to either identify, or control for, all the variables that might influence the crime rate. Studies also rarely account for the competence, motivation and integrity of the individuals engaged in the police activity or program. Some police activies may be successful or unsuccessful, as much, if not more, as a result of the personnel assigned than the strategies employed.

There are also ethical issues to consider. For example, even though research suggests that the arrest of employed suspects in domestic violence cases will reduce recidivism, and that the arrest of unemployed suspects will increase violence and recidivism, should the police use the employment or unemployment of a suspect as a major factor in an arrest decision? If so, would this be considered selective enforcement? Would it be a form of discrimination? In addition, the use of certain strategies may result in becoming more effective in terms of one police goal but less effective in terms of another goal. As noted previously, increasing the level of police presence combined with increasing the enforcement of the law may result in a decline in the crime rate, however, it may also result in a decline in public support or police legitimacy. Managers must attempt to balance the concerns of citizens that they will be treated fairly with the goal of reducing crime. The two most promising approaches to doing this are: (1) an ongoing dialogue between police and the community concerning the most desirable combination of strategies to be utilized; and (2) the integrity, competency and style of individual police officers. Indifference, or abrasive or abusive styles, or the excessive reliance on coercion, is not compatible with the values of a democratic society.

Summary

Police resources include both sworn and nonsworn officers. Sworn officers (those who take an oath to uphold the constitution and follow a code of ethics) are the more important police resource. The resources needed by a police department are usually determined intuitively or by comparing ratios of officers to population. Most police resources are allocated to police operations, which include those activities (e.g., patrol and investigation) that are presumed to have the most impact on the organization's goals. Police resources are invested in one of four possible strategies: presence, law enforcement, education and community building. These strategies are used by the different functions (e.g., patrol and investigations) singly and in combination. The allocation of police resources includes consideration of the purpose of the organization, the strategies to be used, the process to be employed, time and area, and mobility.

Patrol and investigations are linked by the crime response process. The police response to crime can be proactive or reactive and overt or covert. Police patrol can be carried out at the discretion of the officer, randomly, or directed as a result of crime analysis. Research concerning the effectiveness of the police in reducing crime has substantially increased in recent decades but the quality of that research varies; however, the most reliable and valid research provides a basis for allocating police resources and improving police effectiveness.

Discussion Questions

1. Explain the difference between sworn and nonsworn police employees.

2. Explain the comparative method of determining police resources.

3. Identify, define, and give examples of the four major police strategies.

4. Explain how police productivity and competence may influence the crime rate.

5. Explain the following terms and how they apply to the use of police resources: overt, covert, discretionary, random, directed, proactive, and reactive.

6. What is a police crackdown? Explain how crackdowns influence the crime rate.

7. What is situational crime prevention? Give at least five examples of how it is used.

8. Do the police have a role in developmental crime prevention? Explain your answer.

9. Explain how the law enforcement strategy can be used most effectively.

10. Should the police use the employment status of a suspect to determine whether or not to make an arrest in a domestic violence case? Explain your answer.

References

Adams, F. 1964. "Operation 25." In S. Chapman (ed.), *Police Patrol Readings*, pp. 206–214. Springfield, IL: Charles C. Thomas.

"Arresting Statistics." 1994. *Law Enforcement News*, September 30: 3, 10.

Bureau of Justice Assistance. 1993. *Problem-Oriented Drug Enforcement*. Washington, DC: Bureau of Justice Assistance.

Clarke, R. V. 1995. "Situational Crime Prevention." In M. Tonry and D. P. Farrington, *Building a Safer Society: Strategic Approaches to Crime Prevention*, pp. 91–150. Chicago: University of Chicago Press.

Cordner, G. W., L. K. Gaines, and V. E. Kappeler (eds.). 1996. *Police Operations: Analysis and Evaluation.* Cincinnati, OH: Anderson.

"DC's Metro police keep searching for some light at the end of a long tunnel." 1996. *Law Enforcement News,* June 30: 1, 6.

Dodenhoff, P. C. 1996. "The NYPD and Its Compstat Process." *Law Enforcement News* December 31: 1, 4–5.

Elliott, J. F. 1973. *Interception Patrol.* Springfield, IL: Charles C. Thomas.

Hope, T. 1995. "Community Crime Prevention." In M. Tonry and D. P. Farrington (eds.), *Building a Safer Society: Strategic Approaches to Crime Prevention,* pp. 21–89. Chicago: University of Chicago Press.

Jefferis, E. S., Frank, J., Smith, B. W., Novak, K. J., and Travis, L. F. 1998. "An Examination of the Productivity and Perceived Effectiveness of Drug Task Forces." *Police Quarterly* 1: 85-107.

Kennedy, D., Piehl, A. M., and Braga, A. A. 1996. "Youth Gun Violence in Boston: Gun Markets, Serious Youth Offenders and a Use Reduction Strategy." *Law and Contemporary Problems* 59: 147–196.

Krauss, C. 1995. "New York Sees Steep Drop in Rate of Violent Crime." *The New York Times,* December 13: Y, 13.

"Massive retraining effort due for DC cops." 1996. *Law Enforcement News,* February 14: 7.

Moore, M. H. 1995. "Public Health and Criminal Justice Approaches to Prevention." In M. Tonry and D. P. Farrington, *Building a Safer Society: Strategic Approaches to Crime Prevention,* pp. 237–262. Chicago: University of Chicago Press.

Nelson, G. 1964. "Roulette Wheel Helps Village Enforce Laws." In S. G. Chapman (ed.), *Police Patrol Readings,* pp. 228–230. Springfield, IL: Charles C. Thomas.

"Patrol Allocation." 1995. *Telemasp Bulletin: Texas Law Enforcement Management and Administrative Statistics Program 2.* Huntsville, TX: Sam Houston State University, Criminal Justice Center.

Polley, E. 1996. "One Good Apple." *Time,* January 15: 54–56.

Pratt, T. C., Frank, J., Smith, B. W., and Novak, K. J. 2000. "Conflict and Consensus in Multijurisdictional Drug Task Forces: An Organizational Analysis of Personnel Attitudes." *Police Practice and Research: An International Journal* 1: 509-525.

Reaves, B. A. 1999. *Law Enforcement Management and Administrative Statistics, 1997.* Washington, DC: Bureau of Justice Statistics.

Rich, T. R. 1995. "The Use of Computerized Mapping in Crime Control and Prevention Programs." *Research in Action.* Washington, DC: National Institute of Justice.

Sherman, L. W. 1990. "Police Crackdowns." *NIJ Reports,* March/April: 2–8. Washington, DC: National Institute of Justice.

——. 1992. "Attacking Crime: Policing and Crime Control." In M. Tonry and N. Morris (eds.), *Modern Policing,* pp. 159–230. Chicago: University of Chicago Press.

——. 1995. "The Police." In J. Q. Wilson and J. Petersilia (eds.), *Crime.* San Francisco: ICS Press.

Sherman, L. W., Gartin, P., and Buerger, M. E. 1989. "Hot Spots of Predatory Crime." *Criminology* 27: 27–55.

Sherman, L.W., Shaw, J.W., and Rogan, D. P. 1995. *The Kansas City Gun Experiment.* Washington D. C.: U. S. Government Printing Office.

Sherman, L. W., Gottfredson, D. MacKenzie, D., Eck, J., Reuter, P., and Bushway, S. 1997 *Preventing Crime: What Works, What Doesn't, What's Promising.* Washington D. C.: National Institute of Justice.

Smith, B. W., Novak, K. J, Frank, J. and Travis, L. F. 2000. "Multijurisdictional Drug Task Forces: An Analysis of Impacts." *Journal of Criminal Justice* 28: 543-556.

Trembley, R. E., and Craig, W. M. 1995. "Developmental Crime Prevention." In M. Tonry and D. P. Farrington (eds.), *Building a Safer Society: Strategic Approaches to Crime Prevention,* pp. 151–236. Chicago: University of Chicago Press.

Weingart, S. N., Hartmann, F. X., and Osborne, D. 1994. "Case Studies of Community Anti-Drug Efforts." *Research in Brief*. Washington, DC: National Institute of Justice.

Wilson, O. W., and McLaren, R. C. 1972. *Police Administration*, 4th ed. New York: McGraw-Hill.

Civil Liability

Understanding Civil Liability

America is a litigious society, and certainly the police are not immune from such action. Civil liability is a growing concern in American policing, and this trend will not change in the foreseeable future. In many ways civil liability is inherent in the awesome power police have in a democratic society, and civil lawsuits often arise when police officers abuse their power, engage in negligent behavior, or otherwise violate the civil rights of a citizen. The risk of being sued is part of the police occupation, and officers, supervisors, managers and other agents of government understand this fact. However, they may not be exactly clear about how, why, and under what circumstances they may be held liable.

Since this portion of the text diverges from the criminal justice system and discusses the influence of the civil justice system, it is important to briefly describe the differences between these two legal systems. A ***crime*** is an act that causes public injury and is classified as an offense or a wrong against the state, for which a punishment is attached. In contrast, a ***tort*** is an act (other than a breach of contract) that causes injury to a private person or to their property. In contrast to criminal laws, there is no punishment attached to the act; however, the injured party may seek to recover damages from the offending party. The injured party is referred to as the plaintiff, and the party being sued is called the defendant. When referring to civil liability in policing, we are referring to torts or civil wrongs the police commit against members of the public. Barrineau (1994) further explains the basic differences between the criminal justice system and the civil justice system:

Initiation. The state (or the government) initiates a case in the criminal justice system. Therefore, the state assumes the costs associated with criminal prosecution, and the prosecutor in court represents the state. The plaintiff initiates a case in the civil justice system, and therefore the plaintiff assumes the costs associated with civil litigation. A privately retained attorney represents the plaintiff in civil court.

Remedy. The state imposes a punishment against the defendant in the criminal justice system, such as fines, probation, or imprisonment. In contrast, the remedy in a civil case is typically money awarded for damages, and is paid by the defendant to the plaintiff.

Burden of Proof. In order for someone to be found guilty in criminal court, the prosecutor must demonstrate beyond a reasonable doubt that the person committed the act in question. In order for someone to be found liable in civil court, the plaintiff must demonstrate with a ***preponderance of the evidence*** that the defendant committed the act. Preponderance of evidence is significantly less strenuous than beyond a reasonable doubt.

Appeal. In criminal court the defendant enjoys the right to appeal the decision, but the state does not enjoy such a right. In civil trials either party may appeal the verdict.

These basic differences between the systems of justice make civil litigation a more attractive option for many people. Since the burden of proof is significantly less in civil court, it is easier for the plaintiff to prevail. Obviously the potential of receiving compensation from the defendant may further drive the plaintiff to initiate civil proceedings. This has led one scholar to remark, "suing police officials has become a popular sport in the United States" (del Carmen, 1991: 1).

This chapter is designed to provide students and police managers a basic overview of the laws that govern civil liability for police officers. First, this chapter will discuss the actual (and potential) costs and pervasiveness of civil lawsuits against the police, and it will also define important terms. Second, this chapter will describe various avenues for civil litigation, including state law and federal laws. It will also describe who may be the subject of lawsuits and immunity from litigation. Third, this chapter will outline liabilities of police supervisors. Fourth, it will discuss emerging trends in police liability, including encounters with citizens, vehicle pursuits, racial profiling, questioning suspects, and community policing. Fifth, this chapter will provide a discussion of the unintentional cost litigation may have on officers. This chapter concludes with a discussion of how police managers can manage and reduce exposure to civil litigation. Police administrators must be cognizant of the law as it relates to policing innovation, and ultimately, "police executives of the future will have to sift innovations through a civil liability filter" (Kappeler, 2001, p. 200).

Costs of Liability in Policing

There are many different costs associated with police civil liability. Beyond the obvious monetary costs, there are often other ancillary costs associated with retraining officers, purchasing new equipment, and the personal costs associated with officers and supervisors being the target of litigation. Civil litigation has increased in both its frequency and the amount of money paid to plaintiffs.

The number of civil lawsuits against the police continues to grow, and this trend will likely continue. An early report by the International Association of Chiefs of Police indicated there were 1,741 civil suits against the police in 1967. This estimate grew to 3,897 in 1971, an increase of 123 percent. By 1975 the number of suits nearly doubled again (del Carmen, 1991). The frequency of such suits has continued to escalate since that time. Silver (1996) estimated police face more than 30,000 lawsuits per year. However, the true number of civil lawsuits filed against the police is largely unknown, and this has led some to call for the creation of a national, systematic data set in order to fully understand the dimensions of civil liability (Vaughn, Cooper, and del Carmen, 2001). Furthermore, Kappeler (2001) estimated the costs of liability could be as high as $780 billion. Examples of civil liability judgments are outlined in Inside Management 13.1.

These estimates beg the question. What has changed in policing over the past three decades to warrant such profound increases in civil liability? One possible answer is "nothing"; instead, the propensity to sue officers for their actions during encounters with the public may have increased. The increase in lawsuits may be more a function of the public viewing the police (and government in general) as having many resources with which to compensate citizens for even the most meager transgressions. And there may be some truth to this perception. Kappeler (2001) stated that the average jury award for litigation against municipal government is around $2 million. Civil litigation rewards involving the police tend to be somewhat less than this estimate. Ross (2000) conducted an analysis of over 1,500 federal lawsuits alleging failure to train between 1989 and 1999. He reported the average award for the plaintiff was around $492,794, with an additional average of $60,680 in attorneys' fees. A survey of Texas police chiefs found the typical award in police civil liability cases was around $98,100; however, these amounts are often significantly reduced on appeal (Vaughn, Cooper, and del Carmen, 2001).

Of course, many of these cases are settled out of court. Often the decision to settle out of court is a tactical decision that is designed to avoid the risk of paying more money in a jury-awarded decision. In their survey of Texas police chiefs, Vaughn and his colleagues (2001) asked chiefs about their moti-

---

Inside Management 13.1

Examples of Recent Civil Judgments Against the Police

The following is a brief list of recent awards for police misconduct. This list is not meant to be representative of all civil lawsuits but is intended merely to demonstrate the range of police misconduct that can result in litigation.

- Maryland State Police settle racial profiling lawsuit brought by the ACLU. The police agreed to maintain detailed records of motorist stops, to allow ACLU monitoring, to pay four plaintiffs a total of $50,000 plus legal fees of $45,600. *Wilkins v. Md. St. Police*, # MJG-93-468 (D.Md. 1995).

- The 9th Circuit Federal appeals court upheld a $10,000 award to each of two black men stopped in their car for a purported investigative stop and ordered out of the vehicle at gunpoint, when they did not fit details of descriptions of suspects sought. The officer's conduct violated the Fourth Amendment. *Washington v. Lambert*, 98 F.3d 1181 (9th Cir. 1996).

- Women arrestees illegally strip-searched without reasonable suspicion that they possessed weapons or contraband receive $6.01 million settlement from city. *Doe v. Calumet*

City, as cited in *Chicago Sun-Times*, p. 4 (Sept. 11, 1993).

- The U. S. Border Patrol was found liable for the death of six people in a collision with a stolen vehicle smuggling illegal aliens that agents were pursuing at high speed. Plaintiffs' families were awarded $1,011,606.19 in damages. *Murillo v. United States*, SACV940006, U.S. Dist. Ct., C.D. Cal., Feb. 25, 1997, as cited in Los Angeles Daily Journal Verdicts & Settlements, p. 4 (May 23, 1997).

- The city of Los Angeles agreed to pay $10.9 million to settle the first 29 cases against the city in the police department's corruption scandal. The cases represent about one-third of the lawsuits related to the scandal, which has led to the overturning of more than 100 convictions because of tainted evidence or testimony by officers who worked in the department's Rampart Division. APBnews.com, November 7, 2000.

Adapted from: Americans for Effective Law Enforcement. (http://www.aele.org/Civilcase. html)

---

vations to "settle." Sixty percent reported the decision was motivated by the desire to avoid paying more money later. Indeed, there was some truth to this motivation, in that the average settlement was around $55,411 per case (compared to $98,100 awarded by a jury). Other motivations included to make the case "go away" (56 percent), to avoid losing in court (38 percent), to avoid embarrassment (37 percent), "and to compensate the plaintiff even though no police wrongdoing occured" (22 percent). Only 17 percent of police chiefs indicated their decision to settle was in part to compensate the plaintiff for some wrongful act by the police officer. In addition to paying less than if the case proceeded to court, the municipality would not have to devote scarce resources to other costs associated with the litigation, including attorney costs, the costs associated with compensating expert testimony, and officers' time testifying in court.

Though the number of lawsuits filed for improper police behavior has increased, what is seldom reported is the rate that plaintiffs are successful in their quests for compensation. The fact is that most police lawsuits are decided in favor of the officers, although the exact number varies considerably. Early research indicated that only about 4 percent of all claims against the police were found in favor of the plaintiff. More recent research places this figure at about 8 percent (Kappeler, Kappeler, and del Carmen, 1993). In their survey of Texas police chiefs, Vaughn, Cooper, and del Carmen (2001) found chiefs reported losing about 22 percent of all civil suits. In his examination of federal lawsuits decided in Federal District Courts between 1980 and 2000, Kappeler (2001) reported plaintiffs prevailed in between 45.7 and 53.4

percent of all cases. However, it is important to understand "prevail" does not necessarily mean the police were found to be liable, only that there were sufficient grounds to warrant a jury trial; that is, there was found to be a substantive issue before the court. Nonetheless, these civil suits can produce significant damage to the reputation of the police officers and the police departments involved. Further, the cost associated with protecting the officers and departments from lawsuits can be quite high, regardless of the final determination.

Avenues of Liability

In a broad sense, police may be defendants at two different levels. They may be held liable in state courts for violations of state laws, or may be held liable in federal court for violations of constitutional, or federally protected, rights. It is important to understand that defendants may be held liable simultaneously in both arenas for the same action if the action violates both state torts and civil liberties. In civil law, "double jeopardy" claims are irrelevant. In other words, if the officer's actions are negligent under state tort laws, and at the same time a violation of civil rights, the plaintiff may seek relief in both state courts and federal courts. To make matters more confusing, if the action by the officer is also in violation of criminal law, then prosecutors may seek indictments in criminal court as well. In order to understand these different procedures, this chapter will explore the basics of state tort law and federal liability, with particular emphasis on Section 1983 of the U.S. Code.

Civil Liability in State Courts

Officers and supervisors may be defendants in state courts when state torts are violated. Most suits in state court allege wrongful police conduct in which a person is injured because of actions conducted by another person. Generally there are three classifications of state tort laws, including strict liability torts, intentional torts, and negligent torts. Strict liability torts involve the creation of some conditions that are so hazardous that the person engaging in such activity can be reasonably certain that injury or damage will result (Kappeler, 2001). Strict liability torts rarely involve the police and thus will not be discussed in detail here.

Intentional Torts

Intentional torts involve behavior specifically designed to cause some type of injury or harm. The key to intentional torts is the ***culpable state of mind*** of the officer, in that their actions were purposive and designed to bring about some type of injury or property loss. Whereas numerous different activities may be classified as intentional torts, among the most common for police officers is excessive use of force, wrongful death, assault and battery, and false arrest.

Excessive use of force entails the application of physical force that is not in line with the level of resistance faced by the officer. In other words, the application of force was unreasonable. Recall from Chapter 11 the discussion of the use of force policy by the Kansas City Police Department (Inside Management 11.2). Officers are trained to match resistance by citizens with a certain level of force, but this force must be ***proportional*** to the level of resistance by the citizen. If officers use force that is not proportional, given the situation, they may be sued for intentional use of excessive force. Effective training, supervision, and documentation of use of force encounters between the police and the public are essential in order to reduce exposure to civil liability. Similarly, ***wrongful death*** suits may arise when an unjustified police action results in the death of a citizen. The victim's family levies the civil suit, and compensation is sought for pain and suffering, medical and funeral expenses, and loss of future earnings (del Carmen and Smith, 2001). An example of wrongful death may include shooting a fleeing felon in violation of the landmark case of *Tennessee v. Garner* (1985). Garner, a young male, was shot by a police officer while attempting to elude the police by climbing a fence. He was suspected of breaking and entering and was unarmed. The Court held the police may not use deadly force to stop a "fleeing felon" unless the officer has probable cause to believe the person poses a significant threat of death or serious physical injury to the officer or members of the public.

   Assault involves the "intentional causing of an apprehension of harmful or offensive conduct; it is the attempt or threat, accompanied by the apparent ability, to inflict bodily harm on another person" (del Carmen, 1991: 18). This is when officers intentionally cause a person to fear for their safety. An example of this may be that during a custodial investigation, the officer grabs the suspect and threatens him with serious physical injury, such as throwing him out the second-story window (Kappeler, 2001). In contrast, ***battery*** is the harmful or offensive body contact between two people, such as when an officer applies any force to an individual without justification. The basic difference between the two is that assault involves menacing conduct, whereas battery must involve actual contact (del Carmen, 1991).

   Claims of ***false arrest*** arise from an intentional, illegal detention of an individual for prosecution. Typically these suits arise from warrantless arrests, an activity that is very common in modern policing. The legal standard for making an arrest is probable cause, that is, the facts and circumstances would lead a reasonable person to believe a specific person has committed a criminal act. If officers detain a person without sufficient probable cause, this may give rise to an allegation of false arrest.

   Police officers, supervisors, organizations and municipalities are often the target of intentional tort violations, perhaps because of the very nature of their occupation. The police occupy a unique role in society; they are among the few government entities sanctioned to exercise control over the public. Klockars (1985: 12) defined the police as "institutions or individuals given the general right to use coercive force by the state within the state's domestic territory," and Bittner (1970) suggested that this use of coercion and control is the core role of the police. The exercise of physical coercion is not conducted in a vacuum, it is conducted in unstable and dynamic environments. The importance of individual liberty and freedom are culturally stressed values in America (Riksheim and Chermak, 1993), and control by the police can deprive individuals of this valued status. Policing at its core, involves police-citizen contacts. It was estimated that over 21 percent of all U.S. residents over age 16 had at least one contact with the police during 1999, resulting in over 42.8 million enounters (Langan et al., 2001). Given the sheer number of encounters between the police and the public, coupled with the legitimate right to use coercion, it is not surprising these civil suits occur with some frequency. However, actions only become problematic under intentional tort laws when the ***action is unreasonable***

Negligent Torts

Where intentional torts focus on the mental state of an individual, ***negligent torts*** only require ***inadvertent and unreasonable behavior resulting in damage or injury*** (Kappeler, 2001). Negligence may be described as injury that is the result of a lapse of due care so that the ingredients for injury were the result of some action or inaction on the officer's part. Thus, negligence provides liability for unreasonably creating a risk (Levine, Davies, and Kionka, 1993). In order to prove negligence, four criteria must be present:

1. Legal duty to act

2. A breach of duty

3. A proximate causal connection between conduct and harm

4. An actual loss or damage

Legal duty involves those actions on the part of the defendant as prescribed by the courts that require some police action. Thus, there must be a legal basis for the requirement of certain behavior or activity. However, ***breach of duty*** (or failure to conform with duty) is more complex. It must be demonstrated that a reasonably prudent person would believe the officer breached his or her duty to a plaintiff. This breach of duty must cause some type of injury; in other words, but for the actions of the officer, the plaintiff would not have been injured or damaged. Finally, ***actual damage or injury*** must have resulted from this action, including mental, physical, or economic harm (del Carmen, 1991; Hughes, 2001a; Kappeler, 2001; Prosser and Keeton, 1984).

There are a number of typical claims for negligent police action in state courts; however, only several directly related to police management will be outlined here (for a more detailed discussion of negligence claims, see Kappeler, 2001). Several negligent claims directly related to police management are detailed later in this chapter. However, to provide an example of negligence for the purposes of police liability, presented below is a discussion of negligent failure to arrest.

Failure to arrest may be negligent behavior if the plaintiff can prove that the ***officer's inaction caused injury or damage***. Police officers' ability to exercise discretion was discussed in Chapter 11, and discretion involves the ability to choose between a course of action or inaction. Officers often do not make arrests even when there are sufficient legal grounds to do so. Whether discretion is a virtue or a vice is beyond the parameters of the current discussion; however, officers and supervisors should recognize liabilities associated with inaction. An example of negligence may be illustrated by the circumstances surrounding *Thurman v. City of Torrington* (1985). The plaintiff, Tracey Thurman, alleged that Torrington police officers failed to arrest her estranged husband for a pattern of domestic abuse, even though officers observed the abuse in question. After police failed to arrest the suspect, Thurman sustained significant and debilitating injuries from her estranged husband that persist to this day. Though this case was settled in federal court, the ingredients for negligent failure to arrest were also present. The *Thurman* case, along with other factors, gradually led to police departments taking a more legalistic approach to domestic abuse (Sherman, 1992).

Civil Liability in Federal Courts

Recently there has been a tremendous increase in the number of civil liability filings against the police in federal courts. The most typical avenue for redress has come through the "resurrection" of Title 42 of the United States Code, Section 1983 (Barrineau, 1994). The origin of this section can be traced back to the Civil Rights Act of 1871, and was primarily used as a mechanism to control the conduct of officials associated with the Ku Klux Klan (del Carmen, 1991; Kappeler, 2001). Under §1983, citizens can seek relief from officials who violate their constitutional rights under the guise of their governmental positions; 42 USC §1983 reads in part:

> Every person who, under color of any statute, ordinance, regulation, custom, or usage, of any State or Territory or the District of Columbia, subjects, or causes to be subjected, any citizen of the United States or other person within the jurisdiction thereof to the deprivation of any rights, privileges, or immunities secured by the Constitution and laws, shall be liable to the party injured in an action at law, suit in equity, or other proper proceeding for redress. . . .

Thus, 42 USC §1983 does not create any substantive rights. Instead, it outlines a procedure individuals can follow to seek compensation for violations of their constitutional rights. There are two essential components of §1983, namely (1) the defendant must be acting under the color of law, and (2) there must be a violation of a constitutional or federally protected right.

Color of Law

Color of law translates into the ***misuse of power*** possessed by an individual who is a "state actor" and derives his or her power from the state. Police officers are given authority and power by the state. Thus, if officers are performing typical police duties (e.g., making arrests, enforcing traffic regulations, conducting searches and seizures of property), they are, for the purposes of liability, acting under the color of law (Kappeler, 2001). Worrall (1998) indicated that the courts often define the color of law by asking, "Was police power used?" or "Did the department authorize the act?"

Is an officer who is working off-duty security acting under the color of law for the purposes of liability? Can police organizations be liable under §1983 for their actions? In other words, are there circumstances in which police officers may not act under the color of law? Vaughn and Coomes (1995: 398) noted several important exceptions and caveats to this prong of §1983 requirement for liability. In their review of contemporary case law on the topic, they concluded that officers act "under the color of law if they invoke police power, if they discharge duties routinely associated with police work, or if they use their authority to lure potential plaintiffs into compromising positions." Officers are acting under the color of law if they perform certain activities typically associated with policing, including wearing a uniform, identifying themselves as police officers, placing people under arrest, and filing reports. However, this is determined by the plaintiff's point of view, and whether the plaintiff believed the defendant was acting as a public official. However, if an officer, even if in uniform, acts as a private citizen and does not invoke police powers, then he or she is not acting under the color of law for liability purposes. Table 13.1 provides insight into factors that courts consider when determining this prong of §1983. To answer the question posed above, if the officer is working an off-duty assignment under the auspices and direction of the police department, then his or her actions may be done under the color of law. In contrast, if the officer is working off-duty security through a private contract with a private security firm, then he or she is not acting under the color of law.

Table 13.1 Factors to Determine Whether an Officer Acted Under the Color of Law	
Officers act under the color of law if. . .	**Officers do not act under the color of law if. . .**
They identify themselves as a law enforcement agent.	They do not invoke police power.
They perform duties of a criminal investigation.	Their inaction does not constitute state action.
They file official police documents.	They commit crimes in a personal dispute without invoking police power.
They attempt or make an arrest.	They act as federal agents.
They invoke their police powers outside their lawful jurisdiction.	They report the details of alleged crimes as private citizens.
They settle a personal vendetta with police power.	They work for a private security company and do not identify themselves as law enforcement personnel.
They display or use police weapons / equipment.	The department removes the officers' lawful authority.
They act pursuant to a statute or ordinance.	
The department policy mandates they are "always on duty."	
They intimidate citizens from exercising their rights.	
The department supports, facilitates, or encourages the off-duty employment of its officers as private security personnel.	

Adapted from: Vaughn, M S., and Coomes, L. F. 1995. "Police Civil Liability Under Section 1983: When Do Police Officers Act Under the Color of Law?" *Journal of Criminal Justice* 23: 409.

Violations of Constitutional or Federally Protected Rights

The second prong of §1983 involves **rights** protected by the **Constitution** or **federally protected rights**. Therefore, rights provided by the states are not covered in §1983 actions. Typically, plaintiffs will seek redress for violations of a right in one of the amendments outlined in the Bill of Rights or of the equal protection clause of the Fourteenth Amendment. A sample of selected amendments typically applied in §1983 cases is presented in Table 13.2. If an officer (while acting under the color of law) violates an individual's constitutional rights, then §1983 may be used as a remedy.

Table 13.2 Selected Constitutional Amendments

Amendment I

Congress shall make no law respecting an establishment of religion, or prohibiting the free exercise thereof; or abridging the freedom of speech, or of the press; or the right of the people peaceably to assemble, and to petition the Government for a redress of grievances.

Amendment IV

The right of the people to be secure in their persons, houses, papers, and effects, against unreasonable searches and seizures, shall not be violated, and no Warrants shall issue, but upon probable cause, supported by Oath or affirmation, and particularly describing the place to be searched, and the persons or things to be seized.

Amendment V

No person shall be held to answer for a capital, or otherwise infamous crime, unless on a presentment or indictment of a Grand Jury, except in cases arising in the land or naval forces, or in the Militia, when in actual service in time of War or public danger; nor shall any person be subject for the same offence to be twice put in jeopardy of life or limb; nor shall be compelled in any criminal case to be a witness against himself, nor be deprived of life, liberty, or property, without due process of law; nor shall private property be taken for public use, without just compensation.

Amendment VIII

Excessive bail shall not be required, nor excessive fines imposed, nor cruel and unusual punishments inflicted.

Amendment XIV

Section 1. All persons born or naturalized in the United States, and subject to the jurisdiction thereof, are citizens of the United States and of the state wherein they reside. No state shall make or enforce any law which shall abridge the privileges or immunities of citizens of the United States; nor shall any state deprive any person of life, liberty, or property, without due process of law; nor deny to any person within its jurisdiction the equal protection of the laws.

An example of §1983 in action may be instructive. In *Graham v. Connor* (1989), the plaintiff (Graham) asked a friend to drive him to a store to obtain orange juice for his diabetic condition. Upon arrival at the store, Graham observed too many people in line so he hurried out and asked his friend instead to drive him to a friend's house. A police officer, observing Graham's suspicious behavior, stopped the car driven by Graham's friend and detained the plaintiff until he could determine what had happened in the store (even though Graham explained his medical condition). After the officer determined no crime had been committed, he released Graham. However, in the time that Graham was in police custody, he was denied access to means to treat his medical condition, and Graham had sustained injuries as a result of being in police custody. The plaintiff sued the officer for violating his Fourth Amendment rights protecting him from excessive use of force. The Court held that officers might be liable pursuant to §1983 for excessive use of force. In doing so they determined that a standard of ***objective reasonableness*** is to be used in such cases, indicating the force must be considered from the view of the officer at the time of the event and not in twenty-twenty hindsight.

Municipal Liability Under §1983

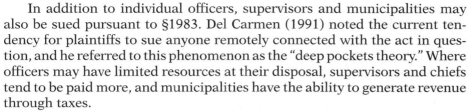

In addition to individual officers, supervisors and municipalities may also be sued pursuant to §1983. Del Carmen (1991) noted the current tendency for plaintiffs to sue anyone remotely connected with the act in question, and he referred to this phenomenon as the "deep pockets theory." Where officers may have limited resources at their disposal, supervisors and chiefs tend to be paid more, and municipalities have the ability to generate revenue through taxes.

In *Monell v. Department of Social Services* (1978), the Court ruled that municipalities were persons under 42 USC §1983, and thus may be party to lawsuits where the rights of plaintiffs were violated as a result of an official policy or custom of a local unit of government (Barrineu, 1994). This decision attaches liability if the violation of constitutional or federally protected rights were part of an "official policy" or custom. Where an official policy is somewhat straightforward, the concept of custom is somewhat elusive. According to the decision in *Bennett v. City of Slidell* (1984: 862), a custom is "A persistent, widespread practice of city officials or employees which, although not authorized by officially adopted and promulgated policy is so common and well settled as to constitute a custom that fairly represents municipal policy." In other words, a custom is a pattern or practice that is understood and known throughout the organization, but it does not occupy an official policy of the department or the municipality. For example, if it is understood among officers that black motorists are differentially targeted for enforcement in a specific area of the city or along a certain stretch of highway, this understanding may elevate itself to a custom for the purposes of liability. In short, if the violation occurred as part of a standard practice associated with policing, the municipality may be liable for such actions.

Defenses to §1983

There are four instances when, where confronted with suits under §1983, defendants can offer defenses for their actions, thus negating the federal lawsuit. First, ***absolute immunity*** is when a civil action is brought against a person or entity protected by this form of immunity; the lawsuit will be dismissed by the court. However, this form of immunity has little application on liability for police officers, and it is typically reserved for the judiciary. The lone exception to this rule is when an officer commits perjury in court. If the officer, while testifying in criminal court, presents incorrect information that violates a person's right, the officer may seek absolute immunity from §1983 lawsuits. However, though immune from civil lawsuits, the act of perjury is a criminal offense for which officers may be charged and convicted in criminal courts (Kappeler, 2001).

Second, ***qualified immunity*** extends to police officers performing duties that are discretionary in nature. This form of immunity addresses the question, Did the officer know his or her conduct was in violation of a constitutional right or a federally protected right? According to Kappeler (2001: 62), "if a court determined that the law was not clearly established or that the officer's conduct was reasonable, the officer is to be afforded immunity from liability." An example of qualified immunity can be demonstrated from the decision in *Wilson v. Layne* (1998). Wilson was the target of a police crackdown that focused on dangerous fugitives. The police invited the media to accompany them and videotape the execution of a warrant on the home of Wilson's parents, where Wilson was believed to be present. Wilson's parents claimed this act violated their Fourth Amendment right to be free from searches and seizures, and sought legal remedies under §1983. The Court held that bringing third parties who were not aiding the execution of the warrant (i.e., the media) into the home was indeed a violation of the Fourth Amendment. However, they also indicated there was no law that clearly established this at the time it took place, and thus the officers were entitled to qualified immunity.

Third, police officers may defend themselves from federal litigation if they can claim there was ***probable cause*** to believe their action was legal. This is particularly important for defenses against false arrest or improper searches and seizures. For example, if officers can demonstrate that probable cause was present that a person had committed a crime or that probable cause existed that justified a search, then redress in federal court is barred (Kappeler, 2001; *Hunter v. Bryant*, 1991). Even if it is later determined that in fact probable cause did not exist but that the officer was acting on good faith, the officer is immune from liability. "Probable cause is so strong a defense in arrest and search and seizure cases that some courts have held that if probable cause is present, the officer is not liable even if malice is involved in the officer's act" (del Carmen, 1991: 57).

Finally, officers may be free from civil liability if they can demonstrate their actions were conducted in ***good faith***. This means the officer could not have ***reasonably known*** their actions were in violation of law or the constitution, such as executing a warrant that they believe to be valid. The factors the court will consider regarding good faith actions include:

1. The officer acted in accordance with agency rules and regulations,

2. The officer acted pursuant to a statute that is reasonably believed to be valid but is later declared unconstitutional,

3. The officer acted in accordance with orders from a superior that are reasonably believed to be valid, or

4. The officer acted in accordance with advice from a legal counsel that is reasonably believed to be valid (del Carmen, 1991: 55–56).

Liability of Police Managers

Police managers and supervisors may be held liable for the actions of their subordinates. According to del Carmen and Smith (2001: 189), liability attaches to a supervisor of police officers if the supervisor:

1. Authorized the act

2. Participated in the act

3. Directed the act

4. Ratified the act (such as when a supervisor learns of an illegal act and approves of it)

5. Was present at the time of the act and could have prevented it (but chose not to), or

6. Created the policy or custom that led to the illegal act

Police supervisors have the obligation to be aware of and understand the activities of their subordinates. Failure to do so may result in liability in civil court for this negligent behavior. There are several specific types of activities in which supervisors are commonly held responsible. The following discussion is based on legal summaries of Kappeler (2001), del Carmen (1991), and del Carmen and Smith (2001).

Negligent hiring occurs when administrators fail to use reasonable methods to hire adequate applicants for the position of police officer. Negligence may occur when administrators fail to adequately screen applicants. If applicants with extensive criminal backgrounds are hired as officers and these officers later cause harm or injury to plaintiffs, then liability may attach. Hughes (2001a) described the facts surrounding *Bryan County (Oklahoma) Commissioner v. Brown* (1997). Two officers of the Bryan County sheriff's office stopped the plaintiff, Jill Brown, and her husband, who were allegedly attempting to avoid a police checkpoint. The plaintiff and her husband were ordered to exit their vehicle, and as they exited, Deputy Burns administered an "arm bar" control technique on Brown and threw her to the ground. This resulted in injuries to her knees, requiring corrective surgery. It was later discovered that Burns had an extensive pre-employment criminal history, including traffic offenses, resisting arrest, public drunkenness, and assault and battery. Brown claimed the sheriff was negligent in his hiring practices (or failed to adequately review Burns' criminal history) and this resulted in her injuries. Although the Supreme Court held that this single act of hiring Burns did not elevate to the level of negligent hiring, it does demonstrate that municipalities may be negligent if a pattern develops or if officers are not adequately trained to perform specific duties.

Negligent failure to train involves the indifference of supervisors to adequately train subordinates to engage in specific activities. Common areas of negligent failure to train include use of less than lethal force, use of deadly force, and making arrests. If damage or injury results from activities in which subordinates did not receive adequate training, then supervisors may be liable for this oversight. Additionally, municipalities may also be held liable for failure to adequately train police officers (see *City of Canton v. Harris*, 1989).

Negligent supervision involves failure of supervisors to provide direction and oversight of employees. Oversight may come in the form of direct observation but may also involve written or oral directives. Negligence may also be demonstrated if the department does not have adequate policies or directions in performance of the policies. This idea of negligent supervision will be revisited later in this chapter in the context of community policing.

Negligent assignment involves assigning officers to a specific duty or task without adequately assessing the subordinate's level of competence to perform such as task. An example of this may be demonstrated from *Gutierrez-Rodriguez v. Cartagena* (1st Cir. 1989). The supervisor assigned a violence-prone officer to lead a drug task force, and during the course of a drug investigation the officer shot a citizen. Because the supervisor was aware of the officer's history of violence, the act of assigning this officer to this particular position amounted to liability under §1983.

Negligent failure to investigate and discipline involves a failure to thoroughly examine cases of police misconduct, or if misconduct is discovered, a failure on the supervisor's part to discipline or correct the conduct. If supervisors were aware of problem behavior, whether other officers brought it to their attention, members of the public did, or they discovered it through their own observations, then supervisors are obligated to remedy the situation or face the possibility of being held liable for negligent behavior. If misconduct or dangerous behavior is brought to the attention of supervisors, then action should be taken, including retraining, administrative discipline, or termination of employment.

Emerging Liability Issues for the Twenty-First Century

Policing in the twenty-first century may present new challenges to police officers, supervisors, and municipalities in the civil liability arena. Changes in technology, information systems, data analysis, and society provide a dynamic environment to which police officers must adapt. As stated earlier, people may become plaintiffs in civil liability suits for violating constitutional or federally protected rights. It is therefore important for officers and police managers to remain current on changes in criminal procedure. This section does not present an exhaustive discussion of these issues, but it is intended to present an overview of contemporary issues confronting modern police organizations. These issues include encounters with citizens, vehicle pursuits (e.g., hot pursuits), racial profiling, questioning of suspects, and community policing.

Encounters with Citizens

American police interact with citizens hundreds of thousands of times each day. Issues of liability become important when officers want to detain citizens against their wishes. In order to detain citizens, officers are required to have a certain level of proof that a crime has been committed or that the citizen was involved in criminal activity. In *U.S. v. Seslar* (1993) three different types of police-citizen encounters were identified:

1. ***Consensual Encounters***. These involve ***voluntary interactions*** between the police and the public, and the questioning by the officer is typically noncoercive. There is ***no legal justification needed*** in these encounters, and because the encounter is consensual, the citizen is free to terminate the encounter at any time and thus there is no seizure under the meaning of the Fourth Amendment.

2. ***Investigative Detentions***. These encounters involve a ***temporary detention*** of the citizen's movement by the police. Officers may detain citizens for questioning when there is ***reasonable suspicion*** to believe the citizen has committed, is committing, or is about to commit a crime. This type of temporary detention has also been referred to as a "Terry Stop," after the landmark Court decision (*Terry v. Ohio*, 1968).

3. ***Arrests***. Arrests involve a **seizure of the citizen** by the police that is characterized as lengthy and highly intrusive, in which there is likelihood that the intent of the detention is to subject the

citizen to criminal prosecution. In order to make an arrest, officers are required to have ***probable cause*** that a crime has been or is being committed (Klotter, 1999).

It is important at this point to clarify several terms. First, ***reasonable suspicion*** involves a lesser degree of certainty on the part of the officer that a person has committed a crime. While there is no steadfast or bright-line rule regarding exactly what reasonable suspicion is, the Court has acknowledged that it is a less demanding standard than what is required for an arrest. While it is difficult (and perhaps unwise) to affix a numeric value to the level of certainty, del Carmen (2001) indicates that reasonable suspicion is about 30 percent certainty. Second, ***probable cause*** exists when the "facts and circumstances within the police officer's knowledge and of which he or she has trustworthy information are sufficient in themselves to justify to a 'man of reasonable caution' the belief that an offense has been or is being committed" (del Carmen, 2001: 75). In other words, the officer has trustworthy evidence that it is more than likely that a particular person has or is about to commit a crime. To put probable cause into the same mathematical analogy as above, the level of certainty is above 50 percent.

Officers must understand these basic typologies of encounters in order to avoid civil liability, and must be prepared to articulate the facts and circumstances available to justify a level of proof. Indeed, officers may consider the "totality of circumstances" when determining reasonable suspicion or probable cause. If an officer detains a citizen beyond their will without the requisite level of proof, then an illegal seizure under the Fourth Amendment may occur, or the intentional tort of false arrest.

Vehicle Pursuits and Negligent Operation of an Emergency Vehicle

Operation of a motor vehicle may be negligent if the officer operates the vehicle in such a way that it causes a dangerous environment that results in injury or damage. For example, if the officer drives "code three" (or at a high rate of speed with lights and sirens) through a populated area, and such action causes a traffic accident, then this may give rise to negligent use of a motor vehicle. Similarly, if officers (or the police department) fail to maintain a motor vehicle in good working order and this failure causes damage or injury, this too may be negligent behavior under state tort law. Often at the beginning of a tour of duty, officers are required to conduct an inspection of the general state of their vehicle. This includes checking tire pressure, making sure the emergency lights and siren are operational, and checking the overall condition of the vehicle (e.g., loose bumpers or material hanging from the vehicle that may cause an accident). This is done in order to insulate the department from civil negligence claims.

It is possible for plaintiffs to seek relief under §1983 for injuries and damage incurred during high-speed pursuits. Inside Management 13.2 outlines a recent ruling by the Supreme Court and discusses the implications for police policy.

Inside Management 13.2

Sacramento v. Lewis, 523 U. S. 833 (1998)

The facts were as follows: A motorcycle approached Deputy Smith (who was responding to a disturbance call) at a high rate of speed. Lewis was a passenger on the motorcycle. Deputy Smith turned on his emergency lights in attempts to stop the motorcycle, but a high-speed vehicle pursuit ensued. At times speeds reached over 100 miles per hour, and Deputy Smith followed the motorcycle closely, only 100 feet behind. The driver of the motorcycle attempted a sharp turn but lost control and jettisoned Lewis from the motorcycle. Deputy Smith struck Lewis with his vehicle, and Lewis was pronounced dead at the scene. Lewis' family alleged pursuant to §1983 that Deputy Smith deprived Lewis of his Fourteenth Amendment substantive due process right to life. They argued that the Deputy was acting under the color of law and that police pursuits were regulated by the use of training and resources provided by the police department, and his actions amounted to reckless indifference. The Supreme Court held that the Deputy did not violate Lewis' constitutional rights, and instead ruled in favor of the defendant (Deputy Smith). Their holding was that the standard of "reckless indifference" was insufficient to warrant a §1983 claim, instead relying on behavior that "shocks the conscience." They went on to note that in police pursuits there is a need to balance the need to capture the fugitive against the safety of persons involved in the chase. Hughes (in press) stated that the Court feared that allowing a person to ignore a lawful order to stop and then sue for damages sustained in a resulting chase would encourage persons to flee from the police. This claim is supported by research indicating that a substantial majority of people who flee the police are not deterred by high-speed pursuits, and would repeat their behavior knowing the police would chase until the vehicle crashed or was stopped. In short, this holding is a position to reduce the number of civil liability claims under §1983, and in doing so to deter citizens from fleeing the police in hopes of recovering damages at a later date.

Adapted from: Dunham, R., Alpert, G. P., Kenn[e]y, D. J., and Cromwell. P. 1998. "High-Speed Pursuit: The Offender's Perspective." *Criminal Justice and Behavior*, 25: 30–45. Homant, R., and Kennedy, D. 1994. "Citizen Preferences and Perceptions Concerning Police Pursuit Policies." *Journal of Criminal Justice*, 22: 425–435. Hughes, T. In Press. "'Maximum Lawman Run Down Flamingo': County of Sacramento v. Lewis and Police Pursuit Liability." *The Justice Professional*.

Racial Profiling

No topic has engendered more debates regarding police behavior and liability than the topic of racial profiling. ***Racial profiling*** involves police-initiated actions that rely on race, ethnicity, or national origin rather than on the individual's behavior (Ramirez, McDevitt, and Farrell 2000). This differential targeting is predicated on the fact that officers often incorrectly believe individuals of certain racial or ethnic groups are more likely to be engaging in criminal behavior. Officers may believe targeting minorities increases their odds of making an arrest, recovering stolen property, or discovering drugs. Furthermore, local police departments often receive a proportion of money seized in drug arrests and asset forfeitures. Thus, proactive traffic enforcement of drug-related crimes is sometimes identified as a priority for departments seeking to subsidize their budget through asset forfeitures. Court decisions that permit these practices provide officers who have a racist predisposition with the opportunity to act them out under the guise of "good police work" (Roberg, Crank, and Kuykendall, 2000). Although the anecdotal evidence today outweighs the empirical evidence regarding the existence and pervasiveness of racial profiling, politicians and police managers alike are attempting to eliminate this improper police behavior. As former President Bill Clinton acknowledged, "racial profiling is in fact the opposite of good police work, where actions are based on . . . stereotypes. It is wrong, it is destructive, and it must stop." (as cited in Ramirez, McDevitt, and Farrell, 2000: 1).

Although racial profiling may be difficult to prove, it does provide the potential for a §1983 claim. Specifically, if it is demonstrated that police officers, while acting under the color of law, differentially target individuals for enforcement and searches based on race or ethnic background, then plaintiffs may claim that their rights to equal protection of the law may have been violated, in opposition to the Fourteenth Amendment. Similarly, if plaintiffs can demonstrate that their detention by officers and searches of their person or vehicles were based on their race or ethnicity, then they may also argue that their right to be free from unreasonable searches and seizures was also violated. This, of course, would be in violation of the Fourth Amendment (see *Wilkins v. Maryland State Police*, 1993).

It may be difficult to imagine that racial profiling would ever be an official organizational policy; however, more likely plaintiffs may demonstrate that the practice fits the definition of "custom" for liability purposes. In 1998 police officers of the Highland Park (IL) Police Department claimed that supervisors instructed their subordinates to engage in an informal policy called NNUT, which reportedly stood for "No N—— Up Town" (racial epithet omitted). According to officers, this custom encouraged officers (acting under the color of law) to single out black and Hispanic motorists who were observed driving in the predominately white suburb (Alter, 2001). If this claim is valid, then plaintiffs may seek compensation under §1983 for violations of civil liberties.

It should be noted that to date the Court has not ruled on whether racial profiling is in fact a violation of the Fourth Amendment or the Equal Protection Clause of the Fourteenth Amendment. However, it is safe to assume the Court would be likely to find traffic stops unconstitutional if the stop was ***based on race alone,*** holding all other characteristics of the citizen's behavior equal. But what is intriguing is whether the Court will allow race to be considered as one factor under the ***totality of circumstances***, a standard the Court often applies in determining probable cause or reasonable suspicion (del Carmen, 2001). It is currently unclear whether race may be used as part of a group of factors to establish probable cause or reasonable suspicion in traffic stops. However, race should never be considered as a factor when stopping citizens, and police managers should institute a system in which the actions of officers are monitored to ensure ethical behavior.

Questioning Suspects

Officers must often take procedural safeguards to ensure that citizens do not incriminate themselves when being questioned. Perhaps the most famous Court ruling relating to police officer behavior was the decision in *Miranda v. Arizona* (1966). The Court determined that the officer must provide the citizen the following warnings:

1. You have the right to remain silent and say nothing.

2. If you make a statement, anything you say can and will be used against you in a court of law.

3. You have the right to have an attorney present.

4. If you cannot afford an attorney, one will be appointed for you prior to questioning, if you so desire.

The majority in *Miranda* determined that the police must provide these warnings whenever there is a ***custodial interrogation***. This involves any questioning initiated by police after a person has been ***taken into custody*** or otherwise ***deprived of freedom in a significant way***. In other words, the citizen must feel that he or she is not free to leave police presence. Interrogation (or questioning) refers to words or actions on the part of the officer that would be likely to elicit incriminating responses from the suspect (Klotter, 1999). The rationale behind the decision is that the nature of the police-citizen encounter is at times so coercive that absent these warnings citizens may not provide voluntary statements to the police, and that citizens may not know their constitutional rights. Failure to provide requisite "Miranda Warnings" may not only result in evidence obtained from the questioning (such as admissions of guilt) being excluded from criminal proceedings, but it may also provide avenues for redress under federal liability statutes.

Community Policing

Community policing is designed to increase the level of discretion of the line officer, as well as the frequency of officer-citizen encounters. Officers will have more ability to make decisions, engage in problem-solving activities, and facilitate partnerships with citizens. The changing role of the police has caused some to wonder if community policing may alter the exposure of police officers and police managers to civil liability. Interestingly, Worrall (1998) found an organization's level of commitment was related to fewer civil liability lawsuits. Recalling the characteristics of community policing, the idea that community policing may decrease liability makes sense theoretically, and Vaughn, Cooper, and del Carmen (2001) outlined these arguments. They include (1) an increase of women and minority voices in police organizations designed to reduce citizens' complaints; (2) improvement in attitudes toward the police; and (3) improvement in confidence in the police and the criminal justice system. In short, because the police and the public are working in partnership with each other, there may be less antagonism and misunderstanding between these two groups.

On the other hand, there are several reasons to believe community policing may increase civil liability for police. First, the number of contacts between the police and the public should increase; this may lead to more opportunities for civil liability. Community policing also exposes police to areas that were, prior to the community policing model, not considered public matters. Hughes (2000), for instance, argues that increased contact with the public in new and diverse matters will logically lead to greater opportunities for civil suits against the police.

Second, discretion and policy creation is shifted to the lowest level of the organization. Therefore, officers will have more opportunity and responsibility in creating and implementing policy or custom on behalf of the organization "under the color of law." This may suggest that control and accountability of police officers will decrease and make direct supervision of these officers more difficult. Indeed, direct supervision and control of officers runs counter to the community-policing philosophy. Similarly, police departments may have to relax the number of policies influencing the behavior of officers.

The 1994 Crime Act pledged an additional 100,000 police officers to the streets in order to conduct community policing. It is plausible that this act may actually contribute to future civil litigation against the police. Police departments are but one of many organizations competing for and retaining qualified individuals, and often private industry can offer compensation that police departments cannot. Often the number of qualified applicants for police jobs is related to the national economy. When the economy is strong, the applicant pool becomes weak and the number of qualified applicants decreases. However, when the economy is weak (such as when the nation is in a recession), the number of qualified individuals seeking employment in policing increases. Although there is no empirical research to support the contention that officers hired under the Crime Act were "of lower quality" than their predecessors, it seems logical that if this were indeed the case, then police exposure to civil liability may increase. Ultimately, of course, police departments should be more concerned about the quality of officers than the quantity of officers.

Increased liability may be demonstrated by considering the New York City experience with their Compstat procedure. The NYPD has realized reductions in crime, and at least some of these benefits can be attributed to their aggressive, zero tolerance model of police services. This style encourages officers to be proactive in their problem solving and make arrests for relatively minor violations of the law. However, Greene (1999) also noted that the number of legal filings alleging violations of civil rights he increased dramatically during the same time period. Many of these complaints involved police abuse of authority or brutality.

Worrall and Marenin (1998: 131–132) recommended several strategies that police managers can employ to manage liability in the community-policing era.

1. Don't oversell community policing to the community and political leadership. In the end community policing is still policing, and policing on some level involves social control. Community policing will require police to educate the community, emphasizing that change does not come easily and mistakes are inevitable. Citizens should be encouraged to give police a chance to right any wrongs before pursuing legal remedies.

2. The police need to problem solve their liability positions after adopting community policing. Police managers should become aware of the areas that are the biggest legal concerns (based on their unique implementation of community policing). They should then dedicate research and training to these areas to reduce their liabilities.

3. Training at all levels of the organization needs to incorporate community policing, including the likelihood of complaints and legal challenges, in an effort to predict, preempt, and deal with them as they occur.

It appears that community policing without the endorsement, cooperation, and blessing of the community could ultimately fail at the hands of civil liability.

Impact on Officers

The potential for civil liability is a part of policing that officers and supervisors must accept. In a recent survey of police officers in Cincinnati, Hughes (2001b) found that 18.5 percent of officers were sued for a job-related matter, and that 74.8 percent of officers personally knew of an officer who had been named in a lawsuit for a job-related matter. At the same time, 86.4 percent felt officers are sued even when they acted properly. This has led some officers to view complaints by the public and lawsuits as just another part of policing.

Although the media tend to focus on plaintiff experiences, it is also important to consider the impact of being the focus of a lawsuit from the officer's perspective. When officers and supervisors are sued for wrongdoing, there may be effects beyond the obvious loss of monetary resources. When named as a defendant in a civil lawsuit, officers may experience heightened levels of stress and anxiety. Pursuant to citizen complaints or civil litigation, officers are often interrogated regarding not only the act in question, but also about past behavior and disciplinary records. Previously, we discussed the fact that officers often report administrative policies, discipline, and a perceived lack of support as important sources of stress. However, these organizational responses, at least in part, may be reactions by supervisors and municipalities to insulate themselves from litigation. Yet officers may perceive this behavior as the organization not "backing" them; they may also think that citizens are just out to "get rich" at the expense of the officers and that "no one respects what the police do." Not only may officers' stress increase but this procedure may also lead to increased cynicism among officers. Case Study 13.1 provides an example of one officer's experience with being sued and subsequent responses by the municipality.

Case Study 13.1
One Officer's Civil Lawsuit Experience

Regardless of the outcome, civil lawsuits impact officers in significant ways. Joan C. Barker conducted extended research with the Los Angeles Police Department, which gave her unprecedented access to conversations and observations into the lives of police officers. Below is one officer's experience of being sued.

"We were on loan to Hollywood because they were having the Christmas parade. So we were working the crowd, people were just arriving and everyone was in a good mood. Lots of people, families and such. And everything was fine when this citizen came over and told us that there was a man down and bleeding. We went to see this guy, and he was down and out. All bloody. He was passed out, and when I leaned over to talk to him,

he woke and said he'd been in a bar and got in a fight and got himself beat up; and then he saw who we were, that we were police, and became all combative. Calling us "pigs" and that sort of thing. He was drunk and not hearing at all what we had to say. He was swearing and spitting at the [pedestrians]. And now there were lots of people, mothers and their children, all coming to this parade."

"Here's this beat-up drunk swearing and carrying on. This guy was saying real foul things, bad language and spitting at the people...and we told him to 'shut up,' but we said it nicer at the time. The first time we did, then later it was just 'shut up.' But we handcuffed him, and he was spitting and kicking out at people, so we thought, 'we can't have this.' So we got out the restraints and tied him so he couldn't kick anymore. Had to pick him up and carry him to where we could get a car for transport. And the sergeant said we should take him to county and get him [treated] and absentee to book him, and we did. Eight hours, eight hours of paperwork because of this guy."

"And that was it. We thought that was it, and then we get summonses. [His partner] and I got the summonses and we didn't even know what they were talking about. It had been five years since the incident. We didn't even recognize the name. It wasn't even familiar to me; I had to go through my officer's notebook to find out what had happened, and then I remembered the guy and what happened. Now, this is what he alleges. He alleges that my partner and I went into this gay bar, and pulled him out and beat him up, because he was gay, and then arrested him. He didn't even know what had happened to him, but that was his story. I actually think he really believes that we did it. I think he really didn't remember what really happened and thought we did it. He alleged this, brought this to a lawyer five years later. Five years! Half a decade. Where are you going to get the witnesses [even] three years later? Just [his partner] and me and the sergeant."

"It was the worst time of my life, to be accused of something and not be able to prove myself innocent. To not even have the opportunity to prove myself because the city was busy covering its ass. [very agitated] I didn't do anything, and everybody knew it. I had a partner and a sergeant, and they took the deposition of [his partner], but

didn't even call the sergeant in. They didn't even need us because they'd already decided. They just paid the fucker thirty-five hundred dollars, and it goes in my package that there was an action against me and the city paid. How does that look?" When the partner was interviewed, he stated:

"After that time I did as little as I could and had as little contact with citizens as possible. I used to work the L car [a one-officer unit that handles reports most of the time], so I was only there if they asked me to be there. And there was a record of that. I didn't do anything else if I could help it. It didn't make any sense to do anything—any real police work. Not patrol. I didn't want to go through that again."

Based on this description, it is apparent that the officers harbored resentment toward the city for settling the lawsuit. By settling out of court, the city avoided additional costs associated with the lawsuit, but it sent a message to the officers (and perhaps other officers in the department) that the officers had done something wrong. This also led to one officer seeking assignments not involving contact with citizens to avoid similar situations. Police managers should be cognizant that lawsuits are a stressful event for officers, and these lawsuits (regardless of the outcome) may increase the level of officer cynicism.

Adapted from: Barker, J. C. 1999. *Danger, Duty and Disillusion*. Waveland Press: Prospect Hts, IL: 128–129.

Civil lawsuits can have an impact even on officers in the police organization who are not identified as defendants. In the wake of a lawsuit, officers may feel the need to engage in fewer interactions with the public, particularly officer-initiated encounters. Officers rationalize this as a normal response to what they feel is an unjust situation, and also rationalize that their own likelihood of being named as a defendant in a lawsuit decreases if they interact with fewer citizens. This phenomenon has been called "laying low" or, more recently, "de-policing."

There is some evidence that de-policing may have recently occurred in Cincinnati. In April 2001, a white Cincinnati police officer shot and killed an unarmed young black male. Whether or not this shooting was justified, it sparked several days of rioting resulting in injuries sustained by citizens and officers alike. In the months that followed, the officer was indicted and a civil lawsuit was filed in federal court alleging that the police department engaged in racial profiling. After the riots, indictment, and lawsuit, there is evidence that officers engaged in a department-wide slowdown in activity. For example, in June 2000, officers made 5,063 arrests for nonviolent crimes (such as disorderly conduct and weapons violations). In June 2001 (after the riots, indictment, and lawsuit), the department made half as many arrests (2,517). Additionally, arrests for violent crimes (such as murder and arson) declined to 487 from 502. This was despite a 20 percent increase from June 2000 in these crimes. Furthermore, traffic citations were down 35 percent. One police officer stated that officers were frustrated with the increase in crime rates but that they also were afraid of being labeled a racial profiler whenever they arrested someone (Cloud, 2001; McLaughlin and Prendergast, 2001).

De-policing has implications for police managers. The most effective way to avoid this phenomenon is to maintain an environment that does not allow it to occur in the first place. Police managers who are confronted with subordinates engaged in de-policing will need to take additional steps to explain to officers that avoiding encounters with the public is not in line with the organizational goals, and is unethical behavior. Effective policing involves maintaining a healthy relationship with citizens. By engaging in de-policing, officers not only alienate citizens who are frustrated with the police, but they also alienate citizens who support the police. Over time, it is likely that de-policing will fade away and that police officer activity will regress to the mean (or return to previous levels). Yet in the meantime the department may sustain irreparable damage to public trust, public support, and the department's reputation.

Managing Risk

Managing the risk of liability is incredibly difficult, and tactics to reduce liability for officers, supervisors, police organizations, and municipalities will certainly vary from place to place. Tactics that are effective in one police department may not be effective in another department. Additionally, the courts are continually revising what actions constitute negligent behavior. While the evolution of civil liability in policing may be an interesting intellectual exercise for the policing scholar, it can be incredibly challenging and frustrating for police officers. However, based on contemporary case law and research, police managers may choose whether the following recommendations are effective ways to reduce their exposure to civil liability:

1. ***Hiring Practices***. Police departments should naturally strive to hire the most competent, qualified, and desirable individuals for the position of police officer. This includes conducting thorough background investigations. In many ways there is a lot of truth behind the old saying, "past behavior is the best predictor of future behavior," and past behavior may provide an indication of activities that have the potential for liability. Departments should ***screen in the most desired candidates***, including factors related to education, intelligence, ethical behavior, and critical thinking. Police departments should actively strive for diversity in terms of minority candidates, and some research has demonstrated that police departments that do so are less likely to incur liability (Worrall, 1998).

2. ***Training***. Officers should be trained not only **how** to do their job, but also what the department is trying to accomplish, and ***why*** their activities contribute to achieving the organizational goals.

This will assist officers in determining the most appropriate courses of action, and may insulate them from civil litigation. Officers should be kept abreast of *updates in civil liability* through in-service training programs. Hughes (2001b) reported that 62.2 percent of Cincinnati police officers felt that increased training protects officers from civil liability. Similarly, officers should be advised of the logic behind the rulings. To this end, police departments should seek the legal advice of experts in the field of civil litigation.

❖ ❖ ❖ ❖

3. *Early Identification of Problem Officers*. In order to reduce the risk of liability, police departments should routinely examine internal records regarding citizen complaints about officer behavior (even if civil litigation does not follow the complaint). Lersch and Mieczkowski (1996: 38) indicated that it is possible to identify officers with chronic problems of officer complaints and misconduct. They recommend early warning systems (as discussed in Chapter 10), which "may assist a department in identifying problem-prone officers before the situation gets out of control." Once problem officers have been identified, managers will need to choose from various methods to correct the problem. This may include *additional training*, or *special assignments* for these officers may reduce the organization's exposure to liability. Managers must also choose to recommend *termination* of employment for officers who negligently expose the police department to civil liability, or officers who engage in unethical behavior. This may also entail state *de-certification* of the status of police officer. Furthermore, supervisors may also collect and present evidence of criminal activity to the prosecutor, who may seek criminal charges against problem officers.

4. *Maintaining Good Relationships with Citizens*. This recommendation goes beyond "good public relations," and in many ways it is the root of community policing. By maintaining a good relationship with citizens, police departments may be able to address problems informally or administratively, without intervention from the courts. Similarly, the police department should strive to maintain a good reputation. The reputation should focus on *even-handed enforcement* of the law and *integrity* during encounters with citizens. Police departments that have a reputation for being "corrupt" or "brutal" may be living a self-fulfilling prophecy. Citizens may view civil litigation as a natural reaction to police departments with a reputation for corruption or brutality. Managers should *promote integrity and nonaggressive behavior* in order to reduce violence between the police and the public.

Finally, Camp (2000: 137) presents an insightful rule for police managers: "Understanding the law is far better than knowing it." Although this may appear to be double-talk, in actuality it makes a lot of sense. Police officers are often well versed in regurgitation of criminal and civil laws but often fail to understand or appreciate what the law actually means, or the logic behind the legal decision of case law. Failure to understand the legal theory and the logic behind civil litigation may doom officers to eventually compromise the law, not out of maliciousness, but merely out of ignorance.

Summary

Civil litigation regarding police behavior has increased over time, both in the number of suits filed and the amount of money paid for damages or injury. People who initiate lawsuits (called plaintiffs) against the police (called defendants) may do so in either state courts or in federal courts. In state courts torts may be brought for intentional as well as negligent behavior. In federal courts, plaintiffs may bring lawsuits against the police if there is a violation of constitutional rights or federally protected rights. Often these lawsuits are filed under 42 USC §1983. In order to be successful in a §1983, the plaintiff must demonstrate that the officer acted under the color of law and that the act violated the plaintiff's civil rights. Acceptable defenses to §1983 lawsuits include absolute immunity, qualified immunity, probable cause, and good faith. Supervisors may be named as defendants in lawsuits for actions committed by their subordinates, and common areas include negligent hiring, failure to train, negligent supervision, negligent assignment, and failure to investigate and discipline. While community policing may decrease the incidence of civil liability in policing, there is an equal chance that civil liability will increase. Regardless of whether plaintiffs prevail in their lawsuits against the police (and most do not), the process can cause negative consequences for police officers, including increased stress and cynicism. Effective risk management for liability included effective hiring practices, effective training, early identification of problem officers, and maintaining good relationships with the community.

Discussion Questions

1. Describe the prevalence of civil liability in policing.

2. Compare and contrast the criminal justice system to the civil system of justice.

3. Describe the costs associated with civil liability.

4. What types of claims may plaintiffs seek in state courts? In federal courts?

5. Describe 42 US §1983. What key components are necessary for a claim under §1983?

6. Under what circumstances do officers act "under the color of law," and why is this important to understand?

7. Describe the defenses to federal lawsuits.

8. Under what circumstances are supervisors exposed to civil liability for the behavior of their subordinates?

9. Will community policing increase or decrease the number of civil liability claims? Support your answer.

10. What steps can officers take to limit their exposure to civil liability? Supervisors? Police organizations? Municipalities?

References

Alter, J. 2001. "Hillary Raises Her Profile: Senator Clinton Takes on Race and Crime—A Subject Much More Complex Than It Seems." Newsweek, June 25: 34.

Barker, J. C. 1999. *Danger, Duty and Disillusion*. Prospect Hts, IL: Waveland Press.

Barrineu, H. E. 1994. *Civil Liability in Criminal Justice*, 2nd ed. Cincinnati: Anderson Publishing.

Bennett v. City of Slidell, 735 F.2d 861 (5th Cir. 1984).

Bittner, E. 1970. *The Functions of Police in a Modern Society*. Washington, DC: USGPO.

Camp, D. D. 2000. "Civil Liability: Executive Preparation." In Doerner, W. G., and Dantzker, M. L. (eds.), *Contemporary Police Organization and Management: Issues and Trends*. Pp. 115–142. Boston: Butterworth/Heinemann.

City of Canton v. Harris, 489 US 378 (1989).

Cloud, J. 2001, July 30. "What's Race Got to Do With It? Despite a Crime Wave, Cincinnati's Cops Pull Back, Underscoring Stakes in the Conflict over Racial Profiling." Retrieved August 16, 2001, from the World Wide Web: http://www.time.com/time/covers/1101010730/cover.html.

del Carmen, R. V. 1991. *Civil Liabilities in American Policing: A Text for Law Enforcement Personnel*. Englewood Cliffs, NJ: Brady.

——. 1994. "Criminal and Civil Liabilities of Police Officers." In Barker, T. and Carter, D. L. (eds.), *Police Deviance*, 3rd ed. Cincinnati: Anderson Publishing.

——. 2001. *Criminal Procedure: Law and Practice*, 5th ed. Belmont, CA: Wadsworth.

del Carmen, R. V., and Smith, M. R. 2001. "Police, Civil Liability, and the Law." In Dunham, R. G. and Alpert, G. P. (eds.), *Critical Issues in Policing*, 4th ed. Pp. 181–198. Prospect Hts., IL: Waveland Press.

Dunham, R., Alpert, G. P., Kenn[e]y, D. J., and Cromwell, P. 1998. "High-Speed Pursuit: The Offender's Perspective." *Criminal Justice and Behavior* 25: 30–45.

Graham v. Connor, 490 US 397 (1989).

Greene, J. A. 1999. "Zero Tolerance: A Case Study of Police Policies and Practices in New York City." *Crime and Delinquency* 45: 171–187.

Gutierrez-Rodriguez v. Cartagena, 882 F.2d 553 (1st Cir. 1989).

Homant, R., and Kennedy, D. 1994. "Citizen Preferences and Perceptions Concerning Police Pursuit Policies." *Journal of Criminal Justice* 22: 425–435.

Hughes, T. 2000. Community Policing and Federal Civil Liability Under 42 USC §1983. Unpublished doctoral dissertation: University of Cincinnati.

——. 2001a. "Board of the County Commissioners of Bryan County, Oklahoma v. Jill Brown: Municipal Liability and Police Hiring Decisions." *The Justice Professional* 13: 143–162.

——. 2001b. "Police Officers and Civil Liability: 'The Ties That Bind'?" *Policing: An International Journal of Police Strategies and Management* 24: 240–262.

——. In press. "'Maximum Lawman Run Down Flamingo': County of Sacramento v. Lewis and Police Pursuit Liability." *The Justice Professional*.

Hunter v. Bryant, 502 U.S. 224, 112 S. Ct. 634 (1991).

Kappeler, V. E. 2001. *Critical Issues in Police Civil Liability*, 3rd ed. Prospect Hts., IL: Waveland Press.

Kappeler, V. E., Kappeler, S. F., and del Carmen, R. V. 1993. "A Content Analysis of Police Civil Liability Cases: Decisions in the Federal District Courts, 1978–1990." *Journal of Criminal Justice* 21: 325–337.

Klockars, C. B. 1985. *The Idea of Police*. Beverly Hills: Sage.

Klotter, J. C. 1999. *Legal Guide for Police: Constitutional Issues*. 5th ed. Cincinnati: Anderson Publishing.

Langan, P. A., Greenfield, L. A., Smith, S. K., Durose, M. R., and Levin, D. J. 2001 "Contacts Between the Police and the Public: Findings from the 1999 National Survey." Washington, DC: Bureau of Justice Statistics.

Lersch, K. M., and Mieczkowski, T. 1996. "Who Are the Problem-Prone Officers? An Analysis of Citizen Complaints." *American Journal of Police* 15: 23–44.

Levine, L., Davies, J., and Kionka, E. 1993. *A Torts Anthology*. Cincinnati: Anderson Publishing.

McLaughlin, S., and Prendergast, J. 2001, June 30. "Police Frustration Brings Slowdown: Arrests Plummet from 2000; Officers Seek Jobs in Suburbs." Retrieved August 16, 2001, from the World Wide Web: http://enquirer.com/editions/2001/06/30/loc_police_frustration.html.

Miranda v. Arizona, 384 U.S. 436, 86 S. Ct. 1602, 16 L. Ed. 2d 694 (1966).

Monell v. Department of Social Services, 436 U.S. 658 (1978).

Prosser, W., and Keeton, P. 1984. *The Law of Torts*. St. Paul, MN: West Publishing.

Ramirez, D., McDevitt, J., and Farrell, A. 2000. *A Resource Guide on Racial Profiling Data Collection Systems: Promising Practices and Lessons Learned*. Washington, DC: Bureau of Justice Assistance.

Riksheim, E. C., and Chermak, S. M. 1993. "Causes of Police Behavior Revisited." *Journal of Criminal Justice* 21:353–382.

Roberg, R., Crank, J., and Kuykendall, J. 2000. *Police and Society*, 2nd ed. Los Angeles: Roxbury Publishing.

Ross, D. L. 2000. "Emerging Trends in Police Failure to Train Liability." *Policing: An International Journal of Police Strategies and Management* 23: 169–193.

Sacramento v. Lewis, 523 U.S. 833 (1998).

Sherman, L. W. 1992. *Policing Domestic Violence*. New York: Free Press.

Silver, I. 1996. *Police Civil Liability*. New York: Mathew Binder.

Tennessee v. Garner, 471 U.S. 1 (1985).

Terry v. Ohio, 392 U.S. 1, 88 S. Ct. 1868, 20 L. Ed. 2d 889 (1968).

Thurman v. City of Torrington, 595 F. Supp. 1521 (1985).

United States v. Seslar, 996 F 2d. 1058 (10th Cir.) 1993.

Vaughn, M. S., and Coomes, L. F. 1995. "Police Civil Liability Under Section 1983: When Do Police Officers Act Under the Color of Law?" *Journal of Criminal Justice* 23: 395–415.

Vaughn, M. S., Cooper, T. W., and del Carmen, R. V. 2001. "Assessing Legal Liabilities in Law Enforcement: Police Chiefs' Views." *Crime and Delinquency* 47: 3–27.

Wilkins v. Maryland State Police, Civil Action No. CCB-93-483, 1993.

Wilson v. Layne, 141 F.3d 111, 1998.

Worrall, J. L. 1998. "Administrative Determinants of Civil Liability Lawsuits Against Municipal Police Departments: An Exploratory Analysis." *Crime and Delinquency* 44: 295–313.

Worrall, J. L., and Marenin, O. 1998. "Emerging Liability Issues in the Implementation and Adoption of Community Oriented Policing." *Policing: An International Journal of Police Strategies & Management* 21: 121–136. 11

Chapter Fourteen

Organization Change and Development

Throughout the book, the authors have emphasized the need for many police departments to become more organic. In general, a more organic or flexible orientation allows the organization to adapt more readily to both internal and external environmental concerns. For many departments, becoming more organic has become synonymous with a move toward community policing. As noted previously, such critical changes, especially in highly traditional, mechanistic departments, not only take time and energy but must be carefully planned and implemented. The focus of this chapter is on understanding change in organizations, the importance of developing an innovative climate if change is to occur, and the types of strategies or methods that can be used to develop and change organizations. Once managers have an adequate understanding of the change and development processes, it is more likely that strategic changes toward organic designs and managerial styles will succeed.

Organization Change

Organization change occurs when an organization adopts new ideas or behaviors (Pierce and Delbeq, 1977). Usually, an innovative idea, such as a new method of management or a new patrol strategy, is introduced and behavioral changes are supposed to follow. Consequently, the ultimate success of any organization change depends on how well the organization can alter the behavioral patterns of its employees. Employee behavior is influenced by factors such as leadership styles, motivational techniques, informal relationships, and organization and job design. Any change in the organization, regardless of how it is introduced, involves an attempt to persuade employees to change their behavior and their relationships with one another. In order to bring about timely change, managers need to consider why people resist change, how resistance can be overcome, the effects of pace on change, and factors influencing police management.

Resistance to Change

Probably the most common characteristic of change is people's resistance to it. Generally, people do not like to change their behavior. Adapting to a new environment or learning a new method or technique often results in feelings of stress and fear of the unknown (e.g., Will I like it? Will I be able to do it well?). The following is a discussion of the major reasons, based on Kerr and Kerr (1972), why resistance to change is so common, using community policing as an example.

Inertia

A great deal of *inertia*, or "doing things as they have always been done," is strongly associated with paramilitary departments. People have what is known as *sunk costs* in their jobs and routines, including time, energy, and experience; these are powerful forces in resisting change. Individuals or groups with many such "investments" sunk into a particular department or job may not want changes, regardless of their merit. Lewis, Rosenberg and Sigler (1999), for example, found that older officers with more seniority and detectives, both of whom tend to have a greater stake in the traditional police structure, had the lowest acceptance rate of community policing. Community policing, of course, requires officers to do many of their old tasks in new ways and to take on new tasks with which they are not familiar. They may be

"asked to identify and solve a broad range of problems; reach out to elements   ❖ ❖ ❖ ❖
of the community that previously were outside their orbit; and put their
careers at risk by taking on unfamiliar and challenging responsibilities"
(Skogan and Hartnett, 1997: 71). These expectations are often beyond the
officers' capabilities and the traditional roles for which they were initially
selected and trained (Lurigio and Rosenbaum, 1994). There is little doubt
that most officers would rather do what they believe they were hired for and
what they perceive to be the "real" police role: crime fighting. Consequently,
community policing is often viewed as "social work," which takes critical
time away from their crime-fighting activities.

Management personnel will have the same inertia factor at work because
they also have been selected and trained to do traditional policing. Although
inertia occurs at all managerial levels, except possibly at the very top where a
new police chief is brought in to implement community policing, the attitudes of sergeants are especially important. Because sergeants have the most
direct influence over the day-to-day activities of street officers, it is crucial
that they "buy into" the new program, promoting the department's new policies and procedures.

In order to do so, sergeants will need to act as facilitators and trainers as
well as supervisors. Mitigating against this facilitating and training role,
however, is the newness of community policing; most sergeants have never
experienced it themselves. They too must learn new skills and behaviors and
what is expected of them. Another mitigating factor is that in "command and
control" departments, supervision tends to be negative—relying primarily on
sanctions for not "going by the book," that is, adhering strictly to departmental rules and regulations (Weisburd, McElroy, and Hardyman, 1988). Of
course, this attitude is antithetical to community policing, in which innovation in solving community problems is of primary concern. However, as
Skogan and Hartnett note:

> Little is supposed to happen in police departments without general orders
> that detail how it is to be done . . . working life . . . is dominated by the need to
> reconstruct or redefine what actually happens in the field, so it appears to fit
> the model. This helps ensure that top managers downtown "don't know what
> really happens on the street"—a derisive charge that rolls easily off the lips of
> street officers and helps legitimate their resistance to strategies devised at
> headquarters. (1997: 73)

Such a managerial approach not only adds to the resistance of new programs
and strategies, but it helps contribute to the police culture as well, where the
relationship between street cops and management cops is often adversarial.
Completing the circle, adversarial relationships between street officers and
management contribute to resistance to management's attempts at change.

Misunderstandings

Resistance to change is likely when organization members do not clearly
understand the purpose, mechanics, or consequences of a planned change
because of inadequate or misperceived communication. A critical problem in
this area is uncertainty about the consequences of change. If employees are
not told how they will be affected by change, rumors and speculation will follow, and resistance and even sabotage may be strong enough to severely limit
the effort to change. When change is imposed on employees, instead of occurring as a result of participation, misunderstandings are more likely to occur.

When police departments attempt to move to community policing, they frequently make the mistake of not clearly articulating what new roles will be created and the effect of those new roles on all involved. For instance, in Houston when evaluators interviewed officers who were assigned to the neighborhood-oriented policing (NOP) program (often referred to by the officers as "nobody on patrol"), they discovered that officers frequently had no idea what the program was about or what they should be doing differently (Sadd and Grinc, 1994). In addition, departments often do not allow officers to participate in the planning and development of the new program. Although rumors generally abound, the first official announcements they hear about it is when the program is unveiled at a downtown press conference by the chief, surrounded by politicians. Because they have not been kept abreast of program development and expectations, what they see from their perspective is an increased workload that will be hard to maintain—that is, more social work activities, while maintaining their current work schedule. In such instances, it is little wonder that officers feel the program is being forced upon them—creating a situation that is not conducive to cooperation.

Group Norms. As discussed previously, groups have an important impact on the behavior and attitudes of their members. **Group norms**, or expected behavior from group members, may be a powerful factor in resistance to change. If individual officers follow the norms strictly (e.g., that only law enforcement activities are important), they will not easily perceive the need for change. If significant departmental changes are to occur, police managers must consider group norms and influences and involve group consensus and decision making in planning for change. The major way to achieve such involvement is to allow for participatory management. For example, in Madison (Wisconsin), where participatory management practices (referred to as quality management) produced more satisfied workers, the planners believed that it was a necessary condition for implementation of community policing (Wycoff and Skogan, 1993). By allowing for general participation, the adversarial relations between street cops and management cops should diminish, and thus increase the chances for successful change.

Balance of Power. One source of stability in organizations is the balance of power among individuals, groups, and units. Changes that are perceived to threaten the autonomy, authority, power, or status of a group or unit will most likely encounter resistance, regardless of their merit. For instance, such resistance was well documented in the team-policing experiments of the 1970s, when departments attempted to decentralize their operations into neighborhood teams (see Sherman, Milton, and Kelley, 1973). Because this approach provided more control and autonomy for lower-level management (sergeants), middle-level management (lieutenants and captains) often resisted the change (by subverting and, in some cases, sabotaging the plans) for fear that they would lose authority, power, and status. Because the failure of most team-policing efforts can be traced, at least in part, to the lack of support by mid-level mangers, it is crucial that police executives plan for their role in the change process. It has been suggested that whether middle managers are part of the problem or part of the solution in changing to community policing will depend on such factors as (1) involving middle managers in planning for change to increase their credibility with subordinates; (2) linking rewards to performance in implementing desired changes; (3) making a serious commitment to train middle managers in the skills necessary to adjust to their new roles; (4) articulating and adhering to a consistent vision for the department; (5) allowing middle managers to make honest and constructive mistakes; and (6) ensuring that community policing strategies have a long-term commitment and will prevail (Geller and Swanger, 1995).

Inside Management 14.1 provides insight into the reasons officers resisted change in New York in that city's attempt to make a transition to community policing. Notice how every reason overlaps, to some degree, with the major reasons for resistance discussed above. These reasons for resistance would be found in most traditional paramilitary police departments.

❖ ❖ ❖ ❖

Inside Management 14.1

Resistance to Organization Change in New York

The following are examples of reasons that some police officers in the New York City Police Department resisted change toward a community policing philosophy. These examples are based on informal discussions with officers. It should be noted, however, that these examples appear to be fairly representative in police departments attempting major organizational change. [Author's note: The department reduced its emphasis on community policing, at least in part, because of this resistance.]

Misunderstanding of Purpose. Early in the process of implementing community policing, many officers do not truly understand (or wish to understand) the philosophy and purpose of community policing.

Failure to See the Need for Change. Some officers believe that community policing is merely a result of the commissioner wanting to try out his ideas in New York City. They see this as a grand management experiment attempted at their expense.

Confusion Over New Roles and Fear of the Unknown. Many officers do not fully understand their new roles or what the department expects of them. Some officers perceive a conflict between their new role, where they are asked to "serve the public," and their traditional role, in which they exerted coercive control over the community. Officers ask, "How can you expect people to work with me to solve their problems when they know I may have to enforce the law against them because their behavior is, at times, someone else's problem?" Some supervisors are also uncertain as to their new roles and what the department expects of them.

Fear of Loss of Status, Security, and Power. Many officers in New York believe they are doing a credible job in controlling crime and see themselves as having achieved a reasonable status in society; they have earned this status by being brave. Community policing, with its re-duced emphasis on adventure and bravery and its enhanced focus on public service, has some officers fearing that their status will be diminished. Some officers also feel that once they align themselves with the community, they will lose much of their power. After all, how can they exercise power over people they must befriend and be accountable to?

Lack of Involvement with Change. Some officers feel that they are simply being told this is the new philosophy and have no sense of participation in the decision. One superior officer stated after a training seminar, "Community policing is the new train—get on or get off." This attitude enhances the feeling that this program is being forced on them, and they have no more intention of changing their philosophy of policing because the commissioner tells them to than they would change their political philosophy if the president told them to.

Vested Interest in the Status Quo. In order to bring back the beat cop in dramatic numbers—a hallmark of community policing—some cops will have to be pried out of their radio cars. They do not like walking a beat, especially in cold or inclement weather. Some believe that after working hard for several years they have earned the right to ride comfortably in radio cars. Others still view foot patrol negatively, because it was once used as punishment or as an assignment for rookies.

Threat to Existing Social Relationships. While foot patrol officers are getting acquainted with merchants and other citizens who live and work in their assigned communities, the radio car cops are busy responding to calls and, as they say, "busting their butts." They are beginning to resent the department's preferential attitude toward the beat cops, and the beat cops themselves, who they feel are not pulling their load and spend their time "schmoozing" with the public. One officer explained, "While I'm out here doing all the grunt work and risking my life, they're playing with the neighborhood kids or attending some community meeting." Another officer observed, "I know a community patrol officer who spends most of his day hiding out in a store. I guess he's getting to know the merchants or helping them solve their problems."

One veteran superior officer said he was saddened by what he saw as a department being "torn in two." The nonbeat cops feel as if they are being treated as second-class citizens; although beat cops are not doing any work or placing their lives at risk, they are looked up to by the department. A prime example they cite is the departmental accolade bestowed on a beat cop who assisted 25 brides-to-be in retrieving their wedding gowns from a shop that abruptly went out of business.

Conflicting Personal and Organizational Objectives. The police department is interested in getting officers to work with the citizens to-

ward solving social problems, thereby improving the quality of life and making their streets safer. Some officers believe, however, that many of the problems brought forth by the public are not worthy of police attention and have little to do with crime. Although proponents of community policing believe that resolving such problems will create an environment less conducive to crime, and thus lower the crime rate, to many officers this is a waste of their time, since the causes of crime go far beyond aesthetic fixes to the immediate neighborhood. Some officers are also candid about their aversion to performing what they perceive as "social work." And they complain that after a while, other officers do not see them as "real cops."

Adapted from: A. L. Pisani, 1992. "Dissecting Community Policing: Part 2." *Law Enforcement News,* May 31: 8, 10. Reprinted with permission from *Law Enforcement News,* John Jay College of Criminal Justice.

Reducing Resistance

The following discussion focuses on methods police managers can use to lessen resistance and institute change in a beneficial and constructive fashion. Because of individual differences, the same method will not reduce resistance in every organization member. In general, however, several methods are valuable in reducing resistance to change: sharing expectations, avoiding coercive tactics, using group decision making, and making changes tentative.

Sharing Expectations

A mutual sharing of expectations, as suggested by the expectation-integration model, between the organization (especially top-level management) and the individual can greatly facilitate understanding and reduce dysfunctional conflicts. Much of the misunderstanding results from too little open communication between the two parties; distrust develops and the change process becomes a traumatic experience, strongly resisted by the rank and file. By contrast, if two-way communication and shared expectations are encouraged, specific reasons for resistance can be discovered and additional explanation or a change in strategy can be made.

Police managers must also be sure that expectations are being shared with all the parties who are to be affected by the change, even if they are not directly involved in it. For instance, in the Flint (Michigan) Police Department's foot-patrol program, conflict arose between motor-patrol and foot-patrol officers. According to Trojanowicz and Bucqueroux:

> They did a great job of educating the community and the officers involved in the program, but they forgot to include motor patrol in the educational process. Traditional officers not only felt neglected but insulted, laying the groundwork for hostility between the two units. (1990:207)

Avoiding Coercive Tactics

✦ ✦ ✦ ✦

Those who resist change are sometimes coerced into accepting it. Strauss and Sayles (1980) accurately interpret the use of coercive tactics as **overcoming resistance**, in contrast to **reducing resistance**. Owing to the traditional, mechanistic design of many police departments, management may assume that whatever is communicated from the top of the pyramid will be readily embraced by the lower echelons. When questions arise or policies are not carried out enthusiastically, uncooperative members may be encouraged to retire or threatened with punishments, such as transfers from an immediate peer group, suspensions, demotions, and even termination.

Such coercive tactics only exacerbate the situation. Resistance may actually become stronger over time, followed by resentment and possibly sabotage. The related decrease in morale will most likely result in lowered levels of performance and possibly increased employee turnover. Thus, although coercive tactics may initially suppress resistance, the long-term effects for both the organization and the individual are likely to be inflammatory and counterproductive. Nevertheless, for political reasons, managers may rely on coercive tactics because they do tend to produce immediate results.

Changes in police departments, particularly major changes, are frequently characterized by the use of centralized decision making and coercive tactics, both associated with the mechanistic model. Management and employees often have an adversarial relationship because coercive tactics are used to implement change. This management perspective seems to be that because many employees do not understand the need for change and will resist it anyway, there is no need to involve them in the process. Instead, they must be forced to go along. Some police managers even hope that coercive tactics will result in the retirement or resignation of those who are opposed to the change. Not only is this approach inhumane, it assumes that only the proponents of change have the "right" vision for the future of the organization, and the opponents can add nothing to the process. This essentially political conception of management is a reflection of segmentalism, as will be discussed later.

However, even though change is usually more effective if coercive tactics are not used, they may be necessary under some circumstances. In police departments, even when there is substantial consensus on the direction the organization should take, there will most likely be resistance. This is due at least partially to the fact that the two or more generations of officers each have their own style of policing. Consequently, in some instances, changes in activity and behavior may have to be mandated. It is important to remember, however, that coercion should be a last resort, and not the basic perspective from which managers should function. Interestingly, as we discovered in Chapter 7, there may even be a need for dual roles (i.e., rapid response and beat/community-policing officer) in most organizations transitioning to community policing, which, if managed creatively, might reduce not only resistance to the changes but the temptation to use coercion as well.

Using Group Decision Making

Kurt Lewin's (1958) initial studies on the development of group methods in decision making revealed that behavioral change is more likely to occur and persist when based on a group rather than an individual decision. This is especially true when the group is important to an individual, who will change attitudes and behavior in order to conform. Lewin further stated that the basis for successful change involves (1) **unfreezing** existing habits and stereotypes, (2) **changing** to new behavioral patterns and attitudes, and (3) **refreezing** or reinforcing the new patterns and attitudes to ensure future conformity. The key to this method is group pressure, which will be especially strong if the participants feel they own the decision and are responsible for it.

According to this analysis, a participative management style can reduce much of the potential conflict and resistance to change. Through the use of task forces, ad hoc committees, group seminars, and other participatory techniques, employees can become directly involved in planning for change. By thoroughly discussing and debating the issues, a more accurate understanding and unbiased analysis of the situation is likely to result. Although the group may still reject a particular decision for change, resistance based on misunderstanding will nevertheless be reduced. In police departments, such a discussion or debate of the issues is essential to overcome initial resistance to change.

Making Changes Tentative

In general, changes should take place on a tentative or trial basis, particularly in traditional, mechanistic departments. If employees do not perceive changes as irreversible, they will feel less threatened and their resistance will be reduced. Strauss and Sayles suggest two distinct advantages to this method:

1. It enables employees to test their own reactions to the new situation and provides them with more facts on which to base their decision.

2. It helps to "unfreeze" their attitudes and encourages them to think objectively about the proposed changes. (1980, 121)

Pace of Change

Planned organization change should occur at an appropriate pace, neither too rapid nor too gradual. The pace is critical; if change is forced through abruptly, it could cause severe resistance that could disrupt the organization over a long period. But if change is so gradual and slow that the employees cannot really see anything "happening," they may return to the more familiar and comfortable ways of the past. Change should be introduced quickly enough to show that something is happening and slowly enough to prevent it from totally disrupting the status quo and being rejected.

Contingency factors play an important role in determining the pace for organization change, as organic organizations can withstand more rapid change than mechanistic ones. For mechanistic police departments, a gradual or medium pace would be the least disruptive route to change and, therefore, the most beneficial. In organic departments whose employees may be more amenable to change, there is no reason why change cannot be introduced rapidly. The advantage of quick change is that it eliminates the need for the series of adjustments that are required by slow change and thus the chance of losing momentum. Of course, managers should also keep in mind that some specific unit(s) within a traditional police department may have characteristics that allow for a more rapid pace of change than that of the overall department.

It is important to remember that because of the highly structured, mechanistic nature of many police departments, the struggle to bring about significant change can be compared to "bending granite" (Guyot, 1979). Therefore, as discussed earlier in the book, it should be expected that a relatively lengthy and sustained effort will be necessary in order to facilitate permanent changes in such organizations. In other words, police managers must pay careful attention to *keeping the change process moving forward* at a fast enough pace, for a long enough period, so that momentum is not lost and change has a reasonable chance to occur. Pace and sustained effort should be recognized as crucial variables in implementing significant change in police departments.

Overcoming Resistance to Change: The Madison Experience

One of the most successful examples of transition from traditional to community policing is the Madison (Wisconsin) Police Department. The use of participatory management smoothed the transition process and helped to overcome initial resistance to the new developments. It is important to understand that this department was one of the early leaders in the movement toward community policing. The change process started in earnest within the department in the early 1980s, well before most of the present-day knowledge gained through research and evaluation was available. Thus, much of what the department accomplished in the way of change was groundbreaking. At the time, the department had approximately 280 commissioned personnel serving a community of approximately 175,000. The organization change process utilized in Madison is presented in Case Study 14.1.

Case Study 14.1 also offers many insights into how to constructively introduce major change in police departments. Many of the methods used in Madison—for example, survey feedback, job enrichment, and team building—are organization-development strategies, which are discussed in the

---

Case Study 14.1

Organization Change in Madison

In the early 1970s, with the appointment of a new chief, the Madison Police Department was operating on a high-control, central-authority model. This traditional style of police management continued through the early years of the chief's tenure but not without a cost to the department and its members in terms of a high degree of distrust, grievances, complaining, stress, and confrontations. In 1981, after a four-month leave of absence, the chief decided that something had to be done regarding the department's internal problems. After discussions with rank-and-file officers, it became clear that a "lack of communication" was a primary concern and that a new management or leadership style was necessary. Consequently, the chief decided to let employees participate more in organizational decisions and to take on the role of facilitator for himself. This decision led to the establishment of the Officers' Advisory Council (OAC) to provide advice to the chief.

The Officers' Advisory Council

The development of the OAC was critical in clearing the way for a major change in leadership style within the department. The council consists of 12 peer-selected employees who serve for a two-year period. The group was originally made up of two officers elected from each patrol shift, two detectives, one sergeant, and one officer-at-large. A majority of the council agreed that all departmental employees should be represented. This was accomplished by adding two "at-large" seats, one for a female and one for a minority representative, and agreeing to keep the special seats in existence even though female and minority employees have been elected to other seats on the council.

The OAC became a top priority and over time was given increased organizational decision-making powers. The OAC developed its ability to gather data and make recommendations using a problem-solving approach. The members meet at least monthly and attempt to develop new ideas and support them with research. They have learned that if they obtain data that support their recommendations, they are likely to see those recommendations put into practice; thus, they have significant input in departmental policies and procedures. It is believed that the OAC's actions now reflect the problem-solving and research orientation of the department's quality-improvement effort.

Committee on the Future

In 1984, a Committee on the Future was formed to look at trends and how they might affect the department in the coming years. The committee was composed of a diverse group of department members who had at least 15 years of service remaining. The intent was to have committee members who had a vested interest in the future direction of the department. A member of the OAC was appointed to serve on this committee in order to link the two groups. After a year of meeting two to four times a month, the committee released a report on the results of its findings and made three major recommendations:

1. Get closer to the people we serve.
2. Make better use of available technology.
3. Develop and improve health and wellness in the workplace.

The report helped the department to establish a vision for the future and become aware of the importance of long-range planning. This thinking about the future caused the department to re-examine its structure, internal practices, and the direction in which it was moving.

Quality Leadership

Early in 1985, almost parallel with the efforts in the police department, the mayor's office initiated a citywide effort to improve the Quality/Productivity (QP) of the city's departments. A four-day seminar conducted by W. Edwards Deming, at the time the leader of the quality movement in this country, was followed by a 15-day training seminar in QP principles and procedures for city employees. Five police employees attended the training sessions, which covered team building, group processes, facilitator skills, and the gathering and use of data.

Following the QP training, the department articulated the management philosophy of quality leadership, which includes the following principles: teamwork for planning; goal setting for operations; data-based problem solving; a customer orientation; employee input in decisions; respect and trust among employees; improvement of systems and processes; policies to support productive employees; encouragement for creativity and risk taking; tolerance for mistakes; and the manager as facilitator rather than commander. Quality leadership, and its emphasis on employee input, became the means to the goal of a healthier workplace and was viewed as a necessary prelude for community policing.

The Experimental Police District

The decision was made to develop a prototype of the new design in one part of the department before attempting to reshape the entire organization. The result was the experimental police district (EPD), the first decentralized police facility in the department. Opened in 1988, the EPD housed approximately one-sixth of the department's personnel and served approximately one-sixth of Madison's population. The charge of the EPD was to promote innovation and experimentation in three areas:

1. Employee participation in decision making about the conditions of work and the delivery of police services

2. Management and supervisory styles supportive of employee participation and of community-oriented and problem-oriented policing

3. The implementation of community-oriented and problem-oriented policing

Planning for the EPD was done by a team of persons representing all areas and ranks of the department. A captain from the chief's office was asked to become an ad hoc member and to serve as a link to the chief's office and the management team. Other links to the group included a patrol officer who was a member of the OAC, a union board member, a woman detective, and a minority (male) patrol officer. This was the first time that management actively involved the union in the development of a major program. The chief reserved the right to choose a team leader and name a team facilitator. Additionally, he established a project-coordinating team to act as a steering committee and assist the project team.

Development of the EPD

As a first step in the planning process, project-team members identified departmental problems that they thought needed to be corrected, such as a lack of meaningful involvement with the community, lack of teamwork or team identity among officers, inflexible management styles and resulting loss of creativity, and lack of communication and information exchange among ranks. Project-team members also conducted department-wide interviews, in which team members met in small groups with all employees to find out what they thought needed to be corrected. The top preferences were voted on by the group and published in an EPD newsletter and sent to all employees. This was the first time that management had allowed employees to survey other employees on issues that heretofore were considered to be strictly management's concern.

To get citizens involved, the project team held eight community meetings in the project area, two in each alderman's district. The first set of meetings in each district was for people whom the department and alderman designated as community leaders. The second set of meetings was open to all concerned citizens. At the meetings, citizens were questioned about their knowledge of and satisfaction with police services, about neighborhood problems and concerns, and about how they felt police could work with them in responding to problems. The group process used at the meetings resulted in a listing of problems rated by priority.

Operation of the EPD

The goals of the EPD managers are to become facilitators and coaches who allow and encourage creativity and risk taking among officers. They have given officers substantial latitude to decide their own schedules, their own work conditions, and how to address neighborhood problems. In other matters, the managers consider the input of employees before making decisions. They try to encourage problem solving by offering ideas, information, and scheduling alternatives. Although things moved slowly at the beginning, the managers began to see increased use of problem solving as a tool.

Adapted from: D. C. Couper and S. H. Lobitz. 1991. *Quality Policing: The Madison Experience*. Washington, D.C.: Police Executive Research Forum, pp. 15–22, 33, 36–37; M. A. Wycoff and W. G. Skogan. 1993. *Community Policing in Madison: Quality From the Inside Out*. Washington, D.C.: National Institute of Justice, December, pp. 20–22, 26–28.

final section of this chapter. In order to apply such strategies and sustain change, however, it is first necessary to create an organizational climate that encourages innovation.

Obstacles to Change Outside of Management's Control

Some factors that may have a direct influence on management's ability to implement organization change may be beyond the control of management. Several of these factors have been briefly discussed in other chapters. First, there are *civil service regulations,* which may limit the selection criteria (e.g., higher educational standards) and promotional practices (e.g., seniority versus ability). Such regulations may hinder progress toward change and may need to be dealt with by management, even to the point of modifying or eliminating them.

Other factors that may affect management's efforts at change include police unions, fraternal organizations, and agency accreditation. Several primary objectives of *police unions* include union recognition, improvements in wages and benefits, clear disciplinary procedures, and better job conditions. *Fraternal organizations* primarily seek recognition and benefits for their members (especially with respect to race, gender, and sexual orientation issues), and these goals may differ from the goals of union or other fraternal units. With respect to wages and benefits, it is clear that if primary emphasis is placed on money issues (hygiene factors) rather than employee satisfaction (motivating factors), change can be made more difficult. It is not suggested that unions should not attempt to increase salaries and benefits, but in those departments where pay and benefit packages are already attractive and competitive, the lower-level needs of employees are essentially being met; therefore, management must work with labor leaders to emphasize the satisfaction of employees' upper-level needs, especially by focusing on how jobs can best be enriched. Attempts to severely limit or impede the disciplinary process can have a significant impact on management's attempts to change the organization's culture as well as to change the work of officers. The importance of working with union leadership to preserve or to establish a fair yet firm approach to discipline cannot be overstated.

Negotiated job conditions through police unions may also play a vital role with respect to how much control management has over changing the content of jobs and even job assignments. As noted in Chapter 4, it is becoming common for unions to negotiate matters that were once the traditional province of police managers, including personnel assignments and allocation of resources. How negotiated job conditions can affect management control with respect to departmental change can be illustrated by a relatively large San Francisco Bay area department that was attempting to implement community policing. One of the foundations of its approach was the "stable" area assignment of a team of officers in order to make them familiar with local residents and better understand their needs. One sergeant—popular with both residents and officers—had served a certain amount of time in a particular beat area and, based on his seniority under the union contract, was eligible to transfer to another area. The sergeant applied for a transfer and was turned down by the chief because his leadership and popularity were too important to the community-policing effort at that time. The sergeant subsequently filed a grievance with the union. Reluctantly, the chief allowed the transfer, lamenting that such a transfer policy would need to be renegotiated in the next union contract if community policing were to succeed. Although the sergeant's right to transfer in this case was unquestionable, the point is that implementing major organization change is complicated and must be well planned, including negotiations with the department's union leaders.

Interestingly, the use of *agency accreditation*, which has been promoted as an attempt to improve police professionalism, may actually hamper organization change and the development of community policing. The Commission on Accreditation of Law Enforcement Agencies (CALEA) originally established 944 standards that had to be met to gain accreditation, implying that such accreditation established a certain standard of professionalism. The standards were later reduced to 897, then to 436 (Commission on Accreditation, 1995), still a staggering number. Most of the standards that apply to patrol work focus on law enforcement, to the virtual exclusion of order maintenance and service functions (Mastrofski, 1990). Furthermore, nearly all the standards require only that a formal policy or procedure be established or that records be maintained; there is no performance-monitoring system set up to determine the extent that such policies and procedures are being followed.

An examination of these standards regarding their applicability to community policing indicated, for the most part, that they were silent or neutral on the subject (Cordner and Williams, 1995, 1996). Such standards may be constraining on departments attempting true community policing, especially with respect to officers' participation, encouraging risk taking, and removing organizational barriers to creativity (Cordner and Williams, 1996: 256). At this time, it would appear that in relatively well-developed departments attempting to implement community policing, accreditation would most likely impede managers in their efforts to promote change. This conclusion would appear to hold until the accreditation process places greater emphasis on problem solving, innovation, and community input than on bureaucratic rules and regulations. However, for less well-developed departments that may not have adequate policies and procedures, accreditation would most likely be beneficial, with the caveat that the agency does not become even more bureaucratic in the process.

Planning for Large-Scale Change: The Chicago Experience

This section will take an inside look at the overall plan for change, as well as the different types of change methods, used by the Chicago Police Department in its attempt to move to community policing. Chicago's attempt at organization change has been the largest-scale effort to date (Skogan and Hartnett, 1997). Beginning in April 1993, the experimental program consisted of five of the 25 police districts in the city, including 54 experimental beats. The experimental districts were referred to as prototypes, and the program would eventually be expanded to include the 20 remaining traditional districts. The program became labeled the ***Chicago Alternative Policing Strategy (CAPS)***, thus giving the department and city its own style of community policing. For the initial implementation of CAPS, 1,500 police personnel of all ranks went through orientation and skill-building sessions, and close to 700 beat meetings, attended by 15,000 people, were held during the first year and a half of the program. By the end of 1995, CAPS would be expanded to encompass the remainder of the city, and nearly 7,500 additional patrol officers would be trained for community policing citywide (Chicago Community Policing Evaluation Consortium, 2000).

Laying the Foundation

The department developed a mission statement and a 30-page supporting report describing the basic philosophy of community policing and identifying, step-by-step, many of the key components of change that were needed for the program to succeed. The report opened with a "rationale for change" that reviewed the limits of the traditional model of policing and argued for a "smarter" approach that would capitalize on the strengths of the city's neighborhoods. It further argued that the department had to be "reinvented" in order to form a partnership with the community, one that stressed crime prevention, customer service, and honest and ethical conduct. (As discussed in Chapter 2, the elements of "reinvention" reflecting the ideals of community policing are becoming more commonly accepted among police middle managers.) The report was mailed to every departmental member, and to help ensure that it would be read, it was included on the reading list from which questions would be drawn for the next promotional exam. It became the basis for planning the eventual citywide implementation of CAPS.

It should further be noted that the department had a traditional paramilitary structure, with many hierarchical levels. The mayor favored the idea of compressing the rank structure and freeing up more personnel for street-level work; he once exclaimed to the researchers, "Captains! Nobody can tell

❖ ❖ ❖ ❖   me what they do!" (Skogan and Hartnett, 1997: 34). The rank of captain was eliminated (although, as we shall see, it was eventually restored), thus flattening the hierarchy by one level. A flattening of the rank-structure promotes the need to decentralize community policing departments, thus helping to push decision-making authority down to the street and neighborhood level.

Key Elements of Change

The organization change process incorporated six key elements, briefly described below:

1. ***The entire department and the city were to be involved***. Rather than forming special community-policing units, the whole department would change, although at differing paces. Whereas community policing roles were developed for all units, including detective, tactical, gangs, and narcotics divisions, only patrol would be utilized until the program was proven to be effective. A commitment to citywide involvement was reflected in the decision to use diverse districts spread throughout the city as prototypes for the program (several of which had high rates of crime), as well as to use existing personnel in the districts. In some experimental community-policing departments, both the districts and the personnel (oftentimes volunteers) were carefully selected. As one executive put it, the department did not "stack the deck in favor of success."

2. ***Officers were to have permanent beat assignments***. In order to develop partnerships with the community and to learn about the neighborhood, officers had to be assigned to one place long enough for residents to get to know and to trust them. Additionally, officers had to have enough free time to allow them to engage in community work. In attempting to resolve the conflict between working with the public and responding promptly to calls for service, officers in each district were divided into ***beat teams*** and ***rapid-response teams*** (see Case Study 14.2). Beat teams were to be dispatched less frequently in order to have time to work on community projects.

3. ***The department was to have a strong commitment to training***. The department invested a significant effort in training officers and their supervisors in the skills required to identify and solve problems in working with the community. The lesson learned from other cities that did not pay proper attention to a strong training component was that those cities never developed serious community-policing programs. By emphasizing training, a message would also be sent to the rank and file that community policing was real and that upper management was committed to the program. The initial training program consisted of orientation sessions followed by skill-building sessions. To further promote the seriousness of the training effort, participants would have to pass a test on the material; those who did not pass would have to repeat the course. This appeared "to have a salutary effect on their attentiveness" (Skogan and Hartnett, 1997: 101).

4. ***The community was to play a significant role in the program***. The foundation of CAPS was the formation of police-community partnerships, focused on identifying and solving problems at the neighborhood level. This community involvement was developed in two ways. First, ***beat meetings*** began, usually monthly, involving small groups of residents and beat officers. The meetings were held in church basements and park buildings throughout the city. Second, ***advisory committees*** were formed at the district level to meet with upper management and district staff; committees included community leaders, school council members, ministers, business operators, and other institutional representatives.

   Interestingly, the primary concerns of the residents in beat meetings were not the types of crime traditionally associated with the police; for example, predatory and violent crimes were identified only 3 percent of the time and fear of crime only 2 percent. The four categories that constituted over 75 percent of all beat meeting discussions were: (1) social disorder at 28 percent (including disturbances and drunkenness, prostitution, truancy, gunfire, and gang problems); (2) physical decay at 23 percent (including abandoned cars and buildings, litter, graffiti, and vandalism); (3) police performance at 15 percent (including harassment and insensitivity, response time, traffic stops, and neighborhood patrols; (4) drug problems at 11 percent (including drug use or sale and use of pay phones).

5. ***Policing was to be linked to the delivery of city services***. Community policing inevitably involves the expansion of the police role to include a broad range of concerns that are outside the scope of traditional policing. Such expansion was considered necessary by management because they realized that although the police could put a lid on many crime-related problems, they could never eliminate them. They wanted to develop problem-solving systems that could keep the lid on even after they had moved on. In addition, the delivery of city services in the prototype districts was linked to community policing through the use of service-request forms. The requests for service generated by officers were closely tracked by city hall, which developed a system to prioritize and track each case.

6. ***There was to be an emphasis on crime analysis***. The geographic analysis of crime was considered a key element of the program. Computer technology was to be used to speed up the collection and analysis of data, which would be used to identify crime problems in the beat area. A user-friendly crime-mapping system was developed for use on computers, with printouts to be distributed at beat meetings and made accessible to the public at each district station. Other planned analytic tools included "beat planners," which were beat officers' notebooks filled with local information. New roll-call procedures were also developed to encourage officers on various shifts to share information about their beats and community resources.

Case Study 14.2

Change and WHAM in Chicago

Management knew that there could be no real change without the support of rank-and-file members at the bottom of the organization. This became known as the "winning hearts and minds" (WHAM) component of organizational change. In order to win the hearts and minds of street officers, the following change methods were used.

Changing the Job

In each prototype district, officer's jobs were changed by dividing them into beat teams and rapid-response teams (those primarily responding to calls-for-service). By using beat teams, a majority of their time could be spent within their assigned geographical area. This new beat integrity, and the freedom from responding to 911 calls, was accomplished by increasing the number of officers who served in the prototype districts by about 13 percent. In addition, a radio-dispatch plan was implemented that allocated selected calls to beat teams. Beat officers were to work with schools, businesses, and residents to identify and solve problems and to act as coordinators for service requests to other city agencies—an integral part of the program. They attended neighborhood meetings to work with existing community organizations, as well as regularly scheduled public beat meetings, thus increasing communication between residents and beat officers. Over time, officers would alternate between beat work and rapid-response cars in order to ensure that community policing did not become confined to special units.

Changing Supervision

The role of sergeants was crucial to CAPS, as prototype beat officers needed direction and mentoring in their new roles; sergeants were also responsible for supervising rapid-response officers as well. Although the sergeants were given some initial CAPS training, it soon became apparent that their role was not clearly defined, and they often felt unsure about what was expected of them. The prototype sergeants were told that their job was to coach officers in their new community roles, but, in reality, they knew as little as the street officers about what that entailed. They soon became disgruntled and felt overworked. Additional training attempted to alleviate this role confusion; it was designed to encourage them to become teachers, coaches, and mentors. These were all new roles in the department and a far cry from the traditional supervisory role of giving orders and signing forms. The additional training consisted of several skill-building sessions with respect to leadership styles, building partnerships, problem solving, and team building.

Avoiding the Social-Work Image

One of the lessons learned from other cities was that separate community policing units did not work. Members of these units inevitably were looked down on by their colleagues as "empty holsters" doing "wave-and-smiling" policing. The prototype districts that were selected joined the program as a unit, "warts and all"; they were not staffed by volunteers, or specially selected officers, supervisors, or even district-level managers (two of whom—out of five—never supported the program). Officers on all three shifts, not just the day shift, made up a beat team. The teams received no special privileges, such as selecting their own working hours or days off. (In New York, for example, the beat officers used flexible schedules to work only the day shift—Monday through Friday—which got the program into significant trouble both internally and externally). Management also made a concerted effort to assure all sworn personnel that community policing was not a "soft on crime" approach. They stressed that officers would not become social workers but rather referral specialists who could help solve problems at the neighborhood level. In addition, it was emphasized that traditional police work would continue to be important and would be rewarded, with a strong emphasis on making arrests where appropriate.

Dealing with the Union

Employee organizations played major roles in departmental policy making in Chicago. Officers were represented in bargaining by the Fraternal Order of Police. There were also unions that represented civilian employees and associations that separately represented sergeants, lieutenants, and captains, who were not allowed to form unions. The program had to be consistent with the union contract; assignments were closely regulated by a union contract based on seniority and were renewable each year through a bidding procedure. Thus, only assignments to specific tasks—for instance, either to beat teams or to rapid-response cars—were under the control of management. As a result, management could not attempt to match officer skills with specific district conditions or guarantee that officers would remain in any job or beat for more than a year. Dring CAPS' first year, a new FOP president was elected and he was included on a policy-planning committee for the future of policing in the city.

He was widely consulted, as were representatives of the civilian employees' unions. Later in the development of CAPS, the FOP's executive committee took the unique step of endorsing the program.

Adapted from: W. G. Skogan and S. M. Hartnett, 1997. Community Policing, Chicago Style. New York: Oxford University Press, pp. 89–95.

In addition to the six key elements developed in the organization plan, Chicago also used a number of change methods to facilitate the organization-wide change process. These methods are described in Case Study 14.2.

Results in Chicago

An early evaluation of the program found evidence of CAPS-related success with physical decay problems in three of the five experimental districts, a decline in gang and drug problems in two districts, and a decline in major crimes in two districts (Hartnett and Skogan, 1999). At the seven-year evaluation, the citywide crime rate showed a continuing substantial decline in robbery, sexual assault, auto theft, burglary, and crimes involving a firearm; however, the marked decline in Chicago's crime rate could be due in part to economic trends or other factors and may not be primarily associated with CAPS.

An especially intriguing finding of the seven-year evaluation is the high level of ongoing citizen involvement in some of the historically most disenfranchised areas of the city. Citizen involvement, as measured by community beat meeting attendance, was higher in predominantly African American beats, in low-income areas, and in areas with higher rates of violent crimes. This would suggest that CAPS has been highly successful at engaging those citizens who would typically avoid forming partnerships with the police. Surprisingly, beat meeting attendance was lowest for white communities, and Latino communities attended at rates between those of African Americans and whites. Overall, attendance rates have increased since 1995 but have remained fairly stable over time; it was found that CAPS was helping to promote better relationships between police and residents in some of the city's poorest communities. Since the development of CAPS citywide, satisfaction with the quality of police services has increased significantly among African Americans and whites, but not as substantially among Latinos (Chicago Community Policing Evaluation Consortium, 2000).

Changes in police management, however, remained problematic. The department continued to gather and distribute the same activity counts as before (calls answered and arrests made); there were no measures of the extent to which officers were involved in problem solving and no indicators of their success. It has proven difficult to develop workable performance measures and incentives that would reflect the new mission. As one watch commander has stated:

Nothing has been implemented—new disciplinary procedures, efficiency ratings. Good officers get disciplined the same as bum officers. Honest mistakes are judged the same as intentional mistakes. They promised a new promotional process—we haven't seen it. It's hypocritical. They wrote it, but they don't abide by it. (Hartnett and Skogan, 1999, p. 10)

There were other indicators of weak leadership and ineffectual change. For instance, at the six-year evaluation it was noted that many of the formal requirements of the program were being met by "going through the motions," and very little police problem solving was occurring. Information was not regularly shared system-wide, and seldom was there face-to-face communication among team members at shift changes. District planning processes had largely been ignored, and most district commanders demanded only nominal CAPS efforts in their districts. Beat team sergeants often did not directly supervise their assigned beat teams; the daily supervision of beat teams remained in the hands of sergeants who had no responsibility for the various components or the ultimate outcomes of any community policing activities. Community policing was often viewed as an additional burden by beat officers and supervisors, who felt they were not given adequate time away from answering calls for service and other traditional duties to problem solve. Many management layers remained untouched by CAPS. Additionally, the rank of Captain, which had been abolished at the launch of CAPS, was resurrected, signaling to many a retreat from the department's commitment to organization reform (Chicago Community Policing Evaluation Consortium, 2000).

By 2000, several organization changes within the department were made to increase district accountability and responsiveness in problem solving. Charged with reorganizing CAPS implementation, the newly established CAPS Project Office performed an audit of CAPS activities in different districts, identifying program weaknesses and providing remedial as well as ongoing training reinforcement. The new Office of Management Accountability was created to centrally gather and analyze citywide data on crime and disorder and to help mobilize resources needed to address chronic crime and disorder problems. Although a significant amount of organization change occurred during the first five years of CAPS, year six marked the department's regression toward old habits. In light of these renewed efforts at sustaining organization change in Chicago, CAPS now has a renewed chance of being more fully implemented (Chicago Community Policing Evaluation Consortium, 2000).

Lessons Learned From Madison and Chicago

Two of the most comprehensive organization change efforts, from traditional policing to community policing, have taken place in Madison and Chicago. The change processes utilized had many similarities and some significant differences. While each relied on a report developed by departmental personnel to lay the foundation for change and to guide the change process, and each attempted to improve communication with rank-and-file officers, Madison spent significantly more time developing a true participatory (quality) leadership style. A comprehensive committee structure was developed in Madison, staffed with personnel from throughout the department whose recommendations for change were generally adopted. This level of employee participation in policing is unparalleled. It is also important to understand that both departments had strong support from their cities' top political leadership. In Madison, quality improvement was a citywide movement, whereas in Chicago, the mayor used the CAPS program to shore up city hall's provision of services throughout the city. Both cities recognized the importance of, and relied heavily upon, the training of their personnel. Finally, both cities started with experimental programs, which, over time, were expanded throughout the department.

One significant difference was that Chicago used regular officers and supervisors ("warts and all") in its prototype districts, whereas Madison selected personnel who were "interested" in the program (effectively volunteers), for its experimental police district; EPD personnel could also decide their own schedules and work conditions. An important consideration regarding the use of regular officers, supervisors, and established beats is that the experimental or prototype programs will not be as likely to generate a "we versus they" mentality between experimental and regular officers. Such an approach can go a long way toward reducing the types of resistance to change discussed earlier and documented in Inside Management 14.1.

One additional caveat should be noted. In Madison, a concerted effort had been made for approximately two decades to recruit highly educated officers, who, most likely, would be supportive of change. If a true commitment to community policing is to take place, and the police role is to be significantly broadened to carry it out, the level of higher education required for police may be an important factor (although the research is mixed in this area; see Chapter 15). In Madison, however, it appears that the history of promoting higher education contributed significantly to establishing a more conducive atmosphere for large-scale organization change.

Although both departments sought input from the external environment, the level of participation from each community differed significantly. Madison developed feedback mechanisms only (mainly surveys), whereas Chicago took the development of citizen communication and input to a new level for police departments. The involvement of beat officers who were geographically stable allowed them to work closely with the community in problem solving. By attending (and often conducting) regularly scheduled public beat meetings, as well as by meeting with various community organizations, officers could get a sense of what residents considered to be the important problems in their areas. Trends in assessments of police service quality through 1999, including performance, responsiveness, and demeanor, all made solid gains since CAPS began in the early 1990s (Chicago Community Policing Evaluation Consortium, 2000).

It would appear that both departments have made substantial gains toward implementing community policing (although Chicago regressed after the five-year mark), but they have done it in different ways. In Madison, employee participation in the change process was a strong point (internal change), whereas in Chicago, the development of partnerships with the community through beat teams was the strong suit (external change). Perhaps the most effective change approach to community policing would be to mix the internal practices of Madison with the external practices of Chicago, while perhaps raising the educational standards for recruits.

Innovation

If constructive and timely change is to take place in police departments, mid- and top-level managers must develop an organization climate that fosters and encourages innovation. ***Innovation*** refers to the ability to develop and use new ideas and methods. Such a climate should be relatively open, trustworthy, and forward looking. Although managers frequently espouse this kind of climate, the rhetoric often outweighs the action when it comes to rank-and-file employees. As Moss-Kanter explains, "The message behind the words of the top is that those below the top should stay out of the change game unless given a specific assignment to figure out how to implement a decision top management has already made" (1983: 100).

Rules for Stifling Innovation

Moss-Kanter also points out that top management often behave as if they were following a set of "rules for stifling initiative." She lists a set of ten rules that are all too frequently followed in organizations (p. 101):

1. Regard any new idea from below with suspicion—because it's new, and because it's from below.

2. Insist that people who need your approval to act first go through several other levels of management to get their signatures.

3. Ask departments (units) or individuals to challenge and criticize each other's proposals. (That saves you the job of deciding; you just pick the survivor.)

4. Express your criticisms freely and withhold your praise. (That keeps people on their toes.)

5. Treat identification of problems as signs of failure to discourage people from letting you know when something in their area isn't working.

6. Control everything carefully. Make sure people count anything that can be counted, frequently.

7. Make decisions to reorganize or change policies in secret and spring them on people unexpectedly. (That also keeps people on their toes.)

8. Make sure that requests for information are fully justified and make sure that it is not given out to managers freely. (You don't want data to fall into the wrong hands.)

9. Assign to lower-level managers, in the name of delegation and participation, responsibility for figuring out how to cut back, lay off, move people around, or otherwise implement threatening decisions you have made. And get them to do it quickly.

10. And above all, never forget that you, the higher-ups, already know everything important about this business.

Rules such as these, according to Moss-Kanter, reflect **segmentalism** in action; that is, a culture and attitude that make it unattractive and difficult for people in the organization to develop innovative solutions to problems. Such a segmentalist approach is a real handicap because it does not allow people to work together, in teams, or to share information (especially across organization levels) that could lead to creative solutions to organization problems. It is important for top-level managers to understand that most organizations have people who are potential innovators, capable of change. The problem, then, is that organizations may not suffer from a lack of potential innovators so much as they do from a failure to provide the necessary power and means to allow their employees to innovate.

Successful Police Innovation

In their study on police innovation in six American cities, Skolnick and Bayley (1986) made several recommendations for promoting police innovation. First, and most important to successful innovation, is ***effective and energetic leadership from the office of the chief.*** Although executive leadership is vital to any enterprise, it is essential to traditional paramilitary, mechanistic police departments. Because such departments tend not to be democratically run, most members are aware of the chief's preferences, demands, and expectations. However, it is not enough simply to espouse certain ideals and values; the chief must become an active, committed exponent of them. The Madison Case Study (14.1) presents an excellent example of how the chief established his values and expectations for the department (e.g., by developing and following Quality Leadership/Productivity principles) and his long-term, unwavering commitment to the change process.

The second requirement for successful innovation is that the ***chief must be able to motivate*** (and sometimes manipulate) departmental personnel into supporting the values that the chief espouses. Some resistance from the old guard, who have strong ties to the status quo, is likely. Because these individuals may retain much influence, police executives often attempt to keep or enlist their support. As a result, chiefs may actually affirm conflicting norms, telling different audiences what each wants to hear. Consequently, nobody in the department knows what the chief stands for and everyone is confused. Preferably, a majority of the officers can be persuaded that the new values are superior. Persuasion is seldom easy, however, especially in departments that have associations and unions resistant to change and innovation (in both Madison and Chicago, the chiefs decided to include union leaders throughout the change process). Nevertheless, Skolnick and Bayley maintain that an innovatively inclined chief can gain the support of the rank and file.

Skolnick and Bayley noted that one of the ways of potentially lessening resistance from the old guard is first to implement change in one part of the department; this strategy was used in both Madison and Chicago. In this way, the department can learn how best to implement change with the least amount of disruption, and those who are resistant have a chance to observe the potential benefits of the change. If the change is not considered to be beneficial for the entire organization, it would simply not be implemented throughout the department.

A third requirement is that the ***integrity of innovation must be defended.*** Once a new value system (one dedicated to the development and use of new concepts and methods) has been established, it will need to be defended from the pull to return to the status quo. Such defense is especially necessary in policing, because police departments tend to be heavily tied to the traditional, bureaucratic ways of doing things. This "pull" back toward the status quo was evident in Chicago during the sixth-year review, and organization adjustments had to be made in an effort to "return" to community-policing initiatives.

The fourth requirement for innovation is ***public support.*** Innovative crime prevention programs that were implemented with community input enjoy strong, often unexpected, support from the public. If properly introduced and explained to the community, police innovations will most likely be widely supported. Because the public was so widely involved in the change process in Chicago, significant gains in public support were readily apparent.

As Skolnick and Bayley pointed out, the need to sustain or defend innovation is critical, as regression toward the status quo in highly mechanistic departments is strong. What methods can police managers use to keep the department on the path toward innovation? Case Study 14.3 examines several types of management techniques that the Madison Police Department employed to gain momentum and sustain innovation in its organization change process.

Case Study 14.3

Sustaining Innovation in Madison

In promoting and sustaining innovation, a vision was created for the department that asked: What is it that we want to be? The management team next asked the following questions relating to the vision: How do we get there? What resources do we need? How will we know when we are making progress?

In carrying out the plan, the department's managers followed these steps:

1. They listened carefully to their employees and their citizen-customers.
2. They tailored a leadership style to meet those needs.
3. They trained all employees in the new philosophy.
4. They empowered and coached managers and supervisors to be quality leaders.
5. They promoted, praised, and gave key assignments to the quality "champions" in the department.
6. They settled in for the long term; they took risks and continually tried to practice what they were preaching.

Some of the techniques used in carrying out the plan are briefly described below.

Training

Early in 1987, the management team completed the quality-productivity (QP) and quality leadership training put on by the city. Some of the subjects covered in the training included:

- Systems thinking
- Leadership systems: thinking and planning
- Running and conducting effective groups
- Interpersonal skills
- Community organizing
- Representing and graphing data
- The nature and variability of statistics

By the fall of that year, all of the department's lieutenants had completed similar training. The chief appeared the last hour of each training day to answer questions and address concerns. This was an attempt by the chief to bridge the gap between theory and practice of the new philosophy, as well as to serve as a role model for the new leadership style. This process was also followed for sergeants, who were trained next. Quality-improvement training then began for all departmental employees, civilian and commissioned. The department also reserved four or five seats in each of the training sessions for other city employees, establishing the importance of teamwork among city agencies.

Promotions

The first effort beyond training to start running the department in accordance with the new philosophy involved the implementation of a new promotion policy. Promotions provide both a symbolic and actual impact on organizational behavior; who is promoted sends a louder message than any words from management. Consequently, the chief sent out a memorandum establishing the importance of the new promotion policy, which stated, in part:

I strongly believe that if we are to "practice what we preach" in our Mission Statement to achieve excellence (i.e., teamwork, respect, problem solving, openness, sensitive and community-oriented policing) . . . . we will have to alter the way in which we lead. . . .The promotions I make from now on are going to people who have strong interpersonal and facilitative skills and who can adjust and adapt to the new needs and demands. . . . In addition to being totally committed to the Mission of the organization, [supervisors and managers] will have to be able to work in a team, become coaches, accept feedback, ask and listen to others in the team, and facilitate their employees' input and growth in the workplace.

Accordingly, subsequent promotions went to those officers who were peer-group leaders and who wished to adopt a quality leadership style.

Some of those promoted would not have been selected in the past; thus, new leaders who would help to implement and sustain innovative policing were being selected.

Quality Coordinator

The position of quality coordinator was established to help maintain the necessary momentum toward change and a culture of quality improvement. The new coordinator was a 34-year-old officer with three years of service. She had a graduate degree in social work and had taught at the college level. She also had a strong background in statistics and research methodology. Her experience before joining the department was in community organizing and organizational development. Her appointment was another example of practicing the new leadership philosophy—that is, by promoting someone with such a nontraditional police background.

Customer Surveys

In order to establish baseline data and to assess the quality and customer satisfaction of the department, a survey was developed. The survey asks citizens to rate police service on a five-point scale from poor to excellent in seven areas: (1) concern, (2) helpfulness, (3) knowledge, (4) quality of service, (5) solving the problem, (6) putting citizens at ease, and (7) professional conduct. An open-ended question at the end asks: How can we improve? About 25 percent of the responses include feedback on this question.

Surveys are mailed each month (with a stamped, self-addressed return envelope) to all persons identified in every fiftieth case-numbered report, including victims, witnesses, complainants, and arrestees. Approximately 160 surveys are mailed out each month, with a return rate of about 35 to 40 percent, all of which are read by the chief. The results are periodically published in the department's newsletter, in which both positive and negative comments regarding improvements are summarized. The newsletter also provides statistical results for the seven areas, including demographic data on respondents, and tabulates satisfaction levels in relationship to the age, race, income, and gender of the respondent.

Managing by Wandering Around

The department believes that leadership involves being seen, and that leaders cannot be seen very well if they spend all their time behind a desk. Accordingly, the department has found that a very simple technique of managing by walking around (MBWA) is a powerful one. For most police managers, MBWA means getting out on the "street," observing and asking or answering questions. In this way, managers learn what their employees need from them to do a quality job, as well as letting them know that they care about quality work and are looking for ways to improve conditions and processes. The chief also started going out on the street at night and taking calls with officers.

Leadership Check-ins

Starting in the summer of 1988, one-day check-ins were held with the lieutenants and three groups of sergeants to assess how the department was doing with quality leadership. The chief and deputy chief asked them to share "success stories" and identify barriers and what they needed to be more effective quality leaders. The chief and deputy chief spent an entire day with each group, listening and gaining valuable insight into what needed to be done to improve the change process.

Adapted from: D. C. Couper and S. H. Lobitz. 1991. *Quality Policing: The Madison Experience*, pp. 59–60, 63–64, 66–68, 80–81. Washington, D. C.: Police Executive Research Forum.

The previous two sections have discussed the organization change process and the importance of establishing and sustaining innovation for lasting change. Case studies of the Madison and Chicago police departments allowed the examination of processes and examples of how change and innovation can take place in a traditional police organization. This final section will examine the role played by organization development (OD) and describe related strategies that can be used for implementing constructive change. Interestingly, several of these strategies, at least to some degree, were successfully applied in both Madison and Chicago.

Organization Development

Organization development (OD) is a process by which intervention strategies, based on behavioral science research, are used to enhance organization effectiveness through planned change. It consists of an organization-wide effort to improve performance by improving the quality of work environments and by positively affecting employee beliefs and attitudes and levels of motivation (Huse and Cummings, 1985). Organization development, then, is a program for introducing planned, systematic change in an organization. Typically, organization members must interact and collaborate with one another in introducing change; this process is directed by a change agent. The change agent uses behavioral science techniques, including questionnaires, interviews, group discussions, and experimentation, to diagnose problem areas and design appropriate change responses. Several characteristics that have traditionally been used to guide change agents in their choice of intervention strategies include the following:

1. The basic building blocks of an organization are groups or teams. Therefore, the basic units of change are groups, not individuals.

2. An always relevant change goal is the reduction of inappropriate competition between parts of an organization and the development of a more collaborative condition.

3. Decision making in a healthy organization is located where the information sources are rather than in a particular role or level of hierarchy.

4. One goal of a healthy organization is to develop generally open communication, mutual trust, and confidence between and across levels.

5. "People support what they help create." People affected by a change must be allowed active participation and a sense of ownership in the planning and conduct of the change. (Beckhard, 1969: 26–27)

The Role of Change Agents

There are three primary forms of change agents in organization development. The first and generally most common is the external change agent brought in to diagnose problem areas and make recommendations for change. The second is an internal change agent, who has a good working knowledge of the organization and is aware of its problems. The third is the combination external-internal change agent, which involves a team approach that attempts to use knowledge and resources that exist both inside and outside of the organization. Each form of change agent has particular advantages and disadvantages.

External Agents

The external agent is generally a professional OD consultant, who has appropriate academic credentials and is well grounded in the theory and practice of organization change and behavioral interventions. External agents are frequently viewed as outsiders who do not understand the "real" workings of police departments, particularly if they have not had police experience and therefore may not be trusted. Because they are usually "hired" by management, rank-and-file employees may feel as though the agent is simply brought in to promote and implement the chief's philosophy and plans. Consequently, it is crucial that external agents establish a high degree of rapport with lower-level employees, as well as management, if they are to have an impact. On the other hand, external change agents tend not to have extensive knowledge about internal relationships and behavior, which means they can approach the organization with an open mind regarding change strategies and directions they deem the most appropriate.

Internal Agents

Internal agents are usually not trained as OD specialists but have a good working knowledge of the department. Persons used in this capacity would normally include mid- to upper-level managers (e.g., lieutenants through assistant chiefs), who have wide-ranging experiences in the organization. Their knowledge can contribute substantially to the change process if used objectively. Insiders, however, are often viewed as being more closely associated with certain groups or individuals who approach change with preconceived notions or hidden agendas. There may be suspicion that the agent's recommendations further his or her personal gain or are what the chief wants rather than what is best for the organization. Consequently, internal change agents may actually have a more difficult time establishing rapport within the organization than external agents. Therefore, if management decides to use insiders, the people who are chosen must be widely respected for their integrity, knowledge, and objectivity.

External-Internal Combination

The combination of external and internal change agents, although difficult to coordinate, offers advantages over both of the other forms. The objectivity and behavioral knowledge of the professional OD consultant is combined with the insider's insights into how the organization is actually run, including both formal and informal relationships and group behavior. This blending of knowledge can substantially contribute to successful change by helping specify appropriate change strategies and identifying where the process should begin and at what pace it should proceed. Finally, this team approach may develop even greater rapport throughout the organization, thus reducing resistance to recommended changes. Of course, in such an arrangement, both cooperation and "turf" problems can develop, actually decreasing the potential for implementing change. Careful attention must be paid to this potential problem in police departments because there is often a built-in suspicion between civilian (outsider) and sworn (insider) personnel. However, if management carefully selects external and internal change agents who complement each other, this approach provides a high probability of success.

OD Intervention Strategies

Organization development interventions are particular types of strategies or methods that change agents and managers use to help improve levels of effectiveness. These strategies can focus either on *structural changes,* which emphasize organization outcomes, or on *behavioral changes,* which emphasize individual outcomes. Changes that focus on the organization's structural characteristics are formal and readily observable, such as span of control, hierarchical levels, and job descriptions. Changes dealing with behavior (both individual and group) are more informal and include attitudes, values, and belief systems. Because behavioral changes require more *emotional involvement* than structural changes, managers need to deal with behavior in a more in-depth, intense manner.

Intervention Depth

In general, *intervention depth* can be defined as the extent of an individual's emotional involvement in the change process (Harrison, 1970). Although emotional involvement is present at any level of intervention, the concept of depth is concerned with the degree to which the intervention is related to one's involvement. As Harrison explains:

> Strategies which touch the more deep, personal, private, and central aspects of the individual or his relationships with others fall toward the deeper end of this continuum. Strategies which deal with more external aspects of the individual and which focus upon the more formal and public aspects of role behavior tend to fall toward the surface of the depth dimension. (1970: 183)

In other words, strategies that deal with the formal aspects of the organization, including structural characteristics and job descriptions, are relatively open and easily manipulable. However, an organization's informal aspects, including individual beliefs and attitudes and interpersonal and group relationships, are relatively hidden and take considerable emotional involvement if they are to be changed. Accordingly, strategies attempting to change individual behavior must be at a deeper level of emotional involvement than strategies dealing with structural considerations, if they are to have lasting impact.

OD Strategies and Intervention Depth

The following discussion of OD strategies will be based on the level of intervention depth required to bring about successful change. The strategies will be grouped according to two targets for change: (1) *structural*, which emphasizes tasks, activities, and role relationships and is concerned with the formal organization and data that are readily available; and (2) *behavioral*, which emphasizes emotional and psychological reactions, is related to the informal organization and the individual, and has private or hidden data that usually must be obtained through behavioral research methods (e.g., surveys, interviews, and observations).

Because certain OD strategies require deeper levels of emotional involvement if they are to be successful, several relevant strategies have been classified into four levels of "depth," from relatively impersonal (i.e., structural) to highly personal (i.e., behavioral). A model of OD strategies, and their degree of intervention depth, is depicted in Figure 14.1. It is important to keep in mind, however, that all these levels overlap to some degree and should not be viewed as mutually exclusive. The OD strategies presented, although by no means an all-inclusive list, provide a sample of available methods that are likely to be of value in implementing change in police organizations.

Level I: Operations Analysis. The first level is concerned with the roles and functions to be performed within the organization, generally with little regard for individual characteristics (e.g., beliefs and attitudes) or for the persons occupying the roles. The change strategy focuses on determining and specifying resources, tasks, authority and power; levels of hierarchy; and other structural characteristics important to the formal operation of the organization. Examples of intervention strategies at this level include survey feedback and organization design changes.

Survey feedback uses questionnaires to collect information from the employees regarding their feelings about the organization. Once collected, the data are analyzed and fed back to managers and employees so that they can evaluate and define problems and develop plans of action. Feeding the information back to employees is generally accomplished through groups, starting with top management and systematically moving down through the lower levels. Another technique that can be useful for feedback and was used in Madison is a generally available departmental newsletter.

Organization redesign changes the structural characteristics of the organization through the manipulation of role relationships and the redistribution of tasks and resources or the power attached to various roles. This strategy includes changing reporting and decision-making relationships between and among individuals and units, as well as increasing or decreasing the span of control and the number of hierarchical levels in the organization. Often, the need for such changes is determined through survey feedback techniques. Examples of organization redesign are apparent in both Chicago, with respect to removing a hierarchical level (although later re-inserted), and Madison, with respect to decentralization and the associated changes in tasks, power, and decision-making relationships of mid- and lower-level managers and supervisors.

Level II: Work Style. The second level is concerned with the selection, training, counseling, and evaluation of individuals in accord with job design and other structural characteristics of the work they perform. Although this strategy is deeper than the preceding one, the focus is on observable performance rather than on the personal characteristics of the individual. Attempts to facilitate change at this level can include both external rewards (e.g., transfers, promotions, and merit pay) and internal rewards (e.g., greater feelings of satisfaction and accomplishment). Two frequently used strategies at this level are management by objectives (MBO) and job redesign, especially job enrichment.

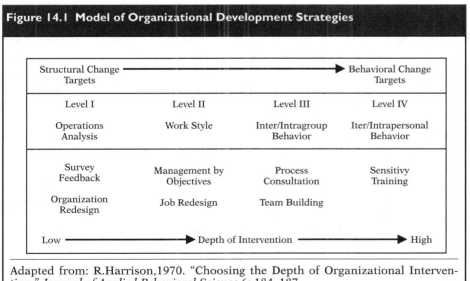

Figure 14.1 Model of Organizational Development Strategies

Structural Change Targets		→	Behavioral Change Targets
Level I	Level II	Level III	Level IV
Operations Analysis	Work Style	Inter/Intragroup Behavior	Iter/Intrapersonal Behavior
Survey Feedback	Management by Objectives	Process Consultation	Sensitivy Training
Organization Redesign	Job Redesign	Team Building	
Low →	Depth of Intervention →		High

Adapted from: R.Harrison,1970. "Choosing the Depth of Organizational Intervention." *Journal of Applied Behavioral Science* 6: 184–187

Management by objectives is an attempt to help resolve conflicts and increase understanding of organization and individual goals and objectives by increasing communication between the two parties. To this end, MBO requires mutual planning by managers and employees in establishing goals and objectives, in measuring job performance in terms of goals and objectives, and in deciding whether performance measures have been met. Additionally, periodic reviews of progress and accomplishments and mutual problem solving occur in the course of work performance. The MBO process frequently goes beyond the manager-employee relationship and deals with work teams in an effort to solve problems. In general, the MBO process involves the following steps:

1. Managers and employees meet to discuss various objectives, which, if met, would contribute to attaining the organizational goal.

2. Managers and employees jointly participate in establishing attainable objectives for the employees.

3. Managers and employees meet at a later date to provide feedback regarding progress toward the objectives.

MBO is very similar to goal-setting theory, described in Chapter 7, with some of the same advantages and disadvantages. For example, if objectives or goals are properly determined (i.e., attainable but challenging, measurable) and constructive feedback is provided at the proper time, employee satisfaction and performance can be improved. However, if goals or objectives are too easy to achieve (sometimes when easily achievable objectives are purposely set in order to win rewards), are too difficult to measure, are used as a controlling technique, or provide too little or negative feedback, MBO can actually be a disincentive for employees and can lead to negative results.

One study of 141 police departments that used some form of MBO over a three-year period found that such processes can help departments motivate managers to improve efficiency and service outputs (Hatry and Greinger, 1986). However, the researchers also discovered several major problem areas that frequently crop up, including vaguely defined objectives, excluding lower-level personnel from the process, not regularly comparing performance with goals, not regularly providing performance feedback, and not providing sufficient training opportunities in the use of MBO. Such results are not too surprising given that mechanistic organizations tend to revert back to traditional methods of operation; thus, the more traditional police departments will have to plan and implement an MBO program very carefully if they are to avoid these types of problems and their negative consequences.

Job redesign to enrich work is based on the premise that work satisfaction and efficiency can be increased if jobs include high levels of variety, autonomy, and feedback. Several steps that can be taken to enrich jobs, based on the jobs characteristics model, were discussed in Chapter 7. As further discussed in Chapter 7, employees who have a relatively strong need for growth are more likely to benefit from job enrichment. Of course, one significant form of job enrichment is community policing, and much of the research discussed previously suggests that employees who have higher-order needs and

higher levels of education are more satisfied in a job with community polic- ✦ ✦ ✦ ✦
ing characteristics.

Level III: Intergroup and Intragroup Behavior. The third level of intervention is concerned with the processes through which performance is
achieved within and among work groups. This level involves factors such as
how the individual perceives his or her role, what is or is not valued, and how
the individual acts toward others—for instance, delegating authority or
reserving decisions, communicating or withholding information, or collabo-
rating or competing with others on work-related issues. Strategies are oriented toward attempts to structure work behavior and working relationships
among individuals and groups. Group processes are diagnosed; change strategies often involve bargaining and negotiating. Changes in group norms,
communications, behaviors, and methods of resolving present and future
conflicts often result. Two of the more common OD strategies at this level
include process consultation and team building.

Process consultation focuses on the "human processes" that occur in an
organization, including individual, interpersonal, and intergroup levels
(Schein, 1969). In process consultation (PC), it is assumed that the group is
the building block of the organization and little can be changed without
group participation and effort. Consequently, intervention efforts are
directed at helping group members diagnose problems and develop and
implement solutions. Typical target areas include communications, roles and
role expectations, problem solving, leadership, intergroup cooperation, and
conflict and competition.

Process consultation typically uses an outside change agent, or process
consultant, to act as a group facilitator to help group members learn the skills
necessary to diagnose problem areas. Thus, the emphasis is on process consultation. The most common reason for such intervention is when there is
conflict among group members or between groups. For example, when
police departments attempt to change toward community policing by first
developing a special unit or district, problems such as misunderstandings,
suspicions, and lack of cooperation may develop with the other operating
units. Problems may also arise within the experimental unit as well, especially between specialists (e.g., detectives) and generalists (e.g., patrol officers), or between foot and patrol officers.

Process consultants can help alleviate these types of conflicts within and
between groups by allowing the members to understand what in the situation
is causing the problem and to work out their own solutions. The consultant
should withdraw from the process when the problems are alleviated and
group members have developed the capacity to diagnose and deal with similar problems that may arise in the future.

Team building includes using intervention methods that will develop
effective teamwork both within and among work groups. The purpose of
team building is to improve work performance by enhancing interpersonal
and problem-solving skills of group members. This process normally begins
with diagnostic meetings, which enable each group member to share his or
her perceptions with other members. The purpose is to obtain and make
known the views of all members; such diagnosis implies the value of openly
confronting certain problems that may only have been discussed privately in
the past. Once problems are identified, the group attempts to reach a consensus on their priorities and to develop an action plan to solve the problems. It

❖ ❖ ❖ ❖   is important that each group member take part in the action plan. In this way, each member has contributed to the decisions and is involved in carrying them out; increased levels of motivation and commitment are likely to result from such a high degree of participation.

Team building can also help facilitate other OD interventions, including organization design, MBO, and job redesign. These change programs are usually implemented through various committees and work groups. The use of team building can help such groups plan high-quality change programs and ensure that the programs are accepted and implemented by organization members.

Interestingly, the Madison Police Department used many of the methods associated with team building, although an outside consultant was not hired; consequently, it should be noted that it *is* possible for police departments to use many of these methods on their own. For example, several team-building methods used in Madison included group meetings to diagnose and assign priority to issues that needed addressing, a group process for brainstorming ideas and voting on the top selections, peer selection, equal representation (including the union) of members to serve on important policymaking groups such as the Officers' Advisory Council, and surveying departmental members regarding their feelings and attitudes about departmental concerns. Because group processes tend to improve through team-building efforts, team building has become increasingly popular as an OD method (Heisler, 1982).

Level IV: Interpersonal and Intrapersonal Behavior. The final and deepest level of intervention focuses on the feelings, attitudes, values, and perceptions that organization members have about one another. Personal feelings, including warmth and coldness, acceptance and rejection, and trust and suspicion, are directly confronted and dealt with in this strategy. Interventions are directed toward helping members feel more comfortable in being themselves and relating to one another. The degree of mutual concern and understanding is expected to increase. The basic strategy at this level is sensitivity training.

Sensitivity training is concerned with individual and individual–group problems and attempts to ***increase the sensitivity of the self and others in the workplace***. Sensitivity training is based on the assumption that poor task performance is related to the ***emotional problems*** of employees who must work together to achieve a goal; by eliminating these problems, task performance can be increased. Sensitivity-training methods include communications workshops, Outward Bound trips, and T-groups, the most common form. The T-group (T for training) generally meets at a site away from the job, under the direction of a professional trainer. The trainer facilitates group discussion, often with no particular agenda, with the expectation that group members will learn about themselves as they deal with others. Participants may include organization "cousins" (people from different work groups in the same organization), members from the same organization "family" (people from the same work group) or "strangers" (people from outside the organization). Police departments, for instance, have used strangers in T-groups, with an emphasis on improving police-community relations through a mutual understanding between the police and minority groups.

Because of the highly personal nature of T-groups, their use and level of effectiveness is controversial in the OD field. After reviewing the research in this area, Huse and Cummings (1985) suggest there are three conditions under which T-groups can improve both individual and group functioning: (1) the T-group must be structured in order that learning can be transferred back to the organization; (2) the more closely the T-group is tied in with an ongoing OD program, the greater its effectiveness appears to be; and (3) when applied to organization behavior, T-groups are more effective in organizations supporting information sharing, openness, and conflict resolution. Because these characteristics are generally not found in police organizations, this approach should be used with an appropriate degree of caution and only by highly qualified trainers.

In the model of OD strategies presented, the ***deeper the level of intervention*** (from level I through level IV), the more significant the impact, either positive or negative, on organization members. For this reason, Harrison suggests two criteria that should be considered in choosing an appropriate strategy: (1) It should intervene at a level no deeper than that required to produce lasting solutions to the problems at hand, and (2) it should intervene at a level no deeper than that at which the energy and resources of the client can be committed to problem solving and to change (1970). Finally, there are some guidelines that can be used by managers who wish to utilize OD strategies in changing their organizations. For instance, Dyer (1989: 7–8) believes that nine conditions must be met if OD strategies are to bring about desired change:

1. Management and all those involved must have high and visible commitment to the effort.

2. Individuals involved must have information in advance that enables them to know what will happen and why they need to do what they are to do.

3. The effort must be connected to other parts of the organization, especially the evaluation and reward systems.

4. The effort must be directed by line managers and assisted by a change agent if necessary.

5. The effort must be based on good diagnosis and consistent with the conditions in the organization.

6. Management must remain committed to the effort throughout all its steps, from diagnosis through implementation and evaluation.

7. Evaluation must take place and consist of more than asking people how they felt about the effort.

8. People must see clearly the relationship between the effort and the organization's mission and goals.

9. The change agent, if used, must be clearly competent.

It is interesting to note that most of these conditions were present in the Madison department in their change toward community policing. Although all of the conditions are important, perhaps the most significant factor was leadership style and the active role played by managers, who must support and direct the effort. It is becoming increasingly evident that significant

❖ ❖ ❖ ❖   organization change will not take place in police departments if the chief and top- and mid-level managers are not enthusiastically behind it.

Summary

Because police organizations operate in relatively unstable environments and need to adapt to changing conditions to be effective, police managers need to have an understanding of the change process and of available methods or strategies to constructively implement change. People have a tendency to resist change in organizations because of inertia, misunderstandings, group norms, and threatened changes in the balance of power. Such resistance can be reduced by sharing expectations, avoiding coercive tactics, using group decision making, and making changes tentative. Determining the appropriate pace of change is also important, especially in departments that tend to be mechanistic. The change processes used in Madison and Chicago were described, including lessons learned from these experiences. If significant change is to occur, an organizational climate that fosters and encourages innovation will need to be developed. Innovation refers to the ability to develop and use new ideas and methods.

Organization development (OD) is a process by which intervention strategies, based on behavioral science research, are used to enhance organization effectiveness through planned change. Different types of change agents have different advantages and disadvantages. Change agents use many types of OD strategies to help implement change and improve organizational effectiveness. A model of OD strategies provides a sample of available methods that are likely to be of value to police organizations. The model is based on four levels of intervention "depth," from relatively impersonal (i.e., aimed at structural changes) to highly personal (i.e., aimed at behavioral changes). It has become clear that active leadership by top- and mid-level managers is critical in attempting to move police organizations toward a more organic, community policing approach.

Discussion Questions

1. Discuss four reasons why employees tend to resist organization change and four methods that may be useful in reducing such resistance.

2. Why is the pace of change so crucial to the success of organization change in policing?

3. Briefly describe the organization change process used in Madison. Do you think the process was successful?

4. Briefly describe the change process used in Chicago. Do you think the process was successful?

5. Describe several major lessons learned regarding the change process with respect to Madison and Chicago.

6. Define innovation. Discuss at least six reasons or "rules" for stifling innovation that are frequently followed by top management.

7. Describe at least five techniques used in Madison to sustain innovation.

8. Define organization development. List at least three characteristics that have been traditionally used by change agents in their choice of intervention strategies.

9. Describe the three forms of change agents. List several advantages and disadvantages associated with each form.

10. List the four levels of OD interventions described in the model and provide an example of at least one strategy that can be used at each level.

❖ ❖ ❖ ❖

References

Beckhard, R. 1969. *Organization Development: Strategies and Models*. Reading, MA: Addison-Wesley.

Chicago Community Policing Evaluation Consortium. 2000. *Community Policing in Chicago, Year Seven: An Interim Report*. Chicago: Illinois Criminal Justice Information Authority.

Commission on Accreditation of Law Enforcement Agencies. 1995. 3rd ed. Standards Manual. Alexandria, VA.

Cordner, G. W., and Williams, G. L. 1995. "The CALEA Standards: What Is the Fit with Community Policing?" *National Institute of Justice Journal*, August: 39–49. Washington, DC: National Institute of Justice.

——. 1996. "Community Policing and Accreditation: A Content Analysis of CALEA Standards." In L. T. Hoover (ed.), *Quantifying Quality in Policing*, pp. 243–261. Washington, DC: Police Executive Research Forum.

Couper, D. C., and Lobitz, S. H. 1991. *Quality Policing: The Madison Experience*. Washington, DC: Police Executive Research Forum.

Dyer, W. G. 1989. "Team Building: A Microcosm of the Past, Present, and Future of OD." *Academy of Management OD Newsletter*, Winter: 6–7.

Geller, W. A., and Swanger, G. 1995. *Managing Innovation in Policing: The Untapped Potential of the Middle Manager*. Washington, DC: Police Executive Research Forum.

Guyot, D. 1979. "Bending Granite: Attempts to Change the Rank Structure of American Police Departments." *Journal of Police Science and Administration* 7: 253–284.

Harrison, R. 1970. "Choosing the Depth of Organizational Intervention." *Journal of Applied Behavioral Science* 6: 181–202.

Hartnett, S. M., and Skogan, W. G. 1999. "Community Policing: Chicago's Experience." *National Institute of Justice Journal* April: 3–11. Washington, DC: National Institute of Justice.

Hatry, H. P., and Greinger, J. M. 1986. *Improving the Use of Quality Circles in Police Departments*. Washington, DC: National Institute of Justice.

Heisler, W. J. 1982. "Patterns of OD in Practice." In D. Robey and S. Altman (eds.), *Organization Development*, pp. 23–29. New York: Macmillan.

Huse, E. F., and Cummings, T. G. 1985. *Organization Development and Change*, 3rd ed. St. Paul, MN: West.

Kerr, S., and Kerr, E. B. 1972. "Why Your Employees Resist Perfectly 'Rational' Changes." *Hospital Financial Management* 26: 4–6.

Lewin, K. 1958. "Group Decision and Social Change." In T. M. Newcomb and L. Harte (eds.) *Readings in Social Management*, pp. 197–211.

Lewis, S., Rosenberg, H., and Sigler, R. T. 1999. "Acceptance of Community Policing Among Police Officers and Police Administrators." *Policing: An International Journal of Police Strategies & Management* 22: 567–588.

Lurigio, A. J., and Rosenbaum, D. P. 1994. "The Impact of Community Policing on Police Personnel: A Review of the Literature." In D. P. Rosenbaum (ed.), *The Challenge of Community Policing*, pp. 147–166. Thousand Oaks, CA: Sage.

Mastrofski, S. 1990. "The Prospects of Change in Police Patrol: A Decade in Review." *American Journal of Police* 9: 1–79.

Moss-Kanter, R. A. 1983. *The Change Masters: Innovations for Productivity in the American Corporation*. New York: Simon & Schuster.

Pierce, J. L., and Delbeq, A. L. 1977. "Organization Structure, Individual Attitudes and Innovation." *Academy of Management Review* 2: 27–37.

Pisani, A. L. 1992. "Dissecting Community Policing—Part 2." *Law Enforcement News*, May 31: 8, 10.

Sadd, D., and Grinc, R. M. 1994. "Innovative Neighborhood Oriented Policing: An Evaluation of Community Policing Programs in Eight Cities." In D. P. Rosenbaum (ed.), *The Challenge of Community Policing: Testing the Promises*, pp. 27–52. Thousand Oaks, CA.: Sage.

Schein, E. 1969. *Process Consultation: Its Role in Organization Development*. Reading, MA: Addison-Wesley.

Sherman, L. W., Milton, C. W., and Kelley, T. V. 1973. *Team Policing: Seven Case Studies*. Washington, DC: Police Foundation.

Skogan, W. G., and Hartnett, S. M. 1997. *Community Policing, Chicago Style*. New York: Oxford University Press.

Skolnick, J. H., and Bayley, D. H. 1986. *The New Blue Line: Police Innovation in Six American Cities*. New York: Free Press.

Strauss, G., and Sayles, L. R. 1980. *Personnel: The Human Problems of Management*, 4th ed. Englewood Cliffs, NJ: Prentice-Hall.

Trojanowicz, R., and Bucqueroux, B. 1990. *Community Policing: A Contemporary Perspective*. Cincinnati, OH: Anderson.

Understanding Community Policing: A Framework for Action. 1994. Washington, DC: Bureau of Justice Assistance, August.

Weisburd, D., McElroy, J., and Hardyman, P. 1988. "Challenges to Supervision in Community Policing." *American Journal of Police* 7: 29-50.

Wycoff, M. A., and Skogan, W. G. 1993. *Community Policing in Madison: Quality From the Inside Out*. Washington DC: National Institute of Justice, December.

Chapter Fifteen

Police Management: Challenges Ahead

Perhaps the most important lesson to be learned from the discussion and research presented throughout the text is that in policing the *capacity for adaptability* is more important than a specific model of policing, or a role definition, mission, vision, or strategic emphasis. For without a high capacity to adapt, efforts to change will either fail, have limited success and ultimately be abandoned, or be claimed as successful when in reality they are not. If an organization has a capacity to adapt, any changes are more likely to be successful. In an adaptable organization, members will be more amenable to change (i.e., shift to a new role or mission or vision or strategy), because the success of any new approach will be determined by realistic implementation and evaluation of programs, appropriate "testing" of new ideas, and a commitment to analyses and responses.

Adaptable Police Agencies

Adaptable organizations in policing would include flexible organization designs (including democratic controls), participatory management, and problem-solving capabilities. They are learning organizations in that they not only conduct evaluations (and know the literature), but they also educate and are educated by their employees and community members. One of the most important characteristics of such an organization is a well-informed, interested clientele. Furthermore, any particular organization response must be based on a commitment first to the **rule of law** and second to the ***informed opinions of community residents and employees***. It is believed that properly defined and implemented, community policing can provide a stimulus for the development of organizations able to deal with change. Consequently, the strengthening of the adaptive capacity of the organization is more important than the philosophy and strategies of community policing because there is substantial historical evidence that new models of policing will emerge in the future.

Adaptable police departments will also be able to better respond to the intrinsic allure of incident-based enforcement actions, which, while appropriate in some situations, are not the only way to alleviate crime and disorder problems in a community. This type of response provides the most immediate gratification, is more "romantic," and is more in keeping with the "dangerous and dramatic" self-image of many police officers, as well as the expectations of many in the community. Although this image is more myth than reality for most officers, it is still very powerful and seductive. For instance, would you rather solve the crime and catch the bad guy, possibly in a dangerous confrontation, or help develop crime prevention programs (through surveys, interviews, and group meetings) in the community? Just as it is easy to drift toward autocratic management styles, it is also easy to drift toward a predominately authoritarian and coercive approach in policing.

If police departments are to function effectively and efficiently, it is clear that they must become more adaptable. At least three prevailing conditions in policing make such adaptation necessary: (1) the realization that police departments function within turbulent community environments, (2) the attraction of more highly educated and demanding individuals into the field, and (3) the increasing diversity of police employees.

With respect to the first condition, in the past, many police departments have not responded well to the changing societal demands made on them, chiefly because of an improper fit between the organization and its turbulent environment; unstable environments require more flexible, less bureaucratic structures that can readily adapt to changing conditions. A recent study on organization change and community policing confirmed the need for police departments to be able to readily adapt to changing community conditions. For instance, in his study of over 200 police departments, Zhao (1996) discovered that changes toward community policing were more likely to be forced on the departments than consciously chosen. He concluded that the changes were most likely in response to external environmental demands (e.g., affirmative action programs and community makeup) rather than to organization considerations.

With respect to the second and third conditions, traditional, mechanistic structures are generally not able to provide a stimulating and diverse atmosphere that will develop and use the full potential of well-educated officers entering the field today. Thus in many departments, there may be an improper fit between the individual and the organization. If departments wish to maintain high-quality personnel, their organization designs and managerial styles will need to become more flexible, democratic, and humanitarian.

Finally, the above discussion on police adaptability, efficiency, and effectiveness provides an impetus for describing how managers might be able to evaluate the "organizational health" of their departments. The following (edited) list, developed by a panel of police experts for the National Institute of Justice, describes six attributes that a ***healthy police department*** would incorporate into its operating practices:

Attribute One. The healthy police organization knows what it wants to accomplish. It has articulated goals that can be expressed in an operational form, not as general as "To serve and protect." The goals can be expressed in operational form, and assessed, meaning that there are measures of things that are reflective of the goals.

Attribute Two. The healthy police organization needs to know its citizens. Are they getting what they want? What they are entitled to? They are not just those who call and complain, or summon the police, but residents in a neighborhood, business, and so on. Finally, there are those we think of as the objects of police control—the offenders—they, too, are people who need to be considered in terms of their experiences with the police. There are a variety of user surveys that could measure transactions with citizens—for example, periodic citizen surveys.

Attribute Three. The healthy police organization knows its business, the demands that are placed upon it. Calls for service are a readily available source of information in this regard. The department needs to know why "business" is increasing or decreasing. Besides calls for service, special efforts also have to be made in terms of measuring proactive efforts, particularly in trying to capture programmatic efforts. For example, problem solving requires not just random responses or responses to individual incidents, but responses that are planned and coordinated to accomplish some objectives.

Attribute Four. The healthy police organization knows what it is doing about the demands of business. It has the ability to monitor resource allocations and officer activities. In terms of community policing, it knows what other agencies and organizations are doing that are pertinent to problems it is trying to deal with.

Attribute Five. A healthy police organization knows its people. Things that would tell us what people get from their jobs, what motivates them about their work, and what demoralizes them. Knowing these things would help drive decisions about supervision, training, recruitment, and job design. In terms of measurement, surveys would need to be conducted within the organization.

Attribute Six. The healthy police organization feeds back information to people and groups who need to know. To do this, you need to know what they need to know, what they want to know, and how they need to get it. Whether it's neighborhood groups that need to know more about the kind of service that they're getting, whether it's victim groups, or whether it's employees, they are all users of information (Travis and Brann, 1997: 4–5).

Core Organization Problems: Back to the Future

The above conditions suggest that police management must be decisively transformed if it is to adequately meet the internal needs of the organization as well as the external demands placed on it. Interestingly, it appears that much can be learned from a futurist of three decades ago, Warren Bennis, who foresaw a fundamental change in the basic philosophy that underlies managerial behavior, including the following:

1. *A new concept of man,* based on increased knowledge of his complex and shifting needs, which replaces an oversimplified, innocent push-button idea of man.

2. *A new concept of power,* based on collaboration and reason, which replaces a model of power based on coercion and threat.

3. *A new concept of organization values*, based on humanistic-democratic ideals, that replaces the depersonalized mechanistic value system of bureaucracy. (Bennis, 1967: 8)

Bennis suggested that the push for these changes "stems from some powerful needs, not only to humanize the organization, but to use the organization as a crucible of personal growth and development for self-realization" (p. 8). Although contemporary management philosophy may not have developed as quickly as Bennis predicted, it is apparent, as indicated throughout the book, that some police departments are decidedly moving in this direction. Considering these changing conditions, Bennis perceived five core problems that would have a vital impact on organizations of the future. These problems appear as critical today as when Bennis first described them; each is briefly discussed below.

1. *Integration* concerns the problem of relating individual needs (incentives, rewards, and motivation) to organization demands. It may be thought of as that ratio between individual needs and organization demands that creates the transaction most satisfactory to both.

2. *Social influence* essentially involves the problem of the distribution of power within the organization. In contemporary police organizations, the distribution of power must be seriously reconsidered in recognition of college-educated officers entering the field, as well as of the highly demanding, complex role responsibilities of the job—particularly community policing—which make authoritarian rule (from the top) obsolete.

3. *Collaboration* is a way of meeting the problem of fragmentation and conflict that results as organizations become more complex. The usual mechanisms for resolving this conflict—avoidance or suppression, annihilation of the weaker party by the stronger, sterile compromises, and unstable collusions and coalitions—are inadequate. Constructive ways of dealing with such conflicts, which minimize suspicion and mistrust, must be discovered. That does not mean, however, that conflict is always avoidable or necessarily harmful; a certain amount of conflict is healthy for an organization and can lead to creative and productive ends.

4. *Adaptation* is necessary to solve the problem created by a turbulent environment. The pyramidal structure of bureaucracy is suitable for organizations whose tasks are highly routine and repetitive. However, because all police departments operate in environments that are uncertain, they must acquire more organic

characteristics so they can adapt to changing demands. Not all police environments are as turbulent as others; the distinction is mainly one of degree. For example, although the environment of a department in a large city may be more turbulent than that of a department in a small city, each must continually adapt to changing external stimuli (such as public opinion, special interest or minority group interests, problem definitions, political influences, and new laws and ordinances), if it is to adequately serve the community.

5. ***Revitalization*** to overcome the problem of stagnation will be an important part of organizations in the future. It will include (1) an ability to learn from experience and to codify, store, and retrieve the relevant knowledge; (2) an ability to "learn how to learn," that is, to develop methodologies for improving the learning process; (3) an ability to acquire and use feedback mechanisms in performance, to develop a "process orientation," in short, to be self-analytical (and self-correcting); and (4) an ability to direct its own destiny.

These qualities have a good deal in common with quality management practices, including continuous improvement and the use of quantitative methods to evaluate progress. For the organization, this is a means of paying attention to its own evolution. Without a process for change and explicit direction, the organization cannot realize its full potential. As suggested earlier in the text, perhaps the use of quality management and leadership concepts is the missing link in attempting to move the police toward more organic models, including community policing.

Table 15.1 summarizes the core problems confronting contemporary organizations and the emerging conditions that appear necessary if police departments are to resolve these problems and meet their prevailing internal and external needs. It is interesting to note that in Bennis' original 1967 table of core problems, he labeled the emerging conditions as being appropriate for the development of organizations in the twentieth century. Inasmuch as these core problems are still applicable, the time frame has been changed to the twenty-first century; hence, they are a "back to the future" reality check for today's organizations attempting to adapt to their turbulent environments.

Obstacles to Change: Lessons Learned

Research on police departments attempting to make the transition to community policing have provided the most recent lessons for police managers with respect to overcoming obstacles to major change and managing the change process. If police departments are to become truly adaptive in nature, how the organization change process is managed becomes crucial. For instance, in a national survey of more than 1,600 agencies (Wycoff, 1995), police chiefs and sheriffs were asked about the lessons they learned from their experiences in attempting to implement community policing. The most frequently mentioned responses were: (a) the need for pre-implementation training of personnel, (b) the importance of taking a long view of the change

Table 15.1 Core Problems Confronting Contemporary Organizations		
Problem	**Bureaucratic Solutions**	**New 21st-Century Conditions**
Integration The problem of how to integrate individual needs and organizational needs.	No solution because of no problem. Individual vastly oversimplified, regarded as passive instrument or disregarded.	Emergence of human sciences and understanding of man's complexity. Rising aspirations. Humanistic democratic ethos.
Social Influence The problem of the distribution of power and sources of power and authority.	An explicit reliance on legal-rational power, but an implicit usage of coercive power. In any case, a confused, ambiguous shifting complex of competence, coercion, and legal code.	Emergence of self-reliance and power sharing. Leadership too complex for one-man rule.
Collaboration The problem of producing mechanisims for the control of conflict.	The "rule of hierarchy" to resolve conflicts between ranks and the "rule of coordination" to resolve conflict between horizontal groups. "Loyalty."	Increased needs for independence and minimization of mistrust and suspicion.
Adaptation The problem of responding appropriately to changes induced by the environment.	Environment stable, simple, and predictable; tasks routine. Adapting to change occurs in haphazard and adventurous ways. Unanticipated consequences abound.	External environment of organization more "turbulent," less predictable. Unprecedented rate of technological change. Increased need for flexible orientation, which allows for adaptation.
"Revitalization" The problem of growth and decay.	Underlying assumption that the future will be certain and basically similar to the past.	Rapid changes in technologies, tasks, manpower, norms and values of society, goals of organization and society all make constant attention to the process imperative.

Adapted from W. Bennis, 1967. "Organizations in the Future." *Personnel Administration,* September–October: 18.

process, (c) the need for support from elected officials and other city agencies, and (d) the importance of listening to and involving the community. Additional important findings from the chiefs and sheriffs included the following: 48 percent thought that implementation would require major changes in organization policies or goals; 56 percent anticipated that rank-and-file employees would resist such change; and 83 percent strongly supported the need for training in community policing and believed that existing training efforts were inadequate.

A comprehensive study of six police departments self-described as engaged in some form of community policing indicated that each agency used four major techniques to promote the change process (Lamm Weisel and Eck, 1994). Departments in Las Vegas, Nevada; Edmonton, Alberta; Philadelphia; Santa Barbara, California; Savannah, Georgia; and Newport News, Virginia, all included the following approaches to change:

- Using participative management styles, including seeking input from line officers into the development of the community-policing effort.

- Changing promotional practices to reinforce officer involvement with community policing efforts.

- Changing performance evaluation systems to support community policing.

- Providing formal training to personnel. (Lamm Weisel and Eck, 1994: 65)

Despite a wide variation in implementation activities among the departments, a remarkable consistency in the attitudes of officers toward community policing was found. At least two-thirds of officers (64 to 80 percent) in each agency believed community policing, as currently practiced or in a varied form, was here to stay. Only about one-quarter (20 to 32 percent) felt it was a fad or on the way out. Interestingly, it was further discovered that the consistent positive views remain regardless of seniority (years of service), education, race, sex, or assignment to a fixed beat. The authors take these findings to mean that resistance to change may be overrated and less pervasive than widely assumed. They suggest that the best approach to changing an organization toward community policing is perhaps to ignore or wait out the relatively small percentage of detractors, and move ahead with the changes. This is an approach supported by some management consultants known as a ***bias for action***; that is, in implementing change, the most critical activity is to move forward and avoid over-concentration on the processes involved.

Additional lessons for overcoming problems associated with change can be gleaned from a study of eight jurisdictions funded by the Bureau of Justice Assistance to implement community policing programs (Sadd and Grinc, 1994, 1996), in this instance referred to as Innovative Neighborhood Oriented Policing (INOP). The eight jurisdictions were Hayward, California; Houston, Texas; Louisville, Kentucky; New York; Norfolk, Virginia; Portland, Oregon; Prince George's County, Maryland; and Tempe, Arizona. The INOP jurisdictions varied greatly, as did the prior experiences of each department with community policing. Since these programs were evaluated after approximately only one year of operation, their overall effectiveness was minimal. Perhaps the most significant findings were that each of the sites experienced common implementation problems, including:

- Minimal involvement of police officers, city agencies, and community residents in program design; consequently, knowledge of the structure and goals of the program and of community policing in general was lacking in all of these groups. As a result, there was considerable resistance on the part of police officers to the substantial role changes being required.

- Similarly, community residents (even those living in INOP areas) were generally unaware of the goals of the INOP projects. Although respondents in most of the INOP sites believed that community organization and involvement had increased since the start of the program, this involvement was limited in scope (i.e., at some sites "involvement" simply meant providing the police with information about crime).

- Community policing was often defined and implemented solely as a police initiative to the virtual exclusion of other city agencies and of the communities it hoped to serve. One of the most important findings of the INOP research is that the education and training of community residents regarding their roles in community policing was almost nonexistent.

The experiences of the eight INOP sites clearly indicated that in attempting to promote organization change toward community policing, departments (and their jurisdictions) need to pay particular attention to three issues: (1) **overcoming patrol-officer resistance,** (2) **generating interagency support** (becoming citywide if possible), and (3) **building community involvement.** The types of change problems described in the INOP programs reflect the reality of attempting to implement community policing programs. As indicated by the Madison department's change efforts, it is a long and oftentimes painful process. But given enough effort, and under the right leadership and conditions, it can be done. As Wycoff and Skogan (1994) found in their evaluation of Madison, "It is possible to change a traditional, control-oriented police organization into one in which employees become members of work teams and participants in decision-making processes." With this in mind, some of the more important lessons in change learned in Madison include the following:

1. It is possible to implement participatory management in a police department, and doing so is very likely to produce more satisfied workers. Some of the possible advantages of a participatory style of management include (a) employees whose input is valued learn to value the input of others (e.g., citizens); (b) employees who are invited to work in team relationships to solve internal problems learn in this way to work with citizens in team relationships to solve problems; (c) people closest to the problems (officers and citizens) have the most information about those problems, and their input is critical for problem definition and resolution; and (d) organization change tends to be more readily accepted by employees who participate in the process of creating it.

2. Decentralization contributed significantly to the creation of the new management style. It also contributed to the development of team spirit and processes, conditions that should facilitate com-

munity policing. Officers who work in the Experimental Police District (EPD) believe the decentralized station improved relationships with the public; they report increased numbers of contacts with citizens in the community and an ever-increasing number of citizens who come to the station for assistance.

3. The managers of the Madison Police Department also thought that the best way to move toward decentralization and community policing was to change one part of the organization (i.e., the EPD) before proceeding with department-wide implementation. Furthermore, it was evident that special attention paid to one part of the organization did not block change elsewhere (i.e., other changes in the organization were not affected by the attention received by the EPD).

   It is important to note, however, that this was not true in the INOP projects, where the special-unit status accorded many of the project officers had a tendency to generate intradepartmental rivalry that led to resentment and resistance (Sadd and Grinc, 1996). Once again, it is clear that both internal and external departmental conditions must be considered prior to attempting major change.

4. During the long time frame of undergoing change and experimentation (i.e., over twenty years), Madison continued to make efforts to recruit highly educated officers whose backgrounds, life experiences, and attitudes increased the likelihood that they would be supportive of change (Wycoff and Skogan, 1994). Although this supposition supports the research, Lamm Weisel and Eck (1994), found that levels of education had no impact on support for community policing. Additional research regarding the relationship between education and change in general, and community policing in particular, is warranted, as the research results tend to be mixed and we cannot be sure of their meaning. However, other things being equal, college-educated recruits clearly remain preferable to recruits with less education.

It appears that lessons learned regarding departmental change toward community policing can be tied directly to: (a) *flexible organization designs,* (b) *participatory management,* (c) *citywide* or *governmental support*, (d) *redefinition of the police role,* including training, reward, and promotional practices, and (e) *involvement of a representative body of citizens.* In the final analysis, whether police departments can overcome the obstacles to implement community policing rests on how much they have learned about change from the research and thus how committed they may be to implementing the above criteria. The type of total commitment required by a department to move in this direction is highlighted in Case Study 15.1, which describes the guidelines followed by the Portland (Oregon) Police Department's change toward community policing.

Case Study 15.1

The Portland Police Department's Guidelines to Change: Implementing Community Policing

The guidelines outlining the change process are categorized as follows: requisite structural changes, the organizational change process, internal resistance to change, and organizational design.

Requisite Structural Changes

1. A quasi-military, command-and-control management structure must be changed to a nonauthoritarian, participatory structure.
2. The criterion for reward must emphasize quality service.
3. Promotion criteria must be based upon a demonstrated ability to carry out community-policing strategies and on competency and leadership ability.
4. Recruitment policies must include seeking qualified candidates who reflect the ethnic and cultural diversity of the community served.
5. Training must include community-policing skills. Role redefinitions must take place concomitant with retraining.

Organization Change Process

1. The chief executive should initiate the change process by enlisting an outside consultant or expert to act as a neutral change agent to assist in developing and coordinating the change process.
2. The chief executive must be committed to the idea that change is necessary and committed to the alternative selected.
3. Goals must be clear.
4. Relevant actors and groups from both inside and outside the organization must be included in the planning and implementation processes.
5. Once the problem is diagnosed, experiments are designed to test the innovation.
6. Successful change requires time and repeated effort.
7. Progress must be monitored to enable midcourse corrections.

Internal Resistance to Change

1. In the case of innovative change in police departments, public support for the change must be garnered to help counter internal resistance.
2. Power must be redistributed within the department; that is, authority must be pushed down to the lowest level of responsibility.
3. Power redistribution must occur through a developmental process of change rather than by sudden and arbitrary appointment.
4. Those directly affected by the change should be brought into the change process at the earliest possible stage.
5. The nature and purpose of the change should be expressed clearly to reduce ambiguity and resistance.
6. Role redefinitions must take place concomitant with retraining.
7. Experiments are carried out to test the innovation. Positive results yielded by the experiments are used to reinforce the change and encourage acceptance at all levels of the organization.

Organization Design

1. The kind of organizational design required to develop the capacity to achieve organizational goals is contingent upon the kind of environment in which the organization operates: Bureaucratic structures are inappropriate for turbulent, unstable task environments.
2. There is no "one best way to organize."
3. The degree of complexity in the organizational design will mirror the degree of complexity in the organization's environment.

Adapted from: E. J. Williams, 1995. *Implementing Community Policing: A Documentation And Assessment of Organizational Change (Portland, Oregon)*, pp. 182-196. Dissertation, Portland State University.

Police Departments as Learning Organizations

As can be seen from the previous discussion, adaptive organizations, by their very nature, must also be learning organizations. If management can develop an environment that promotes continuous learning, the department (and its members) would benefit from its own and other's experiences, including both success and failure. Such a learning environment leads to a

❖ ❖ ❖ ❖

learning organization, which is able to process what it has learned and adapt accordingly. According to Geller (1997), there are many structural and process ideas that would help police departments to become learning organizations. One idea is to create a ***Research and Development (R & D) unit*** that actually does research and development, instead of only statistical descriptions of departmental inputs and outputs. Such a unit would be run by someone who understands R & D and is supported by a respectable budget (generally not the norm). An R & D unit could help foster an appreciation for the practical benefits of prior research in the field and also facilitate internal studies as well. It is virtually impossible to be a learning organization if the use of recent research findings is not part of departmental processes.

Another idea along these lines is to continue to expand ***police-researcher partnerships***, such as those sponsored by the National Institute of Justice. Such partnerships allow the department to get involved in a research project without all the necessary expertise or budget restraints, while learning something about themselves. The innovative neighborhood-oriented policing (INOP) project discussed above would be an example of how such a research project might work, where NIJ provided training and technical assistance tailored to each of the eight sites. Additionally, if a department finds a researcher it really trusts (e.g., at a local or regional university), it could contract with him or her part-time to serve as a research "broker," helping the department to become a better consumer and user of research knowledge. Some departments have acquired this kind of capability by hiring a criminologist to head their R & D units.

Sherman (1998) has taken the above concepts to their ultimate conclusion with his ***evidence-based policing (EBP)*** model, where departments would appoint certified criminologists to be primarily responsible for putting research into practice, and for evaluating the results of those practices. The EBP model is essentially:

Literature/In-House Research → Best Evidence → Guidelines → Outputs → Outcomes → Feedback Loop

EBP consists of using existing published literature and/or in-house research to identify the best guidelines for practice, taking law, ethics, and community culture into account. These guidelines translate into specific measurable outputs, such as number of arrests, calls for service, problems solved, patrol allocation methods, and so on. The varying degrees of success, of these outputs, such as reduced levels of disorder, lower crime rates, or higher quality of life for residents, can then be evaluated. If the outcomes fail to meet expectations (i.e., fall within specified paramaters), the department will use this information (and possibly newly published research) to develop new guidelines. Thus the process repeats itself in a continuous learning, self-improvement mode.

A further idea that would help foster learning would be to ***organize police work around problem solving*** and to take seriously the SARA process for confronting problems. Managers and groups of problem-focused officers, who would be working with the community, could develop procedures to guide their work. For example, checklists could be developed for both police supervisors and community organizers to help ensure that concerns are not cut and that the most viable solutions are sought.

One interesting structural suggestion is to **use middle managers to facilitate critical thinking**. Since middle managers in police departments (e.g., lieutenants and captains) are continually coming under fire in reorganization plans as being unproductive and even counterproductive, it may be constructive to give them something useful to do. Because they are between the policymakers above and the policy implementers below, why not charge them "with facilitating critical thinking about the efficacy of policies and implementation?" (Geller, 1997: 6). If departments were to do this (assuming proper training and ability levels), the performance ratings of middle managers might reflect how well they lead their units and the community constructively to criticize and improve departmental operations. A concomitant idea would be to include, as part of individual and unit performance ratings, **a comparison of employee accomplishments with respect to industry standards in policing** as a way to help promote organization progress.

This idea of matching police performance levels to present-day industry standards and to promoting organization progress is an interesting concept whose time may have already arrived. One municipal police chief in Scottsdale (Arizona), for example, supports the idea that every community should require a "stockholders'" report of its local police department. The report would focus on twelve fundamental questions that should be asked by the community and answered by the department (Heidingsfield, 1996). Inside Management 15.1 takes a look at these questions.

Inside Management 15.1

Community Stockholders' Report on Local PDs

Question 1. Has your department been willing to examine its inner workings by comparing the local way of doing business with national standards of the law enforcement industry? This is a three-year process of national accreditation.

Question 2. Does your department have a simple, easily understood statement of values that are known throughout the department and embody the fundamental notion of ethical behavior and principled decision-making?

Question 3. Has your department been rigorous in its effort to diversify itself by representing community cultures and instilling broad confidence in the police services being delivered?

Question 4. Has your department embraced the concepts of community policing that imply openness, citizen partnership, and joint responsibility for public safety; is the department recognized for its success in this regard?

Question 5. Does the leadership of your department consistently and passionately carry the message to the community and its police officers that disparate treatment for individuals, heavy-handedness, and racism are absolutely not tolerated?

Question 6. Is the maintenance of dignity and respect a theme that is recurrent throughout the department's culture?

Question 7. Is the department willing to be formally evaluated by the community on its ability to deliver service in the best manner possible?

Question 8. Has your department embarked on an organizational campaign to reinforce the concepts and premises of ethics in policing?

Question 9. Does your department have in place an open, formal system to ferret out misconduct and to deal with it decisively and promptly?

Question 10. In its hiring standards, does your department highly value college education and community service, including a commitment to ideals and strength of character?

Question 11. Does your department consistently enjoy the nonpartisan support of its elected and appointed officials?

Question 12. Does your impression of your community's officers include characterizations such as compassionate, skilled, fair, committed to the principles of good public safety, available, and open?

Adapted from: M. J. Heidingsfield. 1996. "Pointed Questions About Your Police Agency." *Law Enforcement News*, September 30: 8. Printed with permission from the *Law Enforcement News*, John Jay College of Criminal Justice.

Managing Change and Adaptability

By now it is clear that the future success and well-being of police departments, not to mention the communities they serve, depend on their ability to deal effectively with change by adapting to environmental concerns. To this end, police managers must be able to determine the need for change, how the change process can be constructively implemented, and whether or not the change has been effective. Police managers need to be able to effectively manage and motivate a diverse group of employees and at the same time understand and respond to public expectations. Thus, managers must be cognizant of the best managerial practices and change strategies available, which can only be accomplished by staying abreast of the contemporary literature and research in policing—and possibly other fields as well. In other words, today's police manager must be a consumer of empirical knowledge, and, at the same time, not be afraid to make changes based on that knowledge. Managing complex police organizations is certainly more sophisticated than in the past; "seat of the pants management" or "doing things as they have always been done management" is not going to get the job done to help departments adapt to their turbulent environments. The authors end the book by making six recommendations that it is believed, if generally followed, will help facilitate organization change and adaptability and allow contemporary police managers to better satisfy both their employees and the citizens they serve.

The first recommendation calls for managers to become, in part, ***clinical scientists*** (as described in Chapter 2), and place greater emphasis on research and evaluation. Only through research and evaluation can the most appropriate management practices be discovered. This calls for a ***spirit of scientific inquiry***; for example, along the lines of the SARA model, or the EBP model described above. Much of the research reviewed in this book should be useful to police managers, either in terms of "what works" or as a general guide. Regardless, police managers who do not base their decisions and policies on research will likely continue to repeat past failures.

The second recommendation calls for managers to act ***as role models in promoting and rewarding integrity and ethical behavior***. It must be made clear that ***integrity is the most valued commodity*** throughout the organization and a more important characteristic than loyalty to peers. If the police are to truly become co-producers of law enforcement with citizens (see below), they must be able to be trusted in order that citizens will feel comfortable in sharing information about their neighborhoods. Along with integrity, managers will need to promote and reward ***non-aggressive behavior that reduces violence*** in the community, and should establish this type of behavior as the model for other officers to follow. In turn, this type of behavior promotes the understanding that many problems in the community can, and should, be solved without resorting to the use of force.

The third recommendation calls for a change in leadership style away from authoritarian toward a ***participatory style.*** Employees (and citizens) are treated with respect, are listened to, are allowed a voice in decision making, and are guided in their activities (rather than simply ordered). The research is clear that organization change is more effective (i.e., less resisted) if those affected by the change are allowed to participate in decisions regarding the change; in fact, with the types of changes necessary to move toward community policing, it is likely that without first developing a participatory leadership style, all other efforts will ultimately fail. In addition, such a mentoring approach must also encourage and facilitate ***teamwork*** and ***open communication*** in working toward goal accomplishment.

The fourth recommendation calls for the recognition of ***citizens as co-producers of law enforcement and problem solving.*** As has been noted, most change efforts directed at the community are simply police initiatives, without real involvement from the community in terms of input, training, or education. Such involvement must also include input and cooperation with other city agencies if community problems are to be solved. It is important that the police build trust in the community by confronting fear and mistrust and by sharing expectations. This partnership, however, must be based on the principle of the rule of law, not on the politics of special interests.

The fifth recommendation calls for ***increased initiative and imagination on the part of practicing managers.*** It is evident that police managers cannot fall into a complacency rut if constructive change is to take place. In order to promote constructive change, today's police managers will not only need to have knowledge of the available research, they must have the ***courage*** to initiate action on what might work best for them, even if it is unconventional. They must also push for the evaluation of these new practices in order to determine if they are successful and whether further refinement or other action is required.

The sixth and final recommendation calls for managers to ***commit themselves to a sustained effort with respect to organization change.*** As previously discussed, implementing major innovations in police departments requires a sustained, long-term effort. Research has indicated, for instance, that community policing efforts are currently only in the preliminary phase of change, and that unreasonably high expectations set forth by managers will be detrimental to the change process. Furthermore, some research (see Zhao, 1996) has found that during the preliminary phase of change, organizational rather than technical rationality should be the primary criterion by which managers should evaluate community policing innovations (e.g., citizens' support and input); targets of change based solely on technical rationality (e.g., reduction of crime rates) will hinder rather than promote the change process.

In the final analysis, if police departments are to adapt appropriately to their environments, police managers must be willing to look to the future and to use creative management methods that are supported by contemporary research rather than to the past and the status quo. Police managers must also expect that in attempting to make major changes, they will need to be committed for the long term and have a bias for action. In this way, police departments will be able to implement significant change and become more adaptable, thus increasing the satisfaction levels of their employees and citizens alike. Consequently, the future role of police managers will be both exciting and challenging, as they have a chance to make a significant impact not only in their organizations but in their communities as well.

Epilogue: September 11th, 2001

The terrorist attacks on September 11, 2001 in New York, Pennsylvania, and Washington, DC occurred while this text was in final production, precluding a full assessment of the implications of this tragic event for police organizations. Beyond the significant impact these unprecedented events had on the citizens of these cities, these events also had an important impact on the management of police departments as well. Police departments, acting as learning organizations, are suddenly being asked to adapt to an ambiguous and changing environment. While the long-term impact of the September 11 events may be unclear, the authors believe there are at least three important consequences for police managers and police departments.

First, there appears to be new widespread respect, admiration and support for civil service positions such as firefighters and police officers. This support, coupled with an economic downturn, may result in more educated and diverse individuals seeking careers in policing. Recruitment of highly qualified officers may thus become easier for police organizations. Second, terrorism and its resultant focus on security will become a new or expanded topic in police training curricula and practices.

Finally, the terrorist attacks may have lessened public concern for discriminatory enforcement practices and violation of civil liberties. As discussed previously, racial profiling has become an emerging issue in American policing, and has thus become a problem for managers. The events may also lead to greater support for aggressive policing styles, particularly when encountering ethnic groups. For instance, shortly following the attacks Nislow (2001), citing a poll conducted by the *Los Angeles Times*, stated 68 percent of those queried said they favored law enforcement "randomly stopping people who may fit the profile of suspected terrorists." This newfound public tolerance of racial profiling might lead to justification for increased police harassment of individuals, based on race. This practice, however, remains unethical behavior that must be eliminated from policing. In light of the aftermath of September 11, it becomes even clearer why the primary task of police managers is to monitor and promote integrity and ethical behavior. Only by adhering to these standards will police and citizens become meaningful co-producers of crime prevention outputs, and thus promote the tenets of community policing.

Summary

Today's police organizations need to become more flexible and adaptable. This is necessitated by at least three prevailing conditions: (1) the realization that police departments function within turbulent community environments, (2) the attraction of more highly educated and demanding individuals, and (3) the increasing diversity of police employees. With respect to these conditions, six attributes were described that may allow police managers to evaluate the "organizational health" of their departments. Five core organization problems that must be addressed in order for constructive change to occur were also considered; these included: (1) integration, (2) social influence, (3) collaboration, (4) adaptation, and (5) revitalization.

Because many departments will attempt to adopt some form of community policing, some important lessons that have been learned with respect to overcoming obstacles to change were described. Further, it was noted that adaptive organizations, by their very nature, are also learning organizations; both structural and process ideas for helping police departments to become

❖ ❖ ❖ ❖   learning organizations were discussed. Finally, six recommendations are made that should help to facilitate organization change and adaptability, which, in turn, should allow contemporary police managers to better satisfy both their employees and the citizens they serve.

Discussion Questions

1. Discuss the meaning of the concept capacity for adaptability; describe the three prevailing conditions in policing that necessitate a change toward adaptable organizations.

2. Briefly describe the six attributes developed by a panel of police experts that relate to the "organizational health" of a police department.

3. Briefly describe the five core problems confronting contemporary organizations. What are the emerging conditions that appear necessary if police departments are to meet their prevailing internal and external needs?

4. Describe the four major techniques used in the study of six police departments to promote the change process; discuss the implications and the meaning of a "bias for action" regarding the change process.

5. Describe several lessons that were learned from the INOP study of eight jurisdictions regarding obstacles to the implementation of community policing.

6. Describe several lessons that were learned regarding obstacles to the implementation of community policing in Madison.

7. What is a learning organization? Describe several approaches, including the evidence-based policing (EBP) model, which might prove useful in helping police departments to become learning organizations.

8. What do you perceive to be the most important role of the police manager in the future? Provide several relevant examples to support your choice.

References

Bennis, W. 1967. "Organizations in the Future." *Personnel Administration*, September/October: 1–19.

Geller, W. A. 1997. "Suppose We Were Really Serious About Police Departments Becoming Learning Organizations?" *National Institute of Justice Journal*, December: 2–8.

Heidingsfield, M. J. 1996. "Pointed Questions About Your Police Agency." *Law Enforcement News*, September 30: 8.

Lamm Weisel, D. L., and Eck, J. E. 1994. "Toward a Practical Approach to Organizational Change: Community Policing Initiatives in Six Cities." In D. P. Rosenbaum (ed.), *The Challenge of Community Policing: Testing the Promises*, pp. 53–72. Thousand Oaks, CA: Sage.

Nislow, J. 2001. "Are Americans Ready to Buy Into Racial Profiling?" *Law Enforcement News* October 15, p. 11.

Sadd, S., and Grinc, R. 1994. "Innovative Neighborhood Oriented Policing: An Evaluation of Community Policing Programs in Eight Cities." In D. P. Rosenbaum (ed.), *The Challenge of Community Policing: Testing the Promises*, pp. 27–52. Thousand Oaks, CA: Sage.

——. 1996. *Implementing Challenges in Community Policing: Innovative Neighborhood-Oriented Policing in Eight Cities*. Washington, DC: National Institute of Justice.

Sherman, L. W. 1998. "Evidence-Based Policing." *Ideas in American Policing Series*. Washington, DC: Police Foundation.

Travis, J., and Brann, J. E. 1997. *Measuring What Matters, Part Two: Developing Measures of What the Police Do*. Washington, DC: National Institute of Justice.

Williams, E. J. 1995. *Implementing Community Policing: A Documentation And Assessment of Organizational Change (Portland, Oregon)*, pp. 182–196. Dissertation, Portland State University.

Wycoff, M. A. 1995. *Research Preview: Community Policing Strategies*. Washington, DC: National Institute of Justice.

Wycoff, M. A., and Skogan, W. G. 1994. "Community Policing in Madison: An Analysis of Implementation and Impact." In D. P. Rosenbaum (ed.), *The Challenge of Community Policing: Testing the Promises*, pp. 75–91. Thousand Oaks, CA: Sage.

Zhao, J. 1996. *Why Police Organizations Change: A Study of Community-Oriented Policing*. Washington, DC: Police Executive Research Forum.

❖ ❖ ❖ ❖

Author Index

Subject Index